Portuguese Morphophonology:
A Generative-Markedness Approach

Arthur Brakel

# Portuguese Morphophonology: A Generative-Markedness Approach

**Volume 2 Nominals**

PETER LANG

Bern · Berlin · Bruxelles · New York · Oxford

**Bibliographic Information published by the Deutsche Nationalbibliothek**
The Deutsche Nationalbibliothek lists this publication in the Deutsche Nationalbibliografie; detailed bibliographic data is available in the internet at http://dnb.d-nb.de.

**Library of Congress Cataloging-in-Publication Data**
A CIP catalog record for this book has been applied for at the Library of Congress

Cover illustration: © Mr. Rizal/Shutterstock.com

ISBN 978-3-0343-3843-1 (Print)
E-ISBN 978-3-0343-4388-6 (E-PDF)
E-ISBN 978-3-0343-4389-3 (EPUB)
DOI 10.3726/b18595

For

LINDA,

who 40 years later continues to make it all worthwhile.

# Table of Contents

# 6 The Morphophonology of Number and Gender: Unproblematic Nominals

## Introduction

**§6.0.0 Nominals Identified:** This chapter addresses the number and gender morphology and phonology related not only to nouns but also to adjectives, articles, demonstratives, pronouns, and infinitives. They are all nominals because, by and large, they share both syntactic and morphological properties. Syntactically, almost all of them can be subjects of verbs, objects of verbs, and objects of prepositions, as Table 6.1 demonstrates:

**Table 6.1** Shared Rolls—Nominals

| Open-Ended Nominals | | | | |
|---|---|---|---|---|
| **Sets** | **Nominals** | **Subject** | **Object of Verb** | **Object of Preposition** |
| 1 | **Noun: *pinguim*** | **os pinguins ficam** | **quero pinguins** | **de pinguins não falo** |
| | 'penguin' | the penguins stay | I want penguins | of penguins I do not speak |
| 2 | **Adjective: *velho*** | **os velhos ficam** | **quero velhos** | **de velhos não falo** |
| | 'old' | the old stay | I want old (items) | I don't speak of old (items) |
| 3 | **Infinitive: *falar*** | **falar não é possível** | **quero falar** | **acabo de falar** |
| | 'to speak' | to speak isn't possible | I want to speak | I have just spoken |

(*Continued*)

Table 6.1 Continued

| Grammatical Nominals | | | | |
|---|---|---|---|---|
| Sets | Nominals | Subject | Object of Verb | Object of Preposition |
| 4 | **Def. Article: *o*** | **o que vai é meu** | **quero o que vai** | **falo de o que vai** |
| | 'the' | the one going is mine | I want the one going | I speak of the one going |
| 5 | **Indef. Article: *um*** | **umas ficam** | **quero umas** | **de umas não falo** |
| | 'a(n)' | some stay | I want some | of some I don't speak |
| 6 | **Demonstrative: *este*** | **este fica** | **quero este** | **deste não falo** |
| | 'this' | this stays | I want this | of this I shall not speak |
| 7 | **Pronoun:[a] *ela*** | **ela fica** | **quero ela** | **dela não falo** |
| | 'she/her' | she stays | I want her (= she) | of her I shall not speak |
| 8 | **Object Prn.[b] *os*** | *** | **quero-os** | *** |
| | 'them' | *** | I want them | *** |
| 9 | **Possessive: *nossos*** | **os nossos ficam** | **quero os nossos** | **dos nossos não falo** |
| | 'ours' | ours stay | I want ours | of ours I shall not speak |

a This pronoun is not strictly nominal since it can occur as an object of prepositions and, in the everyday speech of most Brazilians, as a direct object.
b This object pronoun is accusative. The morphology and phonology of object pronouns includes dative (indirect object pronouns) and reflexive pronouns.

**§6.0.1** Table 6.1 is divided into two sections: Open-ended Nominals and Grammatical Nominals. Sets 1, 2, and 3 (nouns, adjectives, and infinitives) are open-ended both because they are bona fide words—they may begin or end utterances—and because their inventory is open-ended. At any time, new nouns, adjectives, and infinitives may be coined, either from Portuguese sources or from words barrowed from other languages. The grammatical nominals (Sets 4–9) are paradigmatic forms with a closed inventory, and some are restricted to specific semantic and syntactic circumstances. They are essentially nominals, however.

**§6.0.2 Set 1:** There is no controversy as far as the sentences in set 1 of Table 6.1 are concerned since *pinguim* is a noun, and it is an ideal subject, verbal object, and an object of a preposition.

**§6.0.3 Set 2:** *Velho* 'old' is incontrovertibly an adjective, and one might argue that in these sentences some noun has been deleted. In addition, it is of course true that sentences like these would only make sense in the real-world if listeners knew exactly of whom or about what (i.e. some actual noun) the speaker was talking. Still, it is the case that in Portuguese most adjectives can take the place of whatever nouns they might describe, and, once they do, they function as subjects as well as verbal and prepositional objects.[1] And this is precisely one of the two reasons[2] why both nouns and adjectives are nominals.

**§6.0.4 Set 3:** Infinitives function as nouns because they can occur as sentence subjects, direct objects, and objects of prepositions.[3]

---

1 The dividing line between adjectives and nouns in Portuguese is often vague and tenuous. Take two nouns of equal 'noun valence', such as *urso* 'bear' and *amigo* 'friend'. The phrase *amigo urso* turns *urso* into an adjective and means, in Brazilian Portuguese, a friend who is hard to reach, reclusive, i.e. a friend with bear-like skittishness. On the other hand, the phrase *urso amigo* turns *amigo* into an adjective, and the phrase means 'friendly bear'. When two nouns of equal valence are juxtaposed in a particular construction, the first is modified by the second, which performs the role of an adjective. Conversely, take two adjectives also of equal 'adjectival valence': *alto* 'tall' and *baixo* 'short'. The phrase *alto baixo* can identify a person who, relative to most people, is tall, but among the tall this person is relatively short. The phrase *baixo alto* may indicate an individual who is classified as short, but relative to other short people that person is tall. The first word in the phrases with two adjectives becomes a noun which the second adjective modifies.

2 The other reason is adjectives' and nouns' inflection for gender and number.

3 Using note 1's admittedly impressionistic notion of nominal valence, i.e. the extent to which a form is a noun, it turns out that among nouns, adjectives, and infinitives, the latter have, surprisingly, the highest noun valence since they can only function as nouns. Infinitives may not modify a noun the way nouns of equal valence may: cf. *amigos ursos* and **amigos falar* or **ursos dormir,* which, if they meant anything at all, would mean something like 'friends to talk' or 'bears to sleep'. Alone, with no other context, these phrases make no sense. Even when inflected for person and number, Portuguese infinitives are nouns: **subject:** *Eles **irem** me perturba* 'Their going bothers me'; **object of preposition:** *Ao **dormires**, dormirei também* 'Upon your sleeping, I'll sleep as well'; **Direct object:** *Ouviram **sairmos*** 'They heard us leave'. Infinitives, in addition to their inflection for specific grammatical persons, are always [-feminine] and, when not inflected for person and number, can be inflected for nominal plurality, and they can be modified by adjectives: *o pensar rápido* 'quick thinking' or *os caminhares intermináveis* 'the interminable walkings-around'.

**§6.0.5 Set 4** The examples of the definite article as nouns are problematic. One could be justified in assuming that the adjective clause *que vai* has been nominalized and it, rather than the definite article, is the subject of the verb *é*. Likewise, the same phrase (*que vai*) could be seen as the object of *Quero* and the object of the preposition *de*. Another alternative, which would eliminate *o* as subject and object, is to consider structures like *o que vai* as nominalized adjective clauses.

**§6.0.6 Set 5:** The indefinite article shares the same relationship to nouns that adjectives do. Like adjectives it can substitute for the nouns it modifies, and when it does, it too assumes the syntactic role of a noun. In its singular forms, the indefinite article, *um* or *uma,* doubles as a numeral: *um moço* can mean both 'a young person' or 'one young person', *uma moça* may indicate 'one young female person' or 'a young female person'. There is no distinction between singular indefinite articles and singular numerals in Portuguese.

**§6.0.7 Set 6:** This demonstrative (deictic) pronoun appears in its non-feminine, non-plural form and functions as a verbal subject and object, as well as an object of a preposition. Portuguese actually has three different demonstratives, and they perform similarly to adjectives: they modify nouns, they can substitute for nouns, and they are inflected for gender and for number.

**§6.0.8 Set 7:** The 3rd person pronoun (in this case, *ela*[4]) functions in all varieties of Portuguese as a subject or as the object of prepositions. The verbal direct object *ela* has become wide-spread in Brazilian Portuguese, at least in casual speech. Speakers of European Portuguese do not use subject pronouns as direct objects, they would say *Quero-a* for 'I want her'.

**§6.0.9 Set 8** demonstrates the 3rd person direct object pronoun. It cannot occur as either object of a preposition or as a subject. The pronouns of Sets 7 and 8 are high valence nouns insofar as they, like infinitives, never function as adjectives. On top of that, they are never modified by adjectives without a copula: *Ele é velho* 'He is old' but **Ele velho foi comigo* '*Old he went with me'. And whereas *quero-os* means 'I want them', *quero os velhos* only means 'I want the old ones'—the

4 Here the pronoun is inflected for [+feminine] gender and [-plural] number. Like adjectives, nouns, and articles, these 3rd person pronouns can be singular or plural, feminine or non-feminine.

direct object *os* is homophonous but not homologous with the definite article *os*. (See Table 6.18 and §6.2.1.0–.1, §6.2.5.3.0–4.2.)

**§6.0.10 Set 9:** This set demonstrates the use of the possessive *nosso* 'our' clearly nominalized as subject, verbal object, and as object of the preposition *de*. Possessive pronouns have a relatively high adjectival valence since they can be readily modified by adverbs: *O carro é exclusivamente nosso* 'The car is exclusively ours'.

**§6.0.11.0** The other reason for considering nouns, adjectives, definite and indefinite articles, nominative pronouns, demonstratives, possessives, 3rd person direct object pronouns, and infinitives together is that at least some of each category's forms can reflect gender and/or number.[5] Table 6.2 shows how all these forms reflect gender and number:

5 Mateus and D'Andrade have proposed (2000: 69) that '[g]ender is an intrinsic (non-inflectional) property of nouns and that only animate nouns such as *menino* 'young boy' and *menina* 'young girl' alter their forms when denoting a masculine or feminine referent of the same category. This is not correct. Non-inflectional gender is not intrinsic to nominal roots, and it is assigned arbitrarily by specific suffixes. There are myriad nouns whose roots appear to be the same but have widely different referents when they are feminine or non-feminine: *casa* 'house', *caso* 'case'; *fala* 'speech', *falo* 'phallus'; *passa* 'raisin', *passo* 'step', *passe* 'pass [to go somewhere]', and *paço* 'palace' (The latter set of items all have #pas+ as their root). In addition, nouns derived from nominal stems often change gender: *mulher* 'woman' (f.)➔ *mulherio* 'group of women' (-f.); *árvore* 'tree' (f.) ➔ *arvoredo* 'clump of trees' (-f.); *erva* 'grass' (f.) ➔ *herbário* 'herbarium' (-f.); *inverno* 'winter' (-f.) ➔ *invernia* 'wintering' (f.); *tímpano* 'ear drum' *timpanite* 'ear ache' (f.); *grito* 'shout'➔*gritaria* 'shouting'. Clearly, the suffixes' gender determines that of the entire word. Of course there are many words of [-feminine] gender that end in /a/, and a few that end in /o/ but are [+feminine]. Gender in human life and language is less than totally and unambiguously determined.

Table 6.2 Nominal Inflection: Gender and Number

| Sets | | [-feminine] | | [+feminine] | |
|---|---|---|---|---|---|
| | | [-plural] | [+plural] | [-plural] | [+plural] |
| 1 | Noun | **cachorro** | **cachorros** | **cachorra** | **cachorras** |
| | Gloss | pup | pups | bitch pup | bitch pups |
| 2 | Adjective | **cachorro novo** | **cachorros novos** | **cachorra nova** | **cachorras novas** |
| | Gloss | new pup | new pups | new bitch pup | new bitch pups |
| 3 | Infinitives | o dizer | os dizeres | *** | *** |
| | Gloss | the saying | the sayings | *** | *** |
| 4 | Definite Articles | **o cachorro** | **os cachorros** | **a cachorra** | **as cachorras** |
| | Gloss | the pup | the pups | the bitch pup | the bitch pups |
| 5 | Indefinite Article | **um cachorro** | **uns cachorros** | **uma cachorra** | **umas cachorras** |
| | Gloss | a pup | some pups | a bitch pup | some bitch pups |
| 6 | Demonstratives | **esse cachorro** | **esses cachorros** | **essa cachorra** | **essas cachorras** |
| | Gloss | that pup | those pups | that bitch pup | those bitch pups |
| 7 | Pronoun | **ele** | **eles** | **ela** | **elas** |
| | Gloss | he | they | she | they (+f.) |
| 8 | Object Pronouns | **quero-o** | **quero-os** | **quero-a** | **quero-as** |
| | Gloss | I want it | I want them | I want it (+f.) | I want them (+f.) |
| 9 | Possessives | **nosso cachorro** | **nossos cachorros** | **nossa cachorra** | **nossas cachorras** |
| | Gloss | our pup | our pups | our bitch pup | our bitch pups |

**§6.0.11.1** Table 6.2 shows that for all nominals standard orthography reflects plurality with a word-final –s (<z#>). Beyond this, in **Sets 1, 2, 4, 8, 9** the vowel –o (<o#>) indicates [-feminine] gender. In the eight cases where [+feminine] gender can be indicated, –a (<a#>) occurs. On the other hand, potentially word-final –e (in **Sets 6 and 7**) indicates [-feminine] gender, and the indefinite article (**Set 5**) appears to have no morpheme indicating [-feminine] gender. The 3rd person direct object pronouns in **Set 8** appear to be mere sequences of regular gender ([±feminine]) and number [±number].[6] **Set 9:** The 1st person plural form, like all possessive pronouns, reflects the number and gender of the possessed item(s) with the typical gender and number reflections.

**§6.0.12.0** Tables 6.1 and 6.2 use the markedness strategies advanced in Chapter 1 and put to use there, as well as in Chapters 2, 3, 4, and 5. That is, the marked nominal cases are [+feminine] and [+plural], whereas the unmarked cases are [-feminine] and [-plural]. Such an analysis predicts: (A) In representative texts, plural nominals will be less frequent than non-plurals. (B) Non-plural nominals will be more widely interpretable than the plurals. (C) The marked gender ([+feminine]) will occur less frequently than its negation [-feminine]. (D) The marked gender will be restricted to a subset of referents. (E) The unmarked gender will refer to a more general set of referents. That is, [-feminine] may include [+feminine] referents, whereas the converse does not normally obtain: [+feminine] may not, in general, indicate non-feminine entities among particular words' referents.[7] This approach provides an economic and elegant analysis of Portuguese morphophonology.[8]

**§6.0.12.1** Concerning the frequency of the marked cases, the Portuguese phonological dataset used in this study provides a convenient set of texts on which to test these predictions. The definite and indefinite articles and demonstrative pronouns are easily isolable in the corpora and co-occur with and modify or stand in for nouns. Table 6.3 displays their relative frequency in the dataset.

---

6 Table 6.18 shows that they, like the definite articles, have an (often deleted) consonantal root in addition to these gender morphemes.

7 There are [+feminine] epicene nouns that imply both sexes of a species: e.g. *baleias* 'whales', *cobras* 'snakes', *sardinhas* 'sardines'.

8 Mattoso Câmara's (1972) analysis of gender and number anticipates the one used here. Mattoso (64) says 'gender is expressed in Portuguese by means of an *-a* desinence for the feminine as opposed to a Ø desinence for the masculine. This situation is quite similar to the one for number (*-s* in the plural).' Thus, [+feminine] is the marked case for gender, [+plural] the marked case for number.

**Table 6.3** Frequency Count: Marked and Unmarked Gender and Number

| | Gender | | Number | |
|---|---|---|---|---|
| | [-feminine] | [+feminine] | [-plural] | [+plural] |
| **Definite Articles** | 244 | 206 | 348 | 102 |
| **Indefinite Articles** | 38 | 21 | 58 | 1 |
| **Demonstrative Pronouns** | 16 | 5 | 20 | 1 |
| **Totals:** | **298** | **232** | **426** | **104** |
| **% of Totals:** | **56.23%** | **43.80%** | **80.37%** | **19.62%** |
| **Ratio: Unmarked/marked** | **1.29/1** | | **4.1/1** | |

Table 6.3 bears out the prediction of text frequency. Of the 530 nominals counted in the dataset, 298 (56.23%) were [-feminine] and 426 (80.37%) were [-plural]. Beyond their textual frequency, marked and unmarked nominals' ranges of reference are inversely related to their markedness. Two Portuguese proverbs and modifications thereof demonstrate this principle.

**Table 6.4** Proverbs, Gender, and Number

| | Standard Proverb | Modified Proverb |
|---|---|---|
| | [-feminine] (unmarked gender) | [+feminine] (marked gender) |
| 1 | Filho alheio come muito e chora feio | Filha alheia come muito e chora feia |
| | 'Someone else's child eats a lot and cries ugly' | 'Someone else's daughter eats a lot and cries ugly' |
| | [-plural] (unmarked number) | [+plural] (marked number) |
| 2 | (Um) lobo velho não cai em armadilha | Uns lobos velhos não caem em armadilha |
| | '(An) old wolf doesn't fall into (a) trap(s)' | 'Some old wolves don't fall into trap(s)' |

**§6.0.12.2.0** The two standard Portuguese proverbs occur in unmarked cases: Proverb 1 unmarked gender, Proverb 2 unmarked number. In the modified set of proverbs, the subject of Proverb 1 has changed from [-feminine] to [+feminine], and the subject of Proverb 2 has changed from singular to plural.

**§6.0.12.2.1** In the case of Proverb 1, *filho* 'child' can refer to a particular child (either male or female, other than one's own) or children in general. When the noun is *filha* ([+feminine]), it can refer only to a daughter—to a particular daughter, or daughters in general since it is not inflected for plurality. However, it says nothing about other people's [-feminine] (i.e. male) offspring.

**§6.0.12.2.2** In Proverb 2, the noun *lobo*, owing to its unmarked gender, can refer to both male and female wolves, to a particular wolf, and it can be a general statement about old wolves' perspicacity. The [+plural] indefinite article along with form *lobos* says that only some ***subgroup*** of wolves does not fall into traps. *Uns lobos velhos* cannot refer directly to an individual, whereas the [-plural] form can denote both groups and individuals.

**§6.0.12.3** Paragraphs §6.0.11.1–§6.0.12.2.2 and the tables therein confirm the status of [+plural] as the marked number and [+feminine] as the marked gender. What this means is that Portuguese has only one gender (feminine) which stands in contrast with gender's absence or negation, which neither excludes nor identifies [+feminine] referents. Likewise, Portuguese has only one number [+plural], which is opposed by its absence or negation. The absence of plurality in nominals will be morphophonemically represented by <Ø#, inflection for unmarked gender, on the other hand, will be represented by actual morphemes such as <o#, and <e#, as well as by <Ø#. The morpheme <z# indicates plurality's presence in nominals.

## The Morphophonological Structure of Open-Ended Nominals

**§6.1.0** It is obvious from Table 6.2 and the discussion and tables following it that the structure of most nominals is:

**Nominal Pattern 1:**

#stem[9] + {< / +}[10] [±feminine]# < [±plural]#.

Now, using morphophonemic transcription, Table 6.5 shows the structure of the open-ended items in Table 6.2—all of which have monomorphemic roots.

Table 6.5 The Structure of Simple Nominals

| | | [-feminine] | | [+feminine] | |
|---|---|---|---|---|---|
| | | [-plural] | [+plural] | [-plural] | [+plural] |
| 1 | Noun | cachorro | cachorros | cachorra | cachorras |
| | | #kašor̲+<o#<ø# | #kašor̲+<o#<z# | #kašor̲+<a#<Ø# | #kašor̲+<a#<z# |
| 2 | Adjective | (cachorro) novo | novos | nova | novas |
| | | #nɔv+<o#<Ø# | #nɔv+<o#<z# | #nɔv+<a#<Ø# | #nɔv+<a#<z# |
| 3 | Infinitive | falar | falares | *** | *** |
| | | #falar#[a]+e+<Ø# | #falar#+e+<z# | *** | *** |

a For the sake of simplicity and space, the infinitive *falar* appears unanalyzed. Its formal analysis is: #stem++theme vowel#+infinitive deriver#+[-feminine]+<[±plural#, i.e. #fal++a#+r#+e+<Ø#. It has no tense-mood-aspect morpheme because it is not a verb (cf. Volume 3, Vi.0.0)

**§6.1.1** Table 6.5 shows that the plural morpheme is unequivocally <z# for open-ended nominals. It also represents plurality on a significant portion of the grammatical nominals as well (see Tables 6.22, 6.24, 6.25). Indeed, nominal pluralization is largely, but not entirely, unproblematic.[11] Notwithstanding the nominal plural morpheme's

9 'Stem' refers both to mono-morphemic roots to which affixes may be added and to poly-morphemic strings to which even more morphemes may be added. Roots are core morphemes of words. A stem is any string of morphemes to which one may add one or more morphemes. The disjunction containing < and + indicates that gender can be either inflectional (<) or derivational and more tightly bound (+) to particular stems.

10 The disjunction containing both the inflecting boundary (<) and the deriving boundary (+) indicates that gender can be both inflectional and derivational. Number is always inflectional.

11 Chapters 8 and 9 address less tractable pluralizations of open-ended nominals.

unambiguous identity and the transparency of the forms in Table 6.5's Sets 1–3, nominal pluralization impedes a phenomenon addressed in the next section: stem vowel metaphony.

**§6.1.2.0 Number and Stem Vowel Metaphony:** Whereas the structure illustrated in Table 6.5 obtains for all nominals as far as their number is concerned, even for simple nominals such as these, the case is not closed. There is a class of both nouns and adjectives in which the stressed stem vowel /ɔ/ exhibits metaphony between plural and non-plural forms. That is, in the plural their tonic vowel surfaces as [ɔ], whereas in the singular it emerges as [o]. Table 6.6 demonstrates this case of stem vowel metaphony.

**Table 6.6** Vowel Metaphony: [-feminine] Nouns and Adjectives

| Nouns | | | | |
|---|---|---|---|---|
| **Word** | **Singular** | **Plural** | **Morphemic Analysis** | **Gloss** |
| **caroço** | [kă.ˈro.sŭ] | [kă.ˈrɔ.sŭš] | #kaˈrɔs++o#(<z#)[a] | pit(s) |
| **corvo** | [ˈkor.vŭ] | [ˈkɔr.vŭš] | #kɔrv++o#(<z#) | crow(s) |
| **fogo***[b] | [ˈfo.ɣŭ] | [ˈfɔ.ɣŭš] | #fɔg++o#(<z#) | fire(s) |
| **jogo*** | [ˈžo.ɣŭ] | [ˈžɔ.ɣŭš] | #žɔg++o#(<z#) | game(s) |
| **osso*** | [ˈo.sŭ] | [ˈɔ.sŭš] | #ɔs++o#(<z#) | bone(s) |
| **ovo*** | [ˈo.vŭ] | [ˈɔ.vŭš] | #ɔv++o#(<z#) | egg(s) |
| **poço*** | [ˈpo.sŭ] | [ˈpɔ.sŭš] | #pɔs++o#(<z#) | well(s) |
| **miolo** | [mi.ˈo.lŭ] | [mi.ˈɔ.lŭš] | #miɔl++o#(<z#) | brain(s) (matter) |
| **tojo** | [ˈto.žŭ] | [ˈtɔ.žŭš] | #tɔž++o#(<z#) | gorse (shrubs) |
| Adjectives[c] | | | | |
| **grosso*** | [ˈgro.sŭ] | [ˈgrɔ.sŭš] | #grɔs+<o#(<z#) | gross, ill-mannered |
| **novo*** | [ˈno.vŭ] | [ˈnɔ.vŭš] | #nɔv+<o#(<z#) | new |
| **famoso***[d] | [fẵ.ˈmo.zŭ] | [fẵ.ˈmɔ.zŭš] | #fam++ɔz+<o#(<z#) | famous |

a Notice that the morphemic affinity between the gender morpheme and the roots of the nouns is ++ rather than +<. This is because the gender ([-feminine]) is intrinsic to these words' meanings rather than a consequence of their referent's gender. These gender morphemes are deriving morphemes rather than inflecting morphemes. On the other hand, the affinity between the adjectives and their gender morpheme appears as +< because the gender morpheme varies according to the adjectives' referents or the nouns they modify.

b The words bearing asterisks are among the *Aurélio*'s 3,000 most frequent words.

c The adjectives' [+feminine] forms also preserve the /ɔ/ in their surface manifestations, be they singular or plural.

d Adjectives ending in –<u>oso</u> are by far the largest class of adjectives showing the /ɔ/ ⇔ /o/ metaphony. The *Aurélio* lists 1254, 21 of which are among the 3,000 most frequent words.

The words analyzed in Table 6.6 do not exhaust the category of singular/plural root vowel metaphony in Portuguese. They come from a list of 32 nouns (Cunha, 1969: 127) of this type.

**§6.1.2.1** The 4th column of Table 6.6 identifies /ɔ/, rather than /o/, as the vowel underlying both the singular and the plural forms of these words.[12] This tack acknowledges that the vowel in these nouns was a short (i.e. open, lax) vowel in Latin, /ŏ/, which regularly became /ɔ/ in Portuguese (Williams, 1962: 36).[13] In addition, this identification is the cornerstone of a simple rule of stem vowel metaphony:

**Rule 6.1 The Closing of Nominal Class 1 ($N_1$) Vowels:**

$$\begin{pmatrix} \text{-contoid} \\ \text{+dorsal} \\ \text{+wide glottis} \\ \text{+labial} \\ \text{+delayed release} \end{pmatrix} \rightarrow [\text{-wide glottis}] \;/\; \_\_\; C_{1\text{-}2} + \begin{Bmatrix} < \\ + \end{Bmatrix} o\# < [\text{-plural}]\#_{[N1]}$$

The environment or determinant of this rule (i.e. the material to the right of the slash) is for nominals in class $N_1$[14] that are neither plural nor feminine. The non-feminine suffix must be preceded by at least one but no more than two consonants.[15] The disjunction in the determinant indicates that the [-feminine] gender morpheme can be either an inflecting morpheme or a derivational one.[16] The determinand, i.e. the

---

12 From Cunha's (127) and Azevedo's (2005: 59) point of view, the metaphony works the other way: /o/ mutates to /ɔ/ in plural forms.

13 The adjectives ending in –oso derive from Latin /ō/, which should have produced /o/ in modern Portuguese, but these forms acquired /ɔ/ in analogy with forms like *novo* (Williams, 130).

14 Class N nominals are the unmarked case, where virtually nothing happens to the stem regardless of the presence or absence of the plural morpheme. Class $N_1$, as a subset, is the first in an array of nominal subsets susceptible to various morphophonological processes.

15 Nouns such as *aboio* 'float', *comboio* 'train', *apoio* 'support', and *joio* 'darnel' appear to be N class nouns, i.e. nouns with no stressed vowel metaphony. The *Aurélio* and Infopédia consider the tonic vowel in *comboio* to be /ɔ/ in European Portuguese.

16 The only [-feminine] gender morpheme that triggers this metaphony is <o# and +o#.

specification to the left of the arrow indicating a transformation, more than adequately describes a stressed /ɔ/, which in the environment of the determinant loses its lax quality ([+wide glottis]) and becomes [o].

**§6.1.2.2** The words of class $N_1$ constitute a minority category in the nominal sector of the Portuguese lexicon and, quite likely owing to their frequent occurrences, native speakers learn which words undergo this transformation item by item. The adjectives ending in –oso are so common that their metaphony is easily learned. For the nouns, Cunha (127), immediately after his examples of nominal root vowel metaphony, lists another 32 nouns whose root vowel is an invariant /o/ and whose structure is similar (Table 6A.1). Identifying nouns as pertaining to Class N and identifying their root vowels as /o/ obviates their susceptibility to Rule 6.1

**§6.1.2.3** The phenomenon generated by Rule 6.1 can be explained in the following manner: The presence of a [+high] back vowel [ŭ] in a syllable following one containing a non-high back vowel, especially a labial vowel such as [ɔ], will cause the formants of the open vowel to approximate those of [o].[17] In the evolution of Vulgar Latin into modern Portuguese, the word-final vowel, i.e. the morpheme <o# or +o#, indicating [-feminine] gender reduced from [o] to [ŭ] earlier than it did when it was followed by the plural suffix. Words inflected for plurality, i.e. ending in <z#, end with a potentially closed syllable, and a contoidal coda such as this can impede or at least retard the rising of a tautosyllabic vowel.

**§6.1.2.4** Word-final atonic vowels, especially [ŭ], undergo considerable reduction and a high degree of effacement (§3.2.1.2, §3.3.2.8, and Table 3.18b), but such is not the case when the plural suffix follows this [-feminine] morpheme. And the reason for this is that the deletion of a word-final vowel such as [ŭ] may leave a word with a somewhat aberrant syllable coda, i.e. a word-final syllable ending in other than a vowel or /n, r, l, z/ e.g. *povo* 'folk': #pɔv++o#<Ø# ➔ [ˈpo.vŭ] ➔ [ˈpov]. Loss of the vowel in a plural form would end the word with a much more aberrant consonant cluster: *povos* 'peoples': #pɔv++o#<z#

17 Delgado Martins (66) shows that for stressed [ɔ] $F_1$ averages 490Hz and $F_2$ 1,318Hz. Her figures for stressed [o] are: F1 363Hz, F2 787Hz. Posttonic [u] F1 averages 270Hz and F2 858.

→ [ˈpɔ.vʊ̃š] →*[ˈpɔvš], were this gender indicating vowel deleted.[18] The atonic vocalic conservatism of the potentially closed word-final syllable of plural nouns, as opposed to the volatility of the singular forms with their open syllables, contributed to the maintenance of the tonic open vowel in the preceding syllable.

**§6.1.2.5** The data and analysis in §6.1.0–.2.3 account for a huge amount of the phenomena related to nominals' grammatical number, but these data are far from closing the case on Portuguese pluralization and nominal stem vowel metaphony. Nominal gender also plays a role in nominal stem vowel metaphony, and, even in the unproblematic nominals, gender is significantly more complex.

**§6.1.3.0 Simple Nominal Gender:** At their most basic, nouns that refer to animate beings (human or otherwise) are ***inflected*** for gender, which can be [±feminine]. This inflection is systematic insofar as it corresponds to the actual gender of the [+animate] being particular words denote. Table 6.7 contains examples of inflected nouns:

**Table 6.7** Inflected Noun Gender

| | Systematic Gender | | | |
|---|---|---|---|---|
| | [-feminine] | Gloss | [+feminine] | Gloss |
| 1 | aluno | student | aluna | female student |
| 2 | amigo | friend | amiga | female friend |
| 3 | gato | cat | gata | female cat |
| 4 | lobo | wolf | loba | female wolf |
| 5 | macaco | macaque | macaca | female macaque |
| 6 | moço | young person | moça | young woman |
| 7 | pombo | pigeon | pomba | female pigeon |
| 8 | porco | pig | porca | sow[a] |
| 9 | tio | uncle | tia | aunt |

a In addition to meaning 'sow', *porca* is the word for 'hex nut'. Likewise, the word *gata* (item 4) can also indicate the third mast of a ship, *loba* (item 6) can indicate a cape or a perfect hand in a card game, and *macaca* (item 8) can indicate a cow without a calf. The idiomatic uses of these [+feminine] words justifies their entry into the Portuguese lexicon as independent words, and it justifies the assignment of idiomatic or deriving gender morphemes for the words whose meanings cannot be deduced from their parts' sums: #pɔrk++a#, #gat++a#, #lob++a#, and #makak++a#.

18 In an OT analysis, [ˈpovš] would incur more violations than [ˈpɔv], which would incur more than [ˈpɔ.vʊ̃š].

Several of these items, *amigo, moço*, and *porco*, function readily as adjectives. And all but *pombo* are among the *Aurélio*'s 3,000 most frequent words. Save *porco/porca,* these words are Class N nouns, i.e. their [-plural] manifestations undergo no-stem vowel metaphony.

**§6.1.3.1 Stem Vowel Metaphony Revisited:** All $N_1$ stems are exempted from metaphony when they occur with a [+feminine] suffix.[19] Table 6.8 contains examples of this phenomenon:

**Table 6.8** Vowel Metaphony: [± feminine] Nouns and Adjectives[a]

| Noun | | | | |
|---|---|---|---|---|
| **Stem** | **[-feminine]** | **[+feminine]** | **Morphemic Analysis** | **Gloss** |
| **#pɔrk+** | [ˈpor.kŭ] | [ˈpɔr.kă] | #pɔrk+<gender#<number# | pig/sow |
| **ADJECTIVES** | | | | |
| **#grɔs+** | [ˈgro.sŭ] | [ˈgrɔ.să] | #grɔs+<[αfeminine] #(<z#) | crude |
| **#nɔv+** | [ˈno.vŭ] | [ˈnɔ.vă] | #nɔv+<[αfeminine] (<z#) | new |
| **#X++ɔz+** | [fã̆.ˈmo.zŭ] | [fã̆.ˈmɔ.ză] | #fam++ɔz#+<[αfeminine]#(<z#) | famous |
| **Deriving Gender Morphemes (Nouns)** | | | | |
| **#kɔk+** | [ˈko.kŭ] | [ˈkɔ.kă] | #kɔk++gender#<number# | head/ spying |
| **#korkɔv+** | [kŭr.ˈko.vŭ] | [kŭr.ˈkɔ.vă] | #korkɔv++gender#<number# | buck/ hump |
| **#pɔs+** | [ˈpo.sŭ] | [ˈpɔ.să] | #pɔs++gender#<number# | well/ puddle |
| **#pɔzt+** | [ˈpoš.tŭ] | [ˈpɔš.tă] | #pɔz++t++gender#<number# | job/ piece |

a The words in this table are *porco, coxo, grosso, novo, famoso, coco/coca, corcovo/ corcova, poço/poça, posto/posta.*

**§6.1.3.2** The metaphony displayed in Table 6.8 is most prevalent in adjectives, especially given the high-frequency (fn. 13) adjective-forming suffix +ɔz +. The adjectives, and however many nouns of the type *porco* ⇔ *porca* there may be, undergo root vowel metaphony when their roots are inflected for [-feminine] and [-plural]. Rule 6.1 needs no

19 As in the metaphony occasioned by [-feminine, -plural] nominal inflection, the factor suspending metaphony in $N_1$ nominals is <a# and +a#. The formant configuration of <a# and +a# [ă] is such that it would not cause /ɔ/'s formants to drift toward those of /o/.

alteration to account for the non-metaphony of [+feminine] inflected (or derived) $N_1$ words. $N_1$ nominals' metaphony occurs only in the context of [-feminine] items with [-plural] inflection.

**§6.1.3.3 Derivational Gender:** Although there are many nouns similar to those in Tables 6.7 and 6.8, there are many more Portuguese nouns like the final four of Table 6.8. These nouns bear gender morphemes, but the gender morpheme is arbitrarily attached to the nominal stem. These morphemes assign gender to the resultant nouns, but, beyond that, they can actually combine with nominal stems and derive different words using the same stem. Table 6.9 has more representative examples:

**Table 6.9** Derivational Noun Gender[a]

| | [-feminine] | Analysis | Gloss | [+feminine] | Analysis | Gloss |
|---|---|---|---|---|---|---|
| 1 | **maço** | #mas++o# | bundle | **massa** | #mas++a# | dough |
| 2 | **falo** | #fal++o# | phallus | **fala** | #fal++a# | speech |
| 3 | **mato** | #mat++o# | brush | **mata** | #mat++a# | forest |
| 4 | **favo** | #fav++o# | honeycomb | **fava** | #fav++a# | flat bean |
| 5 | **fado** | #fad++o# | fate | **fada** | #fad++a# | fairy |
| 6 | **modo** | #mod++o# | way | **moda** | #mod++a# | style |
| 7 | **fuso** | #fuz++o# | spindle | **fusa** | #fuz++a# | $32^{nd}$ note |
| 8 | **fundo** | #fund++o# | fund | **funda** | #fund++a# | slingshot |

a There is a definite semantic relationship between the [-feminine] and [+feminine] forms in the nouns in rows 3 and 6, and this relationship identifies these words' roots as the same. Even though the other words in the idiomatic gender category evince no sematic parentage between [±feminine] forms, there is no reason to consider the roots different because as idioms these nouns' meanings are always greater than that of the sums of their constituent parts. For example, the root #fav+ has no definite meaning. When it combines with +o# ([-feminine]) the form #fav++o# denotes 'honeycomb', when it combines with +a# ([+feminine]) the form #fav++a# indicates a flat bean. To put it another way, these words' roots have no intrinsic meaning.

The words in Table 6.9 exhibit the property basic to derivation: at least two morphemes are conjoined (here roots and gender morphemes) to form words whose meanings are greater than the sum of the constituent parts (§5.0.1, §5.2.1–3.2). That is, the roots in Table 6.9 do not determine these nouns' referents—their meanings idiomatically emerge from the combination of the roots and their (derivational) gender suffixes. In the course of addressing gender morphemes, it has been, and will continue to be, necessary to distinguish inflectional gender morphemes from deriving gender morphemes.

**§6.1.4.0** In Table 6.7, the gender morphemes <a# and <o# are inflectional. In Table 6.9, the gender morphemes are derivational: +a# for feminine gender and derivational +o# for non-feminine gender. Regardless of its function, the feminine gender morpheme is realized as [ă] owing to its lack of tonicity, and the non-feminine gender morpheme, which is also atonic, is realized as [ŭ], when it occurs (cf. Table 3.18b). Whereas one need have no qualms about identifying /a/ as the phonemic segment that underlies [ă], [ŭ]'s underlying /o/ is somewhat more problematic. Notwithstanding the [-feminine] gender morpheme's pronunciation as [ŭ], which is more lax than the realization of atonic /u/, this morpheme is not <u# or +u# because a word-final atonic /u/ fails to occasion the glide insertion that word-final atonic /o/ and /a/ do when preceded by a stressed /e/ or /ɛ/ (§2A.2.3.2). However, there are certain nouns, as well as adjectives and possessive pronouns, whose [-feminine] gender morpheme is indubitably <u#. Table 6.10 provides examples of these nominals in their [-feminine] and [+feminine] forms.

**Table 6.10 Nominals <u# ⇔ <a#**

| Systematic Gender (Nouns/Adjectives) | | | |
|---|---|---|---|
| | [-feminine] | Gloss[a] | [+feminine] |
| 1 | **ateu** | atheist | **ateia** |
| 2 | **epicureu** | Epicurean | **epicureia** |
| 3 | **europeu** | European | **europeia** |
| 4 | **hebreu** | Hebrew | **hebreia** |
| 5 | **pigmeu** | Pigmy | **pigmeia** |
| 6 | **pireneu** | (of the) Pyrenees | **pireneia** |
| 7 | **plebeu** | plebeian | **plebeia** |
| 8 | **sandeu** | idiot | **sandia** |
| 9 | **judeu** | Jew | **judia** |
| 10 | **ilheu** | islander | **ilhoa** |
| 11 | **reu** | defendant | **ré** |
| Systematic Gender (Possessive Pronouns) | | | |
| 12 | **meu** | mine | **minha** |
| 13 | **teu** | your (familiar) | **tua** |
| 14 | **seu** | 3rd's | **sua** |

a Table 6.10 omits a gloss column for the [+feminine] reflexes of these words because in English there is no special word for the female designee—except for item 9, the slightly old-fashioned term for a female Jew: 'Jewess'.

**§6.1.4.1** The first eleven items clearly demonstrate the lack of an obvious distinction between the traditional categories of noun and adjective. Virtually every one may be regularly and unremarkably used as an adjective or as a noun.[20] Items 1–7 display total regularity between

20 The gender morphemes that attach to stems with the +< affinity such as in the nouns *amigo* 'friend' #amig+<o# or *judeu* 'Jew' #žude+<u# are much more adjectival than those in which the affinity between stem and gender suffix is ++. Whereas the former words readily modify nouns: *autor amigo* 'friendly author' and *autor judeu* 'Jewish author', nouns with the ++ affinity between stem and gender suffix *povo* 'people', *moda* 'style' are extremely reluctant adjectives. When idiomatic gender words modify other nouns, they do so as compounds: *homem-rã* 'frogman' (-f., +f.), *caneta-tinteiro* 'fountain pen' (+f., -f). In these cases, there is no gender agreement between the combined nouns. Similarly, a high valence noun can be used without plural inflection to modify plural nouns. In Eugênio Canesin Dal Molin's abstract of his master's thesis (2013), he writes: 'discutem-se as teorizações **dos autores base,**' which I have translated as 'I discuss these **fundamental**

non-feminine and feminine forms: the use of <a# rather than <u# as the gender morpheme occasions the insertion of /i/ between the stem-final stressed /ɛ/ and the /a/. Items 8–11 show that the [+feminine] reflex of these roots can be idiosyncratic, as do the possessive pronouns in rows 12–14. Nonetheless, Table 6.10 shows that <u# also represents non-feminine gender.[21] In addition to the systematic variation between [+feminine] and [-feminine] in Table 6.10, there is also lexical distinction between nominals inflected with <u#, and words derived with +a# from the same or similar roots as Table 6.11 demonstrates.

**Table 6.11** Idiomatic Gender <u# and +u# vs. +a#

| | [-feminine] Nominals | | | [+feminine] Nominals | | |
|---|---|---|---|---|---|---|
| 1 | **aréu** | #arɛ+<u# | confused | **areia** | #are++a# | sand |
| 2 | **meu** | #me#<u# | mine (pos.) | **meia** | #me++a# | stocking |
| 3 | **seu** | #se#<u# | $3^{rd}$'s | **Seia** | #se++a# | a town in Portugal |
| 4 | **véu** | #vɛl++u#[a] | veil | **veia** | #ven++a# | vein |

a The /l/ of #vɛl+ surfaces in words such as *velar* 'to veil'. The /n/ of #ven+ surfaces in words such as *venoso* 'veined'.

**§6.1.4.2** Similar to the words with idiomatic gender in Table 6.8, the paired items in Table 6.11 have no convincing semantic affinities between [-feminine] and [+feminine]. They seem totally unrelated.[22]

authors' theoretical deliberations.' Canesin Dal Molin uses *base* 'base' as an (uninflected) adjective to modify the *autores* 'authors', i.e. Sigmund Freud and Sándor Ferenczi.

21 The grapheme –u in word-final position is rare in Portuguese. The *Aurélio* contains 1,442 nominals ending in /u/. Wolf et al's reverse dictionary contains 154 nominals ending in /u/, and only five are listed as uniquely feminine. The overwhelming predominance of [-feminine] words among these forms reinforces my assertion that <u# (also +u#) is a [-feminine] gender morpheme and that [+feminine] is the marked gender. Of those 1,442 items, 234 end in –eu—i.e. either /ɛu/ or /eu/.

22 The terms *xareu* [ša.ˈre$^{u}$] and *xaria* [ša.ˈri.ă] may in fact be related. The *xareu* is a migratory fish that spawns offshore in northern Brazil and then migrates south. The inhabitants of Natal use a maritime metaphor to describe the inhabitants of the lower (waterfront) city. They are known as *canguleiros*, i.e. gatherers of *cangulos*, another fish peculiar to those waters. The term *xaria* 'inhabitants of the upper city' might be a collective of *xareu*.

**§6.1.4.3.0** Given the structure #stem+ (<, +) gender#<number# for all nominals, and even distinguishing a deriving [+feminine] gender morpheme +a# from an inflecting <a# as well as deriving [-feminine] gender morphemes +o# and +u#, from inflecting <o# and <u#, there is more to be said about gender morphemes.[23] There are hundreds of nominals with /a/ in the gender slot of their structure, and nonetheless they are intrinsically [-feminine], and, because of this, some of them can denote entities of both genders. Table 6.12 displays the different categories of [-feminine] nominals ending -a.

23 The inflecting and the deriving gender morphemes (e.g. <a# and +, a#, <o#, and +o#) are the same morphemes, but with different binding affinities to their stems.

Table 6.12 [-feminine] Nominals Ending in –a

| Foreign (non Latin) Origin [-feminine] | | | | Native Origin | | | |
|---|---|---|---|---|---|---|---|
| Greek | | Other | | [-feminine] | | [±feminine] | |
| Word | Gloss | Word | Gloss | Word | Gloss | Word | gloss |
| **clima** | climate | **acangapara** | tortoise | **bandarra** | idler | **agrícola** | agricultural |
| **enigma** | enigma | **estafeta** | messenger | **cabecilha** | bandit chief | **alfacinha** | Lisbonite |
| **eremita** | hermit | **champanha** | Champagne | **carapina** | carpenter | **artista**[a] | artist |
| **esquema** | outline | **inca** | Inca | **dia** | day | **belga** | Belgian |
| **gorila** | gorilla | **pijama** | pajama | **guleima** | glutton | **caçula** | last born |
| **lema** | motto | **samba** | samba | **janota** | fop | **caraíba** | Carib |
| **prisma** | prism | **safardana** | low-life | **marialva** | horseman | **colega** | classmate |
| **profeta** | prophet | **chá** | tea | **dinheirama** | big money | **indígena** | indigenous |
| **programa** | program | **xá** | shah | **nada** | nothingness | **patriota** | patriot |
| **sarcoma** | sarcoma | **zabumba** | bass drum | **rapazola** | young man | **suicida** | suicide |

a The *Aurélio* contains 1,820 Portuguese words ending in –ista, all of which are [±feminine].

The 40 items in Table 6.12 were not hard to find. Indeed, it is much easier to find nominals ending in -a that are not feminine than it is to find them ending in either -o or -u that are [+feminine]. The largest class of [-feminine] words ending in +a# (other than the words ending in –ista) are the numerous words of Greek origin (cf. §12.2.4.0). The native words ending in -a that are ambivalent are also legion, and there are words such as *cabeça* 'head', *caixa* 'box, cash register', *guarda* 'guard', and *guia* 'guide (book)' that are gender ambivalent normally [+feminine] but may be [-feminine] when they refer to a male professional: *o cabeça* 'the head of an organization', *o caixa* 'the cashier', *o guarda* 'the guard person', *o guia* 'the guide person'. As numerous as these nominals may be, they nonetheless constitute a minority when compared to the thousands of [+feminine] nominals ending in –a. For this reason, they belong to two subcategories: $N_2$ being the nominals ending in -a that are [-feminine], and $N_3$ being those nominals ending in –a that may refer to or modify both feminine and non-feminine entities. There is, however, yet another gender morpheme: +e# (deriving) <e# (inflecting), which, as Table 6.13 shows, is ambivalent concerning the gender it represents.[24]

**Table 6.13** The Ambivalent Gender Morpheme +e# in Nouns

| | Ambivalent Gender | | | Idiomatic (Static) Gender | | | |
|---|---|---|---|---|---|---|---|
| | [-feminine] | [+feminine] | Gloss | [-feminine] | Gloss | [+feminine] | Gloss |
| 1 | **o agente** | **a agente** | agent | **pente** | comb | **mente**[a] | mind |
| 2 | **o estudante** | **a estudante** | student | **algibe** | cistern | **hecatombe**[b] | hecatomb |
| 3 | **o crente** | **a crente** | believer | **coice** | (a) buck | **foice** | sickle |
| 4 | **o herege** | **a herege** | heretic | **ciclone** | cyclone | **alcione** | halcyon |
| 5 | **o gerente** | **a gerente** | manager | **naipe** | (card) suit | **trempe** | grill |
| 6 | **o intérprete** | **a intérprete** | interpreter | **erre** | the letter r | **torre** | tower |
| 7 | **o cliente** | **a cliente** | client | **crepe** | crepe | **estepe** | steppe |
| 8 | **o delinquente** | **a delinquente** | delinquent | **trote** | hazing | **glote** | glottis |
| 9 | **o ianque** | **a ianque** | Yankee | **pique**[c] | lance | **psique** | psyche |

a The word *menta* 'mint' #ment++a# is also feminine. There is no semantic connection between *mente* and *menta*.
b There is an alternate to *hecatombe* with the prevalent [+feminine] morpheme: *hecatomba*.
c The words *pica* 'prick (penis)' and *pico* 'point' are derived from the same root as *pique* and are semantically related to one another.

24 The <e# or +e# occurring in word-final position is a gender morpheme by virtue of its position in the structure of nominals.

All the forms in Table 6.13 can be inflected for plurality, which locates the e in the gender slot in nominal structure.[25] These nouns and the thousands of nouns that end in -e are derived using this ambivalent gender morpheme. Table 6.14 displays words in which the morpheme +e# distinguishes invariant nouns that either end in +o# or +a#.

Table 6.14 +e# in Contrast with +a# and +o#

| +a# | Gloss | +o# | Gloss | +e# | Gloss |
|---|---|---|---|---|---|
| **boda** | wedding feast | **bodo** | donation | **bode** | billy goat |
| **lança** | lance | **lanço** | cast | **lance** | play |
| **mata** | forest | **mato** | thicket | **mate** | yerba mate |
| **passa** | raisin | **paço** | palace | **passe** | pass |
| **pica** | pica | **pico** | summit | **pique** | pike |
| **porta** | door | **porto** | port | **porte** | load |
| **porra** | club | **porro** | leek | **porre** | drinking spree |
| **topa** | child's toy | **topo** | top | **tope** | collision |

25 Concerning the nouns with ambivalent gender, all have bi-morphemic stems save *ianque* 'Yankee', which is a loan word from English. Ambivalent gender items 1, 2, 3, 5, 7, 8 are formed with the agentive or participial suffix –nt++e#<number. Of these items 1, 2, 3, 5, and 8 are clearly deverbal nouns: *agir* 'to act', *agente* 'one who acts'; *estudar* 'to study', *estudante* 'one who studies'; *crer* 'to believe', *crente* 'one who believes', *gerar* 'to generate or cause', *gerente* 'one who causes' and *delinquir* 'to commit crimes', *delinquente*, 'one who commits crimes'. Item 5, *intérprete*, is also a deverbal noun, built on the same stem as *interpretar* 'to interpret'. Item 4, *herege* has as its stem #ere+ given the existence of words such as *heresia* 'heresy' #ere++zi++a#<number# and *herético* 'heretical' #erɛ++tik+<o#<number#. The stem for ambivalent item 7, *cliente,* in contemporary Portuguese seems not to exist except in this word, which comes straight from Latin. That is, the suffix –*ente* seems to suggest that *cliente* is derived from a verb (cf. *crer* 'to believe' *crente* 'believer'), but there is no corresponding verb for *cliente*. There is only one form derived from *cliente*, *clientela* 'clientele'.

Again, the words in Table 6.14 acquire their meanings through the combination of their roots and their gender morpheme, which makes all these items derived nouns.[26]

**§6.1.4.3.1** The *Aurélio* contains 15,242 nouns that end in -e.[27] A great many adjectives[28] use +e# as their gender morpheme when modifying either [-feminine] or [+feminine] singular or plural nouns as in Table 6.15.

**Table 6.15** Ambivalent -e in Adjectives

| | [-feminine] | | | [+feminine] | | |
|---|---|---|---|---|---|---|
| | [-plural] | [+plural] | Gloss | [-plural] | [+plural] | Gloss |
| 1 | livro verde | livros verdes | green book(s) | casa verde | casas verdes | green house(s) |
| 2 | carro grande | carros grandes | big car(s) | mãe grande | mães grandes | big mother(s) |
| 3 | moço alegre | moços alegres | happy boy(s) | moça alegre | moças alegres | happy girl(s) |
| 4 | boi doente | bois doentes | sick ox(en) | vaca doente | vacas doentes | sick cow(s) |
| 5 | bago edule | bagos edules | edible berry(s) | flor edule | flores edules | edible flowers |
| 6 | morro íngreme | morros íngremes | steep hill(s) | rua íngreme | ruas íngremes | steep street(s) |
| 7 | grupo triste | grupos tristes | sad group(s) | cara triste | caras tristes | sad face(s) |

In Table 6.15, it is obvious that the structure of these adjectives is the same as that for all nominals. The only difference is that these adjectives (and many more like them) do not reflect the gender of the nouns they modify. Put another way, the same form of the adjective can modify either feminine or non-feminine nouns. Because most adjectives are inflected for the gender of whatever noun or entity they modify, their gender morphemes will be <o#, <a#, <e#, <e+ (§6.2.5.6.5) and

26 Several of these words' roots can be roots for verbs when they are followed by the 1st conjugation theme vowel +a#: *lançar* 'to throw', *matar* 'to kill', *passar* 'to pass', *picar* 'to bite', *aportar* 'to come to port', *aporrear* 'to bludgeon', *topar* 'to find'.

27 Compare this with the 32,269 nouns that end in –a and the 30,877 that end in –o. The count of the words ending in –o, did not include those ending in –ção or -são because lexically the forms of many of those words do not end in <o# or +o#<number#.

28 The *Aurélio* often considers its adjectives to double as nouns, so that the figure 15,242 includes many adjectives.

<u#. Others bear gender morphemes that are invariant and, thus, attached to their stems as +e# or +e+. (The latter evanesces in word-final position.)

**§6.1.4.4** There is yet another set of nominal vocabulary where the gender morpheme <e+ is not obvious, at least in the non-feminine non-plural form of these words, as in Table 6.16.

**Table 6.16** Occult <e$_{[\text{-feminine}]}$+< [-plural]#

| | [-feminine] | | | [+feminine] | | |
|---|---|---|---|---|---|---|
| | [-plural] | [+plural] | Gloss | [-plural] | [+plural] | Gloss |
| 1 | burguês | burgueses | bourgeois | burguesa | burguesas | female bourgeois |
| 2 | cantor | cantores | singer(s) | cantora | cantoras | female singer(s) |
| 3 | espanhol | espanhóis | Spaniard(s) | espanhola | espanholas | Spanish woman (women) |
| 4 | general | generais | general(s) | generala | generalas | general(s)'(s) wife (wives) |
| 5 | inglês | ingleses | English | inglesa | inglesas | English woman (women) |
| 6 | pagador | pagadores | payer(s) | pagadora | pagadoras | female payer(s) |
| 7 | professor | professores | teacher(s) | professora | professoras | female teacher(s) |
| 8 | rapaz | rapazes | young man (men) | rapariga | raparigas | young woman (women) |
| 9 | zagal | zagais | live wire person(s) | zagala | zagalas | female live wire(s) |

The feminine forms (both singular and plural) in Table 6.16 are unremarkable when compared with the [+feminine] forms of Tables 6.2, 6.5, 6.8–6.10. And the presence of <e+ is obvious in the plural [-feminine] nouns (sets 1, 2, 5, 6, 7, 8).[29] The only aberrant forms are those of the [-feminine, -plural] category because they have no manifest gender morpheme.

**§6.1.5** Words like the [-feminine, -plural] nouns in Table 6.16 should be analyzed so as to include an underlying word-final gender morpheme <e+ because that would make them susceptible to Rule 3.1 (§3.1.0–1), which assigns regular (unmarked) paroxytone stress to

29 Chapter 9 (§9.3.2.0–l) addresses the loss of /l/ in the plural [-feminine] forms (rows 3, 4, and 9).

the majority of Portuguese words (cf. Table 3.4). Owing to the underlying <e+ in nominals such as these, 22,048[30] nouns and adjectives become regular as far as their stress is concerned, and they have the same underlying structure that other nominals have according to this analysis. Thus, words similar to *burguês*, *general*, and *professor* (items 1, 4, 7 of Table 6.16) would have the following underlying structure: #professor#<e+<[±plural]#, #burgez#<e+<[±plural]#, and #ženeral#<e+<[±plural]#.[31] Rule 6.2a accounts for the emergence of the superficially word-final consonant:

**Rule 6.2a Deletion of Word-Final <e+, +e+, +i+ after /r#, /l#, and /z#:[32]**

$$\begin{bmatrix} < \\ + \end{bmatrix} \begin{pmatrix} +\text{palatal} \\ -\text{contoid} \end{pmatrix} \rightarrow \emptyset \;/\; \#X\,[-\text{contoid}] \begin{pmatrix} +\text{contoid} \\ -\text{surd} \\ -\text{labial} \\ -\text{high} \\ -\text{nasal} \\ -\text{occlusion} \end{pmatrix} \_\_ + <[-\text{plural}]\#$$

30 According to the *Aurélio*, there are 3,557 overtly oxytone nominals ending in –or, 2,652 ending in –al, 1944 ending in –el, 192 ending in –il, 285 ending in –ol, 84 ending in –ul, and 455 ending in –z. Add to these the 11,482 infinitives ending in –ar, the 719 ending in–er, and the 678 ending in –ir for a total of 22,048 nominals for which the gender morpheme is <e+.

31 The stems of all these words are morphologically complex; however, their complexity does not bear on their relationship with the inflecting suffixes <e+<number#.

32 In effect, Rule 6.2a deletes any palatal vowel in the gender morpheme position. It turns out (Appendix 9C) that the vowel /i/ occurs in the gender slot after a mutation in the suffix +ibil#+e+. The final morpheme boundary on the [-feminine] morpheme <e+, etc. could be considered redundant, because it disappears word-finally in circumstances in which the stem-final consonant could close a syllable. However, it does not evanesce in the 'subject' pronoun *ele* 'he' and in the demonstrative *aquele* 'that, 3rd person domain' even though it is inflectional in both cases <e#. Similarly, the deriving suffix +e+ and +e# stand in contrast in stem-final [+nasal] circumstances (cf. Tables 6.17 and 6.21).

Rule 6.2a deletes any instance of a word-final /e+ after stem-final /l, z, r/ (specified as [+contoid], etc.)[33] when they occur in a [-plural] context.[34] It operates on a large class of nominals (nouns, adjectives, and infinitives), and this rule operates because /l, z, r/ are three of the four phonemes that can close a word-final syllable.[35] There are, nonetheless, other nominals whose word-final –e̱ remains in their [-feminine, -plural] forms notwithstanding their stems' ending in /r/, /z/, or /l/. Table 6.17 contains some examples:

**Table 6.17** Nominals Immune to Rule 6.2a[a]

| /re# | | | /ze# | | | /le# | | |
|---|---|---|---|---|---|---|---|---|
| [-plural] | [+plural] | Gloss | [-plural] | [+plural] | Gloss | [-plural] | [+plural] | Gloss |
| donaire | donaires | grace(s) | doze | dozes | dozen(s) | xale | xales | shawl(s) |
| árvore | árvores | tree(s) | crise | crises | crisis (es) | vale | vales | valley(s) |
| freire | freires | friar(s) | frase | frases | phrase(s) | prole | proles | offspring |

a The *Aurélio* contains some 1,881 nouns of this nature: /Vre# 282, /Vze# 1,208, /Vle# 391. The sequence /Vre# contains numerous items whose final e̱ is stressed, both as [ˈɛ] and [ˈe]. They are largely loan words from indigenous Amerindian or African languages.

All the words in Table 6.17 are nouns with intrinsic gender: *árvore*, *crise*, *frase*, and *prole* are [+feminine], whereas *donaire*, *freire*, *doze*, *xale* and *vale* are [-feminine]. The word-final gender morpheme in Table 6.17 is +e#, a deriving morpheme. Save for the nominals ending in #XVn+<e# and +e# (§6.2.3.0–2.1), the inflectional peculiarities of all but the problematic open-ended nominals have been addressed. Before addressing the grammatical nominals, §6.1.6 takes stock of the work up to this point.

---

33 The specification [-surd] eliminates /p, t, k, f, s, š/ as stem-final consonants. Were these consonants stem-final, a following vowel would emerge. The specification [-labial] eliminates /b, m, v/; [-high], /k, g, ž, ɲ/; [-nasal] /n/; [-occlusive], /d/; and [-delayed transition] /ṟ/. In other words, this rule only applies to <e# when it follows a stem-final /l, z, r/.

34 Rule 6.2a deletes the final /e+ in the future subjunctive morpheme and in the infinitive that compounds with finite forms of *haver* 'to have' to form future and conditional tenses (§13.5.2.0–§13.5.3.3). The environment for /e+'s deletion is [-plural] because in the nominal context <Ø# after the gender morpheme identifies [-plural]; however, <Ø# in some verbal contexts identifies 1st and 3rd person singular (See Table 13.11).

35 The +e# (or <e#) always remains on words where /r/ and /z/ are preceded by a consonant, e.g.: *bagre* 'bullhead', *catre* 'cot'; *bronze* 'bronze' and *urze* 'heather'.

**§6.1.6** The open-ended nominals are divided into four classes: N—nouns, adjectives, and infinitives that consist of stems followed by gender and number morphemes and undergo no morphophonemic alterations other than the loss of the gender morpheme <e+ or +e+ word-finally when preceded by /r, l, z/. $N_1$ nominals are those whose tonic /ɔ/ mutates to [o] in singular, non-feminine nominals. $N_2$ are those nominals whose ending, +a# appears on [-feminine] nouns and adjectives. $N_3$ nominals end in +a# and can have [±feminine] referents. $N_4$ nominals [-feminine, -plural] retain +e#, even when the stem-final consonant (/r, l, z, n/) could constitute a syllable coda. Nominal gender is [±feminine], number is [±plural]. The only plural morpheme <z# is inflectional. The gender morphemes are both inflectional and derivational: <o# ([-feminine]) and +o# (usually [-feminine]), <a# ([+feminine]) and +a# (usually [+feminine], but often ambivalent, and sometimes [-feminine]), <u# ([-feminine]) and +u# (usually [-feminine]), <e# (usually [-feminine]) and <e+ ([-feminine]), +e# (idiomatic), +e+ (idiomatic[36]).

## The Morphophonological Structure of Grammatical Nominals

**§6.2.0** Table 6.18 demonstrates the structure of Portuguese grammatical nominals:

**Table 6.18** The Structure of Inflected Paradigmatic Nominals

| | [-feminine] | | [+feminine] | |
|---|---|---|---|---|
| | [-plural] | [+plural] | [-plural] | [+plural] |
| Definite Article | o cachorro | os cachorros | a cachorra | as cachorras |
| | #l+<o><Ø> | #l+<o><z> | #l+<a><Ø> | #l+<a><z> |
| Indefinite Article | um cachorro | uns cachorros | uma cachorra | umas cachorras |
| | #un+<e+<Ø# | #un+<e+<z# | #un+<a#<Ø# | #un+<a#<z# |
| Demonstrative Pronoun | esse cachorro | esses cachorros | essa cachorra | essas cachorras |
| | #es+<e#<Ø# | #es+<e#<z# | #es+<a#<Ø# | #es+<a#<z# |
| Nominative Pronoun | ele | eles | ela | elas |
| | #el+<e#<Ø# | #el+<e#<z# | #el+<a#<Ø# | #el+<a#<z# |
| Objective Pronoun | quero-o | quero-os | quero-a | quero-as |
| | <l+<o#<Ø# | <l+<o#<z# | <l+<a#<Ø# | <l+<a#<z# |
| Possessive Pronoun | nosso cachorro | nossos cachorros | nossa cachorra | nossas cachorras |
| | #nɔs+<o#<Ø# | #nɔs+<o#<z# | #nɔs+<a#<Ø# | #nɔs+<a#<z# |

36 'Idiomatic' = arbitrary.

**§6.2.1.0** These nominals all belong to closed sets or paradigms, i.e. each category contains a relatively small set of items whose memberships are extremely unlikely to increase and whose members are organized according to grammatical persons: 1st, 2nd, and 3rd, singular and plural. The nominative and objective pronouns also include 1st and 2nd person pronouns that are not inflected. And, different from the other nominals, all these forms' use in particular utterances is dependent on actual nouns and their particular gender and number. The use of grammatical nominals also depends on pragmatic circumstances: e.g. whether the noun they stand for has been used before in a particular interchange or discourse as well as the location of speaker, hearer, and the referent of the grammatical nominal in question. And, as the morpheme boundaries indicate, many of them have restricted distribution: the definite articles must precede nominals, and the object pronouns normally follow verbs. Table 6.19 displays the first class of grammatical nominals, the definite and indefinite article.

**Table 6.19** The Structure of Articles

| **The Definite Article—Structure: #l+<gender><[±plural]>** | | | | |
|---|---|---|---|---|
| | **[-feminine]** | | **[+feminine]** | |
| | **[-plural]** | **[+plural]** | **[-plural]** | **[+plural]** |
| **Orthography:** | o | os | a | as |
| **Analysis:** | **#l+<o><Ø>** | **#l+<o><z>** | **#l+<a><Ø>** | **#l+<a><z>** |
| **Realizations:** | [ŭ], [lŭ], [nŭ] | [ŭš], [lŭš] [nŭš] [a] | [ă], [lă], [nă] | [ăš], [lăš], [năš] |
| **The Indefinite Article—Structure: #un+<gender#<[±plural](#)** | | | | |
| **Orthography** | um | uns | uma | umas |
| **Analysis** | **#un#<e+<Ø#** | **#un#<e+<z#** | **#un#<a#<Ø#** | **#un#<a#<z#** |
| **Realizations** | [ũ] | [ũš] | [ũ.mă], [ũ.ă] | [ũ.măš], [ũ.ăš] |

a The [+plural] transcriptions represent pronunciations in isolation, before a pause or before a voiceless consonant.

**§6.2.1.1** The underlying structures of the two forms in Table 6.19 need to be explained. The definite article is preceded by # in order to indicate that it may begin utterances such as *Os estudantes dormem* 'The students sleep'. Because it cannot end an utterance, or even follow the nominal it modifies, the definite article is always followed by >, which indicates that the nominal it specifies must follow (see

Table 5.2b).[37] The indefinite article begins and ends with a word boundary (#) because it can begin and end an utterance: *Uma dormiu* 'One slept' and *Quero umas* 'I want some'.

§6.2.2.0 **The Definite Article:** Superficially, this form appears to be a simple sequence of gender morphemes followed by number morphemes, but its lexical form begins with #l+, which is its root. The definite article as well as the 3rd person nominative pronoun derive from the Latin demonstrative *ĭllum* 'that'. The first half of which (ĭl) became the 3rd person pronoun *ele* (cf. Williams, 139–42), and the second half became *lo* (i.e. *lum*→*lo*). In old Portuguese, the /l/ in the definite article appeared after prepositions ending in consonants: e.g. *sobolo*[38] (from *superlo*) 'above the' (Williams, 93, 142); *hulas provas* (*ub las provas*) 'where [is] the proof?'; after imperatives *Vedela frol* 'Behold the flower'; after inflected participles *passadallas tres partes* '[with] three parts gone by' and after the form *todos* 'all' *todolos dias* 'every day' (Williams, 141).[39] In contemporary Portuguese, the definite article's /l/ emerges when it follows the preposition *por*, which occurs as [pe] in this instance: *Pel<u>a</u> alma de minha mãe* 'by the soul of my mother', *Fico pel<u>o</u> Catete* 'I stay somewhere in the Catete

37 This is the case whether or not the article is inflected for plurality. Remarkably, the specified nominal need not follow directly after the definite or indefinite article. Nominal phrase structure allows many intervening items between articles and nouns: O *amigo* 'the friend', *o meu amigo* 'my friend', *o meu velho amigo* 'my old friend' *o meu querido velho amigo* 'my dear old friend', *o meu muito querido velho amigo* 'my very dear old friend'. Contrariwise, the indefinite article allows some intervening words between it and the noun it modifies. However, noun phrases begin to sound ungrammatical the more intervening items emerge between the indefinite article and the noun in question: e.g. *um amigo* 'a friend', *um meu amigo* a friend of mine', *?*um meu velho amigo* 'an old friend of mine', *?*um meu querido velho amigo* 'a dear old friend of mine', *?*um meu muito querido velho amigo* 'a very dear old friend of mine'. Were the possessive *meu* put at the end of the noun phrases containing the indefinite article, they would cease to be problematic: *um velho amigo meu* 'an old friend of mine' *um querido velho amigo meu* 'a dear old friend of mine', *um muito querido velho amigo meu* 'a very dear old friend of mine' are perfectly acceptable.

38 In modern Portuguese, *sobre o*.

39 *Hu* 'where' has been replaced by *onde*. In contemporary Portuguese, the other phrases are: *vede a flor*; *passadas as três partes*, and *todos os dias*.

neighborhood [in Rio]', *Dorme pelas praias do Recife* '3rd sleeps somewhere along the beaches of Recife'.

**§6.2.2.1** In contemporary speech and writing, the word *mais* 'more' is also used as a preposition: *Quer mais um?* 'Do you want one more?' In some European Portuguese's speech and writing *mais*, with its final /z/, occasions the surfacing of the definite article's underlying #l+; *Ele mai-los outros bebem vinho* 'He plus the others drink wine'.[40]

**§6.2.2.2** The underlying #l+ in the definite article occasions the loss of the /e/ in the preposition *em* 'in, on' and its underlying /n/'s surfacing: *em* + def. article, i.e. #en>#l+<o><Ø> ➔ [nŭ], #en<#l+<a><Ø> ➔ [nă], #en<#l+<o><z> ➔ [nŭš], #en>#l+<a><z> ➔ [năš] (Williams 141). Two rules are necessary to account for these phenomena:

**Rule 6.3 Loss of #e/ in #en>:**

$$\begin{pmatrix}\text{-contoid}\\ \text{+palatal}\\ \text{-high}\\ \text{-wide glottis}\end{pmatrix} \rightarrow \emptyset\ /\ \#\_\_\ \ n>\#l+<[\pm\text{feminine}]\#<[\pm\text{plural}]>$$

Rule 6.3 deletes the /e/ of #en> before the definite article.

**Rule 6.4 Progressive Assimilation of #l+:**

$$\begin{pmatrix}\text{+lateral}\\ \text{-high}\end{pmatrix} \rightarrow \begin{pmatrix}\text{-lateral}\\ \text{+nasal}\end{pmatrix} / \begin{pmatrix}\text{+contoid}\\ \text{+nasal}\end{pmatrix} >\#\_\_\ +[\pm\text{feminine}]\#<[\pm\text{plural}]>$$

After Rule 6.4 changes article-initial #l+ to #n+, Rule 4.1, Like-Segment deletion, deletes the second /n/.

**§6.2.2.3** Finally, in addition to the historical evidence and the (admittedly rare) emergence of the definite article's #l+ in contemporary Portuguese, the presence of underlying #l+ in the definite article gives it

40 The /l/ need not surface, however. Jucá (402) exemplifies the use of *mais* as a preposition with the sentence *Ela esteve aqui mais o filho* 'She was here with her son' where the definite article's #l+ does not emerge. The *Aurélio* considers the word *mais* to be an adverb, adjective, noun, preposition, conjunction, and an indefinite pronoun. All make sense except their notion of 'indefinite pronoun'.

a discrete root, which makes its structure jibe with that of all the other nominals. The definite article is not merely a sequence of gender and number morphemes, and Rule 6.5 governs its forms:

**Rule 6.5 Deletion of #l+ Except After Prepositions:**

$$\#\begin{pmatrix}+\text{lateral}\\ -\text{high}\end{pmatrix} + /\_<[\pm\text{feminine}]><[\pm\text{plural}] \rightarrow \varnothing - \left\{\begin{matrix}\#\text{por}\\ \#\text{maiz}\\ \#\text{en}\end{matrix}\right\} > \_\_$$

**§6.2.2.4** Rule 6.5 deletes the #l+ of the definite article everywhere ***except*** (-) after these three prepositions.[41] It is not useful to write a rule using phonological features to identify these three prepositions, because whatever rule one might concoct to achieve #l+'s preservation, would still have to stipulate that it only occurred consistently after *em* and *por.*

**§6.2.2.5** The transformations entailed in converting *em* + definite article (e.g. #en>#l+<o><z> → #n><o#<z>) parallel those affecting the 3rd person direct object when it follows a verb ending in <n# (§6.2.5.3.2).

**§6.2.3.0 The Indefinite Article:** Table 6.1 shows that the indefinite article can be a noun and can be the subject and object of a verb, and the object of prepositions. When it performs these functions, it is a full-fledged noun with stress on its underlying #u/. The root of the indefinite article is #un#, even though the consonant rarely surfaces as [n] in the indefinite article.[42] In the [-feminine] forms, the /n/'s usual manifestation is the nasal resonance the /u/ receives, although there may be some assimilatory contoidal realizations at the end of the [-feminine, -plural] indefinite article owing to a following stop consonant (§2.2.1.1). However, issues in the Portuguese writing system and in the indefinite article's allomorphy merit the following excursus.

**§6.2.3.1.0** It is a convention of the Portuguese writing system that word-final /n/ is represented as m. Table 6.20 demonstrates this convention, as well as the identity of the stem-final consonant as /n/ in these cases:

---

41 The same form-final consonants that occur in these prepositions (/z/, /n/, /r/ ) also occasion <l+'s preservation in direct object pronouns (§6.2.5.3.0–2).

42 This morpheme #un# has the allomorph #un+, which occurs in the root of *único* 'unique' and *unir* 'to unite', where it surfaces as [un].

**Table 6.20** The Maintenance of Stem-Final /n/ in Selected [+feminine] Forms

| [-feminine] | | | [+feminine] | | |
|---|---|---|---|---|---|
| **[-plural]** | **[+plural]** | **Gloss** | **[-plural]** | **[+plural]** | **Gloss** |
| **botim** | **botins** | ankle boot(s) | **botina** | **botinas** | ankle boot(s)[a] |
| **comum** | **comuns** | common | **comuna** | **comunas** | commune(s) |
| **malandrim**[b] | **malandrins** | low-life (lives) | **malandrina** | **malandrinas** | low-life female(s) |
| **mandarim** | **mandarins** | Mandarin(s) | **mandarina** | **mandarinas** | Mandarins (+f.) |
| **paladim** | **paladins** | paladin(s) | **paladina** (adj.) | **paladinas** (adj.) | paladin(s) (+f.) |
| **vintém** | **vinténs** | 20 reis coin(s) | **vintena** | **vintenas** | group(s) of 20 |

a For women and children (Portugal).
b Both *maladrim* and *paladim* have vowel-final alternates: *malandrino* and *paladino*.

When these words' roots occur with the feminine gender morpheme <a# (or +a# in the case of *botim*, *comum*, and *vintena* to form different words), the /n/ surfaces, be the forms singular or plural. And this should be the case for the indefinite article, but, in fact, it may emerge with a root-final [m] in its [+feminine] forms. Beyond the possibility that pronunciations such as [ˈũ.mă] may have originated owing to the printed word's influence, the usual explanation for this /n/'s realization as [m] is that /u/'s labiality has caused the /n/ to assimilate to its point of articulation and become a labial realized as [m].[43] The informal pronunciation [ˈũ.ă][44] is worthy of remark because words whose stems end in /n/ usually preserve the /n/ in their [+feminine] reflexes as Table 6.20 has demonstrated.

**§6.2.3.1.1** The reason the /n/ of the indefinite article can lose its contoidal articulation leaving nasal resonance on the preceding stressed /u/ comes from this grammatically governed form's ubiquity in ordinary usage. Because of its frequency of occurrence, its vague meaning and, especially, its dependence on the gender and number of the nouns it modifies, the indefinite article's contribution to sentences' semantic content is often minimal, hence its emergent form is reducible. Save

43 See below (§6.2.5.6.3–4) for similar phenomena related to the [+feminine] form of the 1st person possessive pronoun.

44 [ũ.ă] is an acceptable albeit casual pronunciation for this form's use as a definite article, whereas as a pronoun it is much more likely to be [ˈũ.mă].

*comum*, the words in Table 6.20 are hardly common and nowhere near as predictable in their occurrence as indefinite articles are; therefore, there is a premium for greater transparency in their marked, i.e. [+feminine] forms.[45]

**§6.2.3.2.0** The indefinite article's [+feminine] gender marking (singular or plural) is not terribly problematic. It is <a#, the same morpheme that occurs in myriad nominals. The surfacing of /n+/ as [m] or as mere nasal resonance on the #u/ have both phonotactic and pragmatic/semantic explanations. However, the non-feminine forms also present a challenge since their surface manifestations conform neither to the majority of [-feminine] nominals nor to those with an 'occult' <e+ in the [-feminine, -plural] forms of words such as those in Table 6.16. There, the <e+ fails to emerge only in the [-feminine, -plural] forms, whereas with #un- (and in all words ending in Vm, i.e. /vn#<e+, /vn#+e+), <e+ and +e+ fail to surface in both singular and plural [-feminine] forms. The 1,035 nominals whose singular non-feminine forms end in Vm pertain to a minority class of words, and they pertain to such a class by virtue of their ending in Vn#{<,+}e+<[-plural]#. Rule 6.2a for the deletion of <e+ in nominals must be followed by Rule (6.2b), which deletes <e+ and +e+ in all [-feminine] forms of words ending in Xn#{+,<}e+<[±plural]#:

**Rule 6.2b Deletion of Word-Final <e+, +e+, (and +ɛ#) after /n#:**

$$\begin{pmatrix} -\text{contoid} \\ -\text{high} \\ -\text{delayed transition} \\ +\text{palatal} \end{pmatrix} \rightarrow \varnothing \;/\; \#\,X \begin{pmatrix} +\text{contoid} \\ +\text{nasal} \\ -\text{labial} \\ -\text{high} \end{pmatrix} \#_{[\text{-N4}]}$$

Rule 6.2b deletes posttonic /e/ (and /ɛ/ vacuously) after /n# both when the lexical item in question is singular or plural. It operates on the indefinite article only when its gender is [-feminine]. It operates on all nominals—save those nominals in class $N_4$, which maintain word-final /e/ after /n/ as in Table 6.21 below.

45 Because these words are rare in common speech, their articulation is much more likely to be more faithful to their phonemic configuration than common or function words' pronunciation would be.

**§6.2.3.2.1** This analysis of the Portuguese indefinite article (and the two rules of <e+ and +e+ deletion) links its underlying structure to overall nominal structure. This analysis has also made the indefinite article's instantiation as a pronoun (*Quero um* 'I want one') susceptible to the paroxytone stress rule because it is preceded and followed by word boundaries: #un#<e+<[±plural]#. And the reason that <e+ is deleted in the plural [-feminine] forms is because the sequence /nz/ is a fairly common word-internal coda in Portuguese (§4.5.0, Table 4.10).[46]

**§6.2.3.2.2** There is, similar to the words in Table 6.15, a set of words that end in ne, i.e. adjectives and nouns, that do not lose their gender morpheme in singulars or plurals. Table 6.21 contains a representative sample:

**Table 6.21** Nominals Ending in Xn++e# Immune to Rule 6.2b[a]

| [-feminine] Nouns | | | [+feminine] Nouns | | | Ambivalent Adjectives | | |
|---|---|---|---|---|---|---|---|---|
| [-plural] | [+plural] | Gloss | [-plural] | [+plural] | Gloss | [-plural] | [+plural] | Gloss |
| gene | genes | gene(s) | **higiene** | **higienes** | hygiene(s) | **inane** | **inanes** | inane |
| **cânone** | **cânones** | canon(s) | **mitene** | mitenes | mitten(s) | **perene** | **perenes** | perennial |
| **sene** | **senses** | senna(s) | **alcione** | **alciones** | halcyon(s) | **imune** | **imunes** | immune |

a The *Aurélio* contains 291 nouns of this type.

Words of the sort displayed in Table 6.21 are of a somewhat refined, erudite, or recondite nature. Their pre-gender phoneme /n/ is followed by + rather than #, which makes them immune to rule 6.2b. There are at least 291 words of this sort, and they can be added to the 1,881 words already considered immune to rule 6.2a, giving that exceptional class ($N_4$) 2,171 members. The allomorphy of Portuguese articles has been accounted for. Next comes the allomorphy of the pronouns that can be subjects.[47]

**§6.2.4.0** Table 6.22 contains the pronouns that can be verbal subjects:

46 There are at least 1,747 words, many of which are common, with /nz# plurals. Thus, the [-feminine] forms of #un# are not aberrant.

47 Some of which can also be objects of prepositions and direct objects.

**Table 6.22** The Subject Pronouns of Portuguese

| | | | | | |
|---|---|---|---|---|---|
| **Singular** | | | | | |
| **Persons:** | **1st** | **2nd S** | **2nd S** | **2nd F** | **3rd[a]** |
| **[-plural]** | **eu** | **tu** | **você** | **o senhor** | **ele** |
| **Analysis** | #eu# | #tu# | #vɔsˈe#<Ø# | #l+<o><Ø>#seɲor#<e+<Ø# | #el+<e#<Ø# |
| **Gloss:** | I | thou | you | you | he/him |
| **Plural** | | | | | |
| **Persons:** | **1st** | **2nd S** | **2nd S** | **2nd F** | **3rd** |
| **[+plural]** | **nós** | **vós** | **vocês** | **os senhores** | **eles** |
| **Analysis** | #nɔz# | #vɔz# | #vɔsˈe#<z# | #l+<o><z>#seɲor#<e+<z# | #el+<e#<z# |
| **Gloss:** | we | ye | you | you | they/them |

a The 3rd person forms (i.e. [-1st, -2nd] person) are the unmarked case in pronouns. Whereas they are formally specified as [-1st, -2nd], for convenience and out of tradition this treatise refers to them as 3rd person.

For readers unfamiliar with Portuguese, Table 6.22 contains data that require explanation.

**§6.2.4.1 Subject Pronouns:** These items are subject pronouns rather than nominative pronouns because all (save *eu* and *tu*) can also be objects of prepositions.

**§6.2.4.2 2nd Person Pronouns:** The 2nd person pronouns, *tu* and *vós*, are identified as S for 'solidarity'. Their use indicates a special relationship between speaker and addressee. The pronoun *você* and its plural form indicate a 2nd person with whom the speakers do not necessarily have any solidarity.[48] The noun phrases used as forms of address *o*(*s*) *senhor*(*es*) are labelled F to indicate a formal, deferential 2nd person form. This form can be inflected for [+feminine] gender and plurality: *a*(*s*) *senhora*(*s*).

**§6.2.4.3.0 3rd Person Pronouns:** The 3rd person pronouns can be inflected for plurality and for [+feminine] gender and are almost totally transparent. Their number morpheme is <z#, and their [-feminine] gender morpheme is <e#, which, contrary to that morpheme in occult paroxytone nominals (<e+, Table 6.16) does not disappear when word-final. Thus, the 3rd person subject pronoun pertains to class $N_4$ because it does not lose <e# when this morpheme is followed by [-plural], i.e. <Ø#.

**§6.2.4.3.1** The root vowel of the 3rd person subject pronoun does exhibit metaphony, however. In the [+feminine] forms, the root vowel

48 For many Brazilians, it is the unmarked 2nd person. For the Portuguese, *você*(*s*) can have a derogatory connotation.

is /ɛ/, whereas it is /e/ in the [-feminine] forms. The root vowel of the 3rd person pronoun is /e/ rather than /ɛ/ because: (A) The regular reflex of Latin /ĭ/ (*ele* derives from the 1st half of the demonstrative *ĭllum*) is /e/. (B) The <a# of the feminine forms is more likely to exert a lowering on the root's /e/ than an underlying /e/ realized atonically as [ə] or [ĭ] is to exert a raising influence on an underlying /ɛ/. Table 6.23 shows the figures for F1 and F2 of the vowels in question.

**Table 6.23** Formant Values: Tonic /e/ and /ɛ/, Atonic /a/ and /e/[a]

| | Tonic | | Atonic /e/ and /ɛ/ | | Atonic /a/ |
|---|---|---|---|---|---|
| | /e/ | /ɛ/ | [i] | [ə] | [ă] |
| F1 | 333 | 437 | 300 | 416 | 437 |
| F2 | 1,662 | 1,602 | 1,700 | 1,115 | 1,318 |

a Since /e/'s F1 is 333Hz, the F1 (437Hz) of [ă] (post-tonic /a/) would be most likely to cause /e/'s F1 to rise to around 437Hx (i.e. the F1 of /ɛ/). Since /ɛ/'s F2 is 1,662Hz, its lowering to around 1,602 could be occasioned by a following [ă], whereas [i]'s F2 would cause /ɛ/'s F2 to rise. Since [ă]'s F2 is 203Hz higher than [ə]'s, and the lowering of /e/'s F2 from 1,662Hz to 1,602Hz is hardly radical, the evidence points toward the [+feminine] gender morpheme's occasioning the /e/ → /ɛ/ metaphony of the pronominal root. (The frequencies in Table 6.23 are averages of the values Delgado Martins (66, 68) compiled for the vowels in question.)

The same phenomenon occurs in demonstrative pronouns. Rule 6.6a governs subject pronoun root vowel metaphony:

**Rule 6.6a Subject Pronoun Root Vowel Metaphony:**

$$\begin{pmatrix} \text{-contoid} \\ \text{-high} \\ \text{-wide glottis} \\ \text{+palatal} \end{pmatrix} \rightarrow [\text{+wide glottis}] \,/\, \#\_\_\ C < [\text{+feminine}]_{[\text{Pronoun: -1st,-2nd}]}$$

Rule 6.6a changes the root vowel of the 3rd person pronoun from /e/ to /ɛ/ when the pronoun is inflected for feminine gender. This exhausts the subject pronouns' morphophonological peculiarities and processes. Next come the peculiarities of Portuguese demonstratives.

§**6.2.4.3.0** Table 6.24 displays the Portuguese demonstrative pronouns:

**Table 6.24** Portuguese Demonstratives

| | **Inflected** | | |
|---|---|---|---|
| | **1st Person** | **2nd Person** | **[-1st, -2nd]** |
| [-f., -pl.] | este | esse | aquele |
| [-f., +pl.] | estes | esses | aqueles |
| | [ˈeš.tə] / [ˈeš.təš] | [ˈe.sə] / [ˈe.səš] | [ă.ˈke.lə] /[ă.ˈke.ləš] |
| [+f., -pl.] | esta | essa | aquela |
| [+f., +pl.] | estas | essas | aquelas |
| | [ˈɛš.tă] / [ˈɛš.tăš] | [ˈɛ.să] / [ˈɛ.săš] | [ă.ˈkɛ.lă] /[ă.ˈkɛ.lăš] |
| Structure | #ezt+<[±f.]#<[±pl.]# | #es+<[±f.]#<[±pl.]# | #akel+<[±f.]#<[±pl.]# |
| Gloss | this/these | that/those | that/those |
| | **Neuter** | | |
| | isto | isso | aquilo |
| Structure | #izto# | #iso# | #akilo# |

Portuguese demonstrative pronouns are remarkable in many different ways. They are deictic, which means that they refer to items with respect to their location relative to addresser and addressee. The 1st person form can indicate an item pertaining only to the addresser: *este teclado que estou usando* 'this keyboard I'm using', or to an inclusive 1st person plural: *esta bicicleta que estamos montando* 'this bicycle we're riding'. The 2nd person form indicates an item within the realm of the addressee to the exclusion of both 1st and 3rd person: *Esses olhos me fascinam* 'Those eyes [of yours] fascinate me' *essas noções que vocês têm* 'those notions you people have'.[49] The 3rd person ([-1st, -2nd]) forms denote objects that are beyond the reach or scope of either addresser or addressee: *Aquele rapaz fuma* 'That young man [yonder] smokes', *Aqueles picapaus destruíram a porta* 'Those woodpeckers [yonder] destroyed our door'. In addition, Portuguese has neuter demonstratives, as well as one neuter noun: *tudo* 'all'. These forms never modify specific nouns, rather they indicate objects or circumstances whose gender

---

49 At least in speech, Brazilians merge the 1st and 2nd person demonstratives and use *esse*, etc. for both fields of reference.

and number are difficult or impossible to identify: *Que é isto?* 'What is [all] this? What's going on?'; *Isso que você diz é mentira* 'What [all] you say is a lie'. *Aquilo na Arizona horroriza* 'What [went on] in Arizona is horrible', *Quero tudo* 'I want everything' (cf. *Quero todo* 'I want all [of it]'). Because of the small number of neuter forms, [+neuter] is, in this grammar, a lexical characteristic of these words rather than a grammatical gender.[50] As such they have no actual morphological makeup, even though their final vowel /o/ [ŭ] is homophonous with the <o# (or +o#) that indicate non-feminine gender.

**§6.2.4.3.1** The demonstratives are transparent, just like the articles and 3rd person subject pronouns. The <e# remains on [-feminine] forms in singular or plural instantiations. This is not a problem for this grammar because: (A) The root-final consonants of the 1st and 2nd person forms are [+surd]; thus, these forms do not fit the structural description of rule 6.2a so the <e# remains. (B) The gender morpheme <e# remains on the 3rd person form #akel+<e#<Ø# because this form belongs to the $N_4$ class of nominals, i.e. those nominals that do not lose their ambivalent gender morpheme even when the stem-final consonant can close a syllable. The tonic root-vowel of all these forms is /e/, which, like the /e/ of the 3rd person nominative pronoun, lowers to /ɛ/ in the [+feminine] forms of the demonstrative: *esta(s)* [ˈɛš.tă(š)], *essa(s)* [ˈɛ.să(š)], *aquela(s)* [ă.ˈkɛ.lă(š)]. With a couple of additions to rule 6.6a, a new rule (6.6b) can control root vowel metaphony in both subject pronouns and demonstratives:

50 Were neuter nominals more prevalent in Portuguese, one could posit two genders [masculine] and [feminine]. Neuter words' gender would be specified as [-masculine, -feminine]. Indeed, one could be tempted to posit a neuter definite article #lo> for uses such as *O que quero é sair* 'What I want to do is leave', *O do outro dia foi maravilhoso* 'What happened the other day was marvelous'. Because this form [ŭ] is homophonous with the unmarked and default [-feminine, -plural] form of the definite article, such a posit is unnecessary since as the unmarked (non-committal) form of the definite article, it has great latitude in usage and interpretation.

**Rule 6.6b Subject Pronoun/Demonstrative Root Vowel Metaphony:**

$$\begin{pmatrix} \text{-contoid} \\ \text{-high} \\ \text{-wide glottis} \\ \text{+palatal} \end{pmatrix}^{51} \rightarrow [\text{+wide glottis}] \,/\, \#X\_\_\; C_{1\text{-}2} < [\text{+feminine}]_{[\text{Pronoun, Demonstrative}]}\#$$

Rule 6.6b, the new rule of pronominal /e/ metaphony, now allows for up to two consonants following the tonic root vowel and is specified for both pronouns and demonstratives. These two categories are $N_4$ nominals since they preserve the gender morpheme <e# in their [-feminine, -plural] forms. They exhibit stem-vowel metaphony accounted for by Rule 6.6b. This closes the case on Portuguese demonstratives, next in line are the direct object pronouns.

§6.2.5.0 Table 6.25 displays the Portuguese direct object pronouns:

**Table 6.25** The Accusative Pronouns of Portuguese and Their Structure

| Singular | | | | | |
|---|---|---|---|---|---|
| **Persons:** | $1^{st}$ | $2^{nd}$ S | $2^{nd}$ -S | $2^{nd}$ F | $3^{rd}$ |
| **[-plural]** | me | te | o, a | o, a | o, a |
| **Analysis** | <me# | <te# | <l+<o#<Ø# | | |
| **Gloss:** | I | thee | you | you | him/her |
| **Plural** | | | | | |
| **Persons:** | $1^{st}$ | $2^{nd}$ S | $2^{nd}$ –S | $2^{nd}$ F | $3^{rd}$ |
| **[+plural]** | nos[a] | vos | o, a | o, a | o, a |
| **Analysis** | <nɔz# | <vɔz# | <l+<o#<z# | | |
| **Gloss:** | us | eow | you | you | them |

a Notice that the phonemic makeup of the $1^{st}$ and $2^{nd}$ person plural object pronouns is the same as that of the subject pronouns (Table 6.22). The only difference is that the subject pronouns may begin or end an utterance (symbolized by # at their beginning and end), whereas the object pronouns begin with <, which symbolizes both their inability to begin an utterance and their immunity to stress. These pronouns end with # because they can be the final element in a sentence. The root vowel of <nɔz# and <vɔz# always emerges in accusative pronouns as [ŭ] owing to its atonicity.

---

51 Identifying the determinand of rule 6.6b as /e/ along with the specification $C_{1\text{-}2}$ limits Rule 6.6b's application to the $3^{rd}$ person subject pronouns and the demonstratives because they are the only ones containing stem vowel #e/ followed by consonants.

**§6.2.5.1** Just like the 1st and 2nd person subject pronouns, the 1st and 2nd person accusative pronouns are ambivalent as far as the referents' gender is concerned. There is, in addition, no morphological relationship between the singular and plural forms—in all cases they monomorphemic idioms.[52] As always, the 1st and 2nd persons are the marked pronominal cases, whereas the 3rd person forms are unmarked. In their structure, the accusative pronouns bear a < at their beginning to indicate that, at least in the rather formal register examined in this book, accusative pronouns may not begin an utterance.[53]

**§6.2.5.2** In independent clauses of positive declarative and imperative sentences, object pronouns follow verbs and verbals, other than the past participle. When the sentence is negative, object pronouns precede the verb, as they do in dependent clauses—this is the case for negative and positive dependent clauses. Likewise, when an infinitive with an object is itself the object of a preposition, the pronominal object may precede or follow the verb. Table 6.26 demonstrates object pronouns' positioning.

---

52 The pronouns *me* and *te* could be analyzed as <m+ <e# and #t+<e#-, i.e. as inflected for ambivalent gender. However, there is no compelling reason to consider these pronouns polymorphemic.

53 The pronouns *você(s)*, *o senhor*, etc. pertain to the class of open-ended nominals. They may function as both subjects and direct objects. And they are not the only way 2nd persons can be addressed. In Portugal, it is common to use a given name plus the definite article (e.g. o Artur or a Linda, 'the Arthur, the Linda') as the subject in direct address, and one may also use a professional title: *o senhor professor* 'the mister professor' to address an individual.

**Table 6.26** Pronoun Positioning

| Post-verbal[a] | | |
|---|---|---|
| **Grammar** | **Sentence** | **Gloss** |
| Declarative: | **Vejo-te.** | I see you. |
| Imperative | **Levantem-me.** | Pick me up. |
| Infinitive | **Posso ver-te.** | I can see you. |
| Gerundive | **Está ouvindo-nos.** | 3rd is hearing us. |
| **Pre-verbal** | | |
| **Grammar** | **Sentence** | **Gloss** |
| Neg. Declarative: | **Não te vejo.** | I don't see you. |
| Neg. Imperative: | **Não me levantem.** | Don't pick me up. |
| Prep>#infinitive.[b] | **Para te pedir.**[c] | So as to see you. |
| Neg. Gerundive: | **Não nos está ouvindo.** | 3rd isn't hearing us. |
| Dependent Clause: | **Sabes que te quero.** | You know I love you. |

a At least in speech, Brazilians prefer to place 1st and 2nd person object pronouns before verbs, be the verbs declarative, be they imperative. And these pronouns may begin an utterance. However, Brazilians rarely use the 3rd person accusative pronouns, and, to my knowledge, they do not place them at the beginning of a sentence.

b This preverbal position of the direct object pronoun is optional: *para poder pedir-te* is also possible.

c This comes from the Portuguese Nobel Prize–winning author José Saramago (324). Pre-infinitive placement of a direct object clitic may seem more Brazilian than Portuguese, yet this order of constituents is not rare in Saramago's writing.

In Table 6.26, 1st and 2nd person pronouns exemplify the positions accusative clitic pronouns can take because these pronouns, owing to their initial consonants' being (/t/, /m/, /n/), neither undergo morphophonemic variation nor do they occasion any in the verbs they follow.[54] The same cannot be said about the 3rd person pronouns. Their manifestations vary according to their position vis-à-vis the verbs of which they are the object, and they can trigger morphophonemic variation in the verbs as well.

**§6.2.5.3.0** The 3rd person direct object pronouns are homophonous with the definite articles. Both forms have the same root containing only the phoneme /l/, and both reflect the gender and number of the nouns they modify or represent. The only difference between the two

54 When <nɔz# occurs as a reflexive pronoun, it will cause the 1st person plural morpheme <moz# to lose its /z/: *vamo-nos* (Saramago, 234).

forms is the definite article's ability to begin a sentence and its inability to end one, whereas object pronouns may not begin a sentence, but they can end one. In addition, they have similar allomorphy: in specific environments their underlying /l/ surfaces. The definite article's /l/ emerges after specific prepositions, whereas the object pronoun's /l/ emerges after specific verb forms, as in Table 6.27a.

**Table 6.27a** The Allomorphy of <l+<[±feminine]#<[±plural]#

| | Loss of /l/ in <l+<[±feminine]#<[±plural]# | | | |
|---|---|---|---|---|
| | **Post-verbal** | **Gloss** | **Pre-verbal** | **Gloss** |
| 1 | **Como-os.** | I eat them. | **Sabes que os como.** | You know I eat them. |
| 2 | **Leva-a.** | 3rd carries her. | **Quero que a leve.** | I want 3rd to carry her. |
| | **Maintenance of /l/ in <l+<[±feminine]#<[±plural]#** | | | |
| | **Post infinitive** | **Gloss** | **Post 1st plural** | **Gloss** |
| 3 | **Vou comê-los.** | I shall eat them. | **Comemo-los.** | We eat them. |
| 4 | **Vai estudá-los.** | 3rd will study them. | **Estudamo-los.** | We study them. |
| 5 | **Vais ouvi-la.** | You'll hear her. | **Ouvimo-la.** | We hear her. |
| | **Post 2nd –plural** | **Gloss** | **Post 2nd +plural** | **Gloss** |
| 6 | **Ten-lo.** | You have it. | **Tende-lo.** | You [folks] have it. |
| 7 | **Estuda-lo.** | You study it. | **Estudai-lo.** | You [folks] study it. |
| 8 | **Ouve-la.** | You hear her. | **Ouvi-la.** | You [folks] hear her. |

**§6.2.5.3.1** The sentences in rows 1 and 2 demonstrate the loss of underlying <l+ when this pronoun occurs after a verb-final vowel or when it appears before a verb. This is similar to the loss of #l+ in the definite article because it loses its /l/ everywhere—except after the three prepositions that end in /r/ or /z/. And both phenomena arose owing to a general tendency in the evolution of Portuguese from Latin: the loss of intervocalic /l/ in ordinary words: *palum* ➔ *pau* 'stick', *dolōrem* ➔*dor* 'pain', *palam* ➔ *pá* 'shovel', and *pilam* ➔ *pia* 'sink'. In addition to the loss of #l+ and <l+ in intervocalic position, when there is no immediate grammatical relationship between either the definite article or the 3rd person direct object and the word preceding them, the /l/ also disappears, regardless of the words' endings. For example, in the pre-verbal direct object pronouns (row 2 above), the presence of a consonant-final subject before the object, i.e. *Quero que o mar a leve* 'I want the sea to carry her away' and *Quero que o algoz a leve*, 'I want the executioner to take her' the <l+ fails to surface, even though word-final /r/ and /z/

are precisely the phonemes that will occasion the emergence of the direct object's /l/, but only after a verb. In Table 6.27b the fifth column contains analyses of the items examined in both Table 6.27a and 6.27b.

**Table 6.27b** The Allomorphy of <l+<[±feminine]#<[±plural]# and Verbs

| | | | | |
|---|---|---|---|---|
| **Loss of /l/ in <l+<[±feminine]#<[±plural]#** | | | | |
| | **Post-verbal** | **Structure[a]** | **Pre-verbal** | **Structure** |
| 1 | **como-os.** | #komo#<l+<o#<z# | **... que os como.** | #ke><l+<o#<z##komo# |
| 2 | **leva-a.** | #leva#<l+<a#<Ø# | **... que a leve.** | #ke><l+<a#<Ø##lɛve# |
| **Maintenance of /l/ in <l+<[±feminine]#<[±plural]#** | | | | |
| | **Post 1st plural** | **Structure** | **Post 2nd –pl.** | **Structure** |
| 3 | **comemo-los.** | #komemoz#<l+<o#<z# | **ten-lo.** | #tenz#<l+<o#<Ø# |
| 4 | **estudamo-los.** | #eztudamoz#<l+<o#<z# | **estuda-lo.** | #eztudaz#<l+<o#<Ø# |
| 5 | **ouvimo-la.** | #ouvimoz#<l+<a#<Ø# | **ouve-lo.** | #ouviz#<l+<o#<Ø# |
| | **Post 2nd plural** | **Structure[b]** | **Post-infinitive** | **Structure** |
| 6 | tende-lo | #tendez#<l+<o#<Ø# | **... comê-los.** | #komer#+e+<l+<o#<z# |
| 7 | estudai-lo | #eztudadez#<l+<o#<Ø# | **... estudá-los.** | #eztudar#+e+<l+<o#<z# |
| 8 | ouvi-la | #ouvidez#<l+<a#<Ø# | **... ouvi-la.** | #ouvir#+e+<l+<a#<Ø# |

a The verbs' internal structure does not appear in Table 6.27b because their internal structure does not affect the 3rd person pronoun's realization. For these verbs' complete morphemic structure, see Chapters 13–15.
b The rationale for the underlying structure of 2nd person plural verbs appears in §13.1.0–2. For the irregular form, *tendes* see Tables 14.11a and 14.12c.

Rows 1 and 2 show that the /l/ of <l+<[±feminine]#<[±plural]# vanishes after a verb ending in a vowel[55] or whenever this direct object is proclitic. In rows 3–5 and the first two columns of rows 6–8, a verb-final /z/ (A) occasions the preservation of <l+ and (B) disappears after the /l/ has been preserved. In the final two columns of rows 6—8, the /r/ of the infinitive preserves the <l+ and then disappears.[56]

**§6.2.5.3.2** Before advancing the rule that deletes verb-final consonants and the rule that deletes pronoun-initial <l+, one more peculiarity associated with post-verbal <l+<[±feminine]#<[±plural]# must

55 This generalization obtains for gerunds as well: *Vendo-os, resolvemos comprá-los* 'Seeing them, we decided to buy them'.
56 The gender morpheme on the infinitive in these juxtapositions must be deleted by rule 6.2a before a rule that governs <l+'s preservation applies.

be dealt with. When this pronoun follows 3rd person plural verbs, all of which end in the nasal consonant /n/ on the morphophonemic level, the /n/'s nasality is transferred to the pronoun's /l/, as demonstrated in Table 6.27c:

**Table 6.27c** <l+[±feminine]+[±plural] Realized as +n+[±feminine]+[±plural]

| Sentence | Realization | Structure | Gloss |
|---|---|---|---|
| **Comam-nas.** | [ˈkõ.mã̃ᵘ-năš] | #kom++e#<a#<n#<l+<a#<z# | Eat them. |
| **Põem-no aqui.** | [ˈpõʸ.nu.aˈki] | #pon++e#<Ø#<n#<l+ <o#<∅##aki# | They put it here. |

This phenomenon is the progressive nasal assimilation of /l/ by the verb-final /n/, which, when the Portuguese 3rd person plural verbs emerge as phonetic sequences, will be reflected as verb-final nasal diphthongs, as Table 6.27c demonstrates.[57] In order for a morphophonological grammar to account for the emergence of underlying forms, such as those in Table 6.27c, its rules of <l+ deletion, preservation, and progressive nasalization will have to be ordered as are the rules accounting for the nasal allomorphy of the definite article (§6.2.2.2).

**§6.2.5.4.0 Loss of <l+:** Rule 6.7a deletes the <l+ of the 3rd person direct object pronoun when <l+ follows a transitive verb ending in a vowel and when it precedes a verb within a specific verb phrase:

**Rule 6.7a Deletion of <l+:**

$$< \begin{pmatrix} \text{-high} \\ \text{+ lateral} \end{pmatrix} + X \rightarrow\ <\varnothing\ /\ \left\{ \begin{array}{l} [\text{-contoid}]_{[\text{Verb}]}\#\_ \\ [\_\_\_\_\_\ [\text{Verb}] \end{array} \right\}$$

57 In the speech of the folk in Portugal, the third person direct object pronouns emerge with an initial [n] after negatives, as in a folk song I recorded (1971) in Ourondo: *Eu perdi o meu amor, e às escuras não n̲o̲ acho* ' 'I lost my loved one, and in the darkness I can't find him'.

The specification [-high, +lateral] plus the boundary symbols < and + suffice to identify <l+ as the segment undergoing deletion because there are only two lateral phonemes, /l/ and /λ/, in Portuguese.[58] The presence of the morpheme boundary <, which indicates that this form cannot begin an utterance, is necessary in order for Rule 6.7a to apply only to the 3rd person direct object, rather than to the underlying form of definite articles as well. The definite article, which is homophonous and homologous with this pronoun, save for the # at its onset, does not have its #l+ preserved in this context, as Table 6.28 demonstrates.

Table 6.28 The Definite Article in Direct Object Noun Phrases

| | Sentence | Structure[a] | Gloss |
|---|---|---|---|
| 1 | Comem as folhas. | #kom++e#<n##l+<a#<z>#foλ++a#<z# | They eat the leaves. |
| 2 | Põem o chapéu. | #pon++e#<n##l+<o#<∅>#šapɛ++u#<∅# | They put their hat on. |
| 3 | Levas os filhos. | #lɛv++a#<z##l+<o#<z>#fiλ+<o#<z# | You're taking the kids. |
| 4 | Olhamos as rosas. | #ɔλ++a#<moz##l+<a#<z>#r̲oz++a#<z# | We look at the roses. |
| 5 | Vai ler o livro. | #vai##leg++e++r#<e##l+<o#<∅> #livr+ +o#<∅# | 3rd will read the book. |

a The structure of these finite, present tense, verbs is not complete. They lack the tense/mood/aspect morpheme, which is <Ø# in this unmarked tense and mood (Verb Introduction Vi.0.0).

Other than the grammatical affinities symbolized by #< (in the case of a transitive verb plus a direct object) and by ## (in the case of a transitive verb followed by a definite article), the strictly phonological environments and the elements are the same when transitive verbs precede either 3rd person direct object pronouns or definite articles. It is the grammatical affinity (preposition >#article) plus the phonological environment that condition the surfacing of the definite article's #l+.

58 The phoneme /λ/ is the initial segment of the 3rd person indirect object pronoun *lhe*, which has the same patterning constraints that the direct object pronouns have. The pronoun *lhe* adds a new wrinkle to the loss of <l+ in 3rd person direct object pronouns. (§6.2.5.5.1–3.)

A transitive verb ending in a consonant triggers the maintenance of the direct object pronoun's <l+.

**§6.2.5.4.1 <l+ Becomes <n+:** After Rule 6.7 has applied leaving the /l/ after verb-final /n, r, z/ (there are no more verb-final consonants than these), Rule 6.8 will apply:

**Rule 6.8 Progressive Nasal Assimilation of <l+:**

$$< \begin{pmatrix} +\text{lateral} \\ -\text{high} \end{pmatrix} + \rightarrow \begin{pmatrix} -\text{lateral} \\ +\text{nasal} \end{pmatrix} / \ [+\text{nasal}]_{[\text{Verb}]}\_\_\_$$

Rule 6.8 turns <l+ of the direct object pronoun into <n+.

**§6.2.5.4.2 Preservation of <l+:** Once Rule 6.8 applies, Rule 6.9a deletes verb-final /r/ and /z/.[59] Pronoun-initial <l+ will be intact and will emerge.

**Rule 6.9a Verb-final /r/ and /z/ Deletion Before <l+:**

$$\begin{pmatrix} +\text{contoid} \\ -\text{surd} \\ -\text{high} \\ -\text{labial} \\ -\text{nasal} \end{pmatrix}_{[\text{Verb}]} \rightarrow \varnothing \ / \ \_\_ \ <\text{l}+<[\pm\text{feminine}]\#<[\pm\text{plural}]\#$$

There is nothing more to the morphophonological peculiarities associated with direct object pronouns' relationship with transitive verbs. This does not close the case on 3rd person direct object pronouns, however. Indirect object pronouns may combine with direct object pronouns, which occasions both indirect and direct objects' allomorphy.

**§6.2.5.5.0** Table 6.29 displays the Portuguese indirect object pronouns:

59 The grammar deletes verb-final /n/ after the rule of vowel nasalization applies.

**Table 6.29** The Indirect Object Pronouns of Portuguese and Their Structure

| | [-plural] | | [+plural] | |
|---|---|---|---|---|
| | **Orthography** | **Structure** | **Orthography** | **Structure** |
| **1st person** | me | <me# | nos | <nɔz#[a] |
| **2nd person** | te | <te# | vos | <vɔz# |
| **-1st, -2nd** | lhe | <λe#<∅# | lhes | <λe#<z# |

a The reason *nos* and *vos* are transcribed as <nɔz# and <voz# is because they are always atonic, thus they always occur with 'reduced' vowels (Rule 2.3)

Table 6.29 shows that the 1st and 2nd person indirect object pronouns are homophonous and homologous with their direct object pronoun counterparts: their phonological substance is the same, and their grammatical boundaries are the same. For the speakers of European Portuguese, they must not be the first element in an utterance, and they are post-verbal, except when circumstances dictate that they may or must precede a verb (Table 6.27a). Only the 3rd person forms may be inflected for plurality.

**§6.2.5.5.1** When both 3rd person direct and indirect object pronouns occur as objects of the same verb, the indirect object precedes the direct object. When this happens, the indirect object pronouns lose their final segments, as Table 6.30 demonstrates:

**Table 6.30** Indirect and Direct Object Pronouns Combined[a]

| | **Sentence** | **Gloss** | **Structure** | **Pronunciation** |
|---|---|---|---|---|
| 1 | **Vai dar-mo.** | 3rd will give it to me. | **<me#<l+<o#<∅#** | [mŭ] |
| 2 | **Levam-tas.** | They take them to you. | **<te#<l+<a#<z#** | [tăš] |
| 3 | **Procuro-lha.** | I'll find it for 3rd [-plural]. | **<λe#<l+a#<∅#** | [λă] |
| 4 | **Trazem-no-lo.** | They bring it to us. | **<nɔz#<l<o#<∅#** | [nŭ.lŭ] |
| 5 | **Compram-vo-lo.** | They buy it from you folks | **<vɔz#<l<o#<∅#** | [vŭ.lŭ] |
| 6 | **Dão-lha a eles.** | They give it to them. | **<λe#<z#<l+ <a#<∅#** | [λă] |

a These forms do not occur spontaneously in Brazilian speech.

Indeed, not only do the indirect object pronouns (*me*, *te*, *lhe*) lose their final /e#, *nos* and *vos* lose their final /z/. And, beyond this, the direct object pronouns lose their initial <l+, except after <nɔz# and <vɔz#.

These phenomena can be managed in a grammar of Portuguese. The first step is adding [+I.O.] (indirect object) to the determinant deleting <l+ everywhere except after a consonant-final verb is to modify Rule 6.9a. Rule 6.9b deletes the <l+ in cases 1, 2, and 3 of Table 6.30 with no problem, leaving it in cases 4 and 5—as well as 6, where <l+ presents a problem.

**Rule 6.9b Deletion of <l+:**

$$< \begin{bmatrix} -\text{high} \\ +\text{lateral} \end{bmatrix} + \rightarrow \varnothing \,/ \left\{ \begin{matrix} [-\text{contoid}]_{[\text{Verb}]}\,\#\_\_\_ \\ \_\_\_\,[\text{Verb}]\,] \\ \text{I.O.}_{\text{prn}}\ \_\_\_ \end{matrix} \right\}$$

Cases 4, 5, and 6 of Table 6.30 pose the following problems: <l+ is maintained in the 1st and 2nd plural I.O.#<D.O. combinations. But the indirect objects' final /z/ disappears (cf. Rule 6.9a), whereas with the 3rd person plural indirect object pronoun, both the <l+ and the plural morpheme <z# are lost—after which the 3rd person I.O.'s word-final /e/ is lost.

**§6.2.5.5.2** A possible way around this conundrum would be to consider the plural suffix on *lhe* to be a relatively superficial accretion to that form, and in a grammar of Portuguese, there would be no <z# on that form when a direct object pronoun follows it, even if its referent were plural.[60] However, the plural form of *lhe* (*lhes*) is of long-standing in the history of the Portuguese language (Williams, 153–4), and according to the data seen so far, this pronoun-final <z# should preserve the <l+ of the direct object pronoun, which it does not, and it should

60 To consider *lhe* ambivalent in its underlying form as far as its referents' plurality is concerned, one could make an analogy between it and the reflexive pronoun se, and the 3rd person possessive forms, which are indifferent concerning their referents' plurality. That is, *se* can have either singular or plural referents: *Ele lava-se* 'he washes himself' or *Eles lavam-se* 'They wash themselves'. In the sentences *Você tem o seu livro* 'You have your book' and *Vocês tem o seu livro* 'You people have your book', *seu* refers to either a singular or plural verbal subject.

then disappear, which it does.[61] In addition, once rule 6.7b has applied, a phonological grammar of Portuguese needs a rule that would delete the final /z/ of *nos* and *vos* when these forms precede a 3rd person direct object.

**§6.2.5.5.3** And, indeed, there is one in the grammar already—Rule 6.9a, which must be slightly modified to accommodate these data by once more adding I.O. to the determinand.

**Rule 6.9b Final /r/ and /z/ Deletion Before <l+:**

$$\begin{pmatrix} +\text{contoid} \\ -\text{surd} \\ -\text{high} \\ -\text{labial} \\ -\text{nasal} \end{pmatrix}_{\{\text{Verb, I.O.}\}} \rightarrow \varnothing \,/\, \_\_ \; <\text{l}+<[\pm\text{feminine}]\#<[\pm\text{plural}]\#$$

Rule 6.9b still applies to verb-final /r/ and /z/, and it applies to the indirect objects' /z/, be it the plural morpheme <z# or be it the final /z/ of *nos* and *vos*. Now Rule 6.9b would apply after Rule 6.7b, and it would clear both the verbs and the indirect objects of their final /z/s. The grammar still needs a rule that will delete the final /e/ of the indirect object when a direct object follows.

**Rule 6.10 Loss of /e# in *Lhe* and other I.O. Pronouns:**

$$\begin{pmatrix} -\text{contoid} \\ +\text{palatal} \\ -\text{high} \\ -\text{wide glottis} \end{pmatrix} \rightarrow \varnothing \,/\, <\text{PRN}_{[\text{i.o.}]}\#\_\_ \; <\text{PRN}_{[\text{d.o.3rd}]}\#$$

61 Evidently Galician (Portuguese's ancestor, spoken in northwest Spain) has a form *lhe-lo* in which the <l+ is maintained, the <z# is dropped, and the /e# remains (Williams, 154).

Even though there seems to be scant independent phonological motivation for Rule 6.10,[62] it identifies precisely and uniquely the morphological environment in which this particular /e# disappears. Now, however, having established rules for the morphophonological phenomena associated with the direct and indirect object pronouns, the reflexive pronouns come next.

**§6.2.5.5.4** Table 6.31 displays the Portuguese reflexive pronouns:

**Table 6.31** The Reflexive Pronouns of Portuguese and Their Structure

| | [-plural] | | [+plural] | |
|---|---|---|---|---|
| | **Orthography** | **Structure** | **Orthography** | **Structure** |
| 1st person | me | <me# | nos | <nɔz# |
| 2nd person | te | <te# | vos | <vɔz# |
| -1st, -2nd | se | <se# | se | <se# |

Once again the 1st and 2nd person forms are the same as the other object pronouns. The only difference the reflexives demonstrate in Portuguese is that the 3rd person form is *se*, and it occurs unchanged both with singular and plural subjects.[63] The 1st person plural form <nɔz# occasions the loss of verb-final /z/ when it occurs after a 1st person plural form, e.g. *vemo-nos*, #vemoz#<nɔz#, [ˈvẽ.mŭ.nŭš], 'we see each other'. This phenomenon is related to the loss of verb-final /z/ before the <l+ of the direct object, but it is peculiar to the 1st person plural followed by its special reflexive object. The relationship exists in both cases because the segments that occasion the consonantal loss are the voiced coronal non-occlusive, non-fricative /l/ and /n/. On the other hand, the use of direct or indirect object <nɔz# occasions no loss of verb-final /z/: D.O. *Ouvis-nos?* #ouviz#<nɔz# [o.ˈviž.nŭš] 'Do you folks hear us?'; I.O.

---

62 There is no particular phonological reason for this /e/ to disappear. The phoneme /e/ can be found unstressed preceding unstressed /o/, /a/, or /u/ as well as before the #l+ of the definite article: *bebe água*, #bɛbe##ˈagu++a#, [ˈbɛ.βə.ˈa.ɣ$^{u}$ă] '3rd drinks water'; *mede ocos* #mɛde##ok++o#<z# [ˈmɛ.ðə.ˈo.kuš], '3rd measures hollows'; *vende o carro* #vende##l+<o>#Ø##kar̠+o# [ˈvẽ$^{n}$.də.ŭ.ˈka.r̠ŭ] '3rd sells the car'.

63 In fact, as the unmarked reflexive pronoun, some speakers [of Brazilian Portuguese] generalize this pronoun for all reflexives, e.g. *eu se cortei* 'I cut myself' (Bruno Maroneze, critical comment).

*Trazes-nos os pratos*, #trazez#<nɔz##l+<o#<z>#prat++o#<z# [ˈtra.zĭž. nŭ.zŭž.ˈpra.tŭš] 'You bring us our plates'. Owing to this evidence, the rule that deletes the 1st person plural's final /z/ applies only to the reflexive use of that verb. Rule 6.11 deletes /z/ in this and only this form.

**Rule 6.11 Loss of /z/ in Reflexive 1st Person Plural Verbs:**

$$\begin{pmatrix} +\text{fricative} \\ -\text{surd} \\ -\text{high} \\ -\text{labial} \end{pmatrix} \rightarrow \emptyset \,/\, \text{Verb}^{96}{}_{[1^{64}\ +\text{plural}]} \ \_\_\_ \ +\text{Prn}_{[+\text{reflexive}]}$$

The specification in Rule 6.11's determinand identifies /z/ among all the consonants in the Portuguese inventory. In its determinant, the specifications [+1st, +plural] for the verb and the specification [+reflexive] for the pronoun ensure that this rule deletes the final /z/ of a 1st person plural verb when it is followed by the reflexive pronoun *nos*. In sum, the reflexive pronouns have the same referent as their verbs' subjects, and other than *nos*, they neither occasion nor undergo any morphophonological changes, and they have the same collocation constraints the other clitic pronouns do. The next pronominal category is the possessive pronouns.

**§6.2.5.6.0** Table 6.32a contains the possessive pronouns.

---

64 In dealing with clitic pronouns there has been no mention of transitive verbs, which, it must be said, are the major users of clitic pronouns. This omission is because intransitive verbs sometimes occur with clitic pronoun: e.g. *Não se é sério* 'One isn't serious' and *O mais velho, é-o ele* 'The oldest, he's it'.

**Table 6.32a** Portuguese Possessive Pronouns

| Grammatical Person | [-feminine] | | [+feminine] | |
|---|---|---|---|---|
| | [-plural] | [+plural] | [-plural] | [+plural] |
| **+1st –plural** | meu | meus | minha | minhas |
| **+1st +plural** | nosso | nossos | nossa | nossas |
| **+2nd –plural** | teu | teus | tua | tuas |
| **+2nd +plural** | vosso | vossos | vossa | vossas |
| **-1st** | seu | seus | sua | suas |

**§6.2.5.6.1** The possessive pronouns present a noteworthy hybridization of object pronouns and adjectives. Like all adjectives, they agree in number and gender with the items they modify, and like the other pronouns, their stems are mono-morphemic, and they identify the possessor as 1st, 2nd, or 3rd person. Their roots bear no inflection for, nor indication of their ***referents'*** gender—only the gender (and number) of the items possessed. Their different forms do, however, identify singular and plural possessor referents—except in the case of the –1st forms (i.e. 3rd person).

**§6.2.5.6.2** The –1st forms denote referents designated by the 3rd person subject pronouns as well as by the 2nd person non-solidarity pronouns: *você*, *o senhor*, etc. But in oral, face-to-face usage, this pronoun only indicates possession by 2nd person non-intimates.[65]

**§6.2.5.6.3** In Table 6.32b analyzes the possessive pronouns.

**Table 6.32b** Portuguese Possessive Pronouns' Structure

| Grammatical Person | [-feminine]Possessed Item | | Possessed Item [+feminine] | |
|---|---|---|---|---|
| | [-plural] | [+plural] | [-plural] | [+plural] |
| **+1st –plural** | #me++u#<Ø# | #me++u#<z# | #miɲ+<a#<Ø# | #miɲ+<a#<z# |
| **+1st +plural** | #nɔs+<o#<Ø# | #nɔs+<o#<z# | #nɔs+<a#<Ø# | #nɔs+<a#<z# |
| **+2nd -plural** | #te++u#<Ø# | #te++u#<z# | #tu+<a#<Ø# | #tu+<a#<z# |
| **+2nd +plural** | #vɔs+<o#<Ø# | #vɔs+<o#<z# | #vɔs+<a#<Ø# | #vɔs+<a#<z# |
| **-1st [±plural]** | #se++u#<Ø# | #se++u#<z# | #su+<a#<Ø# | #su+<a#<z# |

65 This is essentially different from Spanish usage, where *su*(*s*) refers indifferently to both 3rd person referents and 2nd person referents identified as *usted(es)*. People learning Portuguese after having mastered Spanish may be teased by their interlocutors when they use *seu*, etc. for a referent other than the person in direct address.

**§6.2.5.6.4** In the roots of the [-feminine] forms, one immediately perceives a relationship between the possessive pronouns' roots and clitic pronouns' roots.[66] Except for their morpheme boundaries, the 1st and 2nd person roots are practically the same as the accusative, genitive, and reflexive pronouns although the plural possessive roots end in /s/ rather than /z/. The 3rd person [-feminine] roots have the same phonological makeup as the 3rd person reflexive pronoun *se* (<se#). In all the [+feminine] forms other than the 1st and 2nd plurals, the roots are suppletive. That is, 1st person singular #me+ changes to #miɲ+, the 2nd person singular #te+ changes to #tu+, and the '3rd person' [+feminine] forms #se+ changes to #su+. There is no contemporary phonological reason for this variation.[67]

**§6.2.5.6.5** The [+feminine] morpheme <a# emerges in all the [+feminine] forms, as does the [+plural] morpheme <z# in all [+plural] forms. The 1st and 2nd person plural [-feminine] possessive pronouns have the [-feminine] morpheme <o#,[68] whereas the 1st, 2nd, and '3rd' singulars have the other [-feminine] morpheme, <u#. The only contemporary aberrancy possessive pronouns exhibit is in their exchange of roots between [+feminine] and [–feminine] forms.

**§6.2.5.6.6** Before abandoning the possessive pronouns, their usage deserves attention. Table 6.33 shows how possessives' pre- or post-nominal position as well as how their use with or without the definite article affect their interpretation.

---

66 Of course the possessives are not clitics, as the boundary symbol # both before and after each form indicates. They can be stressed and can occur utterance-initially and finally.

67 The [-feminine, -plural] 1st person singular possessive in Latin was *mĕum*, which became *meu*, whereas its [+feminine] form was *mĕam*, whose tonic vowel rose to /i/ as Vulgar Latin became Portuguese, then /i/ underwent progressive nasalization [ˈmĩ.ă] (Williams, 62). An epenthetic consonant /ɲ/ arose as an onset to the word's second syllable, but even today pronunciations such as [ˈmĩ.ỹă], i.e. without intervocalic contoidal articulation, are common. Latin *tŭum* and *sŭum* probably became *teu* and *seu* out of analogy with *meu*, whereas the [+feminine] *tŭam* and *sŭam* transferred directly into Portuguese as *tua(s)* and *sua(s)*. The forms *nosso* and *vosso* derive from *nostrum* and *vostrum* (Williams, 156). Their preservation of root final /s/ probably derives from the presence of /t/ in the Latin roots.

68 The root vowel /ɔ/ for the 1st and 2nd person plural possessives is always /ɔ/ regardless of these forms' gender or number.

**Table 6.33** Possessives in Action

| | Pre-nominal Possessive | Post-nominal Possessive |
|---|---|---|
| Examples: | **o meu carro** | **o carro teu** |
| Gloss: | 'my car' | your car |
| | Predicate Adjective | Predicate Nominative |
| Examples: | **É minha.** | **É a minha.** |
| Gloss: | It's mine. | It's mine. |

In ordinary possessive declarations, one usually includes a definite article, as in the 1st set of examples. When the possessive pronoun precedes the noun, like any adjective, its function is descriptive. When it follows the noun, it is contrastive: *o carro teu* implies comparison, i.e. with somebody else's car(s). When the possessive is a predicate adjective, it occurs without the definite article and simply describes an object as being possessed. When it occurs with the definite article as a predicate nominative, it also indicates that there are other objects present and the one in question (ideally) belongs to the person who says '*É a minha*'. In predicate nominatives, the definite article reinforces the possessive pronoun's noun valence. The definite article may be used with the possessives and the possessed nouns, except when in direct address: *meu caro amigo* 'my dear friend', *minha senhora* 'my lady'—or when referring to sacred beings: *Nossa Senhora* 'Our Lady' (See Cunha, 150–1.).[69] Before closing this section on grammatical nominals, three more pronouns merit examination—prepositional object pronouns.

**§6.2.5.7.0** The 1st and 2nd person singular as well as the -1st pronouns have unique forms as prepositional objects, as Table 6.34 demonstrates:

**Table 6.34** The Pronominal Objects of Prepositions

| | [-plural] | [+plural] |
|---|---|---|
| 1st person | mim <min# | nós #nɔz# |
| 2nd person | ti <ti# | vós #vɔz# |
| -1st | si <si# | |

69 Portuguese villagers would sometimes address me as *o sô Artur*, using the definite article with my default title.

**§6.2.5.7.1** The prepositional objects *nós* and *vós* are the same as the subject pronouns. The $1^{st}$ and $2^{nd}$ person singular pronouns, obviously related to the $1^{st}$ and $2^{nd}$ person singular object pronouns, are preceded by < since they may only occur after prepositions. In this analysis they are, like the other $1^{st}$ and $2^{nd}$ person singular pronouns, mono-morphemic idioms, applying, as $1^{st}$ and $2^{nd}$ person pronouns do, to [±feminine] referents indifferently.[70] The -$1^{st}$ prepositional pronoun *si* can be used as a strictly $3^{rd}$ person form as either singular or plural: *Guardou o dinheiro para si* '$3^{rd}$ singular kept the money for him/herself', *Guardaram o dinheiro para si* 'They kept the money for themselves'. In addition, European Portuguese speakers use this form for $2^{nd}$ person non-intimates: *A senhora tem um carro só para si?* 'Do you (+feminine, -intimate) have a car all for yourself?' *Vocês não o querem para si?* 'Don't you (±feminine, -intimate) want it for yourselves?' This usage parallels that of the possessive pronouns whose '$3^{rd}$ person' forms are actually -$1^{st}$ person. (§6.2.5.6.2)

**§6.2.5.8** This concludes the analysis of gender (inflectional and derivational) and number (inflectional) of unproblematic nominals. The analysis of problematic nominals' gender and number will be more pertinent after Chapters 7 and 8. It is now time to take stock of the data and analyses in this chapter.

## Conclusions

### Summary

**§6.3.0.0 Introduction:** This chapter has examined the data and provided rules for the morphophonemic phenomena related to unproblematic nominals' gender and number. Nouns, adjectives, and infinitives are open-ended nominals because new nouns, adjectives, and verbs

70 The $1^{st}$ person pronoun *mim* derives from the Latin dative *mĭhĭ* (Williams, 62). The original spelling was *mi*, but eventually Portuguese orthographic pundits acknowledged the progressive nasal assimilation that applied to the vowel /i/ by adding the final m to the word. Whereas Portuguese orthography represents this form-final nasality with m, on a morphophonological level, it is /n/, <min#. The $2^{nd}$ person singular form *ti* comes from the Latin dative *tibi*, which, even in Vulgar Latin was tī (Williams, 144), and it emerged as such when the Vulgar Latin of Western Iberia became Galician and then Portuguese.

may be coined at any time. This is not the case with the remaining nominals included in this study under the heading of grammatical or functional categories, where new forms cannot be formed because the extant ones belong to specific, well defined sets. The restricted categories are grammatical nominals and include subject, accusative, dative, and prepositional pronouns. These forms reflect the grammatical person and number of their referents in particular utterances. Only the 3rd person direct objects also reflect their referents' gender. Except for the object pronouns and the definite article, these forms can be employed as nouns: as sentence subjects, direct or indirect objects, or as objects of prepositions.

**§6.3.0.1 Inflection-Induced Mutations:** Certain nouns, adjectives, demonstratives, and 3rd person subject pronouns undergo root vowel metaphony. Definite articles' and 3rd person accusative pronouns' roots occasion and undergo consonantal deletion as well as assimilation to the nasal ending of grammatically relevant forms (prepositions and verbs). Finite verbs, infinitives, prepositions, and indirect object pronouns undergo modifications when they co-occur with specific grammatical nominals.

**§6.3.0.2.0 Gender and Number:** Using the principles of markedness outlined in Chapter 1, there is one gender for Portuguese, [+feminine], and one number, [+plural]. For [+plural], there is only one morpheme <z#, and for [-plural], the unmarked number, there is no overt morpheme. Gender morphemes are more complicated and can be either inflectional or derivational. Since the structure of ordinary nominals is

$$\#\text{stem} \begin{Bmatrix} < \\ + \end{Bmatrix} [\pm\text{feminine}]\# < [\pm\text{plural}]\#,$$

and since the representation of number is the last item in this structure, [-plural] appears as <Ø# in the representation of singular nominals. The marked nature of [+feminine] and [+plural] is manifest in the database for Portuguese phoneme frequency and distribution counts. Table 6.3 shows that in this study's texts, [-feminine] prevails over [+feminine] by a ratio of 1.29 to 1 and [-plural] prevails over [+plural] by a ratio of 4.1 to 1. The next table (Table 6.4) and its subsequent commentary shows that [-feminine] nominals may have more varied referents than [+feminine] ones, as do [-plural] referents.

**§6.3.0.2.1** Representation of gender is more problematic than that of number. Whereas <a# functions to indicate [+feminine] in all the grammatical forms, +a# may occur in adjectives and nouns of [-feminine] gender. Likewise, <o# and +o# are the major indicators of [-feminine] gender, but +o# can end a [+feminine] word. Likewise, the gender morpheme whose phonological substance is /u/ has two boundary affinities with stems: <u# is [-feminine] inflectional and alternates with various [+feminine] suffixes. The deriving suffix +u# does not alternate and can occur on [±feminine] nouns: *nau* 'ship' [+feminine] and *camafeu* 'cameo' [-feminine]. The gender morpheme whose phonological substance is /e/ has several boundary affinities, both with its stems and with the morphemes following it. It is <e# in those words in which it occurs word-finally (e.g. *mestre* 'teacher', *presidente* 'president', and *freire* 'friar'). These words' stems, and others with similar structures, can be inflected with <a# when [+feminine]: (*mestra*, *presidenta*, *freira*). It is <e+ in those words where it evanesces word-finally but appears when such words are inflected for plurality, and it gives way to <a# when those words are inflected for [+feminine], e.g. *professor, professores, professora* 'teacher'. It is +e# when it emerges word-finally and can indicate [±feminine] gender either in ambivalent adjectives and nouns or in nouns that are arbitrarily [+feminine] or [-feminine].

**§6.3.0.2.2** Directly related to both number and gender inflection is the phenomenon of stem vowel metaphony. A minority of nouns and adjectives displays an alternation between tonic [o] in their [-feminine], [-plural] forms and tonic [ɔ] in their [+plural] or [+feminine] forms. The underlying mutable vowel in these words is /ɔ/, and Rule 6.1 changes it to [o] in their [-feminine] and in their [-plural] forms.

**§6.3.0.2.3** The opposite, i.e. vowel lowering rather than raising, obtains in the subject and demonstrative pronouns. In these forms, the root vowel is /e/ and [ɛ] occurs in the [+feminine] forms owing to the lowering influence word-final [ă] exerts on their tonic vowel.

**§6.3.0.3.0 Nominal Classes:** The largest nominal class is the one containing the nominals that undergo no morphophonological modification whether they bear either an <a#, +a# or an <o#,+o# gender morpheme or whether they are singular (<Ø#) or plural (<z#). These nominals belong to class N. (For a representative sample, see Table 6A.1.)

**§6.3.0.3.1** The first minority class, $N_1$, consists of those nominals (nouns and adjectives) (Table 6.8) susceptible to Rule 6.1, which raises /ɔ/ to /o/ in these nominals' [-plural, -feminine] forms. This class also includes subject 3$^{rd}$ person pronouns and the demonstrative pronouns whose root vowel /e/ mutates to [ɛ] in their [+feminine] forms. Their stems' allomorphy is accounted for by Rule 6.6b. The second minority class is $N_2$, whose ending, +a# appears on [-feminine] nouns and adjectives (Table 6.12). The third minority class ($N_3$) contains those nominals that end in +a# and can have [±feminine] referents (Table 6.12). The fourth minority ($N_4$) among the nominals are those in Table 6.17 whose [-feminine, -plural] forms retain word-final +e#, even when the stem-final consonant (/r, l, z, n/) could constitute a syllable coda.[71] When this study addresses the Portuguese language's more abstruse plurals (Chapter 9), it will posit more minority class nominals.

**§6.3.0.4 Derivation with Gender Morphemes:** Number is always inflectional, whereas gender may be inflectional, but in the great majority of nouns, it is actually derivational—it can make a semantic difference in what a particular stem plus gender morpheme can designate.

**§6.3.0.5 Boundary Symbols:** The four boundary symbols advanced in Chapter 5 appear throughout this chapter to indicate the affinities morphemes have with one another and their distribution. Nouns, adjectives, infinitives, subject pronouns, possessives, indefinite articles, and demonstratives begin and end with #. Since # indicates potential word boundaries, forms bordered by # at both extremities will have a tonic syllable. Internally, words consist of stems that need a gender suffix to be actualized. Stems end in +. The gender suffix can be prefaced by the inflecting boundary <, or by the deriving boundary +. Inflectional and deriving gender morphemes can be word-final; thus, they end in #. Definite articles and object pronouns have a # at only one extremity: definite articles begin with # because they can be utterance-initial; they end with > because they must be followed by a noun phrase. Object pronouns end with # because they may occur utterance-finally, but they begin with < because, at least in the register described here, they do not begin utterances.

---

71 There are many words with similar structures that lose their +e# gender morpheme in their [-plural, -feminine] manifestations. These words belong in the majority nominal category (N), whereas the $N_4$ nominals are immune to rules 6.2a and b.

**§6.3.0.6 Rules:** Beyond the implied simple rewrite rules that assign phonological substance to the morphemes in question (see Appendix B), this chapter advances 15 rules in a grammar designed to account for the phenomena associated with the inflection of simple nominals. (To see these rules in their order of appearance and in action, see Appendices C and D.)

## Findings and Interpretations

**§6.3.1.0 Clarification:** The phenomena illustrated, analyzed, and regulated in this chapter are well-known to students of Portuguese, be they phonologists, syntacticians, or Portuguese language teachers. So, the contribution of this chapter is more in the area of clarification and assertion than it is in discovery. Approaching the data from a markedness perspective has limited the postulates to one gender mark [+feminine] and one number mark [+plural], and these two postulates suffice to account for the morphological reflections of Portuguese gender and number. In both cases, the marked nature of these categories reinforces commonly held notions of marked groupings: they are less frequent and more restrictive in their reference than their unmarked counterparts. With few exceptions (indirect objects, reflexive pronouns, and $1^{st}$ and $2^{nd}$ person plural pronouns), all the grammatical nominals under study here use the same morphemes that adjectives and nouns use to reflect gender and number. They also reflect grammatical person $+1^{st}$, $+2^{nd}$, and $3^{rd}$ (i.e. [$-1^{st}$, $-2^{nd}$]) as well as their plurality or lack thereof.

**§6.3.1.1 Number:** The pluralization of the majority of nouns (Class N) is unremarkable, given that it entails the use of a word-final <z# added to words' ends. The rules in Appendices C and D dealing with plurality, or the lack thereof (Rules 6.1, 6.2a, 6.9a, 6.9b, and 6.11), apply to a minority of nominals in the Portuguese lexicon. Indeed, all of the rules in this chapter apply to minorities, i.e. marked cases in the gamut of unproblematic nominals.

**§6.3.1.2 Gender in Grammatical Nominals:** Even in these simple nominals, gender is a more complicated matter than number is. In the restricted (paradigmatic) nominals when <a# appears, it reflects the [+feminine] gender of the referent, except in the case of the possessive pronouns, demonstratives, and articles where it reflects the gender of the possessed or modified item. When <o> appears (in definite articles and <o# appears in $3^{rd}$ person direct objects), this inflectional suffix reflects the [-feminine] gender of referents, as does <e# in the

demonstrative pronouns and those 3rd person pronouns used as subjects of verbs and objects of prepositions. Indirect object pronouns, reflexive pronouns, and possessives do not reflect their referents' gender. Infinitives' gender is always [-feminine], and adjectives' gender is determined by the nouns they modify. However, nouns' gender, when designating inanimate items, is arbitrary: there is nothing intrinsically feminine in the referents of words such as *perna* 'leg', *calçada* 'sidewalk', *cuecas* 'jockey shorts', or *motocleta* 'motorcycle', nor is there anything intrinsically masculine (i.e. [-feminine]) in the referents of *olho* 'eye', *paralelepípedo* 'paving stone', *vestido* 'dress', or *livro* 'book'. Nonetheless, these words, and countless words like them, bear either a [+feminine] or [-feminine] morpheme. When nouns are modified by articles, adjectives, demonstratives, or possessives, or when they are represented by 3rd person subject or accusative pronouns, overtly and systematically, these pronouns reflect the nouns' arbitrary gender and their number.

**§6.3.1.3 Pronouns:** By examining the Portuguese pronominal system, one bears witness to pronouns' versatility. The 1st person [-plural] form in all the non-nominative, verb related cases is *me* regardless of denotees' gender. The 2nd person [-plural] form begins with /t/ in every case (*tu, te, ti*) regardless of denotees' gender. The 1st and 2nd person [+plural] forms have the same segmental phonemes in all cases (/nɔz/ and /vɔz/) regardless of denotees' gender, but their subject forms, which double as prepositional objects, are surrounded by # (#nɔz# and #vɔz#) and receive stress, whereas the non-subjective forms begin with < and, as bound forms, receive no stress. Because they receive no stress, they are realized as [nũš] and [vũš] in specific circumstances (Table 6.25, fn. a). The possessive pronouns bear an uncanny similarity in their [-feminine] roots to the roots of the reflexive pronouns, and the 3rd person indirect and reflexive pronouns have no indication of their referents' gender, but the indirect object pronouns can reflect their referents' number. These forms' versatility in grammatical function and their phonosthematic similarities (i.e. /t/'s presence in all 2nd person singular forms, /m/'s presence in all but the subjective form of the 1st person singular) contribute to the Portuguese functional nominals' learnability.

## So What?

**§6.3.2.0** As unusual and recondite as some of the phenomena addressed in this chapter may be, their regulation is necessary in a structural framework that purports to generate all the grammatical forms of the Portuguese language.

## Appendix A: Nominal Classes

**§6A.0** Chapter 6 has advanced five categories of nominals in: N, $N_1$, $N_2$, $N_3$, $N_4$. The unmarked category N is the largest set of nominals. Its members' roots undergo no vowel metaphony owing either to [±plural] or [±feminine] inflection. This category also includes the nominals that lose the ambivalent gender morpheme (either <e+ or +e+) when the form is [-feminine, -plural].

**§6A.1.0** The phoneme /ɔ/ is the only root vowel that may be altered by the lack of plural or feminine marking in nouns and adjectives. But there are abundant nominal cases in which [±plural, ±feminine] does not affect the timber of either /o/ or /ɔ/. Table 6A.1 provides a sampling of these nominals.

**Table 6A.1** N Class Words with Immutable Tonic /o/ and /ɔ/

| (stressed /o/)[a] | Gloss | (stressed /ɔ/) | Gloss[b] |
|---|---|---|---|
| **almoço**(s)* | lunch(es)' | **amorfo**(s) | amorphous* |
| **bolo**(s)* | 'cake(s)' | **bode**(s) | billy goats(s) |
| **coco**(s)* | coconut(s) | **coco**(s) | coccus(es) |
| **dorso**(s)* | back(s) | **dobre**(s) | chime(s) |
| **engodo**(s)* | enticement(s) | **escroque**(s) | crook(s) |
| **ferrolho**(s)* | bolt, catch(s) | **foco**(s) | focus(es) |
| **globo**(s)* | globe(s) | **gole**(s) | drop(s) |
| **hoje**(s) | today(s) | **heterodoxo**(s) | heterodox* |
| **iodo**(s) | iodine(s) | **inóxio**(s) | non-noxious* |
| **joio**(s) | darnel(s) | **jóquei**(s) | jockey(s) |
| **lodo**(s) | mud(s) | **lote**(s) | lot(s) |
| **morro**(s)* | hill(s) | **modo**(s) | mode(s) |
| **namoro**(s)* | courtship(s) | **nodo**(s) | node(s)[c] |
| **odre**(s) | wineskin(s) | **ócio**(s) | leisure(s) |
| **piolho**(s)* | louse, lice | **pólo**(s) | pole(s) |
| **rolo**(s)* | cylinder(s) | **roble**(s) | oak(s) |
| **quioco** | person from Quioco | **quilose** | cheilitis |
| **sopro**(s)* | gust(s) | **soco**(s) | wooden clog(s) |
| **topo**(s)* | peak(s) | **tope**(s) | summit(s) |
| **uitoto** | Witoto | *** | *** |

Table 6A.1 Continued

| (stressed /o/)[a] | Gloss | (stressed /ɔ/) | Gloss[b] |
|---|---|---|---|
| **vôo(s)** | flight(s) | **voto(s)** | vote(s) |
| **xoxo(s)** | loud kiss(es) | *** | *** |
| **zorro(s)** | fox(es) | **zote(s)** | stupid* |

a The asterisked items in this column come from Cunha (127).
b The asterisked items in this column are adjectives and, hence, have no plurals in English.
c The very common possessive pronoun, *nosso* 'our', maintains its root's /ɔ/ in all its forms [± plural, ±feminine].

The nominals in Table 6A.1[72] demonstrate that the mutation /ɔ/ → [o] / ___ [<o#, -plural] is not a language-wide phenomenon. It is, rather, restricted to $N_1$ words.

**§6A.1.1** The next subcategory of Nominal Class N are those words that lose a final <e+ in their [-feminine, -plural] forms. With the addition of the infinitives *domar, comer, dormir,* Table 6A.2 demonstrates these forms.

72 Table 6A.1 presents an alphabetical list of [-feminine] paroxytone words whose /o/ or /ɔ/ was in an open syllable, since syllables containing an /o/ or /ɔ/ closed by /n/ in most pronunciations favor [õ] and those ending in /l/ favor [ɔ].

Table 6A.2[a] Occult <$e_{[-feminine]}$#< [-plural]#

| | [-feminine] | | | [+feminine] | | |
|---|---|---|---|---|---|---|
| | [-plural] | [+plural] | Gloss | [-plural] | [+plural] | Gloss |
| 1 | professor | professores | teacher(s) | professora | professoras | female teacher(s) |
| 2 | pagador | pagadores | payer(s) | pagadora | pagadoras | female payer(s) |
| 3 | cantor | cantores | singer(s) | cantora | cantoras | female singer(s) |
| 4 | domar | domares | to dominate[b] | *** | *** | *** |
| 5 | comer | comeres | to eat | *** | *** | *** |
| 6 | dormir | dormires | to sleep | *** | *** | *** |
| 7 | burguês | burgueses | Bourgeois | burguesa | burguesas | female bourgeois |
| 8 | inglês | ingleses | English | inglesa | inglesas | English woman (women) |
| 9 | rapaz | rapazes | young man (men) | rapariga | raparigas | young woman (women) |
| 10 | espanhol | espanhóis | Spaniard(s) | espanhola | espanholas | Spanish woman (women) |
| 11 | general | generais | general(s) | generala | generalas | general(s)'(s) wife (-ves) |
| 12 | zagal | zagais | live wire person(s) | zagala | zagalas | female live wire(s) |

a Table 6.16 reproduced and expanded.
b Pluralized infinitives can be translated into 'acts of'. In this case, 'acts of dominating, eating, sleeping'.

The [-feminine, -plural] words whose surface forms contain no gender morpheme are accounted for by Rule 6.2a, which applies to Class N nominals with stems ending in /r, l, z/.

**§6A.1.2** The final subcategory of Class N nominals are those whose stems end in /n/ and which bear an /a/ in their [+feminine] incarnations, but which bear no /e/ in their [-feminine] instantiations. Table 6A.3 contains representative members of these forms:

Table 6A.3[a] Class N Nominals, Stem-Final /n/

| [-feminine] | | | [+feminine] | | |
|---|---|---|---|---|---|
| [-plural] | [+plural] | Gloss | [-plural] | [+plural] | Gloss |
| botim | botins | ankle boot(s) | botina | botinas | ankle boot(s) |
| comum | comuns | common | comuna | comunas | commune(s) |
| maladrim | malandrins | low-life (lives) | malandrina | malandrinas | low-life female(s) |
| malandrim | mandarins | Mandarin(s) | mandarina | mandarinas | Mandarin female(s) |
| paladim | paladins | paladin(s) | paladina (adj.) | paladinas (adj.) | female paladin(s) |
| vintém | vinténs | 20 Reis coin(s) | vintena | vintenas | group(s) of 20 |
| um | uns | one, some | uma | umas | one, some ([+fem.) |

a Table 6.20 reproduced.

The [-feminine] forms (both singular and plural) of these words are generated by Rule 6.2b.

**§6A.2.0** $N_1$ nouns' tonic stem vowel is /ɔ/, which mutates to /o/ when these nominals (nouns and adjectives) are neither feminine nor plural. Representative words appear in Tables 6.6 and 6.8 (amalgamated here for readers' convenience):

**Table 6A.4** $N_1$ Nominals

| Root Vowel Metaphony; /ɔ/→/o/ [±plural] Nouns | | | | |
|---|---|---|---|---|
| **Word** | **Singular** | **Plural** | **Morphemic Analysis** | **Gloss** |
| **caroço** | [kă.ˈro.sŭ] | [kă.ˈrɔ.sŭš] | #karɔs++o#(<z#) | pit(s) |
| **corvo** | [ˈkor.vŭ] | [ˈkɔr.vŭš] | #kɔrv++o#(<z#) | crow(s) |
| **fogo*** | [ˈfo.γŭ] | [ˈfɔ.γŭš] | #fɔg++o#(<z#) | fire(s) |
| **jogo*** | [ˈžo.γŭ] | [ˈžɔ.γŭš] | #žɔg++o#(<z#) | game(s) |
| **osso*** | [ˈo.sŭ] | [ˈɔ.sŭš] | #ɔs++o#(<z#) | bone(s) |
| **ovo*** | [ˈo.vŭ] | [ˈɔ.vŭš] | #ɔv++o#(<z#) | egg(s) |
| **poço*** | [ˈpo.sŭ] | [ˈpɔ.sŭš] | #pɔs++o#(<z#) | well(s) |
| **miolo** | [mi.ˈo.lŭ] | [mi.ˈɔ.lŭš] | #miɔl++o#(<z#) | brain(s) (matter) |
| **tojo** | [ˈto.žŭ] | [ˈtɔ.žŭš] | #tɔž++o#(<z#) | gorse (shrubs) |
| **Root Vowel Metaphony ($N_1$) /ɔ/→/o/ [±feminine] Nouns and Adjectives** | | | | |
| **Word** | **[-feminine]** | **[+feminine]** | **Morphemic Analysis** | **Gloss** |
| **porco** | [ˈpor.kŭ] | [ˈpɔr.kă] | #pɔrk+<[αfemine] #(<z#) | pig/sow |
| **coxo** | [ˈko.šŭ] | [ˈkɔ.šă] | #kɔš+<[αfemine] #(<z#) | lame |
| **grosso** | [ˈgro.sŭ] | [ˈgrɔ.să] | #grɔs+<[αfemine] #(<z#) | ill-mannered |
| **brioso** | [bri.ˈo.zŭ] | [bri.ˈɔ.ză] | #bri+<[αfemine] #(<z#) | spirited |
| **novo** | [ˈno.vŭ] | [ˈnɔ.vă] | #nɔv+<[αfemine] (<z#) | new |

**§6A.2.1** The final sets of $N_1$ nominals are 3[rd] person subject pronouns and demonstrative pronouns. These words' roots contain an #e/, which mutates to #ɛ/ in the feminine forms, as Tables 6A.5a and 6A.5b demonstrate:

**Table 6A.5a** Subject Pronouns: Root Vowel Metaphony /e/→/ɛ/

| | [-feminine] | | [-feminine] | |
|---|---|---|---|---|
| | [-plural] | [+plural] | [-plural] | [+plural] |
| **Root: #el+** | **#el+<e#<Ø#** | **#el+<e#<z#** | **#el+<a#<Ø#** | **#el+<a#<z#** |
| | **[ˈe.lə]** | **[ˈe.ləš]** | **[ˈɛ.lă]** | **[ˈɛ.lăš]** |
| **Gloss:** | he/him | they/them | she/her | they/them |

**Table 6A.5b** Demonstrative Pronouns: Root Vowel Metaphony /e/→/ɛ/

| | 1st Person: #ezt+ | 2nd Person: #es+ | 3rd Person: #akel+ |
|---|---|---|---|
| [-feminine] | #ezt+<e#(<z#) | #es+<e#(<z#) | #akel+<e#(<z#) |
| Transcription | [ˈeš.tə]([š]) | [ˈe.sə]([š]) | [ă.ˈke.lə]([š]) |
| [+feminine] | #ɛzt+<a#(<z#) | #ɛs+<a#(<z#) | #akɛl+<a#(<z#) |
| Transcription | [ˈɛš.tă]([š]) | [ˈɛ.să]([š]) | [ă.ˈkɛ.lă]([š]) |
| Gloss: | this/these/them | that/those/them | that/those/them |

Notwithstanding this regularity, the Portuguese lexicon is replete with adjectives whose tonic stem vowel /e/ or /ɛ/ is constant regardless of their (inflected) gender. Table 6A.6 contains a sampling of such adjectives.

**Table 6A.6** Adjectives with Immutable Stressed /e/ and /ɛ/

| /ˈɛ/ constant | Gloss | /ˈe/ constant | Gloss |
|---|---|---|---|
| abjeto, -a | abject | faceto, -a | facetious |
| cego, -a | blind | galego, -a | Galecian |
| correto, -a | correct | grego, -a | Greek |
| fero, -a | wild | labrego, -a | rustic |
| mero, -a | mere | ledo, -a | cheerful |
| obeso,[a] -a | obese | leso, -a[b] | wounded |
| obsesso, -a | obsessed | negro, -a | black |
| obsoleto, -a[c] | obsolete | preso, -a | caught |
| reto, -a | straight | teso, -a | tense |
| secreto, -a | secret | | |
| vero, -a | true | | |

a The Houaiss and Avery dictionary transcribes this word with /ɛ/.
b The stressed vowel of *leso, -a* can be either /ˈe/ or /ˈɛ/ (Houaiss and Avery).
c The stressed vowel of *obsoleto, -a* can be either /ˈɛ/ or /ˈe/ (Houaiss and Avery).

**§6A.3** The nominals of Class $N_2$ are those nouns ending in /a/ that are [-feminine], and those of Class $N_3$ are ambivalent as far as the gender of what they denote is concerned. Table 6A.7 demonstrates both classes:

Table 6A.7 [-feminine] Nouns Ending in –<u>a</u>

| Foreign (non-Latin) Origin [-feminine] | | | | Native Origin | | | |
|---|---|---|---|---|---|---|---|
| Class $N_2$ | | | | | | Class $N_3$ | |
| Greek | | Other | | [-feminine] | | [±feminine] | |
| Word | Gloss | Word | Gloss | Word | Gloss | Word | Gloss |
| **clima** | climate | **acangapara** | tortoise | **bandarra** | loafer | **agrícola** | agricultural |
| **enigma** | enigma | **estafeta** | messenger | **cabecilha** | bandit chief | **alfacinha** | Lisbonite |
| **eremita** | hermit | **champanha** | Champagne | **carapina** | carpenter | **artista** | artist |
| **esquema** | outline | **inca** | inca | **dia** | day | **belga** | Belgian |
| **gorila** | gorilla | **pijama** | pajama | **guleima** | glutton | **caçula** | last born |
| **lema** | motto | **samba** | samba | **janota** | fop | **caraíba** | Carib |
| **prisma** | prism | **safardana** | low-life | **marialva** | horseman | **colega** | classmate |
| **profeta** | prophet | **chá** | tea | **dinheirama** | big money | **indígena** | indigenous |
| **programa** | program | **xá** | shah | **nada** | nothingness | **patriota** | patriot |
| **sarcoma** | sarcoma | **zabumba** | bass drum | **rapazola** | young man | **suicida** | suicide |

**§6A.4** Class $N_4$ nominals are those that are immune to both Rule 6.2a and Rule 6.2b and maintain their word-final /e/, which occurs after stem-final /r, l, z, n/ as Table 6A.8 demonstrates:

**Table 6A.8** [a]Word-Final +e#

| Nominals Immune to Rule 6.2a | | | | | | | | |
|---|---|---|---|---|---|---|---|---|
| /re/ | | | /ze/ | | | /le/ | | |
| [-plural] | [+plural] | Gloss | [-plural] | [+plural] | Gloss | [-plural] | [+plural] | Gloss |
| donaire | donaires | grace(s) | doze | dozes | dozen(s) | xale | xales | shawl(s) |
| árvore | árvores | tree(s) | crise | crises | crisis (es) | vale | vales | valley(s) |
| freire | freires | friar(s) | frase | frases | phrase(s) | prole | proles | offspring |
| Nominals Ending in Xn<e# Immune to Rule 6.2b | | | | | | | | |
| [-feminine] Nouns | | | [+feminine] Nouns | | | Ambivalent Adjectives | | |
| [-plural] | [+plural] | Gloss | [-plural] | [+plural] | Gloss | [-plural] | [+plural] | Gloss |
| gene | genes | gene(s) | higiene | higienes | hygiene(s) | inane | inanes | inane |
| cânone | cânones | canon(s) | mitene | mitenes | mitten(s) | perene | perenes | perennial |
| sene | senes | senna | alcione | alciones | halcyon(s) | imune | imunes | immune |

a Tables 6.17 and 6.21 reproduced and amalgamated.

## Appendix B Grammatical Parameters

**§6B.0** Only the functional, paradigmatic nominals can be analyzed into a set of parameters determined by the principles of markedness. Table 6B.1 identifies the parameters underlying the morphemes indicative of nominal number and gender.

**Table 6B.1** Nominative Inflectional Morphology Rewrite Rules

| Number and Gender Morphemes | | | Exceptions | | | |
|---|---|---|---|---|---|---|
| Gender→ | [±feminine] → | {+, <} e#[a] | [-fem.] +a# | Gloss | [+fem.], +o#, +u# | Gloss |
| | [+feminine] → | {+,<} a# | samba [-f.] | samba | foto [+f.] | photo |
| | [-feminine] → | {+,<}o# | capeta [-f.] | devil | tribo [+f.] | tribe |
| | [-feminine] → | {+,<} u# | estafeta [-f.] | relay | nau [+f.] | ship |
| | | | | | | |
| Number → | [±plural] | | | | | |
| | [+plural] → | <z# | | | | |
| | [-plural] → | <Ø# | | | | |

a The /e, a, o, u, z/ of the morphemes in Table 6B.1 as well as the strings of phonemes in Table 6B.2 are shorthand for sufficiently specified matrices of the distinctive features used to identify the 26 phonemes of Portuguese. The Ø represents no phonological substance. In addition, both <e and +e may end in +, i.e. in the latter case they may not be word-final, they must be followed by some morpheme, normally <z#.

Number in Portuguese is [±plural], and for nominals only [+plural] is marked. There are no exceptions to marking nominals for plurality.[73] Gender is [±feminine], but there are morphemes that indicate both [+feminine] and [-feminine]. To complicate matters further, gender morphemes and nouns' gender are laden with exceptions to general patterns.

## The Pronouns

**§6B.1.0** Matrix 6B.1a provides a schematic analysis of all the paradigmatic 'subject', accusative, genitive, reflexive, and prepositional nominals in Portuguese.

73 Chapter 9 examines nominals ending in /z/ that can represent [±plural] referents with no apparent plural morpheme: e.g. *lápis* #ˈlapiz# 'pencil(s)'. Underlyingly, however, they are still marked for plurality when their referent is [+plural]: #ˈlapiz#<z#. Portuguese does not permit the surfacing of contiguous instantiations of the same phoneme (Rule 4.1) so words like *lápis* lose their plural morpheme (Table 9B.5).

**Matrix 6B.1a** Paradigmatic Nominals (Pronouns)

| | 1st | 2nd | F. | Pl. | Acc.[a] | Gen. | Reflex. | Prep. | Morphophonemics |
|---|---|---|---|---|---|---|---|---|---|
| eu | + | - | ± | - | - | - | - | - | #eu# |
| me | + | - | ± | - | + | + | + | - | <me# |
| mim | + | - | ± | - | - | - | - | + | <min# |
| tu | - | + | ± | - | - | - | - | - | #tu# |
| te | - | + | ± | - | + | + | + | - | <te# |
| ti | - | + | ± | - | - | - | - | + | <ti# |
| nós | + | ± | ± | + | - | - | - | + | #nɔz# |
| nos | + | ± | ± | + | + | + | + | - | <nɔz# |
| vós | - | + | ± | + | - | - | - | + | #vɔz# |
| vos | - | + | ± | + | + | + | + | + | <vɔz# |
| você(s) | - | + | ± | ± | + | - | - | + | #vɔ.ˈse#(<z#) |
| o, senhor | - | ± | ± | ± | + | - | - | + | #l+<[αf.]#<[βp.]#se#ɲor#<[αf.]#<[βp.] |
| ele, -a (s) | - | - | ± | ± | - | - | - | + | #el+<[αf.]#<[βp.] |
| o, -a, (s) | - | - | ± | ± | + | - | - | - | #l+<[αf.]#<[βp.] |
| si | - | ± | ± | ± | - | - | - | + | <si# |

a Most Portuguese nouns had their origin in the Latin accusative case. But the only vestiges of the Latin case system occur in the 1st and 2nd person clitic pronouns.

Matrix 6B.1a defines the 15 Portuguese pronouns.[74] The only commonality all 15 share is that they can be used to indicate marked or unmarked gender entities—only the 3rd person subject and accusative pronouns are inflected for their referents' number and gender.

**§6B.1.1.0** Matrix 6B.1b provides a schematic analysis of the Portuguese possessive pronouns.

74 The forms using *senhor* are not as 'pronominal' as the others, because by casting the addressee as a 3rd person, they indicate their deference to their addressee by referring to him/her as 'the gentleman, the lady', etc.

**Matrix 6B.1b** Paradigmatic Nominals (Possessives)

| | Possessor | | Referent | | Possessed | | Case | |
|---|---|---|---|---|---|---|---|---|
| Pronouns | $1^{st}$ | $2^{nd}$ | Fem. | Plural | Fem. | Plural | Gen. | Morphophonemics |
| meu(s) | + | - | ± | - | - | ± | + | #me+<u#(<z#) |
| minha(s) | + | - | ± | - | + | ± | + | #miɲ+<a#(<z#) |
| teu(s) | - | + | ± | - | - | ± | + | #te+<u#(<z#) |
| tua(s) | - | + | ± | - | + | ± | + | #tu+<a#(<z#) |
| nosso(s) | + | ± | ± | + | ± | ± | + | #nɔs+<[αfem]# (<z#) |
| vosso(s) | - | + | ± | + | ± | ± | + | #vɔs+<[αfem]# (<z#) |
| seu(s) | - | ± | ± | ± | - | ± | + | #se+<u#(<z#) |
| sua(s) | - | ± | ± | ± | + | ± | + | #su+<a#(<z#) |

In Matrix 6B.1b, the ± sign indicates either that a particular form is indifferent to the particular parameter or that it is capable of accommodating the parameter by inflection for either [±feminine] or [±plural]. The specification [+genitive] distinguishes the possessive pronouns from all other grammatical nominals. In their morphophonemic representations, all possessive pronouns are bounded by # at their extremities, which means they can both begin and end utterances, and they receive stress.

**§6B.1.1.1** The possessive pronouns are dual entities, they are organized as $1^{st}$, $2^{nd}$, and $3^{rd}$ [±plural] possessors (i.e. referents), and they also reflect the number and gender of the possessed item(s). They are positively specified as [+genitive] because they indicate that the specific grammatical person they denote is the possessor of whatever the form may modify or represent. Possessive pronouns are full-fledged adjectives capable of beginning and ending utterances as well as being nominalized as subjects, direct objects, and objects of prepositions. Matrix 6B.1b shows that possessive roots are suppletive between [±feminine] forms in the [-plural] person category: the roots of the [-feminine] forms are #me+, #te+, #se+, the roots of the [+feminine] forms are #miɲ+, #tu+, and #su+. The $3^{rd}$ person forms, like the prepositional pronoun *si* and the $3^{rd}$ person reflexive pronoun *se*, do not distinguish between [±plural] referents, but they can be used to denote the non-intimate $2^{nd}$ person possessors, e.g. *você(s)* and *o(s) senhor(es)*.

**§6B.1.2.0** Matrix 6B.2 provides a schematic analysis of the Portuguese demonstrative pronouns.

**Matrix 6B.2** Paradigmatic Nominals (Demonstratives)

| | Person | | Def. | Locator | | Demonstrated | | |
|---|---|---|---|---|---|---|---|---|
| Pronouns | $1^{st}$ | $2^{nd}$ | | Fem. | Plural | Fem. | Plural | Morphophonemics |
| este, -a, -s | + | - | + | ± | ± | ± | ± | #ezt+<[αfem]# (<z#) |
| esse, -a, -s | - | + | + | ± | ± | ± | ± | #es+<[αfem]# (<z#) |
| aquele, -a, -s | - | - | + | ± | ± | ± | ± | #akel+<[αfem]# (<z#) |

Matrix 6B.2 indicates that the three demonstratives coordinate with $1^{st}$, $2^{nd}$, and $3^{rd}$ ($-1^{st}$, $-2^{nd}$) grammatical persons that, like all normal adjectives, they agree in number and gender with the nominals they locate in those three grammatical spaces. Their extremities bounded by # indicate that they receive stress and may occur in utterance-initial or utterance-final position. Like the possessives, they are not clitics and can be nominalized subjects, direct objects, and objects of prepositions. They are distinguished from the possessives because they are specified as [+definite], which means that ideally when demonstratives occur, speaker and hearer can locate the nouns they refer to.

**§6B.1.3** Matrix 6B.3 provides a schematic analysis of the Portuguese articles.

**Matrix 6B.3** Paradigmatic Nominals (Articles)

| | Person | | Nominal | | | |
|---|---|---|---|---|---|---|
| Articles | $1^{st}$ | $2^{nd}$ | Fem. | Plural | Definite | Morphophonemics |
| o, a, -s | - | - | ± | ± | + | #l+<[αfem]>(<z>) |
| um, -a, s | - | - | ± | ± | - | #un+<[αfem]# (<z#) |

Matrix 6B.3 indicates that grammatical person has no bearing on the use of articles, that, like all adjectives, they can accommodate both the gender and number of the nominals they identify as definite or indefinite. The clitic ending of the definite article (>) indicates that it cannot end an utterance, whereas the final # of the indefinite article indicates that it can, and that it receives stress. The section that follows elaborates the parameters used to identify the grammatical nominals of Portuguese.

## The Parameters

**§6B.2.0 [±feminine], [±plural]:** The specification [-feminine] indicates what has traditionally been known as masculine. This chapter has argued, however, that [-feminine] does not assign exclusive masculinity to any set of referents, it only indicates that there is at least one [-feminine] individual or item in the particular set being identified. On the other hand, [+feminine] generally rules out any masculine presence, except, of course, in epicene [+feminine] nouns indicating species: e.g. *águias, baleias, onças, trutas, pessoas* 'eagles, whales, wildcats, trout, persons'. The animals designated by these [+feminine] words consist of both male and female entities. Similar relations obtain among [±plural]: [-plural] does not preclude general (collective) referents, but [+plural] generally rules out singular referents. There is more to say about each category immediately below (§6B.2.6.0–1).

**§6B.2.1 Unmarked Case (i.e. subject, i.e. [-accusative, -genitive, -reflexive, -prepositional]):** What is commonly called the nominative case is the unmarked pronominal case in Portuguese because the unmarked subject case enjoys the widest distribution of the pronouns. They occur both at utterances' beginnings and endings, and three of the five pronouns may double as objects of prepositions—this peculiarity indicates that such forms are not strictly nominative. They are, simply, the pronominal unmarked case.

**§6.B.2.2 Accusative Case:** The accusative case is uniquely manifest in the '3rd person' direct object pronouns: <l+<gender#<number#. All the other clitic pronouns (1st person, 2nd person, [±plural], i.e. *me, te, nos, vos*) also occur as accusative, genitive, and reflexive pronouns. And in the speech register described in this treatise they may not begin an utterance.

**§6B.2.3 Genitive Case:** The genitive case identifies both the indirect object pronouns and the possessives. The possessives are genitives since indicating possession is one of the genitive case's primary functions in many languages. However, calling indirect objects genitives requires some explanation, especially because the indirect object pronouns descend from Latin datives. But the genitive case is also used for designating possession and source, which the Portuguese indirect object pronoun can do: (A) **Source:** *Comprei-lhe a casa* 'I bought the house from 3rd'. (B) **Benefit:** this sentence can also mean 'I bought the house for 3rd'. And (C) **possession:** 'I bought 3rd's house'. Sentences like

*Caiu-lhe o relógio* '3rd's watch fell' or *Tiraram-lhe o apêndice* 'They took 3rd's appendix out' indicate possession and source.[75]

**§6B.2.4 Reflexive Case:** The reflexive pronouns (save *se*) are all homophonous and homologous with the other clitic pronouns. Notwithstanding the homophony and homology of reflexive pronouns with the other pronominal clitics, they constitute a different case because these pronouns indicate that verbs' subjects and direct objects have the same referent: e.g. *Deita-se às 11* '3rd puts 3rd to bed at 11', *Vejo-me correndo pelo parque* 'I see myself running through the park'. In addition, because this set's 3rd person pronoun (*se*) is uniquely reflexive, there is no other category for it other than 'reflexive'.

**§6B.2.5 Prepositional Case:** This is a more improvisational, ad hoc case that owes its origin to the existence of three special pronouns, *mim*, *ti*, and *si* that occur only as prepositional objects. All the other pronouns (demonstrative, 'subject' and possessive) may be objects of prepositions.

**§6B.2.6.0 Person and Number:** Grammatical persons (i.e. [±1st, ±2nd]) identify entities that speak for themselves, are directly addressed, or that are talked about. The negation of grammatical person, i.e. the specification [-1st, -2nd] which, used to identify the articles among the clitics, indicates that reference to a specific situation is not necessarily restricted to either of the grammatical persons participating in a particular linguistic act. The marked grammatical persons are 1st and 2nd, which indicate, respectively, the addresser(s) and the addressee(s).[76] Number in Portuguese indicates whether a referent is necessarily multiple i.e. [+plural]. The specification [-plural] indicates that a referent need not be multiple although it may be general, as in the proverbs cited in Table 6.4, and §6.0.12.2.0–2 Every non-defective Portuguese verb has a morphological reflex for the plurals of these grammatical persons, as well as for the familiar 2nd person [-plural], whereas only

75 One might want to argue that another function of the indirect object is benefit: *Dão-me dinheiro* 'They give me money' or *Emprestaram-nos o carro* 'They lent us the car' or prejudice: *Roubaram-me a gravata* 'They stole my tie' or *Sujaste-me a cara* 'You dirtied my face'. However, both possession and source are implied in these sentences, and the benefit and prejudice expressed come from the verbs' meanings rather than from the any meaning the pronoun itself may have.

76 The plural marker appears in parentheses because the 1st and 2nd persons may indicate individuals or pluralities: 'I' or 'we', 'you' and 'you people'.

the present indicative and the preterite have 1$^{st}$ person [-plural] reflexes, and only the preterite has an actual [-1$^{st}$, -2$^{nd}$, -plural] person suffix (§13.2.2).

**§6B.2.6.1 [-1$^{st}$, -2$^{nd}$] Person:** The 3$^{rd}$ person [-plural], is, thus, the unmarked grammatical person. It occasions scant morphological recognition in verb forms, and 3$^{rd}$ person [-plural] utterances can be understood in a gamut of ways. That is, a sentence such as *A gente vai* can mean 'people go, We go, I go'; *Vêem-se clientes pela tarde* can be interpreted to mean 'One sees, we see, they see, (s)he sees clients in the afternoon' or 'Clients see themselves in the afternoon', or 'Clients are seen in the afternoon'.

**§6B.2.7 Definite:** The feature [±definite] distinguishes the Portuguese definite articles from indefinite articles. Compare the sentences *Ouço o pássaro* 'I hear the bird' and *Ouço um pássaro* 'I hear a bird'. In the first sentence, the specific *pássaro* is a referent common to both addresser and addressee(s). In the second, whatever *pássaro* it may be is not necessarily known to either addresser or addressee(s). This parameter also characterizes demonstrative pronouns.

**§6B.3** Table 6B.4 displays the parameters needed to definite the pronominal system of Portuguese:

**Table 6B.4** Analytic Nominal Parameters

| Number | Gender | Person | Case | Reference |
|---|---|---|---|---|
| ±plural | ±feminine | ±1$^{st}$ | ±accusative | ±definite |
| | | ±2$^{nd}$ | ±genitive | |
| | | | ±reflexive | |
| | | | ±prepositional | |

The number and person parameters govern verbal inflection—they are not unique to nouns.

## Appendix C Rules as they Appear in Chapter 6

§6C.0 Appendix C contains the morphophonemic rules as they appear in Chapter 6.

**Rule 6.1 The Closing of Nominal Class 1 ($N_1$) Vowels:**

$$\begin{pmatrix} \text{-contoid} \\ +\text{dorsal} \\ +\text{wide glottis} \\ +\text{labial} \\ +\text{delayed release} \end{pmatrix} \rightarrow [\text{-wide glottis}] \;/\; \_\_\; C_{1\text{-}2} + \begin{Bmatrix} < \\ + \end{Bmatrix} o\#<[\text{-plural}]\#_{[N1]}$$

**Rule 6.2a Deletion of Word-Final <e+ and+e+_ after /r#, /l#, and /z#:**

$$\begin{Bmatrix} < \\ + \end{Bmatrix} \begin{pmatrix} \text{-contoid} \\ \text{-high} \\ \text{-wide glottis} \\ +\text{palatal} \end{pmatrix} \# \rightarrow \emptyset \;/\; \#X\,[\text{-contoid}] \begin{pmatrix} +\text{contoid} \\ \text{-surd} \\ \text{-labial} \\ \text{-high} \\ \text{-nasal} \\ \text{-occlusion} \end{pmatrix} \_\_ + <[\text{-plural}]\#$$

**Rule 6.3 Loss of #e/ in #en>:**

$$\begin{pmatrix} \text{-contoid} \\ +\text{palatal} \\ \text{-high} \\ \text{-wide glottis} \end{pmatrix} \rightarrow \emptyset \;/\; \#\,\_\_\; n>\#l+<[\pm\text{feminine}]\#<[\pm\text{plural}]>$$

**Rule 6.4 Progressive assimilation of #l+:**

$$\begin{pmatrix} +\text{lateral} \\ \text{-high} \end{pmatrix} \rightarrow \begin{pmatrix} \text{-lateral} \\ +\text{nasal} \end{pmatrix} \;/\; \begin{pmatrix} +\text{contoid} \\ +\text{nasal} \end{pmatrix} >\#\_\_ +[\pm\text{feminine}]\#<[\pm\text{plural}]>$$

**Rule 4.1 Like Segment Deletion (Alluded):**

$$\text{Segment}_2 \rightarrow \varnothing \,/\, \text{Segment}_1 \,\_\_\_$$

**Condition:** $\text{Segment}_1 = \text{Segment}_2$

**Rule 6.5 Deletion of #l+ Except After Prepositions:**

$$\# \left( \begin{array}{l} +\text{lateral} \\ -\text{ high} \end{array} \right) + \;/\_ <[\pm\text{feminine}]> <[\pm\text{plural}] \rightarrow \varnothing \;\text{--} \left\{ \begin{array}{l} \#\text{por} \\ \#\text{maiz} \\ \#\text{en} \end{array} \right\} > \;\_\_\_$$

**Rule 6.2b Deletion of Word-Final <e+, +e+, (and +ɛ#) after /n#:**

$$\left( \begin{array}{l} -\text{contoid} \\ -\text{high} \\ -\text{delayed transition} \\ +\text{palatal} \end{array} \right) \rightarrow \varnothing \,/\, \#\, X \left( \begin{array}{l} +\text{contoid} \\ +\text{nasal} \\ -\text{labial} \\ -\text{high} \end{array} \right) \#_{[\text{-N4}]}$$

**Rule 6.6a Subject Pronoun Root Vowel Metaphony:**

$$\left( \begin{array}{l} -\text{contoid} \\ -\text{high} \\ -\text{wide glottis} \\ +\text{palatal} \end{array} \right) \rightarrow [+\text{wide glottis}] \,/\, \#\_\_\; C <[+\text{feminine}]_{[\text{Pronoun, -1st, -2nd}]}$$

**Rule 6.6b Subject Pronoun/ Demonstrative Root Vowel Metaphony:**

$$\left( \begin{array}{l} -\text{contoid} \\ -\text{high} \\ -\text{wide glottis} \\ +\text{palatal} \end{array} \right) \rightarrow [+\text{wide glottis}] \,/\, \#X\_\_\; C_{1\text{-}2} <[+\text{feminine}]_{[\text{Pronoun, Demonstrative}]}\#$$

**Rule 6.7a Deletion of <l+:**

$$< \begin{pmatrix} \text{-high} \\ \text{+lateral} \end{pmatrix} + X \rightarrow\ < \varnothing\ /\ \begin{Bmatrix} [\text{-contoid}]_{[\text{VerbTR}]}\ \#\_\_ \\ \_\_\_\_\_\_\ [\text{Verb}]\ ] \end{Bmatrix}$$

**Rule 6.8 Progressive Nasal Assimilation of <l+**

$$< \begin{pmatrix} \text{+lateral} \\ \text{-high} \end{pmatrix} + \ \rightarrow \begin{pmatrix} \text{-lateral} \\ \text{+nasal} \end{pmatrix}\ /\ [\text{+nasal}]_{[\text{Verb}]}\_\_\_\_$$

**Rule 6.9a Verb-final /r/ and /z/ Deletion Before <l+:**

$$\begin{pmatrix} \text{+contoid} \\ \text{-surd} \\ \text{-high} \\ \text{-labial} \\ \text{-nasal} \end{pmatrix}_{[\text{Verb}]} \rightarrow \varnothing\ /\ \_\_\ <\text{l}+<[\pm\text{feminine}]\#<[\pm\text{plural}]\#$$

**Rule 6.7b Deletion of <l+:**

$$< \begin{pmatrix} \text{-high} \\ \text{+lateral} \end{pmatrix} + \rightarrow \varnothing\ /\ \begin{Bmatrix} [\text{-contoid}]_{[\text{Verb}]}\ \#\_\_\_\_ \\ \_\_\_\_\_\_\ [\text{Verb}] \\ \text{I.O.}_{\cdot\text{prn}}\ \_\_\_ \end{Bmatrix}$$

**Rule 6.9b Final /r/ and /z/ Deletion Before <l+:**

$$\begin{pmatrix} \text{+contoid} \\ \text{-surd} \\ \text{-high} \\ \text{-labial} \\ \text{-nasal} \end{pmatrix}_{[\text{Verb, I.O.}]} \rightarrow \varnothing\ /\ \_\_\ <\text{l}+<[\pm\text{feminine}]\#<[\pm\text{plural}]\#$$

**Rule 6.10 Loss of /e# in *Lhe* and other I.O. Pronouns:**

$$\begin{pmatrix} \text{-contoid} \\ \text{+palatal} \\ \text{-high} \\ \text{-wide glottis} \end{pmatrix} \rightarrow \emptyset \; / \; {<}\text{PRN}_{[\text{i.o.}]}\#\_\_ \; {<}\text{PRN}_{[\text{d..o.3rd}]}\#$$

**Rule 6.11 Loss of /z/ in Reflexive 1st Person Plural Verbs:**

$$\begin{pmatrix} \text{+fricative} \\ \text{-surd} \\ \text{-high} \\ \text{-labial} \end{pmatrix} \rightarrow \emptyset \; / \; \text{Verb}_{[\text{1st, +plural}]} \; \_\_ + \text{Prn}_{[\text{+reflexive}]}$$

## Appendix D The Grammar of Unproblematic Nominal Inflection

**§6D.0** Of all the rules proposed in Chapter 6, the following rules, in the following order, account for all the phenomena examined in this chapter:

**Rule 6D.0 Adjective-Noun Agreement:**[77]

$$[\text{modifier}] \rightarrow \begin{pmatrix} \alpha\text{gender} \\ \beta\text{number} \end{pmatrix} \; / \; \_\_ \; \text{noun} \begin{pmatrix} \alpha\text{gender} \\ \beta\text{number} \end{pmatrix} \_\_$$

77 Rule 6D.0 has been implicit in this study and is formalized now as above. The determinand is the ad hoc category modifier, which includes adjectives, articles, demonstrative and possessive pronouns, which agree in number and gender with the nouns they modify.

**Rule: 13.9 Stress Regular Past Tense Theme Vowel:**

$$[\text{-contoid}]/\ \_\ \ \# \begin{Bmatrix} < \\ + \end{Bmatrix} CV \begin{Bmatrix} \# \\ + \end{Bmatrix} <\ P/N\# \rightarrow [+\text{delayed transition}]$$

**Rule 3.1 Paroxytone Stress:**

$$[\text{-contoid}] \rightarrow [+\text{stress}]\ /\ \#X\ \_\ \left( \begin{bmatrix} +\text{high} \\ \text{-contoid} \end{bmatrix} \right) C_{0\text{-}4} V_{[\text{-high}]} \#(C)\#$$

Condition: The word has no previously assigned stress.

**Rule 6.1 The Closing of Nominal Class 1 ($N_1$) Vowels:**

$$\begin{bmatrix} \text{-contoid} \\ +\text{dorsal} \\ +\text{wide glottis} \\ +\text{labial} \\ +\text{delayed release} \end{bmatrix} \rightarrow [\text{-wide glottis}]\ /\ \_\_\ C_{1\text{-}2} + \begin{Bmatrix} < \\ + \end{Bmatrix}\ o\# < [\text{-plural}]\#_{[N1]}$$

**Rule 6.2a Deletion of Word-Final <e+ and +e+_ After /r#, /l#, and /z#:**

$$\begin{Bmatrix} < \\ + \end{Bmatrix} \begin{bmatrix} \text{-contoid} \\ \text{-high} \\ \text{-wide glottis} \\ +\text{palatal} \end{bmatrix} \# \rightarrow \emptyset\ /\ \#X\ [\text{-contoid}] \begin{bmatrix} +\text{contoid} \\ \text{-surd} \\ \text{-labial} \\ \text{-high} \\ \text{-nasal} \\ \text{-occlusion} \end{bmatrix} \_\_ + < [\text{-plural}]\#$$

**Rule 6.2b Deletion of Word-Final <e+, +e+, (and +ɛ#) After /n#:**

$$\begin{bmatrix}\text{-contoid}\\ \text{-high}\\ \text{-delayed transition}\\ \text{+palatal}\end{bmatrix} \rightarrow \varnothing \;/\; \#\, X \begin{bmatrix}\text{+contoid}\\ \text{+nasal}\\ \text{-labial}\\ \text{-high}\end{bmatrix} \#_{[\text{-N4}]}\underline{\quad\quad}$$

**Rule 6.6b Subject Pronoun/ Demonstrative Root Vowel Metaphony:**

$$\begin{bmatrix}\text{-contoid}\\ \text{-high}\\ \text{-wide glottis}\\ \text{+palatal}\end{bmatrix} \rightarrow [\text{+wide glottis}] \;/\; \#X\underline{\quad} \; C_{1\text{-}2} < [\text{+feminine}]_{[\text{Pronoun, Demonstrative}]}\#$$

**Rule 6.8 Progressive Nasal Assimilation of <l+:**

$$< \begin{bmatrix}\text{+lateral}\\ \text{-high}\end{bmatrix} + \rightarrow \begin{bmatrix}\text{-lateral}\\ \text{+nasal}\end{bmatrix} \;/\; [\text{+nasal}]_{[\text{Verb}]}\underline{\quad\quad}$$

**Rule 6.3 Loss of #e/ in #en>:**

$$\begin{bmatrix}\text{-contoid}\\ \text{+palatal}\\ \text{-high}\\ \text{-wide glottis}\end{bmatrix} \rightarrow \varnothing \;/\; \# \underline{\quad\quad} n > \#l + < [\pm\text{feminine}]\# < [\pm\text{plural}] >$$

**Rule 6.4 Progressive Assimilation of #l+:**

$$\begin{bmatrix}\text{+lateral}\\ \text{-high}\end{bmatrix} \rightarrow \begin{bmatrix}\text{-lateral}\\ \text{+nasal}\end{bmatrix} \;/\; \begin{bmatrix}\text{+contoid}\\ \text{+nasal}\end{bmatrix} > \#\underline{\quad} + [\pm\text{feminine}]\# < [\pm\text{plural}] >$$

**Rule 6.5 Deletion of #l+ Except After Prepositions (6D.2, 4):**

$$\# \begin{pmatrix} +\text{lateral} \\ -\text{high} \end{pmatrix} +/\_ <[\pm\text{feminine}]> <[\pm\text{plural}] \rightarrow \varnothing \text{ - } \begin{Bmatrix} \#\text{por} \\ \#\text{maiz} \\ \#\text{en} \end{Bmatrix} > \_\_\_$$

**Rule 6.11 Loss of /z/ in Reflexive 1st Person Plural Verbs:**

$$\begin{pmatrix} +\text{fricative} \\ -\text{surd} \\ -\text{high} \\ -\text{labial} \end{pmatrix} \rightarrow \varnothing \,/\, \text{Vb}_{\text{trans [1st, +plural]}} \_\_\_ + \text{Prn}_{[+\text{reflexive}]}$$

**Rule 6.9b Final /r/ and /z/ Deletion Before <l+:**

$$\begin{pmatrix} +\text{contoid} \\ -\text{surd} \\ -\text{high} \\ -\text{labial} \\ -\text{nasal} \end{pmatrix}_{[\text{Verb, I.O.}]} \rightarrow \varnothing \,/\, \_\_\_ <\text{l}+<[\pm\text{feminine}]\#<[\pm\text{plural}]\#$$

**Rule 6.7b Deletion of <l+:**

$$< \begin{pmatrix} -\text{high} \\ +\text{lateral} \end{pmatrix} + \rightarrow \varnothing \,/ \begin{Bmatrix} [-\text{contoid}]\#\_\_\_ \\ \_\_\_\_ [\text{Verb}]\,] \\ \text{I.O.}_{\text{prn}} \_\_\_ \end{Bmatrix}$$

**Rule 6.10 Loss of /e# in *Lhe* and other I.O. Pronouns (6D.8):**

$$\begin{pmatrix} \text{-contoid} \\ \text{+palatal} \\ \text{-high} \\ \text{-wide glottis} \end{pmatrix} \rightarrow \emptyset \,/\, <\text{PRN}_{[\text{i.o.}]}\#\_\_ \;\; <\text{PRN}_{[\text{d.o.3rd}]}\#$$

**§6D.1** Two sentences demonstrate the operation of this chapter's grammar of nominal inflection: Sentence 1: *Um agricultor queria o nosso ovo, ele quis levá-lo, mas os filhos comeram-no com aquelas batatas no porão* means 'A farmer wanted our egg, he tried to take it, but his children ate it with those potatoes in the basement.' Sentence 2: *Tiramos-lhas e pusemo-no-las* 'We took them [the clothes] from them and put them on (ourselves)'. The following derivations demonstrate the role these rules play in producing grammatical Portuguese utterances.

## §6D.2 First Clause: Um agricultor queria o nosso ovo 'A farmer wanted our egg'

#un+<gen.#<nu##agrikultor$_{N[-fem.]}$#[78]<e#<Ø##kɛria#

#l+<gen.#<nu>#nɔs$_{N}$+<gen.#<nu# #ɔv++o#<Ø#$_{N1}$

78 The morphological makeup of the words *agricultor* and *queria* does not appear because it is not germane to the matter at hand.

**Table 6D.1** Um agricultor queria

| | **Morphemes** | | | | | | |
|---|---|---|---|---|---|---|---|
| **U.Fs.** | #un# | <gen# | <nu.# | #agrikultor$_{N[\text{-fem.}]}$# | <e+ | <Ø# | #kɛria# |
| **R. 6B.0** | #un$_N$# | <e+ | <Ø# | #agrikultor$_{N[\text{-fem.}]}$ | <e+ | <Ø# | #kɛria# |
| **Stress**[a] | #ˈun$_N$# | <e+ | <Ø# | #agrikultˈor$_{N[\text{-fem.}]}$ | <e+ | <Ø# | #kɛrˈia# |
| **R. 6.1** | *** | *** | *** | *** | *** | *** | *** |
| **R. 6.2a** | #ˈun$_N$# | <e+ | <Ø# | #agrikultˈor$_{N[\text{-fem.}]}$ | Ø | <Ø# | #kɛrˈia# |
| **R. 6.2b** | #ˈun$_N$# | Ø | <Ø# | #agrikultˈor$_{N[\text{-fem.}]}$ | Ø | <Ø# | #kɛrˈia# |
| **R. 6.6b** | *** | *** | *** | *** | *** | *** | *** |
| **R. 6.8** | *** | *** | *** | *** | *** | *** | *** |
| **R. 6.3** | *** | *** | *** | *** | *** | *** | *** |
| **R. 6.4** | *** | *** | *** | *** | *** | *** | *** |
| **R. 6.5** | *** | *** | *** | *** | *** | *** | *** |
| **R. 6.11** | *** | *** | *** | *** | *** | *** | *** |
| **R. 6.9b** | *** | *** | *** | *** | *** | *** | *** |
| **R. 6.7b** | *** | *** | *** | *** | *** | *** | *** |
| **R. 6.10** | *** | *** | *** | *** | *** | *** | *** |
| **Representation** | | #ˈun$_N$+<Ø##agrikultˈor$_{N[\text{-fem.}]}$#<Ø##kɛrˈia# | | | | | |
| **Ø Morpheme Erase** | | #ˈun$_N$##agrikultˈor$_{N[\text{-fem.}]}$###kɛrˈia# | | | | | |

a Rules 13.9 and 3.1.

Rule 6.2a deletes the <e+ from #agrikultor#$_N$<e+<Ø# because it is a class N nominal to which this rule applies when the nominal is not plural. Rule 6.2b deletes the <e# on #un#<gender#<number# because this form is an N class nominal with an /n/ preceding the gender morpheme <e+, which disappears after the rule of paroxytone stress has applied. No more rules apply to this string. The final step in bringing this utterance to its phonetic realization is to clear the representation of Øs and extraneous morpheme boundaries. Then various low-level phonological and phonetic rules can apply producing [ˈũ.ă.ɣri.kuɫ.ˈtor.kə.ˈri.ă].

**§6D.3** Table 6D.2 accounts for the second half of this clause: 'our egg': #l+<gen.#<nu>#nɔs$_N$+<gen.#<nu# #ɔv$_{N1}$++o#<Ø#.

Table 6D.2 o nosso ovo

| Morphemes | | | | | | | | | |
|---|---|---|---|---|---|---|---|---|---|
| U.Fs. | #l+ | <gen# | +<nu> | #nɔs$_N$+ | <gen# | <nu# | #ɔv$_{N1}$+ | +o# | <Ø# |
| R.6B.0 | #l+ | <o# | +Ø> | #nɔs$_N$+ | <o# | <Ø# | #ɔv$_{N1}$+ | +o# | <Ø# |
| Stress | #l+ | <o# | +Ø> | #nˈɔs$_N$+ | <o# | <Ø# | #ˈɔv$_{N1}$+ | +o# | <Ø# |
| R.6.1 | #l+ | <o# | +Ø> | #nˈɔs$_N$+ | <o# | <Ø# | #ˈov$_{N1}$+ | +o# | <Ø# |
| R.6.2a | *** | *** | *** | *** | *** | *** | *** | *** | *** |
| R.6.2b | *** | *** | *** | *** | *** | *** | *** | *** | *** |
| R. 6.6b | *** | *** | *** | *** | *** | *** | *** | *** | *** |
| R. 6.8 | *** | *** | *** | *** | *** | *** | *** | *** | *** |
| R. 6.3 | *** | *** | *** | *** | *** | *** | *** | *** | *** |
| R. 6.4 | *** | *** | *** | *** | *** | *** | *** | *** | *** |
| R. 6.5 | #Ø> | <o# | +Ø> | #nɔs$_N$+ | <o# | <Ø# | #ov$_{N1}$+ | +o# | <Ø# |
| R. 6.11 | *** | *** | *** | *** | *** | *** | *** | *** | *** |
| R.6.9b | *** | *** | *** | *** | *** | *** | *** | *** | *** |
| R. 6.7b | *** | *** | *** | *** | *** | *** | *** | *** | *** |
| R. 6.10 | *** | *** | *** | *** | *** | *** | *** | *** | *** |
| Representation | | #Ø>#o><Ø>#nˈɔs$_N$+<o#<Ø#$_N$#ˈov$_{N1}$++o#<Ø#$_{N1}$ | | | | | | | |
| Ø Morpheme Erase | | (#kɛrˈia#)#o>#nˈɔs$_N$+<o##ˈov+<o# | | | | | | | |

Rule 6.1 shifts the /ɔ/ of #ɔv$_{N1}$+to /o/ because the word is [-feminine, -plural]. It does not change the /ɔ/ of #nɔs$_N$+ because it is an N root immune to any mutations caused by gender or number morphemes. Rule 6.5 deletes the #l+ of the definite article because it does not follow any of the prepositions that occasion its emergence (*por*, *mais*, or *em*). At this point, the boundaries can be erased and various phonetic rules would apply producing [ŭ.ˈnɔ.sŭ.ˈo.vŭ].

§6D.3 The second clause in the sample sentence is: **ele quis levá-lo**, #el+<gen#<nu##kiz##lɛvar#+e+<Ø#<l+<gen#<nu#.

**Table 6D.3** ele quis levá-lo

| | Moprhemes | | | | | | | | | |
|---|---|---|---|---|---|---|---|---|---|---|
| U.Fs. | #el+ | +gen# | <nu# | #kiz# | #lɛvar# | +gen# | <Ø# | <l+ | <gen# | <nu# |
| R.6B.0 | #el+ | <e# | <Ø# | #kiz# | #lɛvar# | +e+ | <Ø# | <l+ | <o# | <Ø# |
| Stress | #ˈel+ | <e# | <Ø# | #kˈiz# | #lɛvˈar# | +e+ | <Ø# | <l+ | <o# | <Ø# |
| R. 6.1 | *** | *** | *** | *** | *** | *** | *** | *** | *** | *** |
| R. 6.2a | #ˈel+ | <e# | <Ø# | #kˈiz# | #lɛvˈar# | Ø | <Ø# | <l+ | <o# | <Ø# |
| R. 6.2b | *** | *** | *** | *** | *** | *** | *** | *** | *** | *** |
| R. 6.6b | *** | *** | *** | *** | *** | *** | *** | *** | *** | *** |
| R. 6.8 | *** | *** | *** | *** | *** | *** | *** | *** | *** | *** |
| R. 6.3 | *** | *** | *** | *** | *** | *** | *** | *** | *** | *** |
| R. 6.4 | *** | *** | *** | *** | *** | *** | *** | *** | *** | *** |
| R. 6.5 | *** | *** | *** | *** | *** | *** | *** | *** | *** | *** |
| R. 6.11 | *** | *** | *** | *** | *** | *** | *** | *** | *** | *** |
| R. 6.9b | #el+ | <e# | <Ø# | #kiz# | #levˈa# | <Ø# | <Ø# | <l+ | <o# | <Ø# |
| R. 6.7b | *** | *** | *** | *** | *** | *** | *** | *** | *** | *** |
| R. 6.10 | *** | *** | *** | *** | *** | *** | *** | *** | *** | *** |
| Representation | | #ˈel+<e#Ø##kˈiz##levˈa#<l+<o#<Ø# | | | | | | | | |
| Ø Morpheme Erase | | #ˈel+<e##ˈkiz##leva#<l+<o# | | | | | | | | |

Rule 6.2a removes the derivational gender morpheme +e+ from the infinitive, an N nominal, since it bears no plural (or person/number) morpheme. Rule 6.5 does not delete the direct object pronoun's initial <l+ because it follows the verb's final /r#, which Rule 6.9b deletes. Phonetic rules may now apply making this clause [ˈe.lə.ˈkiž.ləˈva.lŭ].

**§6D.4** Of course similar rules and fates befall the final clause: **mas os filhos comeram-no com aquelas batatas no porão,** #maz>#l+<gen><nu>#fiλ+<o#<z# #komeran#<l+<gen#<nu##kon>#akel+<gen#<nu##batat++a#<z##en>#l+<gen>#en>l+<o><Ø>#porão#. Table 6D.4 derives the first phrase.

Table 6D.4 mas os filhos

| | Moprhemes | | | | | | |
|---|---|---|---|---|---|---|---|
| U.Fs. | #maz# | #l+ | <gen> | <nu> | #fiλ+ | <o# | <z# |
| R.6B.0 | #maz# | #l+ | <o> | <z> | #fiλ+ | <o# | <z# |
| Stress | #mˈaz# | #l+ | <o> | <z> | #fˈiλ+ | <o# | <z# |
| R.6.1 | *** | *** | *** | *** | *** | *** | *** |
| R.6.2a | *** | *** | *** | *** | *** | *** | *** |
| R.6.2b | *** | *** | *** | *** | *** | *** | *** |
| R. 6.6b | *** | *** | *** | *** | *** | *** | *** |
| R. 6.8 | *** | *** | *** | *** | *** | *** | *** |
| R. 6.3 | *** | *** | *** | *** | *** | *** | *** |
| R. 6.4 | *** | *** | *** | *** | *** | *** | *** |
| R. 6.5 | #maz# | <Ø# | <o> | <z> | #fiλ+ | <o# | <z# |
| R. 6.11 | *** | *** | *** | *** | *** | *** | *** |
| R.6.9b | *** | *** | *** | *** | *** | *** | *** |
| R. 6.7b | *** | *** | *** | *** | *** | *** | *** |
| R. 6.10 | *** | *** | *** | *** | *** | *** | *** |
| Results | #maz##Ø+<o><z>#fiλ+<o#<z# | | | | | | |
| Ø Morpheme Erase | | #maz##<o><z>#fiλ+<o#<z# | | | | | |

The only rule to apply to this phrase is Rule 6.5, which deletes the definite article's #l+. Phonetic rules eventually operate to produce [ˈma. zŭš.ˈfi.λŭš].

**§6D.5** The next part of this clause contains the verb and the 3rd person direct object:

**Table 6D.5** comeram-no

| | Morphemes | | | |
|---|---|---|---|---|
| U.Fs. | #komeran# | <l+ | <gen# | <nu# |
| R.6B.0 | #komeran# | <l+ | <o# | <Ø# |
| Stress | #komˈeran# | <l+ | <o# | <Ø# |
| R.6.1 | *** | *** | *** | *** |
| R.6.2a | *** | *** | *** | *** |
| R.6.2b | *** | *** | *** | *** |
| R. 6.6b | *** | *** | *** | *** |
| R. 6.8 | #komeran# | <n+ | <o# | <Ø# |
| R. 6.3 | *** | *** | *** | *** |
| R. 6.4 | *** | *** | *** | *** |
| R. 6.5 | *** | *** | *** | *** |
| R. 6.11 | *** | *** | *** | *** |
| R.6.9b | *** | *** | *** | *** |
| R. 6.7b | *** | *** | *** | *** |
| R. 6.10 | *** | *** | *** | *** |
| Results | #komeran# <n+<o#<Ø# | | | |
| Ø Morpheme Erase | | #komeran#<n+ <o# | | |

Rule 6.8 causes the progressive assimilation of pronoun-initial <l+ by verb-final /n#. Rule 4.1, like segment deletion, does not apply in this grammar. It is a low-level rule that applies after the rules that turn the verb-final sequence /an/ into [ã̆ᵘ̃] (cf. §8.1.1, §9.0.2.0, §9.1.0–.1, §13.1.7). This sequence is realized as [kŭˈme.rã̆ᵘ̃ˑ.nŭ].

**§6D.6** The penultimate phrase in sentence one is: ##kon>#akel+ <gen#<nu##batat++a#<z#

**Table 6D.6** com aquelas batatas

| | Morphemes | | | | | | |
|---|---|---|---|---|---|---|---|
| U.Fs. | #kon> | #akel+ | <gen# | <nu# | #batat+ | +a# | <z# |
| R.6D.0 | #kon> | #akel+ | <a# | <z# | #batat+ | +a# | <z# |
| Stress | #kon> | #akˈel+ | <a# | <z# | #batˈat+ | +a# | <z# |
| R. 6.1 | *** | *** | *** | *** | *** | *** | *** |
| R. 6.2a | *** | *** | *** | *** | *** | *** | *** |
| R. 6.2b | *** | *** | *** | *** | *** | *** | *** |
| R. 6.6b | #kon> | **#akˈɛl** | <a# | <z# | #batˈat+ | +a# | <z# |
| R. 6.8 | *** | *** | *** | *** | *** | *** | *** |
| R. 6.3 | *** | *** | *** | *** | *** | *** | *** |
| R. 6.4 | *** | *** | *** | *** | *** | *** | *** |
| R. 6.5 | *** | *** | *** | *** | *** | *** | *** |
| R. 6.11 | *** | *** | *** | *** | *** | *** | *** |
| R. 6.9b | *** | *** | *** | *** | *** | *** | *** |
| R. 6.7b | *** | *** | *** | *** | *** | *** | *** |
| R. 6.10 | *** | *** | *** | *** | *** | *** | *** |
| Results | #kon>#akˈɛl<a#<z##batˈat++a#<z# | | | | | | |
| Ø Morpheme Erase | #kon>#akˈɛl<a#<z##batˈat++a#<z# | | | | | | |

Rule 6.6b causes the underlying root vowel of the demonstrative pronoun *aquele* to become lax when inflected for [+feminine]. The phrase emerges as: [kõ.ăˈkɛ.lăž.bă.ˈta.tăž].[79]

**§6D.7** The final phrase of sentence one is: ##en><l+<o#<Ø+#porˈão#

79 The plural morpheme /z/ is realized as [ž] because in *aquelas* it precedes the /b/ of *batatas* and in the latter it precedes the /n/ of *no*—progressive assimilation of voice .

**Table 6D.7 no porão[a]**

| | Morphemes | | | | |
|---|---|---|---|---|---|
| **U.Fs.** | #en> | #l+ | <gen# | <nu# | #porão# |
| **R. 6D.0** | #en> | #l+ | <o# | <Ø# | #porão# |
| **Stress** | #en> | #l+ | <o# | <Ø# | #porˈão# |
| **R. 6.1** | *** | *** | *** | *** | *** |
| **R. 6.2a** | *** | *** | *** | *** | *** |
| **R. 6.2b** | *** | *** | *** | *** | *** |
| **R. 6.6b** | *** | *** | *** | *** | *** |
| **R. 6.8** | *** | *** | *** | *** | *** |
| **R. 6.3** | #n> | #l+ | <o# | <Ø# | #porˈão# |
| **R. 6.4** | #n> | #n+ | <o# | <Ø# | #porˈão# |
| **R. 6.5** | *** | *** | *** | *** | *** |
| **R. 6.11** | *** | *** | *** | *** | *** |
| **R. 6.9b** | *** | *** | *** | *** | *** |
| **R. 6.7b** | *** | *** | *** | *** | *** |
| **R. 6.10** | *** | *** | *** | *** | *** |
| **Results** | #n>#n+<o#<Ø+#porˈão# | | | | |
| **Ø Morpheme Erase** | | #n+<o#<#porˈão# | | | |

a The morphophonology of *porão* has been omitted here because it is of no consequence to the matter at hand.

Rule 6.3 deletes the initial /e/ of *em* #en>, and Rule 6.4 occasions the progressive assimilation of the definite article's initial #l+ after this preposition. Rule 4.1 will eliminate the definite article's /n/when the phonetic rules apply, and this string becomes: [nŭ.pŭ.ˈrã$^{\tilde{u}}$]

**§6D.8** The sentence *Tiramos-lhas e pusemo-no-las* 'We took them [the clothes] from them and put them on (ourselves)' demonstrates the effects of Rules 6.9b (deletion of final /r/ and /z/), 6.7b, (deletion of <l+, 3$^{rd}$ person direct object), 6.11 (loss of 1$^{st}$ person plural's final /z/ before reflexive pronoun), and 6.10 (loss of indirect object pronoun's final /e/). The first clause is #tiramoz#<λe#<z#<l+<a#<z; the second is #e>#puzemoz#<nɔz#<l+<a#<z#.

**Table 6D.8** Tirámos-lhas

| | Morphemes | | |
|---|---|---|---|
| U.Fs | #tiramoz# | <λ+<gen#<nu# | <l+<gen#<nu# |
| R. 6D.0 | #tiramoz# | <λ+e#<z# | <l+<a#<z# |
| Stress | #tirˈamoz# | <λ+e#<z# | <l+<a#<z# |
| R. 6.1 | *** | *** | *** |
| R. 6.2a | *** | *** | *** |
| R. 6.2b | *** | *** | *** |
| R. 6.6b | *** | *** | *** |
| R. 6.8 | *** | *** | *** |
| R. 6.3 | *** | *** | *** |
| R. 6.4 | *** | *** | *** |
| R. 6.9b | *** | *** | *** |
| R. 6.5 | *** | *** | *** |
| R. 6.11 | *** | *** | *** |
| R. 6.9b | #tirˈamoz# | <λ+<e#<Ø# | <l+<a#<z# |
| R. 6.7b | #tirˈamoz# | <λ+<e#<Ø# | <Ø+<a#<z# |
| R. 6.10 | #tirˈamoz# | <λ+<#<Ø# | <Ø+<a#<z# |
| Results | #tirˈamoz#<λ+<#<Ø#<Ø+<a#<z# | | |
| Ø Morpheme Erase | | #tirˈamoz#<λ+<a#<z# | |

Table 6D.8 contains the only incidence of Rule 6.10.

**§6D.9** Once again, when the pertinent phonological and phonetic rules apply, this utterance will appear as [ti.ˈra.mŭž.λă.zi.pŭ.ˈzẽ.mŭ.nŭ.lăš].

**Table 6D.9** e pusemo-no-las

| | **Morphemes** | | | |
|---|---|---|---|---|
| **Underlying** | #e> | #puzemoz# | <noz# | <l+<gen#<nu# |
| **R.6B.0** | #e> | #puzemoz# | <noz# | <l+<a#<z# |
| **Stress** | #e> | #puzˈemoz# | <noz# | <l+<a#<z# |
| **R.6.1** | *** | *** | *** | *** |
| **R.6.2a** | *** | *** | *** | *** |
| **R.6.2b** | *** | *** | *** | *** |
| **R. 6.6b** | *** | *** | *** | *** |
| **R. 6.8** | *** | *** | *** | *** |
| **R. 6.3** | *** | *** | *** | *** |
| **R. 6.4** | *** | *** | *** | *** |
| **R.6.9b** | *** | *** | *** | *** |
| **R. 6.5** | *** | *** | *** | *** |
| **R. 6.11** | #e> | <u>#puzˈemo#</u> | <noz# | <l+<a#<z# |
| **R.6.9b** | #e> | #puzˈemo# | <no# | <l+<a#<z# |
| **R. 6.7b** | *** | *** | *** | *** |
| **R. 6.10** | *** | *** | *** | *** |
| **Results** | #e>#puzemo#<no#<l+<a#<z# | | | |
| **Ø Morpheme Erase** | | #e>#puzemo#<no#<l+<a#<z# | | |

# 7 Nominal Derivation: Suffixes

## Introduction

§7.0.0 The canonical pattern of nominals in Portuguese consists of a stem followed by a gender morpheme, which in turn is followed by a number morpheme (§6.1.0). These post-stem morphemes are nominals' sole inflecting suffixes. Pronouns, demonstratives, possessives, and articles have monomorphemic stems, i.e. roots. And some of the pronouns (*me, mim, tu, te, ti, si, se, lhe, nós, nos, vós, vos*) are entirely monomorphemic and, as such, are gender indifferent. Likewise, there are some nouns that, for all intents and purposes, are monomorphemic, with arbitrary gender, but with no element that one can immediately identify as a gender morpheme, as Table 7.1 demonstrates.

**Table 7.1** Monomorphemic Nouns (Arbitrary Gender)

| [-feminine] | Gloss | [+feminine] | Gloss |
|---|---|---|---|
| **ré** | d string | **ré** | stern |
| **pé** | foot | **fé** | faith |
| **rubi** | ruby | **caxixi** | weak brandy |
| **pó** | powder | **mó** | grindstone |

Notwithstanding the words in Table 7.1 and the monomorphemic pronouns, complexity is the order of the day for the Portuguese lexicon, and nominals' stems are often complex.[1] As a first step in investigating Portuguese word formation, the morphologically complex nominals

1 A stem is a string of one or more morphemes to which another may be added. A root is a single morpheme to which others may be added. For example, take the word *abonamento* 'guarantee'. At is core is the **root** #bon+, which denotes 'good'. To form the word in question, the root acquires both the prefix #a+ and the verb-deriving suffix for the 1st conjugation +a#. The string of three morphemes #a+#bon ++a# is now a verbal stem to which the suffix +ment++o# can be added to form a noun: #a+#bon ++a#+ment++o#. This word can be pluralized, and when it is, its entirety is once more a stem for its plural form: #a+#bon ++a#+ment++o#<z# *abonamentos* 'guarantees'.

formed with the suffixes +izm++o# and +izt++a# are revealing.[2] They unambiguously demonstrate the working of Portuguese suffix based nominal derivation.

**Table 7.2** Transparency and Opacity in Portuguese Nominals

| A: Transparency in Deriving Suffixes | | | | | |
|---|---|---|---|---|---|
| Derived Word and Analysis | | | | Relative[a] | |
| +izt++a# Word | Gloss | Stem | Root | Word | Gloss |
| **sindicalista** | unionist | #sindik++al# | #sˈindik+ | **síndico** | agent |
| **sensualista** | sensualist | #sens++o#+al# | #sens+ | **senso** | sense |
| **contabilista** | accountant | #kont++a++bil# | #kont+ | **conta** | bill |
| **articulista** | columnist | #art++ik++ul+ | #art+ | **arte** | art |
| **transformismo** | transformism | #tranz+#fɔrm+ | #form+ | **forma** | form |
| **B: Transparency Only in Specific Derived Forms** | | | | | |
| **Derived Word and Analysis** | | | | **Opaque Relative** | |
| **+izm++o# Word** | **Gloss** | **Stem** | **Root/Stem** | **Word** | **Gloss** |
| **histrionismo** | buffoonishness | #iztr++ion+ | #iztr++ion+ | **histrião** | buffoon |
| **liberalismo** | liberalism | #libɛr++al# | #libɛr+ | **livre** | free |
| **fatalismo** | fatalism | #fat++al# | #fat+ | **fado** | fate |
| **subjetivismo** | subjectivism | #sub+#žɛk++t++iv+[b] | +žɛk+ | **sujeito** | person |
| **automobilismo** | motoring | #auto+#m ɔb++il# | #m ɔb+ | **move** | moves |
| **rececionista** | receptionist | #re++sɛp++sion+ | +sɛp+ | **recebe** | receives |

a These forms (save #ˈsind+ik+) are nouns that have obligatory gender morphemes that can signal different meanings for specific roots: e.g. *conta* (f.) 'bill' and *conto* (-f.) 'short story'.

b The +t+ in the lexical form of *subjetivismo* is not part of the root. In the obviously related words such as *objetivo, trajetória, projetor* (normally pronounced [ɔb.žɛ.ˈti.vu], [tră.žɛ.ˈtɔ.ri.ă], and [prŭ.žɛ.ˈtor]), the underlying /t/ is always present, and the non-reduction of pretonic root vowels in European Portuguese pronunciation betrays an underlying abutment of the consonants /kt/ immediately following the vowel. The +t+ is also not part of the suffix +iv+, which attaches to stems with no underlying /t/: *passivo* 'passive' (cf. *passar* 'to pass'), *abusivo* 'abusive' (cf. *abusar* 'to abuse). On the other hand, there is a multitude of transparent words where the /t/ is present, and there is no compelling reason to associate it with the words' root: *vingativo* 'revengeful',

2 Just as stems can be morphologically complex, noun-forming suffixes can be morphologically complex. Strictly speaking, most of these suffixes (including +izt++a# and +izm++o#) consist of a bound deriver (+deriver+) plus an intrinsic gender morpheme +a#, +o#, +e#, and +e+. Other suffixes, expecially those that form adjectives, consist of a bound deriver and inflecting morphemes (<[αfeminine]#<[βplural]#). Noun-deriving suffixes largely determine the resultant nouns' gender.

Table 7.2 Continued

*descritivo* 'descriptive' and *unitivo* 'uniting'. Since these are deverbal adjectives (related to *vingar* 'to avenge', *descrever* 'to describe' and *unir* 'to unite'), they are derived from underlying forms containing the verbs' perfective participle morpheme. That is, the perfective participle of verbs such as the previous three would, at the morphophonemic level, be #ving++a#+t++iv+<o#, cf. *vingado* 'avenged', #de+#ezkr++i++t++iv+<o#, cf. *descrito* 'described' and #un++i++t++iv+<o#, cf. *unido* 'united'. There is good reason to identify the participle morpheme as both a deriving suffix (+t+) and an inflecting suffix (<t+) (§13.10.0–3.3).

**§7.0.1** The suffixes +izm++o# and +izt++a# are full-fledged deriving suffixes that produce nominals: +izm++o# only produces nouns, whereas the forms ending in +izt++a# can be used as either nouns or adjectives.[3] Most importantly, these two suffixes readily attach to nominal, i.e. both to noun and adjectival stems, as well as to verbal stems to form transparent nominals whose meanings are motivated by their constituent parts. Whereas words ending in these two suffixes (as well as in other deriving suffixes) are in the main morphologically transparent right down to their roots, many of these same roots, when they occur in other morphological circumstances, may undergo modifications such that their roots (or stems) lose some of their constituent phonemes, or their phonemes undergo systematic changes. The cases in point can be seen in set B of Table 7.2, where words with some deriving suffixes emerge with their roots or stems intact, whereas the related, opaque words evince morphophonemic decay—e.g. bilabial stops become fricatives, or stops go from [+surd] to [-surd], or /g+ → Ø when the stems are followed by gender morphemes or theme vowels.[4]

3 It appears that all words ending in +izm++o# have an +izt++a# counterpart, but the reverse does not obtain: at least for *rececionista,* the dictionaries do not list the reciprocal **rececionismo*. Cunha (70) observes that words such as *protestantismo*, *maometismo*, and *islamismo* 'Protestantism, Mohamadanism, and Islamism' have no +izt++a# counterparts. The words *protestante*, *maometano*, and *islamita* make such coinages unnecessary. The *Aurélio* contains 1,737 +izm++o# words and 1,820 +izt++a# words.

4 Examples of morphophonemic decay abound in Portuguese. The root of *lecionista* and *ler* appears in its entirety (#lɛg+) in neither form, but it does in the obviously related words *legar* 'to bequeath' and *legal* 'legal'. The root of *liberalismo* and *livre,* #libɛr+, loses its /ɛ/ in its related form (*livre*), and its /b/ becomes /v/ in that form. The /t/ of #fat+ that underlies *fatalismo* and *fado* becomes /d/ before the suffix +o#.

§7.0.2 The phenomena evinced in Table 7.2 indicate that a grammar of Portuguese derivational morphology will need to specify: (A) Which stems and roots are susceptible to mutation or deletion of their constituent segments and which are not. (B) Which suffixes occasion (or at least co-occur with) mutations and/or deletions of stems' constituent phonemes. (C) Which suffixes allow the transparent forms of specific stems to emerge. (D) Which suffixes are immutable, i.e. which have only one realization. (E) Which forms have more than one allomorph. In addition, the grammar should identify deriving affixes' relative productivity.

## Derivational Suffixes

§7.1.0 Derivation is the formation of words from the stringing together of morphemes within a set of word boundaries. In the creation of new words, suffixes may attach to stems that form the bases of nouns, adjectives, or verbs. When they do this, (A) they may add a denotation; (B) they may both add a denotation and determine form classes (e.g. noun➔adjective, adjective➔noun, noun➔verb, verb➔noun, verb➔adjective); (C) diminutive or augmentative deriving suffixes, in addition to creating words on their own, may connote a speaker's affect concerning the word's referent; (D) other deriving suffixes may add a semantically based aspect to a verb.[5] This section addresses open-ended nominals: nouns, adjectives and infinitives. After a caveat (§7.1.1), it begins by examining suffixes that create nominals that bear a semantic relationship to other, sometimes morphologically simpler, nouns.[6]

5 'Semantically based' aspect indicates something different from grammatically based aspect, which is reflected in verbal inflectional morphology. The latter in Portuguese is [±perfect] (§13.4.0–2). Semantically based aspect is achieved through derivation, i.e. through the adding of deriving affixes to a verbal root or stem so as to indicate a modality of action not distinguished in the verbal stem: cf. *nevar* 'to snow', *neviscar* 'to snow lightly', *lamber* 'to lick' *lambiscar* 'to nibble'.

6 For a case in point consider the noun *norma* 'norm' and the adjective *normal* 'normal'. The latter is not derived from the former, rather both forms are derived from the root #nɔrm+. *Norma* consists of its root plus the gender and number morphemes: #nɔrm++a#<Ø#. *Normal* consists of the same root plus the adjective-deriving suffix +al# plus the ambivalent gender morpheme +e+: #nɔrm++al#+e+<Ø#.

**§7.1.1** Notwithstanding their semantic relationships with specific nouns, the derived nouns examined in this section, and, indeed, throughout this chapter, cannot always be said to be derived ***directly*** from the semantically related nouns. Words derived by suffixes are mostly the result of the addition of suffixes to stems ***that are not complete words***. The case in point are nominal stems that, when deriving suffixes are added to them, have no gender or number morpheme attached to them. Without the gender morpheme they are not complete words. Thus, the designation 'Noun-to-Noun' is a heuristic label that does not imply that the derived words bear anything more than a semantic, or at times metaphorical, relationship with the related words containing the stems followed directly by a gender morpheme.[7]

**§7.2.0 Noun-to-Noun:** Table 7.3a provides a set of suffixes that form nouns from the stems that occur in related nouns:

**Table 7.3a** Noun to Noun Derivation (Immutable Suffixes)

| | Suffix | Productivity | Related Noun | Gloss | Derivative | Gloss |
|---|---|---|---|---|---|---|
| 1 | +i++o# | Negligible 26 | **mulher (f.)** | woman | **mulherio** | womenfolk |
| 2 | +am++a# | Negligible 29 | **dinheiro** | money | **dinheirama**[a] | a fortune |
| 3 | +um++e# | Very Low 60 | **queixa (f.)** | complaint | **queixume** | lamentations |
| 4 | +ed++o# | Low 87 | **árvore (f.)** | tree | **arvoredo** | clump of trees |
| 5 | +am++e# | Low 104 | **pelo** | fur | **pelame** | pelt collection |
| 6 | +at++o# | Low 199 | **clérigo** | cleric | **clericato** | cleric vocation |
| | | | **carvão** | coal | **carbonato** | carbonate |
| 7 | +it++e# | Modest 268 | **tímpano** | ear drum | **timpanite (f.)** | ear ache |
| 8 | +al#+e+ | Modest 384 | **banana (f.)** | banana | **bananal** | banana grove |

(*Continued*)

7 The suffixes illustrated here for the most part maintain their configurations regardless of what suffixes might follow them. Table 7.3a indicates the [+feminine] gender of specific nouns, both with and without the deriving suffixes—the remaining nouns are [-feminine]. One should note that nouns' gender is determined by the gender morpheme—either that of the unembellished noun or by the gender morpheme pertaining to the deriving suffix.

Table 7.3a Continued

| | Suffix | Productivity | Related Noun | Gloss | Derivative | Gloss |
|---|---|---|---|---|---|---|
| 9 | +ad++o# | High 563 | **conde** | count | **condado** | county |
| | | | **eleitor** | voter | **eleitorado** | electorate |
| 10 | +ˈar#+i++o# | High 601 | **suor** | sweat | **sudário** | shroud |
| | | | **erva** (f.) | herb | **herbário** | herbarium |
| 11 | +ar#+i++a# | High 610 | **papel** | paper | **papelaria** (f.) | paper store |
| | | | **grito** | shout | **gritaria** (f.) | hubbub |
| | | | **velhaco** | rascal | **velhacaria** (f.) | rascally action |
| 12 | +ˈVžin++e+ | High 740 | **bobo** | fool | **bobagem** (f.) | foolish notion |
| | | | **fulo** | African | **fuligem** (f.) | soot |
| | | | **ferro** | iron | **ferrugem** (f.) | rust |
| 13 | +ad++a# | Very High 1343 | **menino** | child | **meninada** (f.) | group of kids |
| | | | **peixe** | fish | **peixada** (f.) | fish dish |
| | | | **colher** (f.) | spoon | **colherada** (f.) | spoonful |
| | | | **jogo** | game | **jogada** (f.) | maneuver |
| | | | **inverno** | winter | **invernada** (f.) | wintering |
| 14 | +eir++a# | Very High 1434 | **alfinete** | pin | **alfineteira** (f.) | pin cushion |
| | | | **figo** | fig | **figueira** (f.) | fig tree |
| | | | **coelho** | rabbit | **coelheira** (f.) | rabbit hutch |
| 15 | +eir++o# | Supreme 1946 | **nevoa** (f.) | fog | **nevoeiro** | brume |
| | | | **formiga** (f.) | ant | **formigueiro** | ant hill |
| | | | **cinza** (f.) | ash | **cinzeiro** | ash tray |
| 16 | +eir++<o# | | **vidro** | glass | **vidreiro** | glazer |
| | | | **abacate** | avocado | **abacateiro** | avocado tree |
| | | | **agulha** (f.) | needle | **agulheiro** | needlemaker |
| 17 | +i++a# | Outlier 5500 | **fidalgo** | noble | **fidalguia** (f.) | nobility |
| | | | **inverno** | winter | **invernia** (f.) | hard winter |

a In standard Portuguese (both Brazilian and European), *dinheirama* is [+feminine]. In European Portuguese folk speech, it is [-feminine] (Morais).

The 17 different suffixes in Table 7.3a do not exhaust the set that can attach directly to stems and form derived nouns. The unpacking of the data in Table 7.3a and in the tables to follow begins by examining the suffixes' productivity, then the roles of gender, meaning, and allomorphy in establishing the data in this and subsequent sections of nominal derivation.[8]

**§7.2.1.0 Productivity:** The source of the numbers in third column of Table 7.3a is the *Aurélio*, whose digital accompaniment can list and enumerate words according to their endings and beginnings. As with the Portuguese phonemes, these suffixes do not share their word-creating burden equally, as Table 7.3b demonstrates:

**Table 7.3b** Relative Productivity: Noun-to-Noun-Deriving Suffixes

| Negligible to Modest Productivity | | | High to Supreme Productivity | | |
|---|---|---|---|---|---|
| Suffix | Occurrences | % of Total | Suffix | Occurrences | % of Total |
| +i++o# | 26 | 0.31 | +ad++o# | 563 | 6.71 |
| +am++a# | 29 | 0.35 | +ˈar#+i++o# | 601 | 7.16 |
| +um++e# | 60 | 0.71 | +ar#+i++a# | 610 | 7.27 |
| +ed++o# | 87 | 1.04 | +ˈVžin++e# | 740 | 8.82 |
| +am++e# | 104 | 1.24 | +ad++a# | 1,343 | 16.00 |
| +at++o# | 199 | 2.37 | +eir++a# | 1,434 | 17.08 |
| +it++e# | 268 | 3.19 | +eir++o# | 1,946 | 23.18 |
| +al#+e# | 384 | 4.57 | +eir+<o# | | |
| | | | +i++a# | Outlier | |
| Totals: | 1157 | 13.78 | | 7,237 | 86.21 |

**§7.2.1.1** As in Chapter 1 (§1.2.1.1), where a minority of segments accounts for an overwhelming majority of segmental tokens, here too a minority (seven suffixes) accounts for 86.21% of the items in this category, whereas the eight negligible to modestly frequent suffixes account for 13.78%. This range of prominence establishes productivity categories for use in the chapters dealing with nominal and verbal derivation. Table 7.3c displays the rankings:

8 Cunha (1970) is the main source of deriving affixes. The *Aurélio*, contains 8,394 words formed with the suffixes in Table 7.3a. Their mean occurrence was 559.60, their SD was 587.32, Z= 2.548. Other than the the suffix +i++a#, there were no outliers. Suffixes 15 and 16 count as allomorphs of one another. The gender in suffix 15 is +o#—an invariant deriving morpheme. That of suffix 16 is inflectional (<o#) and identifies their referents' gender. Together +eir++o# and +eir+<o# have a Z value of 2.36

**Table 7.3c** Productivity Rankings

| | Ranking | Prominence |
|---|---|---|
| 1 | Negligible | -0.50% |
| 2 | Very Low | 0.50–1.0% |
| 3 | Low | 1.0–3.0% |
| 4 | Modest | 3.0–6.0% |
| 5 | High | 6.0–10.0% |
| 6 | Very High | 10.0–20.0% |
| 7 | Supreme | Above 20% |

That is, morphemes used in the derivation of specific form classes will be considered negligibly productive if they account for 0.50% or less of all words formed in their particular category: e.g. the suffix +i++o# (indicating a collectivity) provides tokens for only 0.30% of all the suffixes used to derive nouns related to other nouns. A productivity of 3.0% or less will be in the low category. Very high productivity affixes are those that play a role in 10% to 20% of all words formed by the addition of affixes (prefixes and suffixes). And any productivity beyond 20% that is not an outlier in a particular set of data will assign an affix supreme productivity.[9]

§7.2.2 **Gender:** The suffixes in Table 7.3a (except 16, +eir+<o#) appear with their gender morphemes tightly bound to their stems. This is because gender is intrinsic to suffixes 1–15 and 17. The gender suffixes (+o# [-feminine], +a# [+feminine], and +e# [±feminine]) linked to these deriving suffixes perform according to expectations. Indeed, the only [+feminine] suffixes ending in the +e# or +e+ are number 7, +it++e# and number 12 ˈVžin++e+. The data in Table 7.3a, and in the subsequent tables illustrating the derivation of nouns, show that roots and stems are not intrinsically gendered—they acquire gender thanks to the specific gender suffix at ending the words.

§7.2.3.0 **Meaning:** Compiling the data for Table 7.3a, the suffixes 1–5 (negligible to low productivity) group together according to semantic

9 The frequency of a particular suffix is surely a sign of its productivity. Certainly new words are more likely to be formed by the suffix -eir+<o# than by +it++e#. This notion is testable, but beyond the scope of this study.

criteria—they all indicate collectivity.[10] Likewise, suffixes 7 and 8 were limited, respectively, to physical pathology and collectivity. Suffix 16 +eir+<o# attaches to the roots of words for fruits and vegetables to create names for plants bearing that fruit. The remaining suffixes rarely convey anything resembling constant meaning, i.e. systematic relationships with their stems.

**§7.2.3.1** Suffix 11 +ari++a# can indicate a store selling a particular product cf. *sorvete* 'ice cream (Braz.)' ⇔ *sorvetaria* 'ice cream store', *livro* 'book' ⇔ *livraria* 'book store', *merce* 'merchandise' ⇔ *mercearia* 'general store'. It may indicate a collectivity cf. *gradaria* 'collection of grates'⇔ *grados* 'grates', *velharia* 'a store that sells used items' ⇔ *velhos* 'old',[11] or something typical of a class of people e.g. *taful* 'dandy' ⇔ *tafularia* 'dandyish act'.

**§7.2.3.2** Suffix 12 +ˈVžin++e# can indicate institutionality: cf. *marido* 'husand' ⇔ *maridagem* 'a man's married life', an 'act' cf. *via* 'route' ⇔ *viagem* 'trip', and a particularity: *língua* ⇔ 'language' *linguagem* 'speech'.[12]

**§7.2.3.3** Suffix 13 +ad++a# indicates a collectivity in *meninada* 'group of kids', a 'fish dish' *peixada*, a 'spoon measurement' *colherada*, a 'maneuver' *jogada*, a 'wintering' *invernada*. It can also be used to indicate both a blow *bicada* 'peck' (cf. *bico* 'beak') and an 'amount a bird may carry in its beak'.

**§7.2.3.4** With this cursory glance at word meanings created by this first set of deriving suffixes, there is both systematicity and idiomaticity. The low productivity suffixes are quite consistent in their denotations. As suffixes become more productive, they provide prevalent patterns on which speakers of Portuguese can form words whose meanings may stray from the sum of their constituent parts. That is, speakers can both invent new words or produce words they may never have experienced, but which exist in the language's lexical patrimony. For example, the

---

10 Semantic criteria identify these nouns as collectives. There are nouns ending in the phonemic sequences that are homophonous with these suffixes, but are not these suffixes: e.g. +i++o#≠ /i++o# *câmbio* 'exchange'; +am++a# ≠ /am++a# *aljama* 'handcuff'; #um++e# ≠ /um++e# *lume* 'fire'; +ed++o# ≠ /ed+<o# *enxovedo* 'fool'; +am++e# ≠/am++e# *badame* 'chisel'.

11 *Velharia* can also mean an 'act typical of old people'.

12 This suffix can also attach to $1^{st}$ conjugation verbs. Examples include *tirar* 'to print', *tiragem* 'number printed', *rodar* 'to rotate' *rodagem* 'rotation', *lavar* 'to wash', *lavagem* 'a washing'.

word *dedite* (formed from the stem of *dedo* 'finger' and suffix number 7 [+it++e#]) meaning 'finger irritation' would be recognized immediately understandable, just as *arturedo* (using suffix 4) 'a group of (perhaps standing) people named Artur' would be, given the right context. However, true innovation, i.e. a derived word used for the first time in the history of the language, is harder to come by since there are already abundant words ending in these suffixes. At any rate, derived words' meanings depend on their usage and often transcend the sum of whatever meaning can be attributed to their constituent parts.

**§7.2.3.5** Notwithstanding the semantic criteria used in this study to limit the number of words ending in particular suffixes or segmental sequences in particular form classes, the concern throughout this study is not the semantic correlates of words formed with deriving affixes, it is rather the morphophonological processes and phenomena associated with word-formation, i.e. allomorphy.

**§7.2.4.0 Allomorphy:** The stems and suffixes in Table 7.3a are largely stable as Table 7.3d demonstrates:

**Table 7.3d** Immutable Roots, Stems, and Suffixes

| 7.3a | Stems | Words | Stem + gender | Suffixes | Derivatives | Stem+ Deriver |
|---|---|---|---|---|---|---|
| 1 | #muλer# | **mulher** | #muλer#+e> | +i++o# | **mulherio** | #muλer#+i++o# |
| 2 | #diɲeir+ | **dinheiro** | #diɲeir++o# | +am++a# | **dinheirama** | #diɲeir++am++a# |
| 3 | #keiš+ | **queixa** | #keiš++a# | +um++e# | **queixume** | #keiš++um++e# |
| 5 | #pel+ | **pelo** | #pel++o# | +am++e# | **pelame** | #pel++am++e# |
| 7 | #timpan+ | **tímpano** | #timpan++o# | +it++e# | **timpanite** | #timpan++it++e# |
| 8 | #banan+ | **banana** | #banan++a# | +al#+e# | **bananal** | #banan++al#+e# |
| 9 | #kond+ | **conde** | #kond++e# | +ad++o# | **condado** | #kond++ad++o# |
| 11 | #papɛl+ | **papel** | #papɛl++e# | +ar#+i++a# | **papelaria** | #papel++ari++a# |
| 11 | #grit+ | **grito** | #grit++o# | +ar#+i++a# | **gritaria** | #grit++ar++i++a |
| 11 | #vɛλ++ak+ | **velhaco** | #vɛλ+ak+<o# | +ar#+i++a# | **velhacaria** | #vɛλ++ak++ar#+i++a# |
| 12 | #bob+ | **bobo** | #bob+<o# | ˈVžin++e# | **bobagem** | #bob++ažin++e# |
| 12 | #ful+ | **fulo** | #ful+<o# | ˈVžin++e# | **fuligem** | #ful++ižin++e# |
| 12 | #fɛr̲+ | **ferro** | #fɛr̲++o# | ˈVžin++e# | **ferrugem** | #fɛr̲++užin++e# |
| 13 | #men++in+ | **menino** | #men++in+<o# | +ad++a# | **meninada** | #men++in++ad++a# |
| 14 | #alfinet+ | **alfinete** | #alfinet++e# | +eir++a# | **alfineteira** | #alfinet++eir++a |

Table 7.3d Continued

| 7.3a | Stems | Words | Stem + gender | Suffixes | Derivatives | Stem+ Deriver |
|---|---|---|---|---|---|---|
| 15 | #sinz+ | **cinza** | #sinz++a# | +eir++o# | **cinzeiro** | #sinz++eir++o# |
| 16 | #abakat+ | **abacate** | #abakat++e# | +eir+<o# | **abacateiro** | #abakat+ |
| 17 | #fidalg+ | **fidalgo** | #fidalg+<o# | +i++a# | **fidalguia** | #fidalg++i++a # |
| 17 | #in+#vɛrn+ | **inverno** | #in+#vɛrn++o# | +i++a# | **invernia** | #in+#vɛrn++i++a |

Of the 35 different stems in Table 7.3a, 20 are invariant—regardless of the suffix attached to them. Their underlying phonemes emerge when deriving suffixes, including gender morphemes, are added. The suffixes are, by and large, those that do not normally impede underlying stem segments from mutating or disappearing. Table 7.3e contains the stems that are mutable and suffixes that allow their volatility:

**Table 7.3e** Mutable Roots, Permissive Suffixes

| 7.3a | Stems | Suffixes | Word | Mutations |
|---|---|---|---|---|
| 4 | #arb++or+ | +ed++o# | **arvoredo** | /b+→/v+ |
| 10 | #ɛrb+ | +a# | **erva** | |
| 6 | #klɛr++ik+ | +o# | **clérigo** | /k+→/g+ |
| 14 | #fik+ | +eir++a# | **figueira** | |
| 13 | #žɔk+ | +ad++a# | **jogada** | |
| 6 | #karb++on+ | +eir+<o# | **carvoeiro** | /on+→/o+ |
| 9 | #en+#lɛg++t++or+ | +ad++o# | **eleitorado** | /g+ → /i+ |
| 10 | #sud+ | +or#+e# | **suor** | /d+→Ø |
| 13 | #pizk+ | +ad++a# | **peixe** | /izk+ → +eiš+ |
| 16 | #vitr+ | +as++a# | **vidraça** | /tr+ → /dr+ |

Compare the mutations in Table 7.3e with the stability demonstrated between the stems and the surface forms of these same stems in Table 7.3f:

Table 7.3f Mutable Roots, Restrictive Suffixes

| 7.3a | Stems | Suffixes | Word | Gloss |
|---|---|---|---|---|
| 4 | #arb++or+ | +et++o# | **arboreto** | (planned) tree clump |
| 10 | #ɛrb+ | +ˈari++o# | **herbário** | herbarium |
| 6 | #klɛr++ik+ | +at++o# | **clericato** | priesthood |
| 14 | #fik+ | +ˈase+<o# | **ficáceo** | fig tree related |
| 13 | #žɔk+ | +ɔz+<o# | **jocoso** | funny |
| 6 | #karb++on+ | +at++o# | **carbonato** | carbonate |
| 9 | #lɛg+ | +al#++e+ | **legal** | legal |
| 10 | #sud+ | +sion++e+ | **sudação** | act of sweating |
| 13 | #pizk+ | +ɔz+<o# | **piscoso** | replete with fish |
| 16 | #vitr+ | +in++a# | **vitrina** | display window |

**§7.2.4.1** The data in Tables 7.3d-f clearly demonstrate that there are sets of stems that are stable, sets of stems that are morphophonologically volatile, sets of suffixes that impede stems' morphophonological volatility, and other suffixes that do not. The mutable roots and stems belong to class $R_1$+, a marked minority within the class of all stems. The suffixes that allow the underlying forms of $R_1$+ stems to emerge unaltered shall be designated +$S_1$ since they too constitute minorities within the deriving suffixes. Stems and roots that are stable will be designated R+, and suffixes that do not impede stems' volatility will be designated +S.[13] Before leaving the suffixes illustrated in Table 7.3a, a closer scrutiny of each one will be revealing.

13 In addition to the allomorphy associated with $R_1$+ stems, some of the suffixes from Table 7.3a have allomorphic variation: **Suffix 8, +al#+e+** creates collectives. When it attaches to **words** like *butiá*, *café*, *capim*, *bambu* 'butia palm, coffee, grass, bamboo', the collective derivatives of these words are *butiazal*, *cafezal*, *capinzal*, and *bambuzal*. The roots for these derived words emerge as oxytone words (minus a gender suffix), which may be the motivation for the insertion of /z/ between these **words** and this suffix. On certain words such as *lamaçal* 'quagmire' (cf. *lama* 'mud') and *borraçal* 'quagmire' (cf. *borra* 'sediment'), an /s/ appears between stem and suffix. Indeed, this particular subset of collectives represents a sort of mid point between true derivation and word compounding since the collective suffix, which is not a word, is added directly to words, the last two of which (*lamaçal* and *borraçal*) retain the obvious gender morpheme +a#. When **+ad++a#** attaches to the **word** *rapaz* 'young man', an /i/

**§7.2.5.0 The Suffixes of Table 7.3a:** This section examines the role these suffixes play in the derivation of Portuguese nouns.

**§7.2.5.1 +i++o#** The *Aurélio* lists 3,048 nouns (*substantivos*) that end in /io/.[14] Of those 3,048 words, 1,365 contain deriving suffixes that end in /io/, but many of them pertain to other suffixes, e.g. the adjective-forming suffixes such as +ˈari+<o# (*primário* 'primary'), +ˈɔri+<o# (*simplório* 'stupid'), +tˈisi+<o# (*adventício* 'outsider'). The count in Table 7.3a consists of only those instances in which +i++o# attaches to stems and indicates some sort of array or collectivity: *gentio* 'riff-raff', *casario* 'group of houses', *trio* 'a collection of three'. Among the *Aurélio*'s 3,000 most common words, the only word ending in this suffix is *navio* 'large ship', cf. *nave* 'ship'. The nouns this suffix forms are invariantly [-feminine].

**§7.2.5.2 Collectives +am++a#, +um++e#, +ed++o#, +am++e#** These deriving suffixes attach to stems and are grammatically singular but indicate a semantic plurality. Only *ciúme* 'jealousy' cf. *cio* 'sexual urge' occurs among the 3,000 most frequent words. All but +am++a (Table 7.3a) form [-feminine] nouns regardless of the gender of the simpler noun they are related to.

**§7.2.5.3 +at++o#** This suffix has several uses. It can be used to indicate a profession *pugilato* 'boxing', a developmental stage: *novato* 'novice', or a state of being: *celibato* 'celibacy', as well as chemical compounding: *sulfato* 'sulfate', *silicato* 'silicate'. Table 7.3e shows that it may co-occur with or occasion morphophonemic shifts in stems: /g/⇔/k/, and [ã$^{\text{ũ}}$]⇔/on/. The word *campeonato* 'championship' cf. *campeão* 'champion' is among the 3,000 most frequent words. Nouns formed with this suffix are always [-feminine].

---

appears between the stem and the suffix: *rapaziada* 'group of young men (with whom a person using this word identifies)' or an 'action typical of young men'. **The suffix +ˈVžin++e#** has different vowels (/a/, /i/, /u/) that intercede between it and particular stems, and a word-final realization [ẽ$^{\tilde{y}}$] and a realization as [žĩn] when another deriving suffix is added.

14 The *Aurélio* unfortunately does not rigorously separate adjectives from nouns. Any adjective that can be nominalized is also identified as a noun: e.g. *velho* 'old' (adjective), 'old person', 'father' (noun). This causes noun counts to be somewhat inflated: cf. the 26 nouns formed with +i++o# and the 20 fomed by the adjective-deriving suffix +i+<o# (Table 7.12).

**§7.2.5.4 +it++e#** The suffix of interest here is the one that indicates an irritation such as in Table 7.3's examples and in words such as *acrinite* 'a type of dermatitis' and *falite* 'swollen phallus'. It is also used to designate compounds such as *corticite*, a mixture of sawdust, cork residue, and glue used for paving. The nouns formed with this suffix are always [+feminine].

**§7.2.5.5 +al#+e+** Of interest here is this suffix's function as an indicator of collectivities, e.g. *bananal* 'banana grove', *casal* 'group of houses, couple', cf. *casa* 'house'. Other examples include *tabaco* 'tobacco' ⇔ *tabacal* 'tobacco field', *aveia* 'oats' ⇔ *aveal* 'oat field',[15] *ervilha* 'pea' ⇔ *ervilhal* 'pea-patch', *melão* 'melon' ⇔ *meloal* 'melon patch'. One notices that in the word for 'melon patch' this suffix causes the underlying /n+ #mɛl++on++al#+e+ to evanesce, whereas word-finally the +on++e+ emerges as [ˈã̆ᵘ̃].[16] The nouns this suffix creates are always [-feminine].[17]

**§7.2.5.6 +ad++o#** This suffix indicates some sort of domain or collectivity. It does not seem to cause volatile underlying forms to preserve their segments, cf. #patr++on#+ad++o# ➔ *padroado* and #patr++on#+at++o# *patronato*, both of which mean 'patronage'. Again, this suffix always produces [-feminine] nouns.

**§7.2.5.7 +ˈar#+i++o#** This modestly productive suffix coincides with the emergence of the underlying /d+ in the root of *suor* and the underlying /b+ in the root of *erva*. It is marked for stress on its antepenultimate vowel. The adjective-forming suffix +ˈar#+i+<o# (Tables 7.6a-b.) is homophonous and quite productive. When this suffix forms nouns, they are always [-feminine].

**§7.2.5.8 +ar#+i++a#** In Table 7.3's examples, this suffix does not appear to have a constant meaning. It seems to occasion no morphophonemic alterations *vidro* 'glass' *vidraria* 'glass store' cf. *vitrina* 'display window', although the word *panaria* 'bread box' brings forth the underlying stem of *pão* 'bread', i.e. #pan+. Words formed with this suffix are always [+feminine].

---

15 The root of *aveia* and *aveal* contains a final /n+ that has evanesced in these two words, but emerges in the highly technical term *avenólito* 'a hard intestinal object whose nucleus is an oat seed'.

16 The +on+ occurs in the compound word *meloniforme* 'melon-shaped'.

17 There is also a homophonous adjective forming suffix +al#<e+ (Table 7.6a).

**§7.2.5.9 ˈV++žin++e+** This suffix is the first to show both variation in its form and in the vowels it brings forth between its stems and itself. By far, the suffix's most frequent initial vowel is /a/, which actually occurs in 712 of its 740 word-final occurrences in the *Aurélio*. As in the first example *bobo* ⇔ *bobagem*, the /a/ pertains neither to the suffix nor the root. Similarly the /i/ of *fuligem* and the /u/ of *ferrugem* belong to neither the root nor the suffix. In addition, the underlying form ˈV+žin++e+ is realized as [ˈžẽ$^{\tilde{y}}$] word-finally, but it surfaces as [žĩn] when another deriving suffix is added: *fuligem* ⇔ *fuliginoso* 'sooty', *peluginoso* 'furry' ⇔ *pelugem* 'fur', *voraginoso* 'abyssmal' ⇔ *voragem* 'abyss'. When this suffix is word-final, the word's gender is [+feminine].[18]

**§7.2.5.10 +eir++a#** This highly productive suffix allows underlying forms to undergo the mutations typical of certain consonants and vowels. In Table 7.3a's examples, the underlying /k+ of #fik+ becomes /g+ in both *figo* and *figueira*. This suffix always creates [+feminine] words.[19] With the addition of the gender morpheme, the stem-final /n+ nasalizes the preceding vowel and then disappears. The geminate /aa/ in #avelã++a# meld into one: [ă.və.lã] (Rule 4.1).

**§7.2.5.11 +ad++a#** This very highly productive suffix, like +ad++o# and +eir++a#, does not necessarily impede the ordinary evolution of underlying forms: e.g. #žɔk+ ➔ #žɔg+ in both *jogo* and *jogada*. One can hardly attribute any constant meaning to this suffix. In addition to the earlier examples (§7.2.3.3), a few more are illustrative: *olho* 'eye' ⇔ *olhada* 'glance', *jantar* 'dinner' ⇔ *jantarada*, 'time spent dining', *noite* 'night' ⇔ *noitada* 'spending the night someplace', *neve* 'snow' ⇔ *nevada* 'a period of snowfall'. It always produces [+feminine] nouns.[20]

**§7.2.5.12 +eir++o# and +eir+<o#** Owing to the extraordinary difficulty of separating these two suffixes, they appear together in the

18 The word *personagem* 'personage' can be [±feminine].

19 Notice that the related to [+feminine nouns in Table 7.3a are all [-feminine].

20 The word *limonada* 'lemonade' (cf. *limão* 'lemon') is an exception to this pattern insofar as it preserves the underlying +on+. The *Aurélio* considers *limonada* to be an 'erudite' formation and for that reason it is exempt from the loss of /n+ before this suffix (cf. *feijão* 'bean' #feiž++on++e+ and *feijoada* 'bean dish' #feiž++on++ad++a#).

productivity count. This is because the *Aurélio* ends words formed with both these suffixes in o, even though the first suffix creates invariant [-feminine] nouns,[21] and the second creates nouns that agree in gender and number with their referents, e.g. a 'glazer' could be either a [+feminine] individual, i.e. a *vidreira*, or a [-feminine] one, a *vidreiro.*[22] Similarly, in general the second suffix can be attached to stems indicating fruit (e.g. *abacate* 'avocado', *maçã* 'apple', and *tomate* 'tomato') and the plant that bears such fruit has the same gender as the fruit: *abacateiro* 'avocado tree', *macieira* 'apple tree', *tomateiro* 'tomato plant'. Neither suffix always impedes the normal sound changes associated with underlying stems: *tiçoeiro* 'coal poker' cf. *tição* 'burning coal' #tis++on++e+ and *mamoeiro* 'papaya plant' cf *mamão* 'papaya' #mam++on++e. Indeed, there are at least eleven examples of the preservation of stem-final /n+ in $R_1$+ stems. Thus, the +eir+<o# version of this suffix can have both +S and +$S_1$ characteristics (see Table 7C.1).

§7.2.5.13 **+i++a#** This suffix is an outlier in this particular dataset. The *Aurélio* contains 7,802 nouns that end in *ia.* Word endings such as -ância, -aria, -ária, -ência,-eia, and ícia do not appear in the count since they are suffixes on their own, and their /i/, unlike the /i+ of this suffix, does not receive penultimate stress. In a random set of 777 lexical entries where -ia formed nouns, 29.00% did not qualify as being derived using this suffix. By deducting the numbers associated with the other noun-deriving suffixes and by extrapolating from the sampling and its percentage of +i++a# nouns, the estimated count of actual words derived with this suffix was 5,500—a gross outlier in this set, and in the other sets, since it also derives nouns from adjectival and verbal stems. It is by far the most productive noun-creating suffix, which, in combination with myriad stems, creates words of widely varied meanings. Table 7.3g demonstrates the ubiquity of this suffix, which always produces [+feminine] nouns:

21 Notice that in Table 7.3a the nouns created with +eir++o# are related to [+feminine] nouns.

22 The gender bond <o# to +eir+ stems makes such words virtually indistinguishable from adjectives.

Table 7.3g An Alphabetized Sampling of Words Derived with +i++a#

| +i++a# | Gloss | Underlying Form | Relative | Gloss |
|---|---|---|---|---|
| **agrestia** | rusticity | #a+#grɛzt++i++a# | **agreste** | rustic |
| **bastardia** | illegitimacy | #baztard++i++a# | **bastardo** | bastard |
| **capitania** | captaincy | #kap++it++an++i++a# | **capitão** | captain |
| **diretoria** | head office | #di++rɛk++t++or#+i++a# | **diretor** | head |
| **embrionia** | embryogeny | #en+bri++on++i++a# | **embrião** | embryo |
| **fantasia** | fantasy | #fanta#+z++i++a# | **fantasma** | ghost |
| **grafia** | writing | #graf++i++a# | **grafema** | grapheme |
| **harmonia** | harmony | #arm++on#+i++a# | **harmónio** | harmonium |
| **ironia** | irony | #ir++on#+i++a# | **irónico** | ironic |
| **jerarquia** | hierarchy | #žɛr++ark++i++a# | **jerarca** | high-up |
| **lexia** | words | #lɛg++s++i++a# | **léxico** | lexicon |
| **mania** | mania | #man++i++a# | **fagómano** | glutton |
| **nostalgia** | nostalgia | #nɔz++tal++g++i++a# | **nostálgico** | nostalgic |
| **poesia** | poetry | #poe++z++i++a# | **poema** | poem |
| **quantia** | amount | #kuant++i++a# | **quanto** | how much |
| **raposia** | sly act | #rap++ɔz++i++a# | **raposa** | fox |
| **simpatia** | sympathy | #sin+#pat++i++a# | **simpático** | nice |
| **tecnologia** | technology | #tɛk++no++log++i++a# | **tecnólogo** | tecnologist |
| **ufania** | haughtiness | #ur++em++i++a# | **ufano** | proud |
| **valia** | worth | #val++i++a# | **valor** | value |
| **xerofagia** | dry eating | #šɛro+#fag++i++a# | **xerôfago** | dry eater |
| **zoologia** | zoology | #zoo##lɔg++i++a# | **zoólogo** | zoologist |

The words in Table 7.3g were not hard to come by and reflect the ubiquity of this suffix in the makeup of the Portuguese nominal word stock. All words formed with this suffix are [+feminine]. And words such as *capitania* and *embrionia* indicate that +i++a# is a structure preserving suffix. It allows underlying segments to emerge unchanged—which is not the case if these stems had been followed by gender morphemes: #en++bri++on++e+ → *embrião*; #kap++it++an++e+ → *capitão*. The next category to be examined is the creation of nouns from what appear to be adjectival stems.

**§7.3.0.0 Adjectives to Nouns:** Table 7.4a provides a list of suffixes that form nouns from 'adjectival' roots:

**Table 7.4a** Adjective-to-Noun Formation[a]

| | Suffix | Productivity | Adjective | Gloss | Noun | Gloss |
|---|---|---|---|---|---|---|
| 1 | +ˈisi++e# | Negligible 13 | **mole** | soft | **molície (f.)** | softness |
| 2 | +itud++e# | Very Low 41 | **alto** | high | **altitude (f.)** | altitude |
| 3 | +idon++e+ | Low 83 | **manso** | tame | **mansidão (f.)** | tameness |
| 4 | +ez++a# | Low 155 | **belo** | beautiful | **beleza (f.)** | beauty |
| 5 | +ez++e+ | Low 167 | **mudo** | mute | **mudez (f.)** | muteness |
| 6 | +is++e# | High 427 | **chato** | disagreeable | **chatice (f.)** | disagreableness |
| 7 | +ur++a# | High 513 | **doce** | sweet | **doçura (f.)** | sweetness |
| 8 | +or#+e+ | Very High 685 | **amargo** | bitter | **amargor** | bitterness |
| 9 | +izm++o# | Supreme 1729 | **pacífico** | peaceful | **pacifismo** | pacifism |
| 10 | +dad++e# | Supreme 1779 | **cruel** | cruel | **crueldade (f.)** | cruelty |
| 10a | i++dad++e# | (1685) | **suave** | soft | **suavidade (f.)** | softness |
| 10b | e++dad++e# | (48) | **pio** | pious | **piedade (f.)** | piety |
| 11 | +i++a# | Outlier | **enófilo** | wine-loving | **enofilia (f.)** | love for wine |
| | | | **alegre** | happy | **alegria (f.)** | joy |
| | | | **ancião** | aged | **anciania (f.)** | old age |

a Other than +i++a#, which is an overall outlier, there were no outliers in these data: M= 559.20, SD = 666.88, Z=2.290. The +dad++e# suffix (10a-b)'s Z = 1.83

**§7.3.0.1** The obvious semantic relationship between these adjectives and their corresponding nouns strongly suggests that the nouns are derived from adjectives: e.g. *mudo* 'mute' ⇔ *mutismo* 'muteness', *alegre* 'happy' ⇔ *alegria* 'happiness'. However, similar to the 'nouns derived from nouns', Portuguese deadjectival nouns are not actually derived from adjectives, rather from a set of (largely) R+ stems and roots[23] that can be the base for both adjectives and nouns. Adjectives are followed

23 There are three stems in Table 7.4a that are $R_1$+ forms followed by +S suffixes That is, in addition to *mudez* (line 4), whose underlying /t+ has lost its voicelessness, consider the noun *mutismo* 'mutism', whose /t+ emerges. In addition to *doçura* (line 7), there is *dulcificar* 'to sweeten', whose underlying /ul/ emerges, and the superlative of *cruel* is *crudelíssimo*, which brings the root's underlying /d+ to the surface. The form *cruelíssmo* also occurs, as a less 'erudite' superlative. *Cruelíssimo* is a form derived from *cruel* #kruɛl+ which is a R+ offshoot of the $R_1$+ stem #krud++ɛl#. The suffixes +izm++o# and +ˈisim+<o# as well as the compounding word #fik++a#+r#+e+ (as in *dulcificar*) preserve the underlying forms of the $R_1$+ stems to which they attach. They are $+S_1$ suffixes or, in the case of #fik++a#+r#+e+ an element (in this case, a word) used to form semi-compounds, cf. *ficar* 'to stay, become'.

by inflecting gender suffixes, with a +< affinity. When deriving suffixes are attached, the affinity between stem and suffix (i.e. #root/stem++ deriving suffix) is ++, i.e. a strong deriving affinity.

§7.3.1 **Productivity:** As in the case of Table 7.3a, these suffixes do not share the burden of adjective-to-noun formation equally, as Table 7.4b demonstrates:

**Table 7.4b** Relative Productivity: Adjective-to-Noun-Deriving Suffixes

| Negligible to Modest Productivity | | | High to Supreme Productivity | | |
|---|---|---|---|---|---|
| Suffix | Occurrences | % of total | Suffix | Occurrences | % of total |
| +isi++e# | 13 | 0.23 | +is++e# | 427 | 7.64 |
| +itud++e# | 41 | 0.73 | +ur++a# | 513 | 9.17 |
| +idon++e# | 83 | 1.48 | +or++e+ | 685 | 12.25 |
| +ez++a# | 155 | 2.77 | +izm++o# | 1,729 | 30.92 |
| +ez++e# | 167 | 2.99 | +dad++e# | 1,779 | 31.81 |
| | | | +i++a# | Outlier | |
| Total: | 459 | 8.21 | | 5,133 | 91.79 |

In Table 7.4b of the suffixes (save +izm++o#, and +or#+e+) have intrinsic [+feminine] gender.

§7.3.3 **Meaning:** Cunha (69) is right when he maintains that these suffixes derive nouns related to whatever the particular adjective denotes. Their English counterparts are either Latinate cognates (e.g. 'altit**ude**, beau**ty**, pacific**ism**') or they are formed with the highly productive English noun-forming suffix +nɛs#, e.g. *acridade* 'bitter**ness**'. Contrary to the bulk of denominal derived nouns, there is a systematic semantic relationship between adjectives and the nouns derived from adjectival stems.

§7.3.4.0 **Allomorphy:** The data in and related to Table 7.4a contain morphophonologically stable R+ stems as well as $R_1$+ stems and +S and +$S_1$ suffixes. Table 7.4c contains stable adjectival stems:

Table 7.4c Immutable Stems and Stable Suffixes

| | R+Stems | Adjective | Derivative 1 | Derivative 2 | Derivatove 3 | Derivative 4[a] |
|---|---|---|---|---|---|---|
| 1 | #mɔl+ | mole | molície | molícia | moleza | molúria |
| 2 | #alt+ | alto | altitude | altura | alteza | |
| 3 | #mans+ | manso | mansidão | mansuetude | | |
| 4 | #bɛl+ | belo | beleza | beldade | | |
| 5 | #šat+ | chato | chatice | chateza | chatura | |
| 6 | #amarg+ | amargo | amargor | amargura | | |
| 7 | #suav+ | suave | suavidade | suavizar | | |
| 8 | #pak+ | pacífico | pacifismo | pacifista | | |
| 9 | #alɛgr+ | alegre | alegria | alegrete | alegrinho | |

a The other derived nouns in Table 7.4c are mainly roughly synonymous with the examples from Table 7.4a. However: *alteza* 'highness' was used in addressing nobility, *suavizar* is an infinitive 'to soften', an *alegrete* is a 'small flower pot', and an *alegrinho* is a bird typical of southern Brazil.

The stability of the R+ stems in Table 7.4c allows them to occur with no alteration when followed by either +S or +$S_1$ suffixes.[24] Table 7.4d contains Table 7.4a's mutable stems:

Table 7.4d Mutable ($R_1$+) Stems

| | $R_1$+ Stems | Adjective | +S | +$S_1$ (Noun) | +$S_1$ (Adjective) |
|---|---|---|---|---|---|
| 1 | #duls+ | doce | doçura (f.) | dulçor | dúlcido |
| 2 | #mut+ | mudo | mudez (f.) | mutismo | |
| 3 | #krud+ | cruel | crueldade (f.) | | crudelíssimo |

**§7.3.4.1** The suffixes of Table 7.4a undergo very little morphophonemic alteration. The only exceptions are the low productivity suffix identified as +idon++e#[25] and the supremely productive suffix that has 3 allomorphs: +dad++e#, +idad++e#, and +edad++e#.

24 The underlying /k+ of *pacífico*, etc. (cf. *pacato* 'peace loving') regularly becomes /s+ before palatal vowels. This is (phonological) velar softening, which often occurs in the course of word derivation when the conditions obtain: i.e. when a /k+ or /g+ precedes +e/ or + i(§7.3.5.2).

25 The suffix +idon++e# seems to be a word-final suffix to which no more deriving suffixes may be added. The underlying /on/ of this suffix, which

**§7.3.5.0 Suffixes 1–5, Negligible to Low Productivity:** +ˈisi++e#, +itud++e#, +idon++e+, +ez++a# and +ez++e+ create [+feminine] nouns that convey a more or less abstract notion of whatever the adjective describes. Of them, only +itud++e# and +idon++e+ are $+S_1$ suffixes since they allow underlying roots to emerge without contoidal loss or mutation: e.g. *finitude* 'finality' #fin++itud++e# (cf. *fim* [ˈfĩ] 'end') and *latitude* 'latitude' #lat++itud++e# (cf. *lado* 'side'); *acridão* 'bitterness' #akri++idon++e# (cf. *agrio* 'bitter') and *solidão* 'aloneness' #sɔl++idon++e+ (cf. *só* 'alone'). The only $R_1$+ root in this set is that of *mudez* 'muteness' #mut+ (cf. *mutismo* 'muteness').

**§7.3.5.1 +is++e#** This suffix also creates [+feminine] nouns and, to the extent that it causes root-final /n+ to emerge: *chinfrim* 'shabby' [šĩ.ˈfrĩ], *chinfrinice* 'shabbiness', it is an $+S_1$ suffix.

**§7.3.5.2 +or#+e+** This suffix is obviously related to the suffix +dor#<e+, which is a deverbal nominal-deriving suffix, where it is very productive (Table 7.5a). Other examples of its creating nouns from adjectival roots include: *doutor* 'university graduate' (cf. *douto* 'learned'), *rigor* 'rigor' (cf. *rígido* 'rigid'), and *vigor* 'vigor' (cf. *vigente* 'operative'). This suffix is of the $+S_1$ variety since it allows the underlying form of *doce* 'sweet' #duls+ to emerge in the word *dulçor* 'sweetness', a synonym of *docura*. Words ending in this suffix are always [-feminine].

**§7.3.5.3 +ur++a#** This is an +S suffix that is related to the deverbal noun deriver +dur++a # (Table 7.5a). When it attaches to non-derived adjectives (e.g. *doce* ⇔ *doçura*), it creates [+feminine] abstract nouns

**§7.3.5.4 +izm++o#** This suffix is an $+S_1$deriving suffix that causes underlying segments of $R_1$+ stems to be immune from the sound changes they undergo when attached to +S suffixes. It always creates [-feminine] nouns.

**§7.3.5.5 +dad++e#** This suffix has three allomorphs: +dad++e#, +edad++e, and +idad++e#. The latter form is by far the most frequent, whereas +edad++e# occurs in adjectives whose stem ends in /i/, e.g. *pio* 'pious'➔*piedade* 'piety', *ébrio* 'inebriated'➔*ebriedade* 'inebriation'.

---

emerges as [iˈδã̃$^{ũ}$] in the singular *solidão* 'solitude' and [iˈδõ$^{ỹ}$š] in the plural (*solidões* 'periods of solitude') reflects the allomorphy of other suffixes that appear with similar singular and plural allomorphs. Similar to +idon++e# is the suffix +on++e#, which occurs in the word *sezão* 'intermittent fever' (*sezões*, plural). In a word derived from the underlying form of *sezão* #sez++on++e+ ([səˈzã̃$^{ũ}$]), /on/ emerges: i.e. *sezonismo* 'malaria' (§8.1.1). The infinitive forming suffixes are outliers in these data.

The form +dad++e# can attach to a small number of stems ending in /l/, /n/, and /r/—three of the four consonants that can close a syllable: *leal* 'loyal'→*lealdade* 'loyalty', *ruim* 'terrible'→*ruindade* 'ruinous situation', *úbere* 'fertile'→ *uberdade* 'fertility'. It attaches largely to R+ stems, but when it attaches to $R_1$+ as either +idad++e# or +edad++e#, it performs as an +$S_1$ suffix: *agrio* ⇔ *acridade* 'bitterness', *afável* 'affable' ⇔ *afabilidade* 'affability', *só* 'alone' ⇔ *soledade* 'abandonment'. That is, it allows underlying /k+ to surface in *acridade*, underlying +bil# to surface in *afabilidade*, and underlying /l+ in *soledade*—segments that would have been /gri+, +vɛl+, and Ø had they been followed by a gender morpheme, or /vi+ had they been followed by any +S suffix.

§7.3.5.6 **+i++a#** This most productive outlier always creates [+feminine] nouns. (See Tables 7.3a–b and §7.2.5.13).

§7.4.0 **Deverbal Nouns:** Table 7.5a contains a set of deverbal nouns, i.e. nouns derived from verbal stems that contain reflexes of each verb's theme vowel.[26]

**Table 7.5a** Deverbal Nouns

| | Suffix | Productivity | C | # | Verb | Gloss | Noun | Gloss |
|---|---|---|---|---|---|---|---|---|
| 1 | +is++o# | Negligible | 2nd | 4 | **tolher** | to bar | **tolhiço** | obstruction |
| 2 | +et++e# | Negligible | 1st | 5 | **lembrar** | to recall | **lembrete** | memo |
| 3 | +nd++a # | Negligible 11 | 1st | 2 | **propagar** | to extend | **propaganda** | propaganda |
| | | | 2nd | 9 | **fazer** | to make | **fazenda** | cloth, ranch |
| | | | 3rd | | **agir** | to act | **agenda** | agenda |
| 4 | +ns++a# | Very Low 72 | 1st | 57 | **esperar** | to hope | **esperança** | hope |
| | | | 2nd | 15 | **crer** | to believe | **crença** | belief |
| | | | 3rd | | **diferir** | to defer | **diferença** | deference |
| 5 | +dour++o# | Modest 125 | 1st | 98 | **achar** | to find | **achadouro** | finding site |
| | | | 2nd | 22 | **ferver** | to boil | **fervedouro** | fervor |
| | | | 3rd | 5 | **sumir** | to vanish | **sumidouro** | sink hole |
| 6 | +t++a# | Modest 327 | 1st | 275 | **chegar** | to arrive | **chegada** | arrival |
| | | | 2nd | 52 | **caber** | to fit | **cabida** | opportunity |
| | | | 3rd | | **sair** | to leave | **saída** | exit |

26 The data in Table 7.5a do not close the case on deverbal nouns. Many nouns are derived from perfect participles, but in searching the *Aurélio* they appear among the nouns derived from adjectives since perfect participles double as adjectives.

Table 7.5a Continued

| | Suffix | Productivity | C | # | Verb | Gloss | Noun | Gloss |
|---|---|---|---|---|---|---|---|---|
| 7 | +dur++a# | Modest 377 | 1st | 325 | **ditar** | to dictate | **ditadura** | dictatorship |
| | | | 2nd | 33 | **bater** | to beat | **batedura** | beating |
| | | | 3rd | 19 | **polir** | to polish | **polidura** | polishing |
| 8 | +nsi++a# | High 675 | 1st | 177 | **prestar** | to lend | **prestância** | utility |
| | | | 2nd | 498 | **viver** | to live | **vivência** | way of life |
| | | | 3rd | | **fluir** | to flow | **fluência** | fluency |
| 9 | +ment++o# | Supreme 1907 | 1st | 1,530 | **livrar** | to free | **livramento** | freeing |
| | | | 2nd | 377[a] | **nascer** | to bud | **nascimento** | birth |
| | | | 3rd | | **abrir** | to open | **abrimento** | opening |
| 10 | +dor#<e+ | Supreme 2466 | 1st | 2,223 | **narrar** | to narrate | **narrador** | narrator |
| | | | 2nd | 127 | **reger** | to rule | **regedor** | regulator |
| | | | 3rd | 116 | **fingir** | to feign | **fingidor** | faker |
| 11 | +sion++e+ | Supreme 3303 | 1st | 3,006 | **tentar** | to tempt | **tentação** | temptation |
| | | | 2nd | 3 | **encher** | to bother | **encheção** | bother |
| | | | 2nd | 294 | **vender** | to sell | **vendição** | sale |
| | | | 3rd | | **trair** | to betray | **traição** | treason |
| 12 | +r#+e+ | Outlier 12913 | 1st | 11,482 | **acaba** | 3rd ends | **acabar** | to finish |
| | | | 2nd | 753 | **aprende** | 3rd learns | **aprender** | to learn |
| | | | 3rd | 678 | **late** | 3rd barks | **latir** | to bark |

a There is one deverbal noun ending in –<u>mento</u> preceded by /e/ rather than /a/ or /i/: *adimplemento* 'fulfillment (of a contract)' related to the 3rd conjugation verb *adimplir* 'to fulfill'. Presumably this noun is an erudite construction based on the late Latin *adimplere*, a 2nd conjugation verb.

Table 7.5a is organized as follows: The deriving suffixes appear in the second column, their productivity ratings in the third. The fourth column contains the conjugation classes on which the suffixes appear, and the fifth column contains the number of examples found for each conjugation. Suffixes 1 and 2 only appear in one conjugation class. Suffixes 3, 4, 6, 8, 9, and 11 neutralize 2nd and 3rd conjugation theme vowels: 2nd conjugation (+e#) emerges as +i+ with suffixes 6, 9, and ll;

3rd conjugation merges with 2nd with suffixes 3, 4, and 8.[27] Suffixes 5, 7, 10, and 12 occur with all theme vowels. The remaining columns contain verbs (infinitives) followed by their glosses and nouns derived from those verbs' roots followed by their theme vowels.

**§7.4.1 Productivity:** Again, as in the case of Tables 7.3a and 7.4a, the suffixes do not share the burden of 'adjective-to-noun' formation equally, as Table 7.5b demonstrates:

**Table 7.5b** Relative Productivity Verb-to-Noun-Deriving Suffixes

| Low to Modest Productivity | | | High to Supeme Productivity | | |
|---|---|---|---|---|---|
| **Suffix** | **Occurrences** | **% of total** | **Suffix** | **Occurrences** | **% of total** |
| + is++o# | 4 | 0.04 | ˈV+nsi++a# | 675 | 7.28 |
| +et++e# | 5 | 0.05 | +ment++o# | 1,907 | 20.57 |
| +nd++a | 11 | 0.12 | +dor#+e+ | 2,466 | 26.90 |
| +ns++a# | 72 | 0.78 | +sion+e+ | 3,303 | 35.62 |
| +dour++o# | 125 | 1.35 | +r#+e+ | Outlier | |
| <t++a# | 327 | 3.53 | | | |
| +dur++a | 377 | 4.07 | | | |
| **Totals:** | **921** | **9.93** | | **8,351** | **90.07** |

In this set, except the infinitives, four out of eleven suffixes account for 90.07% of all the deverbal nouns.[28]

**§7.4.2 Gender:** There is a trend in the gender of deverbal nouns: four of the eleven suffixes are [+feminine], six are [-feminine], and one (+dor#<e+) is inflected for the referent's gender. In sheer numbers, the [-feminine] nouns account for 2,299 or 24.8% of the 9,272 deverbal nouns. The inflectible suffix accounts for 26.60%, and the [+feminine] suffixes, for

27 Suffix 11 (+sion++e+) attaches overwhelmingly to 1st conjugation verbs. Very rarely does it attach to 2nd conjugation verbs, only three of which maintain their theme vowel. Many emerge with no theme vowel, and a few shift their theme vowel from 2nd to 3rd conjugation. See Appendix 8B, Tables 8B.5-6.

28 Even though infinitives are statistical outliers and of an order different from the other deverbal nominals, they are present in Tables 7.5a–d because they are full-fledged nouns (Tables 6.1, 6.2, §6.0.4 and fn. 1 and Table 6.5, note a). Indeed, they have the highest valence as nouns because they cannot be marshaled to function as modifiers and their gender is always [-feminine].

48.61%. Of course the supremely productive suffix +sion+e+ is responsible for the exceptionally high number of [+feminine] deverbal nouns.

§7.4.3 **Meaning:** Contrary to the cases for deriving nouns from other nouns or from adjectives, the case for these nouns' being derived directly from verbs is strong. All the suffixed nominals in Table 7.5a have meanings that correspond to the activity the verbs denote. They all indicate some sort of realization of verbal activity. Sometimes the meanings are specific and concrete: *lembrar* 'to remember' ⇔ *lembrete* 'memo', sometimes they are more abstract or general: *prestar* 'to be useful' ⇔ *prestança* 'utility'. Whether the derived meaning is specific or abstract depends on the meaning the verbal stems have.

§7.4.4.0 **Allomorphy:** Whereas the 'denominal' and 'deadjectival' nouns were formed from stems without the gender morphemes of the nouns and adjectives, in all but the first two cases in Table 7.5a the deverbal nouns contain verbs' theme vowels or reflexes thereof.[29] That is, many stems of the words in Table 7.5a are actual, viable verbs.[30] There are 23 stems that occur unaltered when followed by theme vowels (+S suffixes) in Table 7.5a. Table 7.5c shows their structure in words that, were they $R_1$+ stems, would undergo some sort of alteration in their stems' configuration.

29 The stems in Table 7.5a are mainly R+ because the theme vowels are +S deriving suffixes which, in these cases, attach directly to verbal stems. However, the roots of *crer* (4), *caber* (6), *sair* (6), and *trair* (11) are created from $R_1$+ roots (#krɛd+, #kap+, #sal+, and #trad+: cf. *crédulo* 'credulous', *capaz* 'capable', *saliência* 'protrusion', and *tradição* 'delivery'). In these examples, the stems are followed by $+S_1$ suffixes. Their root final consonants either evanesce (/d+, /l+ → Ø) or voice (/p+→ /b+) when followed by +S suffixes.

30 They are formed as follows: #stem++theme vowel#+deriving suffix++[±feminine] #<[±plural]#. Strictly speaking, the structure of a verb is #stem++theme vowel#<tense/mood/aspect#<person/number# (Vi.0.0). Since the verbs that form stems for deverbal adjectives and nouns are 3rd person present indicative, both the <TMA# and the <PN# morphemes are Øs and need not be included in the derivation of deverbal nominals.

Table 7.5c Immutable Roots, Stems, and Suffixes

| R+Stems | Words | Stem + TV | R+Stems | Words | Stem + TV |
|---|---|---|---|---|---|
| #ad+#kab+ | **acabar** | #ad++kab++a# | #lat+[a] | **latir** | #lat++i+ |
| #aš+ | **achar** | #aš++a# | #lenbr+ | **lembrar** | #lenbr++a# |
| #ad+#prɛnd+ | **aprender** | #ad+#prɛnd++e# | #nar̠+ | **narrar** | #nar̠++a# |
| #bat+ | **bater** | #bat++e# | #pɔl+ | **polir** | #pɔl+i+ |
| #šeg+ | **chegar** | #šeg++a# | #prɛzt+ | **prestar** | #prɛzt++a# |
| #di+#fɛr+ | **diferir** | #d+#fɛr+i+[b] | #pro+#pag+ | **propagar** | #pro+#pag++a# |
| #dit+ | **ditar** | #dit++a# | #sum+ | **sumir** | #sum+i+ |
| #enš+ | **encher** | #enš++e# | #tɛnt+ | **tentar** | #tɛnt++a# |
| #ezpɛr+ | **esperar** | #ezpɛr++a# | #tɔλ+ | **tolher** | #tɔλ++e# |
| #fɛrv+ | **ferver** | #fɛrv++e# | #vend+ | **vender** | #vend++e# |
| #finž+ | **fingir** | #finž+i+ | #viv+ | **viver** | #viv++e# |
| #flu+ | **fluir** | #flu+i+ | | | |

a As an R+ stem #lat+ ('bark') undergoes no variation, reguardless of the deriving suffix it occurs with. There is a $R_1$+ root with the same segmental configuration: #lat+ ('side') in which the final /t+ mutates when followed by +S suffixes: *lado* #lad++o# 'side', *ladear* #lat++e++a#+r#+e+ 'to go alongside', cf. *latitude* #lat++i++tud++e# 'latitude' and *lateral* #lat++ɛr++al#+e# 'lateral'.

b The 3rd conjugation theme vowel +i+ is followed by + rather than # because it cannot occur word-finally or before a suffix that consists only of a consonant (§Vi.0.0 fn. 1 and §13A.0).

Compare the data in Table 7.5c with those in 7.5d, where $R_1$+ stems pattern with both +S and +$S_1$ suffixes:

Table 7.5d $R_1$+ Stems, +$S_1$ Suffixes

| $R_1$+ | $R_1$++S[a] | $R_1$++$S_1$# | Word | Gloss |
|---|---|---|---|---|
| #apɛr+ | **abrir** | #apɛr++it++iv++o# | **aperitivo** | opener |
| #ag+ | **agir** | #ag++sion++e+ | **ação** | action |
| #kap+ | **caber** | #kap++as+i+dad++e# | **capacidade** | capacity |
| #krɛd+ | **crer** | #krɛd++i++bil#i+dad++e# | **credibilidade** | credibility |
| #fak+ | **fazer** | #fak++ult++a#+tiv+<o# | **facultativo** | optional |
| #lib+ | **livrar** | #lib++ɛr++a#+sion++e+ | **liberação** | liberation |
| #nat+ | **nascer** | #nat++ur++al#+e# | **natural** | native |
| #sal+ | **sair** | #sal++i++ˈensi++a# | **saliência** | protrusion |
| #trad+ | **trair** | #trad++i++sion++e# | **tradição** | tradition |

a The +S suffixes are all verb-deriving theme vowels.

**§7.4.4.1** Similar to the deadjectival nouns, the suffixes that form the derived nouns in Table 7.5a are not exclusive. That is, they are not the only suffixes to attach to the stems in question to form nouns. Table 7.5e (below) shows that other suffixes may be added to the same verbal stems, often without occasioning drastic changes in meanings from those of the original examples:[31]

31 For example, the word *lembrança* means both 'menory' and 'souvenir', whereas *lembrete* indicates an appointment memorandum; however, the *Aurélio* lists it as synonymous with *lembrança*. The word *crença* meaning 'belief' has near synonyms in *crédito* 'credit' and *crendice* 'superstition'. The words ending in +dour++o# have somewhat more idiomatic meanings: *achadouro* 'finding site', such as a regular fossil finding place; *fervedouro*'s meaning 'fervor' is metaphoric, social agitation, rather than literal boiling; and *sumidouro* as 'sink hole' indicates a material entity, i.e. a place where water and other objects disappear into the ground. The words *fervor* and *fervença* also indicate metaphorical boiling, *achado* means 'a find', and *sumiço* and *sumidura* mean 'disappearance'. The suffix +t++a# when it attaches to *chegar* and *sair* indicates completed action, whereas when it attaches to *caber* and forms *cabida*, it uses a metaphoric extension of the verb's basic meaning of 'fitting', i.e. 'to be one's share or right'. The other words corresponding to *livramento*, *nascimento*, and *saimento* in Table 7.5e's ninth section are synonyms of one another and the original words. The words formed with the suffix ˈV+nsi++a#, which Cunha (70) identifies as 'semi-eruditas', are modeled on Latin forms and of relatively modern coinage. They have a direct and somewhat abstract relationship with their verbal stems' meanings. The near synonyms *prestância*, *prestamento,* and *prestação* can be used interchangeably to mean 'reckoning'; *prestamento* can also mean 'usefulness' as *prestância* also does. However, *prestação* can also mean 'loan payment, installment'. The words formed with +ment++o# are semantically transparent and indicate a realization of the verbs' meaning. Their alternates in column 3 of Table 7.5e are synonyms among themselves and with the words formed using +ment++o#. And, finally, words formed with the suffix +sion++e+ (11a-b) bear a systematic semantic relationship with their stems' meanings—a realization of the verbal activity. Their alternate words in Table 7.5e are their synonyms.

Table 7.5e Verb-to-Noun Formation (Alternatives)

| | Table 7.5 Word | Near Synonymns | Synonymns' Glosses |
|---|---|---|---|
| 1 | tolhiço | tolhimento | impediment |
| 2 | lembrete | lembrança | souvenir |
| 3a | propaganda | propagação | propagation |
| 3b | fazenda*[a] | fazedor | doer |
| | agenda* | agência | agency |
| 4a | esperança | espera | wait, expect, hope |
| 4b | crença* | crendice | belief, superstion |
| | diferença | diferênciacão | differentiation |
| 5a | achadouro | achado | discovery |
| 5b | fervedouro | fervor, fervença | fervor, (a) boiling |
| 5c | sumidouro | sumiço, sumidura | disappearance |
| 6a | chegada | chegamento, chegança | arrival, visitation |
| 6b | cabida* | cabimento | propriety |
| | saída* | saidouro, saimento | starting gate, departure |
| 7a | ditadura | ditatório | dictatorial |
| 7b | batedura | batedeira, batedor | churn, beater |
| 7c | polidura | polidez, polidor | polish, polisher |
| 8a | prestância | prestamento, prestação | rendering, installment |
| 8b | vivência | vivenda | residence |
| | fluência | fluidez | fluidity |
| 9a | livramento* | livrança, liberação, libertação | deliverance, liberation |
| 9b | nascimento* | nascença | birth |
| | caimento* | caída, caidor | fall, entrance to river |
| 10a | narrador | narração, narrativa | narration, narrative |
| 10b | regedor* | regente, regedoria | regent, regent's office |
| 10c | fingidor | fingimento | feigning |
| 11a | tentação | tentamento | temptation |
| 11b | vendição | venda | sale |
| | nutrição | nutrimento | nutriment |

a The forms bearing asterisks have $R_1$+ stems. Only item 9a has +$S_1$ suffixes in these examples.

Tables 7.5b–e have shown that all these suffixes can attach to both transitive and intransitive verbal stems[32] from all three verbal conjugations: 1st conjugation (theme vowel +a#), 2nd conjugation (theme vowel +e#), 3rd conjugation (theme vowel +i+).

**§7.4.4.2** The allomorphy that the cognate suffixes 4 and 8 (+ns++a# and +ˈV+nsi++a#) display and occasion has been accounted for. Suffixes 7 and 10 (+dur++a# and +dor#<e+) also display allomorphy.

**§7.4.5.0 Suffixes of Negligible Productivity: +is++o#, +et++e#, and +nd++a#** The example for suffix 1, +is++o#, does not occur in the *Aurélio*, but it does in the *Morais* dictionary. There is a homophonous suffix, +is+<o#, that forms deverbal adjectives. Suffix 2, +et++e#, is a diminutive suffix which normally attaches to nouns. Suffix 3, +nd++a#, normally merges 2nd and 3rd conjugation theme vowels, but in one case it appears to preserve the 3rd conjugation theme vowel: *vir* 'to come' ⇔ *vinda* 'arrival'.[33]

**§7.4.5.1 Cognate Suffixes of Very Low and High Productivity: +ns++a# and ˈV+nsi++a#:** Suffix (4) +ns++a# is a +S suffix with a long history in the Portuguese language. Suffix (8) ˈV+nsi++a# is the same suffix in a reconstructed key—it copies both its Latin etymon as do its stems, which makes it a +$S_1$ suffix. Words formed with ˈV+nsi++a# reflect their underlying forms perfectly, whereas those formed with +ns++a# do not. Table 7.5f below demonstrates the structure preserving powers of +nsi++a# and the mutative possibilities allowed by +ns++a and a few other +S suffixes:

32 The three verbs providing the stems of nouns formed with +sion++e# are transitive, but intransitive verbs also provide stems for this suffix: *agir* 'to act' *ação* 'action', *estar* 'to be (in a state)' *estação* 'station'.

33 This form may be a derivative of the verb *vir*'s perfective participle and gerund: *vindo*.

Table 7.5f Preservation and Loss of Root Final Consonants

| | Root | Infinitive | Gloss | Root +$S_1$ | Gloss | Root +S | Gloss |
|---|---|---|---|---|---|---|---|
| 1 | #kad+ | **cair** | to fall | **decadência** | decadence | **caimento** | fall |
| 2 | #kred+ | **crer** | to believe | **credência** | credence | **crença** | belief |
| 3 | #fid+ | **fiar** | to trust | **confidência**[a] | confidence | **confiança** | trust |
| 4 | #dɔl+ | **doer** | to ache | **dolência** | affliction | **doença** | illness |
| 5 | #sal+ | **sair** | to emerge | **saliência** | salience | **saimento** | exit |
| 6 | #son+ | **soar** | to sound | **sonância** | sonance | **soante** | sonant |
| 7 | #ten+ | **ter** | to have | **tenência** | vigor | **tença** | pension |
| 8 | #pon+ | **pôr** | to put | **imponência** | grandeur | **poente**[b] | sunset |
| 9 | #pot+ | **poder** | to be able | **potência** | potency | **poderio** | power |

a Whereas the root of *confidência* is #fid+, as a Latinate reconstruction this word does not have a verbal stem. The verb *confidenciar* 'to confide in' is a denominal verb.

b In Portuguese, the verb *pôr* #pon++e#+r#+e+ is used to indicate the setting of the sun, as well as the laying of eggs. The form *poente* for 'sunset' is a present participle of the verb *pôr* used as a noun.

In addition to +ns++a, the +S suffixes include +ment++o, +nt++e#, as well as the theme vowels +a#, +e#, and +i+.

§7.4.5.2.0 **+dour+ +o#** This modestly productive suffix has an allomorph +doir++o# that has the same relationship to verbal stems.[34] That is, they attach directly to verb stems that consist of a root or stem plus the theme vowel. Notwithstanding the transparent lexical forms of *achadouro*, *fervedouro*, and *sumidouro* (#root++TV++dour++o#: #aš++a#+dour++o#, #fɛrv++e#+dour++o#, and #sum++i+dour++o#), other data (§7.4.5.2.1) indicate that +dour++o# is a +S suffix and can occasion (or co-occur with) the morphophonemic modification of $R_1$+ verbal stems.

§7.4.5.2.1 The root of the verb *pôr* 'to put' provides a stem for a –d*ouro* word: *poedouro*, which indicates the place where chickens lay eggs, or an ink- or paint-soaked cloth where pens or brushes can be set (i.e. 'put'). The underlying form of *pôr* is #pon++e#+r#+e+ and that of *poedouro* is #pon++e++dour++o#. The root loses its final /n+ before +S suffixes, and the sequence that is left #po+ is the base on which *poedouro* is formed (as well as *poente* 'sunset' and *poedeira* 'good egg-layer').

34 The *Aurélio* gives –*oiro* alternatives for all the –*ouro* words.

§7.4.5.2.2 Similarly, the *root* of *suor* 'sweat' and *suar* 'to sweat' is a $R_1$+ stem, #sud+ because the /d+ emerges in words such as *sudação* 'sweating', *sudorese* 'excessive sweating' and *sudário* 'shrowd'. The /d+ evanesces both in the verb *suar* 'to sweat' and in the form *suadouro* 'sweat house', which is to be expected given that both the theme vowel +a# and the suffix +dour++o# are class +S suffixes.

§7.4.6 **+t++a#:** This modestly productive suffix is actually a combination of two suffixes: the derivational perfect participle[35] suffix +t+ (§13.10.3.0–3) and the noun-forming suffix +a#, which has a +S relationship with its verbal stems.[36] Thus, the lexical forms of *chegado*, *cabido*, and *saído* are #šeg++a#+t+<o#, #kap++i++t+<o#, and #sal++i++t+<o# so as to reflect their ability to agree in gender (and number) with nouns that they modify when they are used as adjectives. From perfective participle stems, the lexical forms of *chegada*, *cabida*, and *saída* are derived. Lexically they are: #šeg++a#+t++a#, #kap++i++t++a#, and #sal++i++t++a#.[37] Here one sees that the normal deriving theme vowels are +S morphemes because [+surd] occlusive root final consonants in $R_1$+ stems become voiced, and the coronal consonants /n, l, d/ in that position are deleted.

§7.4.7.0 **+dur++a#** This modestly productive suffix is not a combination of the perfective participle morpheme +t+ and +ur++a# because its attachment to verbal stems does not occasion (or co-occur with) the neutralization of 2nd and 3rd conjugation theme vowels the way the +t++a# suffix does. It is a +S suffix since it allows stem-final consonants to

35 The normal designation for this morpheme is 'past participle'. However, it indicates perfectivity more accurately than pastness (§13.10.0).

36 The participial morpheme, if it does not cause the 2nd and 3rd conjugation theme vowels to neutralize in favor of /i/, it at least co-occurs with this neutralization. These emblematic verbs' perfective participles emerge as: *chegado* 'arrived', *cabido* 'fitted', and *saído* 'left', which indicates that the perfective participle morpheme normally occurs as /d/. There are verb conjugations in which this morpheme remains voiceless: e.g. *escrever* 'to write' → *escrito* 'written', *fazer* 'to do' → *feito* 'done', *dizer* 'to say'→ *dito* 'said'.

37 The semantic parentage these nouns have with the perfective participle is obvious. The perfective participle indicates completed action, and it is hardly a stretch to say that deverbal nouns formed from the perfective participle of verbs indicate the realization (if not necessarily total completion) of the action their verbal stems denote.

evanesce: *embotoadura* 'buttoning' (cf. *botão* 'button' #bɔt++on++e+) and *moedura* 'grinding' (cf. *moleiro* 'miller' #mɔl++eir+<o#).

§7.4.7.1 There are many instances in which this morpheme's +d/ evanesces. Table 7.5g contains representative examples:

Table 7.5g +dur++a# Allomorphy

| Derived Nouns | Gloss | Adjective | Gloss | Analysis (Nouns) |
|---|---|---|---|---|
| **abertura** | opening | **aberto** | open | #apɛr+<t++dur++a# |
| **compostura** | composure | **composto** | composed | #kon+#pɔz+<t++dur++a# |
| **cultura** | culture | **culto** | refined | #kult++dur++a# |
| **direitura** | straitness | **direito** | straight | #di+#rɛg+<t++dur++a# |
| **soltura** | release | **solto** | loose | #sɔl+<t++dur++a# |

With the possible exception of *cultura* and *culto* the stems of both the adjectives and the nouns are perfective participles (albeit irregular), which can be used as adjectives. The stem-final /t+ of all these adjectives occasions the deletion of suffix-initial +d/. Provisionally, the rule for this phenomenon is:

**Rule 7.1 Loss of Morpheme-initial +d/:**[38]

$$+\begin{pmatrix}+\text{occlusion}\\ -\text{surd}\\ -\text{high}\\ -\text{labial}\end{pmatrix} \rightarrow \emptyset \,/\, \_\_\_\_ \begin{pmatrix}+\text{occlusion}\\ +\text{surd}\\ -\text{high}\\ -\text{labial}\end{pmatrix} +$$

§7.4.8 **+ment++o#** This highly productive morpheme is also a +S suffix that attaches to stems that include their verbal theme vowels and, in the case of $R_1$+ stems, consonantal mutations occurring in words derived with this suffix bear testimony to that fact:

38 This is a phonotactic constraint. There is no occasion of the sequence /td/ that surfaces in the language.

**Table 7.5h** Consonantal Mutation with +ment++o#[a]

| Mutation | Lexical Form | Word | Gloss |
|---|---|---|---|
| /l+ ➔ Ø | #sal++i++ment++o# | **saimento** | a leaving |
| p+ ➔ /b+ | #kap++i++ment++o# | **cabimento** | propriety |
| /b+➔ /v+ | #lib+ɛr++a#+ment++o# | **livramento** | freeing |
| /k+➔ /g+ | #per+#sɛk++i++ment++o# | **perseguimento** | persecution |

a On the other hand, there are a very few instances in which +ment++o# appears to function as an $+S_1$ suffix: (A) *abonamento* (cf. *aboamento)* 'guarantee' *(*$R_1$+ root #bon+); (B) *fatigamento* (cf. *fadiga*'fatigue'), $R_1$+ root #fat+; (C) *filamento* (cf. *fio* 'filament, thread/wire'), $R_1$+ root #fil+; (D) *lineamento* (cf. *linha*, 'line manufacture, line'), $R_1$+ root #line+; (E) *regulamento*, (cf. *regra* 'regulations, rule'), $R_1$+ root #rɛg+; (6) *turbamento*, (cf. *turvamento* 'opacity/disturbance'), $R_1$+ root #turb+. In all cases, the normal $R_1$+/__+S consonantism obtains in the $2^{nd}$ word of the pair. In the case of pairs (1) and (F), the words are synonyms, whereas in the other cases the $R_1$+/__+S consonantism obtains in related but not synonymous words. The words in which the $R_1$+/__+$S_1$ dynamic obtains are of a slightly more 'refined' nature, which suggests relatively recent coinage.

**§7.4.9 +dor#<c+** This supremely productive suffix is a +S because it does not occasion the emergence of root-final consonants in words such as *caidor* 'place where cattle enter rivers' (cf. *cadente* 'falling'), *livrador* 'liberator' (cf. *liberdade* 'liberty'), *voador* 'capable of flight' (cf. *volátil* 'capable of flight'). Its allomorphy is similar to that of +dur++a# insofar as its initial +d/ disappears after a stem-final /t+: +dor#<e# ➔ +or#<e# as Table 7.5i demonstrates:

**Table 7.5i** +dor#<e+ Allomorphy

| Derived Nouns | Gloss | Nominal | Gloss | Analysis (Nouns) |
|---|---|---|---|---|
| **cultor** | cultivator | **culto** | refined | #kult++dor#<e+ |
| **cantor**[a] | singer | **canto** | song | #kant++dor#<e+ |
| **diretor** | director | **direito** | straight | #di+#rɛg++t++dor#<e+ |
| **genitor** | father | **génito** | created | #žen++it++dor#<e# |
| **produtor** | producer | **produto** | product | #pro+#duk++t++dor#<e+ |

a This word has the doublet *cantador.*

**§7.4.10 Suffix 11 +sion++e+** The examples in Table 7.5a and the counting of words ending in this suffix all contain reflexes of verbs' theme vowels. They do not exhaust this suffix's deriving capacity since +sion++e+ also attaches to verbal stems lacking theme vowels. It is the most problematic of this set insofar as its lexical form is radically different from its word-final realizations. Because of its knotty nature and the difficulty entailed in providing rules to generate its many allomorphs, Chapter 8 addresses this morpheme in detail.

§7.4.11 **Infinitives:** The final suffix to consider in the deverbal noun category is the infinitive-forming suffix +r#+e+. The extreme regularity with which this suffix attaches to verbal stems and its total invariability might make one want to consider it an inflecting suffix, but since it changes its stems' form class from verb to noun, it resides among the deverbal noun deriving suffixes. This suffix presents no allomorphy and, as a +S suffix, it co-occurs with verbs that lose root-final /n, d, l/ and that voice [+surd] occlusive root-final consonants in verbal stems.

## The Formation of Adjectives

§7.5.0 Both nominal and verbal stems can provide the bases to which suffixes attach to form adjectives. Table 7.6a[39] displays the suffixes that form adjectives from nominal stems and roots:

**Table 7.6a** Noun to Adjective

| | Suffix | Productivity | Noun | Gloss | Adjective | Gloss |
|---|---|---|---|---|---|---|
| 1 | +ɛzt++e#*[a] | Negligible 6 | **céu*** | sky | **celeste** | celestial |
| 2 | +oɲ+<o# | Negligible 9 | **medo** | fear | **medonho** | scary |
| 3 | +izk+<o# | Negligible 11 | **mouro** | Moor | **mourisco** | Moorish |
| 4 | +ɛztr++e# | Negligible 16 | **campo** | countryside | **campestre** | rustic |
| 5 | +eng+<o# | Negligible 19 | **mulher** | woman | **mulherengo** | womanizer |
| 6 | +eɲ+<o# | Negligible 35 | **ferro** | iron | **ferrenho** | iron-like |
| 7 | +aik+<o# | Negligible 36 | **prosa** | prose | **prosaico** | prosaic |
| 8 | +lɛnt+<o# | Negligible 45 | **sono** | sleep | **sonolento** | sleepy |
| 9 | +ˈisi+<o# | Very Low 63 | **sarmento** | twig | **sarmentício** | twiggy |
| 10 | +ˈɛ+<u# | Very Low 64 | **ilha** | island | **ilhéu** | Islander |
| 11 | +it++a# | Very Low 71 | **moscovo** | Moscow | **moscovita** | Muscovite |
| 12 | +ɛzk+<o# | Very Low 117 | **quixote** | Quixote | **quixotesco** | Quixotic |
| 13 | +en+<o# | Very Low 120 | **Chile** | Chile | **chileno** | Chilean |

39 The total sampling in Table 7.6a was 22,645 adjectives created by the addition of the tokens for the 29 suffixes listed in the 2[nd] column. Suffixes 28 and 29 were outliers, whereas the remainder (12,357 adjectives) constituted a reliable database: M=457.67, SD = 623.25, Z =2.859. Words formed with suffix 27 had a Z value of 2.47.

Table 7.6a Continued

| | Suffix | Productivity | Noun | Gloss | Adjective | Gloss |
|---|---|---|---|---|---|---|
| 14 | +il#+e+ | Low 149 | **febre** | fever | **febril** | febrile |
| 15a | +ez++e+ | Low 184 | **corte** | court | **cortês** | courteous |
| 15b | +ez+<e+ | | **Líbano** | Lebanon | **libanês** | Lebonese |
| 16 | +ak+<o# | Low 218 | **mania** | mania | **maníaco** | maniac |
| 17 | +ud+<o# | Low 233 | **ponta** | point | **pontudo** | pointed |
| 18 | +ɛnt+<o# | Low 254 | **ciume** | jealousy | **ciumento** | jealous |
| 19 | +ˈari+<o#* | Modest 551 | **reação*** | reaction | **reacionário** | reactionary |
| 20 | +ar#+e+ | Modest 555 | **sol** | sun | **solar** | solar |
| 21 | +in+<o#* | Modest 629 | **cabra*** | goat | **caprino** | goat-like |
| 22 | +izt++a# | High 873 | **varejo** | retail | **varejista** | retailer |
| 23 | + ɔz+<o# | High 1200 | **fama** | fame | **famoso** | famous |
| 24a | +an+<o#$_1$ | High 1207 | **América** | America | **americano** | American |
| 24b | +an+<o#$_2$ | | **Alemânia** | Germany | **alemão** | German |
| 25 | ˈV++tik+<o# | Very High 1801 | **aroma** | aroma | **aromático** | aromatic |
| 26 | +al#+e+* | Very High 1891 | **razão*** | reason | **racional** | rational |
| 27 | ˈV(V$_{[+high]}$)C$_{1-3}$++e+<o# | Very High 2000 | **rosa** | rose | **róseo** | rosy |
| 28 | +ens++e# | Outlier 4584 | **Nicaragua** | Nicaragua | **nicaragüense** | Nicaraguan |
| 29 | ˈVC$_{1-3}$++ik+ <o#* | Outlier 5704 | **Balcãs*** | Balkans | **balcânico** | Balkan |

a The suffixes bearing asterisks are +$S_1$ because the $R_1$+ stems (also asterisked) they attach to are morphophonologically transparent, whereas the nouns that surface with +S suffixes are opaque owing to the mutations one expects of $R_1$+ stems followed by +S suffixes. Several suffixes in this array are +$S_1$.

The glosses in Table 7.6a indicate that, similar to the formation of deadjectival and deverbal nouns, there is a direct relationship between the stems' denotations in the morphologically simple nouns and those in the derived adjectives. The adjectives describe entitities that have the characteristics of the related nouns.[40]

40 Some suffixes may convey speakers' attitudes toward whatever or whoever is the referent. Suffix 12 (+ɛzk+<o#) has acquired a certain derogatory connotation because it often attaches to the stems of nouns with derogatory connotations: *Quixote* (crazed idealism) cf. *quixotesco* 'quixotic', *vilão* 'villian' cf. *vilanesco* 'villianous', *burla* 'mockery' cf. *burlesco* 'burlesque'. This connotation has spread to neutral words, e.g. *livro* 'book'. When knowledge or attitudes are described as *livrescas*, the adjective connotes impracticality.

**§7.5.1 Productivity:** As has been the case in all categories, and as Table 7.6a indicates, the suffixes that derive adjectives from nominal (i.e. non-verbal) stems do not share the adjective deriving function equally. With the outliers eliminated from statistical discussions, Table 7.6b demonstrates that eight of the remaining 27 suffixes account for 86.65% of the data.

**Table 7.6b** Relative Productivity of Noun-to-Adjective-Deriving Suffixes

| | Suffix | Tokens | % | | Suffix | Tokens | % |
|---|---|---|---|---|---|---|---|
| Negligible to Low (1–18) | | | | 15b | +ez#<e+ | *** | *** |
| 1 | +ɛzt++e# | 6 | 0.05 | 16 | +ak+<o# | 218 | 1.76 |
| 2 | +oɲ+<o# | 9 | 0.07 | 17 | +ud+<o# | 233 | 1.89 |
| 3 | +izk+<o# | 11 | 0.09 | 18 | +ɛnt+<o# | 254 | 2.05 |
| 4 | +ɛztr++e# | 16 | 0.13 | Total: Negligible to Low | | 1,650 | 13.35 |
| 5 | +eng+<o# | 19 | 0.15 | Modest to Very High (19–27) | | | |
| 6 | +eɲ+<o# | 35 | 0.28 | 19 | +ˈari+<o# | 551 | 4.46 |
| 7 | +aik+<o# | 36 | 0.29 | 20 | +ar#<e+ | 555 | 4.49 |
| 8 | +lɛnt+<o# | 45 | 0.36 | 21 | +in+<o# | 629 | 5.09 |
| 9 | +ˈisi+<o# | 63 | 0.51 | 22 | +izt++a# | 873 | 7.06 |
| 10 | +ˈɛ+<u# | 64 | 0.52 | 23 | + ɔz+<o# | 1,200 | 9.71 |
| 11 | +it++a# | 71 | 0.57 | 24 | +an+<o#$_{1, 2}$ | 1,207 | 9.77 |
| 12 | +ɛzk+<o# | 117 | 0.95 | 25 | +ˈVtik+<o# | 1,801 | 14.57 |
| 13 | +en+<o# | 120 | 0.97 | 26 | +al#+e+ | 1,891 | 15.03 |
| 14 | +il#+e+ | 149 | 1.21 | 27 | ˈV(V$_{[+high]}$)C$_{1-}$+e+ <o# | 2,000 | 16.19 |
| 15a | +ez#+e+ | 184 | 1.49 | Total: Modest to Very High | | 10,707 | 86.65 |

**§7.5.2.0 Gender:** Contrary to the noun-forming suffixes' arbitrary gender, adjectival suffixes usually end in inflectional gender morphemes, most of which will reflect the gender of whatever the adjective modifies.[41]

41 The unmarked inflectional gender morpheme <o# [-feminine] indicates that the adjectives will reflect nouns' gender. Of course when adjectives of this nature modify [+feminine] nouns, they will end in <a#. Likewise, adjectives ending in <e+, when inflected for [+feminine] gender end in <a#: *francês* 'French [-feminine]' ⇔ *francesa* 'French [+feminine]'. The adjectives will

§7.5.2.1 Seven suffixes in Table 7.6b modify [±feminine] nouns with no change of gender morpheme: (1) +ɛzt++e#, e.g. *planta agreste* 'rural plant' (+f.), *lago agreste* 'rural lake' (-f.); (4) +ɛstr++e# e.g. *casa campestre* 'rustic house (+f.)', *homem campestre* 'rustic man (-f.)'; (11) +it++a# *língua semita* 'semitic language (+f.)', *país semita* 'semitic country (-f.)'; (14) +il#+e+ *luz débil* 'weak light (+f.)' *sol débil* 'weak sun (-f.)'; (15a) +ez#+e+ *moça cortês* 'courteous young woman (+f.)', *velho cortês* 'courteous old man (-f.)';[42] (20) +ar#+e+ *hora regular* 'regular hour (+f.)', *verbo regular* 'regular verb (-f.)'; (22) +izt++a# *lei racista* 'racist law (+f.)', *governo racista* 'racist government (-f.)'; (26) +al#+e+ *ideia sensacional* 'sensational idea (+f.)', *carro sensacional* 'sensational car (-f.)'.

§7.5.3 **Meaning:** Adjectives formed with suffixes describe items (material and abstract) as having a particular relationship to the nouns, i.e. nominal stems, they are derived from. There is no mystery here.

§7.5.4 **Allomorphy:** Table 7.6a contains six $R_1$+ stems, five of which appear Table 7.6c followed by $+S_1$ suffixes that preserve the phonemes in their stems and then followed by +S suffixes that allow their stems to mutate:

**Table 7.6c** $R_1$+ Stems: Stability and Mutuability[a]

| 7.6a | $R_1$ | +S | Word | $+S_1$ | Word | $+S_1$ | Word |
|---|---|---|---|---|---|---|---|
| 1 | #sɛl+ | +u# | céu | +ɛst++e# | celeste | ˈ$VC_{1-3}$++ik+<o# | célico |
| | *** | *** | *** | +ɛbr++e# | célebre | +i+,o# | celio |
| 21 | #kapr+ | +a# | cabra | +iš++o# | capricho | +in+<o# | caprino |
| | | +eir+<o# | cabreiro | +id++e+<o# | caprídeo | +il#+e+ | capril |
| 26 | #radi+ | +o# | raio | +al#+e+ | radial | +ik++al#+e+ | radical |
| | | +a# | raia | | | | |

a The words in Table 7.6c mean: 4th column: 'sky, goat, goatherd, radius, border'; 6th column: 'celestial, of the sky, caprice, related to goats, radial'; 8th column: 'of the sky, pertaining to the sky, goat family, goat farm, radical'.

---

also agree in number with whatever noun they modify. And many adjectives are invariant as far as gender is concerned: *grande homem* 'great man', *grande mulher* 'great woman'; *rapaz pugilista, moça pugilista* 'boy boxer, girl boxer'.

42 Suffix 15b +ez#<e+ admits a feminine suffix: *português* ⇔ *portuguesa* 'Portuguese'; *humor camponês* 'rural humor' ⇔ *festa camponesa* 'rural celebration'.

Table 7.6c shows that these stems are clearly $R_1$+ because when followed by +$S_1$ suffixes they retain their underlying segments, and when they attach to +S suffixes they undergo mutations. It also identifies the suffixes +ɛzt++e#, +ɛbr++e#, +iš++o#, +id++e+<o#, +al#+e+, +ik+<o#, +in+<o#, and +il#+e+ as +$S_1$ suffixes. Table 7.6d provides a further look at the phenomena occasioned by the addition of +S and +$S_1$ suffixes to $R_1$+ stems:

**Table 7.6d** Segmental Mutation $R_1$+ Stems, +$S_1$ and +S Suffixes[a]

| #$R_1$ Stem | +$S_1$ Preservation | | +S Mutations | | |
|---|---|---|---|---|---|
| #ap+ | +ˈari+<o# | **apiário** | +eλ++a# | **abelha** | /p+→ /b+ |
| #et+ | +ˈari+<o# | **etário** | +dad++e# | **idade** | /t+→d+ |
| #eztat+ | +al#+e+ | **estatal** | +o# | **estado** | /t+→/d+ |
| #sabat+ | +in+<o# | **sabatino** | +o# | **sábado** | /t+→/d+ |
| #er++a+t+ | +ik+<o# | **errático** | <o# | **errado** | /t+→/d+ |
| #ɛku+ | +in+<o# | **equino** | +a# | **égua** | /k+→ /g+ |
| #alb+ | +in+<o# | **albino** | <o# | **alvo** | /b+→/v+ |
| #libɛr+ | +in+<o# | **libertino** | +e# | **livre** | /b+→/v |
| #pɛd+ | +al#+e+ | **pedal** | +e+ | **pé** | /d+→Ø |
| #kan+ | +in+<o# | **canino** | <o# | **cão** | /n+→ [ɐ̃] |
| #ɔrg++an+ | ˈVC$_{1-3}$++ik+<o# | **orgánico** | +o# | **órgão** | /n+→ [ɐ̃]+ |
| #ton+ | +al#+e+ | **tonal** | +e+ | **tom** | /n+→ [õ]# |
| #sen+ | +ˈari+<o# | **cenário** | +a# | **ceia** | /n+→Ø |

a The words in Table 7.6d mean: 3rd column: 'related to bees, related to age, of the state, Sabbath-related, erratic, equine, albino, libertine, pedal, canine, organic, tonal, dinner related'; 5th column: 'bee, age, state, Saturday, wrong, mare, white, free, foot, dog, organ, tone, dinner'.

The phenomena entailed in +S suffixation to $R_1$+ stems in Table 7.6d are: (A) voicing before +S suffixes: occlusives /p+, /t+, /k+ mutate to /b+, /d+, /g+; (B) loss of occlusion and addition of friction: /b+ mutates to /v+; (C) loss of contoid nasality: /n+ emerges as nasal resonance on preceding vowels or it disappears completely; (D) vowels and consonants metasticize: #liber+ ⇔ #livr++e#.

**§7.5.5.0** Table 7.6a contains 19 suffixes (+ɛzt++e# to +ɛnt+<o#), whose productivity ranges from negligible to low and 10 (+ˈari+<o# to ˈV(V$_{[+high]}$)C$_{1-3}$ ++e+<o#) whose productivity ranges from modest to very high as well as two outliers: +ens++e# and ˈVC$_{1-3}$++ik+<o#.

§7.5.5.1 +ɛzt++e# The example *celeste* shows that this suffix is a +$S_1$ because it allows the underlying root of *céu* sky #sɛl+ to emerge in this adjective. The gender morpheme is attached to stems with + rather than < because it is invariant.

§7.5.5.2 +oɲ+<o# is a+S. In addition to *medo* ⇔ *medonho*, there is *riso* 'laughter' ⇔ of *risonho* 'merry',[43] *tarde* 'late' ⇔ *tardonho* 'habitually late' and *triste* 'sad' ⇔*tristonho* 'woeful'.

§7.5.5.3 +izk+<o#: attaches to stems such as that of *pedra* 'stone' ⇔ *pedrisco* 'stony', which shows that it is a +S because the stem's /t/ in #pɛtr+ becomes voiced.[44]

§7.5.5.4 **+ɛztr++e#** is a +$S_1$ because it preserves the lexical form of stems to which it attaches: *pedestre* 'pedestrian' #pɛd++ɛztr++e# (cf. *pé* 'foot') and *equestre* 'equestrian' #ɛku++ɛztr++e#, (cf.*égua* 'mare'). Like suffix 1, this suffix's gender morpheme is attached to stems with + rather than < because it is invariant.

§7.5.5.5 **+eng+<o#** is a +S suffix that may attach to adjectives *verde* green *verdoengo* 'greenish', which has a doublet *verdolengo.*[45]

§7.5.5.6 **+eɲ+<o#** There is no evidence to suggest that this is anything other than a +S, which attaches to R+ stems.

§7.5.5.7 **+aik+<o#** Although this suffix is typical of erudite vocabulary (e.g. *deltaico* 'delta-like' and *arcaico* 'archaic'), there is no evidence to suggest it is other than +S because it seems to attach to R+ stems exclusively.[46]

§7.5.5.8 **+lɛnt+<o#** This suffix is an allomorph of the more productive +ɛnt+<o# (§7.5.5.18).

---

43 The underlying form of *riso* is #rid++t+<o# (cf. *ridículo* 'ridiculous'). The base of *risonho* is #rid++t++ oɲ+<o#, which confers oɲ+<o#'s status as +S. For the morphophonemic dynamics that obtain in the sequence d++t+'s (as in #rid++t++) emerging as a /z/ (§8.3.1.2).

44 Compare this with suffix 27 (ˈ$VC_{1\text{-}3}$+e+<o#), which can attach to the lexical form #pɛtr+ to form *pétreo*, which also means 'stony'.

45 The /o/ in these forms may be the product of analogy with words such as *verdor* 'greenness' and *verdoso*, also 'greenish' in which a suffixal /o/ or /ɔ/ follows these words' roots. The /l/ in *verdolengo* is probably a boundary marker between the stem and the suffix. The /l+ may have arisen in analogy with adjectives ending in /l# to which this suffix attaches: e.g. *mole* 'soft', *molengo* 'lazy'; *real* 'royal', *realengo* 'pertaining to royalty'.

46 There are doublets, e.g. *galego* ⇔ *galaico* 'Galician' and *leigo* ⇔ *laico* 'lay'. The forms ending in –aico are Latinate reconstructions.

§7.5.5.9 **+ˈisi+<o#** The adjectival example in Table 7.6a is formed on a R+ stem. However, given adjectives such as *generalício* 'referring to generals' and *factício* 'factitious' (cf. the adjective *geral* 'general' #žen++er++al#<e+ and the participial adjective/noun *feito* 'done, deed, fact': adjective #fak++t+<o#, noun #fak++t++o#), the suffix ˈisi+<o# is $+S_1$ because it conveys $R_1$+ underlying forms to the surface without alteration.

§7.5.5.10 **+ˈɛ+<u#** This suffix appears to have two allomorphs <ɛ++u# as in *ilhéu* 'islander', *tabaréu* 'village-ish' and +e+<u# as in *europeu* 'European', *judeu* 'Jew(ish)'.[47] In addition +ˈɛ+<u# can form words normally considered nouns: e.g. *lebréu* 'harrier' 'rabbit hound'. Given words like *ilhéu* and *lebréu* (cf. their relatives *ínsula* 'island' and *leporino* 'leporine'), this suffix appears to belong to the +S class because it attaches to $R_1$+ stems that undergo the mutations typical of $R_1$+ stems preceding +S suffixes.

§7.5.5.11 **+it++a#** This suffix is invariable, it modifies both [-feminine] and [+feminine] nouns. There is no evidence to indicate that it occurs with $R_1$+ stems and, thus, none to indicate that it either preserves the underlying forms of any $R_1$+ stem nor does it allow a mutation of those stems, ergo +S class.

§7.5.5.12 **+ɛzk+<o#** This is a $+S_1$ because it attaches to underlying stems that surface in some adjectives it derives: cf. *vilanesco* 'villianous', *vilão* 'villian'; *truanesco* 'clownish', *truão* 'clown'; or *laiquesco* 'typical of the laity', *leigo/laico* 'lay'.

§7.5.5.13 **+en+<o#** There is no evidence that this suffix (+S) attaches to other than R+ and no morphophonemic mutations occur in those stems.[48]

§7.5.5.14 **+il#+e+** This is $+S_1$ because it attaches to underlying lexical stems in words such as such as *varonil* 'manly' #var++on++il#+e# (cf. *varão* 'male') and *canil* 'kennel' #kan++il#<e# (cf. *cão* 'dog') and causes stem-final consonants to emerge.

---

47 The [+feminine] forms of words formed with +ˈɛ+<u# end in +o+<a# *ilhoa* and *tabaroa*, e.g. that of *judeu* is *judia* and that of *europeu* +e++u# is *europeia* [e$^{u}$.ro.ˈpɛ$^{i}$.ă]. That is, they are not regular formations.

48 One should not consider words such as *nubígeno* 'cloud producing' to end in +en+<o#. They are compound words ending in the 'element' #žen+<o#. See Tables 12.14a and 12.16a as well as §12B.1.9.0.

**§7.5.5.15 a, b +ez#<e+, +ez#+e+** Both manifestations of this suffix are +S. The gender morpheme of one allomorph is inflectional because the adjectives formed with +ez+<e# acquire the [+feminine] gender morpheme <a# when necessary: *português* ⇔ *portuguesa* 'Portuguese'. Contrariwise, the deriving gender morpheme +e+ occurs on adjectives such as *cortês* 'courteous' and *pedrês* 'spotted', which are invariant in their [±feminine] modification of nouns. Their +e+ appears in their plurals: *corteses* and *pedreses*. The stems of *Português* and *cortês* are R+s; however, the word *pedrês* has a $R_1$+ root #pɛtr+ 'stone' (cf. *pétreo* 'rocky' and *pedra* 'rock') so the voicing of the stem's /t/ in *pedrês* indicates that +ez#+e+ does not impede contoidal mutation of $R_1$+ stems.

**§7.5.5.16 +ak+<o#** When this suffix attaches to a stem ending in /i+, it causes the /i+ to be stressed, regardless of whether it it is stressed in the noun itself: cf. *orgia* [ur.ˈži.ă] 'orgy' and *orgíaco* [ur.ˈži.ă.kŭ] 'orgy-like'; *Síria* [ˈsi.ri.ă] 'Syria' and *siríaco* [siˈri.ă.kŭ] 'Syrian'. When it attaches to roots not ending in /i+, this suffix's +a/ is stressed: *zuraco* 'miserly', *zura* 'miser'.

**§7.5.5.17 +ud+<o#** This +S suffix indicates a prominence of whatever noun stem it attaches to. In addition to the example in Table 7.6a, others abound: *carne* 'flesh' → *carnudo* 'fleshy', *beiço* 'lip' → *beiçudo* 'big lipped', *mão* 'hand' → *mãozudo* 'big handed'.[49]

**§7.5.5.18 +ɛnt+<o# ⇔ +lɛnt+<o#** This +S suffix emerges with stems that have undergone consonantal loss: *luarento* 'moonlit' ⇔ *lunático* 'lunatic' or *suarento* 'sweaty' ⇔ *sudatório* 'sudatory'. The /l/ of the allomorph is probably a transitional sound of some sort because adjectives such as *corpulento* 'corpulent' and *macilento* 'wan' correspond to nouns that also display the /l/: *corpulência* 'corpulence' and *macilência* 'wanness'. There is no reason to connect this /l/ to the root—nor to either of the suffixes since both the suffixes and the roots occur without the /l/, e.g. *corpo* 'body', *corpóreo* 'pertaining to the body', *macio* 'soft', *maciez* 'softness'.[50]

---

49 Notice that the root of *mão* and *mãozudo* is #man+, cf. *manual* 'manual'. The loss of the /n+ in the root is direct evidence that +ud+<o# is a +S suffix.

50 The derivatives *macilento* and *macilência* are quite likely metaphorical extensions of the root #masi+, which indicates softness, e.g. *amaciar* 'to make soft' #ad+#masi++a#+r#+e+. Being wan implies a debilitated overall softness of the physique.

§7.5.5.19 **+ˈar#+i+<o#:** This suffix is lexically marked for stress. The examples in Table 7.6a *reação* ⇔ *reacionário*, as well as pairs such as *mercearia* 'grocery store', *mercenário* 'mercenary', *embrião* 'embryo', *embrionário* 'pertaining to embryos', indicate that this suffix belongs to the $+S_1$ class because when it is attached to $R_1$+ stems such as these, their underlying stem-final /n/ emerges as a contoid.

§7.5.5.20 **+ar#+e+** Most of the adjectives formed with this $+S_1$ suffix are of an erudite nature: e.g. *vincular* 'linking', *ocular* 'ocular', *tubular* 'tubular', *valvular* 'valvular', *lunar* 'lunar', which accounts for their roots being Latinate and for their one-to-one cognates in English erudite vocabulary.[51] That is, the emergence of stem-final /l/ and /n/ in these words indicates that +ar#+e+ preserves the underlying forms of the stems to which it attaches. Its gender morpheme has a + bond with whatever stem it attaches to because these forms do not acquire the [+feminine] morpheme <a#.

§7.5.5.21 **+in+<o#** The adjectives pertaining to animals, e.g. *caprino 'goat-like'*, *canino* 'canine' (cf. *cão* dog), *taurino* pertaining to bulls (cf. *touro* bull) as well as words such as *aprilino* 'pertaining to April' (in Portuguese *abril*), and *velino* 'pertaining to a fine coverlet' (cf. *véu* 'veil') indicate that the $R_1$+ stems to which this $+S_1$ suffix attaches emerge with their lexical roots intact.

§7.5.5.22 **+izt++a#:** This $+S_1$ suffix preserves the underlying forms of the stems to which it attaches. Examples include *populista* 'populist' (cf. *povo* 'folk'), *solista* 'soloist' (cf. *só* 'alone'), *armanzenista* 'store clerk' (cf. *armazem* [ar.mă.ˈzẽ$^{\tilde{y}}$] 'dry goods store') and *bandolinista* 'mandolin player' (cf. *bandolim* [bɐ̃$^{n}$.dŭ.ˈlĩ] 'mandolin'). Stem-final /l+ and /n+ emerge in these derived forms, whereas they evanesce when followed by gender morphemes. Stem-final /b/s are also preserved in words like *arborista* 'tree farmer' and *herborista* 'plant expert' (cf. *árvore* 'tree' and *erva* 'herb').[52]

---

51 On the other hand, when this suffix forms a noun, e.g. *luar* 'moonlight', the root's /n+ vanishes. So as a noun-forming suffix +ar#+e+ is a +S suffix.

52 The suffix +izt++a# also attaches to numerous stems that end in +sion+ (e.g. *impressão* 'impression' ⇔ *impressionista* 'impressionist'). This is, however, no proof that +izt++a# is a $+S_1$ suffix since when *any* deriving suffix is added to +sion+, the latter's underlying form surfaces. For example, theme vowels are +S suffixes, but when the theme vowel is added to the stem of *impressão* #in+#prɛs++sion++a#, +sion+ emerges unchanged: *impressionar* 'to impress'.

**§7.5.5.23.0+ ɔz+<o#;** This $+S_1$ suffix is of high productivity and attaches to lexical roots and stems as the following examples indicate: *fatigoso* 'fatigue inducing', *fadiga* 'fatigue'; *nebuloso* 'nebulous', *névoa* 'fog'; *arenoso* 'sandy', *aréia* 'sand'; *doloroso* 'painful', *dor* 'pain'. The emergence of underlying /t/, /b/, /n/ and /l/ in these examples is testimony to this suffix's $+S_1$ status.

**§7.5.5.23.1** Notwithstanding the evidence indicating that +ɔz+<o# has $+S_1$ properties, it can also occasionally attach to the evolved forms of roots, e.g. *pedroso* 'rocky' (cf. *pedra* 'rock', and *petreóleo* 'petroleum') and *vaidoso* vain (cf. *vaniloqüência* 'vain talking' and *vão* vain).[53] In such cases, it seems that the etymologically faithful root has spawned root mutations of the R+ variety which emerge without the root-final consonants even when $+S_1$ suffixes are attached to them. In other words, the underlying form of *pedroso* is #pɛdr++ɔz+<o# and that of *vaidoso* is #vaid++ɔz+<o# (cf. *vaidade* #vaid++dad++e# 'vanity').

**§7.5.5.24 a, b +an+<o#$_1$, +an+<o#$_2$** As an adjective-deriving suffix, there is no reason to believe that +an+<o#$_1$ attaches to anything other than the lexical roots of the words it forms, and that these roots surface intact. The data indicate that it is $+S_1$.[54] Its related doublet +an+<o#$_2$ is a +S suffix. It undergoes the same leveling in its singular, non-feminine form as do the noun-forming suffixes +sion++e+ and +an+<e# (§8.1.1). The adjectival suffix +an+<o#$_2$ becomes [ˈãᵘ̃] in its singular, non-feminine form, and when the nouns it modifies are [+feminine], it surfaces as [ˈã]: *casa alemã* 'German house', *a mulher meã* 'the average woman'.

**§7.5.5.25 ˈV+tik+<o#** This very highly productive suffix forms adjectives that are largely of an erudite register: e.g. *draconítico* 'related to orbital node', *lavático* 'enema liquid', *jafético* 'a descendant of Jafet', *leptocúrtico* 'typical of a curve sharper than an average curve'. The erudite nature of the words it creates suggests that this is a $+S_1$

53 With this suffix, the underlying form #pɛtr+ can also emerge: like *pedroso*, *petroso* also means 'rocky', which is additional evidence of doublet roots: #pɛdr+ and #pɛtr+.

54 Note that the root of the adjective *mediano* 'mean' is #mɛd+, cf. the noun *média* 'mean'. This particular adjective, however, is one member of a set of adjectival triplets, all of which mean 'mean', 'average', or 'half': *mediano* #mɛd++i ++an+<o#$_1$, *meão* #mɛd++an+<o#$_2$ and *meio* *#mɛd+<o#*. Notice that +an+<o#$_1$ preserves the root in its entirety, whereas the other (+S) endings, +an+<o#$_2$ and <o# do not.

suffix. It is peculiar among the adjective-deriving suffixes in that when it is word-final it causes the final syllable in its stem to be stressed.

**§7.5.5.26.0 +al#+e+**This +$S_1$ suffix is highly productive. The examples in Table 7.6a: *razão* ⇔ *racional* as well as pairs such as *comun* [kũ.ˈnũ] 'common' and *comunal* 'communal' indicate that it can attach to $R_1$+ stems and preserve their segments.

**§7.5.5.26.1** However, doublet adjectives such as *cardeal* and *cardinal* 'cardinal' indicate that the original $R_1$+ stem #kard++in+ has spawned an R+ offspring: #karde+. Likewise, the adjective/noun *pessoal* 'personal, personnel' has a stem #pɛso+, which is the R+ offspring of #pɛrs+on+. The stem-final /n+ emerges unchanged in words like *personalidade* 'personality', *personalizar* 'to personalize'. The stem of *pessoal* 'personal' and 'personnel' has undergone the same fate as *pessoa* 'person', losing both its /r/ and its /n/. And once again this stem #person++al#+e+ has its gender morpheme attached with a + affinity because it is invariant as far as [±feminine] is concerned.

**§7.5.5.27 ˈV($V_{[+high]}$)$C_{1\text{-}3}$+e+<o#:** This +$S_1$ suffix causes stress to be placed on the nucleus of the syllable preceding it. At times this turns out to be the same vowel that would be stressed if these stems ended in a gender (+S) suffix: *rosa* ⇔ *róseo* from Table 7.6a, as well as *pedra* 'rock', *pétreo* 'rocky'; *vidro* 'glass', *vítreo* 'vitreous'; *ouro* 'gold', *áureo* 'golden'. However, pairs such as *mármore* 'marble (noun)' ⇔ *marmóreo* 'marble (adjective)', *fósforo* 'match', *fosfóreo* 'phosphoric' show that with this suffix stress shifts from the lexically assigned, antepenultimate syllable to the new antepenultimate syllable, which is part of the stem rather than the suffix.[55] The examples adduced above demonstrate that this suffix attaches to its lexical roots and brings them to the surface with their segments (although not necessarily their stress) unaltered.

**§7.5.6.0 Outlier Suffixes:** The productivity of the last two suffixes in Table 7.6a was so great compared with that of the other suffixes in this array that the QuickCalc program classifies them as outliers. As productive morphemes (strings thereof) they merit sections in this accounting of adjective formation.

---

55 The reason stress shifts on proparoxytone lexical stems may be a simple phonological constraint: non-compound words may not be stressed earlier than their antepenultimate syllable.

**§7.5.6.1 +ens++e#** The productivity of this (gender invariant) suffix is due to its use in forming adjectives describing inhabitants of, or peculiarities pertaining to places. Take the lexical entry *afogadense*. This obscure adjective merits entry in the *Aurélio*. It indicates inhabitants of or peculiarities pertaining to Afogados da Ingazeira, a municipality of some 36,547 inhabitants in the Brazilian state of Pernambuco. Given words such as *lisbonense* 'peculiar to Lisbon' and *japonense* 'peculiar to Japan' (cf. *Lisboa* and *Japão*), +ens++e# is a +$S_1$ suffix because it attaches to $R_1$+ lexical stems and allows them to surface unaltered.[56]

**§7.5.6.2 ˈ$VC_{1\text{-}3}$ +ik+<o#** This +$S_1$ suffix forms adjectives that are largely of an erudite register, and this helps explain why the lexical forms surface unaltered. There are, nonetheless, some less than totally erudite words that demonstrate definitively that this suffix attaches to lexical stems and causes them to surface with no segmental loss: e.g. *anão* [ã̃ˈnã̃ᵘ̃] 'dwarf' that has the adjective *anânico* 'pertaining to or seeming like a dwarf' and *som* [ˈsõ] 'sound' and the adjective *sónico* 'sonic'. In both cases, the addition of this suffix allows an underlying /n/ to surface. This suffix causes the final syllable in its stem to be stressed.

**§7.6.0 Deverbal Adjectives:** Compared to the suffixes used to turn nominal stems into adjectives, those used to turn verbal stems into adjectives are relatively few, as Table 7.7a demonstrates:

56 Compare *lisbonense* with synonyms *lisboeta* and *lisboano*.

Table 7.7a [a]Deverbal Adjectives

| | Suffix | Prod.[b] | C | Nu. | Verb | Gloss | Adjective | Gloss |
|---|---|---|---|---|---|---|---|---|
| 1 | +tˈisi+ <o# | Negligible 17 | 1st | 10 | **louvar** | to praise | **laudatício** | lauditory |
| | | | 2nd | 2 | *** | *** | *** | *** |
| | | | 3rd | 5 | **nutrir** | to nourish | **nutritício** | nutritious |
| 2 | +dour+ <o# | Negligible 20 | 1st | 8 | **segar** | to mow | **segadouro** | mowing |
| | | | 2nd | 11 | **comer** | to eat | **comedouro** | edible |
| | | | 3rd | 1 | **vir** | to come | **vindouro** | coming |
| 3 | +di+<o# | Negligible 20 | 1st | 10 | **errar** | to wander | **erradio** | wander prone |
| | | | 2nd | 5 | **correr** | to run | **corredio** | prone to run |
| | | | 3rd | 5 | **fugir** | to flee | **fugidio** | prone to flee |
| 4 | +dis+<o# | Low 103 | 1st | 80 | **quebrar** | to break | **quebradiço** | fragile |
| | | | 2nd | 12 | **morrer** | to die | **morrediço** | dying |
| | | | 3rd | 11 | **sumir** | to vanish | **sumidiço** | disappearing |
| 5 | +tˈ ɔri+ <o# | High 309 | 1st | 286 | **apelar** | to appeal | **apelatório** | in appeal |
| | | | 2nd | 23 | **definir** | to define | **definitório** | defining |
| 6 | +tiv+o# | Very High 495 | 1st | 471 | **adular** | to adulate | **adulativo** | adulating |
| | | | 2nd | 4 | **perceber** | to perceive | **perceptivo** | perceptive |
| | | | 3rd | 20 | **partir** | to part | **partitivo** | partitive |
| 7 | +nt++e# | Supreme 1590 | 1st | 1,337 | **tolerar** | to tolerate | **tolerante** | tolerant |
| | | | 2nd | 233 | **doer** | to ache | **doente** | sick |
| | | | 3rd | 20 | **seguir** | to follow | **seguinte** | following |
| 8 | ˈV+bil#+ e+ | Supreme 1657 | 1st | 1,189 | **durar** | to last | **durável** | durable |
| | | | 2nd | 464 | **beber** | to drink | **bebível** | drinkable |
| | | | 3rd | 4 | **punir** | to punish | **punível** | punishable |
| 9 | +t+<o# | Outlier 5763 | 1st | 4,990 | **calar** | to be quiet | **calado** | quiet |
| | | | 2nd | 771 | **responder** | to answer | **respondido** | answered |
| | | | 3rd | 2 | **ir** | to go | **ido** | gone |

a Table 7.7a is structured in the same way as Table 7.5a. Owing to their extreme productivity, the adjectives formed from perfect participles are outliers in the array of suffixes that turn verbs into adjectives. The remaining suffixes have no outliers: M= 534.50, SD = 720.73, Z = 2.127. The highest Z value of these suffixes is that of ˈV+ bil#+e+—1.69. The entire array (including suffix 9) has a Z value is 2.21, and +t+ <o#'s Z value is 2.50.

b Suffixes 1–8 contain no outliers: M=525.88, SD=696.97, Z=2.13.

§7.6.1 **Productivity:** Similar to the other suffixes examined in this chapter, and to the Portuguese phonemes, these nine different suffixes do not share the adjective-producing burden equally, as the productivity figures in Table 7.7a and Table 7.7b demonstrate:

**Table 7.7b** Relative Productivity: Verb-to-Adjective-Deriving Suffixes (Non-outliers)

| | Suffix | # | % of total | | Suffix | # | % of total |
|---|---|---|---|---|---|---|---|
| 1 | +ˈtisi+<o# | 17 | 0.40 | 6 | +tiv+<o# | 491 | 11.57 |
| 2 | +dour+<o# | 20 | 0.47 | 7 | +nt+<e# | 1,590 | 37.47 |
| 3 | +di+<o# | 20 | 0.47 | 8 | ˈtv#+bil#<e# | 1,693 | 39.90 |
| 4 | +dis+<o# | 103 | 2.43 | | | | |
| 5 | +tˈ ɔri+<o# | 309 | 7.28 | | | | |
| | Totals: | 469 | 11.05 | | | 3,774 | 88.95 |

Once again, the bulk (88.95%) of the 4243 adjectives derived from transparent verbal stems are the sum of tokens from three of the eight suffixes. The outlier adjectives, formed from the perfect participle morpheme followed by the gender morpheme, outnumber the entire array of the other derived adjectives in Tables 7.7a and b.

§7.6.2 **Gender:** Again, given that adjectives' gender is determined by the nouns or items they modify, gender is not an issue. Of these deverbal adjectives, only suffixes 7 and 8 are invariant and do not normally acquire an <a# when they modify [+feminine] nouns.

§7.6.3 **Meaning:** Similar to the denominal adjectives, the deverbal adjectives largely have a transparent relationship with their verbs' meanings. They may indicate (A) propensities: +di+<o#, +dis+<o#, ˈtv# +bil#+e+, +nt++e#; (B) completion: participial adjectives; (C) tendencies +dour+<o#.

§7.6.4 **Allomorphy:** Matters of the allomorphy of deverbal adjectives appear both in the sections dedicated to the individual suffixes, but, following this section, the next section addresses the allomorphic phenomena documented in this chapter.

§7.6.5.0 **Suffixes:** Despite their small number, the deverbal adjective-deriving suffixes require extenstive commentary

§7.6.5.1 **+tˈisi+<o#** This negligibly productive +$S_1$ suffix is quite likely cognate with the negligibly productive noun forming suffix +ˈisi+ +e# (Tables 7.4a-b, §7.3.5.0) and the low productivity noun-to-adjective forming suffix +ˈisi+<o# (Tables 7.6a-b, §7.5.5.9). Its initial +t/ in this +$S_1$ not the perfect participle morpheme <t+ or +t+ because it attaches to stems that are not verbs, e.g. *supositício* 'putative', which

is not strictly deverbal.[57] The root #laud+ for the adjective *laudatício* surfaces as [lo$^{u}$v] when it occurs before a +S suffix, as in the verb *louvar* 'to praise'.[58]

§7.6.5.2 **+dour+<o#** This suffix is also a modestly productive deverbal noun deriving morpheme (Tables 7.7a and 7.7b). In this set of negligibly productive suffixes, two of the three examples are worthy of comment. The root of the verb *segar* 'to cut, scythe' is #sɛk+ owing to its emerge as [ˈsɛk] in the verb: *disseca* '3$^{rd}$ dissects', i.e. 'cuts finely and carefully'. The root of these two verbs is obviously a $R_1$+ because /k+ becomes /g+ when followed by +S suffixes such as the theme vowel.[59] The other root worthy of explanation is that of *vindouro*, obviously related to the verb *vir* 'to come'. The highly irregular verb *vir* is one of the eight verbs whose perfective participle is irregular. But *vir*'s perfective participle, *vindo*, is doubly irregular because it is homophonous with its gerund. The underlying form of *vindouro* is #vind++dour+<o#, where the phonotactics of Portuguese (Rule 4.1) cause the second of the geminate consonants to evanesce.

§7.6.5.3 **+di+<o#** Similar to suffix 2, the initial segment +d/ of this suffix is not a reflex of the perfective participle morpheme. The 2$^{nd}$ conjugation theme vowel does not merge with the 3$^{rd}$ in the examples, which it does when the perfective participle morpheme is attached in both strictly verbal perfective participles and those perfective participles used as adjectives (§13.10.3.0–3). No evidence exists to indicate that +di+<o# is anything other than a +S.

§7.6.5.4 **+dis+<o#** For the same reason as above (no theme vowel merger), the initial +d/ of this suffix is not an allomorph of the perfective

---

57 It is related to the verb *supor* 'to suppose' and owes its existence to root suppletion. The lexical form of *supor* is #sub+#pon++e#+r#+e+. The root #pon+ has a suppletive allomorph consisting of #p$V_{[+labial]}$z+ as its preterite forms demonstrate: *pus* 'I put', *puseste* 'you put', *pôs* '3$^{rd}$ put', etc. The perfective participle of *pôr* and its verbal derivatives also contain the root ending in /z/: *posto,* #pɔz++t+<o#. In addition, this form occurs in related words such as *posição* 'position' and *positivo* 'positive'. (§8B.5.1.)

58 The shift of lexical /au/ to superficial /ou/ (or /oi/), occurs in other words as well, as does the shift from /d/ to /v/: cf. *áureo* 'golden' ⇔ *ouro* (or *oiro*) 'gold', *auditivo* 'auditory' ⇔ *ouvir* 'to hear' (cf. *ouço* ⇔ *oiço* 'I hear').

59 The somewhat erudite nature of the word *dissecar* (and its prefix #di+ '2') is what causes the root final /k+ of its root to emerge in this form.

participle morpheme. There appears to be no evidence that this is anything other than a +S.

**§7.6.5.5 +tˈɔri+<o#** The case for the deverbal nature of adjectives ending in this suffix is strong only for 1st conjugation verbs such as *apelar* ⇔ *apelatorio* 'to appeal ⇔appelate' although it does also derive 23 adjectives from 3rd conjugation verbs (*definir* ⇔ *definitório*). These adjectives' structure is #stem++TV++tˈɔri+<o#: #ad+#pɛl++a#+ˈtɔri+<o# and #de+fin++i+tˈɔri+<o#. Other adjectives ending in this suffix preceded by either /e+ or /i+ seem to be formed from nominals rather than from verbs: e.g. *meritório* 'worthy of merit' ⇔ *mérito* 'merit' (cf. *merecer* 'to merit'), *corretório* 'corrective' ⇔ *correto* 'correct' (cf. *corregir* 'to correct'). In addition, this suffix seems to function both as +$S_1$ and as +S: e.g. the synonyms *probatório* (+$S_1$) and *provatório* (+S) 'related to proof' (cf. *provar* 'to prove'). The lexical form of these words' root is #prɔb+, which underlies words such as *provável* 'probable' and *probabilidade* 'probability'

**§7.6.5.6 +tiv+<o#** This very highly productive suffix derives adjectives mainly from 1st conjugation verbs, although Table 7.7a indicates that both 2nd and 3rd conjugation verbs accept this suffix. In addition to those deverbal adjectives ending in +tiv+<o# whose theme vowels appear, this suffix appears in adjectives (and nouns) whose stems may also appear in verbs: e.g. *afetivo* 'affective', *afeto* 'affect', *afetar* 'to affect'; *objetivo* 'objective (noun, adjective)', *objeto* 'object', *objetar* 'to object'. It appears to be a +S suffix because it does not cause the /b+ in #prɔb+ to emerge: #prɔb++a#+tiv+<o# → *provativo* 'constituting proof'.

**§7.6.5.7.0 +nt++e#** This supremely productive suffix was originally an inflecting present participle morpheme. In modern Portuguese, it occurs in deverbal adjectives that evoke verbality: *um cão falante* 'a talking dog', *um homem crente* 'a man who believes', and *um estudante ouvinte* 'an auditing student'. The examples in Table 7.7a show that this suffix may attach to verbs of all three conjugations and allow each conjugation's theme vowel to emerge without alteration.[60] The examples of adjectives formed with +nt++e# used so far: *tolerante*, *doente*, *seguinte*, *falante*, *crente* and *ouvinte* show that +nt++e# allows

60 Some 3rd conjugation verbs merge their theme vowel with the 2nd conjugation theme vowel: e.g. *insistir* 'to insist' *insistente*; *luzir* 'to shine' *luzente*; *inerir* 'to inhere' *inerente*; *fluir* 'to flow' *fluente*; *dormir* 'to sleep' *dormente*; *servir* 'to serve' *servente*.

the consonantal mutuations typical of $R_1$+ verbal stems followed by +S suffixes since the roots of *doente*, *seguinte*, *crente* and *ouvinte* in particular are #dɔl+, #sɛk+, #krɛd+, and #aud+. These mutations indicate that +nt++e# is +S.

**§7.6.5.7.1** There are, however, cases in which this suffix has a +$S_1$ affinity with its roots. Table 7.7c demonstrates the two different affinities between the suffix +nt++e# and its roots:

**Table 7.7c** +S and +$S_1$ Affinities with the Suffix +nt+<e#

| $R_1$+S Affinity | | | | | $R_1$+$S_1$ Affinity | |
|---|---|---|---|---|---|---|
| Verb | Gloss | Root | Adjective | Gloss | Adjective | Gloss |
| doer | to ache | #d ɔl+ | **doente** | sick | **dolente** | grievous |
| pôr | to put | #pon+ | **poente** | setting | **ponente** | setting |
| provir | to arise | #ven+ | *** | *** | **proveniente** | arising |
| saber | to know | #sap+ | *** | *** | **sapiente** | knowing |
| sair | to leave | #sal+ | *** | *** | **saliente** | salient |
| soar | to sound | #son+ | **soante** | resonant | **sonante** | sonorous |
| vagar | to vacate | #vak+ | **vagante** | wandering | **vacante** | vacant |
| ver | to see | #vid+ | *** | *** | **vidente** | seer |

The +nt++e# suffixes with the $R_1$+S affinity to their stems derive adjectives that are somewhat more common than those with their $R_1$+$S_1$ affinity doublets. And those $R_1$++$S_1$ adjectives formed with +nt++e# that have no $R_1$++S doublets are typical of more sophisticated vocabularies.[61] Table 7.7d displays the underlying makeup of deverbal adjectives formed with +nt++e# in its +S and +$S_1$ manifestations:

61 A subclass of both 2nd and 3rd conjugation verbal roots can have their theme vowel expressed with the sequence /ie/, as in *sapiente*, *proveniente*, and *saliente*. At least one root #pɛt+ as in *pedir* 'to ask' (cf. *petição* 'petition') allows both /i/ and /ie/ in the theme vowel position: *pedinte* 'beggar' and *expediente* 'expeditious' (cf. *expedir* 'to dispatch'). The adjectives containing the sequence /ie/ have Latin etymons with the same vocalic sequence, which puts them in a category whose productivity is dubious. That is, such words are more than likely static lexical items rather than the result of a productive morphological process.

Table 7.7d Underlying Affinities with the Suffix +nt+<e#

| $R_1$++S affinity | | | | | $R_1$++$S_1$ Affinity | |
|---|---|---|---|---|---|---|
| Verb | Root | Morph. | Adj. | Morph. | Adj. | Morph. |
| dói | #d ɔl+ | #d ɔl++e# | **doente** | #d ɔl++e#+nt++e# | **dolente** | #d ɔl++e#+nt++e# |
| põe | #pon+ | #pon++e# | **poente** | #pon++e#+nt++e# | **ponente** | #pon++e#+nt++e# |
| soa | #son+ | #son++a# | **soante** | #son++a#+nt++e# | **sonante** | #son++a#+nt++e# |
| vaga | #vak+ | #vak++a# | **vagante** | #vak++a#+nt++e# | **vacante** | #vak++a#+nt++e# |
| vê | #vid+ | #vid++e# | *** | *** | **vidente** | #vid++e#+nt++e# |

§7.6.5.8.0 **Suffix 8: ˈtv++bil#+e+:** This supremely productive suffix attaches to verbal stems of all three conjugations, as Table 7.7a demonstrates. When it attaches to $2^{nd}$ conjugation verbs, the theme vowel merges with that of the $3^{rd}$ conjugation, i.e. it becomes /i/, as the pair *beber* 'to drink', *bebível* 'drinkable' shows. Notwithstanding its composition, this suffix always preserves the stress on the theme vowel or, in words such as *compatível* 'compatible', on a stand-in vowel taking the place of a theme vowel.[62] It not only attaches readily to R+ stems, such as those exemplified in Table 7.7a, but also to $R_1$+ stems and brings them to the surface without any mutations: *audível* #aud++i+bil#+e+ 'audible' (cf. *ouvir* 'to hear'), *legível* #lɛg++e#+bil#+e+ 'legible' (cf. *ler* 'to read'). Some attach to stems that have been altered by regular morphophonemic processes in their derivation: *admissível* 'admissible' (cf. *admitir* 'to admit'), *risível* 'laughable' (cf. *rir* 'to laugh', *ridículo* 'ridiculous'). The R+ and $R_1$+ stems to which this suffix attaches are less of a problem than the suffix itself, since +bil#+e# is a far cry from the suffix's word-final surface form [vɛɫ].[63]

§7.6.5.8.1 Table 7.7e, with superlatives derived from adjectives formed with this suffix (+bil#) in non-word-final position demonstrates that its underlying form is **ˈV+bil#** plus the gender morpheme **+e+:**

62 The adjective *compatível*, as well as several others ending in this suffix, has no corresponding verb.

63 For rules pertaining to the realizations of this suffix, see Appendix 9C.

**Table 7.7e** The Emergence of +bil#[a]

| Infinitive | Gloss | Adjective | Gloss | Superlative | Gloss |
|---|---|---|---|---|---|
| **amar** | to love | **amável** | loveable | **amabilíssimo** | most loveable |
| **mover** | to move | **móvel** | moveable | **mobilíssimo** | most mobile |
| **falir** | to fail | **falível** | fallible | **falibilíssimo** | most fallible |

a The $R_1$+ root #laud+ has also produced an R+ root (§7.6.5.1). In deriving adjectives from this root using ˈtv#+bil#<e# doublets occur: *laudável* 'laudable' and *louvável* 'praiseworthy'. Indeed, when these adjectives become nouns meaning 'laudability' the doublets persist: *louvabilidade* and *laudabilidade*.

The addition of the superlative adjective forming $+S_1$ suffix +ˈisim+ <o# allows the underlying form of this suffix +bil# to emerge, and it motivates the preservation of the root-final /b/ of #mɔb+ to which it is not contiguous.[64]

**§7.6.5.8.2** Whereas most of the adjectives formed with this suffix are transparently deverbal in origin, there are, nonetheless, adjectives formed with **ˈV+bil#+e+** whose provenience is less than obvious. That is, some adjectives formed with this suffix have no corresponding verb, some are formed on verbal roots that have undergone morphophonemic changes, and some are formed from verbal adjectives, as Table 7.7f demonstrates:

64 The supremely productive $+S_1$ noun forming suffix +(i)dad++e#, which is the only noun-deriving suffix that can attach to the adjective forming suffix ˈtv++bil#+e+ shows it to be, clearly, +bil# at its center. Notice here that the nouns formed with +(i)dad++e# are, notwithstanding their length, unmarked as far as their stress is concerned. They conform to the paroxytone stress rule. The suffix +bil# only occasions proparoxytone stress when it is word-final, and followed by the ambivalent gender morpheme. The ambivalent gender morpheme +e+ disappears in standard speech when adjectives formed with ˈtv+bil#+e+ are singular: *marido amável* 'loveable husband', *mulher amável* 'loveable wife'. In its plural form, the +e+ has a reflex at the surface level (cf. *amável* ⇔ *amáveis*, *solúvel* ⇔ *solúveis* 'soluble'—the i̲ in the plural forms comes from the underlying gender morpheme §8.0.1.1).

**Table 7.7f** Aberrant Adjectives Formed with ˈtv+bil#<e#

| No Verb | | Altered ($R_1$+) Root | | Stem + suffix | |
|---|---|---|---|---|---|
| Adjective | Gloss | Adjective | Gloss | Adjective | Gloss |
| **afável** | affable | **fusível** | fusible | **dissolúvel** | soluble |
| **equável** | uniform | **cessível** | (con)cedible | **comestível** | edible |
| **favorável** | favorable | **defensível** | defensible | **combustível** | combustible |
| **formidável** | astounding | | | **adustível** | burnable |
| **horrível** | horrible | | | | |
| **terrível** | terrible | | | | |

**§7.6.5.8.3** The leftmost section of Table 7.7f contains a set of adjectives that obviously end in the suffix +bil#+e+. Their tonic vowel precedes the suffix making these words underlyingly proparoxytone. Even though their overt structure appears to be that of deverbal adjectives, there are no verb counterparts for these adjectives: **afar*, **equar*, **favorar*, **formidar*, **horrir*, or **terrir*.

**§7.6.5.8.4** The three examples in Table 7.7f's central section have doublets derived from verbs: *fundível* (cf. *fundir* 'to melt'), *cedível* 'capable of giving in' (cf. *ceder* 'to give in'), and *defendível* 'defendable' (cf. *defender* 'to defend'). They are related to nominals such as *fuso* 'fusee' (cf. *difuso* 'difuse'), *secesso* 'far off place', and *defensa* 'defense' (cf. *defesa* 'defense'). All the 'no-verb' adjectives have a Latin adjectival etymon that ends in -bile. This array of adjectives with no convincing verbal root suggest that whereas +bil#+e+ is a productive suffix for forming deverbal adjectives, those adjectives that have no contemporary (or etymological) verb are not the result of any word-forming process in Portuguese. They are, simply, static adjectives inherited from Latin.

**§7.6.5.9 Participial Adjectives: +t+<o#** As noted in Tables 7.7a and 7.7b, the *Aurélio* registers 5,761 regularly formed[65] perfective participles

65 At least 27 common verbs have two acceptable perfective participles (Cunha, 306). The irregular perfective participles seem much more like adjectives than verbs, but are used as verbal participles. Take, for example, the verb *soltar* 'to let go' and its irregular perfective participle *solto*. Cunha considers this form an acceptable participle, but both the *Aurélio* and Jucá (*Dicionário de dificuldades)* consider it an adjective. In the active voice sentence *O juiz tinha soltado os réus* 'The judge had released the prisoners', the regular

as adjectives, which they all can be, given the proper syntactic environment. The verbs *calar*, *responder*, and *ir* demonstrate this: *Das duas mulheres a* ***calada*** *é a melhor* 'Of the two women, the ***quiet*** one is the better',[66] *As perguntas* ***respondidas*** *eram fáceis* 'The questions ***answered*** were easy', and *Em tempos* ***idos*** *tudo se entendia* 'In times ***gone by*** everything was understood'. The structure of the largest class of deverbal adjectives is #stem++theme vowel#+t+<o#<[αplural]#. The following phenomena pertain to the participial adjectives it forms: (A) When the underlying form of a verb's root does not emerge in the infinitive form, it does not emerge in the participle: *soar* 'to sound' (cf. *sonoridade* 'sonority') → perfective participle: *soado* 'sounded', *ter* 'to have' (cf. *tênue* 'tenuous') → perfective participle: *tido* 'had', *cair* 'to fall' (cf. *cadente* falling) → perfective participle: *caído* fallen. That is, owing to the loss of root-final consonants, the perfective participal morpheme is a +S suffix. (B) The participial morphemes <t+ (inflecting) and +t+ (adjectival), become voiced when they surface before +S suffixes. (C) The 2nd and 3rd conjugations' theme vowels normally merge (into /i/) when the perfective participle morpheme is added.[67]

**§7.7.0 Allomorphy:** The morphophonological analyses in Chapter 7 rely on the postulation of two classes of stems (R+ and $R_1$+) and two classes of suffixes (+S and +$S_1$). The R+ stems are those that present no consonantal mutations regardless of the suffix that may attach to them. The $R_1$+ stems are those whose final consonants undergo mutations when +S suffixes attach to them. But when +$S_1$ suffixes follow $R_1$+ stems, the stems emerge with their underlying consonants unchanged. The time has come to reexamine these stems and suffixes to see if there

---

participle seems most appropriate. However, in the passive voice version: *Os réus foram soltos pelo juiz* 'The prisoners were released by the judge', the irregular form seems most appropriate. And in a sentence such as *Ela anda com os cabelos soltos* 'She goes around with her hair undone', only the irregular form is used. Another set (Cunha, 307) of eight extremely common verbs admit only irregular perfective participles, as do their derivatives.

66 There is a play on words in this Portuguese proverb. The verb *calar* has two meanings: 'to be quiet' and 'to penetrate'.

67 Sentences of the sort *Eu tinha examinados todos os pormenores* 'I had all the details accounted for' (i.e. the details were in the state of having been examined). As the adjectival perfective participle indicates, the subject of the sentence was not necessarily the agent. In the sentence *Eu tinha examinado todos os pormenores*, the examination is a complete action, the subject did the examining, and the perfective participle is a strictly verbal entity.

might be intrinsic phonological factors that occasion the stems' consonantal mutations. Tables 7.8 and 7.9 contain all the R+, $R_1$+ stems examined in this chapter and the +S, +$S_1$ suffixes that form adjectives from nominal and verbal stems:

**Table 7.8** Nominal Stem + Adjective Suffix

| R+ | | $R_1$+ | +S | +$S_1$ |
|---|---|---|---|---|
| #amˈɛrik+ | #pont+ | #alem+an+$_2$ | +aik+<o# | +ɛzt++e# |
| #arom+ | #prɔs+ | #balk++an+$_2$ | +ak+<o# | +al++e+ |
| #fam+ | #r̲ɔz+ | #kapr+ | +an+<o#$_2$ | +an+<o#$_1$ |
| #fɛbr+ | #sarment+ | #rad++sion+ | +ˈɛ+<u# | +ar#+e+ |
| #fɛr̲+ | #šil+ | #re+#ag++sion+ | +eir+<o# | +ens++e# |
| #iλ+ | #sium+ | #sɛl+ | +en+<o# | +ɛzk+<o# |
| #kanp+ | #sol# | | +eɲ+<o# | +ɛztr++e# |
| #kaz+ | #son+ | | +eng+<o# | +il#+e+ |
| #kišɔt+ | #varež+ | | +ɛnt+<o# | +in+<o# |
| #kɔrt+ | | | +ez+<e+ | +izt++a# |
| #mani+ | | | +it++a# | + ɔz+<o# |
| #med+ | | | +izk+<o# | +ˈari+<o# |
| #mour+ | | | +lent+<o# | +ˈisi+<o# |
| #mozkɔv+ | | | +oɲ+<o# | +ˈVC$_{1-3}$++ik+<o# |
| #muλer# | | | +ud+<o# | +ˈVtik+<o# |
| #nikarˈagu+ | | | | ˈV(V$_{[+high]}$)C$_{1-3}$+e+ <o# |

**Table 7.9** Verbal Stem + Adjective Suffix

| R+ | | $R_1$+ | | +S | +$S_1$ |
|---|---|---|---|---|---|
| #ad+#pɛl++a# | #mor̲++e# | #aud++i+ | #mɔb++e# | ˈV+bil#<e+ | +iv+<o# |
| #adul++a# | #part++i+ | #dɔl++e# | +pɛl++a# | +i+<o# | +tˈɔri+<o# |
| #bɛb+e# | #pun++i+ | #dɔl+ | #pon++e# | +dis+<o# | |
| #dur++a# | #r̲ezpond++e# | +dul++a# | #p ɔz++e# | +ˈisi+<o # | |
| #ɛr̲++a# | #sum++i+ | #kad++i+ | #sɛk++a# | +nt++e# | |
| #fug++i+ | #tɔler++a# | #kap++e# | #sɛk++a# | +dour+<o# | |
| #lud++i+ | | #krɛd++e# | #son++a# | | |
| #kal++a# | | #laud++a# | #vak++a# | | |
| #kebr++a# | | #lɛg++e# | #ven++i+ | | |
| #kom++e# | | #lud+ | #vid++e# | | |
| #kɔr̲++e# | | +mit++i+ | | | |

**§7.7.1** Table 7.10 presents $R_1$+ stems followed by +$S_1$ suffixes and the mutations that occur when they are followed by +S suffixes:

Table 7.10 Pertinent $R_1$+ Consonantal Mutations

| | Roots | Stable | | Mutable | | |
|---|---|---|---|---|---|---|
| | $R_1$+ | $R_1$++$S_1$ [a] | +$S_1$ Suffix | Mutations | $R_1$+ S | +S Suffix |
| 1 | #sud++a# | **sudação** | +sion++e# | d⇔ø | **suor** | +e+ |
| 2 | #pal+ | **palito** | +it++o# | l⇔ø | **pau** | +o# |
| 3 | #ten++e# | **tenente** | +nt++e# | n⇔ø | **ter** | +r#+e+ |
| 4 | #kap+ | **capaz** | +az#+e+ | p⇔b | **caber** | +r#+e+ |
| 5 | #vitr+ | **vitrina** | +in++a# | t⇔d | **vidro** | +o# |
| 6 | #klɛr++ik+ | **clerical** | +al+e+ | k⇔g | **clérigo** | <o# |
| 7 | #karb++on+ | **carbonato** | +at++o# | b⇔v | **carvão** | +o# |
| 8 | #nɔkt+ | **noctámbulo** | +ˈambul+<o# | k⇔i | **noite** | +e# |
| 9 | #elɛg+ | **elegante** | +nt++e# | g⇔i | **eleitor** | +t++or#<e+ |

a The words in column $R_1$++$S_1$ mean: 'sweating, toothpick, lieutenant, capable, store window, clerical, carbonate, nightwalker, and elegant'. Those in column $R_1$++S mean: 'sweat, stick, to have, to fit, glass, cleric, coal, night, and elector'.

**§7.7.2** To prove that the mutations associated with the addition of +S suffixes to $R_1$+ stems entails a morphological rather than a phonological phenomenon, there must be R+ stems that end in the same consonants whose stems undergo no mutations either when +S or +$S_1$ suffixes of similar configurations are added. Table 7.11 provides such data:

Table 7.11 Pertinent R+Consonantal Stability

| | R+ | R++$S_1$# [a] | +S1 Suffix | Constancy | R++S | +S Suffix |
|---|---|---|---|---|---|---|
| 1 | #šup+ | **chupista** | +izt++a# | p⇔p | **chupita** | +it+a# |
| 2 | #r̲e+#trat+ | **retratista** | +izt++a# | t⇔t | **retratinho** | +iɲ+<o# |
| 3 | #fak+ | **faquista** | +izt++a# | k⇔k | **faquinha** | +iɲ++a# |
| 4 | #kub+ | **cubista** | +izt++a# | b⇔b | **cubica** | +ik++a# |
| 5 | #mɔd+ | **modista** | +izt++a# | d⇔d | **modinha** | +iɲ++a# |
| 6 | #fɔg+ | **foguista** | +izt++a# | g⇔g | **foguinho** | +iɲ++o# |
| 7 | #aul+ | **aulista** | +izt++a# | l⇔l | **áulico** | +ik+<o# |
| 8 | #kan+ | **canista** | +izt++a# | n⇔n | **caniço** | +is++o# |

a The words in column R++$S_1$ mean: drunkard, portrait artist, knife-wielder, Cubist, singer of folk songs, locomotive fireman, student, drinker of sugar cane brandy'. Those in column R++S mean: '3rd sips slowly, tiny portrait, little knife, 3rd cubes, urban folk song, a bird (tico-tico rei), class related, thin reed'.

The stem-final consonants in Table 7.11 /p, t, k, b, d, g, l, n/ are precisely those that undergo mutations when they occur in $R_1$ stems followed by +S suffixes (Table 7.10). The suffix +izt++a# is unequivocally +$S_1$ class. Whenever it attaches to a $R_1$+ stem, it conveys the stem's final (pertinent) consonants to the language's surface. However, when +S suffixes attach to these R+ stems, they occasion no mutation of these stems' final consonants. And, conclusively in these data, there is no special stem-internal phonological circumstance that distinguishes either the $R_1$+ stems from R+ stems nor the +$S_1$ suffixes +izt++a# from +S suffixes. They all begin with +i/. It is unlikely that +izt++a#'s VCCV structure, as opposed to the +S suffixes' VCV structure has any bearing on the realization of these stem-final consonants. As far as contemporary Portuguese is concerned, the morphophonological grammar must distinguish between these two classes of stems and of roots.

## Markedness

**§7.8.0** The phenomena depicted in Tables 7.3a–7.7f along with those in 7.10 and 7.11 (i.e. the disappearance of stem-final /d, l, n/, the voicing of /p, t, k/, and the vocalization of stem-final /k, g/ before an occlusive, when their $R_1$+ roots are followed by +S suffixes) entail a loss of markedness. That is, when actual consonants are lost in particular words, the words' stems have lost some of their distinguishing power, they are more opaque. For example, when the [+surd] occlusives loose their voicelessness (i.e. become [-surd]), they lose one mark. When /k/ vocalizes to /i/, there is a loss of three positively specified distinctive features: / k/ → [+contoid], [+dorsal], [+occlusive], [+surd]; /i/ → [-contoid], [+palatal], [-occlusive], [-surd]. When the /g/ vocalizes to /i/, there is a loss of two positive specifications: /g/ → [+contoid], [+dorsal], [+occlusive], [-surd]; /i/ → [-contoid], [+palatal], [-occlusive], [-surd]. All in all, these volatile $R_1$+ (marked) stems lose some of their intrinsic distinctiveness when they are followed by +S suffixes.

**§7.8.1** In adition to $R_1$+ stems' loss of distinctiveness, there is another way in which the data bear out the claim that both the mutable ($R_1$+) stems and the structure preserving (+$S_1$) suffixes are the marked case in both classes. In the data examined in this chapter, $R_1$+ stems total 64, whereas R+ stems total 94; +$S_1$ suffixes total 34, whereas +S suffixes total 67. The $R_1$+ and +$S_1$ classes are marked by virtue of their minority status.[68] To the extent that markedness is inversely related to productivity, data show that the (less marked) +S suffix class is more productive.

**§7.8.2** Table 7.12 contains the +S suffixes that form nominals:

Table 7.12 +S Productivity[a]

| Suffixes | Tokens | Suffixes | Tokens | Suffixes | Tokens |
|---|---|---|---|---|---|
| +ad++a# | 1,343 | +en+<o# | 120 | +ˈ(t) isi+<o# | 80 |
| +ad++o# | 563 | +eɲ+<o# | 35 | +it++a# | 71 |
| +aik+<o# | 36 | +eng+<o# | 19 | +it++e# | 268 |
| +ak+<o# | 218 | +(l) ent+<o# | 299 | +itud++e# | 41 |
| +al#+e #(n) | 384 | +et++e# | 5 | +izk+<o# | 11 |
| +am++a# | 29 | +ez++a# | 155 | +ment++o# | 1,907 |
| +am++e# | 104 | +ez++e# | 184 | +nd++a | 11 |
| +ari++a# | 610 | +ez+<e# | (25) | +ns++a# | 72 |
| +ˈari++o# | 601 | | | +nt++e# | 1,590 |
| +ˈVX+žin++e# | 740 | +i++a# | 5,500 | +oɲ+<o# | 9 |
| ˈV+bil#+e+ | 1,749 | +i++o# | 26 | +or#+e+ | 685 |
| +dad++e# | 1,779 | +i+<o# | 20 | +r#+e# | 12,913 |
| +dour++o# | 145 | +idon++e# | 83 | +tiv+<o# | 491 |
| +ˈɛ+<u# | 64 | +is++e# | 427 | +tˈɔri+<o# | 309 |
| +ed++o# | 87 | +is++o# | 4 | +ud+<o# | 233 |
| +eir++a# | 1,434 | +isi++e# | 3 | +um++e# | 60 |
| +eir+<o# | 1,946 | | | +(d)ur++a# | 890 |
| +eir++o# | | | | | |
| **Totals:** | **11,832** | | **6,880** | | **19,641** |
| **Total Tokens: 38,353** | | | | | |

a The noun-deriving suffixes +i++a# (5,500 tokens) and +r#+e+ (12,913 tokens) are outliers. The remaining 48 +S suffixes had no outiers among them: M=4,437.98, SD = 610.79, Z = 3.05. The most numerous suffixes +eir++o#, and +eir+<o#, with 1,946 tokens have a Z value of 2.47.

68 The stems' markedness cannot be absolutely determined by the numbers in this study. Some sort of text frequency test of R+ and $R_1$+ stems could decide this, but the text(s) that would make such a study revealing must be enormous—much bigger that the texts used here to determine phoneme frequencies.

The token count for Table 7.12 omits the gender suffixes that attach directly to nominal stems, both inflecting and deriving (i.e. arbitrarily assigned) suffixes. Table 7.13 contains the token numbers of those nominals formed with +$S_1$ suffixes:

**Table 7.13** +$S_1$ Productivity[a]

| Suffixes | Tokens | Suffixes | Tokens |
|---|---|---|---|
| +al#+e+ (adj.) | 1,891 | +izm++o# | 1,729 |
| +ar#+e+ | 555 | +izt++a# | 873 |
| +ˈari++o# | 601 | +nsi++a# | 675 |
| +at++o# | 199 | + ɔz+<o# | 1,200 |
| +ens++e# | 4,584 | +sion+e | 3,303 |
| +ɛzk+<o# | 117 | +ˈVC$_{1-3}$ ++ik+<o# | 5,704 |
| + ɛzt++e# | 6 | +ˈVtik+<o# | 1,801 |
| +ɛztr+<e# | 16 | ˈV(V$_{[+high]}$)C$_{1-3}$++e+<o# | 2,000 |
| +il#+e+ | 149 | | |
| **Totals:** | **8,118** | | **17,285** |
| **Total Tokens: 25,403** | | | |

a Remarkably, there are no outliers among the 18 +$S_1$ suffixes: M = 1,363, SD = 1,465.02, Z = 2.65. The highest Z value for these suffixes was that of +ns++e#, 2.20.

**§7.8.3** The suffixes examined in this chapter count in the formation of 63,756 nominals: 39.84% of them are +$S_1$, 60.16% are +S. The numbers indicate that +S formations are the less marked nominals owing to their greater number (50) and the greater number of their tokens. However, the 17 +$S_1$ suffixes are on average more highly productive than the +S suffixes, thanks to their use in coining technical terms and to the great number of +ns++e# adjectives used for describing peculiarities and people pertinent to places.[69]

**§7.9** There is a generalized tendency in nominal derivation. One subset ($R_1$+) loses some of its stems' distinctive power in specific circumstances, i.e. when followed by +S suffixes. Another subset (R+) of stems never undergoes any mutations, regardless of the class of suffixes that attaches to it. And there is a subset of nominal-deriving suffixes (+$S_1$) that impede the mutations $R_1$+ stems undergo when not

69 The average number of words derived from the 50 +S suffixes is 767 per suffix, whereas the average for the +$S_1$ suffixes is 1,494.

followed by $+S_1$ suffixes. The mutation and loss of underlying stem phonemes entails a reduction of the stems' distinctiveness and an increase in their opacity.

§7.10 **Patterns:** Table 7.14 demonstrates once more the consonantal mutations that occur according to whether $R_1$+ stems are followed by $+S_1$ or +S suffixes:

**Table 7.14** $R_1$+Consonantism

| | /b/ / __$+S_1$ | | | /v/ / __+S | |
|---|---|---|---|---|---|
| 1 b⇔v | $R_1$+ Stems | $+S_1$ | Words[a] | +S | Words |
| | #ˈarb++or# | +ɛzs++e# | arboresce | #ˈarb++or#+e# | árvore |
| | #karb++on+ | +at++o# | carbonato | #karb++on++o# | carvão |
| | #ɛrb+ | +ˈari++o# | herbário | #ɛrb++a# | erva |
| | #ˈnɛb+ | +ɔl ++ɛnt+<o# | nebulento | #ˈnɛb++ɔl++a# | névoa |
| 2 k⇔g | /k/ / ___$+S_1$ | | | /g/ / ___ +S | |
| | #fɔrm++ik+ | +ˈari++o# | formicário | #fɔrm++ik++a# | formiga |
| | #klɛr++ik+ | +al#+e+ | clerical | #klɛr++ik+<o# | clérigo |
| 3 p⇔b | /p/ / ___ $+S_1$ | | | /b/ / __ +S | |
| | #kap+ | +az#+e+ | capaz | #kap++e#+ment++o# | cabimento |
| | #sap+ | +nsi++a# | sapiência | #sap++e#+ns++a# | sabença |
| 4 t⇔d | /t/ / ___ $+S_1$ | | | /d/ / ___ +S | |
| | #vitr+ | +in++a# | vitrina | #vitr++o# | vidro |
| | #mut++a# | +sion++e+ | mutação | #mut++a#+ns++a# | mudança |
| 5 l⇔Ø | /l/ / ___ $+S_1$ | | | Ø/ ___ +S | |
| | #pal+ | +it++o# | palito | #pal++o# | pau |
| 6 d⇔Ø | /d/ / ___ $+S_1$ | | | Ø / ___ +S | |
| | #sud++a# | +sion++e# | sudação | #sud++or#+e# | suor |
| | #vid+ | +ɛnt+<e# | vidente | #vid++e#+r#+e# | ver |
| 7 n⇔ ~ | /n/ / ___ $+S_1$ | | | ~ / ___ +S | |
| | #ˈun+ | +ik+<o# | único | #un+<e+ | um |
| 8 n⇔Ø | /n/ / ___ $+S_1$ | | | Ø/ ___ +S | |
| | #kun++i+ | +kult+or#<e# | cunicultor | #kun++i+<o# | coelho |
| | #pan+ | #fik++a#+r#+e# | panificar | #pan++e++t++eir+<o# | padeiro |
| 9 g⇔Ø | /g/ / ___ $+S_1$ | | | Ø/ ___ +S | |
| | #lɛg+ | #lɛg++al#+e+ | legal | #lɛg++e#+r#+e+ | ler |
| 10 k, g⇔i | /g/, /k/ /___ $+S_1$# | | | /i/ ___/t/+S | |
| | #elɛg+ | +ant++e# | elegante | #elɛg++t++or#+e+ | eleitor |
| | #nokt+ | +ˈambul+<o# | noctámbulo | #nokt++e# | noite |

a The words paired in columns 4 and 6 mean, respectively: 'to be tree-like ⇔ tree', 'carbonate ⇔ coal', 'herbarium ⇔ herb', 'cloudy ⇔ cloud', 'ant-related ⇔ ant', 'clerical ⇔ cleric', 'capable ⇔ propriety', 'knowledge ⇔ know how', 'display window ⇔ glass', 'mutation ⇔ move', 'toothpick ⇔ stick', 'persperation ⇔ sweat', 'seer ⇔ to see', 'unique ⇔one', 'rabbit farmer ⇔ rabbit', 'bread making ⇔ baker', 'legal ⇔ to read', 'elegant ⇔ voter', 'sleep walker ⇔ night'.

§**7.11.0** A grammar of Portuguese morphophonology must be able to account for these data. For $R_1$+ stems followed by +S suffixes, it must provide rules for deleting stem-final /d+, /l+, and /n+, for the nasalization of vowels preceding deletable stem-final /n+, for voicing stem-final /p+, /t+, and /k+, for turning $R_1$+ stem-final /b+ into /v+, and to turn stem-final /k+ and /g+ into /i+ before following consonants.

§**7.11.1** Rule 7.1 is a phonotactic constraint that eliminates a morpheme-initial +d/ after a morpheme-final /t+.

**Rule 7.1 Loss of Morpheme-Initial +d/:**

$$+\begin{pmatrix}\text{+occlusion}\\ \text{-surd}\\ \text{-high}\\ \text{-labial}\end{pmatrix} \rightarrow \emptyset \,/\, \underline{\quad} \begin{pmatrix}\text{+occlusion}\\ \text{+surd}\\ \text{-high}\\ \text{-labial}\end{pmatrix} +$$

§**7.11.2** Rule 7.2 accounts for the nasalization of vowels preceding /n+ in $R_1$ stems:

**Rule 7.2 Morphophonemic Nasalization $R_1$ Stems:**

$$+\begin{pmatrix}\text{-contoid}\\ \text{+delayed transition}\end{pmatrix} \rightarrow [\text{+nasal}] \,/\, \underline{\quad} \begin{pmatrix}\text{+nasal}\\ \text{+contoid}\end{pmatrix} + \begin{Bmatrix}+\\ <\end{Bmatrix} [\pm\text{feminine}]\ \#\ <\emptyset\#$$

§**7.11.3** Rule 7.3 accounts for the deletion of stem-final /l, n, d/ in $R_1$+ nominals.

**Rule 7.3 $R_1$+ Stem-Final Coronal Deletion:**

$$\begin{pmatrix}\text{+contoid}\\ \text{-labial}\\ \text{-high}\\ \text{-surd}\\ \begin{Bmatrix}\text{+lateral}\\ \text{+nasal}\\ \text{+occlusion}\end{Bmatrix}\end{pmatrix} \rightarrow \emptyset \,/\, \#R_1 \,/\, \underline{\quad}\,(X)\ +S\#$$

The (X) in these two rules indicates that there may be some (morpho) phonological material between the stem and the +S suffix.[70]

**§7.11.4** Rule 7.3 has, in certain cases (Appendix C, Table 7C.1), a subsequent rule that denasalizes stem-final vowels after the /n+ is deleted.

**Rule 7.4 Stem Vowel Denasalization:**

$$\begin{pmatrix} \text{-contoid} \\ \text{+nasal} \end{pmatrix} \rightarrow [\text{-nasal}] \; / \; \_\_ \; + \; +\text{eir}+ \; <\text{o\#}$$

**§7.11.5** Rule 7.5 voices the final [+surd] occlusives of $R_1$+ stems:

**Rule 7.5 $R_1$+ Stem-Final Occlusive Voicing**

$$\begin{pmatrix} \text{+occlusion} \\ \text{+surd} \end{pmatrix} \rightarrow [\text{-surd}]/[\text{-contoid}]\_ \; +(\text{X})+\text{S}_{\text{R1}}$$

**§7.11.6** Rule 7.6 turns underlying /b/ to /v/:

**Rule 7.6 $R_1$+ /b+ → /v+:**

$$\begin{pmatrix} \text{+labial} \\ \text{+occlusion} \\ \text{-surd} \end{pmatrix} \rightarrow [\;+\text{fricative}] \; / \; <\alpha+> \; \_ \; <\text{-}\alpha+>^{71} \; (\text{S}) + <[\pm\text{feminine}]\#$$

**§7.11.7** Rule 7.7 turns a $R_1$+ stem-final /g+ or /k+ into /i+

70 The word *cabimento* 'propriety' is an example of this phenomenon. The word's root is #kap+ (cf. *capaz* 'capable' and *caber* 'to fit'), and the +S suffix is +ment++o#. The /i/ that intercedes between the root and the suffix may be the reflex of the verb's theme vowel +e#, or it may be a simple transitional vocoid that avoids the abutment of a stem-final /p+ with a suffix-initial +m/.

71 The angle brackets around the morpheme boundaries prefaced by the Greek letter α indicate opposite values, i.e. that the /b/ to /v/ mutation can occur on

**Rule 7.7 Velar Stop Vocoidization:**[72]

$$\begin{bmatrix} +\text{dorsal} \\ +\text{occlusion} \end{bmatrix} \rightarrow \begin{bmatrix} +\text{palatal} \\ +\text{high} \\ -\text{contoid} \end{bmatrix} \;/\; + \_\_ + [+\text{occlusion}]^{R1}$$

§7.12 **Interruption:**At this point, the study of the nominal forming-stems and suffixes and the processes associated with them temporarily ceases. The work so far does not end the deliberations concerning, even, the **formation** of both nouns and adjectives through the use of suffixes. There are, still, diminutive and augmentative suffixal data (Chapter 10) that must be addressed in dealing with nominal formation. Beyond this, Portuguese has a tremendous gamut of prefixes (Chapter 11), many of which operate in conjuction with suffixes to derive many more words. But, before even investigating diminutive and augmentative suffixes and the prefixes, several matters must be resolved. Chapter 8 is dedicated to the morphophonology and allomorphy of the +$S_1$ suffix +sion+, and Chapter 9 addresses the inflectional allomorphy of problematic nominals. Once more, it is time to take stock of the progress up to now.

## Conclusions

### Summary

§7.13.1 **Derivation:** Derivation is the process by which lexical items are formed by stringing together morphemes within a set of word boundaries, most often at the items' extremeties. In the case of nouns and adjectives, suffixes may add a denotation or they may change words' form class (verb→noun, verb→adjective). When, however, nouns and adjectives are derived from non-verbal stems, they are formed by the addition of suffixes to stems that, alone, are not words.

§7.13.2 **Gender:** All adjectives as well as nominals denoting animate beings are ***inflected*** for gender. The genders of nouns' (and certain pronouns') *denotands* and of adjectives' *modificands* determine these

---

morpheme-initial segments, e.g. the +b/ of +bil# and the morpheme-final /b+ of #mɔb+ in pairs such as *contável* 'countable' and *contabilista* 'accountant' and *automobilismo* 'car driving' and *move* '3rd moves'.

72 Rule 7.4 may turn out to be part of a set of constraints that impede sequences of occlusive consonants.

nominals' gender in specific semantic and syntactic situations. That is, these forms have no a-piori gender assigned to them. Convention and tradition have determined that this inflected class of nominals be entered in dictionaries and cited in their [-feminine] forms. And that tradition obtains here, since [-feminine] is the unmarked, rather than masculine, gender. And those adjectives and animate being nouns ending in <o#, <e#, or <e+ have varying gender determined by their semantic and syntactic circumstances.

§7.13.3 Notwithstanding the ubiquity of gender inflected nominals, most nouns' gender is arbitrarily assigned to each stem, and those gender morphemes are derivational because they can be the only element that distinguishes two or even three (often related) words' meanings. Also, in the derivation of words (especially nouns), one cannot always count on the words' meanings to be merely the sums of their constituent parts. This is most patent in those nouns in which the gender morphemes (which have scant meaning in themselves) are the sole factor in determining the referent of an arbitrarily gendered stem.

§7.13.4 **Derivation and Meaning:** The most productive noun-deriving suffixes' relation with the resultant nouns' interpretation can also be arbitrary. There appears to be scant semantic constancy in derivational phenomena—especially when nouns are derived from the same stems but with different suffixes.

§7.13.5 **Noun vs Adjective:** Owing to nouns' and adjectives' structural similarity, the borderline between them is at times tenuous. All adjectives can be nominalized, and many nouns, especially those whose gender morphemes are inflectional, can function as adjectives. The only class of nouns that cannot be used as adjectives is the infinitive. Deverbal nouns and adjectives have a closer semantic relationship with the underlying verb stems, perhaps because they are transparent: they consist of verbal stems followed by theme vowels, to which adjective or noun-deriving suffixes can be added.

§7.13.6.0 **Allomorphy**: The addition of specific suffixes to specific stems can cause certain within-stem consonantal mutations, whereas other suffixes cause no mutation, and other stems appear to be immune to any consonantal mutations. Two postulates account for these phenomena: One subset of stems (R+) is unaffected by the addition of derivational suffixes of any kind. A second subset ($R_1$+) undergoes consonantal mutation when followed by a subset of deriving suffixes (+S).

But these forms are immune to these mutations when a second subset of deriving suffixes (+$S_1$) attaches to them. The $R_1$+ stems and the +$S_1$ suffixes are the marked case in their respective sets.

**§7.13.6.1** The mutations occasioned by the attachment of +S suffixes to $R_1$+ stems are regular occurrences that can be accounted for by five rules. The rules are simple, thanks to the category of stems that undergo mutation and the categories of suffixes that derive nouns and adjectives. The consonantal mutations are not phonologically conditioned since the same stem-final consonants occur in $R_1$+ and R+ stems and the same segments may begin both +S and +$S_1$ suffixes.

## Findings and Insights

**§7.13.7** This chapter's contributions to the understanding of Portuguese morphology include: (A) the derivational status of arbitrarily assigned noun gender morphemes; (B) the genderless nature of all nominal stems as far as derivation is concerned; (C) derivational suffixes' gender-bearing nature; (D) the uniqueness of deverbal nouns and adjectives: actual verbs form these words' stems, whereas other adjectives and nouns are derived from bound stems; (E) the postulation and confirmation of two subsets of stems, the minority that undergoes consonantal mutations and the majority that is immune to these mutations; (F) the postulation and confirmation of two subsets of suffixes, those that occasion consonantal mutations, and those that do not; (G) a formal division between adjectives and the majority of nouns: adjectives and a small subset of nouns are inflected for gender, whereas most nouns are assigned a gender; (H) suffixes' productivity: in every case, a minority of suffixes is responsible for an overwhelming majority of the derived adjectives or nouns in question; (I) the regularity of the consonantal mutations entailed in nominal derivations; (J) markednesss evaluation of the derivational phenomena examined here.

## So What?

**§7.13.8** Beyond providing a minimally complex and somewhat observationally adequate account of how Portuguese nouns and adjectives are derived, Chapter 7 has provided a firm foundation on which to base further deliberations concerning other nominals as well as the the derivation of verbs. Chapter 16 (Verb Derivation) identifies: (A) which stems and roots are susceptible to mutations of their constituent segments and which are not; (B) which suffixes occasion (or at least co-occur with) mutations of stems constituent phonemes; (C) which suffixes allow transparent forms of their stems to emerge; and (D) which suffixes are immutable. That chapter's goal is, once again, to provide the simplest observationally adequate account of verbal derivation.

## Appendix A Rules as they Appear in Chapter 7

**§7A.0** In their order of appearance, these are the rules appearing in Chapter 7.

### Rule 7.1 Loss of Morpheme-Initial +d/:

$$+\begin{pmatrix} +\text{occlusion}\\ -\text{surd}\\ -\text{high}\\ -\text{labial}\end{pmatrix} \rightarrow \emptyset \,/\, \begin{pmatrix} +\text{occlusion}\\ +\text{surd}\\ -\text{high}\\ -\text{labial}\end{pmatrix} +$$

### Rule 7.2 Morphophonemic Nasalization $R_1$+ Stems:

$$+\begin{pmatrix} -\text{contoid}\\ +\text{delayed transition}\end{pmatrix} \rightarrow [+\text{nasal}] \,/\, \_\_ \begin{pmatrix} +\text{nasal}\\ +\text{contoid}\end{pmatrix} + \begin{Bmatrix} + \\ < \end{Bmatrix} [\pm\text{feminine}]\ \#<\emptyset\#$$

### Rule 7.3 $R_1$+ Stem-Final Coronal Deletion:

$$\begin{pmatrix} +\text{contoid}\\ -\text{labial}\\ -\text{high}\\ -\text{surd}\\ \begin{Bmatrix} +\text{lateral}\\ +\text{nasal}\\ +\text{occlusion}\end{Bmatrix}\end{pmatrix} \rightarrow \emptyset\ +\ /\ \_\_\ (X)\ +S_{R1}$$

**Rule 7.4 Stem Vowel Denasalization:**

$$\begin{bmatrix} \text{-contoid} \\ \text{+nasal} \end{bmatrix} \rightarrow [\text{-nasal}] \ / \ \_\_ \ + + \text{eir} + < \text{o}\#$$

**Rule 7.5 $R_1$+ Stem-Final Occlusive Voicing:**

$$\begin{bmatrix} \text{+occlusion} \\ \text{+surd} \end{bmatrix} \rightarrow [\text{-surd}] / \ [\text{-contoid}] \ \_\_ + (\text{X}) + \text{S}_{\text{R1}}$$

**Rule 7.6 $R_1$+ /b+ → /v+:**

$$\begin{bmatrix} \text{+labial} \\ \text{+occlusion} \\ \text{-surd} \end{bmatrix} \rightarrow [\ \text{+fricative}] \ / \ <\alpha+> \ \_ \ <\text{-}\alpha+> \ (\text{S}) \ + <[\pm\text{feminine}]\#$$

**Rule 7.7 Velar Stop Vocoidization:**

$$\begin{bmatrix} \text{+dorsal} \\ \text{+occlusion} \end{bmatrix} \rightarrow \begin{bmatrix} \text{+palatal} \\ \text{+high} \\ \text{-contoid} \end{bmatrix} \ / \ + \ \_\_ + [\text{+occlusion}]^{\text{R1}}$$

## Appendix B The Grammar of Nominal Derviation

**§7B.0** What follows is a viable ordering for the rules of Chapter 7.

**Rule 3.1 Paroxytone stress:**

$$[\text{-contoid}] \rightarrow [+\text{stress}] \,/\, \#X\_\_ \left(\begin{Bmatrix}+\text{high}\\ \text{-contoid}\end{Bmatrix}\right) C_{0\text{-}4}V_{[\text{-high}]}\#(C)\#$$

Condition: The word has no previously assigned stress.

**Rule 7.2 Morphophonemic Nasalization $R_1$ Stems:**

$$+\begin{pmatrix}\text{-contoid}\\ +\text{delayed transition}\end{pmatrix} \rightarrow [+\text{nasal}] \,/\, \_\_ \begin{pmatrix}+\text{nasal}\\ +\text{contoid}\end{pmatrix} + \begin{Bmatrix}+\\ <\end{Bmatrix} [\pm\text{feminine}]\ \#<\text{Ø}\#$$

**Rule 7.3 $R_1$+ Stem-Final Coronal Deletion:**

$$\begin{pmatrix}+\text{contoid}\\ \text{-labial}\\ \text{-high}\\ \text{-surd}\\ \begin{Bmatrix}+\text{lateral}\\ +\text{nasal}\\ +\text{occlusion}\end{Bmatrix}\end{pmatrix} \rightarrow \text{Ø}\ +\ /\ \_\_(X)\ +S_{R1}$$

**Rule 7.4 Stem Vowel Denasalization:**

$$\begin{pmatrix}\text{-contoid}\\ +\text{nasal}\end{pmatrix} \rightarrow [\text{-nasal}] \,/\, \_\_\ +\ +\text{eir}+<\text{o}\#$$

**Rule 7.5 $R_1$+ Stem-Final Occlusive Voicing:**

$$\begin{bmatrix} +\text{occlusion} \\ +\text{surd} \end{bmatrix} \rightarrow [\text{-surd}]/\ [\text{-contoid}]\ \_\_ + (X) + S_{R1}$$

**Rule 7.7 Velar Stop Vocoidization:**

$$\begin{bmatrix} +\text{dorsal} \\ +\text{occlusion} \end{bmatrix} \rightarrow \begin{bmatrix} +\text{palatal} \\ +\text{high} \\ -\text{contoid} \end{bmatrix} /\ +\ \_\_ + [+\text{occlusion}]_{R1}$$

**Rule 7.6 $R_1$+ /b+ → /v+:**

$$\begin{bmatrix} +\text{labial} \\ +\text{occlusion} \\ -\text{surd} \end{bmatrix} \rightarrow [\ +\text{fricative}]\ /\ \ <\alpha+>\ \_\ <-\alpha+>\ \ (S)\ +<[\pm\text{feminine}]\#$$

**Rule 6.2a Deletion of Word-Final <e+, +e+, +i+_ After /r#, /l#, and /z#:**

$$\begin{Bmatrix} + \\ < \end{Bmatrix} \begin{bmatrix} -\text{contoid} \\ +\text{palatal} \end{bmatrix} \rightarrow \varnothing\ /\ \#X\ [\text{-contoid}] \begin{bmatrix} +\text{contoid} \\ -\text{surd} \\ -\text{labial} \\ -\text{high} \\ -\text{nasal} \\ -\text{occlusion} \end{bmatrix} \ \_\_ + <[\text{-plural}]\#$$

**Rule 4.1 Like Segment Deletion**

$\text{Segment}_2 \rightarrow \varnothing\ /\ \text{Segment}_1\ \_\_\_\_$

**Condition:** $\text{Segment}_1 = \text{Segment}_2$

**§7B.1.0** The next two tables demonstrate these rules' operation in the generation of specific morphophonemic phenomena entailed in the derivation of nominals.

**Table 7B.1** Vowel Nasalization, Loss of Root-Final Coronals[a]

| | irmã | carvoeiro | suor | sais |
|---|---|---|---|---|
| U.F. | #irm++an+<a# | #karb++on++eir+<o# | #sud++or#+e+ | #sal#+ e+<z# |
| R. 3.1 | #irm++ˈan+<a# | #karb++on++ˈeir+<o# | #sud++ˈor#+e+ | #sˈal#+ e+<z# |
| R. 7.2 | #irm++ˈãn+<a# | *** | *** | *** |
| R. 7.3 | #irm++ˈã+<a# | *** | #su++ˈor#+e+ | #sˈa++ e+<z# |
| R. 7.4 | *** | #karb++o++eir+<o# | *** | *** |
| R. 7.5 | *** | *** | *** | *** |
| R. 7.7 | *** | *** | *** | *** |
| R. 7.6 | *** | #karv++o++ˈeir+<o# | *** | *** |
| R. 4.1 | #irm++ã# | *** | *** | *** |
| R. 6.2a | *** | *** | #su++ˈor# | *** |
| Ph. | [ir. ˈmã̆] | [kăr.vŭ.ˈeĭ.rŭ] | [su.ˈor] | [ˈsaĭš] |

aThe words in Table 7B.1 mean 'sister, charcoal purveyor, sweat, salts (types of)'. Cf. *irmanar* 'to take as a sibling', *carbono* 'carbon', *sudário* 'sweat rag', *salada* 'salad'.

The stems #irm++an+, #karb++on+, #sud++or#, and #sal++e$_{[fem.]}$+ are R+ followed by +S suffixes that occasion the mutations documented in the table: vowel nasalization, loss of stem-final coronals /n, d, l/ and the /b+'s emergence as /v+.

**Table 7B.2** Voicing of Stem-Final Occlusives, Vocalization of Stem-Final Velar Occlusives[a]

| | vaga | vidro | povo | noites | eleito |
|---|---|---|---|---|---|
| U.F. | #vak++a# | #vitr++o# | #pɔp++o# | #nokt++e$_{[fem.]}$+<z# | #elɛg++t+<o# |
| R. 3.1 | #vˈak++a# | #vˈitr++o# | #pˈɔp++o# | #nˈokt++e$_{[fem.]}$+<z# | #elˈɛg++t+<o# |
| R. 7.2 | *** | *** | *** | *** | *** |
| R. 7.3 | *** | *** | *** | *** | *** |
| R. 7.4 | *** | *** | *** | *** | *** |
| R. 7.5 | #vag++a# | #vidr++o# | #pɔb++o# | *** | *** |
| R. 7.7 | *** | *** | *** | #noit++e$_{[fem.]}$+<z# | #elɛi++t+<o# |
| R. 7.6 | *** | *** | #pɔv++o# | *** | *** |
| R. 4.1 | *** | *** | *** | *** | *** |
| R. 6.2a | *** | *** | *** | *** | *** |
| Ph.[b] | [ˈva.γă] | [ˈvi.δrŭ] | [ˈpo.vŭ] | [ˈnoĭ.təš] | [ə.ˈleĭ.tŭ][c] |

a The words in Table 7B.2 Mean 'opening (at a work site), glass, folk, nights, elected'. They all have $R_1$ stems: cf. *vácuo* 'vacuum', *vitrina* 'display window', *populaça* 'riff-raff', *noctámbulo* 'sleepwalker', *eleger* 'to elect'.

b Phonological processes include the lenition of voiced stops and root vowel metaphony.

c The root vowel of *eleger* 'to elect' is /ɛ/, but the off-glide must cause it to rise and tense to [e] in this past participle.

## Appendix C Suffix Classes

§7C.0 Tables 7C.1–2 demonstrate the +S and +$S_1$ characteristics of the suffixes +eir++a# and +eir+<o#. The tables contain sets of $R_1$+ stem words that are susceptible to Rules 7.1, 7.2, and 7.3—the nasalization of vowels in $R_1$+ stems and the subsequent deletion of stem-final /n+ when followed by +S suffixes, and the deletion of nasality when followed by both suffixes. In addition, they contain examples of $R_1$+ roots in which their final /n+ is preserved owing to the suffix's occasional +$S_1$ properties.

Table 7C.1 +eir++a#: +S and +$S_1$ Manifestations

| $R_1$+ Stems with the +S +eir++a# | | | $R_1$ Stems with +S ++e+ | | |
|---|---|---|---|---|---|
| Words | Glosses | Stems | Relative | Glosses | Lexical Form |
| **botoeira** | button hole | #bɔt++on+ | **botão** | button | #bot+on++e+ |
| **capoeira** | chicken coop | #kap++on+ | **capão** | capon | #kap+on++e+ |
| **carvoeira** | coal bin | #karv++on+ | **carvão** | coal | #karv+on++e+ |
| **ladroeira** | robbery | #ladr+on+ | **ladrão** | thief | #ladr+on++e+ |
| **ratoeira** | animal trap | #rat++on+ | **ratão** | big mouse | #rat+on++e+ |
| **saboeira** | soap vendor | #sap++on+ | **sabão** | soap | #sap++on++e+ |
| **$R_1$+ Stems with the +$S_1$ +eir++a#** | | | **$R_1$ Stems with +S ++e+** | | |
| **atuneira** | tuna salting tub | #atun+ | **atum** | tuna | #atun++e+ |
| **botoneira** | button panel | #buton+ | **botão** | button | #buton++e+ |
| **caganeira** | diarrhea | #kag++an+ | **cagão** | coward | #kag++an+<o# |
| **canhoneira** | gun boat | #kaɲ++on+ | **canhão** | cannon | #kaɲ++on++e+ |
| **chinfrineira** | shabbiness | #šinfrin+ | **chinfrim** | shabby | #šinfrin++e+ |
| **colhoneira** | jock strap | #kɔʎ++on+ | **colhão** | testicle | #kɔʎ++on++e+ |
| **jardineira** | gardener (.f) | #žardin+ | **jardim** | garden | #žardin++e+ |
| **leoneira** | lion's den | #leon+ | **leão** | lion | #leon++e+ |
| **saboneira** | soap dish | #sap++on+ | **sabão** | soap | #sap++on++e+ |
| **timoneira** | rudder axle shaft | #tim++on+ | **timão** | rudder | #tim++on++e+ |

Table 7C.2 +eir++o#: +S and $+S_1$ Manifestations

| $R_1$+ Stems with +S +eir++<o# | | | $R_1$ Stems with +S ++e+ | | |
|---|---|---|---|---|---|
| **algodoeiro** | cotton plant | #algod+on+ | **algodão** | cotton | #algod++on++e+ |
| **botoeiro** | buttonhole | #bɔt++on+ | **botão** | button | #bot++on++e+ # |
| **carvoeiro** | coal tender | #karv++on+ | **carvão** | coal | #karv++on++e+ |
| **colchoeiro** | mattress maker | #kolš++on+ | **colchão** | mattress | #kolš++on++e+ |
| **cordoeiro** | rope maker | #kord++on+ | **cordão** | cord, rope | #kord++on++e+ |
| **dragoeiro** | dragon tree | #drag++on+ | **dragão** | dragon | #drag++on++e+ |
| **feijoeiro** | bean stalk | #feiž+on+ | **feijão** | bean(s) | #feiž++on++e+ |
| **latoeiro** | tinsmith | #lat++on+ | **latão** | tin | #lat++on++e+ |
| **leiloeiro** | auctioneer | #leil++on+ | **leilão** | auction | #leil++on++e+ |
| **limoeiro** | lemon tree | #lim++on+ | **limão** | lemon | #lim++on++e+ |
| **mamoeiro** | papaya tree | #mam++on+ | **mamão** | papaya | #mam++on++e+ |
| **meloeiro** | melon vine | #mel++on+ | **melão** | melon | #mɛl++on++e+ |
| **padroeiro** | protector | #padr++on+[a] | **padrão** | pattern | #padr++on++e+ |
| **pregoeiro** | crier | #preg++on+ | **pregão** | notice | #prɛg++on++e+ |
| **quinhoeiro** | shareholder | #kiɲ++on+ | **quinhão** | share | #kiɲ++on++e+ |
| **saboeiro** | soap maker | #sap++on+[b] | **sabão** | soap | #sap++on++e+ |
| **tamoeiro** | cart part | #tam++on+ | **tamanco** | axel brace | #tam++ank++o# |
| **tiçoeiro** | poker | #tis++on+ | **tição** | hot coal | #tis++on++e+ |
| **traiçoeiro** | traitor(ous) | #tra++i++sion+ | **traição** | treason | #tra++i++sion+ +e+ |
| $R_1$+Stems with $+S_1$ +eir+<o# | | | $R_1$ Stems with +S ++e+ | | |
| **cancioneiro** | song anthology | #kant++sion+ | **canção** | song | #kant++sion++e+ |
| **cantoneiro** | highway worker | #kant++on+ | **cantão** | road section | #kant++on++e+ |
| **invencioneiro** | inventing (adj.) | #invent++sion+ | **invenção** | invention | #in++vent++ sion++e+ |
| **pontoneiro** | pontoon person | #pont++on+ | **pontão** | pontoon | #pont++on++e+ |
| **prisioneiro** | prisoner | #priz++ion+ | **prisão** | prison | #priz++ion++e+ |
| **ratoneiro** | petty thief | #rat++on+ | **ratão** | big mouse | #r̠at++on++e+ |
| **timoneiro** | helmsman | #tim++on+ | **timão** | rudder | #tim++on++e# |
| **vagoneiro** | train conductor | #vag++on+ | **vagão** | train car | #vag++on++e# |

a Cf. *patria* 'fatherland' and *patronato* 'patronage'.
b Cf. *sabonete* 'hand soap' and *saponáceo* 'soapy'

Beyond the overall data in Tables 7C.1–2, the pairs in Table 7C.3 are particularly convincing as far as the varying relationship (+S≈+$S_1$) these suffixes have with the $R_1$+ stems.

**Table 7C.3** Minimal Pairs +S ≠+$S_1$

| **+S Affinity** | | **+$S_1$ Affinity** | |
|---|---|---|---|
| **botoeira** | buttonhole | **botoneira** | button panel |
| **saboeira** | soap vendor | **saboneira** | soap dish |
| **ratoeira** | animal trap | **ratoneiro** | petty thief |

**§7C.1** Tables 7C.4–8 separate the immutable R+ stems from the mutable $R_1$+ stems as well deriving suffixes examined up to now as +S (structure neutral suffixes and structure hiding suffixes), and +$S_1$ (structure preserving suffixes).

**Table 7C4** Nouns ⇔ Nouns

| R+ | $R_1$+ | +S | +$S_1$ |
|---|---|---|---|
| #abakat+ | #elɛg+ | +a# | +al++e# |
| #alfinet+ | #ɛrb+ | +a# $_{(tv)}$ | +ant++e# |
| #ar# | #fat+ | <a# | +at++o# |
| #art+ | #fik+ | +ad++a# | +az#+e# |
| #banan+ | #fɔrm++ik+ | +ad++o# | +ɛnt+<o# |
| #bob+ | #jɔk+ | +ˈažen++e# | +ɛzs++e# |
| #diɲeir+ | #kap+ | +al#+e# | +in++a# |
| #fak+ | #karb++on+ | +am++a# | +it++o# |
| #fɛr̠+ | #klɛr++ik+ | +am++e# | +ˈɔri+<o# |
| #fidalg+ | #kun++i+ | +ari++a# | #+ɔz+<o# |
| #f ɔrm+ | #leg+ | +ˈari++o# | +sion++e# |
| #grit+ | #libɛr+ | +e# | |
| #in+#vern+ | #m ɔb+ | +e# $_{(tv)}$ | |
| #keiš+ | #nokt+ | +ed++o# | |
| #kond+ | #pal+ | +eir++a# | |
| #kont+ | #pizk+ | +eir++o# | |
| #koλer# | #sud+ | +eir+<gen# | |
| #men++in+ | #vitr+ | +i++a# | |

(*Continued*)

Table 7C4 Continued

| R+ | $R_1$+ | +S | +$S_1$ |
|---|---|---|---|
| #muλer# | #ˈarb+ | +i++o# | |
| #papɛl# | #ˈnɛb++ɔl+ | +i+$_{(tv)}$ | |
| #pel+ | +sɛp+ | +it++e# | |
| #pinsɛl# | +žɛk+ | +o# | |
| #sens+ | | <o# | |
| #sindik+ | | +r#+e+ | |
| #sinz+ | | +um++e# | |
| #timpan+ | | | |
| #vɛλ++ak+ | | | |

**Table 7C.5** Adjective ⇔ Nouns

| R+ Stems | $R_1$+ Stems | +S Suffixes | +$S_1$ Suffixes |
|---|---|---|---|
| #alt+ | #duls+ | +dad++e# | +izm++o# |
| #amarg+ | #krud++ɛl+ | +ez++a# | +is++e# |
| #bɛl+ | | +ez++e+ | |
| #in+#prɛs+ | | +i++a# | |
| #kovard+ | | +idon++e+ | |
| #mans+ | | +isi++e# | |
| #m ɔl+ | | +itud++e# | |
| #mut+ | | +or#+e+ | |
| #šat+ | | +or#<e+ | |
| #suav+ | | +ur++a# | |

**Table 7C.6** Verbs → Nouns

| R+ Stems | $R_1$+ Stems | +S Suffixes | +$S_1$ Suffixes |
|---|---|---|---|
| #ag+ | #dɛb+ | +d++a# | +nsi++a# |
| #aš+ | #d ɔl+ | +dour++o# | +sion+e+ |
| #difɛr+ | #fak+ | +et++e# | +t++o# |
| #ezpɛr+ | #fid+ | +is++o# | |
| #fɛrv+ | #kad+ | +ment++o# | |
| #flu+ | #kap+ | +nd++a | |
| #lembr+ | #krɛd+ | +ns++a# | |
| #prɛst+ | #lib++ɛr+ | +r#+e+ | |
| #pro+#pag+ | #pon+ | +t++o# | |
| #šeg+ | #p ɔt+ | | |
| #sub+ | #sal+ | | |
| #sum+ | #son+ | | |
| #sum+ | #ten+ | | |
| #tɔλ+ | | | |
| #viv+ | | | |

# 8 Allomorphy: +sion++e+

## Introduction

**§8.0.0** Chapter 7 (§7.4.10) put off discussing the intricacies associated with +sion++e+ because this supremely productive [+feminine] $+S_1$ suffix is the most problematic of the deverbal noun-deriving suffixes. Owing to its knotty nature, it merits an exclusive chapter which will provide a rationale for its lexical form, as well as for its (and its stems') elaborate allomorphy.[1]

**§8.0.1.0** That +sion++e+'s lexical form is problematic becomes evident immediately. When it occurs word-finally in non-plural forms, it is vastly different from its lexical form. The examples of this form offered in Table 7.5a contain its [-plural] manifestions: *tentação* 'temptation', *vendição* 'act of selling', and *traição* 'treason'. The only indisputable segment common to the lexical form and the surface form of this suffix is /s/ since it begins this word-final realization of the suffix—[ˈsã̆ᵘ̃], a single stressed syllable. Of course, the word-final form's nasal resonance is a likely reflex of the lexical form's /n+. Still, if this suffix is to have one lexical form (+sion++e+), the emergence of the [ã̆] and that of the final [ᵘ̃] must be explained.

**§8.0.1.1** Whereas the singular form of word-final +sion++e+ presents multiple challenges to this morpheme's's underlying configuration, the plurals of words formed with +sione++e+ reflect its underlying form somewhat more faithfully. The examples' plural forms are *tentações*, *vendições*, and *traições*. That is, when the plural morpheme <z# follows +sion++e+, the deriving morpheme mutates to [ˈsõⁱ̃š], once

1 After comparing various non-generative solutions to the patterns evinced by the suffixes +an+, +on+, +sion++e+, Schwindt and Wetzels conclude that 'more in-depth knowledge of the overall phonological grammar of Portuguese is necessary [… to understand] the relation between the lexical base and derived of words like *leão* "lion" ~ *leonino* "lionine," *caminhão* "truck" ~ *caminhoneiro* "truck driver," etc'. (193). To achieve this 'in-depth knowledge' for this allomorphy is the object of this chapter, which relies on the item and process nature of generative morphophonology. Coping with this suffix and its allomorphy will inevitably entail addressing the allomorphy of the deriving suffix +an+ (§7.5.5.24a, b) and the deriving augmentative suffix +on+ (Tables 10.5a, 10.5b, §10.5.11.0-4).

again a word-final stressed syllable. And, once again, the underlying +s# emerges, as does the nasality provisionally associated with the /n+. However, in this allomorph, the suffix's lexical /o/ emerges, nasalized, and the [ĩ] (orthographic e̲) in the plural forms gives credence to the existence of an underlying [+feminine] gender suffix-final +e+, which cannot surface without the plural morpheme's being added. There is, however, nothing in the singular and plural forms to suggest that there is an underlying /i/ in this suffix. But /i/'s presence, as well as that of suffix's /n/, is easily documented once other deriving suffixes (both $+S_1$ and +S) accrete to words superficially ending in ['sã̃ũ] or ['zã̃ũ], as Table 8.1a demonstrates:

**Table 8.1a** Allomorphy of +sion++e+

| **(1) Allomorphs: ['sã̃ũ], ['sõỹš], and [sion][a]** | | | | |
|---|---|---|---|---|
| **Singular** | **Plural** | **Gloss** | **$+S_1$** | **Gloss** |
| **exceção** | **exceções**[b] | exception(s) | **excecional** | exceptional |
| **nação** | **nações** | nation(s) | **nacional** | national |
| **noção** | **noções** | notion(s) | **nocional** | of notions |
| **profissão** | **profissões** | profession(s) | **profissional** | professional |
| **(2) Allomorphs: ['zã̃ũ], ['zõỹš], and [zion]** | | | | |
| **Singular** | **Plural** | **Gloss** | **$+S_1$** | **Gloss** |
| **visão** | **visões** | vision(s) | **visionário** | visionary |
| **adesão** | **adesões** | adhesion(s) | **adesionista** | pro-adhesion |
| **ilusão** | **ilusões** | illusion(s) | **ilusionista** | magician |
| **(3) Post-consonantal Allomorphs: ['sã̃ũ], ['sõỹš], and [sion]** | | | | |
| **Singular** | **Plural** | **Gloss** | **$+S_1$** | **Gloss** |
| **tenção** | **tenções** | plan(s) | **intencional** | intentional |
| **opção** | **opções** | option(s) | **opcional** | optional |
| **contorção** | **contorções** | contortion(s) | **contorcionista** | contortionist |
| **flexão** | **flexões** | flexion(s) | **flexional** | flexional |
| **convulsão** | **convulsões** | convulsion(s) | **convulsionário** | a convulsive |
| **(4) Post-consonantal Allomorphs: ['tã̃ũ], ['tõyš], and [tion]** | | | | |
| **Singular** | **Plural** | **Gloss** | **+S** | **Gloss** |
| **congestão** | **congestões** | congestion(s) | **congestionar** | to congest |
| **questão** | **questões** | question(s) | **questionar** | to question |

a In many pronunciations, the atonic /o/ of [sion], etc. will be reduced to [u], but I have left it as [o] in these transcriptions for clarity's sake.

b Before 1990 this word included a /p/ before the noun-forming suffix: *excepção*. That consonant appears in Brazilian spellings.

There can be no mistaking the parentage (semantic, morphological, and etymological) shared between the singular and plural nouns as well as those to which deriving suffixes accrete to the stems containing +sion+. The additional deriving suffixes (either +$S_1$ or +S) attached to stems ending in +sion++e+ cause its underlying form (minus its gender morpheme +e+) to emerge.[2] There is, thus, no controversy concerning its underlying or lexical form. Conversely, one immediately notices a radical difference between the singular forms (*tentação*, *vendição*, and *traição*) and those in Table 8.1a. The nouns ending in +sion++e+ in Table 8.1a are not obviously deverbal, whereas the former nouns are obviously deverbal owing to the presence of their 1st and (merged) 2nd and 3rd conjugation theme vowels.

**§8.0.1.2** Beyond the challenges that the loss of +sion++e+'s +e+ and /o/ presents to this suffix's [-plural] manifestations and its loss of /i/ and /n+ in all word-final manifestations, Table 8.1a presents further challenges: (A) Are these formations opaquely deverbal? (B) Why does the initial +s/ emerge as +z in Section 2? (C) What happens to the +s/ in Section 4? (D) Does +sion++e+ in circumstances such as these occasion stem allomorphy? In addition, as these matters are cleared up, this chapter will also demonstrate that this +$S_1$ suffix emerges in its lexical form regardless of whether the deriving suffix following it is a +$S_1$ or a +S. Before addressing the questions related to the data in Table 8.1a, an examination of the transparent (unmarked) deverbal noun formation with +sion++e+ provides the basis on which to tackle them.

**§8.0.2** Table 8.2 displays the formation of these transparent deverbal nouns, which parallels that of their related infinitives:

---

2 Likewise, English-speaking readers will recognize similar allomorphy in the English suffix –tion, which occurs both as [šən] in the cognates of words in Sections 1, 3, and 4 of Table 8.1b and as [žən], which occurs in the cognates of Section 2.

Table 8.2 Transparent Deverbal Nouns Formed with +sion++e#[a]

| Verbs: | tentar | encher | trair |
|---|---|---|---|
| Analysis | #tent++a#+r#+e+ | #en+#š++e#+r#+e+ | #tra++i++r#+e+ |
| **Nouns:** | **tentação** | **encheção** | **traição** |
| Analysis | #tent++a#+sion++e+ | #en+#š++e#+sion++e+ | #tra++i++sion++e+ |
| Mutation | [tẽ$^{n}$.tă.ˈsã$^{ũ}$] | [ẽ$^{ɲ}$.šĭ.ˈsã$^{ũ}$] | [tra$^{i}$.ˈsã$^{ũ}$] |
| **Plurals** | **tentações** | **encheções** | **traições** |
| Analysis | #tent++a#+sion++e+<z# | #en++š++e#+sion++e+<z# | #tra++i++sion++e+<z# |
| Mutation | [tẽ$^{n}$.tă.ˈsõ$^{ĩ}$š] | [ẽñ.ˈšə.ˈsõ$^{ĩ}$š] | [tra$^{i}$.ˈsõ$^{ĩ}$š] |

a The words in Table 8. 2 mean: 2$^{nd}$ column: 'to tempt, temptation, temptations'; 3$^{rd}$ column: 'to bother, (a) bother, acts of bothering'; 4$^{th}$ column: 'to betray, treason, acts of treason'.

The analyses in Table 8.2 propose that forms such as these (the vast majority of which derive from 1$^{st}$ conjugation verbs, see Table 7.5a) derive from stems containing both the verbal root and the verbs' theme vowels. The only process they undergo as derived deverbal nouns is the merger of the 2$^{nd}$ conjugation theme vowel with the 3$^{rd}$ conjugation.

## Allomorphy: Forms and Rules

**§8.1.0** Given the assertion that all these suffixal manifestions in transparent nouns derive from +sion++e+, an adequate account of this suffix entails first of all the justification of its manifestation as [ˈsã$^{ũ}$] in most singular nouns since neither of the vocoids matches those in its underlying form. One must also provide a rationale for its plural manifestation as [ˈsõ$^{ĩ}$š] and a justification of its gender morpheme +e+. Once this has taken place, the matters concerning the allomorphy in Table 8.1a will take center stage.

**§8.1.1 Justification of [ã$^{ũ}$]:** One of the salient phenomena in the Portuguese language's evolution from Latin is the loss of morpheme-final intervocalic /n+ in everyday words. This lost intervocalic /n+ usually leaves nasal resonance on the vowel that preceded it: e.g. *bŏnum→bom* [ˈbõ] 'good', *lanam→lã* [ˈlã] 'wool', *germanam→irmã* [ir.'mã̆] 'sister', *manum→mão* 'hand'.[3] This phenomenon was not limited to words' roots, however. It also occurred in suffixes, as Table 8.3 demonstrates:

**Table 8.3** Suffix Fusion

| Latin Word | Suffix | Portuguese | Plural | Suffix | Gloss |
|---|---|---|---|---|---|
| **dant** | -ant | **dão** | *** | +a#<n# | $3^{rd}$ pl. give |
| **capitanem** | -anem | **capitão** | **capitães** | +an+<e# | captain(s) |
| **cantionem** | -tionem | **canção** | **canções** | +sion++e# | song(s) |
| **paganum** | -anum | **pagão** | **pagãos** | +an+<o#$_2$ | pagan(s) |

Table 8.3 shows that certain Latin suffixes, both verbal and nominal, have fused phonologically in Portuguese when they are word-final, and, in the case of nominals, when they are [-plural]. Of interest here are the nominals whose suffixes' singular manifestations all end in [$\tilde{\tilde{a}}^{\tilde{u}}$], but whose plural forms end in [$\tilde{\tilde{a}}^{\tilde{\imath}}\check{s}$], [$\tilde{o}^{\tilde{\imath}}\check{s}$], and [$\tilde{\tilde{a}}^{\tilde{u}}\check{s}$] reflecting their different lexical configurations. The nominals in Table 8.3 (and, many others of this nature) have related words containing additional deriving suffixes that cause +sion+'s +an++e+'s, and +an<o#'s lexical forms to emerge: *capitão→capitania* 'captaincy', *canção→cancioneiro* 'collection of (medieval) songs', *pagão→paganismo* 'paganism'. A set of morphophonemic rules, then, can account for the nominal suffixes' union and manifest vowels ['$\tilde{\tilde{a}}^{\tilde{u}}$] in their singular forms:

3 At times (Tables 7C.2–3) the /n+ left no trace: *lunam* → *lua* 'moon', *bonam* → *boa* 'good (+f.)'.

**Rule 8.1 Suffix Merger in Word-Final Position:**

$$\left\{\begin{matrix} +on+<e+^{4} \\ +an+\{<e+,<o\#\} \\ +(\alpha\ s)ion++e+^{6}\end{matrix}\right\} \rightarrow +(\alpha\ s)an+\left\{\begin{matrix}\alpha+o\#_3\\ <o\#\end{matrix}\right\}^{5} / \_\_ <[\text{-plural}]\#$$

After Rule 8.1's application to these suffixes, the /a/ of this merged suffix receives paroxytone (unmarked, regular) stress, and morphophonemic rules cause the /n+ to nasalize the /a/ and then disappear. The word-final +o# or <o# is reduced to [ŭ] and forms a diphthong with the stressed [ã], and then, as an off-glide of a nasalized vowel, it too becomes a nasal vocoid. To reiterate: the singular endings of the words in question, be they [±feminine], come from a historic fusion of Latin suffixes in their singular forms. These suffixes' plural reflexes replicate their etymons somewhat more faithfully, and, when more deriving suffixes are added to these forms, faithful copies of the suffixes' lexical forms emerge.

---

4 Because it displays the same singular-plural variation as +sion++e+, the augmentative suffix (+on+<e+) appears in Rule 8.1. In addition to the augmentive suffix's ability to indicate a referent that is larger than normal, it can (like other deriving suffixes) change a word's gender, e.g. *faca* 'knife (f.)' ⇔ *facão* 'big knife (-f.)'. This deriving suffix can form nouns from verbs, e.g. *papar* 'to swallow' *papão* 'hob-goblin, i.e. swallower' and *rasgar* 'to tear' *rasgão* '(a) tear'. It can also form nouns from adjectives: *agre* 'bitter' *agrião* 'watercress'. These four nouns form their plurals with [ˈõĩ̆š]. The [+feminine] forms of words with the augmentative suffix +on+ often emerge with the underlying /n+ realized as [n]: *lambão* (-f.)⇔ *lambona* (+f.) 'slob'.

5 This suffix ($+an++o\#_3$) is different from both $+an+<o\#_1$ and $+an+<o\#_2$. See Table 7.6a and §7.5.5.24a,b.

6 The alpha (α) in front of the morpheme-initial /s/ in Rule 8.1's determinand and determinant indicates that only when the original suffix begins with /s/ does it exist in the fused suffix. The alpha also appears before the invariant gender morpheme +o#, which, in this case, is [+feminine]. A suffix whose configuration is +ion++e+ and is [+feminine] occurs in 12 different words and derivatives there of: e.g. *região* 'region (+f.)' (cf. *reger* 'to rule, regulate'), *união* 'union (+f.)' (cf. *unir* 'to unite'), *opinião* 'opinion (+f.)',- (cf. *opinar* 'to opine'). All these nouns form their plurals with [ˈõĩ̆š]. (Words of this nature formed with the other suffixes may be [±feminine] according to their syntactic or semantic circumstances.)

**§8.1.2.0 Justification of Plural [ˈõ$^{\tilde{\imath}}$š]:** Rule 8.1 operates only when these suffixes (including +an+<o#$_2$) occur word-finally with a [-plural] (<Ø#) inflection. Plural inflection on +sion+e+ entails another merger—essentially, +sion++e+<z# merges with the augmentative suffix +on+ <e+<z#:

**Rule 8.2 +sion++e+z#'s Merger:**

+(αs)ion++e+<z# ➔ +(αs)on++e+<z#

The suffix's +o/ receives paroxytone stress, the intervocalic /n+ causes the /o/ to be nasalized, then the /n/ disappears (Rules 7.2 and 7.3). The gender morpheme +e+ reduces to [ĭ] (Rule 2.3), forms a dipththong with the tonic vowel, and aquires nasality.[7]

**§8.1.2.1.0** Several rules governing these mutations have already appeared in this text, as Table 8.4 demonstrates:

**Table 8.4** +sion+e+<Ø# ➔ [ˈsã$^{\tilde{u}}$], +sion+<z# ➔ [ˈsõ$^{\tilde{\imath}}$š]

| | tentação | traições |
|---|---|---|
| Lexical | #tent++a#+sion++e+ | #tra++i++sion++e+<z# |
| R. 8.1 | #tent++a#+san++o# | *** |
| R. 8.2 | *** | #tra++i++son++e+<z# |
| R. 3.1 | #tent++a#+sˈan++o# | #tŕa++i++sˈon++e+<z# |
| R. 7.2 | #tent++a#+sˈãn++o# | #tra++i++sˈõn++e+<z# |
| R. 7.3 | #tent++a#+sˈã++o# | #tra++i++sˈõ++e+<z# |
| R. 2.3 | #tent++ă#+sˈã++ŭ# | #tră++i++sˈõ++ĭ+<z# |
| Syllabification[a] | #.ten.t++ă#.+sˈã++ŭ.# | #.tră++i.++sˈõ++ĭ+<z.# |
| Ph. | [tẽ$^{n}$.tă.ˈsã̃$^{\tilde{u}}$] | [tra$^{ĭ}$.ˈsõ$^{\tilde{\imath}}$š] |

a The rules of syllabification are 4.3a-8. The ones affecting *tentação* and *traição* are 4.4 and 4.6. For the entire array of derivations (Appendices A and B), syllabation rules 4.4–4.6, and 4.8 play a role. Rule 4.3a assigns potential syllable boundaries to words' beginnings and ends, but here all forms are citation forms—represented as being pronounced alone so there is no need for these boundaries. Nor is there a need for Rule 4.7, which deletes certain word-final syllable boundaries in representations of running speech. Syllabification rules do not effect sequences of [-high] vocoids followed by [+high, -delayed transtion] vocoids. These sequences are diphthongs. For the actual rules, see this chapter's Appendix A.

7 Suffixes +an++e+ and +an+<o#$_2$ ([ˈã̃$^{\tilde{\imath}}$š] and [ˈã̃$^{\tilde{u}}$š]) mutate similarly: +a/ becomes nasalized, the /n+ evanesces, +e+ and +o# reduce to <ĭ# and <ŭ#, then they become off-glides and aquire nasality.

§**8.1.2.1.1** Rule 8.3 deletes the morpheme-final /n+ of +sion+ once its word-final mutated vowels have acquired nasality:

**Rule 8.3 Loss of n+:**

$$\begin{pmatrix} +\text{nasal} \\ +\text{contoid} \end{pmatrix} \rightarrow \text{Ø} \; / \; \begin{pmatrix} -\text{contoid} \\ +\text{nasal} \end{pmatrix} \_\_ \; ++\text{S}(<\text{S})\#$$

§**8.1.2.1.2** Rule 8.3 accounts for off-glides' assimilation of nasality following a nasalized vowel.

**Rule 8.4 Progressive Assimilation of Off-Glides:**

$$\begin{pmatrix} -\text{contoid} \\ +\text{high} \\ -\text{del. trans.} \end{pmatrix} \rightarrow [+\text{nasal}] \; / \begin{pmatrix} -\text{contoid} \\ -\text{high} \\ +\text{nasal} \end{pmatrix} \_\_$$

Rule 8.4 applies after stress assignment and after syllabification.

§**8.1.3 Justification of +sion+'s Gender Morpheme as +e+:** The bound morpheme symbol +e+ is invariant and has been arbitrarily assigned to the suffix as a [+f.] morpheme (Table 6.13). It is followed by + because it cannot occur word-finally—it only emerges with plural inflection, and it ends up as a high vocoid that forms an off-glide of the preceding vowel.

§**8.1.4** The initial +s/ of +sion++e+ is the next issue to resolve. Table 7.5a registers the existence of 3,303 deverbal nouns derived with the supremely productive +sion++e+. In addition to those nouns, Table 8.1a contains a set of nouns ending in +sion++e+ whose deverbal provenience is problematic since these nouns lack theme vowels. The *Aurélio* contains 529 nouns of that sort, as Table 8.1b demonstrates:

**Table 8.1b** Nouns Derived with +sion++e—No Theme Vowel

| [ˈsã̄ũ]⇔[ˈsõi̯š] | | [ˈzã̄ũ]⇔[ˈzõĩš] | | [šˈtã̄ũ]⇔[šˈtõi̯š] | |
|---|---|---|---|---|---|
| -epção[a] | 14 | -esão | 14 | -istão | 8 |
| -eção | 86 | -asão | 13 | -estão | 17 |
| -opção | 1 | -isão | 44 | -astão | 5 |
| -ução | 92 | -osão | 12 | -ostão | 4 |
| -upção | 8 | -usão | 42 | -ustão | 7 |
| -ssão | 43 | | | | |
| -nção | 87 | | | | |
| -rção | 31 | | | | |
| -lção | 1 | | | | |
| Totals: | 363 | | 125 | | 41 |
| Total: 529 Words | | | | | |

a The pç junctures are Brazilian spellings. The p is absent in Portuguese dictionaries.

Of the 3,833 nouns derived with +sion++e+, the set in Table 8.1b accounts for 13.83%, whereas 86.17% are transparent nominals with the configuration #stem++tv++sion++e+(<z). These minority nominals will occupy a major portion of this chapter.

§**8.2.0** Sections 1 and 3 of Table 8.1a appear to present no problem since the initial segment of both the singular and the derived forms of this suffix is +s/.[8] Table 8.1a's obviously problematic data are in Section 2, where the suffix's 1st consonant is [z] and Section 4, where the /s/ is either missing or it appears to have emerged as [t].

**§8.2.1.0 Justification of /s/ in Light of +sion++e+'s Allomorphy ['zã̄ũ], [ˈzõĩs] and [zion] (Table 8.1a, Section 2):** The examples in Table 8.1a are essentially different from the transparent formations insofar as they have no manifest theme vowels. These nouns are either formed from roots that can also work as verbal roots or they are formed from verbal stems whose theme vowels undergo deletion early in their derivation.[9]

8 D'Andrade Pardal (1977: 146–170) considered this suffix +ione# and the forms in question to be derived from a unitary base consisting of a verbal root plus its theme vowel, plus the past participle morpheme (+t+), plus +ione#. For a review of his approach, see Appendix C.

9 The second option is how D'Andrade Pardal managed this material.

**§8.2.1.1** One could, of course, attribute all of the allomorphy in Table 8.1a to historical phonology since these words all have Latin etymons, but their forms display a regularity in contemporary Portuguese. They are derived from roots and stems that can perform as verbal stems if followed by theme vowels. Table 8.5 demonstrates these stems' roles in verb and noun formation:

**Table 8.5** Lexical Forms of Class 2 Deverbal Nouns

| Verb | | | | Noun | |
|---|---|---|---|---|---|
| Infinitive | Gloss | Lexical Form | Root | Singular | Lexical Form |
| aderir | adhere | #ad++ɛr++i++r#+e+ | +ɛr+ | adesão | #ad++ɛr++sion++e+ |
| ver | see | #vid++e#+r#+e+ | +vid+ | visão | #vid++sion++e+ |
| iludir | elude | #in+#lud++i+r#+e+ | #lud+ | ilusão | #in+#lud++sion++e+ |

These words' roots all end in [-surd] 'coronal' consonants, specifically /r/ and /d/, and these stem-final segments' voicing transfers to the suffix-initial /s/, after which these consonants disappear. Rules 8.5 and 8.6 produce these results:

**Rule 8.5 +s/ of +sione++e+ Becomes +z/:**

$$\begin{pmatrix} \text{-labial} \\ \text{-high} \\ \text{+ fricative} \end{pmatrix} \rightarrow [\text{-surd}] / \begin{pmatrix} \text{+ contoid} \\ \text{-surd} \\ \text{-nasal} \\ \text{-lateral} \\ \text{-high} \\ \text{-labial} \end{pmatrix} ++ \_\_$$

The determinand in this rule, a non-high, non-labial fricative can be either /s/ or /z/ but no other phoneme in Portuguese. The determinant, which is a non-high, non-labial, non-nasal, non-lateral, voiced contoid, can only be /z/, /d/, or /r/, the last two of which occasion the shift of /s/ to /z/ in +sion++e+. The determinant in Rule 8.5 becomes the determinand in Rule 8.6, which deletes the stem-final consonants.

**Rule 8.6 Loss of /r/ and /d/:**

$$\begin{pmatrix} +\text{contoid} \\ \text{-friction} \\ \text{-surd} \\ \text{-nasal} \\ \text{-lateral} \\ \text{-high} \\ \text{-labial} \end{pmatrix} \rightarrow \varnothing \, / \, \_\_ + + [+\text{fricative}]$$

**§8.2.1.2** Of the roots postulated for the words in Table 8.5, the root-final /r/ of *aderir* is obvious in the infinitive as is the /d/ in *iludir.*[10] Owing to their presence in the infinitival roots, they need no further justification. What remains is to show that the words *ver* 'to see' and *visão* 'vision' have a / d/+ in their root.

**§8.2.1.3** The root #vid+ for *visão* is evident in other words formed from the same root that underlies the infinitive *ver* 'to see': #vid++e#+r#+e+. Related words such as *vidente* 'seer', *evidência* 'evidence, i.e. what can be seen' vouchsafe #vid+ as their root, and it makes sense that #vid+ is also the root of *ver.*[11] The underlying forms of the nouns in Table 8.4 and Rules 8.5 and 8.6 account for 125 realizations of morpheme-initial +z/ in +sion++e+. Before accounting for the juxtaposition of stem-final /r+ and /d+'s to +sion++e+, the emergence of /t+ as the apparent initial segment of this morpheme merits explanation.

**§8.2.2 Justification of +s/ in Light of +sion++e+'s Allomorph [ˈtãũ] (Table 8.1a, Section 4):** A /t/ shows up not because it is the initial segment in these words' suffix, but because these words' stems end in /t+. They are deverbal stems because they are formed from nominal derivatives of the verbs *gerir* 'to manage' and *querer*, whose most common meaning

---

10 The root #lud+, which occurs in *iludir*, underlies *ilusão* and words such as *alusão* 'allusion' and *colusão* 'collusion'. It occurs word-initially in words such as *lúdico* 'pertaining to games' or *ludíbrio* 'mockery'.

11 The first person singular of *ver* (*vejo* 'I see' [ˈve.žŭ]) and its present subjunctive forms *veja*, etc.) have been explained by the presence of /d/ (Williams, 34).

is 'to want', but which, among its myriad uses, can mean 'to seek' or to 'quest'. The root of *congestão*, etc. is the same root that underlies *digerir* 'to digest', which has a nominal form *digesto*, which as an adjective means 'digested'.[12] As a noun, *digesto* can also mean 'digest', i.e. a 'collection of written laws'. The verb *querer*, in addition to *questão* and its derivatives, has nominal forms such as *questório* 'pertaining to questions' and *questuário* 'self-seeking, ambitious'. Table 8.6 analyzes the words in question:

**Table 8.6** Analysis of Aberrant Roots

| congestão | congestionar |
|---|---|
| #kon+#žɛzt++sion++e+<Ø# | #kon+#žɛzt++sion++a#+r#+e+<Ø# |
| **questão** | **questionar** |
| #kɛzt++sion++e+<Ø# | #kɛzt++sion++a#+r++e+<Ø# |

The roots of these forms are 'aberrant' because they are not, strictly speaking, built on the same principle that all the other forms in Table 8.1a are.[13] Beyond this, it is not at all clear that the 'roots' postulated for these forms are monomorphemic. They may be stems systematically formed from the roots of *gerir* and *querer*—indeed, they have a slight semantic and formal relationship with perfect participles. But because these forms have Classical Latin etymons, whatever systematic relationship they have with their verbal relatives is beside the point here. For modern Portuguese, these non-verbal roots form the base of only 41 nominals ending in +sion++e+. To generate words from the strings of morphemes used in section 4 of Tables 8.1a-b, a rule that deletes the /s/ of +sion+ suffices:

12 The form *indigesto* means 'hard to digest'.

13 The other forms, like those of Table 8.1a's Section 2, have the same roots that infinitives do.

**Rule 8.7 Deletion of +s/ After z.t+:**

$$\begin{pmatrix} +\text{fricative} \\ +\text{surd} \\ -\text{labial} \\ -\text{high} \end{pmatrix} \rightarrow \emptyset \,/\, [+\text{fricative}]\,.\begin{pmatrix} +\text{occlusion} \\ -\text{high} \\ -\text{labial} \\ +\text{surd} \end{pmatrix} ++ \_\_$$

Rule 8.7 expresses a phonotactic constraint of Portuguese. In native words, fricatives of any sort cannot follow a syllable-initial /t/. When Rule 8.7 applies to the morphemic strings in question (be they #kon+#žεzt++sion++a#+r#+e+ or #kon+#žεzt++san++o#<Ø#), the forms will become #kon+#žεzt++ion++a#+r#+e+and #kon+#žεzt++an++o#<Ø#. These forms begin to approximate the surface forms of *congestionar* and *congestão*, respectively. The forms #kεzt++sion++a#+r#+e+ and #kεzt++san++o# become *questionar* and *questão* having lost their noun-forming suffix's +s/ owing to Rule 8.7. Having accounted for the loss of +s/ in the 41 words where stem-final /t+ emerges, and having indicated that the root-final [-surd] contoid of the 126 words in which +s/ emerges as [z], Sections 1 and 3 of Table 8.1a must be examined before addressing the absence of theme vowels in the remaining 363 words.

**§8.2.3.0** Even though the /s/ surfaces as [s] in the forms of Table 8.1 Section 1, these forms' deverbal derivation is far from transparent. Table 8.7 contains verbs related to these derived nominals.

Table 8.7 Verbal Roots ⇔ Nominal Roots

| | Verbs | | |
|---|---|---|---|
| | 3rd Person Verb | Gloss | Analysis |
| 1 | **recebe** | $3^{rd}$ receives | #re++sɛp++e# |
| 2 | **excetua** | $3^{rd}$ excepts | #ez++sɛp++t++u++a# |
| 3 | **nota** | $3^{rd}$ notes | #nɔt++a# |
| 4 | **profere** | $3^{rd}$ utters | #pro+#fɛr++e# |
| 5 | **professa** | $3^{rd}$ professes | pro++fɛs++a# |
| 6 | **fende** | $3^{rd}$ separates | #fɛnd++e# |
| | Nouns | | |
| | +sion++e+ | Gloss | Apparent Analysis |
| $1^{I}$ | **receção** | reception | #re++sɛp++sion++e# |
| $2^{I}$ | **exceção** | exception | #ez++sɛp++t++sion++e# |
| $3^{I}$ | **noção** | notion | #nɔt++sion++e# |
| $4^{I}$ | **profissão** | profession | #pro+#fer++sion++e# |
| $5^{I}$ | **profissão** | profession | #pro+#fɛs++sion++e# |
| $6^{I}$ | **fissão** | fission | #fend++sion++e# |

§**8.2.3.1 Rows 1, $1^{I}$ and 2, $2^{I}$:** The root of these words is +sɛp+ ($R_1$+), which does not occur word-initially. The deverbal noun's final /p+ disappears [r̠ ə.sɛ.ˈsã̃ũ], [əš.sɛp.ˈsã̃ũ], but the pretonic /ɛ/ emerges as [ɛ] in EP. The root-final /p+ loses its [+surd] quality when a +S suffix follows (e.g. *recebe* '$3^{rd}$ receives' #re++sɛp++e# [r̠ ə.sə.ˈβə]), which Rule 7.5 (stem-final occlusive voicing) accounts for in this grammar.

**Rule 7.5 $R_1$+ Stem-Final Occlusive Voicing:**

$$\begin{pmatrix} +\text{occlusion} \\ +\text{surd} \end{pmatrix} \rightarrow \text{[-surd]/[-contoid]/ \_ } +(X)+S_{R1}$$

§**8.2.3.2** With +sɛp+ as the root of the words in lines 1 and 2 of Table 8.7, in addition to Rule 7.5, which causes /p+ to lose its [+surd] quality before +S suffixes, the grammar needs another rule that effaces the /p+ in specific environments: e.g. #ez++sɛp++t++u++a#→#ez++sɛ++t++u+<a# '$3^{rd}$ excepts' and #ez++sɛp++sion++e+ → #ez++sɛ++sion++e+ 'exception'.

**Rule 8.8a Loss of Root-Final /p+ (Provisional):**

$$\begin{pmatrix} +\text{occlusion} \\ +\text{labial} \\ +\text{surd} \end{pmatrix} \rightarrow \text{Ø}/\ /\ \_\_++ \begin{pmatrix} +\text{contoid} \\ +\text{surd} \\ -\text{high} \\ -\text{labial} \end{pmatrix}$$

Rule 8.8a deletes /p+ before suffix-initial +s/ and +t/, the only phonemes that are voiceless coronals.

**§8.2.4 Rows 3, 3':** The relationship between *notar* 'to note' and *noção* 'notion' is plausible. The lexical form of *notar* is assuredly #nɔt+ +a#+r#+e+.[14] But deriving *noção* from #nɔt++sion++e+# is problematic because, if the root of *noção* ended in /t+, it would impede the reduction of /ɔ/ to [ŭ] in EP, which is not the case. The word *notação* 'notation', whose underlying form is #nɔt++a#+sion++e+ is semantically (and morphophonologically) closer to *notar* than *noção* is to *notar* .[15]

**§8.2.5 Rows 4, 5, 6; 4', 5', 6':** Related to the final set of words in Section 1 (*profissão* and *profissional*) of Table 8.1a, Table 8.7 contains three related verbs: *proferir* 'to utter, to declare', *professar* 'to profess', and, what appears to be an unlikely relative, *fender* 'to separate'.[16] Were all the nominals in question to be derived from the root of *proferir,* #fɛr+ (cf. *ferir* 'to wound'), a grammar would have to account for the root vowel /ɛ/'s transformation into /i/ and for the loss of root-final /r/. And were the grammar to derive them from the apparent root of *professar,* +fɛs+, it would have to account for the root vowel /ɛ/'s becoming /i/ when +sion+ is added. Likewise, *fender*'s ostensible root #fɛnd+ seems like a dubious candidate to underlie these

14 Cf. *nota* '(a) note' #nɔt++a#<number#. The [+feminine] gender morpheme and the unmarked theme vowel are both /a/.

15 Quite likely the ultimate source of *noção,* with its Latin etymon *notione,* is the Greek root #no+, meaning 'knowledge, perception'. To identify this root as #nɔ+, consider the following words: *noema* 'ideal mental image' #no++em++a# (cf. *fonema* 'phoneme' #fon++em++a#), *noese* 'noesis' i.e. 'cognition', *noética* 'noetics'. Thus, the underlying form of *noção* is #nɔ++ sion++e+.

16 *Fender* occurs as the stem of two prefixed verbs: *defender* 'to defend' and *ofender* 'to offend'.

verbs and nouns given its phonological distance from the derived form *profissão*. *Fender*, however, has derivatives such as *fissão* 'fission', *fissil* 'separable'. This root also underlies a compounding 'element' (§12.0.1) #fisi+ that occurs in words like *fissilíngue* 'fork tongued'. The most plausible root of *profissão* and its derivatives is #fis+, and the words in question are analyzed as #pro+#fis+sion++e+, #pro+#fis+sion++al#+e+, and #fis++sion++e#. The etymon of this root is a suppletive past participle of the Latin verb *fendere* 'to separate' *fissus*.[17] All the meanings of the word *profissão* are metaphoric extentions of the word's primitive meaning when derived from #fis+.

**§8.2.6** Table 8.8 displays the rectified analyes of the problematic nouns in Table 8.7:

**Table 8.8** Non-verbal Roots +sion++e+ Nouns

| | Nouns | | | |
|---|---|---|---|---|
| | +sion++e+ | Gloss | Roots | Revised Analysis |
| 1 | **receção** | reception | +sɛp+ | #re++sɛp++sion++e |
| 2 | **exceção** | exception | +sɛp+ | #ez++sɛp++sion++e+ |
| 3 | **noção** | notion | #nɔ+ | #nɔ++sion++e+ |
| 4 | **profissão** | profession | #fis+ | #pro+#fis++sion++e+ |
| 6 | **fissão** | fission | #fis+ | #fis++sion++e+ |

At this point, suffice it to say that two voiceless stops (/p+ and /t+) can be deleted when followed by +sion+ and that the constraint eliminating any geminate contoids will dispense with the abutting /s/s when #fis+ is followed by +sion+. For this to happen, Rule 8.8a must be modified to Rule 8.8b:

17 On top of the relative ease with which #pro+#fis++sion++e+ can become *profissão* using Rule 8.1b (the suffix neutralization rule), the semantic parentage that *profissão* has with *fender* is at least as close as it is with *proferir* and *professar*. That is, when people join a profession, they professionally **separate** or **distinguish** themselves from people other than those in their profession or of their belief system.

**Rule 8.8b Loss of Stem-Final /p+ /t+:**

$$\begin{pmatrix} +\text{occlusion} \\ \text{-high} \\ +\text{surd} \end{pmatrix} \rightarrow \text{Ø}/\ /\ \_+ + \begin{pmatrix} +\text{contoid} \\ +\text{surd} \\ \text{-high} \\ \text{-labial} \end{pmatrix}$$

The rule now identifies both /p/ and /t/, but not a rule-final /k+. The phenomena examined and dealt with in Tables 8.7 and 8.8 (along with Rule 8.8b) account for the morphophonology of some 144 nominals derived with word-final +sion+e+.

**§8.3.0** The words in Section 3 of Table 8.1a are, perhaps, the least problematic of the entire table.

**Table 8.9** Verbal Roots—Nominal Roots

| Verb | Analysis | Noun | Analysis |
|---|---|---|---|
| **tenta** | #tent++a# | **tenção** | #tent++sion++e+ |
| **opta** | #ɔpt++a#[a] | **opção** | #ɔp++t++sion++e+ |
| **torce** | #tɔrs++e# | **contorção** | #kon+#tɔrs++sion++e+ |
| **flete** | #flɛkt++i+ | **flexão** | #flɛkt++sion++e+ |
| **convulsa** | #kon+#vuls++a# | **convulsão** | #kon+#vuls++sion++e+ |

a The verbs mean '3rd, tries, opts, twists, bends, convulses'. Then nouns meatn 'intent, option, contortion, flexion, convulsion'. The root of the verb *optar* and its derivatives may be simply +t+ since #ɔb+ is a prefix meaning 'put in front, contrary'. It occurs as /ɔb/: *obcecar* 'to obsess, i.e. to render blind'; *objectar* 'to object'; as /ɔ/ *ofuscar* 'to obfuscate', *oscilar* 'to oscillate', *opôr* 'to oppose'. It would not be extravagant to consider *optar* to be #ɔb++t++a#+r#+e+. Special rules could 1) eliminate the /b/ before certain fricatives and stops (*ocasião* could be #ɔb+#kad++sion++e+), and 2) cause /b/ to lose its voice before a voiceless stop. In all of the examples cited in this footnote, the /ɔ/ never reduces to [ŭ] in E.P. pronunciation, which is testimony to the underlying presence of /b+ in tht prefix. (§11.1.2.31, §11.5.2.1.3.)

Of all the words in Table 8.1a, those in Section 3 (related to the words in Table 8.9) are the closest to transparent. They have indubitable morphophonemic and semantic links to the verbs illustrated here. And they share, along with the other nouns in Table 8.1a, the absence of a verbal theme vowel in their stems. Also like the other nouns, +sion+'s attachment to the stems causes the deletion of a stem-final occlusive or fricative consonant.

**§8.3.1.0** By now it is clear that +sion++e+ is a viable lexical form of the suffix under examination, and that stems' final segments condition the realization of +sion++e+'s +s/, which can appear as [s] or as [z] or is lost when preceded by /z.t/. The case is not yet closed, however. Table 8.10 contains another collection of nominals derived with this suffix as well as four other suffixes (+tiv+<o#, +t+, +ent++e#, +dor#<e#), and these forms shall shed more light on this account of stem and suffix allomorphy.

**Table 8.10** Deverbal Nominals Formed by +sion++e#, Deverbal Adjectives formed by +tor#<e#, +t+, +ent++e#, and +tiv+<o#

| Infinitive | Gloss | Nominal | Gloss | Noun | Gloss |
|---|---|---|---|---|---|
| (1) Ø (/d+) ⇔ +z/ | | | | | |
| **corroer** | to rust | **corrosivo** | corrosive | **corrosão** | corrosion |
| **concluir** | to conclude | **conclusivo** | conclusive | **conclusão** | conclusion |
| (2) /nd+ ⇔ +z/ | | | | | |
| **prender** | to capture | **preso** | caught | **prisão** | prison |
| **confundir** | to confuse | **confuso** | confused | **confusão** | confusion |
| (3) /d+ ⇔ +s/ | | | | | |
| **expandir** | to expand | **expansivo** | expansive | **expansão** | expansion |
| **agredir** | to aggress | **agressivo** | aggressive | **agressão** | aggression |
| (4) /z+ ⇔ +s/ | | | | | |
| **seduzir** | to seduce | **sedutor** | seductive | **sedução** | seduction |
| **dizer** | to say | **ditador** | dictator | **dicção**[a] | diction |
| (5) /ž+ ⇔ +s/ | | | | | |
| **dirigir** | to direct | **diretivo** | directive | **direção** | address |
| **agir** | to act | **ativo** | active | **ação** | action |
| (6) /b+ or /v+ ⇔ +s/ | | | | | |
| **receber** | to receive | **recetivo** | receptive | **receção** | reception |
| **absorver** | to absorb | **absorto** | absorbed | **absorção** | absorption |
| (7) Ø ⇔ /n+ | | | | | |
| **reter** | to retain | **retentor** | retainer | **retenção** | retention |
| **convir** | to agree | **conveniente** | convenient | **convenção** | convention |

a According to Infopédia, the cç sequence represents the pronunciation [ks] in this word (10 June 2019).

In Table 8.10, the adjectives and nouns are obviously related to the infinitives, but once again the suffixes attach to stems with no intervening theme vowels or vestiges thereof. As above (§8.2.1.1), juxtapostions of stem-final contoids and the +s/ of +sion++e+ account for the +s/'s realizations. Thus, the purpose of examining these phenomena is no longer that of justifying the suffix's allomorphy, its purpose is, rather, to examine both the allomorphs of +sion+e+, +tiv+<o# and +tor+<e# and their provenience vis à vis the roots in each set: (A) infinitives, (B) nominals (either an adjective or a noun), and (C) nouns. The following data indicate that rules can derive acceptable phonotactic patterns and eventual grammatical realizations from the underlying strings of morphemes.

**§8.3.1.1 Table 8.10, Set 1—Ø (/d+) ⇔ +z/ +sion++e+:** The nominals (including the nouns formed with +sion++e+) bear the same relationship with their stems that the nouns in Table 8.5 do. That is, their roots contain a final /d+, which disappears before +S suffixes. These words' /d+ surfaces when followed by the $+S_1$ suffix +nt+ +e#: *corrodente* 'gnawer' and *concludente* 'concluding'. Thus, the lexical forms of *corrosão* and *conclusão* are #kon+#rɔd++sion++e+ and #kon++klud++sion++e+, and Rules 8.5 and 8.6 apply to voice their +s/ and delete their /d+.

**§8.3.1.2** The /z/ of the adjectival forms is another matter. There are 491 deverbal adjectives ending in -tivo (+tiv+<o#),[18] 50 that end in +siv+<o#, and 39 that end in +ziv+<o#. The forms beginning with +s/ and +z/ are allomorphs of +tiv+<o#. In the case of the two adjectives included in Set 1, their underlying forms could be #kon+#rɔd++tiv+<o# and #kon+klud+tiv+<o#. A rule such as 8.9 below would change the +t+ to +s+.

18 Or +t++iv+<o#, where the +t+ is the perfective participle morpheme.

**Rule 8.9 +t+→ +s+/ d+ ___:**[19]

$$\begin{pmatrix} +\text{occlusion} \\ +\text{surd} \\ -\text{high} \\ -\text{labial} \end{pmatrix} \rightarrow \begin{pmatrix} -\text{occlusion} \\ +\text{fricative} \\ -\text{high}\text{[20]} \end{pmatrix} / \_\, ++ \begin{pmatrix} +\text{occlusion} \\ -\text{surd} \\ -\text{labial} \end{pmatrix}$$

Once Rule 8.9 applies, Rule 8.6 affects these forms just as it does words ending containing +sion++e+: the +s/ becomes /z/, then the /d/ evanesces.

§8.3.2.0 **Set 2) /nd+ ⇔ +z/:** The roots of these two sets of words, plus those of many similar ones, all end in /d+. They are #fund+ and #prɛnd+, and the nouns in question would have the lexical forms #kon+#fund++sion++e+ and #prɛnd++sion+e#. Rules 8.5 and 8.6 voice the +s/ and delete the /d+ making the forms #kon+#fun++zion++e+ and #prɛn++zion+e#. After this, Rule 8.10 deletes the stem-final /n/ when, across morpheme boundaries, a /z/ follows.

**Rule 8.10 Stem-Final Nasal Deletion:**

$$[+\text{nasal}] \rightarrow \emptyset \,/\, \_\_\_ \;\; ++ \begin{pmatrix} +\text{fricative} \\ -\text{surd} \\ -\text{high} \\ -\text{labial} \end{pmatrix}$$

---

19 Rule 8.9 is a morphophonemic rule with a modicum of phonetic motivation. The stem-final /d+ is a voiced stop, which is more sonorant than [+surd] stop. The +t/'s mutation to +s/, a voiceless fricative approximates the sort of sonority one would need a segment to have following a voiced occlusive (See Vol. 1, PS 4). So it is natural that a [+surd] occlusive (a highly non-sonorant segment) would 'weaken' following an occlusive. (The voicing of +sion++e+'s +s/ is another example of this phenomenon.)

20 The conditioning segment must be /d+ because stems ending in /p+ or /k+ do not occasion this lenition of +t/.

This rule is similar to Rule 8.5, which deletes /d/ and /r/ before a fricative when the intervening affinity between stem and suffix is ++.[21]

**§8.3.2.1** The /i/ of the root of *prisão* and its further derivatives (e.g. *prisioneiro* 'prisoner'), where the vowel is not /e/ but /i/, is not a rule-governed synchronic phenomenon. According to Williams (42), pretonic /e/ rose to [ĭ] eventually becoming /i/ in modern Portuguese. Compare *lecionar* 'to teach' and *lição* 'lesson'. Rather than write a rule for /ɛ/→/i/ in *prisão* and *lição*, it is probably better to consider nouns such as *prisão* and *lição* to be derived from roots that are different from their related verbs. For the former, its root could be #prind+ instead of #prɛnd+, for *lecionar* and *lectivo* 'scholastic', the prevalent root would be #lɛg+, but the special root for *lição* would be #lig+.

**§8.3..2.2** One could consider the participial adjectives *confuso* and *preso* to be suppletive, irregular participles.[22] However, *preso* and *confuso* could be lexically #prend++t+<o# and #kon+#fund+t+<o#, and Rule 8.9, the same rule that changes /t/ to /s/ for Set 1, would operate here, then rules 8.4 and 8.5 would voice the +s/ then delete the /d+, after which the nasal deletion rule (8.10) would delete the /n+.

**§8.3.3.0 Set 3:** What makes Table 8.10's Set 3 worthy of examination is that, if the analyses of Sets 1 and 2 are correct, the roots of these two words (and others like them) end in /d+: +pand+ and +grɛd+. However, even though the root-final /d+ vanishes in the derived nominals, their suffixes' initial consonants do not lose their [+surd] quality.

**§8.3.3.1** The first phonologist to advance a systematization of this phenomenon was D'Andrade Pardal (1977). He proposed that words such as these (and many others such as those in Table 8.1a) would have a lexical form in which the theme vowel bore an asterisk indicating

21 There are examples galore of /n/'s occurring before /s/ not withstanding the ++ morpheme affinity: *atenção* 'attention' #ad+#ten++sion++e+, *função* 'function' #fund++sion++e#, and *ascensão* 'assention' #adz++sɛnd++sion++e#. Likewise, there are /nz/ junctions in words like *onze* '11', or *gonzo* 'hinge', where there is no morpheme boundary between the /n/ and the /z+.

22 Both *prender* and *confundir* have regular participles: *prendido* and *confundido* that have a slightly higher verbal valence than *preso* and *confuso*. Because the regular participles are inflectional, they would not appear in the lexicon. They would emerge through explicit syntactic and/or semantic specifications. Their analysis would be #prend++e#<to# and #kon+#fund++i +<to#.

that somewhere in their derivation the theme vowel would be lost.[23] Table 8.11 displays the steps in their order of application generating the forms in question.

**Table 8.11** Steps in Deriving Suffixes Unaffected by Stem-Final /d+

| | **expansivo** | **agressivo** |
|---|---|---|
| **U.F.:** | #ez++pand[a]++i++tiv++o# | #ad++grɛd++i++tiv++o# |
| **R. 8.5** | *** | *** |
| **TV→ Ø[b]** | #ez++pand++tiv++o# | #ad++grɛd++tiv++o# |
| **R. 8.9** | #ez++pand++siv++o# | #ad++grɛd++siv++o# |
| **R. 8.6** | #ez++pan++siv++o# | #ad++grɛ++siv++o# |
| **Ph.** | [əš.pẵ$^{n}$.'si.vŭ] | [a.ɣrɛ.'si.vŭ] |
| | **expansão** | **agressão** |
| **U.F.:** | #ez++pand++i++sion++e+ | #ad++grɛd++i++sion++e+ |
| **R. 8.5** | *** | *** |
| **TV→ Ø** | #ez++pand++sion++e+ | #ad++grɛd++sion++e+ |
| **R. 8.9** | *** | *** |
| **R. 8.6** | #ez++pan++sion++e+ | #ad++grɛ++sion++e+ |
| **Ph.** | [əš.pẵn.'sẵ$^{\tilde{u}}$] | [ă.ɣrɛ.'sẵ$^{\tilde{u}}$] |

a The /d+ in these roots only appears in the verbs themselves. No derived nominal of either verb contains a /d+.
b Theme vowel deletion.

All the rules, save TV→Ø, in Table 8.11 have been written and defended in the preceding paragraphs. TV→ Ø (Rule 8.11) needs to be written and examined closely.

§8.3.3.2 D'Andrade Pardal proposed a solution similar to this one:

**Rule 8.11 Theme Vowel Deletion Verb Subset 3 (Table 8.10):**

$$TV\begin{pmatrix}\alpha\ 2^{nd}\\ \beta\ 3^{rd}\end{pmatrix} \rightarrow \emptyset\ /\ ++\ \_\_\ \begin{Bmatrix}\alpha\ \#\\ \beta\ +\end{Bmatrix} +$$

23 For all the forms examined (§8.3.1.0–2) consisting of root+nominal-deriving suffix, D'Andrade Pardal would have posited an underlying but deletable theme vowel.

Rule 8.11 deletes either a 2nd or a 3rd conjugation theme vowel[24] when it is followed by another suffix bound to it with either a #+ or a ++ affinity.

**§8.3.4.0 Set 4:** The verbal roots of *seduzir* and *dizer* appear with a final /z/ in their infinitives, and this is worthy of remark because both the adjectival suffixes and the noun suffix +sion+e+ do not acquire voicing when attached to the roots of these words. One needs to dig deeper than the infinitives and delve into the Portuguese word stock to ascertain the roots of these forms, both of which end in /k+. Table 8.12 demonstrates the existence of /k/ in their roots.

**Table 8.12** /z+ ⇔ /k+[a]

| Root[b] | /z/ infinitive | /k/ infinitive | /k/ noun |
|---|---|---|---|
| #duk+ | conduzir | educar | duque |
| #dik+ | dizer | indicar | indicação |
| #fak+ | fazer | facultar | faculdade |
| #trak+ | trazer | atracar | atracação |

a The verbs *fazer* and *trazer* and derivatives thereof appear with *conduzir* and *dizer* in Table 8.12 to show that the /k+→/z+ phenomenon occurs with both 3rd and 2nd conjugation verbal roots.
b The roots' glosses are: 'lead, say, do, bring'. The infinitives are: 'to conduct, to say, to do, to bring'. The /k/ infinitives mean: 'to educate, to indicate, to facilitate, to moor'. The /k/ nouns mean: 'duke, indication, faculty, mooring'.

The roots' /k+ turns into /z+ when it is followed by a +S suffix beginning with a front vowel. When it is followed by a non-front vowel, it remains /k+.[25]

---

24 These two examples are minorities within a minority of the adjectives ending in +tiv+<o#. There are only twenty 3rd conjugation verbs that form adjectives with +tiv+<o# following their theme vowel, nine of which exhibit the phenomena examined here. There are only eight 2nd conjugation verbs that exhibit the same phenomenon of a verbal stem ending in /d+ that is deleted without the suffix's initial consonant's becoming voiced: e.g. *apreender* 'to apprehend' *apreensivo* 'apprehensive' and *apreensão* 'apprehension'. Clearly this minority pertains to a subset of verbs susceptible to Rule 8.11. This tiny subset will require a diferent ordering of rules in the grammar (see Table 8B.6)

25 There is scant phonetic motivation for this rule, although the pattern of /k/ ⇔ /s/ alternation also exists both in Portuguese and in English: electric

**§8.3.4.1** Table 8.13 displays the lexical form of the adjectives and nouns formed from these roots plus the steps necessary to turn them into forms on which the rules of Portuguese phonology can work to generate these words' actual realizations:

**Table 8.13** The Loss of /k+

| Nominals | | |
|---|---|---|
| | **sedutor** | **ditador** |
| Lexical | #sɛ+#duk++t++dor#<e + | #dik++t++a#+dor#<e+ |
| /k+→Ø[a] | #sɛ+#du++t++dor#<e+ | #di++t+<a#<dor#<e+ |
| R. 7.1 | #sɛ+#du++t++or#<e+ | *** |
| Ph. | [sə.ðu.ˈtor] | [di.tă.ˈðor] |
| **Nouns** | | |
| | **sedução** | **dicção** |
| Lexical | #sɛ+#duk++sion++e+ | #dik++sion++e+ |
| /k+→Ø | #sɛ+#du++sion++e+ | *** |
| R. 7.1 | *** | *** |
| Ph. | [sə.ðu.ˈ sã̃$^{\tilde{u}}$] | [dik.ˈsã̃$^{\tilde{u}}$][b] |

a This rule deletes /k+ and other root-final consonants before deriving suffixes beginning with +t/ or +s/, §8.3.6.1, Rule 8.12.)
b This word is immune to the rule that deletes /k+. See footnote 19.

The +t+ included in the lexical forms of these nominals is the perfect participial morpheme +t+, which appears in the stems of words related to *sedutor* and *ditador*. The verb *ditar* 'to dictate' has the same root #dik+ 'say' as *dizer*, but in this case, the /k+ is followed by +t+ #dik++t++a#+r#+e+. The verb *produzir* 'to produce' is related to *produto* 'product', whose underlying form is #pro+#duk++t++o#. In both words, the +t+ causes the root final /k+ to evanesce.

**§8.3.5 Set 5:** The words in this section are similar to those of Set 4 insofar as none of them actually evinces their root-final consonant, /g+, directly. Owing to velar softening, g+ appears as /ž/ in the infinitives and has no reflex in the derived words. Table 8.14 demonstrates their affinity with words in which the phoneme /g/ appears root-finally.

⇔ electricity, *eléctrico* ⇔ *eletricidade*, faculty ⇔ facilitate, *faculdade* ⇔ *facilitar*.

Table 8.14 /g/ ⇔ /ž/[a]

| Root[b] | /ž/ infinitive | /g/ infinitive | /g/ noun |
|---|---|---|---|
| #rig+ | dirigir | obrigar | rigor |
| #rɛg+ | reger | regular | régua |
| #ag+ | agir | embriagar[c] | embriaguez |

a The verb *reger* and the related infinitive and noun show that velar softening occurs before /e/ as well as /i/.
b The glosses are: 'control, control, act' (roots); 'to direct, to rule, to proceed' (/ž/ infinitives); 'to obligate, to regulate, to inebriate' (/g/ infinitives); 'rigor, ruler, inebriation' (/g/ nouns).
c The component parts of *embriagar* are #en+#bri+#ag++a#+r#+e+. The prefix #en+ indicates inwardness (Cunha, 63, 64). The form #bri+ is the root of *brio* meaning 'vivacity, spirit'. The form #ag+ indicates a procedure. The remainder of the word contains the expected suffixes for 1st conjugation infinitives. So *embriagar* literally means 'to proceed to fill with spirit'.

In Table 8.14, the roots' /g+ turns to /ž+ when it is followed by a +S suffix consisting of a front vowel. When it is followed by a non-front vowel, it remains /g+.[26] Only one step, the loss of root-final /g/, is necessary to ready these forms for the phonological component of a grammar of Portuguese:

26 The noun forming +S suffix +ez#<e+, notwithstanding its palatal vowel, does not occasion velar softening: e.g. *embriaguez* 'drunkenness' as well as *português* 'Portuguese', *gaguez* 'stuttering' (cf. *gago* 'stutterer'), *caduquez* 'senilitiy' (cf. *caduco* 'senile'), *burguês* bourgeois (cf. *burgo* 'town'), *norueguês* 'Norwegian' (cf. *Noruega* 'Norway'), *dinamarquês* 'Danish' (cf. *Dinamarca* 'Denmark'). This suffix must be marked as not occasioning velar softening.

**Table 8.15** The Loss of /g+[a]

| Nominals | | |
|---|---|---|
| Word | **diretivo** | **ator** |
| Lexical | #di+#rɛg++tiv+<o# | #ag++t++dor#<e# |
| /g+ → Ø | #di+#rɛ++tiv+<o# | #a++t++dor#<e# |
| R. 7.1 | *** | #a++t++or#<e# |
| Ph. | [di.rɛ.ˈti.vu] | [a.ˈtor] |
| **Nouns** | | |
| Word | **direção** | **ação** |
| Lexical | #di+#rɛg++sion++e+ | #ag++sion++e+ |
| /g+ → Ø | #di+#rɛ++sion++e+ | #a++sion++e+ |
| R. 7.1 | *** | *** |
| Ph. | [di.rɛ.ˈ sã͂ᵘ] | [a.ˈsã͂ᵘ] |

a The words in Table 8.14 mean, respectively: 'directive, actor, direction/address, action'.

Once again, a root-final occlusive consonant, this time /g+ disappears in the course of a derivation. Once Set 6 is examined, a rule for this phenomenon follows.

§8.3.6.0 **Set 6**: Earlier, this chapter (Table 8.7, §8.2.3.1) provided an analysis of *receber* and other derivatives of its root +sɛp+. The formation of nominals and nouns in *–ção* from roots ending in labials proceeds in a manner similar to those in Sets 1–5 of Table 8.10. Table 8.16 shows the emergence of Set 6's roots in related words.

**Table 8.16** Roots Ending in Labials

| Root | Gloss | Labial Infinitive | Gloss | /p+, /v+ word | Gloss |
|---|---|---|---|---|---|
| +sep+ | ??? | **receber** | to receive | **recepisse**[a] | receipt |
| | | | | **recipiente** | recipient |
| #sɔrv+ | suck | **absorver** | to absorb | **sorvo** | sip |

a This word appears in the *Aurélio* and the *Morais* dictionary, but not in the *Dicionário Infopédia*.

The derivation of the nominals in question is once again a straightforward matter, as Table 8.17 demonstrates:

**Table 8.17** The Loss of /p/ and /v/

| Adjectives | | |
|---|---|---|
| Word | **recetivo** 'receptive' | **absorto** 'absorbed' |
| Lexical | #re++sɛp++tiv+<o# | #ab+#sɔrv++t+<o# |
| /p+→Ø | #re++sɛ ++tiv+<o# | #ab+#sɔr++t+<o# |
| Ph. | [r̠ə.sɛ.'ti.vu] | [a.'sor.tu] |
| **Nouns** | | |
| | **receção** 'front desk' | **absorção** 'absorption' |
| Lexical | #re++sɛp ++sion++e+ | #ab+#sɔrv++sion++e+ |
| /p+, /v+→ Ø | #re++sɛ ++sion++e+ | #ab+#sɔr++sion++e+ |
| Ph. | [r̠ə.sɛ.'sã$^{\tilde{u}}$] | [ab.sɔr.'sã$^{\tilde{u}}$] |

**§8.3.6.1** Sections §8.3.4.0–6.0 have used the unspecified Rules to delete stem-final consonants. This rule is:

**Rule 8.12 Deletion of Root-Final /k, g, p, v, b/:**

$$\begin{pmatrix} +\text{contoid} \\ \begin{Bmatrix} [+\text{dorsal}] \\ [+\text{labial}] \end{Bmatrix} \end{pmatrix} \rightarrow \emptyset \;/\; \_\_ \;+\,+ \begin{Bmatrix} [+\text{occlusion}] \\ [+\text{fricative}] \end{Bmatrix}$$

Rule 8.12 performs a function similar to that of Rule 8.6, which deletes root-final /d+, /r+, and /t+ before fricative-initial suffixes. The data show that stem-final /d+ provides a voicing environment for subsequent fricatives, whereas the stem-final velars and labials do not transfer voice to following fricatives or occlusives. Indeed, the root-final labial and velar consonants do not cause a contiguous stop consonant to spirantize, as /d+ and some cases of root-final /r+ do. Instead, they evanesce after preventing the reduction of a preceding pretonic vowel.

**§8.3.7 Set** 7: The final set of words in Table 8.10 displays two infinitives obviously related to the derived adjectives and nouns that evince the presence of an underlying /n/ in their roots, and, consequently, in the infinitives' roots as well (§14.2.2.1.1–3.3). Since the lexical presence of /n/ in both forms is established, the derivation of Set 7's adjectives and nouns is totally transparent and uncomplicated:

Table 8.18 Straightforward Derivation

| Nominals | | |
|---|---|---|
| Word | **retentor** 'retainer' | **conveniente** 'convenient' |
| Lexical | #re+#ten ++t++dor#<e+ | #kon+#ven ++ient+<e#[a] |
| R. 7.1 | #re+#ten ++t++or#<e+ | *** |
| Ph. | [r̲ə.tẽ$^{n}$.'tor] | [kõ$^{ŋ}$.vẽ.ni 'ẽ$^{n}$.tə] |
| **Nouns** | | |
| Word | **retenção** 'retention' | **convenção** 'convention' |
| Lexical | #re+#ten++sion++e+ | #kon+#ven ++sion++e+ |
| Ph. | [r̲ə.tẽ$^{n}$.'sã$^{ũ}$] | [kõ$^{ŋ}$.vẽ$^{n}$.'sã$^{ũ}$] |

a One might be tempted to consider the /i/ in *conveniente* to be a reflex of the 3rd conjugation theme vowel. Tentantively, +ient++e# and +ent++e# aappear to be allomorphs of +nt++e#. This is because +ient++e# attaches both to 3rd conjugation verbal roots such as those of *convir* or *sair* (*saliente*), as well as to 2nd conjugation verbal roots such as *saber* 'to know' *sapiente* 'knowing' *receber* 'to receive' and *recipiente* 'recipient'. It also attaches to nouns: *paz* 'peace' *paciente* 'patient (adj.)', and to adjectives: *eficaz* 'efficacious' *eficiente* 'efficient', where no theme vowel is available.

The +t+ in the underlying form of *retentor* is the same participial morpheme that occurs in *sedutor* and *condutor*, which causes Rule 7.1 to delete the +d/ of the suffix +dor#<e+:

§8.3.8 The grammar of the allomorphy of +sion+ is complete. One may, at this point, wish to consult Appendices A and B to review all the rules advanced and invoked in this chapter as well as to see them in action in derivation of representative nominals derived with this suffix.

# Conclusions

## Summary

§8.4.0 **Summary:** This chapter's purpose has been to account for the allomorphy of the +$S_1$ suffix +sion++e+, in word-final and word-medial position as well as that of the stems to which it attaches. The presence of the verbal stem's theme vowel (+a#, +e#, +i+) provides the neutral environment in which this suffix may appear in its entirety—both as a word medial suffix to which a deriving +$S_1$ or +S suffix has been added, and as a word-final suffix that undergoes mutations when it surfaces.

§8.4.1.0 **Allomorphy:** Word-finally this suffix mostly emerges as [ˈsã$^{ũ}$], in [-plural] forms and as [ˈsõ$^{ĩ}$š] in [+plural] forms. The [-plural] forms owe their origin to a merger of various nominal-deriving suffixes (Rule 8.1) and to: (A) the nasalization of the merged form's initial +ˈa/ to [ˈã̆]; (B) the reduction of the suffix's final +o# to [ŭ]; (C) to the loss of the intervocalic /n+; (D) the [ŭ]'s formation of an off-glide [ˈã̆ᵘ]; and (E) the progressive nasalization of the off-glide [ˈã̆ᵘ̃]. The plural form [ˈsõĩš] owes its configuration to similar phenomena: word-finally +sion++e+<z# essentially merges with the augmentative suffix +on+<e+<z#, carrying with it its initial +s/ and its invariant ([+feminine]) gender morpheme: +son++e+. These processes produce: (F) a tonic paroxytone vowel [ˈo], (G) regressive assimilation from /n+ to [õ], (H) the reduction of post-tonic +e+ to [ĭ], (I) the loss of intervocalic /n+, (J) diphthongization [ˈõĭ] → [õĩ], and (K) progressive assimilation of [õ]'s nasality [ˈõĩ].

§**8.4.1.1** This suffix's initial segment +s/ surfaces as [z] when it directly follows a stem-final /d+ or /r+, which disappears once +s/ loses its voicelessness owing to progressive assimilaton. The initial +s/ disappears when it directly follows a stem-final sequence /z.t+. Elsewhere, it emerges as [s]: (A) when it derives a noun from a verb whose theme vowel is not deleted; (B) when it attaches to stems ending in segments other than /d+ and /r+.

§**8.4.2 Stem Classes:** Chapter 8 has established five classes of nominals derived with the suffix +sion++e: Class 1 consists of the transparent nouns formed from the sequence #stem++theme vowel#+sion++e+(<z#), which is the majority, i.e. the unmarked case of nouns formed with this suffix. Class 2 nouns consist of verbal roots with no theme vowel preceding +sion++e+. Class 3 nouns are formed from participial stems. Class 4 nouns derive from a lexical entry containing a 2nd or 3rd conjugation theme vowel that evanesces in their derivation. Class 5, because of the nouns' varied underlying patterns, is the least frequent and the most highly marked of the classes of deverbal nouns formed with +sion++e+.

§**8.4.3 Other Allomorphy:** In the course of working with the allomorphy associated with +sion+ and that of the stems to which it attaches, it was necessary to investigate allomorphy associated with the nominal forming suffixes +tiv+<o# (adjectives) and +dor+<e# (adjectives and nouns). Evidence indicates that allomorphs of these suffixes [ˈsi.vŭ] and [ˈtor] are created owing to the particular consonant that ends a stem, and that these suffixes also occasion alterations in stems when they attach directly to them, i.e. without an intervening theme vowel.

## Findings and Insights

§8.4.4 **Patterns:** The discovery of regularity in the remarkable allomorphy associated with +sion+ has uncovered a canonical pattern for this suffix's attachment to stems. The overwhelming majority (86.17%) of its word-final occurrences has the structure #stem++TV# +sion++e+. Only 13.83% of the words ending in this suffix do not surface with the theme vowel. Some of them are formed from (irregular) past participles, others from stems and roots that could accept a theme vowel, some from stems and roots that are peculiar to the particular formations.

§8.4.5 **Minorities:** The discovery of the rule-governed nature of this suffix's allomorphy and its (and the other two suffixes') effects on stems has entailed the postulation of special stems and a set of suffix-specific rules. Whereas the majority of words formed with word-final +sion+ +e+ contain theme vowels, minorities may contain no theme vowel, deletable theme vowels, or the participial morpheme. The grammar also entails considerable morphophonemic modification of stems, and it is hardly elegant. But the phenomena entailed in the creation of nouns with this suffix is hardly straightforward, even in the secure ground of the forms' canonical deverbal formation.

## So What?

§8.4.6.0 This account of a thorny problem in Portuguese morphophonology entails both a set of 22 rules and significant manipulation of the stems to which +sion++e+ attaches. It remains to be seen if this is the most elegant solution possible, which Appendix C proposes in its review of Ernesto D'Andrade Pardal's account of the same phenomena. Beyond this, now that the morphophonology of the word-final manifestations of +sion++e+ has been identified, these deliberations may proceed to account for the less straightforward nominal inflection, both pluralization and gender, announced in Chapter 6 (§6.1.1, §6.1.2.5).

## Appendix A Rules as they Appear in Chapter 8

§8A.0 This is the order in which Chapter 8 has proposed or invoked rules to govern the allomorphy associated with the suffix +sion+.

### 8.1 Suffix Merger in Word-Final Position:

$$\left\{\begin{matrix} +\text{on}+<\text{e}+ \\ +\text{an}+\{<\text{e}+,<\text{o}\#\} \\ +(\alpha\ \text{s})\text{ion}+\ +\text{e}+ \end{matrix}\right\} \rightarrow +\ (\alpha\ \text{s})\text{an}+ \left\{\begin{matrix} \alpha+\text{o}\#_3 \\ <\text{o}\# \end{matrix}\right\} /\ \_\_\ <[\text{-plural}]\#$$

### 8.2 +sion++e++z#'s Merger:

+(s)ion++e+<z# → +(s)on++e+<z#

### 2.3 Atonic Vowel Reduction::

$$\begin{pmatrix} \text{-contoid} \\ \text{-high} \\ \alpha\text{labial} \\ \text{-del. trans.} \end{pmatrix} \rightarrow \begin{pmatrix} +\text{wide glottis} \\ \text{-palatal} \\ \alpha\text{high} \\ \text{-low} \end{pmatrix} /\ \_\_\_\_\ \left( \begin{matrix} +\text{contoid} \\ \left\{\begin{matrix} [\text{-nasal}] \\ [\text{-lateral}] \\ [\text{-occlusion}] \end{matrix}\right\} \end{matrix} \right).$$

### 7.1 Loss of Morpheme-initial +d/:

$$+\begin{pmatrix} +\text{occlusion} \\ \text{-surd} \\ \text{-high} \\ \text{-labial} \end{pmatrix} \rightarrow \emptyset\ /\ \begin{pmatrix} +\text{occlusion} \\ +\text{surd} \\ \text{-high} \\ \text{-labial} \end{pmatrix} +$$

### Rule 7.2 Morphophonemic Nasalization $R_1$ Stems:

$$+\begin{pmatrix} \text{-contoid} \\ +\text{delayed transition} \end{pmatrix} \rightarrow [+\text{nasal}]\ /\ \_\_\ \begin{pmatrix} +\text{nasal} \\ +\text{contoid} \end{pmatrix} + \left\{\begin{matrix} + \\ < \end{matrix}\right\} [\pm\text{feminine}]\ \#\ <\emptyset\#$$

### 8.3 Loss of /n+:

$$\begin{pmatrix} +\text{nasal} \\ +\text{contoid} \end{pmatrix} \rightarrow \emptyset/ \begin{pmatrix} \text{-contoid} \\ +\text{nasal} \end{pmatrix} /\ \_\_\ +\ +\ \text{S}<\text{S}\#$$

**4.3 Syllable Boundary 1;**

$$\emptyset \rightarrow .\ /\ \left\{ \begin{array}{l} \#\_X \\ X\_\# \\ X>\_\ C \end{array} \right\}$$

**4.4 Syllable Boundary 2;**

$$\emptyset \rightarrow .\ /[\text{-contoid}]\ \_\_\ [+\text{contoid}] \left\{ \begin{array}{l} [\text{-contoid}] \\ C_2 \end{array} \right\}$$

**4.5 Syllable Boundary 3:**

$$\emptyset \rightarrow .\ / \begin{bmatrix} \text{-contoid} \\ \alpha\text{high} \end{bmatrix} \_\_ \left( \left\{ \begin{array}{l} \text{-contoid} \\ \alpha\text{high} \\ +\text{delayed transition} \end{array} \right\} \right)$$

**4.6 Syllable Boundary 4:**

$$\emptyset \rightarrow .\ /\ C_4\_\_ \left( \begin{array}{l} +\text{contoid} \\ \left\{ \begin{array}{l} +\text{nasal} \\ +\text{occlusion} \\ +\text{fricative} \end{array} \right\} \end{array} \right).$$

**4.8 Vowel Epenthesis After Syllable-Final Occlusives:**

$\emptyset \rightarrow$ [-contoid] / [+occlusion].___

[-contoid] = /e/ [ĭ, ə] Portugal; /i/ [ĭ] Brazil

**8.4 Progressive Assimilation of Off-Glides:**

$$\begin{pmatrix}\text{-contoid}\\ \text{+high}\\ \text{-del. trans.}\end{pmatrix} \rightarrow [\text{+nasal}] \;/\; \begin{pmatrix}\text{-contoid}\\ \text{-high}\\ \text{+nasal}\end{pmatrix} \;\text{—}$$

**8.5+s/ of +sione++e+ Becomes +z/:**

$$\begin{pmatrix}\text{-labial}\\ \text{-high}\\ \text{+fricative}\end{pmatrix} \rightarrow [\text{-surd}] / \begin{pmatrix}\text{+contoid}\\ \text{-surd}\\ \text{-nasal}\\ \text{-lateral}\\ \text{-high}\\ \text{-labial}\end{pmatrix} \;++\;\_\_$$

**8.6 Loss of /r/ and /d/:**

$$\begin{pmatrix}\text{+contoid}\\ \text{-surd}\\ \text{-nasal}\\ \text{-lateral}\\ \text{-high}\\ \text{-labial}\end{pmatrix} \rightarrow \text{Ø} \;/\; \_\_ ++ [\text{+fricative}]$$

**8.7 Deletion of +s/ After /z.t+:**

$$\begin{pmatrix}\text{+fricative}\\ \text{+surd}\\ \text{-labial}\\ \text{-high}\end{pmatrix} \rightarrow \text{Ø}/. \begin{pmatrix}\text{+occlusion}\\ \text{–high}\\ \text{-labial}\\ \text{+surd}\end{pmatrix} \;++\;\_\_$$

**7.5 $R_1$+ Stem-Final Occlusive Voicing:**

$$\begin{pmatrix} +\text{occlusion} \\ +\text{surd} \end{pmatrix} \rightarrow [\text{-surd}]/[\text{-contoid}]\ \_\ +(X)+S_{R1}$$

**8.8a Optional Loss of Root-Final /p+ (Provisional):**

$$\begin{pmatrix} +\text{occlusion} \\ +\text{labial} \\ +\text{surd} \end{pmatrix} \rightarrow \varnothing / /\ \_\ ++ \begin{pmatrix} +\text{contoid} \\ +\text{surd} \\ \text{-high} \\ \text{-labial} \end{pmatrix}$$

**Rule 8.8b Loss of Stem-Final /p+ and /t+:**

$$\begin{pmatrix} +\text{occlusion} \\ \text{-high} \\ +\text{surd} \end{pmatrix} \rightarrow \varnothing / /\ \_\ ++ \begin{pmatrix} +\text{contoid} \\ +\text{surd} \\ \text{-high} \end{pmatrix}$$

**8.9 +t+ → +s+ / d+:**[27]

$$\begin{pmatrix} +\text{occlusion} \\ +\text{surd} \\ \text{-high} \\ \text{-labial} \end{pmatrix} \rightarrow \begin{pmatrix} \text{-occlusion} \\ +\text{fricative} \\ \text{-high} \end{pmatrix} /\ \_\ ++ \begin{pmatrix} +\text{occlusion} \\ \text{-surd} \\ \text{-labial} \end{pmatrix}$$

27 Rule 8.9 is essential to generating the allomorphs of the suffix +t+iv+<o# (§8.2.7.1.1) and in the derivation of irregular participial adjectives, e.g. *confuso* 'confused' and *preso* 'captured'. It does not operate in the derivation of allomorphs of +sion+, so it does not appear in the sample derivations in Appendix B.

### 8.10 Stem-Final Nasal Deletion:

$$[+\text{nasal}] \rightarrow \varnothing \,/\, \underline{\quad} \;\; ++ \begin{pmatrix} +\text{fricative} \\ -\text{surd} \\ -\text{high} \\ -\text{labial} \end{pmatrix}$$

### 8.11 Theme Vowel Deletion Verb Subset 3 (Table 8.10):

$$\text{TV} \begin{pmatrix} \alpha\ 2^{\text{nd}} \\ \beta\ 3^{\text{rd}} \end{pmatrix} \rightarrow \varnothing \,/\, ++ \underline{\quad} \begin{Bmatrix} \alpha\ \# \\ \beta\ + \end{Bmatrix} +$$

### 8.12 Deletion of Root-Final /k, g, p, v, b/:

$$\begin{pmatrix} +\text{contoid} \\ \begin{Bmatrix} +\text{dorsal} \\ +\text{labial} \end{Bmatrix} \end{pmatrix} \rightarrow \varnothing \,/\, \underline{\quad} \; ++ \begin{pmatrix} \begin{Bmatrix} [+\text{occlusion}] \\ [+\text{fricative}] \end{Bmatrix} \end{pmatrix}$$

### 8.13 +d/ → Ø /t+ ___:

$$\begin{pmatrix} +\text{occlusion} \\ -\text{surd} \\ -\text{labial} \\ -\text{high} \end{pmatrix} \rightarrow \varnothing \,/ \begin{pmatrix} +\text{occlusion} \\ -\text{labial} \\ -\text{high} \end{pmatrix} ++ \; \underline{\quad}$$

### 3.1 Paroxytone stress

$$[-\text{contoid}] \rightarrow [+\text{stress}] \,/\, \#X \, \underline{\quad} \; \left( \begin{pmatrix} +\text{high} \\ -\text{contoid} \end{pmatrix} \right) C_{0\text{-}4}V_{[-\text{high}]}\#(C)\#$$

**Condition:** The word has no previously assigned stress.

## Appendix B The Grammar of +sion++e+'s Allomorphy

§8B.0 Save the reordering in Table 8B.6, this is the grammar with which Chapter 8's rules govern the allomorphy associated with the suffix +sion+.

### 8.0 Theme Vowel Shift, 2nd Conjugation:

$$TV^{2nd} \rightarrow TV^{3rd} \,/\, \_\_ \left\{ \begin{matrix} +\text{sion}+ \\ +\text{on}+ \end{matrix} \right\}$$

This rule did not appear in the text of Chapter 8. It accounts for the shift of 2nd conjugation theme vowels in a minority of transparent + sion+and [+feminine] +on+ nominals derived from 2nd conjugation verbs (Table 8B.5).

### 8.1 Suffix Merger in Word-Final Position:

$$\left\{ \begin{matrix} +\text{on}+<\text{e}+,\ \beta+\text{e}_{[\text{f.}]}+ \\ +\text{an}+\{<\text{e}+,<\text{o}\#\} \\ +(\alpha\ \text{s})\text{ion}+\beta+\text{e}_{[\text{f.}]}+ \end{matrix} \right\} \rightarrow +\ (\alpha\ \text{s})\text{an}+ \left\{ \begin{matrix} \beta+\text{o}\#_3 \\ <\text{o}\# \end{matrix} \right\} / \_\_ <[\text{-plural}]\#$$

Rule 8.1 merges the three suffixes in non-plural forms. The +on+ that occurs in words such as *região* 'region [+fem.]' and *união* 'union [+fem.]' is followed by the [+fem.]deriving gender morpheme +e+ and preceded by the theme vowel: +e# in *região,* cf. *rege* '3rd regulates'; +i+ in *união,* cf. *unir* 'to unite'. The +o# that emerges in the resultant nominals is the deriving +$o_3$+, i.e. [+feminine]. Conversely, +on+ followed by <e+, even though it merges with +an+ is inflected, and the derived nominals reflect this when they designate [+feminine] entities: *rufião* 'ruffian' cf. *rufiona* 'female ruffian'.

### 8.2 +sion++e++z#'s Merger:

+sion++e+<z# → +son++e+<z#

When followed by the plural morpheme, +sion+ only loses its /i/.

**8.11 Theme Vowel Deletion Verb Subset 3:**

$$\text{TV}\begin{pmatrix} \alpha 2^{\text{nd}} \\ \beta 3^{\text{rd}} \end{pmatrix} \rightarrow \varnothing \;/\; ++ \,\_\, \begin{Bmatrix} \alpha\# \\ \beta+ \end{Bmatrix} +$$

A subset of 2nd and 3rd conjugation verbs loses its theme vowel before deriving suffixes. (Table 8B.2)

**8.5 +s/ of +sione++e+ Becomes +z/:**

$$\begin{pmatrix} \text{-labial} \\ \text{-high} \\ \text{+fricative} \end{pmatrix} \rightarrow [\text{-surd}]/ \begin{pmatrix} \text{+contoid} \\ \text{-surd} \\ \text{-nasal} \\ \text{-lateral} \\ \text{-high} \end{pmatrix} ++ \,\_$$

When the +s/ abuts a stem-final /d+ or /r+, it acquires voice.

**8.6 Loss of /r/ and /d/:**

$$\begin{pmatrix} \text{+contoid} \\ \text{-surd} \\ \text{-nasal} \\ \text{-lateral} \\ \text{-high} \\ \text{-labial} \end{pmatrix} \rightarrow \varnothing \;/\; \_\, ++[\text{+fricative}]$$

After causing the +s/ to lose its [+surd] quality, stem-final /r+ and /d+ evanesce.

**3.1 Paroxytone Stress:**

$$[\text{-contoid}] \rightarrow [+\text{stress}] \;/\; \#X\,\_\; \left(\begin{bmatrix}+\text{high}\\ \text{-contoid}\end{bmatrix}\right) C_{0\text{-}4}V_{[\text{-high}]}\#(C)\#$$

**Condition:** The word has no previously assigned stress.

All nominals ending in an allomorph of +sion+ are paroxytones.

**Rule 7.2 Morphophonemic Nasalization $R_1$ Stems:**

$$+\begin{bmatrix}\text{-contoid}\\ +\text{delayed transition}\end{bmatrix} \rightarrow [+\text{nasal}] \;/\; \_\_ \begin{bmatrix}+\text{nasal}\\ +\text{contoid}\end{bmatrix} + \begin{Bmatrix}+\\ <\end{Bmatrix}[\pm\text{feminine}]\ \# <\text{Ø}\#$$

Stem-final /n+ of deriving suffixes, when followed by +S# suffixes, causes the previous vowel to acquire nasality.

**8.3 Loss of /n+:**

$$\begin{bmatrix}+\text{nasal}\\ +\text{contoid}\end{bmatrix} \rightarrow \text{Ø}/ \begin{bmatrix}\text{-contoid}\\ +\text{nasal}\end{bmatrix} \;/\; \_\_ ++\ S<S\#$$

In the environment created by Rule 7.2, Rule 8.3 deletes the suffix-final /n+ once it has caused the previous vowel to nasalize

**8.10 Stem-Final Nasal Deletion:**

$$[+\text{nasal}] \rightarrow \text{Ø} \;/\; \_\_\ ++ \begin{bmatrix}+\text{fricative}\\ \text{-surd}\\ \text{-high}\\ \text{-labial}\end{bmatrix}$$

Rule 8.10 accounts for the loss of /n+ in words such as *confusão* 'confusion', where their stem-final /d+ (cf. *confundir* 'to confuse') has occasioned the voicing of +sion++e's +s/.

**4.4 Syllable Boundary 2:**

$$\emptyset \rightarrow .\ /[\text{-contoid}]\ \_\_\ [+\text{contoid}] \left\{ \begin{matrix} [\text{-contoid}] \\ C_2 \end{matrix} \right\}$$

This rule establishes a syllable boundary whenever a vowel is followed by a consonant that is syllable initial, i.e. followed by a vowel or followed by /l/ or /r/.

**2.3 Atonic Vowel Reduction:**

$$\begin{pmatrix} \text{-contoid} \\ \text{-high} \\ \alpha\text{dorsal} \\ \text{-del. trans.} \end{pmatrix} \rightarrow \begin{pmatrix} +\text{wide glottis} \\ \text{-palatal} \\ \alpha\text{high} \\ \text{-low} \end{pmatrix} \ / \ \_\_\_\_ \ \left( \begin{pmatrix} +\text{contoid} \\ \left\{ \begin{matrix} [\text{-nasal}] \\ [\text{-lateral}] \\ [\text{-occlusion}] \end{matrix} \right\} \end{pmatrix} \right).$$

**4.5 Syllable Boundary 3:**

$$\emptyset \rightarrow .\ /\ [\text{-contoid}]\ \_\_ \begin{pmatrix} \text{-contoid} \\ \left\{ \begin{matrix} \text{-high} \\ +\text{delayed transition} \end{matrix} \right\} \end{pmatrix}$$

Rule 4.5 establishes syllable boundaries between contiguous vowels provided the second vowel is stressed or a non-high vowel, stressed or atonic. It accounts for +sion+'s bi-syllabicity when it occurs unchanged, i.e. *constituc<u>io</u>nal* 'constitutional'.

**Rule 4.6 Syllable Boundary 4:**

$$\emptyset \rightarrow .\ /\ C_4\_\_ \begin{pmatrix} +\text{contoid} \\ \left\{ \begin{matrix} +\text{nasal} \\ +\text{occlusion} \\ +\text{fricative} \end{matrix} \right\} \end{pmatrix}$$

This rule puts a syllable boundary between two abutting consonants provided the second consonant is not /r/ or /l/ (Tables 8B.3 and 8B.6).

**8.8b Loss of Stem-Final /p+ and /t+:**

$$\begin{pmatrix} \text{+occlusion} \\ \text{-high} \\ \text{+surd} \end{pmatrix} \rightarrow \text{Ø/ / \_\_++} \begin{pmatrix} \text{+contoid} \\ \text{+surd} \\ \text{-high} \end{pmatrix}$$

This rule deletes stem-final segments that may have precluded the reduction of atonic vowels (Tables 8B.3 and 8B.6).

**8.7 Deletion of +s/ After /z.t+:**

$$\begin{pmatrix} \text{+fricative} \\ \text{+surd} \\ \text{-labial} \\ \text{-high} \end{pmatrix} \rightarrow \text{Ø / [+fricative].} \begin{pmatrix} \text{+occlusion} \\ \text{–high} \\ \text{-labial} \\ \text{+surd} \end{pmatrix} \text{++ \_\_}$$

The only fricative that occurs syllable-finally /z/ so no further specification is needed for it to operate is /z/.

**8.4 Progressive Assimilation of Off-Glides:**

$$\begin{pmatrix} \text{-contoid} \\ \text{+high} \\ \text{-del. trans.} \end{pmatrix} \rightarrow \text{[+nasal] /} \begin{pmatrix} \text{-contoid} \\ \text{-high} \\ \text{+nasal} \end{pmatrix} \text{\_\_}$$

Rules 4.4–4.8 do not insert syllable boundaries between non-high vowels followed by high, unstressed vowels, so the reflexes of the gender morphemes +o# and +e+ ([ŭ] and [ĭ]) are off-glides which acquire the nasality /a/ and /o/ have owing to rules 7.1 and 8.3.

**Rule 8.12 Deletion of Root-Final /k, g, p, v, b/:**

$$\begin{pmatrix} +\text{contoid} \\ \begin{Bmatrix} +\text{dorsal} \\ +\text{labial} \end{Bmatrix} \end{pmatrix} \rightarrow \emptyset \;/\; \_\_ \;+\!+\; \begin{pmatrix} \begin{Bmatrix} +\text{occlusion} \\ +\text{fricative} \end{Bmatrix} \end{pmatrix}$$

/p+ → Ø is optional

Rule 8.12 deletes underlying stem-final dorsal and labial stops occurring before deriving suffixes beginning with occlusives or fricatives (Tables 8B.4 and 8B.5).

**Rule 4.8 Vowel Epenthesis After Syllable-Final Occlusives:**

Ø → [-contoid] / [+occlusive]__.

[-contoid] = /e/ [ĭ, ə] Portugal; /i/ [ĭ] Brazil

Rule 4.8 adds an epenthetic vowel to occlusives that are on the verge of emerging in syllable-final position. The actual vowel's prominence varies from region to region and speaker to speaker, as well as according to the particular care speakers might be taking in their diction, e.g. in formal as opposed to familiar registers (Table 8B.3).

**§8B.1.0** In this part of Appendix B, derivational tables demonstrate the generation of nominals containing the suffix +sion+.

**Table 8B.1** Derivation of Transparent Nouns Ending in +sion+

| | **pegação** | **benzeções** | **abrição** |
|---|---|---|---|
| U.Fs. | #pɛg++a#+sion++e+<Ø# | #benz++e#+sion++e+<z# | #abr++i++sion++e+<Ø# |
| 8.0 | *** | *** | *** |
| 8.1 | #pɛg++a#+san++o+<Ø# | *** | #abr++i++san++o+<Ø# |
| 8.2 | *** | #benz++e#+son++e+<z # | *** |
| 8.11 | *** | *** | *** |
| 8.5 | *** | *** | *** |
| 8.6 | *** | *** | *** |
| 3.1 | #pɛg++a#+sˈan++o+<Ø# | #benz++e#+sˈon++e+<z# | #abr++i++sˈan++o+<Ø# |
| 7.2 | #pɛg++a#+sˈãn++o+<Ø# | #benz++e#+sˈõn++e+<z# | #abr++i++sˈãn++o+<Ø# |
| 8.3 | #pɛg++a#+sˈã++o+<Ø# | #benz++e#+sˈõ++e+<z# | #abr++i++sˈã++o+<Ø# |
| 8.10 | *** | *** | *** |
| 4.4 | #pɛ.g++a.#+sˈã++o+<Ø# | #benz++e.#+sˈõ++e+<z# | #a.br++i.++sˈã++o+<Ø# |
| 2.3 | #pĭ.g++ă.#+sˈã++ŭ+<Ø# | #benz++ĭ.#+sˈõ++ĭ+<z# | #ă..br++i.++sˈã++ŭ+<Ø# |
| 4.5 | *** | *** | *** |
| 4.6 | *** | #ben.z++ĭ.#+sˈõ++ĭ+<z# | *** |
| 8.8b | *** | *** | *** |
| 8.7 | *** | *** | *** |
| 8.4 | #pɛ.g++ă#+sˈã++$^{ŭ}$+<Ø# | #benz++ĭ#+sˈõ++$^{ĭ}$+<z# | #ă.br++i.++sˈã++$^{ŭ}$+<Ø# |
| 8.12 | *** | *** | *** |
| 4.8 | *** | *** | *** |
| Ph. | [pə.ɣă.ˈsã̆$^{ŭ}$] | [bẽ$^{n}$.zĭ.ˈsã̆$^{ŭ}$] | [ă.βri.ˈsã̆$^{ŭ}$] |

**§8B.1.1.0** The deverbal nouns in Table 8B.1 are transparent, i.e. they emerge with their theme vowels unchanged. *Pegação* is a slang term meaning 'groping' or 'sexually scoring'. It is derived from the verb *pegar* 'to grab, nab'. *Benzeção* means 'repeated blessings' and its stem is *benze* '3rd blesses'. The word *bênção* 'blessing', derived from the same root, is more common. *Abrição* means 'repeated acts of opening'. All three nouns are of recent, rather spontaneous, coinage and demonstrate that the process of deverbal noun formation with this suffix is still productive.

§**8B.1.1.1** *Benzeções* is not susceptible to Rule 8.11, which merges theme vowel +e# with theme vowel +i+. Conversely, owing to the sequence /nz+, Rule 4.6 inserts a syllable boundary between these consonants. The other rules that apply here apply in all forms derived with +sion+ followed by a gender morpheme.

Table 8B.2 Loss of Theme Vowels +e# and +i+, Voicing of +s/

| | coesões | provisão | provisional |
|---|---|---|---|
| U.Fs. | #ko++ɛr++i++sion++e+<z# | #pro+vid++e#+sion++e+<Ø# | **#pro+vid++e#+sion+al#+e+<Ø#** |
| 8.0 | *** | *** | *** |
| 8.1 | *** | #pro+vid++e#+san++o+<Ø# | *** |
| 8.2 | #ko++ɛr++i++son++e+<z# | *** | *** |
| 8.11 | #ko++ɛr++son++e+<z# | #pro+vid++san++o+<Ø# | #pro+vid++sion+al#+e+<Ø# |
| 8.5 | #ko++ɛr++zon++e+<z# | #pro+vid++zan++o+<Ø# | #pro+vid++zion+al#+e+<Ø# |
| 8.6 | #ko++ɛ++zon++e+<z# | #pro+vi++zan++o+<Ø# | #pro+vi++zion+al#+e+<Ø# |
| 3.1 | #ko++ɛ++zˈon++e+<z# | #pro+vi++zˈan++o+<Ø# | #pro+vi++zion+ˈal#+e+<Ø# |
| 7.2 | #ko++ɛ++zˈõn++e+<z# | #pro+vi++zˈãn++o+<Ø# | *** |
| 8.3 | #ko++ɛ++zˈõ++e+<z# | #pro+vi++zˈã++o+<Ø# | *** |
| 8.10 | *** | *** | *** |
| 4.4 | #ko++ɛ++.zˈõ++e+<z# | #pro+.vi++.zˈã++o+<Ø# | #pro+.vi++.zio.n+ˈa.l#+e+<Ø# |
| 2.3 | #kŭ++ĭ.++zˈõ++ĭ+<z# | #prŭ.+vi.++zˈã++ŭ+<Ø# | #prŭ.+vi.++ziŭ.n+ˈa.l#+ĭ+<Ø# |
| 4.5 | #kŭ++ĭ.++zˈõ++ĭ+<z# | #prŭ.+vi.++zˈã++ŭ+<Ø# | #prŭ.+vi.++zi.ŭ.n+ˈa.l#+ĭ+<Ø# |
| 4.6 | *** | *** | *** |
| 8.8b | *** | *** | *** |
| 8.7 | #kŭ++.ĭ++zˈõ++$^{ĩ}$+<z# | #prŭ.+vi++.zˈã++$^{ũ}$<Ø# | #prŭ.+vi.++zi.ŭ.n+ˈa.l#+ĭ+<Ø# |
| 8.4 | *** | *** | *** |
| 8.12 | *** | *** | *** |
| 4.8 | *** | *** | *** |
| Ph. | [kŭ.ĭ.ˈzõ$^{ĩ}$š] | [prŭ.vi.ˈzã$^{ũ}$] | [prŭ.vi.si.ŭ.ˈnaɫ] |

§**8B.2** The nouns in Table 8B.2 mean 'cohesions, provision, provisional' and are derived from the verbal roots of *coerir* 'to cohere' and *prover* 'to provide'.[28] These forms, and many like them, undergo Rule 8.11, which causes their theme vowel's deletion and enables Rule 8.5, which voices +sion+'s initial segment. After that, Rule 8.6 accounts for the root-final consonants' deletion.

**Table 8B.3** Loss of +sion+'s +s and Stem-Final /t+

| | sugestão[a] | fluxão | opções |
|---|---|---|---|
| U.Fs. | #su++žɛzt++sion++e+<Ø# | #flukt++sion++e+<Ø# | #ɔp++t++sion++e+<z# |
| 8.0 | *** | *** | *** |
| 8.1 | #su++žɛzt++san++o+<Ø# | #flukt++san++o+<Ø# | *** |
| 8.2 | *** | *** | #ɔp++t++son++e+<z# |
| 8.11 | *** | *** | *** |
| 8.5 | *** | *** | *** |
| 8.6 | *** | *** | *** |
| 3.1 | #su++žɛzt++sˈan++o+<Ø# | #flukt++sˈan++o+<Ø# | #ɔp++t++sˈon++e+<z# |
| 7.2 | #su++žɛzt++sˈãn++o+<Ø# | #flukt++sˈãn++o+<Ø# | #ɔp++t++sˈõn++e+<z# |
| 8.3 | #su++žɛzt++sˈã++o+<Ø# | #flukt++sˈã++o+<Ø# | #ɔp++t++sˈõ++e+<z# |
| 8.10 | *** | *** | *** |
| 4.4 | #su++.žɛzt++sˈã++ŭ+<Ø# | *** | *** |
| 2.3 | #su.++žĭzt++sˈã++ũ+<Ø# | #flukt++sˈã++ŭ+<Ø# | #ɔp++t++sˈõ++ĭ+<z# |
| 4.5 | *** | *** | *** |
| 4.6 | #su.++žĭz.t++sˈã++ŭ+<Ø# | #fluk.t.++sˈã++ŭ+<Ø# | #ɔp.++t.++sˈõ++ĭ+<z# |
| 8.8b | *** | #fluk.++sˈã++ŭ+<Ø# | #ɔp.++sˈõ++ĭ+<z# |
| 8.7 | #su.++žĭz.t++ˈã++ŭ+<Ø# | *** | *** |
| 8.4 | *** | #fluk.++sˈã++$^{\text{ŭ}}$+<Ø# | #ɔp.++sˈõ++$^{\text{ĭ}}$+<z# |
| 8.12 | *** | *** | *** |
| 4.8 | *** | #flukə.++sˈã++$^{\text{ŭ}}$+<Ø# | #ɔpə.++sˈõ++$^{\text{ĭ}}$+<z# |
| Ph. | [su.ɣəš.ˈtã̃$^{\text{ŭ}}$] | [flu.kə.ˈsã̃$^{\text{ŭ}}$] | [ɔ.pə.ˈsõ$^{\text{ĭ}}$š] |

a So as not to complicate matters, the prefix #sub+ appears without its final /b+ (see Table 11.1c and §11.1.3.5).

§**8B.3** The words in Table 8B.3 mean 'suggestion, fluxion, options'. They are not derived from verbal roots, but from forms related to roots

28 Their roots are +ɛr+ and #vid+ cf. *inerir* 'to inhere' and *vidente* 'seer'. The prefix of *coerir* and its relatives is #kon+, but in this form the prefix loses its final /n+. See Tables 11.7, 11.8, §11.1.3.11 and Rules 11.2 and 11.3.

that occur in verbs: #sug+ in *sugerir* 'to suggest' (cf. *sugesta* 'suggestion, Brazilian slang'), #flu+ in *fluir* 'to flow' (cf. *fluctívago* 'rider of waves'). The verb *optar* #ɔp++t++a#+r#+e+ seems not to have an actual root, at least according to this analysis. As a prefix, #ɔp+ occurs in words such as *operar* #ɔp++ɛr++a#+r#+e+ 'to operate' (cf. *moderar* 'to moderate' root #mɔd+ from *modo* 'mode'). Three rules (8.8b, 8.7, and 4.8) function for the first time in this set. Rule 8.7 occasions the loss of +s/ after /zt/.[29] Rule 8.8b occasions the loss of (in this case) stem-final /t+ before +s/. Rule 4.8 may insert an epenthetic vowel between the root and the suffix in the surface forms of *fluxão* and *opções*.

**Table 8B.4** Loss of Root-Final /nd+ /k+, /p+

| | fusão | eduções | receções |
|---|---|---|---|
| U.Fs. | #fund++i++sion++e+<Ø# | #e+#duk++i++sion++e+<z# | #re++sɛp++e#+sion++e+<z# |
| 8.0 | *** | *** | *** |
| 8.1 | #fund++i++san++o#<Ø# | *** | *** |
| 8.2 | *** | #e+#duk++i++son++e+<z# | #re++sɛp++e++son++e+<z# |
| 8.11 | #fund++san++o#<Ø# | #e+#duk++son++e+<z# | #re++sɛp++son++e+<z# |
| 8.5 | #fund++zan++o#<Ø# | *** | *** |
| 8.6 | #fun++zan++o#<Ø# | *** | *** |
| 3.1 | #fun++zˈan++o#<Ø# | #e+#duk++sˈon++e+<z# | #re++sɛp++sˈon++e+<z# |
| 7.2 | #fun++zˈãn++o#<Ø# | #e+#duk++sˈõn++e+<z# | #re++sɛp++sˈõn++e+<z# |
| 8.3 | #fun++zˈã++o#<Ø# | #e+#duk++sˈõ++e+<z# | #re++sɛp++sˈõ++e+<z# |
| 8.10 | #fu++zˈã++o#<Ø# | *** | *** |
| 4.4 | #fu++.zˈã++o#<Ø# | #e+#.duk++sˈõ++e+<z# | #re++.sɛp++sˈõ++e+<z# |
| 2.3 | #fu.++.zˈã++ŭ#<Ø# | #ĭ+#.duk++sˈõ++ĭ+<z# | #rĭ.++.sɛp++sˈõ++ĭ+<z# |
| 4.5 | *** | *** | *** |
| 4.6 | *** | *** | #rĭ.++.sɛp++.sˈõ++ĭ+<z# |
| 8.6b | *** | *** | ***[a] |
| 8.7 | *** | *** | *** |
| 8.4 | #fu.++.zˈã++$^{\text{ŭ}}$#<Ø# | #ĭ+#.duk++sˈõ++$^{\text{ĭ}}$+<z# | #rĭ.++.sɛp++.sˈõ++$^{\text{ĭ}}$<z# |
| 8.12 | | #ĭ+#.du++sˈõ++$^{\text{ĭ}}$+<z# | #rĭ.++.sɛ++.sˈõ++$^{\text{ĭ}}$<z# |
| 4.8 | *** | *** | *** |
| Ph. | [fu.ˈzã̆$^{\text{ŭ}}$] | [ĭ.δu.ˈsõ$^{\text{ĭ}}$s̆] | [r̠ĭ.sɛ.ˈsõ$^{\text{ĭ}}$s̆] |

a Rule 8.8b could have deleted root final /p+.

29 Which, in this case, is both syllable-initial and syllable-final.

**§8B.4** The words in Table 8B.4 mean 'fusion, extracts, and receptions'. This table contains the first use of Rule 8.10, which deletes stem-final /n+ before suffix-initial +z/. Rule 8.12 functions here to delete stem-final /t+ and /p+ after Rule 2.3 has caused pretonic vowels not followed by tautosyllabic occlusive contoids to reduce.

**Table 8B.5** Non-verbal Root, Loss of Root Consonant, Pretonic Non-reduction, Theme Vowel Shift

| | ação | acionar | varrições |
|---|---|---|---|
| U.Fs. | #ag++sion++e+<Ø# | #ag++sion+a++r#+e+<Ø# | #var̲ ++e/#+sion++e+<z# |
| 8.0 | *** | *** | #var̲ ++i++sion++e+<z# |
| 8.1 | #ag++san++o+<Ø# | *** | *** |
| 8.2 | *** | *** | #var̲ ++i++son++e+<z# |
| 8.11 | *** | *** | *** |
| 8.5 | *** | *** | *** |
| 8.6 | *** | *** | *** |
| 3.1 | #ag++sˈan++o+<Ø# | #ag++sion+ˈa++r#+e+<Ø# | #var̲ ++i++sˈon++e+<z# |
| 7.2 | #ag++sˈãn++o+<Ø# | *** | #var̲ ++i++sˈõn++e+<z# |
| 8.3 | #ag++sˈã++o+<Ø# | *** | #var̲ ++i++sˈõ++e+<z# |
| 8.10 | *** | *** | *** |
| 4.4 | *** | #ag++sio.n+ˈa++.r#+e+<Ø# | #var̲ ++i++.sˈõ++e+<z# |
| 2.3 | #ag++sˈã++ŭ+<Ø# | #ag++siŭ.n+ˈa++.r#+ĭ+<Ø# | #vă.r̲ ++i++.sˈõ++ĭ+<z# |
| 4.5 | *** | #ag++si.ŭ.n+ˈa++.r#+ĭ+<Ø# | *** |
| 4.6 | #ag++.sˈã++ŭ+<Ø# | #ag++.si.ŭ.n+ˈa++.r#+ĭ+<Ø# | *** |
| 8.8b | *** | *** | *** |
| 8.7 | #ag++.sˈã++$^{\breve{u}}$+<Ø# | #ag++.siŭn+ˈa++r#+ĭ+<Ø# | *** |
| 8.4 | #ag++.sˈã++$^{\breve{u}}$+<Ø# | #ag++.si.ŭn+ˈa++r#+ĭ+<Ø# | #vă.r̲ ++i++.sˈõ++$^{\breve{\imath}}$+<z# |
| 8.12 | #a++.sˈã++$^{\breve{u}}$+<Ø# | #a++.si.ŭn+ˈa++r#+ĭ+<Ø# | *** |
| 4.8 | *** | *** | *** |
| Ph. | [a.ˈsã̃$^{\breve{u}}$] | [a.si.ŭ.ˈnar] | [vă.r̲ i.ˈsõ$^{\breve{\imath}}$š] |

**§8B.5.0** The words in Table 8B.5 mean 'action/stock share, to activate, sweepings'. The words *ação* and *acionar* provide two more examples of the presence of occlusive consonants in syllable-final position (in this case, /g/), which impedes the reduction of pretonic vowels. Rule 8.12's following Rule 2.3 allows for this outcome. In the phonology section, low level iterations of Rule 4.4 operate to establish the syllable boundary between /a/ and /s/.

**§8B.5.1** The word *varrição* is a Brazilianism with synonyms such as *varredura* and *varredela*. In São Paulo state, it also denotes the action of collecting coffee beans fallen to the ground before the coffee harvest actually begins in earnest. Its form is accounted for by Rule 8.0, which also applies to nine other 2nd conjugation stems whose theme vowel shifts from +e# to +i+ before +sion+ and other suffixes: *absorver*➔*absorvição* 'to absorb, absorption'; *põe*➔*posição* '3rd puts, position' (29 derivatives); *bater*➔*batição* 'to beat, beating'; *correr*➔*corrição* 'to run, act of running'; *lambe*➔*lambição* 'to lick, act of licking'; *meter*➔*metição* 'to insert, insertion'; *vender*➔*vendição* 'to sell, act of selling'; *perder*➔*perdição* 'to lose, perdition'.

**Table 8B.6** Ordering Shift

| | tenções | cessão | expansionista |
|---|---|---|---|
| U.Fs. | #tɛnd++e#+sion++e+<z# | #sɛd++e#+sion++e+<Ø# | #ez++pand++i++sion++izt++a# |
| 8.0 | *** | *** | *** |
| 8.1 | *** | #sɛd++e#+san++o#<Ø# | *** |
| 8.2 | #tɛnd+e#+son++e+<z# | *** | *** |
| 8.6 | *** | *** | *** |
| 3.1 | #tɛnd+e#+sˈon++e+<z# | #sɛd++e#+sˈan++o#<Ø# | #ez++pand++i++sion++ˈizt++a# |
| 7.2 | #tɛnd+e#+sˈõn++e+<z# | #sɛd++e#+sˈãn++o#<Ø# | *** |
| 8.3 | #tɛnd+e#+sˈõ++e+<z# | #sɛd++e#+sˈã++o#<Ø# | *** |
| 8.5 | *** | *** | *** |
| 8.11 | #tɛnd+sˈõ++e+<z# | #sɛd++sˈã++o#<Ø# | #ez++pand++sion++ˈizt++a# |
| 8.10 | *** | *** | *** |
| 4.4 | #tɛndsˈõ++e+<z# | #sɛd++sˈã++o#<Ø# | #ez+pand++sio.n++ˈizt++a# |
| 2.3 | #tɛndsˈõ++ĭ+<z# | #sɛd++sˈã+ŭ#<Ø# | #ĭz++pand++siŭ.n++ˈizt++ă# |
| 4.5 | *** | *** | #ĭz++pand++si.ŭ.n++ˈizt++ă# |
| 4.6 | #tɛn.dsˈõ++ĭ+<z# | #sɛd++sˈã+ŭ#<Ø# | #ĭz++pan.d++si.ŭ.n++ˈiz.t++ă# |
| 8.8b | #tɛn.sˈõ++ĭ+<z# | #sɛ++sˈã+ŭ#<Ø# | #ĭz++pan++si.ŭ.n++ˈiz.t++ă# |

(*Continued*)

Table 8B.6 Continued

| | tenções | cessão | expansionista |
|---|---|---|---|
| 8.7 | *** | *** | *** |
| 8.4 | #tɛn.sˈõ++$^{\tilde{\imath}}$+<z# | #sɛ++sˈã+$^{\tilde{u}}$#<Ø# | *** |
| 8.12 | *** | *** | *** |
| 4.8 | *** | *** | *** |
| Ph. | [tẽ$^{n}$.ˈsõ$^{\breve{\tilde{\imath}}}$š] | [sə.ˈsã̆$^{\breve{\tilde{u}}}$] | [əš.pã̆n.si.ŭ.ˈniš.tă] |

**§8B.6** The words in Table 8B.6 mean ‘intension, grant, expansionist’ They are deverbal nouns plausibly derived from the verbs *tender* ‘to lean’, *ceder* ‘to cede’, and *expandir* ‘to expand’. The roots of these verbs all end in /d+, which (Tables 8B.2 and 8B.4) normally entails the voicing of +sion+’s +s/ when the root and suffix abut. And the root-final /d+ evanesces in these cases, which Rule 8.6 accounts for. The only solution in the framework presented here is to reorder the rules, placing Rule 8.5 before 8.11 at a later point in the derivation (shaded lines). Otherwise, these derivations are unremarkable.

## Appendix C D’Andrade Pardal’s Analysis of Deverbal Noun Formation: Suffix +sion++e+

**§8C.0** This appendix examines selected analyses in D’Andrade Pardal’s proposed grammar of deverbal nominals using the suffix identified in this treatise as +sion++e+. Its purpose is to show that the tenets generative phonologists used at the time Pardal finished his work were too unconstrained to provide a plausible grammar of the phenomena associated with this suffix.

**§8C.1** D’Andrade Pardal’s analysis was original and insightful within the relatively unconstrained version of generative phonology in vogue at that time. He sought to derive all the nouns in question from a single underlying pattern, but his postulates are sometimes at odds with Portuguese phonotactics, and at times they only exist to support his deriving all forms from the same underlying pattern. All this is to say D’Andrade Pardal’s **approach** (a grammar of its time) rather than his **effort** was inadequate. However, without D’Andrade Pardal’s work, insight concerning this suffix would be harder to come by, and any efforts to propound a grammar for this suffix would be much more strenuous. Thank you for your work and insight, Ernesto D’Andrade Pardal, may you rest in peace.

**§8C.2.0** Table 8C.1 contains lexical items representative of the output of his grammar, as well as of the grammar propounded in this chapter.

Table 8C.1 D'Andrade Pardal's Data

| Verb | Gloss | Adjective | Gloss | Noun | Gloss |
|---|---|---|---|---|---|
| (1) /t/ ⇔ /s/ | | | | | |
| **permitir** | to permit | **permissivo** | permissive | **permissão** | permission |
| **delatar** | to betray | **delatável** | betrayable | **delação** | betrayal |
| (2) /d/ ⇔ /s/ | | | | | |
| **expandir** | to expand | **expansivo** | expansive | **expansão** | expansion |
| **agredir** | to aggress | **agressivo** | aggressive | **agressão** | aggression |
| (3) /z/ ⇔ /t/ ⇔ /s/ | | | | | |
| **seduzir** | to seduce | **sedutor** | seductive | **sedução** | seduction |
| **dizer** | to say | **ditador** | dictator | **dicção** | diction |
| (4) /ž/ ⇔ /t/ ⇔ /s/ | | | | | |
| **dirigir** | to direct | **directivo** | directive | **direcção** | address |
| **agir** | to act | **ator** | ator | **ação** | action |
| (5) Ø ⇔ /t/ ⇔ /s/ | | | | | |
| **criar** | to create | **criativo** | creative | **criação** | creation |
| **perder** | to lose | **perdedor** | losing | **perdição** | perdition |
| **parir** | to whelp | **paridora** | fertile | **pariçao** | parturition |
| (6) /d/ ⇔ /z/ | | | | | |
| **dividir** | to divide | **divisor** | divisor | **divisão** | division |
| **confundir** | to confuse | **confuso** | confused | **confusão** | confusion |
| (7) /r/ ⇔ /z/ | | | | | |
| **aderir** | to adhere | **adesivo** | adhesive | **adesão** | adhesion |
| **adquirir** | to acquire | **adquisitivo** | acquisitive | **adquisição** | acquisition |
| (8) ø ⇔ /z/ | | | | | |
| **corroer** | to rust | **corrosivo** | corrosive | **corrosão** | corrosion |
| **incluir** | to include | **inclusive** | inclusive | **inclusão** | inclusion |
| (9) /b/ or /v/ ⇔ ø | | | | | |
| **receber** | to receive | **recetivo** | receptive | **receção**[a] | reception |
| **descrever** | to describe | **descritivo** | descriptive | **descrição** | description |
| (10) ø ⇔ /n/ | | | | | |
| **reter** | to retain | **retentor** | retainer | **retenção** | retention |
| **convir** | to agree | **conveniente** | convenient | **convenção** | convention |

a In D'Andrade Pardal's day, the nominals' orthographic forms contained the root final /p+: *receptivo* and *recepção*.

This review examines two types of nominal derivation with the suffix in question: an apparently transparent set and an opaque set, which will suffice to demonstrate the cumbrous and contrived nature of this pioneering attempt at devising a grammar of deverbal nouns formed with this suffix.

**§8C.2.1** In his analysis, nouns such as those in Section 5 have underlying forms consisting of (A) a verbal root, (B) a theme vowel, (C) the participle morpheme (+t+), plus the noun-deriving suffix +ion+e+: [Noun[V[V root + TV] PP] +ion+e+].[30] Indeed, this is the lexical pattern he proposes for all the types of nouns in Table 8C.1. The words in Section 5 demonstrate the emergence of the underlying theme vowels. D'Andrade Pardal justifies the suffix's underlying vowels by citing words resulting from the addition of another deriving suffix, e.g. +izm+o#: *criação*➔*criacionismo* 'creationism'. The presence of /t/ in *criativo* indicates that the participle morpheme is part of the stem to which +ion+e+ attaches. Table 8C.2 demonstrates the five steps his account needs to derive the nominals *criação*, *perdição*, and *parição* from their participial bases.

**Table 8C.2** Straightforward Derivation à la D'Andrade Pardal

| Lexemes | #kri+a+t+ion+e+ | #pɛrd+e+t+ion+e+ | #par+i++t+ion+e+ |
|---|---|---|---|
| **(1) Theme Vowel Neutralization:** +e# ➔ +i+/ ____ Participle | | | |
| | *** | #pɛrd+i+t+ion+e+ | *** |
| **(2) Paroxytone Stress:** | | | |
| | #kri+a+t+i'on+e+ | #pɛrd+i+t+i'on+e+ | #par+i+t+i'on+e+ |
| **(3) Dental Softening:** /t/ ➔ /s/ / ___/i/V | | | |
| | #kri+a+s+i'on+e+ | #pɛrd+i+s+i'on+e+ | #par+i+s+i'on+e+ |
| **(4) Deletion of /i/:** /i/ ➔ Ø/ +___ 'V | | | |
| | #kri+a+s+'on+e+ | #pɛrd+i+s+'on+e+ | #par+i+s+'on+e+ |
| **(5) Evolution of +on+e+ to +ão#**[a] | | | |
| | **[kri.ă.'sɐ̃ᶷ]** | **[pər.di.'sɐ̃ᶷ]** | **[pă.r.i.'sɐ̃ᶷ]** |

a This 'rule' is an abbreviation of a large set of rules (D'Andrade Pardal 32–40). One may take them for granted in the remainder of this exposition.

30 Since morpheme boundaries were not an issue in D'Andrade Pardal's system, in this review single boundaries, both represent his approach and save space in some of the tables.

**§8C.2.2 Step 1:** The neutralization of $2^{nd}$ and $3^{rd}$ conjugation theme vowels, where +e# merges with +i+, is much more general. In addition to its occurring before the participle morpheme of regular (and many irregular) verbs, it occurs in the imperfect indicative (cf. $2^{nd}$ conjugation *comes* 'you eat', *comeste* 'you ate', and *comias* 'you used to eat' with $3^{rd}$ conjugation *sair* 'to leave', *saíste* 'you left', *saías* 'you used to leave'), and before certain other deriving suffixes such as +ment++o#, e.g. *manter* 'to maintain' *mantimento* 'maintenance' (§13.3.3.0-3.).

**§8C.2.3 Step 2:** This suffix is always tonic when it is a word's last derivational morpheme, and it is not normally stressed when another deriving morpheme follows it.

**§8C.2.4 Step 3:** D'Andrade Pardal's rule of dental softening (114, 169) is the following:

**Rule 8C.1 Dental Softening, SPE Features:**

$$\begin{bmatrix}-\text{sonorant}\\ +\text{anterior}\\ +\text{coronal}\\ -\text{voice}\end{bmatrix} \rightarrow [+\text{continuant}] \ / \ [+\ \text{sonorant}]\ \_\_\ + \begin{bmatrix}-\text{consonantal}\\ +\text{high}\\ -\text{round}\end{bmatrix} [+\text{syl.}]$$

Rule 8C.1 would have to be restricted to apply to strings of segments containg the participle morpheme because there are ample examples of its failure to apply on a purely phonological level: cf. *garantir* 'to guarantee' and *garantia* 'guarantee', *apático* 'apathetic' *apatia* 'apathy', *hematólogo* 'hematologist' *hematia* 'erythrocyte', as well as *doente* 'sick', *doentio* 'sickly', *valente* 'brave', *valentia* 'bravery'. In all of these cases, there is a morpheme boundary between the /i/ and the following vowel, but the preceding /t+ fails to spirantize because it is not the morpheme +t+.

§**8C.2.5 Step 4:** There are several (unacknowledged) exceptions to D'Andrade Pardal's rule (120, 169):

$$i \rightarrow \emptyset \ / \ + \ \_\_ \begin{pmatrix} \text{vowel} \\ +\text{stress} \end{pmatrix}$$

which was designed to delete /i/ when it precedes a stressed vowel across a morpheme boundary, as in Table 8C.2. *rebelião* 'rebellion' and the 132 others like it in the *Aurélio*. The lexical form of this word would be #re+bεl+i+on+e+ (cf. *rebelar*, to rebel). Similarly, the *Aurélio* contains 460 words ending in *–ial* similar to *superficial* 'superficial' and *familial* 'familial'. The /i/ preceding the suffix +al+, whose vowel is stressed does not disappear—notwithstanding such suffixes' structural similarity to that of the rule: e.g. #super#fis+i+ˈal+e+, #famili+ˈal#+e+.

§**8C.2.6** The generation of the transparent forms in Table 8C.2's Section 5 is straightforward; however, Rules 3 and 4, while essential for the success of D'Andrade Pardal's derivation, have scant motivation elsewhere in Portuguese phonotactics. That is, there are 368 nominals in the *Aurélio* that are immune to the dental softening rule. This is not to say that a rule could not be written to generate the dental softening D'Andrade Pardal postulates—such a rule would simply have to be restricted to the participle morpheme. The rule of /i/ deletion before a stressed vowel would have to be made much more specific so as to allow for the exceptions pointed out. The other rules, and those implied in Step 5 of Table 8C.2, are independently motivated. And one must admit that his analysis accounts for a tremendous amount of data.

§**8C.3.0** Whereas for Table 8C.2 the output of the grammar is relatively transparent, the forms in Table 8C.3 are opaque.

Table 8C.3 D'Andrade Pardal's Derivation of /z/-initial Suffixes[a]

| **Words** | **divisão (cf. dividir)** | **adesão (cf. aderir)** | **corrosão (cf. corroer)** |
|---|---|---|---|
| **Lexemes** | /divid+i*+t+ion+e+ | #adɛr+i*+t+ion+e+ | #kon+rǫd+e*+t+ion+e+[b] |
| **(1) Theme vowel neutralization:** +e# → +i+/ ____ Participle | | | |
| | *** | *** | #kon+rǫd+i*+t+ion+e+ |
| **(1a) Deletion of theme vowels with asterisk*** | | | |
| | /divid+t+ion+e+ | #adɛr+t+ion+e+ | #kon+rǫd+i+tion+e+ |
| **(1b) Stem-final /d/ becomes /z/ after a vowel and followed by +t+** | | | |
| | /diviz+t+ion+e+ | *** | #kon+rǫz+t+ion+e+ |
| **(1c) Stem-final /r/ becomes /z/ before +t+** | | | |
| | *** | #adɛz+t+ion+e+ | *** |
| **(1d) A +t+ following a /z/ is deleted** | | | |
| | /diviz+ion+e+ | #adɛz+ion+e+ | #kon+rǫz+ion+e+ |
| **Steps 2–5 from Table 8C.2** | | | |
| | **[di.vi.ˈzã̃$^{\tilde{u}}$]** | **[ă.ðe.ˈzã̃$^{\tilde{u}}$]** | **[kŭ.r̲ o.ˈzã̃$^{\tilde{u}}$]** |

a The words in Table 8C.3 appear in sections 6, 7, and 8 of Table 8C.1. The rules used for these words also work for Section 8's *incluir* and its relatives *excluir* 'to exclude', *ocluir* 'to occlude' and *concluir* 'to conclude' since their root is +klud+—cf. *excludente, concludente*. Thus, when all these verbal stems acquire the suffix in question, they occasion /z/'s emergence instead of /s/.
b The /d+ of the *corrosão*'s lexical form is motivated by its appearance in the word *corrodente* 'corrosive agent'.

**§8C.3.1 Step 1a:**[31] Step 1a allows the underlying forms in Table 8A.3 to conform to D'Andrade Pardal's postulated base for all words derived with this suffix. In addition, it juxtaposes the stem-final voiced consonant with the +t+ of these words' participle. Placing asterisks after these theme vowels establishes a class of deverbal nouns in which the theme vowel disappears when the nominal suffix in question is added.

**§8C.3.2.0 Step 1b:** There is scant phonetic motivation for Rule 1b, except that two stops rarely abut in Portuguese. However, at least in the analysis advocated in this book, /z/ regularly closes syllables before following word-internal syllable-initial consonants (see Tables 4.3, 4.5, 4.10, 4.26). In addition, /d+ emerges as [d] before both /s/ and /z/: *adsorção* 'absorption' #ad+#sɔr++sion++e+_ and *adscrever* 'to ascribe' #ad++zkrɛv++e#+r#+e+. D'Andrade Pardal's spirantization of

31 Since Rules 1 and 2–5 have been demonstrated above, only the new ones, 1a-1d need commentary here.

/d+ and progressive assimilation of +t+ are strategems whose only use is to propel these forms toward the surface. They represent no phonologically motivated pattern in the language.

§8C.3.2.1 Beyond this, D'Andrade Pardal's postulated ontogeny of words such as these is contra-historical. In Vulgar Latin's evolution into Portuguese, a syllable-final consonant, which was also morpheme-final, often evanesced leaving an off-glide in its place: *acceptare* ➔ *aceitar* 'to accept', *recipere—recepta*➔*receita* 'receipt', *altero*➔*outro* 'other', *factum*➔*feito* 'deed', *captivum* ➔ *cautivo* 'captive'. This is by far the more natural evolution of potentially syllable-final consonants in the passage from Latin to Portuguese, and, as one can see, the erstwhile presence of syllables closed originally by consonants and later by glides is structure-preserving—the syllable initial and morpheme-initial consonant remains. In addition, the syllable/morpheme-final consonant loses its contoidal property, which is exactly the opposite of what D'Andrade Pardal proposed in the derivation of these words—the morpheme-final consonant occasions the loss of a morpheme-initial consonant in Step 1d.

§8C.3.3 **Step 1c**: At this point, D'Andrade Pardal has /r/ becoming /z/ before a +t+, which again flies in the face of Portuguese phonotactics because /r/ occurs predominantly before /t/ (Table 4.26). There is, of course, a notable /r/ ⇔ /z/ alternation in Portuguese, as Table 8C.4 demonstrates:

**Table 8C.4** Unconditioned Alternation /r/ ⇔ /z/

| Root with /r/ | Gloss | Root with /z/ | Gloss |
|---|---|---|---|
| **querer** | to want | **quiseste** | you wanted |
| **adquirir** | to acquire | **adquisitivo** | acquisitive |
| **direi** | I shall say | **dizer** | to say |
| **farei** | I shall do | **fazer** | to do |
| **trarei** | I shall bring | **trazer** | to bring |

But there is nothing in these words to condition this alternation.[32] And, beyond this, there are 52 examples of /r/'s preceding the +t+ of a past

32 The etymons of *dizer*, *fazer*, and *trazer* are *dicere*, *facere* and *trahere*. The roots that form the future indicative tense (#dir+, #far+, #trar+) are probably Vulgar Latin innovations (Williams, 207).

participle: e.g. *morto* from *morrer* 'to die', *torto* from *torcer* 'to twist', *coberto* from *cobrir* 'to cover', *liberto* from *liberar* 'to free'. Again, a contra-natural, deus-ex-machina morphophonemic sound change makes this analysis work.

**3C.2.4 Step 1d:** Similar to the critique of Step 1a, a rule that deletes /t/ after a morpheme-final /z/, which was originally a /d/ or an /r/, is totally contrary to the overwhelming Portuguese phonotactic pattern. The phoneme /z/ is the second most frequent syllable-final consonant (Table 4.26), and it occurs most frequently before /t/.

**§8C.4.0 Concerning Section 2 of Table 8C.1,** D'Andrade Pardal advances the following steps to derive *expansão* 'expansion' from the stem of *expandir* 'to expand', *agressão* 'agression' from the stem of *agredir* 'to agress', and *gestão* 'management' from the stem of *gerir* 'to manage'. What is problematic in this set of words is that the verbal stems end in /d/ and /r/, which in the previous set of words occasions the emergence of /z/ in their suffixes, whereas here the suffix-initial segment is /s/. Table 8A.5 omits the already familiar steps and shows those necessary to achieve the resultant words.

Table 8A.5 D'Andrade Pardal's Derivation of /s/-initial Suffixes

| Words | expansão | agressão | gestão |
|---|---|---|---|
| Lexemes | #ez+pand+i*+t+ion+e | #ad+grɛd+i*+t+ion+e | #žɛr+i*+t+ion+e$_{\text{[-step 5]}}$ |
| (1, 1a) Theme vowel neutralization: and deletion | | | |
| | #ez+pand+t+ion+e | #ad+grɛd+t+ion+e | #žɛr+t+ion+e |
| (2a) Insert /s/ in +gred+ roots | | | |
| | *** | #ad+grɛsd+t+ion+e | *** |
| (3a) /d+ → /s+ | | | |
| | #ez+pans+t+ion+e | #ad+grɛss+t+ion+e | *** |
| (4a) Stem-final /r+ becomes /z+ before +t+ | | | |
| | *** | *** | #žɛz+t+ion+e |
| (5a) A +t+ following an /s/ is deleted | | | |
| | #ez+pans+ion+e | #ad+grɛss+ion+e | *** |
| (6a) Deletion of like segments | | | |
| | *** | #ad+grɛs+ion+e | *** |
| Rules 2–5 from Table 8C.2 | | | |
| | [əš.pã̆$^{n}$.ˈsã̆$^{\tilde{u}}$] | [ă.ɣrɛ.ˈsã̆$^{\tilde{u}}$] | [žəš.ˈtã̆$^{\tilde{u}}$] |

**§8C.4.1 Lexemes:** Again, these lexical forms have their theme vowels flagged for deletion, i.e. they would be the same class of nouns as those in Table 8C.3 were it not for their need for lexeme-specific rules, such as those in steps 2a through 6a in Table 8C.5. Of special note is the last lexeme #žɛr+i*+t+ion+$e_{[\text{-step 5}]}$, marked as immune to Step 5, although such marking was not necessary since at the stage in the derivation where forms undergo Step 5, the consonantal abutment is /zt/ rather than /st/.[33]

**§8C.4.2 Step 2:** D'Andrade Pardal's rule (137) is Ø → /s/ / [[X e___ $d]_V]_{N, A}$, which is certainly an ad hoc rule peculiar to only the four verbs whose root is +grɛd+. This rule serves no other purpose in the language beyond the derivation of these nouns and is contrary to any phonotactic process in the language.

**§8C.343 Step 3:** Likewise, there is no independent motivation for turning the morphophoneme /d/ into /s/. This step's sole purpose is to edge underlying forms toward the surface.

**§8C.4.4 Step 4:** A rule that turns syllable- and morpheme-final /r/ into /z/ is contrary to Portuguese phonotactic patterns.

**§8C.345 Step 5:** Had D'Andrade Pardal considered the potential syllable-final fricative to be /z/ rather than /s/ (26), a step that deletes a /t/ preceded by an /s/ could have been at least argued for because the sequence /st/ at the morphophonemic level does not occur, again at least in the analysis proposed in this book, and could rightly undergo deletion.

**§8C.4.6 Step 6:** This is a general rule of Portuguese: like segments reduce to a single instantiation (§4.4.1.2.2).[34]

**§8C.5** These examples do not come close to exhausting D'Andrade Pardal's efforts to account for the various nouns ending in ['sã͂ᵘ] or ['zã͂ᵘ] and their derivatives. They are pitfalls entailed in his effort to derive all the forms ending in this suffix from a unitary base, in this case [Noun[V[V root + TV] PP] +ion+e+]. D'Andrade Pardal's need for diacritics to indicate a vast number of theme vowels that delete, for special (and unmotivated) rules for different classes of roots, for

33 In addition, this form is immune to step 1d, which deletes +t+ after /z+.

34 Rule 4.1 does not obtain for sequences of /a/ in Iberian Portuguese. Iberian Portuguese contrasts pretonic /a/ with /aa/: *a casa* 'the house' is realized as [ă.'ka.ză], whereas *à casa* 'to the house' #a>#l++a>#kaz++a# emerges as [a.'ka.ză].

consonantal abutments, and for /r/ ⇔ /z/ alternation caused him to establish, implicitly, only two different classes of nouns formed with the suffix in question plus several sub-classes. The real problem with his analysis comes from his need to establish ad hoc rules to generate the forms that actually occur. Non-unitary bases for subcategories of these deverbal nouns operate with rules that reflect phonological processes and do not play tendentiously with the bases nor with the forms intervening between the bases and the phonetic outcomes.

# 9 The Morphophonology of Number and Gender: Problematic Nominals

## Introduction

**§9.0.0** Chapter 6 has addressed the phenomena related to the pluralization of all but the 'problematic' nominals. Chapter 8 has proposed an account for the morphophonemic patterns associated with the suffix +sion+e+ in its word-final and word-internal instantiations. To begin the final treatment of problematic nominals, Table 9.1 (i.e. Table 6B.1) presents gender and number morphemes and exceptions in their employment:

**Table 9.1** Nominative Morphology: Gender and Number

| Number and Gender Morphemes | | | Exceptions | | | |
|---|---|---|---|---|---|---|
| Gender→ | [±f.] → | {+,< } {e+,<} | [-f.] +a# | Gloss | [+f.], +o#, +u# | Gloss |
| | [+f.] → | {+,<} a# | **samba** [-f.] | samba | **foto** [+f.] | photo |
| | [-f.] → | {+,<} o# | **capeta** [-f.] | devil | **tribo** [+f.] | tribe |
| | [-f.] → | {+,<} u# | **estafeta** [-f.] | courrier | **nau** [+f.] | ship |
| | | | | | | |
| Number → | [±plural] | | | | | |
| | [+plural] → | <z# | | | | |
| | [-plural] → | <Ø# | | | | |

**§9.0.1** Table 9.1 demonstrates that grammatical gender in Portuguese is a more complicated category than number, singular or plural, with [+plural] being the marked case signaled by <z#. As an inflectional morpheme, <z# applies to every nominal. Gender is likewise binary: it is either [+feminine] or [-feminine], and unmarked gender is, simply, not exclusively feminine. However, gender can be an inflectional or derivational phenomenon. And vowel /e/ occurs in four different relationships with nominal stems. These relationships are: +e+ a

word-final derivational, ambivalent, and deletable gender morpheme; +e# a word-final derivational, ambivalent, and non-deletable gender morpheme; <e+ a word-final inflectional, ambivalent, and deletable gender morpheme; and <e# a word-final inflectional, ambivalent, and non-deletable gender morpheme. In addition, the other morphemes that signal predominately [-feminine] (+o#), or [+feminine] (+a#) sometimes occur on nouns of the opposite gender.

**§9.0.2.0** Tables 9.2a–c contain representative examples of nominals whose inflectional phenomena are such that they merit the adjective 'problematic':

**Table 9.2a** Problematic Nasal Phenomena

| Nouns | | | | Adjectives | | | |
|---|---|---|---|---|---|---|---|
| -pl. | +pl. | +fem. | Gloss | -pl. | +pl. | +fem. | Gloss |
| **estação** | **estações** | *** | season(s) | **chorão** | **chorões** | **chorona(s)** | weepy |
| **patrão** | **patrões** | **patrona(s)**[a] | bosses | **ancião** | **anciãos** | **anciã(s)** | agèd |
| **irmão** | **irmãos** | **irmã(s)**[b] | sibling(s) | **comum** | **comuns** | ± | common |
| **cão** | **cães** | **cadela(s)** | dog(s) | **ruim** | **ruins** | ± | bad |
| **guardião** | **guardiães** | **guardiã(s)** | guardian(s) | **marrom** | **marrons** | ± | brown |
| **origem** | **origens** | *** | origin(s) | **bom** | **bons** | **boa** | good |
| **pinguim** | **pinguins** | ± | penguin(s) | **jovem** | **jovens** | ± | young |
| **tom** | **tons** | - | tone(s) | **tremecém** | **tremecéns** | ± | 3 month |

a There is another [+feminine] form of this word: *patroa*, which is an affectionate term for 'wife'.

b Other [+feminine] forms containing a word-final stressed [ã] include: *anciã, pagã, cidadã, escrivã, guardiã, louçã, sacristã, vilã, anã, cristã, cortesã, alemã, catalã, aldeã, anfitriã, campeã, castelã, cirugiã, ermitã, tabeliã*—respectively: 'old woman, pagan, citizen, scribe, guardian, pretty, sacristan, village, dwarf. Christian, courtesan, German, Catalan, villager, hostess, champion, hermit, notary'.

**Table 9.2b** Problematic Lateral Phenomena

| Nouns | | | | Adjectives | | | |
|---|---|---|---|---|---|---|---|
| -pl. | +pl. | +f. | Gloss | -pl. | +pl. | +f. | Gloss |
| **donzel** | **donzéis** | **donzela(s)** | virgin(s) | **civil** | **civis** | ± | civil |
| **funeral** | **funerais** | *** | funeral(s) | **útil** | **utéis** | ± | useful |
| **barril** | **barris** | *** | barrel(s) | **igual** | **iguais** | ± | equal |
| **sol** | **sóis** | *** | sun(s) | **cruel** | **cruéis** | ± | cruel |
| **bulbul** | **bulbuis** | ± | bubul(s) (bird) | **crível** | **críveis** | ± | believable |
| **bagual** | **baguais** | **baguala(s)** | wild horse(s) | **azul** | **azuis** | ± | blue |
| **cônsul** | **cônsules** | **consulesa(s)** | consul(s) | **espanhol** | **espanhóis** | **espanhola(s)** | Spanish |

Table 9.2c Problematic word-final /z# Phenomena

| Nouns | | | | Adjectives | | | |
|---|---|---|---|---|---|---|---|
| -pl. | +pl. | +f. | Gloss | -pl. | +pl. | +f. | Gloss |
| nunes | nunes | *** | odd number(s) | simples | simples | ± | simple |
| maricas | maricas | *** | fairy, (ies) | grátis | grátis | ± | free |
| tebas | tebas | ± | big shot(s) | traquinas | traquinas | ± | naughty |
| trombelas | trombelas | ± | sourpuss(es) | somenos | somenos | ± | inferior |
| ónus | ónus | *** | onus(es) | piegas | piegas | ± | maudlin |
| bónus | bónus | *** | bonus(es) | reles | reles | ± | no good |
| ónix | ónix | *** | onix(es) | tortelos | tortelos | ± | cross-eyed |

Tables 92a-c show that plural and gender inflection entail morphophonemic phenomena associated with nasality, with word-final /l#, and with word-final /z#.

§9.0.2.1 **Morphophonemics and Nasality:** Chapter 8 has shown that the word-final, non-plural instantiation of +sion++e+ as [ˈsã̃ũ] comes from the merger of four suffixes: +sion++e+, +on++e+, and +an++e+/+an+<o# (Rule 8.1). The plural morpheme added to words ending in +sion++e+ occasions another merger in which the sequence /ion+ merges with the suffix +on+, and the gender morpheme +e+ (indicating [+feminine]) remains and emerges because it is followed by <z#, i.e. it is not in word-final position. To achieve the word-final singular and plural forms of such words requires five steps: (A) Paroxytone stress applies to their suffixes' first vowel. (B) The intervocalic /n+ causes the stressed vowel's nasalization. (C) The gender morphemes' posttonic position causes their vowels (/o/ and /e/) to rise to [ŭ] and [ĭ]. (D) Their posttonic/postvocalic position causes them to form off-glides once the /n+ evanesces. (E) Finally, these vocoids' status as off-glides allows them to undergo progressive assimilation of the previous vowel's nasality.

§9.0.2.2 The second set of nasal phenomena in Table 9.2a (nouns typified by *origem*, *pinguim*, and *tom*; adjectives typified by *comum*, *ruim*, *marrom*, *bom*, and *jovem*) are more problematic than they might seem. One could be tempted to consider them totally regular, with word-final m and pre-plural n as mere spelling conventions, but their forms are more complicated owing to the underlying presence of gender morphemes, and metatheses entailing the gender morpheme and the stressed vowel of certain deriving suffixes.

§9.0.3 **Morphophonemics and Laterals (Table 9.2b):** Nominals whose [-feminine, -plural] forms end in /l# normally lose the /l# when inflected for plurality. All the adjectives, except *espanhol*, can modify either [-feminine] or [+feminine] nouns indifferently, be they [±plural]. The three nouns denoting live beings (*donzel*, *bagual*, and *consul*), like *espanhol*, have [+feminine] forms whose /l# does not evanesce when pluralized (*donzelas*, *bagualas*, *consulesas*, and *espanholas*). The plural forms of the [-feminine] nouns and adjectives all evince the presence of the ambivalent gender morpheme +e+. The only nominals that merit special attention vis à vis their plural forms are those whose singular forms end in /il#, both stressed and atonic.

§9.0.4 **Morphophonemics and /z# (Table 9.2c):** The final anomaly in plural formation are the nominals that end in orthographic s̱, z, or x (/z#). Whereas they may refer to singular or plural, feminine or non-feminine entities, none of them emerges with an overt plural or gender morpheme. These nominals' structure is aberrant within the category of nominals.

## Nasal Phenomena: Deriving Suffixes and Number

§9.1.0 Whereas the underlying structure #stem++TV+sion++e+ of words typified by the example *estação* has been amply justified, those of the remaining four nouns and two adjectives whose [-feminine, -plural] forms end in [ˈã$^{\tilde{u}}$] have not. Table 9.3 provides evidence to indicate that the suffixes +on+ and +an+ plus gender morphemes attach to roots, establish stems, and eventually form nouns.

**Table 9.3** Suffix Configuration: Evidence[a]

| | Analysis | | Analysis |
|---|---|---|---|
| **patrão** | #patr++on+<e+<Ø# | **guardião** | #guard+i+an+<e+<Ø# |
| patrões | #patr++on+<e+<z# | guardiães | #guard+i+an+<e+<z# |
| patronato | #patr++on++at++o# | guadiania | #guard++i++an++oi++a#<Ø# |
| patronear | #patr++on++e++a#+r#+e+ | **ancião** | #ansi++an+<o#<Ø# |
| patronal | #patr++on++al#+e+ | anciãos | #ansi++an+<o#<z# |
| **irmão** | #irm++an+<o#<Ø# | anciania | #ansi++an++i++a#<Ø# |
| irmãos | #irm++an+<o#<z# | ancianidade | #ansi++an++idad++e#<Ø# |
| irmanar | #irm++an++a#+r#+e+<Ø# | **chorão** | #šɔr++on+<e+<Ø# |
| mano,-a | #(ir)m++an+<o#<Ø# | chorões | #šɔr++on+<e+<z# |
| | | chorona | #šɔr++on+<a#<Ø# |

a The words in Table 9.3 mean: (1st column): 'boss, boses; reformatory, to patronize, patronal; sibling, siblings; to unite, bro or sis'; (3rd column): 'guardian, guardians guardianship; old person, old people, old age, old age; weepy, weepy (+pl.), weepy (+f.)'.

In all cases the word-final, [-plural] realization of the suffixes +on++e+, +an+<o#, and an+<e# is ['ã̆$^{\breve{u}}$]. However, the addition of a deriving suffix (or in the case of *chorona*, the [+feminine] inflecting suffix), causes the stem-final suffixes to emerge with their underlying phonemes. Thus, their merger in word-final, non-plural position is confirmed.

§**9.1.1 [-plural] Forms:** Table 9.4 contains the derivations of the singular and plural forms of the nominals:

**Table 9.4** Derivations of [-plural] Forms

| | patrão | irmão | guardião | estação |
|---|---|---|---|---|
| Lex | #patr++on+<e+ | #irm++an+<o# | #guard+i+an+<e# | #ezt++a#+sion++e+ |
| R. 8.1 | #patr++an+<o# | *** | #guard+i+an+<o# | #ezt++a#+san++o# |
| R. 3.1 | #patr++'an+<o# | #irm++'an+<o# | #guard+i+'an+<o# | #ezt++a#+s'an++o# |
| R. 7.2 | #patr++'ã̆n+<o# | #irm++'ã̆n+<o# | #guard+i+'ã̆n+o# | #ezt++a#+s'ã̆n++o# |
| R. 2.3 | #pătr++'ã̆n+<ŭ# | #irm++'ã̆n+<ŭ# | #guărd+i+'ã̆n+<ŭ# | #ĭzt++ă#+s'ã̆n++ŭ# |
| R. 8.3 | #pătr++'ã̆+<ŭ# | #irm++'ã̆+<ŭ# | #guărd+i+'ã̆+<ŭ# | #ĭzt++ă#+s'ã̆++ŭ# |
| R. 4.4 | #pă.tr++'ã̆+<ŭ# | #irm++'ã̆+<ŭ# | #guărd+i+'ã̆+<ŭ# | #ĭzt++ă#+.s'ã̆++ŭ# |
| R. 4.5 | *** | *** | #guărd+i+.'ã̆+<ŭ# | *** |
| R. 4.6 | *** | #ir.m++'ã̆+<ŭ# | #guăr.d+i+.'ã̆+<ŭ# | #ĭz.t++ă#+.s'ã̆++ŭ# |
| R. 8.4 | #pă.tr++'ã̆+<$^{\breve{u}}$# | #ir.m++'ã̆+<$^{\breve{u}}$# | #guăr.d+i+.'ã̆+<$^{\breve{u}}$# | #ĭz.t++ă#+.s'ã̆++$^{\breve{u}}$# |
| Ph. | [pă.'trã̆$^{\breve{u}}$] | [irm' ã̆$^{\breve{u}}$] | [guărδi.'ã̆$^{\breve{u}}$] | [əš.tă.sã̆$^{\breve{u}}$] |

It hardly should come as a surprise that many of the rules used for +sion+e+'s realization as [sã̆$^{\breve{u}}$] generate these forms' suffixes

§**9.1.2 [+plural] forms:** Table 9.5 demonstrates the derivation of the plurals of all these forms.

Table 9.5 Pluralizations

| | patrões | irmãos |
|---|---|---|
| Lex. | #patr++on+<e+<z# | #irm++an+<o#<z# |
| R. 8.1 | *** | *** |
| R. 8.2 | *** | *** |
| R. 3.1 | #patr++ˈon+<e+<z# | #irm++ˈan+<o#<z# |
| R. 7.2 | #patr++ˈõn+<e+<z# | #irm++ˈã̆n+<o#<z# |
| R. 2.3 | #pătr++ˈõn+<ĭ+<z# | #irm++ˈã̆n+<ŭ#<z# |
| R. 8.3 | #pătr++ˈõ+<ĭ+<z# | #irm++ˈã̆+<ŭ#<z# |
| R. 4.4 | #pă.tr++ˈõ+<ĭ+<z# | #irm++ˈã̆+<ŭ#<z# |
| R. 4.5 | *** | *** |
| R. 4.6 | *** | #ir.m++ˈã̆+<ŭ#<z# |
| R. 8.4 | #pă.tr++ˈõ+<$^{ĩ}$+<z# | #ir.m++ˈã̆+<$^{ũ}$#<z# |
| Ph. | [pă.ˈtrõ$^{ĩ}$š] | [ir.ˈmã̆$^{ũ}$š] |
| | guardiães | estações |
| Lex. | #guard+i+an+<e+<z# | #ezt++a#+sion++e+<z# |
| R. 8.1 | *** | *** |
| R. 8.2 | *** | #ezt++a#+son++e+<z# |
| R. 3.1 | #guard+i+ˈan+<e+<z# | #ezt++a#+ˈson++e+<z# |
| R. 7.2 | #guard+i+ˈãn+<e+<z# | #ezt++a#+ˈsõn++e+<z# |
| R. 2.3 | #guard+i+ˈãn+<ĭ+<z# | #ezt++a#+ˈsõn++ĭ+<z# |
| R. 8.3 | #guard+i+ˈã+<ĭ+<z# | #ezt++a#+ˈsõ++ĭ+<z# |
| R. 4.4 | *** | #ezt++a#+ˈ.sõ++ĭ+<z# |
| R. 4.5 | #guard+i+.ˈã+<ĭ+<z# | *** |
| R. 4.6 | #guar.d+i+.ˈã+<ĭ+<z# | #ez.t++a#+ˈ.sõ++ĭ+<z# |
| R. 8.4 | #guar.d+i+.ˈã+<$^{ĩ}$+<z# | #ez.t++a#+ˈ.sõ++$^{ĩ}$+<z# |
| Ph. | [g$^{u}$ăr.δiˈ.ã̆$^{ĩ}$š] | [əš.tă.ˈsõ$^{ĩ}$š] |

Given the grammar advanced in Chapter 8, these derivations are unremarkable.

**§9.2.0 Non-merging Nasal Phenomena:** Table 9.6 contains representative samples of the other nasal phenomenon associated with nominal plurality:

Table 9.6 Stem-Final Nasal Manifestations

| Nouns | | | | Adjectives | | | |
|---|---|---|---|---|---|---|---|
| -pl. | +pl. | +f. | Gloss | -pl. | +pl. | +f. | Gloss |
| álbum | álbuns | *** | album | bom | bons | boa | good |
| batom | batons | *** | lipstick | comum | comuns | ± | common |
| origem | origens | + | origin(s) | jovem | jovens | ± | young |
| pinguim | pinguins | ± | penguin(s) | marrom | marrons | ± | brown |
| tom | tons | *** | tone(s) | ruim | ruins | ± | bad |
| vintém | vinténs | *** | 20 réis coin | tremecém | tremecéns | ± | 3 month |

At first, blush pluralization of these forms appears to be a non-problem. One need only add an s (i.e. a <z#) to the singular forms to accommodate both nouns and adjectives to their [+plural] circumstances. And the shift from word-final m to pre-plural n could be no more than a spelling convention. But there is enough morphophonemic evidence to indicate that the nasal segment ending these words is /n+, as Table 9.7 demonstrates:

Table 9.7 Morphophonemic Evidence for Stem-Final /n+

| Simple Word | Derived Word | Analysis | Gloss |
|---|---|---|---|
| bom | boníssimo | #bon++ˈisim+<o# | very good |
| comum | comunismo | #komun++izm++o# | communism |
| jovem | juvenil | #žuven++il#+e+ | juvenile |
| origem | original | #ori++žin++al#+e+ | original |
| ruim | ruina | #ruin++a# | ruin |
| tom | tonal | #ton++al#+e+ | tonal |

It is clear from the data in Table 9.7 that the roots of these words end in /n+ because once a deriving suffix is added, [n] emerges in related words. Table 9.8 (i.e. Table 6.20) contains a set of words that end in m in their singular [-feminine] forms, but evince a stem-final /n+ in related or inflected [+feminine] forms:

Table 9.8 More Evidence for Stem-Final /n+

| [-f.] | | | [+f.] | | |
|---|---|---|---|---|---|
| **botim** | **botins** | ankle boot(s) | **botina** | **botinas** | ankle boot(s) |
| **malandrim** | **malandrins** | low-life(s) | **malandrina** | **malandrinas** | low-life female(s) |
| **mandarim** | **mandarins** | Mandarin(s) | **mandarina** | **mandarinas** | Mandarin female(s) |
| **vintém** | **vinténs** | 20 réis coins | **vintena** | **vintenas** | group(s) of 20 |

The stress patterns of these and other similar [-feminine] (or [±feminine]) forms once more confirm the presence of a stem-final /n+ in words such as these.

**§9.2.1** As Table 9.9 demonstrates, words whose [-plural] forms end in –m can emerge as oxytones and paroxytones:

Table 9.9 Apparent Oxytones and Paroxytones)[a]

| Oxytones | | Paroxytones | |
|---|---|---|---|
| **batom** | **mandarim** | **álbum** | **origem** |
| **botim** | **pinguim** | **fórum** | **babugem** |
| **comum** | **tom** | **cécum** | **acerugem** |
| **malandrim** | **vintém** | **jovem** | **virgem** |

a The apparent oxytones mean: 'lipstick, ankle boot, common, low-life, Mandarin, penguin, tone, and 20 coin'. The apparent paroxytones mean 'album, forum, caecum, young, origin, slobber, wax application, virgin'.

However, Chapter 3 (§3.1.2.0–1) demonstrates that there are many apparent oxytones that are actually occult paroxytones. That is, words like *hospital*, *senhor*, and *atroz* ('hospital', 'sir', and 'atrocious') contain an underlying gender morpheme (+e+ or <e+) that only emerges in their plural forms: *hospitais*, *senhores*, and *atrozes*. This gender morpheme (a vowel) allows these words to be assigned stress on their penultimate syllable by Rule 3.1. With the addition of these word-final morphemes, these words and the 'oxytones' in Table 9.9 conform to the general nominal pattern: #stem+gender+number#. That is, they all have a gender morpheme, here either +e+ (ambivalent or arbitrary

gender) or <e+ (inflected gender), that this morpheme would be deleted in both singular and plural forms once Rule 3.1 had applied. Rule 6.2b accounts for this morpheme's deletion in all the words of Table 9.9:

**Rule 6.2b Deletion of Word-Final <e+ and +e+ After /n#;**

$$\begin{pmatrix} \text{-contoid} \\ \text{-high} \\ \text{-wide glottis} \\ \text{+palatal} \end{pmatrix} \rightarrow \varnothing \,/\, \#\, X \begin{pmatrix} \text{+contoid} \\ \text{+nasal} \\ \text{- labial} \\ \text{- high} \end{pmatrix} \_\_\_ \#_{[\text{- N4}]}$$ [1]

Table 9.10a contains the underlying forms of selected m-final nominals and derives their surface manifestations:

**Table 9.10a** Derivations of Nominals with Arbitrary or Ambivalent Gender

| | comum | comuns | batom | batons |
|---|---|---|---|---|
| U.F. | #komun#+e+<Ø# | #komun#+e+<z# | #baton#+e+<Ø# | #baton#+e+<z# |
| R. 3.1 | #komˈun#+e+<Ø# | #komˈun#+e+<z# | #batˈon#+e+<Ø# | #batˈon#+e+<z# |
| R. 6.2b | #komˈun#<Ø# | #komˈun#<z# | #batˈon#<Ø# | #batˈon#<z# |
| R. 7.2 | #komˈũn#<Ø# | #komˈũn#<z# | #batˈõn#<Ø# | #batˈõn#<z# |
| R. 2.3 | #kŭmˈũn#<Ø# | #kŭmˈũn#<z# | #bătˈõn#<Ø# | #bătˈõn#<z# |
| R. 8.3 | #kŭmˈũ#<Ø# | #kŭmˈũ#<z# | #bătˈõ#<Ø# | #bătˈõ#<z# |
| R. 4.4 | #kŭ.mˈũ#<Ø# | #kŭ.mˈũ#<z# | #bă.tˈõ#<Ø# | #bă.tˈõ#<z# |
| R. 4.5 | *** | *** | *** | *** |
| R. 4.6 | *** | *** | *** | *** |
| Ph. | [kŭ.ˈmũ] | [kŭ.ˈmũ$^n$š] | [bă.ˈtõ] | [bă.ˈtõ$^n$š] |

(*Continued*)

1 The noun class $N_4$ is that class of noun that maintains a final /e/ (+e#) whose stems end in /r+, /l+, /z+, and /n = /n+ (See Table 6.21.).

Table 9.10a Continued

| | ruim | ruins | vintém | vinténs |
|---|---|---|---|---|
| U.F. | #ruin#+e+<Ø# | #ruin#+e+<z# | #vinten#+e+<Ø# | #vinten#+e+<z# |
| R 3.1 | #ruˈin#+e+<Ø# | #ruˈin#+e+<z# | #vintˈen#+e+<Ø# | #vintˈen#+e+<z# |
| R 6.2b | #ruˈin#<Ø# | #ruˈin#<z# | #vintˈen#<Ø# | #vintˈen#<z# |
| R.7.2 | #ruˈĩn#<Ø# | #ruˈĩn#<z# | #vintˈẽn#<Ø# | #vintˈẽn#<z# |
| R. 2.3 | *** | *** | *** | *** |
| R. 8.3 | #ruˈĩ#<Ø# | #ruˈĩ#<z# | #vintˈẽ#<Ø# | #vintˈẽ#<z# |
| R. 4.4 | *** | *** | *** | *** |
| R. 4.5 | #ruˈ.ĩ#<Ø# | #ruˈ.ĩ#<z# | *** | *** |
| R. 4.6 | *** | *** | #vin.tˈẽ#<Ø# | #vin.tˈẽ#<z# |
| Ph. | [r̲u.ˈĩ] | [r̲u.ˈĩš] | [vĩ.ˈtẽ$^{\tilde{\imath}}$][a] | [vĩ.ˈtẽ$^{\tilde{\imath}}$š] |

a The dipthongization of stressed [ẽ] in *vintém* is due to analogy. Third person plural forms of present indicative 2[nd] conjugation verbs have the morphemic structure +e# <Ø#<n#, in which unstressed /e/ and /n/ become juxtaposed and ultimately realized as (posttonic) [ẽ$^{\breve{\imath}}$]. There is no reduced gender morpheme in the verbs or in the word *vintém*, so the rising diphthong in these forms can be explained through analogy with the nominal endings in which an tonic [ĭ], originally a gender morpheme, forms an off-glide on the words' final atonic syllable.

All of the gender morphemes have a #+ (deriving) relationship with their stems because they are either arbitrarily [-feminine] as nouns, or they are ambivalently gendered as adjectives. The unmarked gender morpheme of *bom* ⇔ *boa*, *maladrim* ⇔ *malandrina*, and *mandarim* ⇔ *mandarina* is <e+, which indicates pure inflection and the acceptability of <a# when circumstances call for a [+feminine] inflection on words such as these.

**§9.2.2.0** Whereas the apparent oxytones of Table 9.9 are occult paroxytones, the apparent paroxytones (e.g. *álbum*, *jovem*, and *origem*) are occult proparoxytones (§3.1.6.2.0): #ˈalbun#+e+<Ø#, #žˈɔven#+e+Ø#, and #orˈi++žin#+e+<Ø#, and their roots are marked for stress in the lexicon. One notices that *origen*'s underlying structure differs from that of the other nominals insofar as it ends in /in# rather than /en#. The explanation of this postulate merits its own subsection.

**§9.2.2.1** The root of *origem* is #orˈi+ on the basis of words such as *oriundo* 'originating from' and *oriente* 'orient'. Its suffix +žin# is manifest in the derived adjective *original* 'original' and on similar pairs: *margem* 'margin' ⇔ *marginal* 'marginal', *virgem* 'virgin' ⇔ *virginal* 'virginal', *vagem* 'string bean' ⇔ *vaginal* 'vaginal'.[2] There is yet another wrinkle to words ending in –em in their singular forms and –ens in their plurals.

§9.2.2.2.0 Whereas the words ending in –im, -um, and –om end in tonic monophthongal nasal vowels, those ending in –em and their plurals contain nasalized diphthongs: [ŭ.ˈri.žẽ$^{\tilde{\imath}}$] ⇔[ŭ.ˈri.žẽ$^{\tilde{\imath}}$š], [ˈmar.žẽ$^{\tilde{\imath}}$]⇔[ˈmar.žẽ$^{\tilde{\imath}}$š], [ˈvir.žẽ$^{\tilde{\imath}}$]⇔[ˈvir.žẽ$^{\tilde{\imath}}$š], [ˈva.žẽ$^{\tilde{\imath}}$]⇔[ˈva.žẽ$^{\tilde{\imath}}$š]. Table 9.10b demonstrates the generation of such forms:

**Table 9.10b** Derivations of Nominals with Stem-Final +žin+

| | **origem** | **origens** | **originário** |
|---|---|---|---|
| U.F. | #orˈi++žin#+e+<Ø# | #orˈi++žin#+e+z # | #ori++žin#+ˈari+<o## |
| R. 3.1 | *** | *** | *** |
| R. 9.1b | #orˈi++žen#+i+<Ø# | #orˈi++žen#+i+z | *** |
| R. 7.2 | #orˈi++žẽn#+i+<Ø# | #orˈi++žẽn#+i+z | *** |
| R. 8.3 | #orˈi++žẽ#+i+<Ø# | #orˈi++žẽ#+i+z | *** |
| R. 4.4 | #o.rˈi++.žẽ#+i+<Ø# | #o.rˈi++.žẽ#+i+z | #o.ri++.ži.n#+ˈa.ri+<o## |
| R. 4.5 | *** | *** | *** |
| R. 4.6 | *** | *** | *** |
| R. 2.3 | #ŭ.rˈi++.ž#ẽ+i+<Ø# | #ŭ.rˈi++.ž#ẽ++i+z# | #ŭ.ri++.ži.n#+ˈa.ri+<ŭ## |
| R. 9.2 | #ŭ.rˈi++.ž#ẽ+ĩ+<Ø# | #ŭ.rˈi++.ž#ẽ++ĩ+z# | *** |
| Ph. | [ŭ.ˈri.žẽ$^{\tilde{\imath}}$] | [ŭ.ˈri.žẽ$^{\tilde{\imath}}$š] | [ŭ.ˈri.ži.ˈna.ri$^{\breve{u}}$] |
| | **virgem** | **virgens** | **virginiano** |
| U.F. | #vˈir++žin#+e+<Ø# | #vˈir++žin#+e+z# | #vir++žin#++i++an+<o# |
| R. 3.1 | *** | *** | #vir++žin#++i++ˈan+<o# |
| R. 9.1b | #vˈir++žen#+i+<Ø# | #vˈir++žen#+i+z# | *** |
| R. 7.2 | #vˈir++žẽn#+i+<Ø# | #vˈir++žẽn#+i+z# | *** |
| R. 8.3 | #vˈir++žẽ#+i+<Ø# | #vˈir++žẽ#+i+z# | *** |
| R. 4.4 | *** | *** | #vir++ži.n#++i++ˈa.n+<o# |
| R. 4.5 | *** | *** | #vir++ži.n#++i++ˈ.a.n+<o# |
| R. 4.6 | #vˈir++.žẽ#+i+<Ø# | #vˈir++.žẽ#+i+z# | #vir++.ži.n#++i++ˈ.a.n+<o# |
| R. 2.3 | *** | *** | #vir++.ži.n#++i++ˈ.a.n+<ŭ# |
| R. 9.2 | #vˈir++.žẽ#+ĩ+<Ø# | #vˈir++.žẽ#+ĩ+z# | *** |
| Ph. | [ˈvir.žẽ$^{\tilde{\imath}}$] | [ˈvir.žẽ$^{\tilde{\imath}}$š] | [vir.ži.ni.ˈa.nŭ] |

2 The words *origem*, *margem*, *virgem*, and *vagem* are all [+feminine].

**§9.2.2.2.1** Whereas the roots of *origem* and *virgem* are occult paroxytones and, thus, lexically stressed, the stems of their derivatives *originário* 'native' and *virginiano* 'Virgo' lose their stress because no (non-compound) word can receive stress before its antepenultimate syllable. The suffix +ˈari+<o# is lexically stressed. Only *virginiano* is susceptible to Rule 3.1. Rules 9.1a and 9.2a are new.

**Rule 9.1a Metathesis:**

$$\begin{pmatrix} +\text{palatal} \\ +\text{high} \\ \text{-del. tran.} \end{pmatrix}_1 \begin{pmatrix} +\text{contoid} \\ +\text{nasal} \\ \text{-labial} \\ \text{-high} \end{pmatrix} \# + \begin{pmatrix} +\text{palatal} \\ \text{-high} \\ \text{-del. tran.} \end{pmatrix}_2 + \begin{Bmatrix} <\emptyset\# \\ <z\# \end{Bmatrix} \rightarrow 2C\#1$$

Rule 9.1a shifts the word-final atonic sequence /ine/ to /eni/. Rules 7.2 and 8.3 cause the resulting vowel to nasalize and the /n# to disappear.

**Rule 9.2a Nasalization (Progressive/Regressive Assimilation):**

[-contoid] → [+nasal] / .X ___ [+nasal]___.

A vocoid acquires nasality when it occurs before a nasal segment in the same syllable. Rule 9.2a accounts for both this nasalization and that occasioned by syllable codas containing nasal consonants.

## Word-Final /l+ and Number

**§9.3.0** Table 9.11a reviews the phenomena associated with [±plural] when words end with /l# in their [-feminine, -plural] forms:

Table 9.11a Number and Word-Final /l#

| Nouns ([-f.]) | | | Adjectives ([±f.]) | | |
|---|---|---|---|---|---|
| -plural | +plural | Gloss | -plural | +plural | Gloss |
| **bagual** | **baguais** | wild horse(s) | **igual** | **iguais** | equal |
| **funeral** | **funerais** | funeral(s) | **viável** | **viáveis** | viable |
| **donzel** | **donzéis** | virgin(s) | **cruel** | **cruéis** | cruel |
| **barril** | **barris** | barrel(s) | **civil** | **civis** | civil |
| **sol** | **sóis** | sun(s) | **útil** | **utéis** | useful |
| **bulbul** | **bulbuis** | bulbul(s) | **mongol** | **mongóis** | Mongol |
| **cônsul** | **cônsules** | consul(s) | **azul** | **azuis** | blue |

**§9.3.1** The pattern entailed in pluralization of words whose [-feminine, -plural] forms emerge with word-final /l# is that the /l# evanesces in the plural form. And similar to what happens with the nasal suffixes (§9.1.1 and Tables 9.4 and 9.5), the gender morpheme +e+ reduces to [ĭ] and forms an off-glide on the stems' final vowel.[3] Table 9.11b demonstrates how some of these forms can be generated:

3 With one exception, *cônsul*, whose /l# remains in the plural and in its [+feminine] form *consulesa*. The [+feminine] suffix +ez++a# is to one degree or another honorific. It can indicate royalty: *duquesa* 'duchess', *princesa* 'princess', *marquesa* 'marquise', *condesa* 'coutess'; hierarchy: *prioresa* 'sister superior', *condestabresa* 'female constable'; or a life-style: *jogralesa* 'female bard', *vampiresa* 'female vampire'.

Table 9.11b The Emergence and Deletion of Stem-Final /l#[a]

| | funeral | funerais | gaivel | gaivéis |
|---|---|---|---|---|
| U.F. | #funeral#+e+<Ø# | #funeral#+e+<z# | #gaivɛl#+e+<Ø# | #gaivɛl#+e+<z# |
| R. 3.1 | #funer'al#+e+<Ø# | #funer'al#+e+<z# | #gaiv'ɛl#+e+<Ø# | #gaiv'ɛl#+e+<Ø# |
| R. 6.2a | #funer'al#+Ø+<Ø # | *** | #gaiv'ɛl#+Ø+<Ø# | *** |
| R. 9.3 | *** | #funer'a#+e+<z# | *** | #gaiv'ɛ#+e+<z# |
| R. 2.3 | *** | #funer'a#+ĭ+<z # | *** | #gaiv'ɛ#+ĭ+<z# |
| R. 4.4 | #fu.ne.r'al#+Ø+<Ø# | #fu.ne.r'a#+ĭ+<z | #gai.v'ɛl#+Ø+<Ø# | #gaiv'ɛ#+ĭ+<z# |
| Ph. | [fu.nə.'raɫ] | [fu.nə.'ra$^{ĭ}$š] | [ga$^{ĭ.}$'vɛɫ] | ['ga$^{ĭ}$.'vɛ$^{ĭ}$š] |
| | **sol** | **sóis** | **azul** | **azuis** |
| U.F. | #sɔl++e+<Ø# | #sɔl++e+<z# | #azul#+e+<Ø# | #azul#+e+<z# |
| R. 3.1 | #s'ɔl++e+<Ø# | #s'ɔl++e+<z# | #az'ul#+e+<Ø# | #az'ul#+e+<z# |
| R. 6.2a | #s'ɔl++Ø+<Ø# | *** | #az'ul#+Ø+<Ø# | *** |
| R. 9.3 | *** | #s'ɔ++e+<z# | *** | #az'u#+ĭ+<z# |
| R. 2.3 | *** | #s'ɔ++ĭ+<z# | *** | #az'u#+ĭ+<z# |
| R. 4.4 | *** | *** | #a.z'ul#+Ø+<Ø# | #a.z'u#+ĭ+<z# |
| Ph. | ['sɔɫ] | ['sɔ$^{ĭ}$š] | [ă.'zuɫ] | [ă.'zu$^{ĭ}$š][b] |

a The words in this table mean: 'funeral(s), batter(s), sun(s), blue'.
b A diphthong of of /'ui/ is facultative.

§**9.3.2.0** The only new phenomenon in these data is the loss of /l# in the plurals. This can be managed by Rule 9.3:

**Rule 9.3 The Loss of Word-Final /l# in Pluralizations:**

$$[+\text{lateral}]\ /\ \_\#\left\{\begin{matrix}<\\+\end{matrix}\right\}\ e+\ \#<z\# \rightarrow \emptyset$$

Rule 9.3 is a strictly morphophonemic rule that deletes stem-final /l# (the only lateral capable of ending a word) when followed by either +e+

or <e+ and the plural morpheme. None of these examples is susceptible to metathesis (Rule 9.1); however, Table 9.11c contains forms that are susceptible to that rule, plus another phonological constraint:

**Table 9.11c** The Emergence and Deletion of Stem-Final #l# (2)

| | **barril** | **barris** | **útil** | **utéis** |
|---|---|---|---|---|
| U.F. | #bar̲il#+e+<Ø# | bar̲il#+e+<z# | #ˈutil#+e+<Ø# | #ˈutil#+e+<z# |
| R. 3.1 | #bar̲ˈil#+e+<Ø# | #bar̲ˈil#+e+<z# | *** | *** |
| R. 9.1b | *** | *** | *** | #ˈutel#+i+<z# |
| R. 6.2 | #bar̲il#<Ø# | *** | #ˈutil#<Ø# | *** |
| R. 9.3 | *** | #bar̲ˈi#+e+<z# | *** | #ˈute#+i+<z# |
| R. 2.3 | #băr̲il#<Ø# | #băr̲ˈi#+ĭ+<z# | *** | *** |
| R. 4.4 | #bă.r̲il#<Ø# | #bă.r̲ˈi#+ĭ+<z# | #ˈu.til#<Ø# | #ˈu.te#+i+<z# |
| R. 4.1 | *** | #bă.r̲ˈi#<z# | *** | *** |
| Ph. | [bă.r̲iɫ] | [bă.ˈr̲is] | [ˈu.tiɫ] | [ˈu.te$^{ĭ}$š] |

§**9.3.2.1** The loss of (intervocalic) /l# in the plural manifestations of words such as these resembles the loss of intervocalic /n# in suffixes such as +sion+, +on+, +an+ when followed by overt gender morphemes, i.e. when pluralized. And the loss of intervocalic /n/, /l/ (and /d/) are well-documented phenomena in the evolution of Portuguese from Latin.[4] The metathesis evinced in the derivation of the adjective *úteis* can be accounted for with a modification of Rule 9.1a:

4 In a totally ad hoc and ahistorical analysis of words ending in /l#, Villalva and Conçalves propose that 'the plural of /pɐpɛl+/ [*papel* 'paper'] can be obtained by semi-vocalization of the final consonant of the root but only if it is an athematic root' (168). The authors maintain that the distinction between athematic and thematic roots accounts for the difference between word-final /l#s that disappear in plural forms and those that persist. They cite *aval* 'personal guarantee' and *fel* 'bile' as thematic because *avales* and *feles* are acceptable plurals. They fail to acknowledge that *avais* and *féis* are also acceptable plurals. In addition, whereas /l# vocalizes word-finally (to [ŭ]) in Brazilian Portuguese, it emerges as [l] between vowels before a deriving suffix: cf. *Brasil* [bra.ˈzi$^{ŭ}$] and *brasileiro* [bra.zi.ˈle$^{ĭ}$.rŭ] 'Brazilian'. There is no case in which /l/ in any of its incarnations mutates to a palatal off-glide.

**Rule 9.1b Metathesis:**

$$\begin{pmatrix}\text{+palatal}\\ \text{+high}\\ \text{-del. tran.}\end{pmatrix}_1 \begin{pmatrix}\text{+contoid}\\ \left\{\begin{matrix}\text{+nasal}\\ \alpha\text{lateral}\end{matrix}\right\}\\ \text{-high}\\ \text{-labial}\end{pmatrix} \# + \begin{pmatrix}\text{+palatal}\\ \text{-high}\\ \text{-del. tran.}\end{pmatrix}_2 + \left\{\begin{matrix}<\text{Ø}\#\\ \\ \alpha<\text{z}\#\end{matrix}\right\} \rightarrow 2\text{C}\#1$$

Rule 9.1b causes the metathesis on plural adjectives such as *débil, fácil, volátil, difícil* 'weak, easy, capable of flight, difficult', whose underlying penultimate syllable is not stressed as well as on all word endings consisting of /in++e+.

## Genderless Numberless Nominals

**§9.4.0** Table 9.12 displays those nominals (Table 9.2c) that have no overt inflection for number or for gender.

**Table 9.12** Analysis of Genderless Numberless Nominals

| Nouns | | | |
|---|---|---|---|
| **-plural** | **Analysis** | **+plural** | **Analysis** |
| **nunes** | #nunez#<Ø#<Ø# | **nunes** | #nunez#<Ø#<z# |
| **maricas** | #marikaz#<Ø#<Ø# | **maricas** | #marikaz#<Ø#<z# |
| **tebas** | #tebaz#<Ø#<Ø# | **tebas** | #tebaz#<Ø#<z# |
| **trombelas** | #trombelas#<Ø#<Ø# | **trombelas** | #trombelas#<Ø#<z# |
| **ónus** | #onuz#<Ø#<Ø# | **ónus** | #onuz#<Ø#<z# |
| **bónus** | #bonus#<Ø#<Ø# | **bónus** | #bonus#<Ø#<z# |
| **ónix** | #ɔnikz#<Ø#<Ø# | **ónix** | #ɔnikz#<Ø#<z# |
| **Adjectives** | | | |
| **-plural** | **Analysis** | **+plural** | **Analysis** |
| **simples** | #sinplez#<Ø#<Ø# | **simples** | #sinplez#<Ø#<z# |
| **grátis** | #gratiz#<Ø#<Ø# | **grátis** | #gratiz#<Ø#<z# |
| **traquinas** | #trakinaz#<Ø#<Ø# | **traquinas** | #trakinaz#<Ø#<z# |
| **somenos** | #somenoz#<Ø#<Ø# | **somenos** | #somenoz#<Ø#<z# |
| **piegas** | #piegaz#<Ø#<Ø# | **piegas** | #piegaz#<Ø#<z# |
| **reles** | #rɛlez#<Ø#<Ø# | **reles** | #rɛlez#<Ø#<z# |
| **tortelos** | #tɔrtɛloz#<Ø#<Ø# | **tortelos** | #tɔrtɛloz#<Ø#<z# |

**§9.4.1** None of the items in Table 9.12 has a gender morpheme, which allows them to denote or modify [±feminine] entities with no change in their forms. Likewise, they modify or denote [+plural] items with no overt plural morpheme. Still, these words are all paroxytones that are accounted for in the following iteration of Rule 3.1:

**Rule 3.1b Paroxytone Stress Iteration:**

[-contoid] ➔ [+stress] / #X __$C_{0\text{-}4}$VC(C)#

Beyond these words' stress, Rule 4.1 eliminates the final /z# in these words when it is followed by <z#. (See Table 9B.5.)

## Feminine Gender and the Problematic Nominals

**§9.5.0** There need be no further consideration of those adjectives and nouns that designate [±feminine] and [±plural] entities indifferently. What remain are the [+feminine] forms of specific suffixes and word endings containing nasal consonants and those few nominals whose [-feminine, -plural] forms superficially end in /l# and whose /l# remains when the words acquire a final <a#. The first case to be examined is the reflection of [+feminine] gender on the deriving morphemes containing nasal consonants.

**§9.5.1.0** Table 9.13a displays the nasalizing suffixes other than +sion+ +e+ that merge in their [-plural, -feminine] forms and their (standard) realizations in both [-feminine] and [+feminine] forms.

**Table 9.13a** Standard Feminine Inflection-Deriving Suffixes

| [-f.] | | [+f.] | | | |
|---|---|---|---|---|---|
| Analysis | Realization | Analysis | Realization | Example[a] | *Aurélio* |
| +on+<e# | ['ã̆$^{ũ}$] | +on+<a# | ['õ.nă] | patrona | 187 |
| +an+<o# | ['ã̆$^{ũ}$] | +an+<a# | ['ã̆] | irmã | ?[b] |
| +an+<e# | ['ã̆$^{ũ}$] | +an+<a# | ['ã̆] | guardiã | ? |

a The [-feminine] reflexes of two of these words (*patrão* and *irmão*) appear among the *Aurélio*'s 3,000 most used words. The [+feminine] forms do not appear.
b A count of the word-final incidence of ã is not feasible because the *Aurélio*'s search application does not distinguish word-final ã from a.

The rules postulated to account for the nasalization and deletion of /n+ in the singular and plural [-feminine] manifestations of these suffixes (cf. Table 9.5) and the elimination of geminate segments also account for the feminine forms of nominals such as these:

**Table 9.13b** [+feminine] Derivations

| | patrona | irmã | guardiã |
|---|---|---|---|
| | **#patr++on+<a#** | **#irm++an+<a#** | **#guard+i+an+<a#** |
| R. 8.2 | *** | *** | *** |
| R. 3.1 | #patr++ˈon+<a# | #irm++ˈan+<a# | #guard+i+ˈan+<a# |
| R. 7.2 | *** | #irm++ˈãn+<a# | #guard+i+ˈãn+<a# |
| R. 8.3 | *** | #irm++ˈã+<a# | #guard+i+ˈã+<a# |
| R. 4.1 | *** | #irm++ˈã# | #guard+i+ˈã# |
| R. 2.3 | #pătr++ˈon+<a# | #irm++ˈã# | #guard+i+ˈã# |
| Ph. | [pă.ˈtro.nă] | [ir.ˈmã̃] | [g$^{u}$ar.δiˈã̃] |

The augmentative suffix +on+, when it admits a [+feminine] inflection, on at least 187 different words (*Aurélio*), is immune to the nasal deletion rule. With this exception, there are no new rules or wrinkles necessary to derive the [+feminine] forms of the suffixes +on+, +an+<o#, and #an+<e#. However, this does not close the case on [+feminine] manifestations of these suffixes.

**§9.5.1.1** Because of the word-final fusion of +on+, +an+<o#, and +an+<e# in the [-plural, -feminine] forms, Portuguese speakers have taken the fused manifestations to be the starting point for pluralization and for [+feminine] inflection. They have produced various alternatives for plural and [+feminine] forms. Tables 9.14a and 9.14b display [+plural] and [+feminine] alternations:

**Table 9.14a** Variation in [+feminine] [+plural Forms[a]

| [-feminine, -plural] | | Stems | [+plural] | | |
|---|---|---|---|---|---|
| Nominal | Gloss | Analysis[b] | -ãos | +ães | +ões |
| alão | mastiff | #al++an+ | ✓* | ✓ | ✓ |
| alazão | sorrel | #alaz++an+ | *** | ✓* | ✓ |
| aldeão | villager | #alde++an+ | ✓* | ✓ | ✓ |
| anão | dwarf | #an++an+ | ✓* | *** | ✓ |
| ancião | agèd | #ansi++an+ | ✓* | ✓ | ✓ |
| castelão | castellan | #kaztel++an+ | ✓* | *** | ✓ |
| corrimão | railing | #kɔriman+ | ✓* | *** | ✓ |
| deão | dean | #de++an+ | ✓* | *** | ✓ |
| ermitão | hermit | #ɛrm++it++an+ | ✓* | ✓ | ✓ |
| folgazão | idler | #fɔlg++a#+zan+ | ✓ | *** | ✓ |
| hortelão | gardener | #ɔrt++el++an+ | ✓* | *** | ✓ |
| rufião | ruffian | #rufi++an+ | *** | ✓* | ✓ |
| sultão | sultan | #sultan+ | ✓ | ✓* | ✓ |
| verão | summer | #vɛr++an+ | ✓* | *** | ✓ |
| vilão | villian | #vil++an+ | ✓* | *** | ✓ |

a These data (save *anão* and *folgazão*) come from Cunha (126).
b These analyses are based on etymologies and on at least one of the items' plural manifestations.

*Verão* is the only item in this set that is among the *Aurélio*'s 3,000 most common words—the rest are quite rare. The asterisked checks in Table 9.14a indicate the etymologically faithful realizations, and the data show that by far –ões is the default realization of plural forms of this sort of nominal regardless of the words' etymologies. Its status as default most assuredly comes from the high frequency of word-final +sion++e+ and +on+, whose normal plurals are always –ões. Since all these words (except *corrimão* and *verão*) indicate living, animate beings, they admit feminine inflections (cf. Cunha, 134–5), which emerge as:

Table 9.14b Alternate Reflections of [+feminine] Gender

| [-feminine, -plural] | | Stems | [feminine, -plural] | | | | |
|---|---|---|---|---|---|---|---|
| Nominal | Gloss | Analysis[a] | -ã | -oa | -a | -ana | -ona |
| alão | mastiff | #al++an+ | ?[b] | *** | *** | *** | *** |
| alazão | sorrel | #alaz++an+ | ✓ | *** | *** | *** | *** |
| aldeão | villager | #alde++an+ | ✓ | *** | *** | *** | *** |
| anão | dwarf | #an++an+ | ✓ | *** | *** | *** | *** |
| ancião | agèd | #ansi++an+ | ✓ | *** | *** | *** | *** |
| anfitrião | host | #anfi++tri++on+ | ✓ | ✓ | *** | *** | *** |
| bom | good | #bon+ | *** | ✓ | *** | *** | *** |
| campeão | champion | #kanp++e++on+ | ✓ | *** | *** | *** | *** |
| castelão | castellan | #kaztel++an+ | ✓ | ✓ | *** | *** | ✓ |
| cirugião | surgeon | #sirurži++an+ | ✓ | *** | *** | *** | *** |
| cortesão | courtier | #kɔrt++e++zan+ | ✓ | *** | *** | *** | *** |
| deão | dean | #de++an+ | ? | *** | *** | *** | *** |
| ermitão | hermit | #ɛrm++it++an+ | ✓ | ✓ | *** | *** | *** |
| faisão | pheasant | #faiz++an+ | ✓ | ✓ | *** | *** | *** |
| folgazão | idler | #fɔlg++a#+zan+ | ✓ | *** | *** | *** | ✓ |
| hortelão | gardener | #ɔrt++el++an+ | *** | ✓ | *** | *** | *** |
| ladrão | thief | #ladr++on+ | *** | ✓ | ✓ | *** | ✓ |
| leitão | suckling pig | #leit++on+ | *** | ✓ | *** | *** | *** |
| maganão | free spirit | #magan++on+ | *** | *** | *** | *** | ✓ |
| melão | melon | #mɛl++on+ | *** | ✓ | *** | *** | *** |
| patrão | boss | #patr++on+ | *** | ✓ | *** | *** | ✓ |
| rufião | ruffian | #rufi++on+ | *** | *** | *** | *** | ✓ |
| sultão | sultan | #sul'tan# | *** | *** | *** | ✓ | *** |
| vilão | villain | #vil++an+ | ✓ | ✓ | *** | *** | *** |
| Totals: | | | 13 | 11 | 1 | 1 | 6 |

a These analyses are based on etymologies and on at least one of the items' plural manifestations.
b The *Aurelio* does not list a [+feminine] inflection on certain words.

**§9.5.1.2.0** These words can be problematic either in their [+plural, -feminine] manifestations or in their [+feminine] manifestations (whose plural forms occasion no further morphophonemic phenomena) or in both manifestations. In the [+feminine] category, 11 items have only one feminine form, six have two, and two have three. Beyond this, two items have no [+feminine] form indicated in the *Aurélio*.

**§9.5.1.2.1 ['ã̆]#:** As the most frequent manifestation of [+feminine] gender in this category of nominal, these nominals' stems end in +an+ followed by either <e# or <o# when whatever they designate is [-feminine] and followed by <a# in their [+feminine] instantiations. The plurals in Table 9.14a with etymologically sound –ãos endings have a feminine form ending in –ã.

**§9.5.1.2.2 ['õ.nă]#:** Of the six items that have –ona as a [+feminine] reflex, four (*ladrão⇔ladrona, manganão⇔manganona, patrão⇔patrona, rufião⇔rufiona*) are based on the augmentative suffix +on+. The forms *castelona* and *folgazona* parallel the alternate plural of these words as *castelões* and *folgazões*, where speakers assumed an augmentative +on+ rather than +an+ as the deriving suffix.

**§9.5.1.2.3 [ă]# and ['ã̆.nă] #:** These singletons are aberrancies. Concerning the form *ladra* 'female thief', the *Aurélio* considers the forms *ladro* and *ladra* to be primarily adjectives, which can be used as nouns, just as *ladrão* and *ladrona* may be. The form *sultana*, meaning either the sultan's favorite wife or the sultan's female offspring, probably maintains its underlying +an+ because of its exotic designation in Lusophone culture.

**§9.5.1.2.4.0 ['o.ă]#:** This [+feminine] suffix is the second most frequent in Table 9.14b, after ['ã̆]. It contains the sole [+feminine] morpheme to occur on the following stems: #bon+, #leit++on+, #ɔrt++al++an+, and #mɛl++on+.[5] It also occurs as a [+feminine] reflex of +on+ in other words (*anfitrioa, ladroa, patroa, viloa*) and of +an+ in (*casteloa, horteloa, viloa*).

**§9.5.1.2.4.1** The *Aurélio* contains 41 entries in which the ending –oa is related to nominals whose [-feminine, -plural] manifestations indicate the presence of the nasal-final suffixes +on+ and +an+. It also contains some words ending in this sequence whose [-feminine] counterparts contain no nasal consonant. And it contains some nouns that are derived using the suffix +o++a#, as Table 9.14c demonstrates:

5 Its appearance on #mɛl++on+ is derivational rather than inflectional. Whereas the *Aurélio* only considers *meloa* to be a 'big melon', the *Morais* dictionary considers it an 'adjective' that describes a 'large squash that looks like a melon'. The *Morais* goes on to identify *meloa* as a noun that indicates: a large melon, a small round melon, any whitish melon with dark stripes. In my own experience with melons in Portugal, people have insisted that *meloas* are different from *melões*, but I have failed to perceive said differences.

Table 9.14c –oa Nominal Endings with no +an+ or +on+ Relative

| Inflected Nominals | | | Derived Nominals | | | |
|---|---|---|---|---|---|---|
| [-f.] | [+f.] | Gloss | [+f.] | Gloss | [-f.] Relative | Gloss |
| **capiau** | **capioa** | ruralite | **macacoa** | mild illness | **macaco** | monkey |
| **diabo** | **diaboa** | devil | **retanchoa** | cropping | **retanchar** | to crop |
| **ilhéu** | **ilhoa** | islander | **tanoa** | tannery work | **tanoeiro** | tanner |
| **melro** | **melroa** | ouzel | **tonoa** | barrel repair | **tonel** | barrel |
| **parvo** | **párvoa** | fool | | | | |
| **tabaréu** | **tabaroa** | villager | | | | |

**§9.5.1.2.4.2** The best way to incorporate the nominal ending –oa into a morphophonological grammar of Portuguese is to consider the adjectives and nouns that admit this sequence of morphemes (+o++a#) as their [+feminine] manifestation to be lexically determined rather than to try to derive such forms from nominals containing the suffix +an+ (either +an+<e# or +an+<o#) or +on+, since its parentage is closer to random than to regular. And, beyond this, there are roots to which it directly attaches. Even the word *boa* 'good [+feminine]' should be considered a lexical item. At this point, the [+feminine] manifestations of words with deriving suffixes +on+<e#, +an+<e#, and +an+<o#$_2$ have been accounted for. The final consideration of problematic nominals are those ending in /l# in their [-feminine, -plural] forms that acquire a word-final <a# when inflected for [+feminine] gender.

## Stems Ending in /l# with a [+feminine] Reflex Ending in <a#

**§9.6.0** There appear to be only three nominals whose [-feminine, -plural] forms end in /l# and whose [+feminine, -plural] forms end in <a: *bagual⇔baguala*, *donzel⇔donzela*, and *espanhol⇔espanhola*. Whereas the stem-final /l# evanesces in the [-feminine, +plural] forms, it remains in the [+feminine, +plural] forms: *baguais⇔bagualas*, *donzéis⇔donzelas*, and *espanhóis⇔espanholas*. The difference between these three nominals and the great bulk ending in /l# that do not distinguish [+feminine] gender and whose /l# evanesces in plural forms lies in their gender morpheme. The undifferentiating set's gender morpheme is +e+, which is neutral, whereas the words in the set in question are inflected for gender with <e#, which indicates [-feminine]

gender and can be replaced by <a# when circumstances call for it. In all three cases, dictionaries agree that these words are first adjectives then nouns.[6]

**§9.6.1** Why these three nominals have allowed [+feminine] inflection may be because they indicate (perhaps especially in their [+feminine] forms) slightly charged characteristics or entities: wild, skittish horses in a traditional equestrian culture (Argentina, Uruguay, Rio Grande do Sul); virginal and upper class females in phallocratic cultures; females of the majority population in the Iberian Peninsula. Beyond this, the reasons for their peculiarities are anybody's guess.

## Conclusions

### Summary

**§9.7.0 Subject Matter:** Having addressed the phenomena peculiar to the noun-deriving suffix +sion+ in Chapter 8, Chapter 9 has endeavored to systematize and regulate the allomorphy of the word-final suffixes

6 The *Morais* identifies *bagual* as an ambivalent gender adjective indicating a wild horse or an unsociable person. As a noun it designates a wild horse. The *Aurélio* understands it to be an ambivalent adjective that may indicate skittishness (colts, recently broken colts, wild horses, people). It may also describe overly big objects. As a noun it indicates a wild horse. Even though the *Aurélio* describes *bagual* as gender ambivalent, it has a separate entry for *baguala*. Both the *Morais* and the *Aurélio* consider the word to be peculiar to southern Brazil. According to *Morais*, the adjective *donzel* means 'docile, naïve, pure, bland, virgin'. As a noun it indicates a male virgin, a noble youth yet to be dubbed a knight, or a page. *Donzela* as an adjective describes an unmarried virgin female. As a noun it also identifies unmarried virgin women, or young noblewomen. The *Aurélio* defines *donzel* the adjective as indicating purity or naïveté. As a noun it is restricted to indicating the noble youth who has not yet been dubbed a knight. For the *Aurélio* a original definition of *donzela* was 'young noblewoman' and nowadays it indicates female virgins. *Morais* considers the adjective *espanhol* as describing whatever it may be that is related to Spain. As a noun it indicates a Spaniard or the Spanish language. *Espanhola* was how Brazilians referred to the Spanish flu of 1918. The *Aurélio* defines *espanhol* as an adjective or noun similarly to how the *Morais* defines it. Likewise, *espanhola* indicates the flu of 1918, but as an adjective it identifies a cow with large, unusual horns.

+on+, +an+<e#, and +an+<o#, which can be inflected for gender, whereas +sion+ cannot—it occurs with the [+feminine] suffix +e+. In addition, Chapter 9 has addressed the nominals ending orthographically in –m, (morphophonemically in /n++e+) which lose their final +e+ in both singular and plural forms after the +e+ has occasioned paroxytone stress on what ends up being the word-final syllable. It has also provided a grammar for the pluralization of nominals and adjectives whose [-plural] forms end in /l#—be that /l# a part of a deriving suffix, e.g. +al#+e+ *pessoa* 'person' ⇔ *pessoal* 'personal, personnel', be it a simple stem-final consonant: e.g. *azul* 'blue' #azul#+e+, *anzol* 'fishhook' #anzɔl#+e+. In addition, it has provided a rationale for the set of nominals (both adjectives and nouns) that maintain the final /l# in plural forms as well as those bearing the inflectional [+feminine] morpheme <a#. It has also provided an analysis and rationale to explain and generate those nominals that have no overt plural or gender marking.

§9.7.1 **Aberrancies:** Whereas number is the more tractable of the two categories under investigation here, significant numbers of nominals formed with the suffixes +on+, +an+<o# and +an+<e+ admit more than one plural form (Table 9.14a). Concerning these forms' gender, the augmentative suffix +on+ can be followed by the inflecting suffix <e+ in [-feminine] manifestations, and by <a# in its [+feminine] manifestations. When it is followed by <a#, the final /n+ normally emerges in both [±plural] forms. The suffix +an+ (either as +an+<o# or +an+<e+), when followed by <a# is usually realized as [ˈã]. There is one set of [+feminine] markings, +o++a#, whose emergence is seemingly arbitrary and must be entered lexically rather than grammatically determined.

## Findings and Interpretations

§9.8 **Grammar**: Thirteen rules (Appendix B) account for the phenomena entailed in the allomorphy of these problematic nominals. Of these 13, seven are very general rules of Portuguese: 3.1 paroxytone stress, 2.3 atonic vowel reduction, 6.2a deletion of +e+ and <e+ after word-final /r#, /l#, /z#, 6.2b after word-final /n#, 4.4 and 4.6 syllable boundary insertion, and 4.1 like segment deletion. Another two rules come from Chapter 8: 8.1 is responsible for the merger of four suffixes

(+on+, +an+<o#, +an+<e#, +sion++e+, +ion++e+) in word-final position. Rule 8.3 deletes suffix-final /n+ after it has nasalized the preceding vowel. The remaining rules are original with this chapter: Rule 9.1b causes the posttonic sequence of vowels /iCe/ to metathesize around morpheme-final /n + and /l+. Rule 9.2a causes oral vocoids in the same syllable as a nasalized vocoid to acquire nasality. Rule 9.3 causes word-final /l# to be deleted in pluralized forms.

## So What?

§9.9 It is not surprising that these problematic nominals should be subject to the same phenomena that occur in unproblematic words (stress, vowel reduction, syllable division, deletion of word-final +e+ and <e+, like segment deletion). And it is not surprising that certain phenomena (morphophonemic nasalization and consonant deletion) pertain only to the matters at hand. It was somewhat surprising that [+plural] is the only truly inflectional (nominal) morpheme in Portuguese, whereas [+feminine] in certain cases is lexically determined as a derivational suffix. Chapters 6, 8, and 9 have accounted for all the phenomena associated with nominal gender and number in Portuguese.

## Appendix A The Rules as they Appear in Chapter 9

### 8.1 Suffix Merger in Word-Final Position:

$$\left\{\begin{array}{l} +on+<e+ \\ +an+\{<e+,<o\#\} \\ +(\alpha\ s)ion++e+ \end{array}\right\} \rightarrow +\ (\alpha\ s)an+\alpha+o\#_3\ /\ \_\_\ \left\{\begin{array}{l} <[-plural]\# \\ <o\# \end{array}\right\}$$

### 3.1 Paroxytone Stress:

$$[-contoid] \rightarrow [+stress]\ /\ \#X\ \_\_\ \left(\begin{bmatrix} +high \\ -contoid \end{bmatrix}\right)\ C_{0\text{-}4}V_{[-high]}\#(C)\#$$

**Condition:** The word has no previously assigned stress.

### 6.2a Deletion of Word-Final <e+ and+e+_ After /r#, /l#, and /z#:

$$\begin{Bmatrix} < \\ + \end{Bmatrix} \begin{pmatrix} \text{-contoid} \\ \text{+palatal} \end{pmatrix} \rightarrow \emptyset \;/\; \#X\,[\text{-contoid}] \begin{pmatrix} \text{+contoid} \\ \text{-surd} \\ \text{-labial} \\ \text{-high} \\ \text{-nasal} \\ \text{-occlusion} \end{pmatrix} \_\_ + < [\text{-plural}]\#$$

### 7.2 Morphophonemic Nasalization $R_1$ Stems:

$$+\begin{pmatrix} \text{-contoid} \\ \text{+delayed transition} \end{pmatrix} \rightarrow [\text{+nasal}] \;/\; \_\_ \begin{pmatrix} \text{+nasal} \\ \text{+contoid} \end{pmatrix} + \begin{Bmatrix} + \\ < \end{Bmatrix} [\pm\text{feminine}]\# \; <\emptyset\#$$

### 2.3 Atonic Vowel Reduction:

$$\begin{pmatrix} \text{-contoid} \\ \text{-high} \\ \alpha\text{dorsal} \\ \text{-del. trans.} \end{pmatrix} \rightarrow \begin{pmatrix} \text{+wide glottis} \\ \text{-palatal} \\ \alpha\text{high} \\ \text{-low} \end{pmatrix} \;/\; \_\_\_\_ \; \left( \begin{pmatrix} \begin{Bmatrix} [\text{-nasal}] \\ [\text{-lateral}] \\ [\text{-occlusion}] \end{Bmatrix} \\ [\text{+contoid}] \end{pmatrix} \right).$$

### 8.3 Loss of /n+:

$$\begin{pmatrix} \text{+nasal} \\ \text{+contoid} \end{pmatrix} \rightarrow \emptyset / \begin{pmatrix} \text{-contoid} \\ \text{+nasal} \end{pmatrix} \;/\_\_ \;+ + \; S<S\#$$

### 4.4 Syllable Boundary 2:

$$\emptyset \rightarrow \;.\; /[\text{-contoid}] \_\_ [\text{+contoid}] \begin{Bmatrix} [\text{-contoid}] \\ C_2 \end{Bmatrix}$$

**4.5 Syllable Boundary 3:**

$$\emptyset \rightarrow . \; / \; [\text{-contoid}] \; \_\_ \left(\begin{array}{l} \text{-contoid} \\ \left\{\begin{array}{l} \text{-high} \\ \text{+delayed transition} \end{array}\right\} \end{array}\right)$$

**4.6 Syllable Boundary 4:**

$$\emptyset \rightarrow . \; / \; C_4\_\_ \left(\begin{array}{l} \text{+contoid} \\ \left\{\begin{array}{l} \text{+nasal} \\ \text{+occlusion} \\ \text{+friction} \end{array}\right\} \end{array}\right)$$

**8.4 Progressive Assimilation of Off-Glides:**

$$\left(\begin{array}{l} \text{-contoid} \\ \text{+high} \\ \text{-del. trans.} \end{array}\right) \rightarrow [\text{+nasal}] \; / \left(\begin{array}{l} \text{-contoid} \\ \text{-high} \\ \text{+nasal} \end{array}\right) \_\_$$

**8.2 +sion++e++z#'s Merger:**

+(s)ion++e+<z# → +(s)on++e+<z#

**6.2b Deletion of Word-Final <e+, +e+, (and +ε#) After /n#:**

$$\left(\begin{array}{l} \text{-contoid} \\ \text{-high} \\ \text{-delayed transition} \\ \text{+palatal} \end{array}\right) \rightarrow \emptyset \; / \; \# \, X \left(\begin{array}{l} \text{+contoid} \\ \text{+nasal} \\ \text{-labial} \\ \text{-high} \end{array}\right) \#_{[\text{-N4}]}$$

**9.1a Metathesis:**

$$\begin{pmatrix} +\text{palatal} \\ +\text{high} \\ -\text{del. trans.} \end{pmatrix}_1 \begin{pmatrix} +\text{contoid} \\ +\text{nasal} \\ -\text{labial} \\ -\text{high} \end{pmatrix} \# + \begin{pmatrix} +\text{palatal} \\ -\text{high} \\ -\text{del. trans.} \end{pmatrix}_2 + \begin{Bmatrix} <\emptyset\# \\ \\ <z\# \end{Bmatrix} \rightarrow 2C\#1$$

**9.2a Nasalization (Progressive/Regressive Assimilation):**

$[-\text{contoid}] \rightarrow [+\text{nasal}]$ / .X ___ $[+\text{nasal}]$_____.

**9.3 The Loss of Word-Final /l# in Pluralizations:**

$$[+\text{lateral}] \,/\, \_\# \begin{Bmatrix} < \\ + \end{Bmatrix} e+ \#<z\# \rightarrow \emptyset$$

**9.1b Metathesis:**

$$\begin{pmatrix} +\text{palatal} \\ +\text{high} \\ -\text{del. trans.} \end{pmatrix}_1 \begin{pmatrix} +\text{contoid} \\ \begin{Bmatrix} +\text{nasal} \\ \alpha\text{lateral} \end{Bmatrix} \\ -\text{high} \\ -\text{labial} \end{pmatrix} \# + \begin{pmatrix} +\text{palatal} \\ -\text{high} \\ -\text{del. trans.} \end{pmatrix}_2 + \begin{Bmatrix} <\emptyset\# \\ \\ \alpha<z\# \end{Bmatrix} \rightarrow 2C\#1$$

**Rule 4.1 Like Segment Deletion:**

$\text{Segment}_2 \rightarrow \emptyset \,/\, \text{Segment}_1$ ____

Condition: $\text{Segment}_1 = \text{Segment}_2$

**Rule 3.1b Paroxytone Stress Iteration:**

$[-\text{contoid}] \rightarrow [+\text{stress}] \,/\, \#X \_\_C_{0\text{-}4}VC(C)\#$

# Appendix B The Grammar of Problematic Nominals' Inflection

## 8.1 Suffix Merger in Word-Final Position:

$$\left\{\begin{matrix}\text{+on+<e+}\\ \text{+an+\{<e+,<o\#\}}\\ \text{+(}\alpha\text{ s)ion+ +e+}\end{matrix}\right\} \rightarrow \text{+ (}\alpha\text{ s)an+} \left\{\begin{matrix}\alpha\text{+o\#}_3\\ \text{<o\#}\end{matrix}\right\} / \_\_ \text{<[-plural]\#}$$

## 3.1 Paroxytone Stress (Invoked):

$$\text{[-contoid]} \rightarrow \text{[+stress]} / \text{\#X} \_\_ \left(\begin{bmatrix}\text{+high}\\ \text{-contoid}\end{bmatrix}\right) C_{0\text{-}4}V_{[\text{-high}]}\text{\#(C)\#}$$

## 9.1b Metathesis:

$$\begin{pmatrix}\text{+palatal}\\ \text{+high}\\ \text{-del. trans.}\end{pmatrix}_1 \begin{pmatrix}\text{+contoid}\\ \left\{\begin{matrix}\text{+nasal}\\ \alpha\text{lateral}\end{matrix}\right\}\\ \text{-high}\end{pmatrix} \text{\# +} \begin{pmatrix}\text{+palatal}\\ \text{-high}\\ \text{-del. trans.}\end{pmatrix}_2 + \left\{\begin{matrix}\text{<Ø\#}\\ \\ \alpha\text{<z\#}\end{matrix}\right\} \rightarrow \text{2C\#1}$$

## 6.2a Deletion of Word-Final <e+ and +e+ as well as +i+[7] After /r#, /l#, and /z#:

$$\left\{\begin{matrix}<\\ +\end{matrix}\right\} \begin{pmatrix}\text{-contoid}\\ \text{+palatal}\end{pmatrix} \rightarrow \text{Ø} / \text{\#X [-contoid]} \begin{pmatrix}\text{+contoid}\\ \text{-surd}\\ \text{-labial}\\ \text{-high}\\ \text{-nasal}\\ \text{-occlusion}\end{pmatrix} \_\_\text{+ <[-plural]\#}$$

7 See Tables 9C.1a and 1b.

**Rule 6.2b Deletion of Word-Final <e+, +e+, (and +ɛ#) After /n#:**

$$\begin{pmatrix} \text{-contoid} \\ \text{-high} \\ \text{-delayed transition} \\ \text{+palatal} \end{pmatrix} \rightarrow \varnothing \;/\; \#\, X \begin{pmatrix} \text{+contoid} \\ \text{+nasal} \\ \text{-labial} \\ \text{-high} \end{pmatrix} \#_{[\text{-N4}]}$$

**9.3 The Loss of Word-Final /l# in Pluralizations:**

$$[\text{+lateral}] \;/\; \_\# \begin{Bmatrix} < \\ + \end{Bmatrix} e+\ \#<z\# \rightarrow \text{Ø}$$

**7.2 Morphophonemic Nasalization $R_1$ Stems:**

$$+\begin{pmatrix} \text{-contoid} \\ \text{+delayed transition} \end{pmatrix} \rightarrow [\text{+nasal}] \;/\; \_\_ \begin{pmatrix} \text{+nasal} \\ \text{+contoid} \end{pmatrix} \begin{Bmatrix} + \\ < \end{Bmatrix} +\ [\pm\text{feminine}]\#\ <\text{Ø}\#$$

**2.3 Atonic Vowel Reduction:**

$$\begin{pmatrix} \text{-contoid} \\ \text{-high} \\ \alpha\text{dorsal} \\ \text{-del. trans.} \end{pmatrix} \rightarrow \begin{pmatrix} \text{+wide glottis} \\ \text{-palatal} \\ \alpha\text{high} \\ \text{-low} \end{pmatrix} \;/\; \_\_\_\_ \; \left( \begin{pmatrix} \begin{Bmatrix} [\text{-nasal}] \\ [\text{-lateral}] \\ [\text{-occlusion}] \end{Bmatrix} \\ [\text{+contoid}] \end{pmatrix} \right).$$

**8.3 Loss of /n+:**

$$\begin{pmatrix} \text{+nasal} \\ \text{+contoid} \end{pmatrix} \rightarrow \text{Ø}/ \begin{pmatrix} \text{-contoid} \\ \text{+nasal} \end{pmatrix} \;/\; \_\_\ +\ +\ S<S\#$$

**4.4 Syllable Boundary 2:**

$$\emptyset \rightarrow . / [\text{-contoid}] \_\_ [+\text{contoid}] \begin{Bmatrix} [\text{-contoid}] \\ C_2 \end{Bmatrix}$$

**4.6 Syllable Boundary 4:**

$$\emptyset \rightarrow . / C_4 \_\_ \begin{pmatrix} +\text{contoid} \\ \begin{Bmatrix} +\text{nasal} \\ +\text{occlusion} \\ +\text{friction} \end{Bmatrix} \end{pmatrix}$$

**Rule 9.2a Nasalization (Progressive/Regressive Assimilation):**

[-contoid] → [+nasal] / .X ___ [+nasal].

**Rule 4.1 Like Segment Deletion:**

$\text{Segment}_2 \rightarrow \emptyset / \text{Segment}_1$ ___.

**Condition:** $\text{Segment}_1 = \text{Segment}_2$

**Table 9B.1a** Derivations of [-plural, -feminine] Forms:[a] +on+<e+, +an+<o#, +an+<e#

| | ladrão | anão | alazão |
|---|---|---|---|
| U.F. | #ladr++on+<e+<Ø# | #an++an+<o#<Ø# | #alaz++an+<e#<Ø# |
| R. 8.1 | #ladr++an+<o#<Ø# | *** | #alaz++an+<o#<Ø# |
| R. 3.1 | #ladr++ˈan+<o#<Ø# | #an++ˈan+<o#<Ø# | #alaz++ˈan+<o#<Ø# |
| R. 9.1b | *** | *** | *** |
| R. 6.2a | *** | *** | *** |
| R. 6.2b | *** | *** | *** |
| R. 9.3 | *** | *** | *** |
| R. 7.2 | #lădr++ˈãn+<o#<Ø# | #ăn++ˈãn+<o#<Ø# | #alaz++ˈãn++o#<Ø# |
| R. 2.3 | #lădr++ˈãn+<ŭ#<Ø# | #ăn++ˈãn+<ŭ#<Ø# | #ălăz++ˈãn++ŭ#<Ø# |
| R. 8.3 | #lădr++ˈã+<ŭ#<Ø# | #ăn++ˈã+<ŭ#<Ø# | #ălăzˈã+<ŭ#<Ø# |
| R. 4.4 | #lă.dr++ˈã+<ŭ#<Ø# | #ă.n++ˈã+<ŭ#<Ø# | #ă.lă.zˈã+<ŭ#<Ø# |
| R. 4.6 | *** | *** | *** |
| R. 9.2 | #lă.dr++ˈã+<ũ#<Ø# | #ă.n++ˈã+<ũ#<Ø# | #ă.lă.zˈã+<ũ#<Ø# |
| R. 4.1 | *** | *** | *** |
| Ph. | [lă.ˈδrã̆ŭ] | [ã̆.ˈnã̆ŭ] | [ă.lă.ˈzã̆ŭ] |

a The words in Tables 9B.1a-c mean 'thief/thieves', 'dwarf/dwarves', and 'sorrel horse(s)'.

**Table 9B.1b** Derivations of [+plural, -feminine] Forms +on+<e+<z#, +an+<o#<z#, +an+<e#<z#

| | ladrões | anãos | alazães |
|---|---|---|---|
| U.F. | #ladr++on+<e+<z# | #an++an+<o#<z# | #alaz++an+<e#<z# |
| R. 8.1 | *** | *** | *** |
| R. 3.1 | #ladr++ˈon+<e+<z# | #an++ˈan+<o#<z# | #alaz++ˈan+<e#<z# |
| R. 9.1b | *** | *** | *** |
| R. 6.2a | *** | *** | *** |
| R. 6.2b | *** | *** | *** |
| R. 9.3 | *** | *** | *** |
| R. 7.2 | #ladr++ˈõn+<e+<z# | #an++ˈẵn+<o#<z# | #alaz++ˈẵn++e#<z# |
| R. 2.3 | #lădr++ˈõn+<ĭ+<z# | #ăn++ˈẵn+<ŭ#<z# | #ălăz++ˈẵn++ĭ#<z# |
| R. 8.3 | #lădr++ˈõ+<ĭ+<z# | #ăn++ˈẵ+<ŭ#<z# | #ălăzˈẵ+<ĭ#<z# |
| R. 4.4 | #lă.dr++ˈõ+<ĭ+<z# | #ă.n++ˈẵ+<ŭ#<z# | #ă.lă.zˈẵ+<ĭ#<z# |
| R. 4.6 | *** | *** | *** |
| R. 9.2 | #lă.dr++ˈõ+<ĩ+<z# | #ă.n++ˈẵ+<ũ#<z# | #ă.lă.zˈẵ+<ĩ#<z# |
| R. 4.1 | *** | *** | *** |
| Ph. | [lă.ˈðrõ$^{ĩ}$š] | [ẵ.ˈn ẵ$^{ũ}$š] | [ă.lă.zˈẵĩš] |

**Table 9B.1c** Derivations of [+plural, +feminine] Forms +on+<a#, +an+<a#, +an+<a#

| | ladronas | anãs | alazãs |
|---|---|---|---|
| | #ladr++on+<a#<z# | #an++an+<a#<z# | #alaz++an+<e#<z# |
| R. 8.1 | *** | *** | *** |
| R. 3.1 | #ladr++ˈon+<a#<z# | #an++ˈan+<a#<z# | #alaz++ˈan+<a#<z# |
| R. 9.1b | *** | *** | *** |
| R. 6.2a | *** | *** | *** |
| R. 6.2b | *** | *** | *** |
| R. 9.3 | *** | *** | *** |
| R. 7.2 | #ladr++ˈõn+<a#<z# | #an++ˈẵn+<a#<z# | #alaz++ˈẵn+<a#<z# |
| R. 2.3 | #lădr++ˈõn+<ă#<z# | #ăn++ˈẵn+<ă#<z# | #ălăz++ˈẵn++ă#<z# |
| R. 8.3 | *** | #ăn++ˈẵ+<ă#<z# | #ălăzˈẵ+<ă# |
| R. 4.4 | #lă.dr++ˈo.n+<ă#<z# | #ă.n++ˈẵ+<ă#<z# | #ă.lă.zˈẵ+<ă# |
| R. 4.6 | *** | *** | *** |
| R. 9.2 | *** | #ă.n++ˈẵ+ã<#<z# | #ă.lă.zˈẵ+<ã# |
| R. 4.1 | *** | #ă.n++ˈẵ#<z# | #ă.lă.zˈẵ# |
| Ph. | [lă.ˈδrõ.năš] | [ẵ.ˈnẵš] | [ă.lă.ˈzẵš] |

**Table 9B.2a** Derivations of Nominals with Arbitrary or Ambivalent Gender /un#+e+, /on#++e+, /in#++e+, /en#+e+[a]

| | bebum | bebuns | tom | tons |
|---|---|---|---|---|
| U.F. | #bɛb++un#+e+<Ø# | #bɛb++un#+e+<z | #ton#+e+<Ø# | #ton#+e+<Ø# |
| R. 8.1 | *** | *** | *** | *** |
| R. 3.1 | #bɛb++ˈun#+e+<Ø# | #bɛb++ˈun#+e+<z# | #tˈon#+e+<Ø# | #tˈon#+e+<Ø# |
| R. 9.1b | *** | *** | *** | *** |
| R. 6.2a | *** | *** | *** | *** |
| R. 6.2b | #bɛb++ˈun#<Ø# | #bɛb++ˈun#<z# | #tˈon#<Ø# | #tˈon#<Ø# |
| R. 9.3 | *** | *** | *** | *** |
| R. 7.2 | #bɛb++ˈũn#<Ø# | #bɛb++ˈũn#<z# | #tˈõn#<Ø# | #tˈõn#<Ø# |
| R. 2.3 | #bĭb++ˈũn#<Ø# | #bĭb++ˈũn#<z# | *** | *** |
| R. 8.3 | #bĭb++ˈũ#<Ø# | #bĭb++ˈũ#<z# | #tˈõ#<Ø# | #tˈõ#<Ø# |
| R. 4.4 | #bĭ.b++ˈũ#<Ø# | #bĭ.b++ˈũ#<z# | *** | *** |
| R. 4.6 | *** | *** | *** | *** |
| R. 9.2 | *** | *** | *** | *** |
| R. 4.1 | *** | *** | *** | *** |
| Ph. | [bə.ˈβũ] | [bə.ˈβũ$^{n}$š] | [ˈtõ] | [ˈtõ$^{n}$š] |

a The words in Table 9B.3 mean 'drunkard(s)' and 'tone(s)'.

**Table 9B.2b** Derivations of Plural Nominals with Arbitrary or Ambivalent Gender /un#+e+<z#, /on#++e+<z#, /in#++e+<z#, /en#+e+<z#[a]

| | **fim** | **fins** | **retém** | **reténs** |
|---|---|---|---|---|
| U.F. | #fin#+e+<Ø# | #fin#+e+<z# | #reten++e+<Ø# | #reten#+e+<z# |
| R. 8.1 | *** | *** | *** | *** |
| R. 3.1 | #fˈin#+e+<Ø# | #fˈin#+e+<z# | #retˈen++e+<Ø# | #retˈen++e+<z# |
| R. 9.1b | *** | *** | *** | *** |
| R. 6.2a | *** | *** | *** | *** |
| R. 6.2b | #fˈin#<Ø# | #fˈin#<z# | *** | *** |
| R. 9.3 | *** | *** | *** | *** |
| R. 7.2 | #fˈĩn#<Ø# | #fˈĩn#<z# | #retˈẽn++e+<Ø# | #retˈẽn++e+<z# |
| R. 2.3 | *** | *** | #rĭtˈẽn++ĭ+<Ø# | #rĭtˈẽn++ĭ+<z# |
| R. 8.3 | [fˈĩ] | [ˈfĩš] | #rĭtˈẽ#+ĭ<Ø# | #rĭtˈẽ++ĭ+<z# |
| R. 4.4 | *** | *** | #rĭ.tˈẽ#+ĭ<Ø# | #rĭ.tˈẽ++ ĭ +<z# |
| R. 4.6 | *** | *** | *** | *** |
| R. 9.2 | *** | *** | #rĭ.tˈẽ#+ĩ<Ø# | #rĭ.tˈẽ++ ĩ+<z# |
| R. 1.1 | *** | *** | *** | *** |
| Ph. | [fˈĩ] | [ˈfĩ$^{ɲ}$š] | [r̠ə.ˈtẽ$^{i}$] | [r̠ə.ˈtẽ$^{iɲ}$š] |

a The words in Table 9B.2b mean ‘end(s)’ and ‘retention(s)’.

**Table 9B.3a** The Emergence and Deletion of Stem-Final /l# (1)[a]

| | **banal** | **banais** | **cartel** | **cartéis** |
|---|---|---|---|---|
| **U.F.** | #banal#+e+<Ø# | #banal#+e+<z# | #kart++εl#+e+<Ø# | #kart++εl#+e+<z# |
| **R. 8.1** | *** | *** | *** | *** |
| **R. 3.1** | #banˈal#+e+<Ø# | #banˈal#+e+<z# | #kart++ˈεl#+e+<Ø# | #kart++ˈεl#+e+<z# |
| **R. 9.1b** | *** | *** | *** | *** |
| **R. 6.2a** | #banˈal#+Ø+<Ø# | *** | #kart++ˈεl#+Ø+<Ø# | *** |
| **R. 6.2b** | *** | *** | *** | *** |
| **R. 9.3** | *** | #banˈa#+e+<z# | *** | #kart'ε#+e+<z# |
| **R. 7.2** | *** | *** | *** | *** |
| **R. 2.3** | #bănˈal#+Ø+<Ø# | #bănˈa#+ĭ+<z# | #kărt++ˈεl#+Ø+<Ø# | #kărt++ε#+ĭ+<z# |
| **R. 8.3** | *** | *** | *** | *** |
| **R. 4.4** | #bă.nˈal#+Ø+<Ø# | #bă.nˈa#+ĭ+<z# | *** | *** |
| **R. 4.6** | *** | *** | #kăr.t++ˈεl#+Ø+<Ø# | #kăr.t++ε#+ĭ+<z# |
| **R. 9.2** | *** | *** | *** | *** |
| **R. 4.1** | *** | *** | *** | *** |
| **Ph.** | [bã̆.ˈnaɫ] | [bã̆.ˈna$^{\text{ĭ}}$š] | [ˈkăr.ˈtεɫ] | [kăr.ˈtε$^{\text{ĭ}}$š] |

a The words in Table 9B.3a mean 'banal' and 'cartel(s)'.

**Table 9B.3b** The Emergence and Deletion of Stem-Final /l# (1)[a]

| | atol | atóis | taful | tafuis |
|---|---|---|---|---|
| U.F. | #at ɔl#+e+<Ø# | #atɔl#+e+<z# | #taful#+e+<Ø# | #taful#+e+<z# |
| R. 8.1 | *** | *** | *** | *** |
| R. 3.1 | #atˈɔl#+e+<Ø# | #atˈɔl#+e+<z# | #tafˈul#+e+<Ø# | #tafˈul#+e+<z# |
| R. 9.1b | *** | *** | *** | *** |
| R. 6.2a | #atˈɔl#+Ø+<Ø# | *** | #tafˈul#+Ø+<Ø# | *** |
| R. 6.2b | *** | *** | *** | *** |
| R. 9.3 | *** | #atˈɔ#+e+<z# | *** | #tafˈu#+e+<z# |
| R. 7.2 | *** | *** | *** | *** |
| R. 2.3 | #ătˈɔl#+Ø+<Ø# | #ătˈɔ#+ĭ+<z# | #tăfˈul#+Ø+<Ø# | #tăfˈu#+ĭ+<z# |
| R. 8.3 | *** | *** | *** | *** |
| R. 4.4 | #ă.tˈɔl#+Ø+<Ø# | #ă.tˈɔ#+ĭ+<z# | #tă.fˈul#+Ø+<Ø# | #tă.fˈu.l#+ĭ+<z# |
| R. 4.6 | *** | *** | *** | *** |
| R. 9.2 | *** | *** | *** | *** |
| R. 4.1 | *** | *** | *** | *** |
| Ph. | [ă.ˈtɔɫ] | [ă.ˈtɔ$^{I}$š] | [tă.ˈfuɫ] | [tă.ˈfu.ĭš]/ [tă.ˈfu$^{I}$š] |

a The words in Table 9B.3b mean 'atoll(s)' and 'foppish'.

**Table 9B.4a** Derivation of Atonic+in++e+[a]

| | virgem | virgens | vagem | vagens |
|---|---|---|---|---|
| U.F. | #vˈir++žin#+e+<Ø # | #vˈir++žin#+e+z# | #vˈa++žin#+e+<Ø# | #vˈa++žin#+e+z# |
| R. 8.1 | *** | *** | *** | *** |
| R. 3.1 | *** | *** | *** | *** |
| R. 9.1b | #vˈir++žen#+i+<Ø# | #vˈir++žen#+i+z# | #vˈa++žen#+i+<Ø# | #vˈa++žen#+i+z# |
| R. 6.2a | *** | *** | *** | *** |
| R. 6.2b | *** | *** | *** | *** |
| R. 9.3 | *** | *** | *** | *** |
| R. 7.2 | #vˈir++žẽn#+i+<Ø# | #vˈir++žẽn#+i+z# | #vˈa++žẽn#+i+<Ø# | #vˈa++žẽn#+i+z# |
| R. 2.3 | *** | *** | *** | *** |
| R. 8.3 | #vˈir++žẽ#+i+<Ø# | #vˈir++žẽ#+i+z# | #vˈa++žẽ#+i+<Ø# | #vˈa++žẽ#+i+z# |
| R. 4.4 | *** | *** | #vˈa++.žẽ#+i+<Ø# | #vˈa++.žẽ#+i+z# |
| R. 4.6 | #vˈir++.žẽ#+i+<Ø# | #vˈir++.žẽ#+i+z# | *** | *** |
| R. 9.2 | #vˈir++.žẽ#+ĩ+<Ø# | #vˈir++.žẽ#+ĩ+z# | #vˈa++.žẽ#+ĩ+<Ø# | #vˈa++.žẽ#+ĩ+z# |
| R. 4.1 | *** | *** | *** | *** |
| Ph. | [ˈvir.žẽ$^{\tilde{\imath}}$] | [ˈvir.žẽ$^{\tilde{\imath}}$š] | [ˈva.žẽ$^{\tilde{\imath}}$] | [ˈva.žẽ$^{\tilde{\imath}}$š] |

a The words in Table 9B.4a mean 'virgin(s)' and 'string bean(s)'.

**§9B.0** According to this analysis, the words *virgem* and *vagem* are proparoxytones on the lexical level, which makes them immune to Rule 3.1 since they already have a stressed syllable. In addition, words such as *virgem* and *vagem* are Class $N_4$ nominals (§6.2.3.2.0) immune to Rule 6.2b, which causes the +e+ to be deleted word-finally after /n+ in other words.

**Table 9B.4b** Derivation of Tonic and Atonic word-final +il#+e+[a]

| | atril | atris | ágil | ágeis |
|---|---|---|---|---|
| U.F. | #atr++il#+e+<Ø# | #atr++il#+e+<z# | #ˈaž[b]++il#+e+<Ø# | #ˈaž++il#+e+<z# |
| R. 8.1 | *** | *** | *** | *** |
| R. 3.1 | #atr++ˈil#+e+<Ø# | #atr++ˈil#+e+<z# | *** | *** |
| R. 9.1b | *** | *** | *** | #ˈaž++el#+i+<z# |
| R. 6.2a | #atr++ˈil#+Ø+<Ø# | *** | #ˈaž++il#+Ø+<Ø# | *** |
| R. 6.2b | *** | *** | *** | *** |
| R. 9.3 | *** | #atr++ˈi#+e+<z# | *** | #ˈaž++e#+i+<z# |
| R. 7.2 | *** | *** | *** | *** |
| R. 2.3 | #ătr++ˈil#+Ø+<Ø# | #ătr++ˈi#+ĭ+<z# | *** | *** |
| R. 8.3 | *** | *** | *** | *** |
| R. 4.4 | #ă.tr++ˈil#+Ø+<Ø# | #ă.tr++ˈi.#+ĭ+<z# | #ˈa.ž++il#+Ø+<Ø# | #ˈa.ž++e#+i+<z# |
| R. 4.6 | *** | *** | *** | *** |
| R. 9.2 | *** | *** | *** | *** |
| R. 4.1 | *** | #atr++ˈi#+<z# | *** | *** |
| Ph. | [ă.ˈtriɫ] | [ă.ˈtriš] | [ˈa.žiɫ] | [ˈa.že$^{ĭ}$š] |

a The words in Table 9B.4b mean 'lectern(s)' and 'agile'.
b The actual root of *ágil* is #ag+. This transcription considers velar softening to have taken place.

**§9B.1** On the other hand, the word *atril*, and the many like it, are regularly formed paroxytones that are susceptible to Rule 6.2a. In the course of their plurals' derivation, the tonic /i/ and the post-tonic [ĭ] (/i/) are juxtaposed after the /l# has disappeared. Rule 4.1, which eliminates geminates in favor of the 1st segment, is the final step in their becoming realizable words. This rule also obtains for those apparent numberless and genderless nominals, as Table 9B.5 demonstrates.

Table 9B.5 Derivation of Inflectionless Nominals[a]

| | Singular | Plural | Singular | Plural |
|---|---|---|---|---|
| | **ónix** | **ónix** | **reles** | **reles** |
| U.F. | #ɔnikz#<Ø# | #ɔnikz#<z# | #rɛlez#<Ø# | #rɛlez#<z# |
| R. 8.1 | *** | *** | *** | *** |
| R. 3.1 | #ˈɔnikz#<Ø# | #ˈɔnikz#<z# | #rˈɛlez#<Ø# | #rˈɛlez#<z# |
| R. 9.1b | *** | *** | *** | *** |
| R. 6.2a | *** | *** | *** | *** |
| R. 6.2b | *** | *** | *** | *** |
| R. 9.3 | *** | *** | *** | *** |
| R. 7.2 | *** | *** | *** | *** |
| R. 2.3 | *** | *** | #rˈɛlĭz#<Ø# | #rˈɛlĭz#<z# |
| R. 8.3 | *** | *** | *** | *** |
| R. 4.4 | #ˈɔ.nikz#<Ø# | #ˈɔ.nikz#<z# | #rˈɛ.lĭz#<Ø# | #rˈɛlĭz#<z# |
| R. 4.6 | *** | *** | *** | *** |
| R. 9.2 | *** | *** | *** | *** |
| R. 4.1 | *** | #ˈɔnikz# | *** | #rˈɛlĭz# |
| Ph. | [ˈɔ.niks] | [ˈɔ.niks] | [ˈr̲ɛ.ləš] | [ˈr̲ɛ.ləš] |

a The words in Table 9B.5 mean 'onyx' and 'picayune'.

## Appendix C Pluralization and the Adjective-Deriving Suffix +bil#

§9C.0 Chapter 7 deals at length with the supremely productive adjective deriving suffix +bil# (§7.6.5.8.0–4; Tables 7.7a-b *et passim*) without providing a set of rules to govern its emergence word-finally, where it undergoes extreme mutations. In stem-final position, the morpheme consists of +bil#+e+<number#. Using the rules established in this chapter for aberrant inflection, plus rules specific to this suffix, Table 9C.1 provides a grammar for the allomorphy of +bil+ when it occurs word-finally and with the plural morpheme <z#.[8]

8 The two deverbal adjectives exemplified in Table 9C.1a-b mean 'tractable' and 'fallible'.

Table 9C.1a The Adjective-Forming Suffix +bil# ➔ Word-Final /vɛl/ and /vɛ$^{i}$z/

| | **tratável** | **tratáveis** |
|---|---|---|
| U.F. | #trat++ˈa#+bil#+e+<Ø# | #trat++ˈa#+bil#+e+<z# |
| R. 8.1 | *** | *** |
| R. 3.1 | *** | *** |
| R. 9.1b | #trat++ˈa#+bel#+i+<Ø# | #trat++ˈa#+bel#+i+<z# |
| R. 9C.1 | #trat++ˈa#+bɛl#+i+<Ø# | # trat++ˈa#+bɛl#+i+<z# |
| R.6.2a | #trat++ˈa#+bɛl#<Ø# | *** |
| R.6.2b | *** | *** |
| R. 9.3 | *** | #trat++ˈa#+bɛ++i+<z # |
| R. 7.2 | *** | *** |
| R. 2.3 | #trăt++ˈa#+bɛl#<Ø# | #trăt++ˈa#+bɛ++i+<z# |
| R. 8.3 | *** | *** |
| R. 4.4 | #tră.t++ˈa#+.bɛl#<Ø# | #tră.t++ˈa#+.bɛ++i+<z # |
| R. 4.6 | *** | |
| R. 9.2 | *** | *** |
| R. 4.1 | *** | *** |
| R. /b/--> /v/ | #trat++ˈa#+vɛl++Ø+<Ø# | #tră.t++ˈa#+.+ve++i+<z |
| Ph. | [trăˈta.vɛɫ] | [trăˈta.vɛ$^{\breve{\imath}}$š] |

Table 9C.1b The Adjective Forming Suffix +bil# ➔ Word-Final /vɛl/ and /vɛiz/

| | **falível** | **falíveis** |
|---|---|---|
| U.F. | #fal#+ˈi#+bil#+e+<Ø# | #fal#+ˈi#+bil#+e+<z# |
| R. 8.1 | *** | *** |
| R. 3.1 | *** | *** |
| R. 9.1b | #fal#+ˈi#+bel#+i+<Ø# | #fal#+ˈi#+bel#+i+<z# |
| R. 9c.1 | #fal#+ˈi#+bɛl#+i+<Ø# | #fal#+ˈi#+bɛl#+i+<z# |
| R. 6.2a | #fal#+ˈi#+bɛl#<Ø# | *** |
| R. 6.2b | *** | *** |
| R. 9.3 | *** | #fal++ˈi#+bɛ++i+<z# |
| R. 7.2 | *** | *** |
| R. 2.3 | #făl#+ˈi#+bɛl#<Ø# | #făl++ˈi#+bɛ++i+<z# |

Table 9C.1b Continued

| | falível | falíveis |
|---|---|---|
| R. 8.3 | *** | *** |
| R. 4.4 | #fă.l#+ˈi#+.bɛl#<Ø# | #fă.l++ˈi#+.bɛ++i+<z# |
| R. 4.6 | *** | *** |
| R. 9.2 | *** | *** |
| R. 4.1 | *** | [fa.lˈi.bɛĭz] |
| R. 9C.2 | #fă.l#+ˈi#+.vɛl#<Ø# | #fă.l++ˈi#+.vɛ++i+<z# |
| Ph. | [fă.ˈli.vɛɫ] | [fă.ˈli.vɛĭš] |

§**9C.1** The singular and plural forms of this suffix emerge exactly as the normal words with word-final /l#. What needs to be accounted for is its mutation from +bil# to [vɛɫ. The evidence alluded to above shows that the underlying form of this adjective forming suffix is +bil#.

§**9C.1.2.0** The +bil# Rule (9C.1) changes the /e/ of +bel+ to /ɛ/ when this suffix is followed by the ambivalent gender morpheme +e+:

**Rule 9C.1 (+bil+ Rule):**

$$\begin{pmatrix} \text{-delayed transition} \\ \text{+palatal} \\ \text{-high} \end{pmatrix} \rightarrow \begin{pmatrix} \text{+wide glottis} \\ \text{-high} \end{pmatrix} / + \begin{pmatrix} \text{-surd} \\ \text{+labial} \\ \text{+occlusion} \end{pmatrix} \_\_ \begin{pmatrix} \text{+lateral} \\ \text{-high} \end{pmatrix} ++e+$$

§**9C.2.1** Other than the unavoidable fact that the forms +bil# and +vɛl# are obviously allomorphs of the same morpheme, there seems to be scant phonetic motivation[9] for Rule 9C.1. It seems that this phenomenon is peculiar to this morpheme.

§**9C.2.2** The shift from +b/ to +v/ is not restricted to this suffix, however, but the suffix is so ubiquitous (1,700 words ending in /vɛl/ [27 of which are among the most common], 497 ending in /bilidade/ [three among the most common]), that a rule for the /b/ to /v/ phenomenon is well-motivated by the data:

9 Syllable-final /l/ will occasion lax vowels [ɛ] and [ɔ] as syllable nuclei.

**Rule 9C.2 +b/ to +v/ in +bɛl+:**

$$+\begin{pmatrix} +\text{labial} \\ -\text{surd} \\ +\text{occlusion} \end{pmatrix} \rightarrow [+\text{fricative}]\ /\ \_\_\text{ɛl}\#+\text{e}+$$

# 10 Derivations with Diminutives and Augmentatives

## Introduction

**§10.0.0** Chapters 7–9 demonstrate that speakers of Portuguese use nominal-deriving suffixes to create words from specific stems. These suffixes apply to stems to create words of varying gender and words pertaining to different form classes: e.g. the root #žɔk+ is used to create (**A**) a verb ***joga*** #žɔk+<Ø#+a# ‘$3^{rd}$ plays’, (**B**) a [-feminine] noun **jogo** #žɔk++o# ‘game’, (**C**) a [+feminine] noun ***jogada*** #žɔk++a#+t++a# ‘maneuver’, (**D**) yet another [+feminine] noun **jocosidade** #žɔk++ɔz+idad++$e_{[fem.]}$# ‘playfulness’, (**E**) and an adjective **jocoso** #žɔk++ɔz+<o# ‘fun-loving’. The words ***jocosidade*** and ***jocoso*** (with their +$S_1$ suffixes: +idad++e# and +ɔz+<[αfeminine]#) pertain to a somewhat erudite level of discourse, whereas ***joga***, ***jogo***, and ***jogada*** (with their +S suffixes +a#, +o#, and +t++a#) are much more every-day. Words derived by suffixes such as these may pertain to different levels of speech, but they do not indicate their users’ affect concerning what is denoted.

**§10.0.1** Diminutive and augmentative suffixes may, at first blush, seem to be essentially different from the nominal-deriving suffixes studied so far. This is because people use the most common diminutive and augmentative suffixes to convey affect (Villalva, 2009: 2; Villalva and Gonçalves, 2016: 169, 171–3) concerning a specific individual, thing, or concept. On the other hand, notwithstanding the essential difference between the derivational suffixes that create words from stems and the diminutive and augmentative suffixes that can convey affect, augmentative and diminutive suffixes also derive independent words from stems that form other words. In this sense they are deriving suffixes, or, as Villalva and Gonçalves would have it, they are ‘morphological predicator[s]’ (169) rather than modifiers or evaluatives, i.e. affect conveyers. On the other hand, unlike other deriving suffixes, only very rarely are they instrumental in changing the form class or gender of a particular stem or root. When they accrete to adjectives, the resultant words reflect the gender and number of whatever noun the adjective modifies or stands for.[1]

**§10.0.2.0** Admittedly, the most common diminutive and augmentative suffixes' usual role is to convey Portuguese speakers' affect concerning specific nominals. In addition to Table 10.1's illustration of 'spontaneous' diminutive and augmentative forms, it also illustrates gender preservation in diminutive and augmentative forms of nominals.[2]

**Table 10.1** Gender Preservation in Spontaneous Diminutives and Augmentatives

| Proper Nouns | | | | | |
|---|---|---|---|---|---|
| Diminutives | | | | Augmentatives | |
| Name | Gloss | Diminutive | Gloss | Augmentative | Gloss |
| **Artur** | Arthur | **Arturzinho** | Artie | **Arturzão** | big Art |
| **Guilherme** | William | **Guilhermino** | Willy | **Guilhermão** | big Bill |
| **Gilberto** | Gilbert | **Gilbertinho** | little Gil | **Gilbertão** | big Gil |
| **Maria** | Mary | **Mariazinha** | little Mary | **Mariona** | big Mary |
| **Dora** | Dora | **Dorinha** | little Dora | **Dorona** | big Dora |
| **Linda** | Linda | **Lindinha** | Lindy | **Lindona** | big Linda |
| Common Nouns | | | | | |
| Noun | Gloss | Diminutive | Gloss | Augmentative | Gloss |
| **livro** | book | **livrinho** | cute book | **livrão** | fantastic book |
| **trabalho** | work | **trabalhinho** | nice little task | **trabalhão** | great job |
| **carro** | car | **carrinho** | little car | **carrão** | monster car |

1 Diminutive suffixes can attach to adverbs, and as diminutive adverbs they convey no gender.

2 The term 'spontaneous' indicates the entirely facultative diminutive and augmentative versions of particular names and words. Opting for diminutive or augmentative forms conveys speakers' unique take on specific words' referents. Spontaneous augmentatives and diminutives are different from derived diminutive and augmentative forms because the latter are independent lexical items whose meanings and connotations usually transcend the sum of their constituent parts: cf. *carrinho* 'little, cute, cherished automobile' (*carro* 'automobile') and *azeitinho* 'castor oil' (*azeite* 'olive oil').

Table 10.1 Continued

| | | | | | |
|---|---|---|---|---|---|
| **fita** | ribbon | **fitinha** | cute ribbon | **fitona** | big, wide ribbon |
| **gazela** | gazelle | **gazelinha** | little gazelle | **gazelona** | big ugly gazelle |
| **janela** | window | **janelinha** | tiny window | **janelona** | big ugly window |
| **Adjectives** | | | | | |
| **Adjective** | **Gloss** | **Diminutive** | **Gloss** | **Augmentative** | **Gloss** |
| **calado** | quiet | **caladinho** | very quiet | **caladão** | taciturn |
| **bonito**[a] | pretty | **bonitinho** | very cute | **bonitão** | beyond pretty |
| **petulante** | petulant | **petulantinho** | pettily petulant | **petulantão** | horribly petulant |
| **quente** | hot | **quentinho** | very hot | **quentão** | hot drink |
| **feio** | ugly | **feiínho** | cutely ugly | **feião** | really ugly |
| **fresco** | cool | **fresquinho** | nicely cool | **frescalhão** | really cool |

a The world *bonito* is, in fact, a word derived from the root #bon+, meaning 'good', and the diminutive suffix *–ito*: #bon++it+<[αfeminine]#<[αplural]#.

**§10.0.2.1** The proper noun section of Table 10.1 contains three normally male names and three normally female names.[3] The male diminutive and augmentative names end in <o#, the inflectional [-feminine] gender morpheme, whereas the female diminutives and augmentatives end in <a#, the inflectional [+feminine] gender morpheme. The same obtains for the common nouns: when the original noun is [-feminine], the diminutives and augmentatives are normally [-feminine]. When they are [+feminine], so are the diminutives and augmentatives. All of the adjectives listed in Table 10.1 could occur inflected for [+feminine] gender: e.g. *caladinha*, *bonitinha*, *petulantinha* in their diminutive forms and *caladona*, *bonitona*, and *petulantona* in their augmentative forms; however, tradition has it that adjectives' citation form is [-feminine], even in their diminutive forms.

**§10.0.2.2** The glosses offered for the nominals in Table 10.1 only approximate the affect diminutive and augmentative accretions can convey.

3 The [+feminine] cognate of **Guilherme** (**Guilhermina**) is formed from the diminutive of the ordinary masculine name and has [+feminine] gender.

Normally the affect is positive when the diminutive *–inho* is added to a word,[4] whereas the affect associated with augmentatives is more varied. For example, the word *cavalinho*, when it means 'little horse' or 'horsy' it connotes positive feelings toward the referent, whereas *cavalão* can be used to indicate positive or negative feelings about a big horse, but it can also designate an abnormally tall individual or a boor—the latter obviously connotes negative affect. In Brazilian Portuguese, the word *cachorro* 'pup' is commonly used to indicate all dogs. To refer to a specific dog with the diminutive *cachorrinho* conveys positive affect toward the dog, whereas to call it a *cachorrão* can suggest a 'scary dog'.[5] On the other hand, the augmentative suffix on *carrão* can convey both positive and negative affect, just as to refer to such a car as a 'monster' car in English can transmit positive or negative affect depending on the speakers' vocal qualifiers that can also convey their attitude toward that type of car. The three modalities of the adjective: *fresco* ⇔ *fresquinho* ⇔ *frescalhão* demonstrate the varied connotations the two suffixes can express. The diminutive conveys positive affect, and the augmentative (doubly augmentative with ıaλı followed by ıonı<e#) 'really cool' augments the adjective's intrinsic positive affect. Beyond this, *frescalhão* can mean 'well preserved', but it can also mean 'rascally'.[6]

**§10.0.2.3** Because speakers opt to use diminutives and augmentatives both positively and negatively in specific pragmatic contexts, it is impossible to say that they are consistently complementary or derogatory. A grammar of Portuguese morphophonology can only describe and analyze the items and the processes associated with lexical-grammatical forms such as diminutives and augmentatives, leaving the study of their use as conveyers of positive or negative affect to Portuguese speakers and students of speech acts.

---

4 But the affect diminutives convey can be negative or condescending. When I was researching my dissertation at the Centro de Estudos Românicos at the University of Coimbra, Professor Paiva Boléo (the director of that center) approached me after I had been working there for several months and conceded that my efforts might yield a *trabalhinho* 'a little piece' (cf. *trabalho* 'work'). My irony failed me at that point, so I replied defensively and said that the fruit of my labor would be a *trabalhão* 'a massive work'.

5 I vividly remember Brazilian children expressing their fear of a somewhat feisty dachshund under my care by calling it a *cachorrão*.

6 In at least the 1970s and 1980s, the word *frescão* (also an augmentative) was used to indicate an air-conditioned commuter bus in Rio.

§**10.0.2.4** Readers already versed in Portuguese will have noticed that Table 10.1 illustrates the most common diminutive forming morpheme *-(z)inh-* and the most common augmentative morpheme *–(z)ão*. There are, however, many other suffixes Portuguese grammarians refer to as diminutives and augmentatives. To deal with this subset of deriving suffixes researchers need to know: (A) What are the morphemes that make diminutive and augmentative forms of adjectives and nouns? (B) How can one characterize diminutive and augmentative nominals' underlying forms? (C) Which words containing diminutive and augmentative suffixes are lexical items (idioms)? (D) And which forms come about merely to convey Portuguese speakers' affect concerning a word's referent? This investigation begins with the diminutive morphemes.

## Diminutives

§**10.1.0** Using traditional orthography rather than morphophonemic analysis, Table 10.2a displays the 23 items Cunha (66) classifies as diminutive suffixes as well as their token frequency in the *Aurélio*:

Table 10.2a Diminutive Morphemes[a]

| Cunha | Aurélio | | | Cunha | Aurélio | | |
|---|---|---|---|---|---|---|---|
| Suffixes | [-fem.] | [+fem.] | Total | Suffixes | [-fem.] | [+fem.] | Total |
| -ebre | 6 | *** | 6 | -ico, -a | 85 | 86 | 171 |
| -zito, -a | 4 | 8 | 12 | -ola | *** | 172 | 172 |
| -usco, -a | 12 | 5 | 17 | -ino, -a | 60 | 166 | 194 |
| -icho, -a | 15 | 9 | 24 | -ote, -a | 195 | 133 | 328 |
| -ucho, -a | 18 | 9 | 27 | -ilho, -a | 149 | 194 | 343 |
| -ito, -a | 28 | 13 | 41 | -ela | *** | 365 | 365 |
| -isco, -a | 38 | 11 | 49 | -ete | 373 | *** | 373 |
| -acho, -a | 44 | 17 | 61 | -im | 386 | *** | 386 |
| -elho, -a | 40 | 33 | 73 | 'vX(c)ulo, a | 268 | 204 | 472 |
| -zinho, -a | 63 | 23 | 86 | -eto, -a | 191 | 329 | 520 |
| -eco, -a | 70 | 48 | 118 | -inho, -a | 328 | 391 | 719 |
| -ejo, -a | 103 | 16 | 119 | | | | |
| Totals: | 441 | 192 | 633 | | 2,035 | 2,040 | 4,075 |
| Total Occurrences in the *Aurélio* = 4,708 | | | | | | | |

a The mean of the entire dataset was 203.30, SD=196.90, Z= 2.78. There were no outliers. Similarly the [-feminine] diminutive forms (M=117.90 SD=124.32, Z =2.73) had no outlier. Likewise, the [+feminine] diminutives (M=111.60, SD=128.09, Z= 2.71) had no outlier.

**§10.1.1.** There is a basic difference between the diminutive nominals in Table 10.1 and those created by the suffixes in Table 10.2a. In the former table, the diminutive suffixes add no denotation to the stems, they transmit speakers' affect and impressions according to their whims and proclivities. Words bearing the diminutive morphemes in Table 10.2a (which include the affect-conveying suffix *–inho*, *-a*) actually do appear in dictionaries, as their appearance in the *Aurélio* attests. To the extent that these suffixes create specific lexical items, they are deriving suffixes.

**§10.1.2** Again, invoking the productivity scale (Table 7.3b) Table 10.2b displays the diminutive morphemes' relative productivity:

**Table 10.2b** Diminutive Morphemes' Productivity

| Negligible To Low | | | | Moderate To Very High | | | |
|---|---|---|---|---|---|---|---|
| Suffix | *Aurélio* | % | Productivity | Suffix | *Aurélio* | % | Productivity |
| -ebre | 6 | 0.13 | Negligible | -ico, -a | 171 | 3.66 | Moderate |
| -zito, -a | 12 | 0.26 | Negligible | -ola | 172 | 3.68 | Moderate |
| -usco, -a | 17 | 0.36 | Negligible | -ino, a | 194 | 4.15 | Moderate |
| -icho, -a | 24 | 0.51 | Very Low | -ote, -a | 328 | 7.01 | High |
| -ucho, -a | 27 | 0.58 | Very Low | -ilho, -a | 343 | 7.34 | High |
| -ito, -a | 41 | 0.88 | Very Low | -ela | 365 | 7.81 | High |
| -isco, -a | 49 | 1.05 | Low | -ete | 373 | 8.00 | High |
| -acho, -a | 61 | 1.30 | Low | -im | 386 | 8.25 | High |
| -elho, -a | 73 | 1.56 | Low | ˈvX-(c)ulo, a | 472 | 10.10 | Very High |
| -zinho, -a | 96 | 2.05 | Low | -eto, -a | 520 | 11.12 | Very High |
| -eco, -a | 118 | 2.52 | Low | -inho, -a | 719 | 15.38 | Very High |
| -ejo, -a | 119 | 2.54 | Low | | | | |
| Totals: | 633 | 13.54 | | | 4,043 | 86.46 | |

**§10.1.3** In this set of diminutive endings, the twelve least productive account for only 13.62% of all the tokens of diminutive words in the *Aurélio*. The three very highly productive suffixes account for 36.60% of the data. Once again a minority of significant items (the 11 suffixes of moderate to very high productivity) accounts for the overwhelming majority (86.46%) of tokens in a particular significant category.

**§10.1.4** Tables 10.2a and 10.2b use traditional orthography rather than morphophonemic analysis in listing these diminutive morphemes.

The vocabulary formed with these morphemes demonstrates their status as deriving morphemes. Whereas they rarely determine the form class of the words/stems to which they attach, they convey denotations that are not present in the stems or in non-diminutive related words that bear no deriving suffix other than a gender morpheme. Once again the deliberations address the morphemes in the order of their productivity: the least shall be the first, and the last shall be the most productive.

**§10.2.0 –ebre:** This suffix is the least productive of all the diminutives. The six words ending in the suffix *-ebre* include *casebre* #kaz++ɛbr++e# 'hovel', a derivative of *casa* 'house'.[7] Here this suffix derives a [-feminine] noun from the root #kaz+. This word's meaning is more than 'little house', which qualifies +ɛbr++e# as a deriving suffix. This suffix also derives adjectives such as *célebre*, *fúnebre*, and *mulíebre* 'famous, funereal, woman-like' which are ambivalent, modifying both [±feminine] objects.

**§10.2.1.0 –zito, -a:** The actual diminutives[8] in the *Aurélio* total three: *cãozito* 'little dog', *jardinzito* 'little garden', and *florzita* "little flower', which are not new lexical items or idioms. They are simply words with diminutive morphemes that portray speakers' attitudes toward particular referents as well as idiosyncratic choices for the specific diminutive suffix (one could chose to form diminutives of *cão*, *flor* and *jardim* with the diminutive compounding element *zinho, -a)*. The suffix /z+it+<[αfeminine]# is an allomorph of the more (but still very low) productive suffix +it+<[αfeminine]#. Its initial /z/ is actually a transitional segment that emerges when +it+ follows a segment that can be word-final, i.e. a segment followed by the morpheme boundary #. Both allophones of +it+<[αfeminine]#, trigger a process of gender agreement

7 The English words 'house' and 'hovel' are etymologically, lexically, and semantically further apart than the Portuguese words *casa* and *casebre*. However, *casebre*'s meaning is greater than the sum of its parts and thus merits a dictionary entry, just as hovel does in English dictionaries. The English glosses provide an early clue into certain diminutives' lexical independence.

8 The *Aurélio* contains more [+feminine] instantiations of this suffix than [-feminine]: eight e.g. *afrizita* 'black tourmaline' and *andaluzita* 'aluminum silicate' vs four e.g. *quartzito* 'quartzite' and *queluzito* 'manganese ore'. These are lexical items. However, the +it++o# and +it++a# endings cited for this suffix do not really convey diminutiveness.

with the gender morpheme of the original noun, as Table 10.3 (below) demonstrates. In the examples supplied by the *Aurélio*: *cão* and *jardim* are [-feminine] (#kã̃$^{\breve{u}}$#, from #kan++e+ and #žardin#+e+), *flor* is [+feminine] (#flor#+$e_{[+fem.]}$+), so the gender morpheme <o# emerges on the suffix of the first two examples, whereas <a# emerges on the second—and the gender morphemes of the original word disappear. Rule 10.1a is a general rule of diminutive formation:

**Rule 10.1a Eliminate Stem-Internal Gender Morphemes in Diminutives:**

[±fem.] →Ø / {+, <} __#+diminutive+<[αfem.]#[9]

That is, once the suffixes' inflecting suffix agrees with the 'diminutivized' word, the word's original gender morpheme evanesces.

**§10.2.1.1** The other phenomenon entailed in this diminutive is the insertion of /z/ between the original words' stems and certain other (productive) suffixes. Rule 10.2 applies to these suffixes:

**Rule 10.2a /z/ Insertion for Diminutive Suffixes:**

$$\emptyset \rightarrow /z/ \;/\; \left\{\begin{matrix}[+\text{contoid}]\\ [\pm\text{feminine}]\end{matrix}\right\} \#\_\_ \; + \left\{\begin{matrix}\text{it}+\\ \text{iɲ}+\end{matrix}\right\} <[\alpha\text{feminine}]$$

**§10.2.1. 2** As they stand, Rules 10.1a and 10.2a are provisional. To account for gender agreement for both diminutive and augmentative forms, Rule 10.1a must contain disjunctions (§10.6.7.1), and Rule 10.2 acquires the augmentative suffix +on+ (§10.7.1.5).[10]

---

9 Not all diminutive forms are of the configuration +diminutive+<[αfeminine]#. Some admit deriving gender morphemes, as the suffix –<u>usco</u>, -<u>a</u> demonstrates (§10.2.2.0–2).

10 One of the examples, *cãozito*, has not lost its gender morpheme, which is realized as an off-glide [kã̃$^{\breve{u}n}$.'zi.tŭ]. The gender morpheme +o# may be preserved, and when it is, it occasions the insertion of /z/ between it and these diminutives. In my (1972) dialectal research in Portugal, the only instance of #z+it<o# occurred in the village of Ourondo. At a café one of my informants asked the barista to add a *cheirozito* (which he pronounced [tše$^{i}$.r$^{\breve{u}}$.'zi.t$^{\breve{u}}$]) to his coffee. His request was for a small amount of *bagaço* 'white brandy' to be added to the coffee. In more urban areas, this addition was known as a *cheirinho* 'a whiff'. For more on these matters, see sections §10.2.2.9.0–3 (-zinho, a), §10.2.2.22.0–2 (-inho, -a), and §10.5.11.0–.4.

**§10.2.2.0 –usco, -a:** Cunha's examples are the noun *chamusco* 'singeing' (cf. *chama* 'flame' and *chamusca* 'act of singeing') and the adjective *velhusco* 'happily old' (cf. *velho* 'old'). Other examples of this suffix occur in adjectives such as *pardusco* 'brownish' (cf. *pardo* 'brown'), *vermelhusco* 'ruddy' (cf. *vermelho* 'red'). The [+feminine] noun *farrusca*, which the *Aurélio* identifies as a combination of *ferro* (iron) plus the suffix *–usca*, means 'rusty sword' or 'blot'. It has a doublet adjective *farrusco*, which means 'dirty' and can, of course, be inflected for feminine gender.[11] This deriving suffix ends with the inflecting gender morpheme when it forms an adjective.

**§10.2.2.1** The nouns *chamusca* and *chamusco* are both derived from the root #šam+ followed by the deriving suffix +uzk+, which in turn is followed by the deriving gender morphemes +a# and +o#. That is, these two nouns are formed from bi-morphemic stems consisting of a root followed by a diminutive suffix, which in turn is followed by the two deriving gender morphemes. The adjectives, on the other hand, are structured as: #stem++uzk+<[αfeminine]#.

**§10.2.2.2** The existence of two different words formed from the same stem followed by the same diminutive suffix but of different genders, i.e. *chamusco* 'singeing' and *chamusca* 'the act of singeing' is related to the principle described in (Tables 6.8 and 6.9; §6.1.3.3). Gender suffixes themselves can be deriving suffixes whose addition to specific stems can create specific lexical items. This phenomenon obtains in words formed with the diminutive +uzk+ as well as other deriving diminutive suffixes yet to be examined.

**§10.2.2.3 –icho, -a:** This negligibly productive suffix appears in words such as *cornicho* 'cornice', *capricho* 'caprice', and *rabicho* 'queue'. These words derive from the same roots as *corno* 'horn', *cabro* 'billy goat', and *rabo* 'tail'. Cunha's examples are *governicho* (cf. *governo* 'government') and *barbicha* (cf. *barba* 'beard'), which mean, respectively, 'bad government' and 'thin scraggly beard'. That this suffix adds

11 *Farrusca* may have originally been a [+feminine] form of the adjective marshalled by usage to be a noun, since both *espada* 'sword' and *nódoa* 'stain' are [+feminine]. That is, sword owners and blot detectors are probably prone to referring to their familiar objects by these objects' characteristics rather than by the nouns that denote them modified by adjectives. Sancho Panza refers to his mule as his *rucío* 'gray', and in English spotted horses are known as pintos or piebalds, which originated as adjectives.

both connotation and denotation to its stems and that it can cause an underlying root to emerge without the mutation of a root-final /pr+ (cf. #kapr++o# ⇔ #kapr++o#+iš++o# ⇔ #kabr++a#, i.e. *capricho* and *cabra* 'goat', cf. *cabro* 'billy goat') qualifies it as a +$S_1$ deriving suffix. Because it appears to preserve the gender of related nouns, its lexical form will be **+iš+<[αfeminine]#**. The underlying forms of *barbicha* and *capricho* will be #barb++a#+iš+<[αfeminine]# and #kapr++o#+iš+<[αfeminine]#. Rule 10.1a will delete the stems' gender morpheme once the diminutive's inflecting gender morpheme agrees with that of the stem.[12]

**§10.2.2.4 –ucho, -a:** In accordance with Rule 10.1a Cunha offers the nouns *papelucho* 'paper scrap' (cf. *papel* 'paper' [-feminine]) and *casucha* 'tumbled down house' (cf. *casa* 'house' [+feminine]), and adjectives such as *trancucho* 'half drunk' (a Spanish loan word), *galucho* 'recruit (i.e. 'without rank')' (cf. *gala* 'official ornamentation') and *capucho* 'Capuchin' (cf. *capa* 'cape'). These and 23 other words appear in the *Aurélio*. The form *capucha* 'hooded cloak' (#kap++a#+uš+<[αfeminine]#) also appears. The idiomatic nature of these derived nouns and adjectives qualify this suffix as a deriving suffix that reflects the original nouns' gender, but whose adjectives agree in gender with whatever the adjectives modify or represent. This +S suffix is +uš+<[αfeminine]#. The underlying form of a noun like *casucha* contains the stem's gender morpheme +a#: #kaz++a#+uš+<[αfeminine]#, the underlying form of adjectives, e.g. *galucho* have the diminutive suffix attached directly to their stems #gal++uš+<[αfeminine]#.

**§10.2.2.5.0 –ito, -a:** The Aurélio contains 558 nominals ending in *–ito* that could possibly be diminutives and 747 ending in *–ita*. Those ending in *–ito* largely indicate scientific terms: e.g. *aerolito* 'meteorite', *clorito* 'a salt made from chloric acid'; geological terms: e.g. *coralito* a 'calcareous coral skeleton', *fulgurito* 'melted rock or sand'. Of 222 randomly examined words, there were 11 bona fide diminutives—4.95%, which, extrapolating to the dataset, yield 28 tokens. Those ending in *–ita* overwhelmingly indicate chemical terms: e.g. *acanita* 'silver sulfate', *enstatita* 'magnesium silicate'; advocates: e.g. *ebionita* 'advocate of Judaic law', *eremita* 'hermit'; membership: e.g. *semita* 'Semite', *ismaelita* 'Shiite'. Out of 222 randomly selected examples in the *–ita*

12 Such agreement is automatic since the designation [αfeminine] signals agreement with the preceding gender morpheme within that word's boundaries.

dataset there were four bona fide diminutives—1.80% of the sampling. Extrapolation suggests that the *Aurélio* contains 13 diminutives ending in *–ita*.

**§10.2.2.5.1** The examples Cunha gives, *casita* and *rapazito*, are spontaneous diminutives of *casa* 'house' and *rapaz* 'young fellow'. Noun deriving use of +it++o# appears in words such as *mosquito* 'mosquito' (cf. *mosca* 'fly'), *arenito* 'sandstone' (cf. *areia* 'sand'), and *cabrito* 'kid' (cf. *cabro* 'billy goat', *cabra* 'goat'). This is not a +$S_1$ suffix, even though it transports the underlying /n+ of *areia* #aren++a# to *arenito* and *bom* #bon#+e+ to surface realizations in the adjective: *bonito* 'pretty' (#bon++it+<[αfeminine]#). This happens because usually deriving suffixes preserve stem-final /n+. Indeed, +it+ does not preserve the /p/ in the root of *cabro* (#kapr+) when it forms *cabrito*. When it creates a spontaneous diminutive form of a noun, it preserves the noun's original gender (Rule 10.1a), but the examples of actual derivation indicate that it attaches to roots: *mosca* #mozk++a# ⇔ *mosquito* #mozk++it++o#, *areia* #aren++a# ⇔ *arenito* #aren++it++o# and provides the resultant words with gender. The form *senhorita*, in addition to being an obsequious form of direct address for young women, can mean 'short woman' or 'unmarried young woman', whereas *senhorito* indicates a young dandy, a refined swimmer, or, in Portuguese slang an unworthy individual.

**§10.2.2.6 –isco, -a:** Cunha's examples are *chuvisco* 'drizzle' (cf. *chuva* 'rain') and *talisca* 'chip, splinter' (cf. *tala* 'splint' and *talo* 'stem'). Both of Cunha's examples show the combination of roots plus this suffix forms specific words. Of the 49 examples found in the *Aurélio*, *malvaísco* 'marsh mallow', *pedrisco* 'small volley of rocks', and *marisco* '(edible) marine invertebrate' are other examples of this suffix's being used to form new words from specific roots (cf. *malva* 'mallow', *pedra* 'rock', *mar* 'sea'). This deriving suffix is of the +S variety since in the word *pedrisco* it allows the root's /tr+ to mutate to /dr+. This suffix can combine with either +o# or +a# to form specific words.[13] It attaches to roots rather than to gendered stems: e.g. *chuvisco* #šuv++izk++o#.

**§10.2.2.7.0 –acho, -a:** Cunha's examples are: the nouns *fogacho* 'dynamite blast' (cf. *fogo* 'fire') and *riacho* 'brook' (cf. *rio* 'river'). As a noun forming, deriving suffix it consists of +aš+ followed by either gender morpheme, as the words *bolacha* 'cookie' (cf. *bolo* 'cake'), *plumacho*

13 The *Morais* dictionary lists both *rabisco* and *rabisca*, but it considers them to be synonyms.

'(decorative) plumage' (cf. *pluma* '[decorative] feather'), *velacho* 'foresail' (cf. *vela* 'sail') demonstrate. The word *bombacho(s)* 'small water pump(s)' (cf. *bomba* 'pump') stands in contrast with *bombachas* 'gaucho pants' to confirm that the gender morphemes associated with this suffix are derivational.

**§10.2.2.7.1** This suffix also appears in adjectives: *verdacho* 'greenish' (cf. *verde* 'green') and [+animate] nominals *folacho* 'milquetoast' (cf. *fole* 'bellows'). In its formation of adjectives, this suffix ends in the [αfeminine] gender morpheme, e.g. *folacho* #fol++aš+<[αfeminine]#.

**§10.2.2.7.2** Another noun derived with this suffix is *populacho* 'riff-raff' (cf. *povo* 'folk', *popular* 'popular, of the people'). In these examples, the diminutive suffix is followed by the deriving gender morpheme +o#. The form *populacho* rather than **povacho* (cf. *povinho* 'mass[es]') indicates that +aš+ is a $+S_1$ deriving suffix because it preserves the underlying form #pɔp+ rather than the mutated root #pɔv+ before +S suffixes: e.g. *povo* 'folk', *povoado* 'town', *povoar* 'to populate'.

**§10.2.2.8 –elho, -a:** Cunha gives *folhelho* 'husk' (cf. *folha* 'leaf') and *rapazelho* 'urchin' (cf. *rapaz* 'young male') as examples of this suffix. In the first case, it creates a unique lexical item, whereas in the second it is a diminutive pure and simple, which one can translate into English as 'urchin', but it may merely mean 'young boy'. On the other hand, the *Aurélio* contains words such as *trabelho* 'tightening block' (cf. *trave* 'brake [+fem.]'), *fedelho* 'brat' (cf. *feder* 'to stink'), *bedelho* 'door stop',[14] and *grupelho* 'small faction' (cf. *grupo* 'group'). This suffix also occurs with the [+feminine] deriving morpheme +a# in words such as *parelha* 'a team of two horses' (cf. *par* 'pair [-feminine]') and *guedelha* 'small grapevine, unkempt long hair'.[15] These words' appearance in the *Aurélio* gives them a lexical status rather than that of spontaneous diminutives. And this confers derivational status to +eλ+. Both gender morphemes can attach to this diminutive such that the resultant words' genders may be different from that of their non-diminutive counterparts: e.g. *folhelho* #foλ++eλ++o#, *parelha* #par++eλ++a#. Of course when it forms adjectives, this

14 There may be a relationship between the root of *bedelho* 'door stop' and *badalo* 'bell clapper', but this relationship is tenuous at best.

15 *Guedelha* has the variant *gadelha*, but a clear meaning for #gad+ or #ged+ and their relation to any other words is unlikely. These words and their endings may be more examples of accidental homophony as far as the suffix in question is concerned.

suffix is followed by the inflecting gender morpheme <[αfeminine]# as in *parelho* 'similar': #par#+eλ+<[αfeminine]#. There is no evidence that it is anything other than a +S suffix.

**§10.2.2.9.0 -zinho, -a:** Cunha gives two examples of *-zinho*: *cãozinho* 'little dog' (cf. *cão* 'dog') and *ruazinha* 'little street' (cf. *rua* 'street'). Whereas *ruazinha* has no entry in the *Aurélio*, that dictionary lists *cãozinho* as one of two diminutive forms of the word *cão*. Neither *cãozinho* nor *ruazinha* means anything more than the sum of each word's parts; thus, they need not be lexical items.[16] On the other hand, words like *comezinho*, and *pãozinho* are examples of this diminutive form's word generating capabilities. The former contains the same root as *comer* 'to eat' and means 'palatable', the latter contains #pan+, which is the root of *pão* 'bread' and *panificação* 'bread making'. In Brazil, the word *pãozinho* indicates a (non-sweet) roll. Feminine gender entries in the *Aurélio* include *aguiazinha* 'eaglet' (cf. *águia* 'eagle'), *lãzinha* 'fine, light wool weave', and *tardezinha* 'late afternoon' (cf. *tarde* 'afternoon' and *tardinha* also 'late afternoon').

**§10.2.2.9.1** Whereas Cunha considers *-zinho* to be a diminutive morpheme that can be separate from *-inho* (Table 10.2b and §10.2.2.22.0-1), this form quite likely originated as an allomorph of *-inho*. Its initial /z/ occurs in spontaneous diminutive formations on proper names: Edgar + iɲ+<o# ➔ Edgarzinho, Raquel + iɲ+<a# ➔ Raquelzinha, Esman + iɲ+<o# ➔Esmanzinho. This interstitial /z/ may also appear when a proper noun's gender morpheme is preserved: Maria ⇔ Mariazinha (cf. Mariínha) and Eusébio ⇔ Euzebiozinho.

**§10.2.2.9.2** Villalva (2009) has found (3) that when speakers are asked to form diminutives of a wide array of words, natives of Lisbon prefer +ziɲ+ to +iɲ+ for words unlikely to occur as diminutives: For example, when requested to form a diminutive of *electrocardiograma*, 85.6% of her informants opted for *electrocardiogramazinho*. This is because words formed with *zinho*, -a, are compound words rather than derived words, and no operation need occur on the first set of elements. (§12.4.0–12.4.3.1.)

**§10.2.2.9.3** When the noun's gender morpheme appears along with the allomorph *-zinho*, the diminutive acquires a certain amount of autonomy. So much so that the words formed become compounds rather

16 It may be that the existence of different diminutive forms motivated the inclusion of *cãozinho* in the *Aurélio*.

than nominals with diminutive suffixes. Two of the examples cited above, *cãozinho* and *pãozinho,* demonstrate their compound nature when pluralized: *cãezinhos* 'little dogs' (cf. *cão* 'dog' ⇔ *cães* 'dogs') and *pãezinhos* 'rolls' (cf. *pão* 'bread' ⇔ *pães* 'loaves of bread'). In addition, words such as *bordel* 'bordello' and *igual* 'equal' can have diminutive forms: *bordelzinho* and *igualzinho* 'exactly alike'. Their plural forms also reflect their inflection twice: *bordéizinhos* and *iguaizinhos*'.[17] Other common nouns that end in stressed syllables form compound diminutives: *amor* 'love'→ *amorzinho* 'sweetie-pie'→*amorezinhos* 'sweetie-pies'; *chá*→*chazinho*(s) 'tea, nice tea'.[18] These words' first elements (*amor* and *chá*) appear as they would in their normal plural forms, without the diminutive suffix. In addition, when *zinho, -a,* combines with stems to form specific adjectives, gender appears both on the stem and the suffix: *bonzinho* 'nice [-feminine]' ⇔ *boazinha* 'nice [+feminine]' (cf. *bom* 'good [-feminine]', *boa* 'good [+feminine]'). In the case of compounding, the lexical entry for this particular morpheme is #ziɲ+<[αfeminine]#<[αplural]# because it flexibly agrees in number and gender with whatever it modifies or represents.[19] This diminutive form has, in fact, become an independent word indicating a person.[20] (§12.4.0–3.1.)

**§10.2.2.10 –eco, -a:** Cunha gives *livreco* 'cheap book' (cf. *livro* 'book') and *soneca* 'cat nap' (cf. *sono* 'sleep') as examples. Other examples include *jornaleco* 'low quality newspaper' (cf. *jornal* 'newspaper'), *folheca* 'snow flake' (cf. *folha* 'leaf'), *rabeca* 'fiddle', *boneco* 'doll',[21] *marreco* 'teal'. This is not a +$S_1$ suffix even though it brings the underlying /n+ of *bom* 'good' ['bõ] #bon+ to the surface. This is because

17 The plural morpheme +z# of these words disappears since it is followed by a word-initial #z/. (§9.4.0.)

18 Not every speaker of Portuguese will include the +e+ in the plural of *amorzinho*. When I taught a workshop in phonology in Curitiba (Brazil), students told me they would simply say *amorzinhos*. The Portuguese whom I queried included the +e+.

19 At this point it is unclear whether, in the unlikely event that proper nouns are pluralized, diminutives such as Raquelzinha and Edgarzinho would be realized as Raqueizinhas and Edgarezinhos.

20 In its feminine form *zinha*, it can have a derogatory connotation (personal communication Elizabeth Martins).

21 Since the word *boneco* represents effigies of animate nouns, it can be [±feminine]. Normally *bonecas* are girls' playthings and *bonecos* are males', which one might translate into English as 'action figures' rather than 'dolls'.

most deriving suffixes attached to /n+ will preserve it in the resultant derived word. This suffix of course creates specific words from roots that appear in other words. The suffix itself is +ɛk+, and the gender morpheme following it can be either +a# or +o#, and this combination of diminutive suffix and deriving gender morphemes produces words whose meanings are greater than the sums of their constituent parts. Take, e.g., the word *caneca* 'mug' #kan++ɛk++a# (cf. *cano* 'tube, pipe'). It has a [-feminine] counterpart *caneco* #kan++ɛk++o#, which indicates a taller than average mug. In this case, the specific gender morpheme attached to the stem (#root++diminutive++[±feminine]#) determines the words' denotations.

**§10.2.2.11 –ejo, -a:** Cunha's examples are *lugarejo* 'one horse town' (cf. *lugar* 'place') and *animalejo*, which the *Aurélio* lists as the simple (but irregular) diminutive of *animal* 'animal'. This +S suffix is most often followed by +o# regardless of the gender of the related non-diminutive form: *bodejo* 'a bleat' (cf. *bode* 'billy goat'), *molejo* 'set of springs' (cf. *mola* 'spring [+feminine]'). Followed by +a#, it occurs in *torneja* 'axle pin' (cf. *torno* 'pin, lathe'), where, at least in this case, the noun-forming lexical entry for this suffix is +ež+, and for nouns it attaches to roots, e.g. *molejo* #mɔl++ež++o# and *torneja* #tɔrn++ež++a#. Once again, the gender morphemes in the nouns formed with this suffix are derivational. Any adjectives, e.g. *andejo* 'wandering (adj.)' (cf. *andar* 'to walk') and *sertanejo* 'backlander' (cf. *sertão* 'backlands'), formed with this suffix will be inflected for the gender of the nouns modified or represented. This is the last diminutive suffix of low productivity. The next 11 suffixes range from moderate to very high productivity.

**§10.2.2.12.0 –ico, -a:** The *Aurélio* contains some 7,857 entries ending in the letters –ico and another 771 ending in -ica. Only a tiny percentage of these are diminutives.[22] In a sampling of 370 randomly chosen entries, there were four bona fide diminutives ending in –ico. In a sampling of 222 entries ending in –ica there were 38 bona fide diminutives. Thus, 6.93% of the -ico and –ica tokens in the *Aurélio* are likely to be diminutives.

**§10.2.2.12.1** Cunha's examples are *burrico* 'little burro' and *marica(s)* 'effeminate, homosexual male'. This suffix appears in words

22 That is, the adjective forming ending *–tico* appears in 1,877 different entries, *-fico* in 523, *-lógico* in 491. Nouns ending in *–tica* numbered 268, in *–fica* 5, and in *–lógica* 2.

such as *mulherico* 'effeminate, cowardly male' (cf. *mulher* 'woman'), *jerico* 'burro', and *fanico* 'swoon, small profit',[23] *veranico* 'mild spring' or 'intensely hot period in the rainy season' (cf. *verão* 'summer') and *manjerico* 'basil' (cf. *manjarona* 'marjoram' and *manjar* 'tidbit'). It occurs in feminine forms such as *canjica* 'grits' or 'coconut milk dish' (cf. *canja* 'chicken soup'), or *pelica* 'kid leather' (cf. *pele* 'skin'). The nouns this suffix creates are not the mere sums of their constituent parts. There is no reason to consider it a +$S_1$ deriving suffix even though it allows underlying stem-final /n+ to surface (e.g. *verão⇔veranico*). Words that the sequence +ik+<[αfeminine]# forms maintain their original gender except when they indicate individuals of a specific gender (e.g. *mulher* [+feminine] ⇔ *mulherico* [-feminine]) in which case they agree with the designated individual's gender. The lexical form of *pelica* (e.g.) is #pεl++$e_{[+fem.]}$#+ik+[<αfeminine]#.

**§10.2.2.13 –ola:** Cunha offers *fazendola* 'small ranch' and *rapazola* 'grown boy, childish man' showing that this suffix can attach to stems of words of both genders: *fazenda* 'ranch', *rapaz* 'young male'. *Fazendola* is of course feminine, but despite its suffix's ending in **–a**, *rapazola* is non-feminine as is *mariola* 'rogue, errand boy' (cf. Maria or Mário).[24] Other ([+feminine]) words formed with this suffix are *radiola* 'radio-record-player' (cf. *rádio*, *vitrola* or *electrola* 'victrola'), *gloriola* 'vain glory' (cf. *glória* 'glory'). This +S deriving suffix determines that the nouns (save *rapazola* and *mariola*) it forms will be [+feminine], e.g. *rádio* #radi++o# ⇔ *radiola* #radi++ɔl++a#. Its lexical form is +ɔl++a#.

**§10.2.2.14.0 -ino, -a#:**[25] The *Aurélio* has 551 nominal entries ending in *–ino* and 1,202 ending in *–ina*. For the [-feminine] form, 259

23 There are no obvious manifestations of these two words' roots in other words. They seem to be sui generis lexical items. Their endings may only be accidentally homophonous with the diminutive suffix +ik+<[αfeminine]#

24 *Mariola* also has a [+feminine] instantiation meaning 'banana candy'. It can also be an (invariant) adjective indicating a person with bad character.

25 This diminutive suffix is homophonous and homologous with the moderately productive (629 tokens) +$S_1$ adjective forming suffix +in+<o#. (See Tables 7.3d, 7.6a–d §7.5.5.21.) At times it can be hard to distinguish the diminutive suffix from the adjective forming +in+<[αfeminine]#<[αnumber]#. The word *gasparino* means 'the smallest portion of a Brazilian lottery ticket that can be purchased'. The word comes from a 19th Century politician's name—Gaspar da Silveira Martins, who instituted the fractioning of lottery tickets. Is the suffix in this word a diminutive or is it an adjective-deriving suffix?

randomly selected entries yielded 28 diminutive suffixes, i.e. 10.81% of those entries. For the –ina entries, 370 entries yielded 51 bona fide diminutive entries (13.78%). Extrapolating to the entire dataset suggests that there are some 60 diminutives formed with *–ino* and 166 formed with *–ina*.

**§10.2.2.14.1** Cunha's examples of this suffix are the adjective *pequenino* 'very small' (cf. *pequeno* 'small') and the noun *cravina* 'pink (a flowering plant)' (cf. *cravo* 'carnation'). The *Aurélio*'s examples include *concertino* 'little concert' (cf. *concerto* 'concert') *vivaldino* 'wise guy' (cf. *vivo* 'lively'), and *tenorino* 'high pitched tenor'. Many –ino words are Italian loans: e.g. *maestrino* 'composer of light music' and *figurino* 'model, dandy'. The scientific term *gravitino* is a diminutive designating the 'S-particle of a graviton'. This suffix performs as an ordinary (non-deriving) diminutive for proper nouns: Alexandre→Alexandrino/a, Guilherme→Guilhermino/a, Vítor→Vitorino, Augusto→Augustino.

**§10.2.2.14.2** When this suffix appears in the feminine form, the ratio of diminutives to non-diminutives is much higher, and the diminutive forms are obvious. The diminutive morpheme +in+ coupled with the [+feminine] morpheme +a# constitute a deriving suffix that determines the resultant words' gender—regardless of the related nouns' gender: e.g. *campina* 'meadow' (cf. *campo* 'field'), *lamparina* 'oil lamp' (cf. *lampa* or *lâmpada* 'lamp'), *concertina* 'concertina' (cf. *concerto* 'concert'), *prantina* 'copious weeping' (cf. *pranto* 'weeping'). The [+feminine] manifestation of this suffix attaches to words' roots: e.g. *campina* #kanp++in++a#. The underlying form of the adjective forming suffix, as well as that of the diminutives of proper nouns, is +in+<[αfeminine]#, that of the deriving diminutive is +in++a#.

**§10.2.2.15 –ote, -a:** Cunha's examples are *velhote* and *velhota*, which Houaiss and Avery define as 'oldster' (male and female), (cf. *velho* 'old').[26] This highly productive +S suffix combines with stems to form many lexical items: *raigota* 'hang nail' (cf. *raiz* 'root', *arraigado* 'rooted'), *palhota* 'straw covered dwelling' (cf. *palha* 'straw'), *fatiota* 'men's suit' (cf. Portuguese *fato* 'men's suit', *fatia* 'piece'), and *filhote* 'native' or 'pup' (cf. *filho* 'offspring'), *grandote* 'very big' (cf. *grande* 'big'), *picote* 'perforation' (cf. *pico* 'sharp point'), *serrote* 'hand saw' (cf. *serra* 'saw'), and *camarote* '(theater) box' (cf. *câmara* 'chamber').

26 Houaiss and Avery also list the diminutives *velhinho* and *velhinha* and define them as 'very old' or 'little old' males and females.

Once again a diminutive suffix derives nouns and adjectives: When it attaches to adjective and proper noun stems, its lexical form is +ɔt+ <[αfeminine]#. Take, e.g., the adjective *puxado* 'expensive' and the diminutive *puxadote* 'very expensive'. This adjective is structured as #puš++a#+t+<o#++ɔt+<e#. If this word modified a [+feminine] noun, it would end with the [+feminine] morpheme: *puxadota*. #puš++a#<t+ <o#++ɔt+<a#.[27] To derive common nouns this suffix occurs with the deriving gender morphemes +a# and +e# as in the words *picote* #pik++ɔt++e# 'rough cloth, stitch, scalloped fringe on paper' and *picota* #pik++ɔt++a# 'pillory, nautical lever' and *serrote* #sɛr̲++ɔt++e# 'hand saw [-feminine]' and *serrota* #sɛr̲++ɔt++a# 'hill'. This evidence indicates that the deriving gender morpheme that attaches to stems followed by +ɔt+ determines the resultant nouns' meanings and their gender—more or less independent of what the related nouns' meanings and genders may be.

**§10.2.2.16 –ilho, -a:** Cunha's words demonstrating this highly productive suffix are *pecadilho* 'peccadillo' (cf. *pecado* 'sin') and *tropilha* 'a group of six horses following a lead mare' (cf. *tropa* 'troop[s]'). Other examples of this suffix include: *cabecilha* 'leader [±feminine]' (cf. *cabeça* 'head'), *farroupilha* 'ragamuffin [±feminine]' (*farrapo* 'rag'), and *boquilha* 'cigarette holder, mouthpiece' (cf. *boca* 'mouth') as well as *barbilho* 'muzzle, barbel' (cf. *barba* 'beard, chin'), *novilho* 'yearling calf' (cf. *novo* 'new, young'), *trocadilho* 'pun' (cf. *trocar* 'to exchange'), and *pacotilha* 'free baggage' (cf. *pacote* 'carton [-feminine]'). This +S suffix occurs with both gender morphemes so its lexical form is +iλ+ +[±feminine]. It attaches directly to genderless stems: *tropilha* #trɔp+ +iλ++a#, *pacotilha* #pak++ɔt++iλ++a#.

**§10.2.2.17 -ela:** Cunha gives *ruela* 'lane' (cf. *rua* 'street') and *viela* 'ally, lane' (cf. *via* 'route') as examples of this highly productive suffix. Other examples include: *cidadela* 'citadel' (cf. *cidade* 'city'), *chupadela* '(a) suck' (cf. *chupar* 'to suck'), *rodela* 'a round slice' (cf. *roda* 'wheel'), *costela* 'rib' (cf. *costa* 'back'). This is a +S deriving suffix that produces [+feminine] nouns from nominal stems. Its lexical form is +ɛl++a#, and the lexical form of, e.g., *rodela* would be #r̲ɔt++ɛl++a#. Whereas it seems to attach mainly to the stems of [+feminine] nouns, it imposes

---

27 The word *fiote* as an adjective can mean 'elegant'. As a noun this word as well as *fiota* are vulgarities meaning 'anus'.

[+feminine] gender on a few of the words it forms, e.g. *cliente* 'cliente' ⇔ *clientela* 'clientele'; *parente* 'relative' ⇔ *parentela* 'extended family'.[28]

**§10.2.2.18 –ete:** Cunha offers *artiguete* 'small, worthless article' (cf. *artigo* 'article') and *lembrete* 'mnemonic device' (cf. *lembrar* 'to remember') as examples of this highly productive suffix. His first example illustrates the derogatory use of a diminutive suffix—*artiguete* is simply a modification of *artigo* and need not be an independent lexical item, whereas *lembrete* (cf. *lembrança* 'souvenir') has a meaning that is not deducible from its constituent parts; thus, it is an actual lexical item. Other examples of this highly productive suffix include: *escudete* 'escutcheon' (cf. *escudo* 'shield'), *florete* 'fencing foil ([-feminine])' (cf. *flor* 'flower [+feminine]'), *foguete* 'rocket' (cf. *fogo* 'fire'), and *sabonete* 'hand soap' (cf. *sabão* 'soap'). This +S suffix usually derives [-feminine] nouns. Its lexical form is +ɛt++e#. The only instance of a word with this suffix indicating a [+feminine] referent is in the name Rosinete 'little Rosina'. #ṟɔz+in+<a#+et++e# . The underlying form of *sabonete* is #sap++on++et++e#.[29]

**§10.2.2.19 -im:** Cunhas's examples are *espadim* 'rapier' (cf. *espada* 'sword [+feminine]') and *fortim* 'fort' or 'block house' (cf. *forte* 'fortress [-feminine]'). Other words include *espelhim* 'shiny white plaster' (cf. *espelho* 'mirror'), *coxim* 'pad, bolster' (cf. *coxa* 'thigh [+feminine]'), and *folhetim* 'serialized novel' (cf. *folha* 'leaf [+feminine]', *folheto* 'pamphlet'). This +S suffix derives non-feminine nouns from nominal stems: its lexical form is +in++e+, and the underlying form of, e.g., *coxim* is #kɔš++in++e+<Ø#.

**§10.2.2.20.0 ˈVX+(c)ulo, -a:** Cunha considers this diminutive suffix different from the other diminutives insofar as it is peculiar to more erudite vocabulary, as the examples adduced in this section will largely demonstrate.[30] Beyond this, it is the only diminutive suffix to not bear stress. Its representation includes ˈVX+ to indicate that this

28 One may prefer to consider the suffix a non-diminutive collective in the case of words like *clientela* and *parentela*.

29 This suffix's failure to preserve the /p+ of *sabonete*'s root #sap+ constitutes further proof that it, as well as +on+, are +S suffixes.

30 Indeed, as readers may wish to check, most of the diminutives are Latinate reconstructions, but some are of fairly recent coinage. All of them conform to the patterns identified in this chapter, however. And these patterns motivate a set of rules to generate the documented words, as well as any spontaneous neologisms ending in this suffix.

suffix (like the adjective-deriving suffixes +tik+<o#, +e+<o#, and +ik+<o#) assigns stress to the vowel that precedes it in the derived word—be that vowel the root vowel or not. In addition, when the stressed vowels are mid vowels they are limited to /ɛ/ and /ɔ/. These are some of Cunha's examples: *nódulo* 'nodule' (cf. *nó* 'knot, node'), *glóbulo* 'globule' (cf. *globo* 'globe'), *partícula* 'particle' (cf. *parte* 'part'), *nótula* 'commentary' (cf. *nota* 'note'), and *régulo* 'kinglet' (cf. *rei* 'king'). It is clearly a +$S_1$ deriving suffix that usually preserves the related non-diminutive noun's gender. Its underlying form for noun formation is ˈVX+(k)+ul+<[αfeminine]#, and the underlying forms of, e.g., *partícula* and *régulo* are #part++$e_{[+fem.]}$ #+ul+<[αfeminine]# and #reg++$e_{[-fem.]}$+ +ul+<[αfeminine]#.

**§10.2.2.20.1.0** In the case of *partícula* and several other derived nouns: e.g. *cutícula* 'cuticle' [cf. *cute* 'skin'], *avícula* 'little bird' [cf. *ave* 'bird'], *corbícula* 'little basket [on bees' legs]', [cf. *corbe* 'basket'] two operations take place. The gender morpheme on *parte*, *cute*, *ave*, and *corbe* is +$e_{[+fem.]}$#, which determines these diminutives' gender.[31] In addition, the gender morpheme in words such as these mutates to /i/. And in cases such as these (and some others), a /k/ emerges between the stem and +ul+.

**§10.2.2.20.1.1** The mutation of the gender morpheme +$e_{[+fem.]}$# to /i/ does not apply in all cases: e.g. *mole* 'huge mass [+feminine]' ⇔ *molécula* 'molecule', *trave* 'beam [+feminine]' *trabécula* 'small beam', *nuvem* 'cloud [+feminine]' and *nubécula* 'white spot on the cornea'. In these cases, the gender morpheme +$e_{[+fem.]}$# is not lost, but, similar to the adjective-deriving suffixes +tik+<o#, +e+<o#, and +ik+<o#, this suffix, with or without /k/, causes stressed mid vowel lenition, in these cases from +e# to [ɛ]. Thus, this suffix's configuration accounts for the assignment of proparoxytone stress, and Rule 3.4 accounts for mid vowel lenition in nominals whose final deriving morpheme is +ul+.

**§10.2.2.20.1.2** The intricacies related to this very unusual diminutive form are such that an appendix (Appendix C) is the most fitting

31 There are at least four cases in which the gender of diminutives ending in +ul+ is not determined by their stems' gender: *canícula* 'dog star' (cf. *cão* [-feminine] 'dog'), *valécula* 'depression' (cf. *vale* [-feminine] 'valley'), *cenáculo* 'supper club' (cf. *ceia* [+feminine] 'supper'), and *dilúculo* 'early light' (cf. *luz* [+feminine] 'light').

venue to present them. For now, Rules 10.3, .4, and Rules 10.3-5, which are justified in Appendix C, appear here:

**Rule 10.3 /k/ Insertion in Diminutives Formed with +ul+:**

$$\text{Ø} \rightarrow /\text{k}/\ /\ \left\{ \begin{array}{l} \text{-contoid} \\ \begin{pmatrix} \text{+contoid} \\ \text{-occlusion} \\ \text{-surd} \\ \text{-labial} \\ \text{-high} \end{pmatrix} \end{array} \right\} /\ \#X \left\{ \begin{array}{c} + \\ \# \end{array} \right\} \_\_\ \ \text{+ul+X\#}$$

Rule 10.3 inserts a /k/ before diminutive suffix +ul+ when the suffix follows a stem-final vowel, and when it follows stems ending in /z, n, r, l/.

**Rule 10.4 +e$_{[+fem.]}$, +a#, +o$_{[+fem.]}$# →/ˈi/ / ___ /+ul+<a#:**

$$\text{+[+feminine]} \left\{ \begin{array}{c} \# \\ + \end{array} \right\} \rightarrow \begin{pmatrix} \text{+high} \\ \text{+palatal} \\ \text{+stress} \end{pmatrix} /\ \_\_\_ \begin{pmatrix} \text{+contoid} \\ \text{+dorsal} \\ \text{+surd} \\ \text{+occlusion} \end{pmatrix} \text{+ul+} < \text{a\#}$$

Rule 10.4 accounts for the shift of [+feminine] gender morphemes to /i/ in a minority of words.

**Rule 10.5 +o# → /a/ / ___ /+ul+<o#:**

$$+ \begin{pmatrix} \text{-contoid} \\ \text{+dorsal} \\ \text{-high} \\ \text{+labial} \\ \text{+wide glottis} \end{pmatrix} \# \rightarrow \begin{pmatrix} \text{+low} \\ \text{-labial} \end{pmatrix} /\ \_\_\_ \begin{pmatrix} \text{+contoid} \\ \text{+dorsal} \\ \text{+surd} \\ \text{+occlusion} \end{pmatrix} \text{+ul+}$$

Rule 10.5 accounts the shift from +o# to /a/ in another minority (Table 10.3).

**§10.2.2.20.2.0 Similarities:** Like the other diminutive nominal formations, the gender of words formed with this suffix is mainly determined by their stems' original gender. In addition, a subset of the stems loses the gender morpheme once the suffix has acquired [±feminine] gender. Another subset preserves the gender morpheme in the diminutive forms, but similar to the suffixes +it+<o# and +iɲ+<o#, a transitional consonant emerges—not only after a gender morpheme but also after stem-final consonants: /z, n, l, r/.

**§10.2.2.20.2.1** Also similar to the other diminutives, this suffix both creates (less than spontaneous) diminutives in which the diminutive form indicates a smaller than usual size referent, as well as unique lexical items whose meanings are greater than the sum of their parts. Table 10.3 displays both phenomena:

**Table 10.3** Diminutives and Idioms Formed with +ul+

| Actual Diminutives | | | Diminutive Idioms | | | |
|---|---|---|---|---|---|---|
| Stem | Gloss | Diminutive | Stem | Gloss | Idiom | Gloss |
| **tubo** | tube | **túbulo** | **pele** | hide | **película** | film |
| **nota** | note | **nótula** | **uva** | grape | **úvula** | uvula |
| **floco** | flake | **flócula** | **nó** | knot | **nódulo** | nodule |
| **lente** | lens | **lentícula** | **mole** | mass | **molécula** | molecule |
| **canal** | canal | **canalículo** | **parte** | part | **partícula** | particle |

Table 10.3 omits glosses for the actual diminutives because they only indicate diminution of the particular referent. The idioms formed by this suffix certainly originated as metaphors but are now sufficiently different from their sources. Both the actual diminutives and their idiomatic counterparts in Table 10.3 (and in this entire section) appear in the *Aurélio*, quite likely because of this suffix's unusual nature among diminutive suffixes.

**§10.2.2.20.3.0 Differences:** In addition to not normally forming pet names,[32] diminutives formed by +ul+ are proparoxytones, which no

32 For example, *Artúrculo for Artur or *Líndula for Linda. In a personal communication, Maria Inês Carneiro informs me that she would accept the nickname Maria Inéscula.

other diminutive suffix generates. And their proparoxytone mid vowels emerge as [ɛ] and [ɔ].

**§10.2.2.20.3.1** In the cases where nominals' original gender morphemes remain in diminutives formed by +ul+, there are, in addition to the [+feminine] gender morpheme's acquisition of stress and mid-vowel lenition, other mutations. For one subset of stems, +$e_{[+fem]}$# mutates to /i/, in another subset of stems +o# mutates to +a#. Thus, a grammar that accounts for the allomorphy associated with this suffix must postulate at least two sets (and two subsets) of stems: Stem class 1's gender morpheme +o# mutates to /ˈa/. Stem class 2's gender morpheme +$e_{[+fem]}$# mutates to /i/. Stem class 3 loses its gender morpheme once the diminutive word has acquired word-final gender. Stem class 4 preserves its gender morpheme.[33]

**§10.2.2.21 -eto, -a:** The words *esboceto* 'small outline' (cf. *esboço* 'outline') and *saleta* 'small room' (cf. *sala* '[living] room') appear in Cunha as well as in the *Aurélio*. Notwithstanding these words' appearance in dictionaries, they are mere diminutives rather than independent words. Words such as *libreto* 'libretto' (cf. *livro* 'book'),[34] *dueto* 'duet' (cf. *duas* 'two [+feminine])', *terceto* 'three line stanza' (cf. *terço* 'third'), and *coreto* 'bandstand' (cf. *coro* 'chorus') demonstrate the rather erudite or specialized nature of words formed with this suffix when it occurs with +o#. However, the words ending in *–eta* (+et++a#) are much more numerous than their non-feminine counterparts: *cambeta* 'bow-legged ([±feminine])' (cf. *cambar* 'to totter'), *maçaneta* 'door knob' (cf. *maçã* 'apple'), *camiseta* 'undershirt' (cf. *camisa* 'shirt'), *sapateta* 'slipper' (cf. *sapato* 'shoe').[35] This +S deriving suffix has the lexical form +et+, and it occurs with deriving gender morphemes to form specific words.

---

33 Perhaps because of the protean nature of diminutives ending in +ul+, most of these diminutive nominals have their roots in Latin words, and, notwithstanding this suffix's ubiquity, it rarely appears in neologisms. This suffix does not occur spontaneously nor does it normally form pet names for people. Still, the names Rômulo 'Romulus' and Úrsula are formed with this suffix.

34 Cf. *livreta* and *livrete* #livr+et++a#, #livr++et++e#, both of which can mean 'notebook'.

35 Other words that assume the feminine gender when formed with **–eta** include: *chapeleta* 'hat' (cf. *chapéu* 'hat [-f.]'), *papeleta* 'loose paper, poster' (cf. *papel* 'paper [-f]'), *corneta* 'cornet' (cf. *corno* 'horn' [-f.]).

The lexical forms of *maçaneta* and *sapateta* are #masan++et++a# and #sapat++et++a#, that of *terceto* is #ters++et++o#.

**§10.2.2.22.0 –inho, -a:** The *Aurélio* contains 412 words ending in *–inho* and 445 in *–inha* that are plausible diminutives. In both sets, 222 randomly chosen words indicate that 82.00% of the [-feminine] words were bona fide diminutives and 79.83% of the [+feminine] words were likewise. Thus, the *Aurélio* contains some 328 [-feminine] diminutives and 391 [+feminine] diminutives.

**§10.2.2.22.1** Cunha's examples are *toquinho* 'a slight touch' (cf. *tocar* 'to touch') and *vozinha* 'a weak voice' (cf. *voz* 'voice'). Neither of these words appears in the dictionaries consulted in this study, which suggests that they are spontaneous diminutives, modifications of their roots #tɔk+ and #vɔk+ which mean 'touch' and 'voice', respectively. However, lexical examples formed with this suffix abound: *raínha* 'queen' (cf. *rei* 'king'), *alfacinha* 'native of Lisbon' (cf. *alface* 'lettuce'),[36] *joaninha* 'lady bug' (cf. Joana 'Joanne'), *madrinha* 'god mother' (cf. *madre* 'mother superior' and *padrinho* 'god father'), *estorninho* 'starling' (cf. *estorno* '[an] offset'). It forms adjectives such as *daninho* 'mischievous' (cf. *dano* 'damage'), *setemesinho* 'a premature baby' (cf. *sete meses* 'seven months's gestation').

**§10.2.2.22.2 –inho** is the default diminutive suffix (Villalva, 2009) and can occur with almost all lexical nominals—as well as with some adverbs, as Cunha points out.[37] It preserves the gender of proper and common nouns, and the adjectives it forms agree in number and gender with whatever they modify or represent. The underlying form of *joaninha* would be #žoan++a#+iɲ+<[αfeminine]#, that of *estorninho* #eztɔrn++o#+iɲ+<[-feminine]#. In both cases, the stems' gender morphemes get deleted. Adjectives such as *daninho* would be formed by directly adding +iɲ+<[-feminine]# to their roots: #dan++iɲ+<[αfeminine]#. (See also §10.2.2.5.0–1.)

**§10.3.0** Matrix 10.1 contains, in the order of their productivity, the morphemes' analyses and their properties:

36 Whereas *alface* 'lettuce' is [+feminine], the term *alfacinha* 'native of Lisbon' is ambivalent and can refer to [±feminine] entities.

37 His examples are *agorinha* 'right now', *cedinho* 'very early', *depressinha* 'really quickly', *devagarinho* 'very slowly'. He includes *sozinho* 'all alone' and *adeusinho* 'bye bye'. When the adverb ends in /a# (*agora, depressa*), their diminutives end in /a# also. When they end in /o# or /r# (*cedo, devagar*) their diminutives end in /o#.

**Matrix 10.1** Diminutive Morphemes

| | Analysis | $+S_1$ | ±feminine | Proper Noun |
|---|---|---|---|---|
| 1 | +ɛbr++e# | - | *** | - |
| 2 | +zit+<o# | - | - | ? |
| 3 | +uzk+<o# | - | + | - |
| 4 | +iš+<o# | + | - | - |
| 5 | +uš+<o# | - | - | + |
| 6 | +it+<o# | - | + | + |
| 7 | +izk+<o# | - | + | - |
| 8 | +aš+<o# | + | + | - |
| 9 | +eλ+<o# | - | + | - |
| 10 | #ziɲ+<o# | - | - | + |
| 11 | +ɛk+<o# | - | + | - |
| 12 | +ež+<o# | - | + | - |
| 13 | +ik+<o# | - | - | + |
| 14 | +ɔl++a# | - | *** | - |
| 15a | +in+<o# | - | - | + |
| 15b | +in++a# | - | *** | - |
| 16 | +ɔt+<o# | - | + | ? |
| 17 | +iλ+<o# | - | + | - |
| 18 | +ɛl++a# | - | *** | + |
| 19 | +et++e# | - | *** | + |
| 20 | +in++e+ | - | *** | ? |
| 21 | 'VX (k)+ul+<o# | + | - | ? |
| 22 | +et+<o# | - | + | ? |
| 23 | (z)+iɲ+<o# | - | - | + |

**§10.3.1 Gender:** The analysis of the diminutive morphemes addressed in this chapter identifies all the forms (save #2 +zit+ and #10, #ziɲ+) as discrete suffixes. The latter form is a word compounding element that can be inflected for gender, +zit+ is an allomorph of suffix 6 +it+. The remaining morphemes are all suffixes that can attach to stems that consist of a monomorphemic root or of multi-morphemic stems. Suffix 15 has two allomorphs: 15a agrees in number and gender with its referent, whereas 15b is intrinsically linked to the [+feminine] morpheme +a#. Suffixes 1, 14, 15b, 18, 19, and 20, like the non-diminutive, non-augmentative-deriving suffixes (Table 7.3a), co-occur with specific gender morphemes (+ + affinity between deriving suffixes and gender morphemes) and, thus, determine the gender of the diminutive nouns they form. The remaining suffixes (3–13, 15a, 16, 17, 21, 22, 23) followed by the unmarked gender morpheme <o# can: (A) acquire gender from their stems, (B) be inflected for number and gender according to the gender of whatever nouns they denote or (as adjectives) modify, (C) co-occur with deriving gender morphemes (either +o# or +a#).

**§10.3.2 +$S_1$:** Only three diminutive suffixes (4, 8, and 21[38]) qualify as +$S_1$ suffixes because they impede the consonantal mutation typical of words ending with +S suffixes.

**§10.3.3 [±feminine]:** Nouns formed with suffixes 3, 6, 7, 8, 9, 11, 12, 16, 17, 21, 22 can, at times, occur with different deriving gender morphemes such that minimal pairs can be formed: e.g. *chamusco ≠ chamusca*, *caneco ≠ caneca*, *arbúsculo ≠ arbúscula*. Those marked with dingbats (***) determine the gender of the resultant diminutive without regard for the gender of the original noun.

**§10.3.4 Proper Nouns:** The positively specified suffixes can attach to proper nouns to form pet names. The negatively specified ones do not. And those specified with a question mark are doubtful—they may or may not.

**§10.4.0** Returning to §10.0.2.4 and the desiderata therein,[39] concerning the diminutives one can say: There are 23 morphemes that can form diminutives of nouns and adjectives. Of these forms 21 are bona fide deriving suffixes. Diminutive suffixes, like other deriving suffixes, begin and end with the morpheme boundary +. Only three are +$S_1$ suffixes. Some copy the gender of the nouns of which they form diminutives. Some impose gender on the resultant nouns. Some allow deriving gender morphemes to attach and create independent lexical items whose only formal difference is their gender morpheme. When diminutives attach to adjectives or are added to existing adjectives, the

38 Any derived word indicating a [+animate] referent is capable of being inflected (boundary affinity +<) for [αfeminine] and count as an adjective.

39 (A) What are the morphemes that make diminutive and augmentative forms of adjectives and nouns? (B) How can one characterize diminutive and augmentative nominals' underlying forms? (C) Which words containing diminutive and augmentative suffixes are lexical items (idioms)? (D) And which forms come about merely to convey Portuguese speakers' affect concerning a word's referent?

resultant words' gender is determined by whatever the adjective modifies or represents.

**§10.4.1** This section has shown that diminutive suffixes can: (A) provide pet names for animate creatures and express affect concerning particular [-animate] referents; (B) form words that reflect their referents' gender; (C) form adjectives that, like other adjectives, can be inflected for number and gender according to the genders and numbers of the nouns they modify or represent; (D) form stems to which deriving gender morphemes attach so as to form novel lexical items; (E) carry a specific gender morpheme and create specific words from nominal stems. **Table 10.4a** illustrates and analyzes these patterns:

**Table 10.4a** [a]Patterns of Nominal Formation with Diminutive Suffixes[a]

| | | | | | | |
|---|---|---|---|---|---|---|
| **Section 1: Form Spontaneous Diminutives, Copy Gender** | | | | | | |
| **Pattern:** | **#root++[±feminine]#+diminutive+<[αfeminine]#** | | | | | |
| | [-feminine] | | | [+feminine] | | |
| | kilo | +it+ | kilito | voz | +iɲ+ | vozinha |
| | Vitor | +in+ | Vitorino | Rosina | +et++e# | Rosinete[b] |
| **Section 2: Derive Noun, Copy Gender** | | | | | | |
| **Pattern:** | **#root++[±feminine]#+diminutive+<[αfeminine]#** | | | | | |
| | [-feminine] | | | [+feminine] | | |
| | rabo | +iš+<o# | rabicho | pele | +ik+<a# | pelica |
| | papel | +uš+<o# | papelucho | folha | +ɛk+<a# | folheca |
| | rio | +aš+<o# | riacho | camisa | +et+<a# | camiseta |
| | pico | +ɔt++e# | picote | palha | +ɔt+<a# | palhota |
| | mar | +izk+<o# | marisco | tala | +izk+<a# | talisca |
| | globo | 'Vx++ul+<o# | glóbulo | nota | 'Vx++ul+<a# | nótula |
| **Section 3: Derive (Nuanced) Adjectives** | | | | | | |
| **Pattern:** | **#stem++diminutive+<[αfeminine]#** | | | | | |
| | pardo | +uzk+<o# | pardusco | verde | +aš+<o# | verdacho |
| | pequeno | +in+<o# | pequenino | grande | +ɔt++e# | grandote |
| | dano | +iɲ+ <o# | daninho | sertão | +ež+<o# | sertanejo |
| | par | +eʎ+<o# | parelho | capa | +uš+ <o# | capucho |

(*Continued*)

Table 10.4a Continued

| | | | | | | | |
|---|---|---|---|---|---|---|---|
| **Section 4: Create Stem, Receive (Deriving) Gender Morpheme** | | | | | | | |
| **Pattern:** | **#root++diminutive++[±feminine]** | | | | | | |
| | [+feminine] | | [-feminine] | | [-feminine] | | [+feminine] |
| | chama | +uzk++o# | chamusco | | ferro | +uzk++a# | ferrusca |
| | cano | +εk++o# | caneco | | cano | +εk++a# | caneca |
| | pedra | +izk++o# | pedrisco | | sapato | +et++a# | sapateta |
| | areia | +it++o# | arenito | | bolo | +aš++a# | bolacha |
| | barba | +iλ++o# | barbilho | | torno | +ež++a# | torneja |
| | folha | +eλ++o# | folhelho | | par | +eλ++a# | parelha |
| | mola | +ež++o# | molejo | | pacote | +iλ++a# | pacotilha |
| **Section 5: Create Word, Provide Gender** | | | | | | | |
| **Pattern:** | **#stem++[diminutive++[±feminine]]#** | | | | | | |
| | [+feminine] | | [-feminine] | | [-feminine] | | [+feminine] |
| | casa | +εbr++e# | casebre | | rádio | +ɔl++a# | radiola |
| | coxa | +in++e# | coxim | | campo | +in++a# | campina |
| | câmara | +ɔt++e# | camarote | | parente | +εl++a# | parentela |

a English glosses for Table 10.3 (left to right): Section 1: kilo⇔sweet kilo, voice⇔little voice, and proper nouns; Section 2: tail⇔queue, skin⇔kid leather, paper⇔paper scrap, leaf⇔snow flake, river⇔brook, shirt⇔undershirt, point⇔perforation, straw⇔thatched hut, sea⇔seafood, splint⇔crevice, globe⇔globule, note⇔commentary; Section 3: brown⇔brownish, green⇔greenish, small⇔teeny-tiny, big⇔really big, damage⇔noxious, backlands⇔of the backlands, pair⇔similar, cape⇔cape-wearing; Section 4: flame⇔singeing, iron⇔rusty sword, pipe⇔tall mug, pipe⇔mug, stone⇔stone shower, shoe⇔slipper, sand⇔sandstone, cake⇔cookie, beard⇔barbel, pin⇔axel pin, leaf⇔husk, pair⇔team of 2 horses, spring⇔set of springs, package⇔tax free luggage; Section 5: house⇔hovel, radio⇔radio phonograph, thigh⇔cushion, field⇔meadow, chamber⇔theater box, relative⇔extended family.

b This is actually a double diminutive. The name Rosa 'Rose' is the stem of the diminutive Rosina. Rosinete's structure is #rɔz++a#+in+<[αfeminine]#+εt++e#.

**§10.4.2** The nouns in sections 1 and 2 of Table 10.3 have the same underlying structure: #root++[±feminine]#+[diminutive]+<[αfeminine]#. These diminutives are always formed from stems rather than roots, which the underlying structure reflects by including both their roots and their gender suffixes within word boundaries (# X #).[40] These

40 The gender morphemes in the stems of these two classes of nouns are derivative because they can change the meaning of words: cf. *rio* 'river' ⇔ *ria* 'tidewater basin', *pico* 'peak' ⇔ *pica* 'lance'. Likewise, the gender of a name will indicate a particular person. Someone named 'Guilhermino' is inevitably different from someone named 'Guilhermina'.

diminutive suffixes are intrinsically genderless, but they are necessarily followed by an inflectional gender morpheme (<[αfeminine]#) that agrees with the gender of the original nouns, which the α (alpha) symbol indicates. Rule 10.1a will eliminate the stems' gender morphemes once agreement has been made:

§**10.4.3** The adjectives (Section 3) formed with diminutive suffixes have no gender morpheme attached to their stems since gender plays no role in identifying adjectives. Instead, these words consist of their stems followed by the diminutive suffix to which an inflecting gender morpheme attaches and agrees with the gender of whatever noun is being modified or represented, as is the case with all adjectives.

§**10.4.4** In Section 4's non-diminutive words, gender morphemes attach arbitrarily to stems formed by nominal roots.[41] The second set: *caneco⇔caneca* demonstrates the deriving nature of the gender morpheme in this class of diminutive lexical items.

§**10.4.5** The examples in Section 5 are cases in which the diminutive suffixes attach directly to the words' roots and carry with them, as many ordinary derivational suffixes do, a particular gender morpheme which they impose on the resultant noun.

## Augmentatives

§**10.5.0** Table 10.5a contains the suffixes employed in forming augmentatives (cf. Cunha, 65).[42] They appear in the ascending order of their productivity:

41 In the case of *pacote* the root is followed by diminutive suffix: #pak++ɔt+. The 'diminutive' *pacotilha* is a double diminutive: #pak++ɔt++iλ++a#.

42 Cunha's list contains five more suffixes; however, four of these suffixes are, simply, combinations of augmentative suffixes: -alhaz, +aλ++az#+e+; *-arraz*, +ar̲++az#+e+(7 and 8); *-alhão*, +aλ++on+{<e+,<a#} (10 and 11); *-arrão* +ar̲++on+{<e+,<a#} (7 and 11). The sequence +eir++on+{<e+,<a#} is a combination of the deriving suffix +eir+ plus augmentative suffix 11.

**Table 10.5a** Augmentative Suffixes

| | Suffix | Analysis | | Suffix | Analysis |
|---|---|---|---|---|---|
| 1 | -anzil | +an+z+il#+e+ | 7 | -arra | +aɾ̲++a# |
| 2 | -ast(r)o, -a | +azt(r)+<[αfem.]# | 8 | -az | +az#+e+ |
| 3 | -ázio | +ˈazi++o# | 9 | -aço, -a | +as++[αfeminine] |
| 4 | -uço, -a | +us+<[αfem.]# | 10 | -alho,- a | +aλ++o, +a# |
| 5 | -orra | +ɔɾ̲++a# | 11 | -ão, -ona | +on+<e+,<a# |
| 6 | -aréu, -a | +ar#+ˈɛ+<u# | | | |

Table 10.5b rates the productivity of 11 bona fide augmentative suffixes according to the tokens in the *Aurélio*:

**Table 10.5b** Augmentative Suffixes' Productivity[a]

| Suffix | [-f.] | [+f.] | % | Productivity | Suffix | [-f.] | [+f.] | % | Productivity |
|---|---|---|---|---|---|---|---|---|---|
| -anzil | 1 | | 0.09 | Negligible | -az | 68 | | 6.02 | High |
| -ast(r)o | 9 | 2 | 0.97 | Very Low | -alho,- a | 93 | 52 | 12.83 | Very High |
| -ázio | 14 | | 1.24 | Low | -aço, -a | 114 | 50 | 14.51 | Very High |
| -uço, -a | 8 | 9 | 1.50 | Low | -ona | | 288 | 25.49 | Outlier |
| -orra | | 18 | 1.59 | Low | -ão | 357 | | 31.59 | Outlier |
| -aréu, -a | 16 | 3 | 1.68 | Low | | | | | |
| -arra | | 28 | 2.47 | Low | | | | | |
| Total | 116 | 60 | 15.57 | | | 564 | 390 | 84.42 | |
| Total | 176 | | | | | 954 | | | |
| | Total Augmentatives 1,130 | | | | | | | | |

a Both *–ão* and *–ona*, independently and combined, were outliers in these data. The remaining augmentative suffixes (M=32.38, SD=35.45, Z=2.55) had no outliers among themselves.

Statistical analysis of the data in Table 10.5b shows that the augmentative suffix +on+{<e+,<a#} (the source of both –ão and –ona) is both an outlier among augmentatives and by far the default augmentative suffix in Portuguese.[43] In its [±feminine] instantiations, +on+ constitutes

43 The *Aurélio* lists 5,934 nouns ending in –ão; however, 4,071 of those nouns contain allomorphs of +sion+. This leaves 1,863 potential augmentative words. In an examination of 370 randomly selected augmentative possibilities, there were 71 augmentatives, 19.19% of the items. The number 357 in Table 10.5b represents 19.19% of the total count. Similarly, with the –ona listings the *Aurélio* contains 423 items. In a sampling of 222 randomly

57.08% of the *Aurélio*'s augmentative tokens. And once again a minority (five of the eleven) augmentative suffixes accounts for 84.42% of this dataset. The following paragraphs examine these suffixes one by one.

**§10.5.1 +an+z+il#+e+:** What Cunha calls a single suffix consists of three morphemes: two deriving morphemes followed by the ambivalent gender morpheme. (The segment /z/ is a transitional sound between /n+ and +i/.) The morphemes +an+ and +il+ appear and have been analyzed elsewhere: +an+ in §7.5.5.24 and +il# in §7.5.5.14 Neither of these suffixes is an augmentative, but together they combine in the sole example: *corpanzil* 'bulky body' (cf. *corpo* 'body'), which is an independent, i.e. derived, noun.

**§10.5.2 +azt(r)+<[αfeminine]#:** Cunha lists *medicastro* 'quack' (cf. *médico* 'physician') and *poetastro* 'bad poet' (cf. *poeta* 'poet') as examples of this suffix. Both of these suffixed words need not be considered anything other than spontaneous deprecatory modifications of their stems' meanings. In the *Aurélio*, one finds *criticastro* 'bad critic', *pulhastro* 'person without dignity' (cf. *pulha* 'ne'er do well').[44] This suffix has an allomorph +azt+<[αfeminine]# that occurs in kinship terms such as *madrasta* 'step mother' (cf. *madrinha* 'god-mother' or *padrasto* 'step father' cf. *padrinho* 'god-father'). This suffix indicates less than standard examples of animate (human) referents and, notwithstanding these and other entries in the *Aurélio* and *Morais* dictionaries, it rarely forms words whose denotations are different from the sum of their meaningful parts, i.e. these words are not idioms. In addition to the inferiority its presence implies for professions, whenever +azt(r)+<[αfeminine]# is added to a kinship term, it indicates a lack of genetic relationship. Since it designates animate beings, its gender morpheme is inflectional: e.g. #fiλ++azt(r)+<[αfeminine]#.[45]

**§10.5.3+ˈazi++o#:** Cunha's examples are *copázio* 'a filled large glass' (cf. *copo* 'glass') and *gatázio* 'nails, claws' (cf. *gato* 'cat'), both of which are true lexical items hence derived words. One also finds *balázio* 'large

---

selected tokens, there were 151 bona fide augmentatives or 68.02% of the sampling. The number 288 in Table 10.5b represents 68.02% of the total number of nominals ending in –<u>ona</u>.

44 The *Morais* contains *filhastro* 'step child' (cf. *filho* 'offspring') and considers it provincial in usage. It indicates a child from a spouse's previous marriage rather than an adopted child.

45 The term *cadastro* 'land office' is not formed with this suffix. It is a loan word from French *cadastre*.

bullet' (cf. *bala* 'bullet') and the adjective *durázio* 'hard-shelled [of fruit]' (cf. *duro* 'hard'). The latter also qualifies as a word derived with this augmentative suffix whereas *balázio* does not. This suffix attaches directly to roots: noun: #gat++ˈazi++o#, adjective: #dur++ˈazi+<[αfeminine]#.

**§10.5.4 +us+<[αfeminine]#:** Cunha's examples are the adjective *dentuço* 'buck toothed' (cf. *dente* 'tooth') and the noun *carduça* 'a rough carder' (cf. *carda* 'carder'). In the first case, the adjective *dentuço* designates a buck-toothed individual rather than a remarkable tooth. In its [+feminine] form, the noun *dentuça* is a folk term indicating a dental arch with large or protruding teeth, and it names two species of fish. This suffix's gender may be determined by the person it designates (a male or female buck toothed person) or by the noun it modifies (*carda* is [+feminine]). Other terms include and *carapuça* 'cap' (no apparently related word) and *marouço* 'rough sea' (cf. *mar* 'sea'). When this suffix creates an adjective, it attaches to the root: #dent++us+<[αfeminine]#. In forming a noun, it attaches to the stem and copies the gender morpheme #kard++a#+us+<[αfeminine]#.

**§10.5.5 +ɔr̠++a#:** Cunha's examples are *beiçorra* 'big lip' (cf. *beiço* 'lip') and *cabeçorra* 'big head' (cf. *cabeça* 'head'). Neither of Cunha's examples is an independent word, but these forms not only indicate abnormally large size, they also suggest a certain ugliness pertaining to the referent. Among the words ending in this suffix one finds: *ganchorra* 'mooring hook' (cf. *gancho* 'hook'), *machorra* 'infertile woman' (cf. *macho* 'male'), and *modorra* 'prostration' (cf. *modo* 'way', *moda* 'style'). The latter are all independent words. Again, this +S suffix attaches to roots and creates [+feminine] words: e.g. #beis++ɔr̠++a#.

**§10.5.6 +ar#+ ˈɛ+<u#:** Cunha's examples are *povaréu* 'rabble' (cf. *povo* 'folk') and *fogaréu* 'bonfire' (cf. *fogo* 'fire'), and both of these qualify as independent words. To these words add: *tabaréu* 'villager, bumpkin' (cf. *taba* 'village'). Like +an+z+il#+e+, this suffix is a compound of two deriving suffixes +ar# (§7.5.5.19 Tables 7.3a-b) and +ɛ++u# (§7.5.5.10, Tables 7.6a-b). Again, two deriving suffixes combine to form an augmentative. Although +ar# is a +$S_1$ suffix, when it occurs with +ˈɛ+<u# to form an augmentative, the combination becomes a +S suffix that attaches to roots: e.g. *fogaréu* #fɔk++ar#+ˈɛ++u#, and for that reason the /k+ in #fɔk+ acquires voicing.[46]

---

46 The [+feminine] inflections for those nominals that indicate living beings, e.g. *tabaréu* 'bumpkin' and *aréu* 'confused' vary in their [+feminine] forms: *tabaroa* and *areia*.

**§10.5.7 +ar̲++a#:** Cunha's examples of this suffix are *bocarra* 'big mouth' (cf. *boca* 'mouth') and *naviarra* 'big ship' (cf. *navio* 'ship'). They are not independent words. Rather they are examples of an augmentative suffix used to indicate a large (or affectively charged) instantiation of their stems' standard referent. Among the plausible augmented stems one can find *bimbarra* 'large wooden lever'. (cf, *bimba* 'child's penis'), *gambiarra* 'ramp to stage at a theater' (cf. *gâmbia* 'leg'), and *zanguizarra* 'tumult' (cf. *zanga* 'disagreement, anger'). The last three words are independent lexical items owing to the specificity of their meanings. This suffix determines the resultant nouns' gender ([+femi nine]) and attaches directly to roots: e.g. *naviarra* #navi++ar̲++a#.

**§10.5.8 +az#+e+:** This augmentative suffix both modifies nouns as Cunha's example *lobaz* 'big wolf' (cf. *lobo* 'wolf') shows, and it creates nouns and adjectives such as Cunha's *roaz* 'given to gnawing' (cf. *roer* 'to gnaw') shows. The *Aurélio* lists 68 words (adjectives and nouns) formed with it, e.g. *dicaz* 'severely critical' (cf. *indicar* 'to indicate'),[47] *mordaz* 'mordant' (cf. *morder* 'to bite'), *lambaz* 'gluttonous, deck swab' (cf. *lamber* 'to lick'). All these words are independent lexical items. This suffix includes the ambivalent gender morpheme +e+ so the same forms indicate both [±feminine] referents: e.g. *coelho roaz* 'rabbit given to gnawing' and *capivara roaz* 'capivara given to gnawing'. This suffix occurs on the Portuguese name for Satan: cf. Satanás ⇔ Satã. The lexical form of *capaz* 'capable' is #kap++az#+e+ (cf. *caber* 'to fit' and *cabimento* 'socially fitting, proper' as well as *capacidade* 'capicity'). Its causing underlying [+surd] stops to surface suggests that +az#+e+ is a +$S_1$ suffix.

**§10.5.9.0 +as+,+a#, +o# <o#:** Cunha's examples of +as++a# are *barbaça*, which probably should be *barbaças,*[48] 'bearded man' (cf. *barba* 'beard, chin') and *barcaça* 'barge' (cf. *barca* 'ferry'). Both of these examples constitute lexical items. His examples of +as+<o# are *animalaço* 'large animal'[49] (cf. *animal* 'animal') and *ricaço* 'very rich

---

47 The words *dicaz* and *indicar* quite likely have the same root as *dizer* 'to say', and the preservation of the underlying /k+ suggests that +az+ is a +$S_1$ suffix. Compare words like *capaz* 'capable' and *tenaz* 'tenacious', where underlying root-final consonants emerge without mutation. See also Tables 7.3e, 7.3f, 7.6d, 7.8–10, and §7.2.4.1.

48 The dictionaries only list *barbaças*. It is not out of the question that *barbaça* is a legitimate augmentative form of *barba*, however.

49 This word can be used metaphorically to indicate a 'blockhead'.

person' (cf. *rico* 'rich'). The augmentative of *animal* is not a separate lexical item, it merely indicates a subjective judgment of a particular animal (or, metaphorically, a human being). To show that +as+ is, in fact, an augmentative suffix after which a deriving gender morpheme may occur, consider the minimal pair: *vinhaça* 'low quality wine' and *vinhaço* 'grape squeezings'.

**§10.5.9.1 +as++a** In addition to *vinhaça*, words such as *linhaça* 'linseed, flaxseed (cf. *linha* 'line, thread'), *fogaça* 'bread cooked in embers' (cf. *fogo* 'fire'), *vidraça* 'pane (of glass)', (cf. *vidro* 'glass'), *arruaça* 'street brawl' (cf. *rua* 'street') indicate that one allomorph of this suffix is +as++a#, and it determines the resultant words' gender ([+feminine]). All these forms are lexical items derived by this augmentative suffix followed by +a#. Words such as *vinhaça* and *vidraça* indicate that this suffix attaches directly to roots: #viɲ++as++a# and #vitr++as++a#, and the root-final /tr+'s mutation to /dr+ points to its status as an +S suffix.

**§10.5.9.2 +as++o#** In addition to the word *vinhaço*, among the words formed with +as++o# one finds *balaço* 'gunshot' (cf. *bala* 'bullet'), *bagaço* 'grindings' (cf. *bago* 'berry'), *melaço* 'viscous liquid' (cf. *mel* 'honey'), *estilhaço* 'shard' (*estilha* 'fragment'), *andaço* 'small epidemic, dysentery' (cf. *andar* 'to go about'). In the case of *balaço* and *estilhaço*, it is clear that the suffix +as++o# determines their gender since the related, non-augmentative, words are [+feminine].

**§10.5.9.3 +as+<o#** When this suffix forms words designating animate beings, its gender morpheme is inflectional: *ricaço* ⇔ *ricaça* #r̲ik++as+<[αfeminine]# 'filthy rich' (cf. *rico* ⇔ *rica*), *animalaço* ⇔ *animalaça* 'blockhead', and *soberbaço* ⇔ *soberbaça* 'ridiculously vain person' (cf. *soberbo* 'vain').

**§10.5.10 +aλ++o, +a#:** Cunha does not include this suffix among the augmentatives, but they abound: *cabeçalho* 'heading' (cf. *cabeça* 'head'), *chocalho* 'cowbell' (cf. *chocar* 'to collide, to scare'), *vergalho* 'dried penis (of horses or steers)' (cf. *verga* 'flexible rod'), *gargalho* 'mass of phlegm' (cf. *garganta* 'throat'), *fornalha* 'furnace' (cf. *forno* 'oven), *muralha* 'bulwark' (cf. *muro* 'wall'), *migalha* 'crumb' (cf. *migas* 'bits of bread'), *mortalha* 'shroud' (cf. *morte* 'death'). All of these augmentative formations are words in their own right. This suffix attaches to roots, after which the deriving gender suffixes can determine the words' final configuration and meaning: *farfalho* '(a) rustling' ≠ *farfalha* 'a collection of rustlings'. The lexical form of *cabeçalho* is #kabes++aλ++o# and that of *fornalha* is #forn++aλ++a#.

**§10.5.11.0 +on+<e#, <a#** This set of morphemes is both the default augmentative suffix and an outlier—both [±feminine] forms together and each separately (note a, Table 10.5b). Cunha's examples are *caldeirão* 'big pot' (cf. *caldeira* 'caldron') and *paredão* 'high wall' (cf. *parede* 'wall').[50] These augmentatives have metaphoric extensions such as 'deep place in a river bed' and 'river bank', but they are, originally, simple augmentations of their stems' denotations. When this suffix derives deverbal nouns, it occurs in its [-feminine] instantiation: *achadão* 'bargain' (cf. *achar* 'to find'), *podão* 'pruning instrument' (cf. *podar* 'to prune'), *ferrão* 'spike, stinger' (cf. *ferro* 'iron', *ferrar* 'to sting'). Data such as these show that +on+ can be a deriving suffix in its own right.

**§10.5.11.1** When it creates words designating animate beings, it can be inflected for gender: *lambão* ⇔ *lambona* 'messy eater' (cf. *lamber* 'to lick'), *trintão* ⇔ *trintona* 'person in their thirties' (cf. *trinta* 'thirty'), *fregona* 'lowly female servant' (cf. *fregar* 'to rub' and *esfregão* 'a scrubbing'), *matrona* 'matron' (cf. *maternal* 'maternal'), *poltrona* 'lazy woman' (cf. *poltrão* 'lazy'), *solteirona* 'old maid' (cf. *solteirão* 'a confirmed old bachelor'), *chorona* 'female given to crying' (cf. *chorar* 'to cry' and *chorão* 'crybaby, weeping willow').

**§10.5.11.2** In addition the [+feminine] reflex of this suffix can be a deriving suffix: e.g. *acordeona* 'a type of accordion' (cf. *acordeão* 'ordinary accordion'), *gaifona* 'satire' (cf. *gaiato* 'rascal'), *marafona* 'rag doll' (cf. *marafa* 'low life').

**§10.5.11.3** Similar to the diminutive suffixes +it+, +iɲ+, and +ul+, this suffix can occur with a transitional consonant inserted between it and its stems.

Table 10.6 Lists examples found in the *Aurélio*:

50 Certainly this word, for Cunha's generation, brings to mind the Cuban revolution and the firing squads in which 'enemies of the state' were put up against the *paredón*—the nasty wall. The word *orelhão* 'phone cowl' (cf. *orelha* 'ear') was used in Brazil during the 1970s.

**Table 10.6a** Insertion of /z/ Before +on+

| | Ordinary Nominals | | Augmentatives | | |
|---|---|---|---|---|---|
| | Stem | Gloss | [-feminine] | Gloss | [+feminine] |
| 1 | **bom** | good | **bonzão** | very good | ?[a] |
| 2 | **folga** | leisure | **folgazão** | playful | **folgazona** |
| 3 | **mau** | bad | **mauzão** | really bad | **mauona**[b] |
| 4 | **jataí** | honey bee | **jataizão** | big bee | *** |
| 5 | **mar** | sea | **marzão** | rough sea | *** |

a There seems to be no [+feminine] augmentative, such as **boazona*. The *Aurélio* lists *boazuda* as a folk form meaning something like 'extremely attractive female'.
b Searching the internet one finds disquisitions on *mauzão*, *malzão*, and *malzona*, but not *mauzona or màzona*. In most Brazilian pronunciations, *mauzona* and *malzona* would be homophonous. See eliza-souza.blogspot.com/2011/11/to-malzona.html, www.dicio.com.br./mauzão, www.infopedia.pt.dicionarios/lingua-portuguesa/malzão. All accessed on 3 November 2017. See also dicionarioinformal.com.br/diferençaentremauzona/malvada. This source maintains that *mauzona* is the feminine form of *mauzão*. Accessed 10 December 2019.

**§10.5.11.4** Quite likely items 4 and 5 will have no [+feminine] instantiation given that the word *mar* is only [-feminine] in Portuguese, and the honey bees people normally see are workers, i.e. neuter. The [-feminine] augmentative of *mau* is remarkable since it appears to be inflected twice for [-feminine] (<u# and <o#, cf. *má* 'bad' [+feminine]), which is similar to true compound forms (§12.0.1–3, §12.1.0, §12.2.0, *et passim*). However, the [-feminine] inflected form becomes the stem of the [+feminine] form.

**§10.6.0 Double Augmentatives:** Cunha lists among his augmentative suffixes a set of double augmentatives (see fn. 42, current chapter), which, save +ar̲#+az#+e+, are actually reasonably frequent. Table 10.7 lists them in the order of their frequency (productivity) according to the *Aurélio*:

**Table 10.7** Double Augmentatives

| Suffix | Analysis | [-f.] | [+f.] | Total | Productivity |
|---|---|---|---|---|---|
| -alhaz | +aλ++az#++e+ | 3 | | 3 | Negligible |
| -arraz | +ar̲++az#++e+ | 5 | | 5 | Negligible |
| -arrão, -ona | +ar̲++on+{<e+,<a#} | 36 | 14 | 50 | Moderate |
| -eirão, -ona | +eir++on+{<e+,<a#} | 43 | 20 | 63 | Moderate |
| -alhão, -ona | +aλ++on+{<e+,<a#} | 53 | 26 | 79 | High |
| Totals: | | 140 | 60 | 200 | |

These items have all been counted among the single augmentative suffixes (+az# and +on+). In total (200) they constitute 17.70% of all (1,130, Table 10.5b) augmentative words, a weighty percentage. They merit examination before concluding this section of Chapter 10.

**§10.6.1 +aλ++az#+e+:** This compound suffix is a concatenation of the augmentative suffixes +aλ+ and +az#+e+. Cunha's example is *facalhaz* 'big knife' (cf. *faca* 'knife'). This word does not designate an object different from a knife; thus, it is not really a case of nominal derivation. The words *tracalhaz* (a folk term for huge portion of food[51]) and *parpalhaz* 'quail' are examples of this suffix's deriving capabilities.[52] The lexical form of *tracalhaz* is #trak++aλ++az#+e+.

**§10.6.2+ ar̲++az#+e+:** This compound suffix is a combination of the augmentative suffixes addressed in §10.5.7 and §10.5.8 plus the ambivalent gender morpheme +e+. Cunha's example is *pratarraz* 'big plate' (cf. *prato* 'plate'). This word is an affective modification of the original lexical item, not an independent word. This double suffix occurs in the word *aguarrás* 'spirits of turpentine' cf. *água* 'water'.[53] This word's lexical form would be #aku++a#+ar̲++az#+e+. The abutment of +a# and +a/ will occasion the deletion of the second of two like segments (Rule 4.1). The augmentative word, owing to its two derivational augmentative suffixes, will necessitate stress reassignment from the word's stem #'aku++a# since stress on a vowel four syllables prior to a non-compound word's final vowel is ungrammatical.

**§10.6.3 +ar̲++on+<e, <a#:** Cunha's examples of this. concatenation of augmentative suffixes (§10.5.7 and §10.5.11.0–4), are: *gatarrão* 'big cat' (cf. *gato* 'cat') and *homenzarrão* 'huge man' (cf. *homem* 'man'). These augmentative forms do not qualify as independent lexical items, they merely indicate large or charged exemplars of their stems' referents

---

51 The *Aurélio* provides an alternate form of this word: *tracanaz*, but gives no root for either form. The root may be #trak+, which underlies the verb *tragar* 'to gulp down'. If this analysis is correct, this suffix belongs to the $+S_1$ category since it preserves the underlying /k+ of the root, whereas the +a# theme vowel (a +S suffix) allows /k+ to voice.

52 The term *parpalhaz* is peculiar to northeast Portugal. According to *Morais*, there are several variants of this term.

53 A variant of this suffix occurs in *beberraz* 'drunk' (cf. *beber* 'to drink'). However, the vowel of the compound suffix is lost because this deverbal nominal #bɛb++e#+ar̲++az#+e+ deletes the +a/ and preserves the theme vowel +e#.

(spontaneous augmentatives). De-adjectival nouns like *secarrão* 'a very dry individual' (cf. *seco* 'dry'), *mansarrão* 'a peace-loving individual' (cf. *manso* 'tame'), *santarrão* 'hypocrite' (cf. *santo* 'saint') count as independent, i.e. derived, lexical items mainly because they are the result of this augmentative suffix's creating nouns from adjectival roots. The words this double augmentative suffix forms normally designate animate beings so its gender morpheme is inflectional: cf. *secarrão* ⇔ *secarrona*. This string of suffixes attaches to roots: #mans++ar̲++on+<[αfeminine]#.[54]

**§10.6.4 +eir++on+<e, <a#:** This double suffix consists of two deriving suffixes +eir+ (Table 7.3a, §7.2.0) and +on+ plus the inflectional gender suffixes. Cunha's examples are *asneirão* 'egregious fool' (cf. *asno* 'ass', *asneira* 'foolish act') and *toleirão* 'egregious fool' (cf. *tolo* 'foolish'). Whereas the second word betrays a speaker's judgment of a specific fool, the first, metaphoric in origin, stands on its own as an independent word indicating something other than a literal (animal) jackass or a foolish act or concept indicated by the word *asneira*. Because words formed with this double suffix designate animate beings, their gender is inflectional, and in their [+feminine] instantiations the +on+ emerges: *aseneirona* 'egregious female fool'. This concatenation of suffixes attaches to roots: e.g. #tɔl++eir++on+<[αfeminine]#.

**§10.6.5+aλ++on+{<e+,<a#, +e+, +a#}:** Cunha's examples are *grandalhão* 'very large person' (cf. *grande* 'big') and *vagalhão* 'large concavity' (cf. *vaga* 'open space'). The gender of *grandalhão* is inflectional (underlying #grand++aλ++on+<e+). When it is inflected for [+feminine] gender, the word emerges as *grandalhona* #grand++aλ++on+<a#. The second example is a case of derivation (underlying #vak++aλ++on++e+) because the word acquires the [-feminine] gender arbitrarily assigned to +on+.[55]

**§10.6.6.0** Matrix 10.2 contains the augmentative morphemes, their analyses, and their properties:

---

54 The underlying form of *homenzarrão* contains a transitional, non-suffixal /z/, similar to that of *corpanzil* (§10.5.1): #ɔmin+z+ar̲++on+<e#. This transitional /z/ also appears with the diminutive suffixes +it+ and +iɲ+. (§10.2.1.0, §10.2.2.9.0–3.)

55 Its allowing the root final /k+ to mutate to /g+ confirms this suffix's status as +S.

Matrix 10.2 Augmentative Suffix Properties

| | Morphemes | $+S_1\#$ | Doubles | ±fem. | Proper. Noun |
|---|---|---|---|---|---|
| 1 | +an+z+il#+e+ | - | —[a] | - | - |
| 2 | +azt(r)+<[αfeminine]# | - | - | - | - |
| 3 | +ˈazi++o# | - | - | - | - |
| 4 | +us+<[αfeminine]# | - | - | - | - |
| 5 | +ɔr̲++a# | - | - | + | - |
| 6 | +ar#+ɛ<u#, <a# | - | — | ? | - |
| 7 | +ar̲++a# | - | +* | + | - |
| 8 | +az++e+ | + | +** | - | - |
| 9 | +as+<[αfeminine]# | - | +** | - | - |
| 10 | +aλ+<[αfeminine]# | - | +* | + | - |
| 11 | +on+<[αfeminine]# | - | +** | + | + |

a The dash (–) associated with suffixes 1 and 6 indicates that they are compounds of non-augmentative suffixes. All the compounding augmentatives' positive specifications are followed by asterisks and can occur as word-final augmentative suffixes. The ones followed by single asterisks occur as the first element in a compound augmentative suffix. Those with two asterisks occur as the second augmentative in a compound. In these compound suffixes, the second element carries or acquires the appropriate gender morpheme.

Augmentative suffixes have the following properties:

**§10.6.6.1 Derive Nouns:** All the augmentative suffixes (save 5, +azt(r)+) can be instrumental in the creation of independent words. Words formed by +azt(r)+ are not idioms, i.e. this suffix only attaches to [+animate, +human] stems, and it always indicates the less than authentic nature of the particular referent: *filhasto* 'step son', *criticastro* 'bad critic'.

**§10.6.6.2 Derive Adjectives:** As in the case of the diminutive suffixes, adjectives with augmentative suffixes that designate [+animate] beings (i.e. males and females) reflect their gender with inflecting gender morphemes.

**§10.6.6.3 Double Suffixes:** All the suffixes identified with asterisks as potential members of double augmentatives may be the final augmentative morpheme; however, suffixes +ar̲+ and +aλ+ are always the first suffix, and +az+, +as+, and +on+ are always the second .

**§10.6.6.4 [αfeminine]:** When an augmentative suffix occurs in an adjective or in a nominal indicating an animate being (Suffixes 2, 4, 6, 9, 10, 11), there is always agreement with the referent's gender. Since suffix 1 only occurs on one word, there is no evidence to say that it does anything other than preserve the non-derived noun's gender: #kɔrp++ o#.

**§10.6.6.5 [±feminine]:** Suffixes 3 +ˈazi++o#, 5 +ɔɾ++a#, and 7 +aɾ ++a# always occur with non-inflecting gender morphemes when they are word-final, and, thus, they impose gender on the resultant word. The first morpheme in double augmentatives, however, bears no gender morpheme because gender morphemes only occur word-finally in non-compound lexical items. Suffix 8, contains the deriving variable gender morpheme +e+, which evanesces in [-plural] forms.

**§10.6.6.6 +$S_1$** Only one suffix (9 +az+) qualifies as a +$S_1$. Another example of its consonant-preserving (+$S_1$) nature is the word *sequaz* 'follower' #sɛk++u++az#<e# (cf. *seguir* 'to follow' #sɛk++i++r#+e# [sə.ˈɣi.rə] and *sequência* #sɛk++u++ˈen.si++a# [sə.ˈkʷẽⁿ.si.ă].'sequence').

**§10.6.6.7 Proper Nouns:** The only augmentative suffix that appears to adhere to proper nouns is 11 +on+.

**§10.6.7.0** Table 10.8 summarizes the patterns documented:[56]

56 English glosses for Table 10.8: **Pattern 1**: sea⇔rough sea, carder⇔rough carder, folk⇔rabble, woman⇔terrible woman, low-life⇔especially bad low life, daughter⇔step daughter, wolf⇔bad wolf, dregs⇔ashes, body⇔bulky body, street⇔demonstration, plate⇔big plate; **Pattern 2**: woman⇔remarkable woman, lip⇔ugly lip, bullet⇔big bullet, ship⇔terrible ship, chest (furniture)⇔big chest, dog⇔riff-raff, wave⇔ground swell, hook⇔mooring hook; **Pattern 3**: thistle⇔thistle color, water⇔turpentine; **Pattern 4**: tooth⇔buck toothed, (native) village⇔of a native village, lay person⇔extremely ignorant, straw⇔clown, weeping⇔cry baby, hard⇔hard shelled; **Pattern 5**: wine⇔grape silage, wine⇔low quality wine, Christian soldier in Muslim service⇔a rustling, Christian soldier in Muslim service⇔a collection of rustlings.

Table 10.8 Patterns of Nominal Formation with Augmentative Suffixes

| Pattern 1: Form Augmentatives, Copy Gender | | | | | | | |
|---|---|---|---|---|---|---|---|
| #root++[±feminine]#+augmentative+<[αfeminine]# | | | | | | | |
| [-fem.] | Suffix(es) | | [-fem.] | | [+fem.] | Suffix | [+fem.] |
| mar | +us+ | | marouço | | carda | +us+ | carduça |
| povo | +ar++ˈε+<u# | | povaréu | | mulher | +on+ | mulherona |
| pulha | +aztr+ | | pulhastro | | filha | +ast+ | filhasta |
| lobo | +az#+e+ | | lobaz | | borra | +aλ+ | borralha |
| corpo | +an+z+il#+e+ | | corpanzil | | rua | +as+ | arruaça |
| prato | +ar̲++az#+e+ | | pratarraz | | | | |
| Pattern 2: Form Augmentatives, Supply Gender | | | | | | | |
| #root++agumentative++[-fem.]# | | | | | #root++agumentative++[+fem.]# | | |
| [+fem.] | Suffix | | [-fem.] | | [-fem.] | Suffix | [+fem.] |
| mulher | +on+e+ | | mulherão | | beiço | +ɔr̲++a# | beiçorra |
| bala | +ˈazi++o# | | balázio | | navio | +ar̲++a# | naviarra |
| arca | +az#+e+ | | arcaz | | cão | +aλ++a# | canalha |
| vaga | +aλ++on++e+ | | vagalhão | | gancho | +<ɔr̲++a# | ganchorra |
| Pattern 3: Create Noun, Copy Gender | | | | | | | |
| #root++[±feminine]#+augmentative+<[αfeminine]# | | | | | | | |
| [-fem.] | Suffix | | [-fem.] | | [+fem.] | Suffix | [+fem.] |
| cardo | +on+ | | cardão | | água | +ar̲++az# | aguarrás |
| Pattern 4: Form Adjectives | | | | | | | |
| #stem++augmentative+<[αfeminine]# | | | | | | | |
| [-fem.] | Suffixes | | [αfem.] | | [+fem.] | Suffixes | [αfeminine] |
| dente | +us+ | | dentuço | | taba | +ar++ε++u# | tabaréu |
| leigo | +as+ | | leigaço | | palha | +as+ | palhaço |
| choro | +on+ | | chorão | | duro | +ˈazi+ | durázio |
| Pattern 5: Create Stem, Receive Gender | | | | | | | |
| #root++augmentative++[±feminine] | | | | | | | |
| [-fem.] | Suffixes | | [-fem.] | | [+fem.] | Suffixes | [+fem.] |
| vinho | +as++o# | | vinhaço | | vinho | +as++a# | vinhaça |
| farfã | + aλ ++o# | | farfalho | | farfã | +aλ++a# | farfalha |

§10.6.7.1 **Patterns 1 and 3:** The Pattern 1 nouns are structured similarly to those in Sections 1 and 2 of Table 10.4a. In this case, their structure is #root++[±feminine]#+[augmentative]+<[αfeminine]#, and they are formed from stems that include the gender morpheme, whether the morpheme be clearly derivational as in the case of Pattern

1's *carda* 'carder' (cf. *cardo* 'thistle') or inflectional, as in the case of *filha* 'daughter', the [+feminine] form of *filho* 'offspring'. As examples of the cases at hand, the underlying forms of Pattern 1's *mulherona* and Pattern 3's *aguarrás* will be #muλer#+$e_{[+fem.]}$++on+<[αfem.]#<[αplural]# and #aku++a#+ar̲++az#+e+<[αplural]#. With the addition of a disjunction, Rule 10.1b will eliminate the stems' gender morphemes once agreement has been made on a following diminutive or augmentative suffix:

**Rule 10.1b Eliminate Stem-Internal Gender Morphemes in Diminutives and Augmentatives:**

$$[\pm \text{fem.}] \rightarrow \varnothing \; / \left\{\begin{matrix} + \\ < \end{matrix}\right\} \_\#+ \left\{\begin{matrix} \text{diminutive}^{57} \\ \text{augmentative} \end{matrix}\right\} + <[\alpha\text{fem.}]\#$$

§10.6.7.2.0 **Pattern 2:** In all cases save that of +on+, these suffixes co-occur with specific gender morphemes: +a#, +o# and ambivalent +e+. These gendered augmentative suffixes attach to roots and supply gender, e.g. *balazio* #bal++ˈazi++o#. And this happens regardless of the related (non-augmentative) nouns' genders.

**§10.6.4.7.2.1** Mattoso Câmara (1964: 60) maintains that in the use of augmentatives 'their pejorative aspect [...] becomes intensified when a word's gender is changed.' Mattoso Câmara included *mulherão* as an example of this phenomenon; however, this assertion did not jibe with the usage in Belo Horizonte—nor did it jibe with the *Morais* dictionary's definition of the term: 'a greatly desirable woman'. Many native speakers concur that *mulherão* conveys a complimentary connotation, whereas *mulherona* conveys a negative one.[58] Table 10.9 contains examples of [+feminine] to [-feminine] gender shift which convey positive connotations.

57 The subset of stems that preserve stems' gender morphemes in diminutives formed by +ul+ is immune to this rule.

58 According to the *Aurélio*, the augmentative terms *mulherão*, *mulherona*, *mulheraça*, and *mulheraço* are synonyms designating women of remarkable appearance regardless of the augmentative form's gender.

Table 10.9 Gender Shift with +on+

| Word (+fem.) | Gloss | Augmentative (-fem.) | Augmentative Gloss |
|---|---|---|---|
| **água** | water | **aguão** | much water (rain) |
| **canoa** | canoe | **canoão** | wonderful canoe |
| **cara** | face | **carão** | friendly, smiling face |
| **chuva** | rain | **chuvão** | a big rain |
| **cultura** | cultivation | **culturão** | great cultivation |
| **família** | family | **familião** | great family |
| **festa** | party | **festão** | wonderful party |
| **lavoura** | tillage | **lavourão** | wonderful tillage |
| **noite** | night | **noitão** | wonderful night |

Of the Words in Table 10.9, *festão* and *noitão*, besides being ordinary, positively charged augmentatives also mean, respectively: 'festoon' and 'late at night'. That is, these two words can also occur as idioms rather than mere augmentative versions of ordinary words. In these and similar cases, the suffix +on+ attaches directly to roots and bears the gender morpheme <e+: *mulherão* #muλer#+on+<e+<Ø# and *familião* #fam'ili++on+<e+<Ø#. The +on+<e+ suffix causes stress to fall on the augmentative suffix, regardless of where it fell on the original word: antepenultimate stress: *família* ⇔ final stress *familião;* penultimate stress*: cara* ⇔ final stress *carão.*

**§10.6.7.3 Pattern 4:** These adjectives are formed with augmentative suffixes attached to stems or roots that have no gender morpheme attached. Likewise, the augmentatives have no intrinsic gender. That is, these words' stems are followed by the augmentative suffix to which an inflecting gender morpheme attaches and agrees with the gender of whatever noun is being modified or represented, as is the case with all adjectives.

**§10.6.7.4 Pattern 5:** Gender morphemes attach arbitrarily to stems formed from nominal roots followed by augmentative suffixes. The words *vinhaço* and *vinhaça*, *farfalho*, and *farfalha* demonstrate the deriving nature of the gender morpheme in this class of diminutive lexical items.

# Conclusions

## Summary

§10.7.0: Chapter 10 has examined the role diminutive and augmentative suffixes play both in communicating speaker affect (e.g. intimacy, scorn, appreciation, evaluation) concerning living beings, things, and ideas. It has also shown that these suffixes perform the roll of deriving suffixes—both diminutive and augmentative suffixes can derive nouns and adjectives whose denotations transcend the sum of their constituent parts. The source of these derived nominals may be nominal or verbal stems.

## Findings

**§10.7.1.0 Numbers:** There are at least twice as many diminutive suffixes (22–3) as there are augmentative suffixes (11). The number of diminutive tokens in the *Aurélio* (4,676) is 4.14 times that of the augmentative tokens (1,130). In both cases, a minority of the suffixes (both diminutive and augmentative) accounts for a vast, even overwhelming, number of lexical items. And the most productive augmentative suffix occurs so often that both its [-feminine] and [+feminine] instantiatons constitute outliers in this array of suffixes.

**§10.7.1.1 Gender:** Both diminutive and augmentative suffixes may attach to stems containing gender morphemes, in which case the resultant words' gender is the same as that of their stems. Both diminutive and augmentative suffixes can be composites of deriving suffixes and companion gender morphemes, in which case they determine the resultant nouns' gender. Both can form deverbal and denominal adjectives. And both can occur as the final element in a stem to which the deriving gender morphemes +o# and +a# can be attached so as to form words with unique, idiomatic meanings whose distinction is arbitrary and derives solely from the presence of particular gender morphemes.

**§10.7.1.2 Patterning:** One striking difference between diminutive and augmentative suffixes is that the latter regularly combine to form double augmentatives. In these combinations, certain suffixes (that on their own can end words) are restricted to the first position: +a$\underline{r}$+ and +aλ+. Others are restricted to word-final position: +as+, +az+, and +on+.

**§10.7.1.3.0 Allomorphy:** The data have shown that three of the diminutive suffixes Cunha has listed (*–zito, -a, –zinho, -a, and -culo, -a*), may occur as allomorphs of the suffixes +it+, +iɲ+, and +ul+—just as –*zão* is an allomorph of the augmentative suffix +on+. There are specific circumstances in which the /z/ emerges between the stems and suffixes +it+, +iɲ+, and +on+: when the stems can end in /l#, /r#, and /n#, or when the original word's gender morpheme is not deleted. The consonant /k/ appears between nominal stems ending in vowels or /z, n, r, l/ and the suffix +ul+. The latter suffix also occasions proparoxytone stress and the lenition of tonic mid vowels.

**§10.7.1.3.1 Allomorphy and Lexicalization:** The allomorph of +iɲ+ realized as [ˈzĩ.ɲũ] has become a free form insofar as words like *zinho, -a* are used to indicate specific individuals. In many words, e.g. *hotelzinho, pãozinho, bonzinho*, the diminutive suffix forms compounds since both elements in the word reflect either plurality: *hoteizinhos, pãezinhos*, or gender *bonzinho* ⇔ *boazinha*. (§12.3.4.0.)

**§10.7.1.4 Grammar:** At first it may seem that in the cases wherein diminutive and augmentative forms of words are actual lexical items, there should be no need for rules to form them because such lexical items would be listed with their specific concatenations of morphemes. Nonetheless, those lexical items formed from strings of morphemes that include a pre-diminutive or pre-augmentative gender morpheme, as well as spontaneous diminutive and augmentative forms of proper and common nouns, will require Rule 10.1b. This rule deletes the inner stem's gender morpheme after the suffix-final's inflectional gender morpheme has been made to agree with the original nouns' gender. That is, spontaneous diminutives and augmentatives like *gatinha* 'female kitten' and *carrão* 'big car'[59] are formed from juxtapositions of the nouns *gata* #gat+<a# and #kar̲++o# with the suffixes +iɲ+ and +on+: #gat+<a#+iɲ+<[αfeminine] and #kar̲++o#+on+<e+ Rule 8.1 (see Appendix A) will change the latter form to #kar̲++o#+an++o#. Agreement of gender will occur automatically, after Rule 10.1b.

59 Both words also have metaphoric extensions: *gatinha* can indicate an extremely attractive adolescent female, and a *carrão* is some sort of instrument fishermen use to bring their boats ashore.

**Rule 10.1b Eliminate Stem-Internal Gender Morphemes in Diminutives and Augmentatives:**

$$[\pm \text{fem.}] \rightarrow \emptyset \,/\, \left\{ \begin{matrix} + \\ < \end{matrix} \right\} \_\#+ \left\{ \begin{matrix} \text{diminutive} \\ \text{augmentative} \end{matrix} \right\} + <[\alpha\text{fem.}]\#$$

This rule operates to change these, and words with similar structures, to forms such as: #gat++iɲ+<a# and #kar̲++an+<o#.

**§10.7.1.5 /z/ Insertion:** The evidence suggests that /z/ insertion between stems and diminutive or augmentative suffixes occurs only when +it+, +iɲ+ form certain diminutives and, and +on+ forms certain augmentatives. Rule 10.2b tentatively accounts for this phenomenon:

**Rule 10.2b: /z/ insertion for diminutive and augmentative suffixes:**

$$\emptyset \rightarrow /z/ \,/\, \left\{ \begin{matrix} [+\text{contoid}] \\ [+\text{feminine}] \end{matrix} \right\} \;\#\_\_ + \left\{ \begin{matrix} +\text{it}+ \\ +\text{iɲ}+ \\ +\text{on}+ \end{matrix} \right\}$$

## So What?

**§10.7.2** Diminutive and augmentative suffixes are a minority within the nominal deriving array of suffixes, but, paradoxically, they are quite productive. Virtually every speaker of Portuguese forms diminutives and augmentatives in their spontaneous speech. Diminutive and augmentative morphology are as grammatically intrinsic to Portuguese as are gender, number, tense, mood, and aspect.

## Appendix A Rules as they Appear in Chapter 10

**§10A .0** In the course of Chapter 10, the following list of rules reflect the order in which they have appeared or been mentioned.

Rule **10.1a Eliminate Stem-Internal Gender Morphemes in Diminutives:**

[±fem.] →Ø / {+, <} __#+diminutive+<[αfem.]#

**Rule 10.2a: /z/ insertion for diminutive suffixes:**

$$\emptyset \rightarrow /z/ \;/\; \left\{\begin{matrix}[+\text{contoid}]\\ [\pm\text{feminine}]\end{matrix}\right\} \#\_\_ \;+\left\{\begin{matrix}\text{it}+\\ \text{iɲ}+\end{matrix}\right\} <[\alpha\text{feminine}]$$

**Rule 3.4 Proparoxytone Stress and Lenition Occasioned by +tik+<o#, +e+<o#, +ik+<o#, and +ul+<o#:**

$$\begin{pmatrix}\text{-contoid}\\ \alpha\text{-high}\\ \alpha\text{-low}\end{pmatrix} \rightarrow \begin{pmatrix}+\text{delayed transition}\\ \alpha\text{wide glottis}\end{pmatrix} / \_\_\; C_{1\text{-}3} \;+ \begin{pmatrix}+\text{tik}+\\ +\text{e}+\\ +\text{ik}+\\ +\text{ul}+\end{pmatrix} <\text{o}\#$$

**Rule 10.3 /k/ Insertion in Diminutives Formed with +ul+:**

$$\emptyset \rightarrow /k/ \;/\; \left\{\begin{matrix}\text{-contoid}\\ \begin{pmatrix}+\text{contoid}\\ \text{-occlusion}\\ \text{-surd}\\ \text{-labial}\\ \text{-high}\end{pmatrix}\end{matrix}\right\} /\,\#X \left\{\begin{matrix}+\\ \#\end{matrix}\right\} \_\_\; +\text{ul}+X\#$$

**Rule 10.4 +e$_{[+fem.]}$ # → /i/ / ___ /+ul+<a#:**

$$+\begin{pmatrix}\text{-contoid}\\ +\text{palatal}\\ \text{-high}\\ +\text{wide glottis}\end{pmatrix}_{[+\text{fem.}]} \# \rightarrow \begin{pmatrix}+\text{high}\\ +\text{palatal}\end{pmatrix} \;/\; \_\_\_ \begin{pmatrix}+\text{contoid}\\ +\text{dorsal}\\ +\text{surd}\\ +\text{occlusion}\end{pmatrix} +\text{ul}+$$

Rule **10.5 / ___ /+ul+<o#:**

$$+\begin{pmatrix}\text{-contoid}\\ \text{+dorsal}\\ \text{-high}\\ \text{+labial}\\ \text{+wide glottis}\end{pmatrix}\# \rightarrow \begin{pmatrix}\text{+low}\\ \text{-labial}\end{pmatrix} / \_\_\_ \begin{pmatrix}\text{+contoid}\\ \text{+dorsal}\\ \text{+surd}\\ \text{+occlusion}\end{pmatrix} \text{+ul+}$$

Rule **4.1 Like Segment Deletion (Provisional):**

$$\text{Segment}_2 \rightarrow \varnothing \,/\, \text{Segment}_1 \_\_$$

**Condition:** $\text{Segment}_1 = \text{Segment}_2$

Rule **10.1b Eliminate Stem-Internal Gender Morphemes in Diminutives and Augmentatives:**

$$[\pm\text{fem.}] \rightarrow \varnothing \,/ \begin{Bmatrix}+\\ <\end{Bmatrix} \_\#+ \begin{Bmatrix}\text{diminutive}\\ \text{augmentative}\end{Bmatrix} + <[\alpha\text{fem.}]\#$$

Rule **8.1b Suffix Merger in Word-Final Position:**

$$\begin{pmatrix}+\text{on}+\{<\text{e}+,\ <\text{o}\#\}\\ +\text{an}+\{<\text{e}+,<\text{o}\#\}\\ +(\alpha\ \text{s})\text{ion}+\ +\text{e}+\end{pmatrix} \rightarrow +(\alpha\ \text{s})\text{an}+\ +\text{o}\#_3/\ \_\_\ <[\text{-plural}]\#$$

Rule **10.2b /z/ Insertion for Diminutive and Augmentative Suffixes:**

$$\varnothing \rightarrow /\text{z}/ \,/ \begin{Bmatrix}[+\text{contoid}]\\ [\pm\text{feminine}]\end{Bmatrix} \#\_\_ + \begin{Bmatrix}+\text{on}+\\ +\text{it}+\\ +\text{iɲ}+\end{Bmatrix}$$

Although it was never mentioned, Rule 3.1 (Paroxytone Stress) is necessary for all diminutives save those formed by the suffix +ul+.

Rule **3.1 Paroxytone Stress:**

$$[\text{-contoid}] \rightarrow [+\text{stress}] \;/\; \#X \,\_\_\; \left(\begin{bmatrix}+\text{high}\\ \text{-contoid}\end{bmatrix}\right) C_{0\text{-}4}V_{[\text{-high}]}\#(C)\#$$

**Condition:** The word has no previously assigned stress.

## Appendix B The Grammar of Diminutive and Augmentative Formation

§10B.0 The following derivations demonstrate the order in which specific rules apply in the derivation of selected diminutives and augmentatives:

### Rule Order

Rule **10.5 +o# → /a/ / ___ /+ul+<o#:**

$$+ \begin{pmatrix}\text{-contoid}\\ +\text{dorsal}\\ \text{- high}\\ +\text{labial}\\ +\text{wide glottis}\end{pmatrix} \# \rightarrow \begin{pmatrix}+\text{low}\\ \text{-labial}\end{pmatrix} \;/\; \_\_\_ \begin{pmatrix}+\text{contoid}\\ +\text{dorsal}\\ +\text{surd}\\ +\text{occlusion}\end{pmatrix} +\text{ul}+$$

Rule **10.1b Eliminate Stem-Internal Gender Morphemes in Diminutives and Augmentatives:**

$$[\pm\text{fem.}] \rightarrow \emptyset \;/\; \begin{Bmatrix}+\\ <\end{Bmatrix}\_\#+ \begin{Bmatrix}\text{diminutive}\\ \text{augmentative}\end{Bmatrix} + <[\alpha\text{fem.}]\#$$

Rule **3.4 Proparoxytone Stress and Lenition Occasioned by +tik+<o#, +e+<o#, +ik+<o#, and +ul+<o#:**

$$\begin{bmatrix}\text{-contoid}\\ \alpha\text{-high}\\ \alpha\text{-low}\end{bmatrix} \rightarrow \begin{bmatrix}\text{+delayed transition}\\ \alpha\text{wide glottis}\end{bmatrix} / \_\_\ C_{1\text{-}3} + \begin{bmatrix}\text{+tik+}\\ \text{+e+}\\ \text{+ik+}\\ \text{+ul+}\end{bmatrix} <o\#$$

Rule **10.3 /k/ Insertion in Diminutives Formed with +ul+:**

$$\varnothing \rightarrow /k/\ /\ \left\{\begin{matrix}\text{-contoid}\\ \begin{bmatrix}\text{+contoid}\\ \text{-occlusion}\\ \text{-surd}\\ \text{-labial}\\ \text{-high}\end{bmatrix}\end{matrix}\right\} /\ \#X \begin{Bmatrix}+\\ \#\end{Bmatrix} \_\_\ \text{+ul+X\#}$$

Rule **10.4 +e$_{[+fem.]}$ # → /i/ / ___ /+ul+<a#:**

$$+\begin{bmatrix}\text{-contoid}\\ \text{+palatal}\\ \text{-high}\\ \text{+wide glottis}\end{bmatrix}_{[+\text{fem.}]} \# \rightarrow \begin{bmatrix}\text{+high}\\ \text{+palatal}\end{bmatrix} /\ \_\_\ \begin{bmatrix}\text{+contoid}\\ \text{+dorsal}\\ \text{+surd}\\ \text{+occlusion}\end{bmatrix} \text{+ul+}$$

Rule **10.2b /z/ Insertion for Diminutive and Augmentative Suffixes:**

$$\varnothing \rightarrow /z/\ /\ \begin{Bmatrix}[\text{+contoid}]\\ [\pm\text{feminine}]\end{Bmatrix} \#\ \_\_ + \begin{Bmatrix}\text{+on+}\\ \text{+it+}\\ \text{+iɲ+}\end{Bmatrix}$$

Rule **8.1b Suffix Merger in Word-Final Position:**

$$\left(\begin{array}{l} +\text{on}+\{<\text{e}+,\ <\text{o}\#\} \\ +\text{an}+\{<\text{e}+,<\text{o}\#\} \\ +(\alpha\ \text{s})\text{ion}+\ +\text{e}+ \end{array}\right) \rightarrow +(\alpha\ \text{s})\text{an}+\ +\text{o}\#_3/\ \_\_\ <[\text{-plural}]\#$$

**Rule 3.1 Paroxytone Stress:**

$$[\text{-contoid}] \rightarrow [+\text{stress}]\ /\ \#\text{X}\ \_\ \left(\left\{\begin{array}{l} +\text{high} \\ \text{-contoid} \end{array}\right\}\right) \text{C}_{0\text{-}4}\text{V}_{[\text{-high}]}\#(\text{C})\#$$

**Condition:** The word has no previously assigned stress.

## Sample Derivations

**Table 10B.1** Diminutives Formed with +iɲ+ and +it+[a]

| | bichinho | quilito | barquinha |
|---|---|---|---|
| U.F. | #biš++o#+iɲ+<[αf.]# | #kil++o#+it+<[αf.]# | #bark++a#+iɲ+<[αf.]# |
| Agree | #biš++o#+iɲ+<o# | #kil++o#+it+<o# | #bark++a#+iɲ+<a# |
| R. 10.5 | *** | *** | *** |
| R. 10.1b | #biš++iɲ+<o# | #kil++it+<o# | #bark++iɲ+<a# |
| R. 3.4 | *** | *** | *** |
| R. 10.3 | *** | *** | *** |
| R. 10.4 | *** | *** | *** |
| R. 10.2b | *** | *** | *** |
| R. 8.1 | *** | *** | *** |
| R. 3.1 | #biš++ˈiɲ+<o.# | #kil++ˈit+<o# | #bark++ˈiɲ+<a# |
| Ph. | [biˈšĩ.ɲŭ] | [ki.ˈli.tŭ] | [băr.kĩ.ɲă] |

a The examples in Table 10B.1 mean 'little animal' (often a term of endearment), 'sweet kilo', and 'small boat'.

The only diminutive-specific rule is 10.1b, that deletes the original stem's gender morpheme.

**Table 10B.2** Diminutives Formed with +ul+[a]

| | **cúmulo** | **flóculo** | **bárbula** |
|---|---|---|---|
| U.F. | #kum++e#+ul+<[αf.]# | #flɔk++o#+ul+<[αf.]# | #barb++a#+ul+<[αf.]# |
| Agree | #kum++e#+ul+<o# | #flɔk++o#+ul+<o# | #barb++a#+ul+<a# |
| R. 10.5 | *** | *** | *** |
| R. 10.1b | #kum++ul+<o# | #flɔk++ul+<o# | #barb++ul+<a# |
| R. 3.4 | #kˈum++ul+<o# | #flˈɔk++ul+<o# | #bˈarb++ul+<a# |
| R. 10.3 | *** | *** | *** |
| R. 10.4 | *** | *** | *** |
| R. 10.2b | *** | *** | *** |
| R. 8.1 | *** | *** | *** |
| R. 3.1 | *** | *** | *** |
| Ph. | [ˈkũ.mu.lŭ] | [ˈflɔ.kulŭ] | [ˈbar.bu.lă] |

a The words in Table 10B.2 mean 'culmination', 'little flake', and 'barbule'.

In addition to Rule 10.2, these words require Rule 3.4 to assign proparoxytone stress to the diminutives.

**Table 10B.3** Diminutives Formed with +ul+ (/k/ Insertion, Gender Morpheme Mutation)[a]

| | **animálculo** | **plebécula** |
|---|---|---|
| U.F. | #anim ++al#+e#+ul+<[αfem.]# | #plɛb+e$_{[+fem.]}$#+ul+<[αfem.]# |
| Agree | #anim ++al#+e#+ul+<o# | #plɛb+e$_{[+fem.]}$#+ul+<a# |
| R. 10.5 | *** | *** |
| R. 10.1b | #anim ++al#+ul+<o# | *** |
| R. 3.4 | #anim ++ˈal#+ul+<o# | #plɛb+ˈɛ$_{[+fem.]}$#+ul+<a# |
| R. 10.3 | #anim ++ˈal#k+ul+<o# | #plɛb+ˈɛ$_{[+fem.]}$#k+ul+<a# |
| R. 10.4 | *** | *** |
| R. 10.2b | *** | *** |
| R. 8.1 | *** | *** |
| R. 3.1 | *** | *** |
| Ph. | [ã̆.nĩ.ˈmaɫ.ku.lŭ] | [plə.ˈβɛ.ku.lă] |

a These words mean 'microscopic animal' and 'extreme low class'. *Animálculo* is obviously a modern coinage given the recent invention of the microscope.

Only *animálculo* undergoes Rule 10.1b and loses its stem-final gender morpheme. Both undergo Rule 7.1, which assigns proparoxytone stress and causes +e# to be realized as [ɛ] in *plebécula*. And, since both /l/ and [ɛ] precede a word boundary, both forms acquire a /k/ between their stems and suffixes.

**Table 10B.4** Diminutives Formed with +ul+ (/k/ Insertion, Gender Morpheme Mutation)[a]

| | **tentáculo** | **partícula** |
|---|---|---|
| U.F. | #tent++o#+ul+<[αfem.]# | #part++e$_{[+fem.]}$ #+ul+<[αfem.]# |
| Agree | #tent++o#+ul+<o# | #part++e$_{[+fem.]}$ #+ul+<a# |
| R. 10.5 | #tent++a#+ul+<o# | *** |
| R. 10.1b | *** | *** |
| R. 3.4 | #tent++ˈa#+ul+<o# | #part++ˈɛ#+ul+<a# |
| R. 10.3 | #tent++ˈa#k+ul+<o# | #part++ˈɛ#k+ul+<a# |
| R. 10.4 | *** | #part++ˈi#k+ul+<a# |
| R. 10.2b | *** | *** |
| R. 8.1 | *** | *** |
| R. 3.1 | *** | *** |
| Ph. | [tẽ$^{n}$.ˈta.ku.lŭ] | [par.ˈti.ku.lă] |

a These words mean 'tentacle' and 'particle'.

Rules 10.5 and 10.4 account for the gender vowels' shifts: +o# → +a# and +ɛ# → +i#. Agreement occurs before the rules apply, so +ul+'s gender morpheme has become <o#.

**Table 10B.5** Augmentative +on+ [αfeminine], <a#[a]

| | amigão | chorona |
|---|---|---|
| U.F. | #amik++o++on+<[αfem.]# | #šɔr++on+<a# |
| Agree | #amik++o++on+<e+ | *** |
| R. 10.5 | *** | *** |
| R. 10.1b | #amik++on+<e+ | *** |
| R. 3.4 | *** | *** |
| R. 10.3 | *** | *** |
| R. 10.4 | *** | *** |
| R. 10.2b | *** | *** |
| R. 8.1 | #amik++an+<o# | *** |
| R. 3.1 | #amik++ˈan+<o# | #šɔr++ˈon+<a# |
| Ph. | [ã̆.mi.ˈγã$^{\tilde{u}}$] | [šŭ.ˈrõ.nă] |

a These words mean 'great friend' and 'weepy female'.

Rule 8.1b merges suffixes +on+, +an+, and +(s)ion+ word-finally, non-plural circumstances. The other rules that apply to these forms nasalize the tonic vowels (Rule 7.2), reduce +o# to +ŭ# (Rule 2.3), delete the /n+ in [-feminine] circumstances (Rule 8.3), and assign nasality to word-final +ŭ# following [ã̆] (Rule 9.2). And in European Portuguese voiceless occlusives regularly lose their [+surd] quality intervocalically before +S suffixes (§5.4, Table 5.1), and their occlusion may evanesce once they are voiced (§2A.3.1.0, Rule 2.5).

**Table 10B.6** Augmentative +on+ [+plural], [αfeminine][a]

| | marzões | colherona |
|---|---|---|
| U.F. | #mar#+e++on+<[αfem.]#<z# | #kɔλer++e$_{[+fem.]}$+on+<[αfem.]# |
| Agree | #mar#+e++on+<e+<z# | #kɔλer++e$_{[+fem.]}$+on+<a# |
| R. 10.5 | *** | *** |
| R. 10.1b | #mar#+on+<e+<z# | # kɔλer++on+<a# |
| R. 3.4 | *** | *** |
| R. 10.3 | *** | *** |
| R. 10.4 | *** | *** |
| R. 10.2b | *** | *** |
| R. 8.1 | *** | *** |
| R. 3.1 | #mar++ˈon+<e+<z# | # kɔλer++ˈon+<a# |
| Ph. | [marˈzõ$^{\tilde{\imath}}$š] | [kŭ.λə.ˈrõ.nă] |

a These words mean 'rough seas' and 'big spoon'.

The other rules operating on these forms are the same as those operating on the words of Table 10B.2, save Rule 8.1, which only affects singular nominals.

**Table 10B.7** Augmentative[a]

| | festão | folgazona |
|---|---|---|
| U.F. | # fɛzt++on+<e+ | #fɔlg+a#+on++<a# |
| Agree | *** | *** |
| R. 10.5 | *** | *** |
| R. 10.1b | *** | *** |
| R. 3.4 | *** | *** |
| R. 10.3 | *** | *** |
| R. 10.4 | *** | *** |
| R. 10.2b | *** | #fɔlg+a#z+on++<a# |
| R. 8.1 | #fɛzt++an+<o# | *** |
| R. 3.1 | #fɛzt++'an+<o# | #fɔlg+a#z+'on++<a# |
| Ph. | [fəš.'tã̆ũ̆] | [fɔɫ.gă.'zõ.nă] |

a These words mean ‘great party’ and ‘lazy woman’.

In the case of *festão* [-feminine] (cf.*festa* [+feminine], #fɛzt++a#), the augmentative suffix attaches directly to the word’s root. Thus, +on+’s gender morpheme <e+ has no gender morpheme to agree with and, thus, emerges in the resultant augmentative as [-feminine].

## Appendix C The Intricacies of the Diminutive Suffix +ul+

**§10C.1** The *Aurélio* contains 205 nominals plausibly ending in the diminutive suffix +ul+<o# and often preceded by /k/ (79 in –ula, 136 in –ulo), and §10.2.2.20.3.1 has advanced four subclasses of diminutives formed by the addition of +ul+. In addition to the insertion of /k/ between these diminutive nouns’ stems and their suffix, when Class 1 diminutives’ +o# appears before +ul+, the gender morpheme +o# mutates to [a] as Table 10C.1 demonstrates.

**Table 10C.1** +o# ➔ [ˈa] / ___+ul+<o#

| +o# | Gloss | +o# ➔ [ˈa] | Gloss |
|---|---|---|---|
| **espeto** | spit | **espetáculo** | spectacle |
| **pino** | zenith | **pináculo** | pinnacle |
| **tento** | attention | **tentáculo** | tentacle |
| **concepto**[a] | growing organism | **conceptáculo** | reproductive organ container |

a Infopédia lists this word as 'antiquated'. And the morpheme-final /p+ in *conceptáculo* represents an optional pronunciation.

**§10C.2** Table 10C.2 contains a representative sampling of Class 2 [+feminine] diminutive nouns formed with +ul+ that entail a shift of gender morphemes +e# and +a# to /ˈi/:

**Table 10C.2** The Emergence of /k/ Before +ul+([+feminine])[a]

| | Diminutives | | Related Words | |
|---|---|---|---|---|
| | Noun | Analysis | Noun | Analysis |
| 1 | **clavícula** | #klav++e$_{[+fem]}$#+ul+<a# | **clave** | #clav++ e$_{[+fem]}$# |
| 2 | **febrícula** | #fɛbr++ e$_{[+fem]}$#+ul+<a# | **febre** | #fɛbr+ e$_{[+fem]}$# |
| 3 | **gotícula** | #got++ a#+ul+<a# | **gota** | #got++ a# |
| 4 | **lentícula** | #lent++ e$_{[+fem]}$#+ul+<a# | **lente** | #lent++ e$_{[+fem]}$# |
| 5 | **manícula** | #man++o$_{[+fem]}$#+ul+<a# | **mão** | #man++o$_{[+fem]}$# |
| 6 | **película** | #pɛl++ e$_{[+fem]}$#+ul+<a# | **pele** | #pɛl++ e$_{[+fem]}$# |
| 7 | **quadrícula** | #kuadr++ a#+ul+<a# | **quadra** | #kuadr++a# |

a The diminutives and related words mean, respectively: 'clavicle⇔clef, slight fever⇔fever, tiny drop⇔drop, small lens⇔lens, protective glove⇔hand, membrane⇔hide, small block⇔block'.

Table 10C.2 demonstrates the relationship between (A) stems' gender and the resultant gender of their diminutive forms, (B) the mutation of [+feminine] gender morphemes to /i/, and (C) the emergence of /k/ between vowel-final stems and +ul+. Table 10C.2 also shows that in addition to attaching to gendered and non-gendered stems, +ul+ can attach to compounding elements such as #mani+ and #kuadri+, which also emerge in compound words such as *manipresto* 'dexterous' and *quadriciclo* 'four wheeled vehicle'. The /i/ in *gotículo* is a transitional vowel that appears after the root #got+ in the word *gotímetro* #got+ #mɛtr++o# 'eye dropper'.

**§10C.3.0** Contrary to the (marked) examples in Tables 10C.1 and 2, the emergence of +ul+<[αfeminine]# without the /k/ entails the loss of the gender morpheme or a lack thereof in Class 3 +ul+ diminutives, as Tables 10C.3a–b demonstrate:

**Table 10C.3a** Diminutives in +ul+ Formed From Stems with Unmarked Gender[a]

| | Final C | Gender | Diminutive | Stem | Analysis |
|---|---|---|---|---|---|
| 1 | /b+ | +o# | túbulo | tubo | #tub++o# |
| 2 | /d+ | +o# | acídulo[b] | ácido | #asid++o# |
| 3 | /f+ | Ø | estrófulo | estrof-[c] | #eztrɔf+ |
| 4 | /g+ | Ø | cíngulo | cing-[d] | #sing+ |
| 5 | /k+ | +o# | flóculo | floco | #flɔk++o# |
| 6 | /m+ | +e# | cúmulo | cume | #kum++e# |
| 7 | /n+ | +o# | gránulo | grão | #gran++o# |
| 8 | /p+ | Ø | escrúpulo | escrup- | #ezkrup+ |
| 9 | /r̲+ | Ø | gárrulo | garr-[e] | #gar̲+ |
| 10 | /t+ | Ø | capítulo | capit-[f] | #kap++t+ |
| 11 | /v+ | +o# | acérvulo | acervo | #ascrv++o# |
| 12 | /š+ | Ø | esdrúxulo | esdrux- | #ezdruš+ |

a The diminutives and related words mean, respectively: 'small tube⇔tube, slightly acidic⇔acid, a type of rash⇔place, sash⇔gird, little flake⇔flake, heap⇔peak, granule⇔grain, scruple⇔hesitation, garrulous⇔throat, chapter⇔head, small heap⇔heap, weird⇔weird'.
b Items 2, 9, and 12 are adjectives.
c The diminutives in rows 3, 4, and 12 appear to be formed from what are, in effect, polysyllabic roots rather than from stems consisting of a root or stem plus a gender morpheme. The stem #eztrɔf+ appears in words like *estrofe* 'line of verse' and *estrófico* 'versified'. Perhaps the root of this word is #trof+ as in *troféu* 'trophy' and *trófico* 'related to nutrition'. For *escrúpulo* and *esdrúxulo*, the stems may include the suffix +ul+ since related (derived) words always contain this sequence: e.g. *escrupulizar* 'to evoke scruples' and *escrupuloso* 'scrupulous', *esdruxulizar* 'to make weird' and *exdruxularia* 'weird thing'. There is no evidence to suggest that +krup+ and +druš+ are roots.
d The root for *cíngulo* also appears in *cingir* 'to surround, to gird'.
e This root appears in words related to *garrotar* 'to garrote'.
f Words related to *capítulo* include *capitão* 'captain' and *capital* 'capital'.

The phonemes that end the stems of all the words in Table 10C.3a and 10C.3b (below) are precisely those that never emerge as syllable final.

**§10C.3.1** The [+feminine] diminutives in Table 10C.3b are all nouns, and in general follow the same pattern: the diminutive forms bear the same gender as the stem—when the stem has a gender.

Table 10C.3b Diminutives in +ul+ Bearing [+feminine] Gender[a]

| Final C | Gender | Diminutive | Stem | Analysis |
|---|---|---|---|---|
| /b+ | +a# | bárbula | barba | #barb++a# |
| /d+ | +$e_{[+fem.]}$# | glândula | glande | #gland++$e_{[+fem.]}$# |
| /f+ | Ø | escrófula | escrof-[b] | #ezkrof+ |
| /g+ | +a# | calígula | cáliga | #k'alig++a# |
| /k+ | *** | *** | *** | *** |
| /m+ | +a# | anímula | ánima | #'anim++a# |
| /n+ | +a# | fáunula | fauna | #faun++a# |
| /p+ | +a# | pápula | papa | #pap++a# |
| /ɾ̠+ | *** | *** | *** | *** |
| /t+ | +a# | nótula | nota | #nɔt++a# |
| /v+ | +a# | úvula | uva | #uv++a# |
| /š+ | *** | *** | *** | *** |

a The diminutives and related words mean, respectively: 'barbule⇔beard, glandule⇔gland, scrofula⇔??, little sandal⇔sandal, little soul⇔soul; small fauna⇔fauna, small pimple⇔concentrate, small note⇔note, uvula⇔grape.'
b Like the stems of *escrúpulo* and *esdrúxulo*, the stem of *escrófula* is at least bimorphemic: #ezkrof++ul+ since when it occurs with other suffixes its instantiations always include /ul/, e.g. *escrofulária* 'figwort', *escrofuloso* 'scrofulous'. The gender morpheme on the noun *escrófula* is the arbitrarily assigned deriving morpheme +a#.

**§10C.3.2** As one would expect, owing to the marked nature of [+feminine] gendered nouns, the [+feminine] +ul+ diminutives are both fewer in number (209) than their [-feminine] counterparts (263) and more restricted in their distribution—none occurs after /k+, /ɾ̠+, and /š+. Other than with the word *escrófula*, Rule 10.1b obtains with the diminutive suffix +ul+<[αfeminine]# when circumstances do not require the insertion of /k/ between the stem and the suffix.

§10.4.0 Class 4 diminutives are those whose +$e_{[+fem.]}$# remains but is realized as ['ɛ]:

Table 10C.4 Gender Morpheme Maintenance (With Lenition)

| Diminutive | Gloss | Stem Word | Gloss |
|---|---|---|---|
| **molécula** | molecule | **mole** | 'huge mass' |
| **nubécula** | mist | **nuvem** | cloud |
| **plebécula** | lower class | **plebe** | commoner |
| **trabécula** | small brake | **trave** | brake |

Whereas all the stem words in Table 10C.4 are [+feminine], the diminutive *valécula* 'depression' has a [-feminine] stem word *vale* 'valley' ([-feminine]), but emerges as [+feminine], conceivably out of analogy with the [+feminine] words of this class.

**§10C.4.0** The vocalic patterns entailed in the use of the 'erudite' +$S_1$+ diminutive suffix +ul+ are both similar to those of the other diminutive suffixes, and they are unique among diminutive suffixes but similar to the adjective-deriving suffixes +tik+<o#, +e+<o#, and +ik+<o#. However, the insertion of /k/ between these diminutives' stems and the suffix +ul+ is peculiar to this suffix.

**§10C.4.1** In the four classes of diminutives in +ul+ examined above, only Class 3 does not add an interstitial /k/ between its stems and this suffix. Class 3 is, so far, the only class that fails to preserve a vestige of the stem words' gender phonemes. There is one more set of diminutives where gender morphemes leave no trace other than the gender reflected at the end of +ul+. But in this case, the /k/ appears between stem and suffix.

**Table 10C.5** The Emergence of /k/ before +ul+([-feminine])

| | Diminutives | | Stem Words | |
|---|---|---|---|---|
| | Noun | Analysis | Noun | Analysis |
| 1 | **arbúsculo** | #arbuz++ul++o# | **arbusto** | #arbuz++t++o# |
| 2 | **arbúscula**[b] | #arb++uz++ul+<a# | **árvore** | #arb++or#+ $e_{[+fem]}$ # |
| 3 | **carbúnculo** | #karb++on++ul+<o# | **carvão** | #karb++on++e+ |
| 4 | **furúnculo** | #furun++ul++o# | **furungar** | #furun+g+a#+r#+e+ |
| 5 | **porciúncula**[c] | #pɔrt++sion++e++ul+<a# | **porção** | #pɔrt++sion++e+ |
| 6 | **animálculo** | #anim++al#+e++ul+<o# | **animal** | #anim++al#+e+ |
| 7 | **férculo** | #fer++ul++o# | **feral** | #fer++al#+e+ |

a The diminutives and related words mean, respectively: 'small bush⇔bush, small tree⇔tree, carbuncle⇔coal, boil⇔meddle, tiny portion⇔portion, tiny animal⇔animal, pagan litter⇔funereal'.

b The terms *arbúsculo* and *arbúscula* are obviously related to one another. Whereas both have the root #arb+, the former is related to *arbusto* #arb++uzt++o# 'bush' and the latter to *árvore* 'tree'. They are both formed from the stem *arbus* #'arb++uz# 'oak genus', but they carry the gender of their semantic relative.

c Another mutation that +ul+'s addition to stems seems to trigger is /o/ ➔ /u/ in stem-final suffixes +sion+ and +on (examples 3 and 5).

The characteristic diminutives and stem words in Table 10C.5 share with the items in Tables 10C.1, 2, and 4 is their stem-final segments' ability to occur syllable finally. The stem-final segments in Tables 10C.3a-b cannot occur syllable finally. Thus, Rule 10.3 accounts for /k/ insertion:

**Rule 10.3 /k/ Insertion in Diminutives Formed with +ul+:**

$$\emptyset \rightarrow /k/ \,/\, \left\{ \begin{array}{l} -\text{contoid} \\ \left( \begin{array}{l} +\text{contoid}\\ -\text{occlusion}\\ -\text{surd}\\ -\text{labial}\\ -\text{high}\end{array}\right)\end{array}\right\} / \#X \left\{\begin{array}{c}+\\ \#\end{array}\right\} \_\_ \; +ul+X\#$$

Rule 10.3 inserts a /k/ before diminutive suffix +ul+ when the suffix follows a stem-final vowel, and when it follows stems ending in /z, n, r, l/.

§**10.5.0** The final allomorphic issue in that part of the grammar that is responsible for the generation of diminutives formed by the suffix +ul+ is the shift of [+feminine] gender morphemes +e$_{[+fem.]}$#, +a# and +o# to /i/ (Table 10C.2) in a minority of words and the shift from +o# to /a/ in another minority (Table 10C.1). Rule 10.4 accomplishes that.

**Rule 10.4 +e$_{[+fem.]}$, +a#, +o$_{[+fem.]}$# →/ˈi/ / ___ /+ul+<a#:**

$$+[+\text{feminine}] \left\{\begin{array}{c}\#\\ +\end{array}\right\} \rightarrow \left(\begin{array}{l}+\text{high}\\ +\text{palatal}\\ +\text{stress}\end{array}\right) / \_\_ \left(\begin{array}{l}+\text{contoid}\\ +\text{dorsal}\\ +\text{surd}\\ +\text{occlusion}\end{array}\right) +ul+<a\#$$

§**10.5.1** Rule 10.5 accounts for the shift from stem-final +o# to /ˈa/ in Class 1+ul+ diminutives (Table 10C.1).

**Rule 10.5 +o# → /a/ / ___ /+ul+<o#:**

$$+\begin{pmatrix}\text{-contoid}\\ \text{+dorsal}\\ \text{-high}\\ \text{+labial}\\ \text{+wide glottis}\end{pmatrix}\#\rightarrow\begin{pmatrix}\text{+dorsal}\\ \text{-labial}\\ \text{+stress}\end{pmatrix}\;/\,\_\_\_\;\begin{pmatrix}\text{+contoid}\\ \text{+dorsal}\\ \text{+surd}\\ \text{+occlusion}\end{pmatrix}\text{+ul+}$$

# 11 Derivation with Prefixes

## Introduction

**§11.0.0** Whereas deriving suffixes can both determine the placement of stress on the resulting words and can create adjectives, nouns, and verbs from the same stems, the addition of a prefix to a word, stem, or root does not, in itself, determine the resultant words' form classes or their stress assignment. That is, when ***only*** prefixes are added to nouns, adjectives, and infinitives, the resultant forms remain nouns, adjectives, and infinitives.[1] Some of the prefixes exhibit allomorphy, but as far as stems are concerned, prefixation alone does not occasion segmental mutations.[2]

**§11.0.1** Still, prefixation is derivational to the same extent as the addition of diminutive and augmentative suffixes. This is due to the basic spontaneity with which speakers may employ common diminutives and augmentives to indicate whatever affect they may feel about an individual, animal, or object. Likewise, speakers (writers) may prefix words to suit the semantic conditions in which they find themselves at a specific time. One can say: *Preciso* ***repensar*** *este assunto* 'I need to ***rethink*** this matter' or *Deves* ***desatar*** *este nó* 'You need to ***untie*** this knot'. These particular verbs are prefixed by #re+, #dez+, and (English) #ʊn+. *Repensar* and 'rethink' need not appear in a dictionary because a competent listener or reader can readily understand their meanings.[3] Like the words with diminutive and augmentative suffixes, words with these prefixes need only appear in the dictionary when their meaning

---

1 The adverb 'only' appears in italic boldface because prefixes often work in conjunction with suffixes to turn nominals into verbs, e.g. *covarde* 'coward' → *acovardar* 'to act in a cowardly fashion' #a+#kovard++a#+r#+e+. In this example, the prefix #a+ works in conjunction with the theme vowel +a# to form the verb. (§16.9.3.0–1.)

2 Specific stems of words that come from the Greek occasion proparoxytone stress, which may fall on their prefixes and/or on their compounding elements. (§12.2.5.1.0–1.)

3 The *Aurélio* contains entries for both *repensar* and *desatar*. The latter has copious metaphoric interpretations, whereas the former need not appear. One can say the same about the *American Heritage Dictionary*'s entries for 'rethink' and 'untie'.

transcends the sum of their constituent parts: e.g. ***reportar*** 'to report' (cf. *porto* 'port'), ***descansar*** 'to rest' (cf. *cansar* 'to tire'), ***unsell*** 'to persuade not to believe in the advisability, worth, or truth of something'.[4]

**§11.0.2** Although the examples above (*reportar*, *descansar*, and *unsell*), show that prefixation can create idioms (i.e. independent lexical items whose meanings may be greater than the sums of their parts' meanings), meaning is not the primary focus of this chapter. Still, whereas the relationship of morphological form to meaning is tenuous, it is nonetheless a factor in determining the derivational nature of both suffixes and prefixes. Thus disquisitions on prefixation and meaning appear in Appendix 11A.

## Prefixes and Productivity

**§11.1.0.** Table 11.1a and b contain an extensive but not totally exhaustive inventory of the prefixes found in Portuguese words:[5]

4 However, both the *Aurélio* and *The American Heritage Dictionary of the English Language,* are replete with prefixed words that are immediately intelligible.

5 Most of these 'prefixes' appear in Cunha (62–4). Scare quotes appear around the word prefixes in the preceding sentence because many of the items Cunha includes are 'elements', i.e. morphemes that can actually function in the formation of compounds and which can be roots of independent words, or words themselves. Cunha separates the Latinate prefixes from those of Greek origin, whereas here they appear in a single table. Some are united when they emerge as homophones in Portuguese. Some extremely low-frequency prefixes are not addressed or analyzed, and morphophonological analyses of Portuguese words of Arabic origin only appear when they are inflected for gender and number with Portuguese morphemes or when they acquire Latinate deriving affixes.

**Table 11.1a** Prefixes of Negligible to Very Low Productivity[a]

| Prefix | Tokens | % | Productivity | Prefix | Tokens | % | Productivity |
|---|---|---|---|---|---|---|---|
| justa- | 6 | 0.02 | Negligible | meta- (α) | 82 | 0.26 | Negligible |
| soto- | 15 | 0.05 | Negligible | ec (α) | 92 | 0.29 | Negligible |
| intro- | 21 | 0.07 | Negligible | ab- | 102 | 0.32 | Negligible |
| intra- | 21 | 0.07 | Negligible | ante- | 110 | 0.35 | Negligible |
| supra- | 23 | 0.07 | Negligible | pos- | 122 | 0.39 | Negligible |
| anto- | 27 | 0.08 | Negligible | apo- (α) | 133 | 0.42 | Negligible |
| ultra- | 33 | 0.10 | Negligible | eu- (α) | 136 | 0.43 | Negligible |
| vice- | 38 | 0.12 | Negligible | epi- (α) | 141 | 0.45 | Negligible |
| arc-(α) | 43 | 0.13 | Negligible | hiper- (α) | 143 | 0.45 | Negligible |
| retro- | 44 | 0.14 | Negligible | hipo- (α) | 144 | 0.45 | Negligible |
| anfi-(α) | 52 | 0.16 | Negligible | ad- | 147 | 0.46 | Negligible |
| extra- | 55 | 0.17 | Negligible | para- | 165 | 0.52 | Very Low |
| endo-(α) | 58 | 0.18 | Negligible | dia- | 196 | 0.62 | Very Low |
| cata-(α) | 68 | 0.21 | Negligible | ob_ | 203 | 0.64 | Very Low |
| cis- | 69 | 0.21 | Negligible | peri | 259 | 0.82 | Very Low |
| orto- | 69 | 0.21 | Negligible | ana- | 265 | 0.84 | Very Low |
| pró-(α) | 78 | 0.25 | Negligible | sin- | 269 | 0.85 | Very Low |
| **Total Tokens = 3,429, Percentage of Total Prefix Tokens = 10.84** | | | | | | | |

a Total Tokens in Tables 11.1a–b: 31,639. M=632.80, SD=1,335.51, Z=3.13. The prefix a- (#a+) is an outlier with a Z value of 5.48. There is no outlier within the prefixes of Table 11.1a: M=100.85, SD=73.89. Z=295.

**Table 11b** Prefixes of Low to Supreme Productivity

| Prefix | Tokens | % | Productivity |
|---|---|---|---|
| inter- | 374 | 1.18 | Low |
| trans- | 384 | 1.21 | Low |
| per- | 393 | 1.24 | Low |
| dis- | 427 | 1.35 | Low |
| sub- | 429 | 1.36 | Low |
| anti- | 506 | 1.60 | Low |
| pre- | 591 | 1.87 | Low |
| pro- | 979 | 3.10 | Moderate |
| de- | 1,040 | 3.29 | Moderate |
| ex-* | 1,591 | 5.03 | Moderate |
| con- | 1,870 | 5.91 | Moderate |

(*Continued*)

Table 11b Continued

| Prefix | Tokens | % | Productivity |
|---|---|---|---|
| en- | 2,610 | 8.24 | High |
| re- | 2,924 | 9.35 | High |
| in- | 2,959 | 9.35 | High |
| des- | 3,189 | 10.07 | Very High |
| a-* | 7,944 | 25.11 | Supreme (Outlier) |
| **Total** | **28,210** | **89.16** | **Low-Supreme** |

**§11.1.1** Tables 11.1a–b list the prefixes in standard orthographic form. Those preafixes followed by an alpha (α) are of Greek origin, and those followed by an asterisk are amalgams of Greek and Latinate prefixes. Those with no diacritic mark are Latinate prefixes. The 34 preafixes of negligible (0.02% to 0.46%) and very low (0.50% to 0.99%) productivity appear in Table 11.1a, those of low to supreme productivity in Table 11.1b.[6] Those of negligible to very low productivity account for only 10.84% of the tokens, whereas the low to supreme productivity prefixes account for 89.16% of all the tokens.

**§11.1.2.0** Table 11.1c contains Table 11.1a's prefixes along with the various phonemic shapes they take as prefixes:

6 The token count in the low to supreme data range from 374 to 7,945. Beginning with #inter+, I no longer counted the instantiations of each prefix. For total entries less than 600 and more than 300 (#inter+ 374), I examined 222 randomly selected (six sets of 37) entries and counted the bona fide prefixed words. I used these counts' percentages of 222 to estimate the prefixed tokens in each specific dataset. For those whose count exceded 600, I examined 370 (10 sets of 37) entries and tallied the bona fide prefixes and used that percentage of 370 to calculate the percentage of prefixes in the entire set.

Table 11.1c Prefix Allomorphy: Negligible and Very Low Productivity

| | Orthography | Analaysis | Allomorphs | | | | Orthography | Analaysis | Allomorphs | |
|---|---|---|---|---|---|---|---|---|---|---|
| 1 | **justa-** | #žuzta+ | [žuzta/ | | | 18 | **meta- (α)** | #meta+ | [meta/ | [meˈta/ |
| 2 | **soto-, sota-** | #soto+ | [soto/ | [sota/ | | 19 | **ec (α)** | #εk+ | [εk/ | [ˈεk/ |
| 3 | **intro-** | #intro+ | [intro/ | | | 20 | **ab** | #ab+ | [ab/ | |
| 4 | **intra-** | #intra+ | [intra/ | | | 21 | **ante-** | #ante+ | [ante/ | |
| 5 | **supra-** | #supra+ | [supra/ | | | 22 | **pos-** | #poz+ | [poz/ | |
| 6 | **anto-** | #anto+ | [anto/ | | | 23 | **apo- (α)** | #apɔ+ | [apɔ/ | [aˈpɔ/ |
| 7 | **ultra-** | #ultra+ | [ultra/ | | | 24 | **eu- (α)** | #eu+ | [eu/ | |
| 8 | **vice-, vis,** | #vise+ | [vise/ | [viz/ | [vizo/ | 25 | **epi- (α)** | #εpi+ | [εpi/ | |
| 9 | **arc-(α), arqui-, arci-, arce-** | #arki+ | [arki/ | [ark/ | [arˈkε/ | 26 | **hiper- (α)** | #iper+ | [ˈiper/ | [iˈper/ |
| | | #arse+ | [arsi/ | | | 27 | **hipo- (α)** | #ipɔ+ | [ip/ | [iˈpɔ/ |
| 10 | **retro-** | #retro+ | [retro/ | | | 28 | **ad-** | #ad+ | | |
| 11 | **anfi-(α)** | #anfi+ | [amfi/ | | | 29 | **para-** | #para+ | | |
| 12 | **extra-** | #eztra+ | [eztra/ | | | 30 | **dia-** | #dia+ | | |
| 13 | **endo-(α)** | #endo+ | [endo/ | [enˈdo/ | | 31 | **ɔb-** | #ɔb+ | | |
| 14 | **cata-(α)** | #kata+ | [kata/ | [kaˈta/ | | 32 | **peri-** | #peri+ | | |
| 15 | **cis-** | #siz+ | [siz/ | [si/ | | 33 | **ana-** | #ana+ | | |
| 16 | **orto-** | #ortɔ+ | [orto/ | [orˈtɔ/ | | 34 | **sin-** | #sin+ | | |
| 17 | **pró-(α)** | #ˈprɔ+ | [ˈprɔ/ | | | | | | | |

Table 11.1c also identifies the prefixes as Latinate or Hellenic in origin. It also presents alternate spellings of some prefixes and morphophonemic analyses of the prefixes and half phonetic/half phonemic transcriptions of the allomorphs of specific prefixes. One by one, these prefixes are:

**§11.1.2.1 'Prefix'[7] #žuzta+:** Despite Cunha's having included this form as a prefix (63), and the *Aurélio*'s similar identification of it as such, there is sufficient evidence to suggest that one should consider it an independent word. Alone *justa* can mean 'joust' as well as 'individual serving of wine' or 'police'. It forms the root of *justar* 'to joust' as well as that of *justador* 'one who jousts'. The words formed by the addition of another stem: *justafluvial* 'next to a river', *justalinear* 'line-by-line', *justamarítimo* 'next to the sea' and *justapor* 'juxtapose' are compounds. The root of *justa* #žuzt+ appears in the adjective *justo* 'just, legitimate' as well as in verb compounds such as *justificar* 'to justify'.

**§11.1.2.2 'Prefix' #soto+:** Cunha considers this form to have two allomorphs: #sot++a# and #sot++o#. The former is an independent word, coming from Catalan through Spanish and means both 'queen' (in a deck of cards) as well as 'time off' and 'calm, open sea'. *Sota* can be non-feminine when it means 'rider', 'footman', or 'underling'. It combines with *vento* 'wind' as *sotavento* 'downwind' and with *piloto* 'pilot' to form *sota-piloto* 'sub-pilot'. As *soto* it combines with *capitão* 'captain' as *soto-capitão* 'first mate'. The infinitive *sotopor* 'to put underneath' should be considered a compound. Both *sota* and *soto* seem to indicate 'a step below' some fixed point.

**§11.1.2.3 #intro+:** This prefix attaches infinitives such as *introduzir* 'to introduce' (cf. *conduzir* 'to conduct'), *intrometer* 'to stick in' (cf. *meter* 'to insert'), and *introverter* 'to turn inward'), (cf. *verter* 'to pour'). Of course nominal derivatives of these words exist: e.g. *introdução* 'introduction' and *condução* 'conduction'.

**§11.1.2.4 #intra+:** This is an erudite prefix used for biological terms such as *intracraneano* 'intra-cranial' (cf. *crâneo* 'cranium'), *intramarginal* 'between the extremities [of the nerves of leaves and

7 The quotation marks around the word prefix identify the items Cunha and others have considered prefixes. There is evidence that that the morphemes in question can function at least as prepositions and often as independent words, which makes words formed with these morphemes more akin to compounds than to derived words.

flowers]', (cf. *marginal* 'marginal'). It is also used in *intramuros* 'intramural' (cf. *muro* 'wall'), and *intratextual* 'within a text' (cf. *texto* 'text').

**§11.1.2.5 'Prefix' #supra+:** Again, this item is used in erudite formations such as *supracitado* 'above mentioned' (cf. *citar* 'to quote'), *supramundano* 'other worldly (cf. *mundano* 'worldly'). Even though both Cunha and the *Aurélio* consider *supra-* a prefix, it forms the root of the word *supremo* 'supreme'. This form's ability to become a root, e.g. in the word *suprir* 'to supply, add' indicates that the words to which #supra+ attaches are compounds rather than derived forms.

**§11.1.2.6 'Prefix' #antɔ+:** This is the first of many elements of Greek origin to be examined in this dataset. It originally indicated a flower. As with many Hellenic compounding elements, it can have two allomorphs: one bearing stress, *antófago* 'flower eater', *antólogo* 'collection of Greek orthodox hymns' and one without stress *antologia* 'anthology', *antogênese* 'flower formation'. When this form occurs with #fag+<o# and #lɔgo#, both of which are of Greek origin, the /ɔ/ of #antɔ+ bears stress because these stems require a word-internal preceding vowel to be stressed. The words formed with this element are much more akin to compound words than they are to derived words. Indeed, the forms #fag+<o# and #lɔg++o# can occur word-initially: *logomania* 'excessive wordiness' and *fagoterapia* 'eating therapy', which indicates that they are, in essence, compounding morphemes in Portuguese.

**§11.1.2.7 'Prefix' #ultra#:** This putative prefix has acquired the status of independent lexical item or 'word' because it appears as a noun, *ultra,* meaning an 'expounder of radical or advanced ideas', which has the derived form *ultraísmo* 'vanguard [Spanish language] poetry'. It also occurs as the root of *ultraje* 'outrage' and *ultriz* 'female avenger'. Thus, compound adjectives such as *ultracurto* 'excessively short' and *ultramarino* 'overseas' need not occur in the lexicon because their meanings are equal to the sums of their consitituent parts: #ultr++a##kurt+<o# and #ultr++a##mar#+in+<o#.

**§11.1.2.8 #vise+:** Cunha (63) advanced three allomorphs for this prefix: #vise+, #viz+ and #vizo+. The prefix in the form of #vise+ is common to both English and Portuguese: *vice-presidente* 'vice president' and *vice-cônsul* 'vice consul'. The allomorph #viz+ occurs in the word *visconde* 'viscount' and derivatives as well as in the word *vislumbrar* 'to lighten weakly, to glimpse'

**§11.1.2.9 'Prefix' #arki+:** This morpheme of Greek origin has six allomorphs: the most frequent is #arki+ *arquiabade* 'arch-abbot' (cf. *abade* 'abbot'). The others are #arkˈɛ+ *arquétipo* 'arch-type' (cf. *tipo* 'type'), #arke+ *arqueólogo* 'archeologist',[8] #arse+ *arcebispo* 'arch-bishop' (cf. *bispo* 'bishop'), #arsi+ *arcipreste* 'chief priest' (cf. the archaic word *preste* 'priest'), and #ark+ *arcanjo* 'archangel' (cf. *anjo* 'angel'). This morpheme also occurs as a root in the words *arquivo* 'archive' #arki++iv++o# (cf. *cursivo* 'cursive' #kurs++iv++o# and *anarquia* 'anarchy' and *oligarquia* 'oligarchy'). Because it can be the root of various lexical items, it is a compounding morpheme rather than a prefix.

**§11.1.2.10 #rɛtrɔ+:** This prefix has two allomorphs: #rɛtrɔ+ as in *retrocesso* 'a receding' (cf. *ceder* 'to cede' and *retroflexo* 'retroflex'). It occurs as #r̲ɛtrˈɔ+ as in *retrógrado* 'retrograde'.[9]

**§11.1.2.11 'Prefix' #anfi+:** This Greek origin element is instrumental in forming erudite words such as *anfibolia* 'double meaning', (cf. *hipérbole* 'hyperbole'), *anfigonia* 'issue of two individual organisms', (cf. *gonocorismo* 'sexual dimorphism'), and in the more familiar *anfiteatro* 'amphitheater' (cf. *teatro* 'theater'). It has two allomorphs /aɱfi] and /aɱfˈi], as the words *anfíbio* 'amphibian' (cf. *biologia* 'the study of life') and *anfígamo* 'having two gametes' (cf. *gameta* 'gamete'). The *Morais* dictionary includes the word *anfíbalo* 'cape, bathrobe'.

**§11.1.2.12 'Prefix' #eztra+:** This is another form that appears at the beginning of words, but should be considered either an independent word or, at the very least, a compounding element rather than a bound

8 The second element (*tipo* and *logo*) in these words occasions antepenultimate stress.

9 The word *grado* 'will, degree', when it acquires a prefix or when it is the second element in compounds, can occasion stress on a preceding form's final vowel: *tardígrado* 'tardigrade, given to lateness' (cf. *tardio* 'late'), *saltígrado* 'given to hopping' (cf. *salto* 'leap'), *centígrado* 'centigrade' (cf. *cento* '100'), *plantígrado* 'plantigrade, i.e. one who walks on soles' (cf. *planta* 'sole of foot'). In this case, a Latinate stem #grad+ occasions, like many other stems (Table 12.12a), proparoxytone stress. When the preceding affix has only one vowel, i.e. *mal* 'poorly', the resultant form *malgrado* 'against one's will' does not receive proparoxytone stress. The reason the vowel preceding /grado/ in *emigrado* 'émigré' and *imigrado* 'imigré' is that this /grado/ is not #grad++o# but #Xgra++t+<o#. The root of the latter words is #migr+ as in *migrar* 'to migrate' whose lexical forms are #ek+ #migr++a#+t+<o# and #in+#migr++a#+t+<o#. Because of their structure, these words' stress is assigned by the paroxytone stress rule (Rule 3.1).

prefix. It is used as an abbreviation of *extraordinário* 'extraordinary', but it (*extra*) is independent when used to indicate 'part-time help' or 'theatrical walk-ons'. Words like *extranumerário* 'unregistered worker' (cf. *numerário* 'on the list'), or *extravagante* 'extravagant' (cf. *vagar* 'to wander'), and *extraviar* 'to lose one's way' (cf. *via* 'path') should be considered compounds rather than derived forms.

**§11.1.2.13 #endɔ+:** This Greek origin prefix has two allomorphs: /endɔ] and /endˈɔ] and occurs in bio-medical terms such as *endógamo* 'endogamous' (cf. *gameta* 'gamete') and *endocéfalo* 'without apparent head' (cf. *cefálico* 'relative to the head').[10]

**§11.1.2.14 #kata+:** This Greek origin prefix has two allomorphs: #kata+ as in words such as *cataplasma* 'poultice' (cf. *plasma* 'plasma'), and as #katˈa+ in words like *catástrofe* 'catastrophe' (cf. *troféu* 'trophy').

**§11.1.2.15 #siz+:** This prefix occurs in words like *cisatlántico* 'across the Atlantic' (cf. *Atlántico* 'Atlantic ocean') and *cisaplino* 'across the Alps' (cf. *alpino* 'alpine'). It does not seem to have any allomorphs of phonemic configuration, other than the assimilation and palatalization of its final /z+ when it occurs syllable-finally, e.g. *cisbordo* 'lateral door on a ship'.

**§11.1.2.16 'Prefix' #orto+:** This Greek origin form occurs as #orto+ in words such as *ortobiose* 'normal life' (cf. *biólogo* 'biologist' and *ortofonia* 'speech therapy', *fonologia* 'phonology'), and it occurs as #ortˈɔ+ in words like *ortógrafo* 'expert speller' (cf. *telégrafo* 'telegraph[er]' and *ortónimo* 'correct name', *anônimo* 'anonymous'). Chapter 12 also addresses #orto+ as a compounding element (cf. Tables 12B.9).

**§11.1.2.17 #prɔ+:** This negligibly productive prefix of Greek origin is listed separately from the moderately productive Latinate #pro+. It occurs as #prˈɔ+: *próclise* 'put before' (cf. *ênclise* 'put after'), *prólogo* 'prologue' (cf. *logomaquia* 'debate over words' origins') and as #prɔ+: *profeta* 'prophet' and *programa* 'program' (cf. *gramática* 'grammar').

---

10 One of the reasons *céfalo* does not occasion stress on the final vowel of #endɔ+ is that this stem already is a proparoxytone. Portuguese non-compound words cannot be stressed more than three syllables from the words' end. Likewise, when the suffix +ik+<o# is added to #sɛfal+ (*cefálico*), it causes the word's stress to shift one syllable toward the end owing to the same constraint.

**§11.1.2.18 #meta+:** This Greek origin prefix has two allomorphs: #meta+ and #met'a+. It occurs as #meta+ in words like *metacrítica* 'critique of criticism' (cf. *crítica* 'criticism' and *metamorfose* 'metamorphosis', *morfema* 'morpheme') as well as #met'a+ in *metátese* 'metathesis' (cf. *tese* 'thesis' and *metáfrase* 'paraphrase' and *frase* 'sentence').

**§11.1.2.19 #ɛk+:** This Hellenic prefix is separate from the very highly productive Latinate #ez+. It occurs as #ɛk+ in words like *ecfonema* 'excited raising of voice' (cf. *fonema* 'phoneme' and *eczema* 'eczema'). It occurs as #'ɛk+ in words like *écloga* 'eclogue' cf. *logorréia* 'compulsive speaking' and *éctipo* 'manufactured copy' (cf. *tipo* 'type').

**§11.1.2.20 The prefix #ab+:** This Latinate prefix is one of the sources of the prefix #a+, which is the most productive of all prefixes. It has two allomorphs: #ab+ and #abs+, the latter of which appears before the letters c̲ (when it represents /s/): *absceder*[11] 'to abscess' (cf. *exceder* 'to exceed') and before /t/: *abstração* 'abstraction' (cf. *atração* 'attraction' and *tração* 'traction'). The former occurs in words such as *absorver* 'to absorb' (cf. *sorver* 'to sip') and *abdicar* 'to abdicate' (cf. *indicar* 'to indicate').

**§11.1.2.21 'Prefix' #ante+:** This form is also a preposition that means 'facing, in the presence of' e.g. *ante tal evidência* 'in the face of such evidence'. Since Portuguese prepositions are bound forms insofar as they must have an overt object, one can say that the form *ante* is a preposition #ante>, which makes words such as *antebraço* 'forearm' (cf. *braço* 'arm') and *antenome* 'professional title' (cf. *nome* 'name'). These are compound words rather than derived words.

**§11.1.2.22 'Prefix' #pɔz+:** This 'prefix' also is a preposition, which has the doublet *após* meaning, as *pós* does, 'after'. It occurs in words like *poscênio* 'backstage' (cf. *cena* 'scene') and *pospelo* 'against the direction of fur's growth' (cf. *pelo* 'fur'). Its prepositional nature is acknowledged orthographically in hyphenated words like *pós-data* 'PS' (cf. *data* 'date') and *pós-graduação* 'post-graduation' (cf. *graduação* 'undergraduate studies'). It has no phonemic allophones, but of course this prefix's final /z/ occurs as [z] when a vowel follows, e.g. *pós-eleitoral* 'post-electoral'. It is voiceless preceding [+surd] consonants

---

11 The speakers of Portuguese who pronounce *nascer* 'to be born' as [năš'ser] would pronounce *absceder* [ăβš.sə.'ðer] or [ă.βəš.sə.'ðe.rə].

and palatalized syllable-finally in those pronunciations where speakers palatalize syllable final /z/. Words it occurs in are compounds.

**§11.1.2.23 #apo+:** This Greek origin prefix has two allomorphs: #apɔ+ as in *apoplexia* 'apoplexy' (cf. '*plexo*' 'plexis') and *apotegma* 'pithy saying' (cf. *tema* 'theme'). It occurs as #apˈɔ+ in words like *apólogo* 'fable' (cf. *logotipo* group of letters in a common type') and *apófase* 'negation' (cf. *fase* 'phase').

**§11.1.2.24 #eu+:** This Greek-origin prefix occurs in words such as: *eufonia* 'euphony' (cf. *fone* 'sound'), and *eutrofia* 'good nutrition' (cf. *distrofia* 'poor nutrition').

**§11.1.2.25 #ɛpi+:** This Greek-origin prefix has two allomorphs: #ɛpi+ as in *episcópio* 'opaque projector' (cf. *telescópio* 'telescope') and *epizona* 'superficial zone' (cf. *zona* 'zone'); and as #epˈi+, which occurs in words such as *epígrafe* 'epigraph' (cf. *grafia* 'writing') and *epícrise* 'complete understanding of a crisis' (cf. *crise* 'crisis').

**§11.1.2.26 #ipɛr+:** This Greek-origin prefix has two allomorphs: #ipɛr+ as in *hiperdosagem* 'high dosage' (cf. *dose* 'dose') and *hipertenso* 'hypertense' (cf. *tenso* 'tense'). These forms are hybrids: their prefix is of Greek origin, whereas their stems are Latinate. When this prefix occurs with specific Greek-origin stems, it emerges as #ipˈɛr+ in words like *hipérbato* 'hyperbaton'[12] and *hipérbole* 'hyperbole' (cf. *metábole* 'paraphrase').

**§11.1.2.27 #ipɔ+:** This Greek-origin prefix has two allomorphs: #ipɔ+ as in *hipoderme* 'subcutaneous tissue' (cf. *dermitologia* 'dermitology') and *hipoteca* 'mortage' (cf. *discoteca* 'discotheque'). It occurs as well as #ipˈɔ+ in *hipócrita* 'hypocrite' (cf. *critério* 'criterion') and *hipótese* 'hypothesis' (cf. *tese* 'thesis').

**§11.1.2.28 #ad+:** This Latinate prefix occurs both as #ad+ and as #a+, the latter of which is the most productive prefix. Among its 147 manifestations as /ad/ there is *aderir* 'to adhere' (cf. *coerir* 'to cohere'), *adjazer* 'to abut' (cf. *jazer* 'to lie'), *admirar* 'to admire', (cf. *mirar* 'to look'), *adquisiço* 'acquisition' (cf. *inquisição* 'inquisition'), and *advir* 'to happen' (cf. *vir* 'to come'). Words formed with #ad+ often have doublets lacking the /d/: *aquisição* means the same as *adquisição*, whereas *avir* means 'to conciliate, adjust, to get out of a difficulty' rather than just 'to happen'.

12 There seems to be no plausible reflex of the roots of *hipérbato* and *hipérbole*.

**§11.1.2.29 #para+:** This Greek-origin prefix has two allomorphs: #para+ and #par'a+, which occur, respectively, in words such as *paradoxo* 'paradox' (cf. *ortodoxo* 'orthodox'). As #par'a+ it occurs in words such as *parágrafo* 'paragraph' (cf. *ortografia* 'correct spelling') and in *paráclase* 'displacement, fault (geologic terms)' (cf. *litóclase* 'a natural fracture in a rock').[13]

**§11.1.2.30 #dia+:** This Greek-origin prefix has two allomorphs: #dia+ and #di'a+. The former occurs in words such as *dialeto* 'dialect' (cf. *léxico* 'lexicon' and *diapasão* 'tuning fork'),[14] the latter in words such as *diálogo* 'dialogue' (cf. *loquaz* 'talkative') and *diáfora* '[exploitation of] homophony' (cf. *metáfora* 'metaphor').

**§11.1.2.31 #ɔb+:** This prefix has two allomorphs: #ɔb+ and #ɔ+: As #ɔb+ it occurs in words like *obcecar* 'to blind' (cf. *cego* 'blind'), *oblongo* 'oblong' (cf. *longo* 'long'), and *obstruir* 'to obstruct' (cf. *instruir* 'to instruct'). As #ɔ+ it occurs in words such as *ocorrer* 'to occur' (cf. *correr* 'to run'), *ofensivo* 'offensive' (cf. *defensivo* 'defensive'), and *opor* 'to oppose' (cf. *impor* 'to impose'). It appears that the prefix's /b/ is lost when it occurs before labials or velar stop consonants in common words: (cf. *ocorrer* 'to occur' and *obcláveo* 'upside down clef').

**§11.1.2.32 #peri+:** This Greek-origin prefix has two allomorphs: #peri+ and #per'i+. The former occurs in words such as *periferia* 'periphery' and *periórbita* 'periorbit' (cf. *orbe* 'globe, eye'), the latter in words like *período* 'period' (cf. *sínodo* 'synod') and *perímetro* 'perimeter' (cf. *metro* 'meter').

**§11.1.2.33 #ana+:** This Greek-origin prefix has two allomorphs: #ana+ and #an'a+: The former appears in words such as *analfabeto* 'illiterate' (cf. *alfabeto* 'alphabet') and *anagrama* 'anagram' (cf. *telegrama*

---

13 This prefix has homophones in the Portuguese preposition *para* 'for' (an amalgamation of two Latin prepositions *per* and *ad*) and in the 3rd person present tense form of *parar* 'to stop'. Both the preposition and the verbal root are elements that form compound words: *parabens* 'congratulations (i.e. for the good)' and *para-raios* 'lightning rod (i.e. lightning stopper'). Whereas only the Greek prefix has two allomorphs, one must take care in distinguishing the three homophonous manifestations of these forms.

14 There seems to be no plausible reflex of *–pasão* for a comparison.

'telegram'); the latter in words like *análogo* 'analogous' (cf. *catálogo* 'catalog').[15]

**§11.1.2.34 #sin+:** Given that this prefix's final phoneme is a nasal consonant, its realization is contingent on whether or not it is followed by a consonant, whose point of articulation it will assume. That is, this prefix of Greek origin occurs as [sĩm] in words such as *simpatia* 'sympathy' (cf. *empatia* 'empathy'), as [sĩn] *sintético* 'synthetic' (cf. *antitético* 'antithetic') and as [sĩŋ] in words like *sincrónico* 'synchronic' (cf. *anacrónico* 'anachronic'). Of course when it occurs before a vowel its realization is [sĩn] as in the word *sinalefa* 'synaloepha', i.e. the merger of two syllables into one' and *sinopse* 'synopsis' (cf. *autopse* 'autopsy'). This prefix can be stressless (#sin+) as above or stressed (#sˈin+): *síntese* 'synthesis' (cf. *antítese* 'antithesis') and *síncope* 'syncope' (cf. *apócope* 'apocope').

**§11.1.3.0** The 16 prefixes in Table 11.1b account for 89.16% of all prefixed tokens found in the *Aurélio*. Table 11.1d analyzes them and displays the various orthographic and phonemic configurations they may take in their combinations with stems and roots.

**Table 11.1d** Prefixes: Low to Supreme Productivity

| | Orthography | Analaysis | Allomorphs | | | | Orthography | Analaysis | Allomorphs | |
|---|---|---|---|---|---|---|---|---|---|---|
| 1 | inter- | #inter+ | [inter/ | | | 9 | de- | #de+ | [de/ | |
| 2 | trans-, tras-, tra-, tres- | #tranz+ #trez+ | [tranz/ [tre/ | [traz/ | [tra/ | 10 | ex-, es-, e-* | #ez+ | [ez/ | [e/ |
| 3 | per- | #per+ | [per/ | | | 11 | con-. com-, co- | #kon+ | [kon/ | [ko/ |
| 4 | dis- | #diz+ | [diz/ | [di/ | | 12 | en- em- | #en+ | [en/ | [e/ |
| 5 | sub- | #sub+ | [sub/ | [suz/ | [su/ | 13 | re- | #r̲e- | [r̲e/ | |
| 6 | anti- | #anti+ | [ẵnti+ | [ẵnˈti+ | | 14 | des- | #dez+ | [dez/ | |
| 7 | pre- | #prɛ+ | [prɛ/ | | | 15 | in-, im-, i-, | #in+ | [in/ | [i/ |
| 8 | pro- | #prɔ+ | [pro/ | | | 16 | a-* | #a+, | [a/ | |

**§11.1.3.1 #inter+:** This Latinate prefix occurs in words such as *intercalar* 'to put between' (cf. *calar* 'to penetrate') and *interrogar* 'to interrogate' (cf. *rogar* 'to beg'). Whereas Cunha (63) considers the form /entre/ to be an allomorph of #inter+, this form is, for all intents

15 The stressed /a/ of *anárquico* 'anarchical' and *hierárquico* 'hierarchical' owe their proparoxytone stress to the suffix +ik+ (§7.5.6.2, §3.1.6.0, Table 3.9b, Rule 3.4).

and purposes, the preposition #entre>, and the words it forms are compounds whose meanings can, but need not, transcend the sums of their constituent parts: e.g. *entreabrir* 'to open slightly', *entrecerrar* 'to close slightly', *entrecortar* 'to intersect', *entremear* 'to intermingle', *entrever* 'to glimpse', *entreposto* 'warehouse'.

**§11.1.3.2 'Prefix' #tranz+:** This Latinate morpheme has four allomorphs: #tranz+, #traz+, #tra+, and #trez+. The form #tranz+ occurs in words like *transatlántico* 'ocean-liner' (cf. *Atlántico* 'Atlantic Ocean'), *transbordar* 'to switch conveyance' (cf. *abordar* 'to get on board'), *transferir* 'to transfer' (cf. *ferir* 'to wound'). As #traz+ this prefix occurs in words such as *trasfegar* 'to decant' (cf. *ofegar* 'to pant' and *trasladar* 'to move from one space to another'), (cf. *lado* 'side'). As #tra+ it occurs in words like *traduzir* 'translate' (cf. *conduzir* 'to conduct' and *traficar* 'to traffic', cf. *ficar* 'to remain'). The prefix as #trez+ occurs in words like *tresfolegar* 'to gasp' (cf. *fôlego* 'breath') and *trescalar* 'to emit a penetrating stench' (cf. *calar* 'to penetrate'). Essentially synonymous doublets formed with different allomorphs of this morpheme include: *transbordar* = *trasbordar*, *trasladar* = *transladar*. This form has become a verbal root, i.e. in the word *transar* [trã$^{\tilde{n}}$ˈzar], which, among other meanings, indicates 'to be in agreement'. Rather than a mere prefix, #tranz+ is a compounding element.

**§11.1.3.3 #per+:** This prefix begins words like *perceber* 'to perceive' (cf. *receber* 'to receive'), *perene* 'perennial' (cf. *ano* 'year' and *bienal* 'bi-annual'), *persuadir* 'to persuade' (cf. *dissuadir* 'to dissuade'), and *pernoitar* 'to spend the night' (cf. *noite* 'night').

**§11.1.3.4 #diz+:** This prefix has two allomorphs #diz+ and #di+, and the latter has two origins, both Latin and Greek. The #di+ of Greek origin can occur as #di+ and as #ˈdi+: *dígrafo* 'digraph' (cf. *grafema* 'grapheme') and as #di+ in *digrama* also *'digraph'*. The prefixes of Latin origin are not stressed. The form #di+ occurs in words like *dilatar* 'to widen' (cf. *lateral* 'lateral') and *diminuto* 'diminutive' (cf. *miúdo* 'small'), *digerir* 'to digest' (cf. *ingerir* 'to ingest' and *sugerir* 'to suggest'). As #diz+ it occurs in *discursar* 'to speak in public' (cf. *cursar* 'to study'), and *dispartir* 'to distribute' (cf. *partir* 'to break').

**§11.1.3.5 #sub+:** This Latinate prefix has five allomorphs: #sub+, #sob+, #so+, #su+, and #suz+. As #sub+ it begins words such as *subjugar* 'to subjugate' (cf. *jugo* 'yoke')[16] and *subterrâneo* 'underground' (cf.

16 The words *sojugar* and *sojigar* are folk doublets of *subjugar*.

*coterrâneo* 'person from the same region'). As #sob+ (which also occurs as a preposition meaning 'below') it begins words like *sobalçar* 'to raise from low to very high' (cf. *alçar* 'to raise') and *sobestar* 'to be below' (cf. *estar* 'to be'). As #so+ it occurs in words like *sobraçar* 'to tuck under one's arm' (cf. *braço* 'arm'), *soterrar* 'to cover with dirt' (cf. *enterrar* 'to bury'), and *socorrer* 'to save' (cf. *recorrer* 'to find recourse'). As #su+ it occurs in words like *suplicar* 'to beg' (cf. *aplicar* 'to apply') and *suportar* 'to support' (cf. *aportar* 'to come to port'). As #suz+ it occurs in *suspender* 'to suspend' (cf. *depender* 'to depend') and *sustentar* 'to sustain' (cf. *tentar* 'to try, tempt'). There seems to be little systematicity in the employment of these allomorphs other than to say that the more recent coinages use #sub+, which, in these cases, is semantically transparent. The words using #suz+ or #su+ have Latin etymons, and those using both #so+ and #sob+ are words that underwent the sound changes typical of Latin's phonological evolution into Portuguese. That is, the short /ŭ/ of Latin became /o/ in Portuguese, and the form-final /b/ was regularly dropped (Williams, 92).

**§11.1.3.6 #anti+:** This Greek-origin prefix has two allomorphs: #anti+ and #ant'i+. The former is by far the more common and occurs in words such as *antipatia* 'antipathy' (cf. *empatia* 'empathy') and *anticívico* 'sociopath' (cf. *cívico* 'civic'). The latter allomorph occurs in words like *antífrase* 'antiphrasis' (cf. *frase* 'phrase') and *antítese* 'antithesis' (cf. *tese* 'thesis').

**§11.1.3.7 #prɛ+:** This Latinate prefix occurs in hyphenated words such as *pré-adolescente* 'pre-adolescent', which are, owing to their two stressed syllables ['prɛ] and ['sẽ$^{n}$], compound words. As an ordinary prefix it creates idioms such as *preparar* 'to prepare' (cf. *parar* 'to stop') and *preferir* 'to prefer' (cf. *ferir* 'to wound'). It occurs in all sorts of transparent words, e.g. *predizer* 'to predict' (cf. *dizer* 'to say') and *prever* 'to foresee' (cf. *ver* 'to see').

**§11.1.3.8 #pro+:** This moderately productive prefix is of combined Greek and Latin origin. It occurs in words like *produzir* 'to produce' (cf. *induzir* 'to induce'), *programa* 'program' (cf. *telegrama* 'telegram'), and *professar* 'to profess' (cf. *confessar* 'to confess').

**§11.1.3.9 #de+:** This moderately productive prefix is also an extremely ubiquitous Portuguese preposition. As a prefix it occurs in words like *deter* 'to detain' (cf. *ter* 'to have'), *declarar* 'to declare' (cf. *claro* 'clear'), *denotar* 'to reveal, denote' (cf. *notar* 'to notice'), *depenar* 'to pluck feathers' (cf. *pena* 'feather'), and *devorar* 'to devour' (cf. *voraz* 'voracious').

**§11.1.3.10.0 #εz+:** This moderately productive prefix has two main allomorphs #εz+ and #ε+. As #εz+ it appears in words like *exasperar* 'to exasperate' (cf. *áspero* 'rough'), *exibir* 'to exhibit' (cf. *inibir* 'to inhibit'), *exonerar* 'to exonerate' (cf. *honorar* 'to honor'), *exumar* 'to exhume' (cf. *póstumo* 'posthumous'). In the previous words, this morpheme's final /z/ emerges as [z] in all pronunciations because, since it occurs pre-vocalically, i.e. it is in syllable-initial position. When it occurs syllable-finally, its voicing reflects that of a following consonant, and, in pronunciations where syllable-final /z/ is palatalized, it is palatalized. Examples of [z] or [ž] include: *esburacar* 'to riddle with holes' (cf. *buraco* 'hole'), *esganar* 'to strangle' (cf. *enganar* 'to deceive'), *esmurrar* 'to strike' (cf. *murro* 'blow with a fist'), *esverdear* 'to turn green' (cf. *verde* 'green'). Examples with syllable-final [s] or [š] include, *escabrear* 'to bother' (cf. *cabra* 'goat'), *esfarelar* 'to crumble' (cf. *farelo* 'crumb'), *espalhar* 'to strew' (cf. *palha* 'straw'), *exclamar* 'to exclaim' (cf. *reclamar* 'to complain'), *estágio* 'stage in development' (cf. *contágio* 'contagion'), *exceder* 'to exceed' (cf. *conceder* 'to concede').

**§11.1.3.10.1** The allomorph #ε+ often appears before word-initial /l, m, n, r, f, v, ž/: e.g. #εz+#l/ *eleger* 'to elect' (cf. *legar* 'to bequeath'), *elaborar* 'to eleborate' (cf. *labor* 'labor'), *eliminar* 'to eliminate' (cf. *liminar* 'at the edge'); #εz+#m/ *emigar* 'to *emigrate*' (cf. *migrante* 'migrant'), *emanar* 'to emanate' (cf. *manar* 'to spurt'); and #εz+#r/ *erradicar* 'to eradicate' (cf. *radical* 'radical').

**§11.1.3.10.2** Were these, and words like them, the only cases of the disappearance of this prefix's final /z+, it would be a simple matter to consider their lexical forms to be #ez+#lεg++e#+r#+e+, #ez++lab++or#+a#+r#+e+, #ez++lim++in#+a#+r#+e+, #ez++migr++a#+r#+e+, #ez+#man++a#+r#+e+, #ez+#rad++ik#+a#+r#+e+ and to write a rule that eliminates the prefix's /z+ before word-initial /l, m, r/. However, there are cases of #ez+'s emergence before /l/ and /m/ e.g. *esladroar* 'to pull out new shoots', *eslagartar* 'to clear plants of caterpillars', *esmochar* 'to de-horn', *esmigalhar* 'to crumble'. On top of this, its allomorph #ε+ can appear before word-initial /d, f, v/: *educar* 'to educate' (cf. *duque* 'duke'), *editar* 'to edit' (cf. *ditar* 'to proscribe'), *efeito* 'effect' (cf. *feito* 'deed'), *efluir* 'to flow out' (cf. *fluir* 'to flow'), *evadir* 'to evade' (cf. *invadir* 'to invade'), *evidência* 'evidence' (cf. *vidente* 'seer'), *evacuar* 'to evacuate' (cf. *vácuo* 'empty').

**§11.1.3.10.3** If grammarians were absolutely intent on writing rules for phenomena such as these, they could set up a class of words that cause the /z+ of #ez+ to disappear in specific environments. But by far the simplest solution to the allomorphy of #εz+ is to consider #εz+ and #ε + to be lexical variations of the same prefix and acknowledge that they are peculiar to specific, long-standing lexical items. Beyond this, the words formed with the initial #ε+ are importations from Latin. New words are not coined using the #ε+ allomorph of the prefix #εz+. In the case of neologisms, this prefix's vowel would emerge as [e] or [ə] with the various allophones of /z/ emerging according to is phonotactic circumstances.

**§11.1.3.11 'prefix' #kon+:** This form is also a highly frequent preposition in Portuguese. As a preposition it usually translates as 'with' in English. As a prefix it has two allomorphs: #kon+ and #ko+. It occurs as #kon+[17] in words like *complicar* 'to complicate' (cf. *aplicar* 'to apply'), *condizer* 'to speak well of' (cf. *dizer* 'to say'), *conformar* 'to conform' (cf. *formar* 'to form'), and *congelar* 'to congeal' (cf. *gelar* 'to freeze'). It occurs as #ko+ before stem-initial liquids /l/ and /r/: *coligar* 'to join' (cf. *ligar* 'to link'), *colidir* 'to collide' (cf. *elidir* 'to elide'), *corregir* 'to correct' (cf. *dirigir*[18] 'to direct'), *correlatar* 'to correlate' (cf. *relatar* 'to relate'). The form #ko+ also occurs before vowel-initial stems as in the words: *coerir* 'to cohere' (cf. *inerir* 'to inhere') and *coordinar* 'to coordinate' (cf. *ordinal* 'ordinal'), *cooperar* 'cooperate' (cf. *operar* 'to operate'), and *coagir* 'to force' (cf. *agir* 'to act'). It can appear hyphenated as in the form *co-tutor* 'fellow tutor' (cf. *tutor* 'tutor').

**§11.1.3.12 #en+:** This is a descendent of the very highly productive prefix #in+, and both prefixes are also related to the Portuguese preposition #en> 'in, on'. In current Portuguese, there are doublets in which #en+ and #in+ stand in contrast with one another: *endentar* 'to mesh' ⇔ *indentar* 'to make a tooth-like depression', *enformar* 'to give form to' ⇔ *informar* 'to inform', *entesar* 'to stiffen, intensify' ⇔ *intensar* 'to intensify'. Its final nasal occurs as [n] in words beginning with the vowel #a/, e.g. *enamorar* 'to inspire love' (cf. *amor* 'love') and *enaltecer* 'to hold on high' (cf. *alto* 'high'), and its final consonant assimilates

17 When the prefix final /n/ occurs before a consonant, any contoidal articulation it may have conforms to the following consonants' point of articulation.

18 The lexical forms of these two words are #kon+#rεg++i++r#+e+ and #di++rig++i++r#+e+, respectively. An /r/ after /n/ emerges as [ɽ], whereas it is [r] after a vocoid or after occlusives and labial fricatives.

to following stop and fricative consonants according to the overall Portuguese pattern in which syllable-final nasals assimilate to the point of articulation of following consonants. This prefix loses its /n+ before nasals: *emundecer* 'to become quiet' #en+#mut++ɛs++e#+r#+e+ and *enegrecer* 'to blacken' #en+#negr++ɛs++e#+r#+e+.

**§11.1.3.13 #re+**: This highly productive prefix occurs in words like *reação* 'reaction' (cf. *ação* 'action'), *resistir* 'to resist' (cf. *assistir* 'to attend'), *ressair* 'to come out once more' (cf. *sair* 'to emerge'). The words cited above suggest some sort of precedent action that mirrors or motivates the action these prefixed infinitives denote. But whatever precedence to the actual action (or reflection of such action) the words above may suggest, the following examples denote a more tenuous semantic relationship between the prefix #re+ and the denotations of words formed with it: *receber* 'to receive' (cf. *perceber* 'to perceive'), *receitar* 'to prescribe' (cf. *aceitar* 'to accept'), *recensear* 'to census' (cf. *censo* 'census'), *reclamar* 'to complain' (cf. *exclamar* 'to exclaim'), *recheio* 'stuffing' (cf. *cheio* 'full'). Precedence is totally absent from formations such as *recru* 'overly raw' (cf. *cru* 'raw'), *refrear* 'to brake' (cf. *frear* 'to brake'), *refulgir* 'to shine intensely' (cf. *fulgor* 'brilliance'), and *recolher* 'to shelter' (cf. *colher* 'to collect'). That is, words formed with the prefix #re+, like those formed with the other prefixes, may have meanings that transcend the sum of their constituent parts. However, this prefix consistently denotes repeated action when it precedes another prefix as in words like: *reconsertar* 'to repair once more' (cf. *consertar* 'to repair' and *acertar* 'to be correct'), *reembolsar* 'to reimburse' *embolsar* 'to pocket' (cf. *bolsa* 'bag, pocket'), and *repercutir* 'to produce repercussions,' (cf. *percutir* 'to tap, percuss' and *discutir* 'to argue').

**§11.1.3.14 #in+:** This prefix has two main allomorphs: #in+, #i+. It occurs as #in+ ([ĩn] or [in]) before vowels: *inabitável* 'uninhabitable', (cf. *hábito* 'habit'), *inelegível* 'unelectable, ineligible' (cf. *elegível* 'eligible'), *inibir* 'to inhibit' (cf. *proibir* 'to prohibit'), *inoperante* 'out of order' (cf. *operar* 'to operate'), and *inútil* 'useless' (cf. *útil* 'useful'). The prefix-final /n+, when articulated as a contoid, conforms in point of articulation to the consonants it precedes. This prefix emerges as #i+ before laterals, rhotics, nasals: *ilegal* 'illegal' (cf. *legal* 'legal'), *irresponsável* 'irresponsible' (cf. *responsável* 'responsible'), *imoral* 'immoral' (cf. *moral* 'moral').

**§11.1.3.15 #dez+:** This prefix is actually a combination of two Latin prepositions, #de+ and #ɛks+. It occurs in words such as *desarmar* 'to disarm' (cf. *arma* 'arm'), *descorar* 'to forget something memorized', (cf. *decorar* 'to memorize'), *desdizer* 'to belie' (cf. *dizer* 'to say'), *desnarigar* 'to remove the nose' (cf. *nariz* 'nose'), *desuso* 'out of use' (cf. *uso* 'use'). It often occurs on already prefixed words: e.g. *desavexar* 'to relieve vexation' (cf. *vexar* and *avexar* 'to vex'), *desembarcar* 'to disembark' (cf. *embarcar* 'to embark' and *barco* 'boat'), *desiludir* 'to take away illusions' (cf. *iludir* 'to elude' and *aludir* 'to allude'), *desofuscar* 'to de-obfuscate' (cf. *ofuscar* 'to obfuscate' and *fosco* 'clouded'), *desultrajar* 'to avenge' (cf. *ultrajar* 'to offend'). When this prefix occurs before another prefix, it always denotes an undoing.

**§11.1.3.16.0 #a+:** Getting a reliable count of this prefix's tokens was problematic because more Portuguese words begin with /a/ than with any other phoneme.[19] Paring down 17,996 instances to 7,945 entailed eliminating from the count all those tokens with prefixes that also begin with /a/ (e.g. #antɔ+, #ab+ #apɔ+). This yielded 14,625 entries. The examination of 370 a-initial tokens yielded 169 words that began with an a that was not a prefix. Thus, 45.68% were not tokens containing #a+. Extrapolating, of the 14,625 tokens, 6,681 were not #a+ tokens, which leaves approximately 7,944 that were, and that number of tokens constitutes an outlier among all the prefixes.

**§11.1.3.16.1** This very supremely productive prefix is an amalgam of the Latinate prefixes #ab+ and #ad+ as well as the Greek prefix #a+—all reduced to #a+ in the course of Portuguese's evolution from Vulgar Latin. The #a+ of Latinate origin is ubiquitous in the formation of Portuguese transitive verbs, but has no constant meaning other than (the often redundant) verbal transitivity, as in Table 11.2:

19 In the *Aurélio*, more words begin with /a/ (total entries 17,996) than with any other phoneme. The closest runner up to words beginning with the letter a were those beginning with c. Every instance of a represents the phoneme /a/, whereas c can represent the phonemes /s/ and /k/ as well words beginning with ch (/š/).

**Table 11.2** Prefix #a+ and the Derivation of Verbs and Adverbs

| Transitive Verbs | | | |
|---|---|---|---|
| Derived Verbs | Gloss | Stem | Gloss |
| **abiscoitar** | to take away | **biscoito** | biscuit |
| **acalorar** | to heat | **calor** | heat |
| **adietar** | to take up dieting | **dieta** | diet |
| **afear** | to make ugly | **feio** | ugly |
| **agarrar** | to grab | **garra** | claw |
| **ajuizar** | to pass judgment | **juizo** | judgment |
| **alargar** | to widen | **largo** | wide |
| **amassar** | to amass | **massa** | mass |
| **aninhar** | to nestle | **ninho** | nest |
| **apalavrar** | to make a pact | **palavra** | word |
| **aquietar** | to calm down | **quieto** | quiet |
| **arrimar** | to get in order | **rima** | rhyme |
| **assentar** | to establish | **sentar** | to sit, seat |
| **aterrorar** | to terrorize | **terror** | terror |
| **avergonhar** | to shame | **vergonha** | shame |
| **axicarar** | to turn into a cup | **xícara** | cup |
| **azoar** | to upset | **zoar** | to buzz |
| **Adverbs** | | | |
| Prefixed by #a+ | Gloss | Stem | Gloss |
| **abaixo** | downward | **baixo** | low |
| **acaso** | perchance | **caso** | case |
| **adentro** | inward | **dentro** | inside |
| **adiante** | forward | **diante** | facing |
| **amanhã** | tomorrow | **manhã** | morning |
| **assim** | thus | **sim** | yes |

There are many sources of this particular prefix. The preposition *a* 'to, at', the Latinate prefixes #ab+ and #ad+ and the Greek prefix #a+. The latter is the privy of erudite speech and vocabulary. It indicates the lack of whatever a stem may denote: *anormal* 'abnormal' (cf. *normal* 'normal'), *atípico* 'a-typical' (cf. *típico* 'typical'), *afasia* 'aphasia' (cf. *disfasia* 'speech impediment'). As these examples show, it attaches both to Greek stems (+fasia# and #tip+) and Latinate stems: (#norm++al+ +e+).

## Prefixes and Their Markedness

§**11.2.0** Owing to their rarity, the negligibly productive prefixes convey more information when used and are the most highly marked of the prefixes. The prefixes of very low productivity may be the next highly marked, those of low productivity less informative and less marked, and so forth up to the very highly productive ones, which are the least marked owing to their frequency and the imprecision in their denotations (low information content). To see if there are phonological correlates to this proposed hierarchy, Table 11.3 contains all the prefixes in their respective categories. They are correlated with the number of segments in their basic lexical form and with the number of positive specifications their segments entail.

**Table 11.3** Productivity and Segmental Markedness

| Negligible Productivity | | | | Very Low Productivity | | | |
|---|---|---|---|---|---|---|---|
| Prefix | % | Segments | marks | Prefix | % | Segments | Marks |
| #žuzta+ | 0.02 | 5 | 13 | #para+ | 0.52 | 4 | 7 |
| #soto+ | 0.05 | 4 | 10 | #dia+ | 0.62 | 3 | 5 |
| #intro+ | 0.07 | 5 | 10 | #ɔb+ | 0.64 | 2 | 5 |
| #intra+ | 0.07 | 5 | 9 | #peri+ | 0.82 | 4 | 9 |
| #supra+ | 0.07 | 5 | 12 | #ana+ | 0.84 | 3 | 4 |
| #antɔ+ | 0.08 | 4 | 9 | #sin+ | 0.85 | 3 | 7 |
| #ultra+ | 0.10 | 5 | 10 | **Average** | | **3.17** | **6.17** |
| #vise+ | 0.12 | 4 | 9 | **Low Productivity** | | | |
| #arki+ | 0.13 | 3 | 7 | #inter+ | 1.18 | 4 | 10 |
| #retro+ | 0.14 | 5 | 8 | #tranz+ | 1.21 | 5 | 9 |
| #anfi+ | 0.16 | 4 | 9 | #per+ | 1.24 | 3 | 6 |
| #eztra+ | 0.17 | 5 | 8 | #diz+ | 1.35 | 3 | 6 |
| #endo+ | 0.18 | 4 | 7 | #sub+ | 1.36 | 3 | 8 |
| #kata+ | 0.21 | 4 | 10 | #anti+ | 1.60 | 4 | 8 |
| #siz+ | 0.21 | 3 | 7 | #pre+ | 1.87 | 3 | 6 |
| #ortɔ+ | 0.21 | 4 | 9 | **Average** | | **3.57** | **7.57** |
| #pr'ɔ+ | 0.25 | 3 | 8 | **Moderate Productivity** | | | |
| #meta+ | 0.26 | 4 | 8 | #pro+ | 3.10 | 3 | 7 |
| #ɛk+ | 0.29 | 2 | 5 | #de+ | 3.29 | 2 | 3 |
| #ab+ | 0.32 | 2 | 4 | #ɛz+ | 5.03 | 2 | 3 |

*(Continued)*

Table 11.3 Continued

| Negligible Productivity | | | | Very Low Productivity | | | |
|---|---|---|---|---|---|---|---|
| #ante+ | 0.35 | 4 | 7 | #kon+ | 5.91 | 3 | 9 |
| #pɔz+ | 0.39 | 3 | 9 | Average | | 2.5 | 5.5 |
| #apɔ+ | 0.42 | 3 | 8 | High and Very High Productivity | | | |
| #eu+ | 0.43 | 2 | 4 | #en+ | 8.24 | 2 | 3 |
| #ɛpi+ | 0.45 | 3 | 7 | #re- | 9.35 | 2 | 2 |
| #iper+ | 0.45 | 4 | 8 | #in+ | 9.35 | 2 | 4 |
| #ipɔ+ | 0.45 | 3 | 9 | #dez+ | 10.07 | 3 | 5 |
| #ad+ | 0.46 | 2 | 3 | Average | | 2.25 | 3.5 |
| Average | | 3.05 | 6.68 | Supreme Productivity | | | |
| | | | | #a+ | 25.11 | 1 | 1 |
| | | | | Average | | 1 | 1 |

The first two columns of each section of Table 11.3 contain the prefixes and the token percentages from Tables 11.1a–b. The left hand section contains the prefixes of negligible productivity, whereas the right hand section contains those whose productivity ascends from very low to supreme productivity. The third column in each section contains the number of segments making up each prefix, and the bottom line of the third column displays the average number of segments in prefixes of that category. One notices that the average number of segments rises from suffixes with negligible productivity through low productivity prefixes. Then, in the categories from low to supreme productivity, both the average number of segments and the average markedness in each category diminishes.

**§11.2.1** The fourth column of each section registers the total number of positive specifications the segments in each prefix entail. The least productive prefix, #žuzta+, has the highest number (13) of phonological marks: the /ž/ has four positive specifications [+contoid, +fricative, +high, +palatal], the /u/ three [+labial, +dorsal, +high], the /z/ two [+contoid, +fricative], the /t/ three [+contoid, +occlusion, +surd], and the /a/ one [+dorsal]. Contrariwise, the most productive prefix #a+ has one positive specification: [+dorsal]. Again, in the low to supreme productivity prefixes there is the expected synergistic relationship between phonological simplicity and morphological productivity as well as between low and high information content: the more productive a form is, the less specific information it transmits.

## Prefixal Allomorphy

**§11.3 Stress Allomorphy:** Footnotes 2 and 9 of this chapter indicate that certain stems of Greek (and one of Latin) origin can occasion a stress on specific prefixes. In the 50 prefixes included in this study, all bona fide prefixes can occur pretonically, but one finds that certain prefixes' final vowels become stressed when they attach to specific stems. This makes these words proparoxytones, i.e. they belong to a minority stress pattern. Table 11.4 contains a small sampling of prefixes that emerge as pretonic in paroxytone words and with a tonic syllable in proparoxytone words.

**Table 11.4** Prefix Stress Allomorphy

| Prefix | Paroxtyone | Gloss | Proparoxytone | Gloss |
|---|---|---|---|---|
| #anfi+ | **anfiteatro** | amphitheater | **anfíbio** | amphibean |
| #kata+ | **catafilo** | scaley leaf | **catálogo** | catalog |
| #meta+ | **metacarpo** | metacarpus | **metáfora** | metaphor |
| #ipɛr+ | **hiperagudo** | very sharp | **hipérbole** | hyperbole |
| #sin+ | **sintaxe** | syntax | **síndico** | corporate lawyer |
| #epi+ | **epigeu** | above ground | **epígeno** | epigenetic |

The stress patterns evinced in Table 11.4 are occasioned by the second element in each word. As final elements in prefixed and semi-compound words: *-bio*, *-logo*, *-fora*, *-bole*, *-dico*, and *–geno* cause the vowel that precedes them to be stressed.[20]

**§11.4.0 Segmental Allomorphy**: In addition to the prefixes that, in conjunction with specific stems, acquire stress, there are 12 prefixes[21] that display allomorphy. Table 11.5 contains these prefixes and their allomorphs:

20 For an extensive treatment of this phenomenon, see §12.2.0 and §12.2.5.1.0-2.1.

21 The 'prefixes' identified as components of compound words are not included.

Table 11.5 Segmental Allomorphy in True Prefixes[a]

| Nasal Assimilation and Deletion | | | | | | |
|---|---|---|---|---|---|---|
| Prefix | Phonemic Shapes | | | Emergence | Assimilation | Deletion |
| #in+ | #in+ | #i+ | *** | inoperante | impor | ilógico |
| #kon+ | #kon+ | #ko+ | *** | conter | comparar | coerir |
| #sin+ | #sin+ | *** | *** | sinalefa | simpatia | *** |
| Sibilant Assimilation and Deletion | | | | | | |
| #ez+ | #ez+ | #e+ | *** | exúbere | expor | eleger |
| #tranz+ | #tranz+ | #tra+ | *** | transação | transferir | traduzir |
| Occlusive Preservation and Deletion | | | | | | |
| #sub+ | #sub+ | #suz+ | #su+ | sublocar | suspender | superar |
| | #sob+ | #so+ | *** | sobestimar | soportar | soterrar |
| #ɔb+ | #ɔb+ | #ɔ+ | *** | obter | opor | ofuscar |
| #ab+ | #ab+ | #abz+ | *** | abdicar | absconder | aproximar |
| Other Allomorphy | | | | | | |
| #vise+ | #vise+ | #viz+ | *** | vice-cônsul | visconde | |

a The words in Table 11.5 mean: (fourth column): 'broken down, to contain, stamping die, weened, transaction, sublet, undervalue, obtain, abdicate, vice counsul'; (fifth column): 'impose, compare, sympathy, expose, transfer, suspend, put up with, oppose, abscond, viscount'; (sixth column): 'illogical, to cohere, Ø, to elect/ choose, to translate, overcome, bury, cloud, come close'.

**§11.4.1 Nasal Allomorphy #in+ and #kon+:** When the prefix-final /n/ in #in+, #kon+, and #sin+ precedes occlusives and fricatives, it normally assimilates to those segments' points of articulation. The rule for this phenomenon, which has been alluded to at various junctures (Ch. 2, fn. 18, §2.2.1.1 and Ch 4, fn., 7 and §4.4.1.1), is:

**Rule 11.1 Nasal Assimilation:**

$$\begin{pmatrix} +\text{nasal} \\ +\text{contoid} \end{pmatrix} \rightarrow \begin{pmatrix} \alpha\text{labial} \\ \beta\text{dorsal} \\ \gamma\text{palatal} \end{pmatrix} \; / \_\_ \; \begin{pmatrix} +\text{contoid} \\ \alpha\text{labial} \\ \beta\text{dorsal} \\ \gamma\text{palatal} \end{pmatrix}$$

Rule 11.1 operates regardless of the morphemic environment. That is, it causes nasal consonants to assimilate to the following consonants when there is no morpheme boundary between them, as in Table 11.6:

**Table 11.6** Syllable-Final Nasal Assimilation

| Word | Gloss | Phonemic Transcription | Assimilation | Phonetic[a] |
|---|---|---|---|---|
| ombro | shoulder | /onbro/ | /n/→ [m] | [ˈõ$^{m}$.brŭ |
| entre | between | /entre/ | /n/→ [n] | [ˈẽ$^{n}$.trə] |
| finge | 3$^{rd}$ pretends | /finže/ | /n/→ [ɲ] | [ˈfĩ$^{ɲ}$.žə] |
| tanque | tank | /tanke/ | /n/→ [ŋ] | [ˈtã̂$^{ŋ}$.kə] |

a The raising of the syllable-final nasal consonants in the fourth column indicates that they are not as forcefully articulated as they are in syllable-initial position.

**§11.4.2** Beyond the weakened contoidal realization of syllable-final /n/, when it occurs preconsonantally contoidal articulation can totally disappear and leave only nasal resonance on the vowels that precede them. Whereas the deletion of prefix-final nasal contoids is optional in the circumstances identified in Tables 11.5 and 11.6, the deletion of the final /n+ in #in+ and #kon+ before vocalic nasalization has taken place is obligatory in specific morphophonological environments. Tables 11.7 and 11.8 identify these environments:

**Table 11.7** Total Obligatory Effacement of Prefix-Final /n+ in # in+

| Environment | Word | Phonemic[a] | Phonetic | Gloss |
|---|---|---|---|---|
| #in+#r | irresponsável | #in+#responsavɛl# | [i.r̠əš.põ$^{n}$.ˈsa.vɛɫ] | 'irresponsible' |
| | irreduzível | #in+#reduzivɛl# | [i.r̠ə.δu.ˈzi.vɛɫ] | 'non-reducible' |
| #in+#l | ilegal | #in+#legal# | [i.lə.ˈγaɫ] | 'illegal' |
| | ileso | #in+#lezo# | [i.ˈle.zŭ] | 'unscathed' |
| #in+#m | imoral | #in+#moral# | [ĩ.mu.ˈraɫ] | 'immoral' |
| | imediato | #in+#mediato# | [ĩ.mə.δiˈa.tu] | 'immediate' |
| #in+#n | inovar | #in+##nɔvar# | [ĩ.nŭ.ˈva.rə] | innovate |
| | inato | #in+##nato# | [ĩ.ˈna.tŭ] | innate |

(*Continued*)

Table 11.7 Continued

| Environment | Word | Phonemic | Phonetic | Gloss |
|---|---|---|---|---|
| #kon+#r | **correlatar** | /kon+#relatar# | [kŭ.r̲ə.lă.ˈta.rə] | to correlate |
| | **corresponder** | #kon+#rezponder# | [kŭ.r̲eš.põ$^{n}$.ˈde.rə] | to correspond |
| #kon+#l | **colaborar** | #kon+#laborar# | [kŭ.lă.βŭ.ˈra.rə] | to colaborate |
| | **coligar** | #kon+#ligar# | [kŭ.li.ˈɣa.rə] | to connect |
| #kon+#m | **comedir** | #kon+#medir# | [kŭ.mə.ˈδi.rə] | to regulate |
| | **cometer** | #kon+#meter# | [kŭ.mə.ˈte.rə] | to put together |
| | | **Pre-vocalic Effacement** | | |
| #kon+#a | **coagir** | #kon+#ažir# | [kŭ.ă.ˈži.rə] | to force |
| #kon+#e | **coeducar** | #kon+#ez+#dukar# | [kŭ.ĭ.δu.ˈka.rə] | to co-educate |
| #kon+#ɛ | **co-erdar** | #kon+#ɛrdar# | #ko.er.ˈδa.rə] | to co-inherit |
| #kon+#i | **coincidir** | #kon+#insidir# | #kŭ.ĩn.si.ˈδi.rə] | to coincide |
| #kon+#ɔ | **cooperar** | #kon+#ɔb+#pɛrar# | #kŭ.ŭ.pə.ra.rə] | to co-occupy |
| #kon+#u | **co-utilisar** | #kon+#utilizar# | #kŭ.u.ti.li.ˈza.rə# | to use together |

a Since the phenomenon under examination here is prefixation, stems' morphophonological details do not appear.

Rule 11.2 deletes the /n+ of prefixes #in+ and #kon+ when they appear before word-initial nasals, laterals, and rhotics:

**Rule 11.2 Pre-contoid Nasal Effacement (#kon+ and +in#):**

$$\begin{Bmatrix} +\text{contoid} \\ +\text{nasal} \end{Bmatrix} \rightarrow \emptyset \,/\, \_\_ \;+\;\# \begin{Bmatrix} +\text{contoid} \\ -\text{fricative} \\ -\text{occlusion} \end{Bmatrix} X\;\#$$

In the context of the Portuguese phonological system, specification of contoids as neither occlusive nor fricative identifies the laterals, nasals, and rhotics. The morphological environment +# X # identifies the nasal consonant as a prefix-final segment.[22]

22 This rule seems to apply only to #in+ and #kon+. There are no convincing cases of #sin+'s appearing before word-initial /r, l, n/.

§**11.4.3** Table 11.7 provides ample illustrations of prefix-final /n+'s deletion before a set of contoidal segments (/l, r, m/), i.e. neither fricative nor occlusive. However, the /n+ of #kon+ also elides before word-initial vocoids, which, as Table 11.8 shows, is a structure-preserving environment for #in+:

**Table 11.8** Emergence of Prefixal /n+ as [n]

| Environment | Word | Phonemic | Phonetic | Gloss |
|---|---|---|---|---|
| #in+#a | **inamável** | /in+#amávɛl/ | [ĩ.nă.ˈma.vɛɫ] | unlovable |
| #in+#ɛ | **inere** | #in+#ɛre# | [ĩ.ˈne.rə] | 3$^{rd}$ inheres |
| #in+#e | **inexato** | #in+#ezato# | [ĩ.nə.ˈza.tŭ] | not exact |
| #in+#i | **iniludivel** | #in+#in+#ludívɛl# | [ĩ.ni.lu.ˈdi.vɛɫ] | unavoidable |
| #in+#ɔ | **inoperante** | /in+#ɔperante/ | [ĩ.nu.pə.ˈrã̆$^{n}$.tə] | out of order |
| #in+#u | **inumano** | /in+#umano/ | [ĩ.nu.ˈmã̆.nu] | inhuman |

§**11.4.4** As the data in Tables 11.7 and 11.8 indicate, Rule 11.2 does not close the case on these two prefixes. Because #in+'s /n+ perdures before word-initial vowels, whereas #kon+'s /n+ evanesces in that environment. The grammar needs a rule that would delete the /n+ of #kon+. And in a morphophonemic grammar, this rule would have to apply ***before*** the rule of vocalic nasalization and the rule of nasal contoidal assimilation (Rule 11.1). This rule is:

**Rule 11.3 #kon+'s Loss of /n+:**

$$\begin{Bmatrix} +\text{contoid} \\ +\text{nasal} \end{Bmatrix} \rightarrow \emptyset \ / \ \_\_ \ +\# \ [\text{-contoid}] \ X \ \#$$

As its title indicates, Rule 11.3 applies only to the prefix #kon+.

§**11.4.5** Prefixes #in+ and #kon+ present allomorphy that can only be regulated by appealing to morphophonological conditions in which specific categories of word-initial segments (non-obstruents, and vowels with a # boundary before them) occasion /n+'s disappearance.

**§11.4.5.0 #tranz+:** Table 11.1b identifies #tranz+ as a prefix of low productivity. The bulk of its realizations (76.56%) emerge as [trã̆$^{n}$z],[23] and the three other allomorphs constitute the remaining 23.44% of its occurrences: /traz+ (11.72%), #trez+ (8.85%), #tra+ (2.86%). The majority allomorph appears before every word-initial phoneme, save #z/, which rarely begins a word.

**§11.4.5.1 [trăz]:** The distribution of [trăz] is less wide-spread, occurring before word-initial /p, b, g, f, v, l, m, n, a, o/. There seems to be no conditioning factor in any of the words it forms, so it makes no sense to posit a rule deleting the /n/ in this manifestation of #tranz+. This form may have come about owing to its homophony with the preposition *tras* 'sequentially after' e.g. *hora tras hora* 'hour after hour'.

**§11.4.5.2 [trez]:** In examining attestations of allomorph #trez, one must take care not to confuse it with *três* 'three', which also occurs as the first element in certain compounds, e.g. in *tresdobrar* 'to fold into three parts'. This particular allomorph of #tranz+ appears in words such as *trescalar* 'to emit a stench', *tresmalhar* 'to separate from the flock', *tressuar* 'to sweat profusely', and *tresloucar* 'to go stark raving mad'.

**§11.4.5.3 [tră]:** The allomorph #tra+ is again quiet rare, but it does occur in common words such as *tradição* 'tradition', *traição* 'treason', *trafegar* 'to traffic', *trajeto* 'trajectory' and *travesso* 'mischievous'.

**§11.4.5.4** There seems to be no conditioning factor for any of the truncated versions of #tranz+. The other allomorphs are lexical variants of that prefix and occur in words that have long belonged to the Portuguese lexicon—#tranz+ is the only form of this prefix to occur in neologisms. So, concerning this prefix's nasal-less allomorphs, no over all patterns emerge such that one might write a plausible rule, which indicates that these allomorphs are simple lexical variants of one another.

**§11.5.0 Sibilant Allomorphy**: There are six prefixes that end in /z+: #siz+, #pɔz+, #tranz+, #diz+, #ɛz+ and #dez+. The forms #siz+, #pɔz+, and #dez+ seem to have no phonemic allomorphs. These prefixes' /z+ agrees in voicing with following consonants, and may be palatalized before consonants by speakers who perform this operation. The occurrence

23 Of course the form-final /z+ behaves as other instantiations of /z/ do when syllable-final.

of the allomorphs #ɛz+ and #ɛ+ is both sufficiently complicated and historically based such that any rule that would delete its /z+, in the myriad situations where #e+ emerges, would be baroque at best. Thus, these two forms of the prefix are lexical varieties of one another. The allomorphy of #diz+ is somewhat more manageable.

**§11.5.1** When the /z+ of #diz+ emerges syllable-finally, e.g. *discursar* 'to give a speech', *disgregar* 'to separate', it agrees in voicing with the following consonant as expected. When it appears before a word-initial #s/, it disappears: e.g. *dissabor* 'emotional wound' (cf. *sabor* 'taste'). And it disappears before the segments /ž, l, m, r, f, v/: *digerir* 'to digest' (cf. *ingerir* 'to ingest'), *dilapidar* 'to destroy' (cf. *lapidar* 'to stone'), *diminuto* 'small' (cf. *minuto* 'minute'), *dirigir* 'to direct' (cf. *corregir* 'to correct'), *diferir* 'to defer' (cf. *ferir* 'to wound'), and *divulgar* 'to divulge' (cf. *vulgo* 'common folk'). A rule can account for this loss of /z+ in #diz+:

**Rule 11.4 Loss of /z+ in the Prefix #diz+:**

$$\begin{pmatrix} +\text{fricative} \\ -\text{high} \\ -\text{labial} \\ -\text{surd} \end{pmatrix} + \rightarrow \varnothing \, / \, \_ \; \# \begin{pmatrix} +\text{contoid} \\ -\text{occlusion} \\ \left\{ \begin{matrix} \begin{pmatrix} -\text{surd} \\ -\text{dorsal} \end{pmatrix} \\ +\text{labial} \end{matrix} \right\} \end{pmatrix}$$

Rule 11.4's determinant accounts for the deletion of the /z+ of #diz+ ***except*** before all Portuguese vocoids and occlusives. This rule eliminates the /z+ before the non-occlusive labials /m, f, v/ and as well as before the [-surd, -dorsal, -occlusive] contoids /n, l, r, ž/.[24] And when this /z+ occurs before #s/, it assimilates in voicing and then disappears according to Rule 4.1, like segment deletion. Similar to the allomorphy of #ɛz+, one wonders whether this phenomenon merits a rule rather than mere lexical listing.

---

24 In a few scientific or professional terms of largely modern origin, #diz+ appears as [diž] before /l/-initial words: e.g. *dislalia* 'speech impediment' and *dislogia* 'pathololgical lack of reason'. In words of a less recondite nature, the /z+ disappears.

**§11.5.2.0 Occlusive Preservation and Deletion:** The prefixes #ad+ and #ab+, despite their final occlusive consonants, are sources of the very highly productive #a+, which as a separate morpheme displays no allomorphy. Other than its etymological descendent #a+, the prefix #ad+ has no allomorphy, whereas the suffix #ab+ sometimes acquires a /z/: *abster* 'to abstain' (cf. *ter* 'to have'), *absconder* 'to abscond' (cf. *esconder* 'to hide'), *absceder* 'to absess' (cf. *ceder* 'to cede').

**§11.5.2.1.0** The *Aurélio* contains 107 words beginning with the sequence abs. Of those 107, 62 are cases of stem-initial #s/ followed by a vowel, e.g. *absurdo* 'absurd' (cf. *surdo* 'deaf'), *absorver* 'to absorb' (cf. *sorver* 'to sip'), *absogro* 'a spouse's great grandfather' (cf. *sogro* 'father-in-law'), *absência* 'absense' (cf. *essência* 'essence'). There are 32 cases in which word-initial abs is followed by a stem-initial #t/, e.g. *abstento* 'refuser of an inheretence' (cf. *tento* 'care'), *abstrair* 'to abstract' (cf. *trair* 'to betray'). And there are 12 in which this sequence is followed by c, six of which represent /s/: *abcidar* 'to separate oneself' (cf. *trucidar* 'to immolate') and six which represent /k/, *absconso* 'secret', (cf. *esconso* 'hidden').

**§11.5.2.1.1** The incidences of abs preceding c (/s/) seem to be due to a spelling convention since at least five of the six examples also appear without the s (e.g. *abceder* ≈ *absceder* 'superate'), *abscisão* ≈ *abcisão* 'abscission'. On the other hand, there are no examples of #ab+'s occurring before a /t/—the s (/z/) always appears in this environment, and there are no incidences of #ab+'s occurring before a /k/. Thus, this appearance of /z/ is a rule-governed phenomenon:

**Rule 11.5 The Prefix #ab+'s Acquisition of /z/:**

$$\#ab+ \rightarrow \#abz+ \ / \_\_ \begin{pmatrix} +\text{occlusion} \\ +\text{surd} \\ \text{-labial} \end{pmatrix}$$

**§11.5.1.2** As #ab+ this prefix occurs before word-initial /d, l, n, ž, r/ : *abdicar* 'to abdicate' (cf. *indicar* 'to indicate'), *abluir* 'to bathe' (cf. *diluir* 'to dilute'), *abnegar* 'to deprive one's self' (cf. *negar* 'to deny'), *abjurar* 'to renounce' (cf. *jurar* 'to swear'). The *Aurélio* contains the doublets *abrenunciar [ă.βrə.nũ$^{n}$.si.ˈa.rə]* and *ab-renunciar* [ăβ.ɾə.nũ$^{n}$.siˈa.rə] 'to reject disapprovingly'. In the first case, the /b+ of #ab+ forms an onset cluster with word-intial /r/, in the second case it attaches to the independent word *renunciar* 'to renounce', where the phoneme /r/'s word-initial position has caused it to be realized as [r̠] and where it reverts to [r] when it becomes the second segment in an onset consonant cluster.

**§11.5.2.1.3** The prefix #ɔb+'s emergence with its final /b+ cannot be documented in words beginning with vowels other than #o+, e.g. *obovado* 'having a peak broader than the base' (cf. *ovo* 'egg') or beginning with the consonants /p, b, g, š, m, r/. In certain rather recondite usages, such as the words *ob-piramidal* 'pyramid-shaped' and *ob-rogar* 'to oppose' (cf. *rogar* 'to plead'), traditional orthography provides a hyphen between the prefix and the stem to emphasize this form's status as a prefix to an actual word.[25] Elsewhere, before word-initial /t, d, k, f, v, s, z, ž, n, l/, the prefix and stems are not hyphenated. Examples include *obter* 'to obtain' (cf. *ter* 'to have'), *obdurar* 'to harden' (cf. *durar* 'to last'), *obcónico* 'inverted cone' (cf. *cónico* 'conical'), *obfirmar* 'to be constant'[26] (cf. *afirmar* 'to affirm'), *obviar* 'to obviate' (cf. *aviar* 'to make ready'), *obcecar* 'to obsess' (cf. *cegar* 'to blind'), *obscuro* 'obscure' (cf. *escuro* 'dark'), *objeto* 'object' (cf. *projeto* 'project'), *obnubilar* 'to cloud over' (cf. *nubiloso* 'cloudy'), *obliterar* 'to obliterate' (cf. *literário* 'literary'). On the other hand, #ɔb+'s /b+ normally evanesces both before the word-initial labials: /p, f, m/: *oprimir* 'to oppress' (cf. *reprimir* 'to repress'), *ofender* 'to offend' (cf. *defender* 'to defend'), *omitir* 'to omit' (cf. *permitir* 'to permit'). However, it also may disappear before stem-initial /t, d, k/: *ótimo* 'wonderful' (cf. *íntimo* 'intimate'), *odontose* 'tooth-loosening' (cf. *dente* 'tooth'), and *ocorrer* 'to occur' (cf. *recorrer* 'to appeal to'). Like #ab+ and #sub+ this prefix can acquire a /z/ before word-initial #t+: *ostentar* 'to show' (cf. *tentar* 'to [at]tempt'). Were it not for the loss of #ɔb+'s final /b+ and its acquisition of /z/ in the last word, linguists might reasonably propose a rule in which its /b+ disappears before [+labial] contexts, but the data point once again to these allomorphs' being lexical variants of one another and to the productive allomorph's being the one that preserves the prefix-final /b+.

**§11.5.2.1.4.0 #sub+:** There appear to be no restrictions to the prefix #sub+'s occurrence, other than before /ɲ/ and /λ/, whose occurrence

25 *Ob-piramidal* is not an everyday word, nor is *ob-rogar*.

26 According to the *Aurélio*, this word is no longer used. It does not appear in Infopédia.

word-initially is so rare as to make any prefixation highly unlikely. Its allomorphy is illustrated in Table 11.1c and §11.1.3.5

**§11.5.2.1.4.1 [sob]:** The allomorph #sob+ emerges in words such as *sobalçar* 'to raise [from low to] very high', *sobestar* 'to be lower', *sobgrave* 'less than deep register', *sobnegar* 'to cover up', and *sobpor* 'to put below'. In these and similar words, /sob/ could be instances of the preposition *sob* 'under' rather than of the prefix #sub+, which shares a common etymon with the preposition.[27]

**§11.5.2.1.4.2 [suz]:** In the forms where this suffix's final /b+ is lost, the most frequent allomorph is #suz+, whose occurrence seems to be restricted to stems that begin with #p/, #s/, and #t/: *suspeitar* 'to suspect' (cf. *peitar* 'to bribe'), *susceptível* 'susceptible' (cf. *decepção* 'deception') and *suster* 'to sustain' (cf. *conter* 'to contain'). The form #su+ never occurs before vowels, and its distribution before word-initial consonants is restricted to /d, f, p, r, s, ž/: *súdito* 'vassal' (cf. *dito* 'said'), *sufocar* 'to suffocate' (cf. *enfocar* 'to focus'), *suportar* 'to support' (cf. *aportar* 'to bear'), *surribar* 'to spade' (cf. *riba* 'edge'), *suceder* 'to happen' (cf. *ceder* 'to cede'), and *sugerir* 'to suggest' (cf. *digerir* 'to digest').

**§11.5.2.1.4.3 [sŭ]:** Finally, the form #so+ is relatively unrestricted, occurring before vowels #a/ and #ɛ/: *soabrir* 'to open slightly' (cf. *abrir* 'to open'), *soeguer* 'to raise slightly' (cf. *erguer* 'to raise') and before word-initial consonants /f, k l, m, n, p, r, t, v, ž/: *sofraldar* 'to raise' (cf. *fralda* 'shirt tail'), *socalcar* 'to stomp down' (cf. *calcar* 'to step'), *solevar* 'to raise slightly' (cf. *levar* 'to carry'), *someter* 'to submit' (cf. *meter* 'to insert'), *sonegar* 'to cover up' (cf. *negar* 'to deny'), *sopontar* 'to underline with dots' (cf. *apontar* 'to point'), *sorrir* 'to smile' (cf. *rir* 'to laugh'), *sotrancar* 'to cling' (cf. *trancar* 'to lock'), *soverter* 'to subvert' (cf. *verter* 'to pour'). Once again, there appears to be no identifiable context in which these allomorphs emerge so it seems best to consider them to be lexical variants of the prefix #sub+.

**§11.5.3 #vise+, #viz+ #vizo+:** The productive form of this negligibly productive prefix is the longer form, and the apocopated form appears only in six words, four of which are derivatives of *visconde* 'vicount'.

27 In addition, the words *sobnegar* and *sobpor* have the doublets *sonegar* 'cover up' and *supor* 'suppose'. The prefixes in these doublets are indubitably allomorphs of the prefix #sub+ rather than the preposition *sob*.

The form #vizo+ only appears in one: *vizo-rei* 'viceroy', a synonym of *vice-rei*. These forms are lexical varients of one another.

## Conclusions

### Summary

**§11.6.0 Prefixal Derivation:** This chapter began by pointing out that prefixation is essentially different from suffixation as far as the derivation of lexical items is concerned. Prefixation alone does not create specific form classes or alter stress. It accounts for semantic modification of specific roots and stems.

**§11.6.1 Productivity:** This chapter examines 50 separate prefixes whose relative frequency in the *Aurélio* is often estimated rather than as a result of piecemeal counting. This method has managed to identify which prefixes are of negligible, very low, low, moderate, high, very high, and supreme productivity. And, starting with those prefixes of negligible productivity, it examines the allophony and use of each prefix in contemporary Portuguese.

**§11.6.2 Regularity:** The chapter concludes with examinations and tentative systematization of the allomorphy of true prefixes. One set of prefixes of (largely) Greek origin, when attached to specific stems, acquires stress, which makes the words they form proparoxytones. Some Latinate prefixes undergo segmental allomorphy, some of which is conditioned by word-initial consonants and vowels and can be expressed in rules. Other prefixes' allomorphy is either so spotty, so infrequent, or so haphazard that one would be wise not to hazard rules to account for their appearance. Such suffixes' allomorphy comes from the history of Portuguese and is not productive in modern Portuguese.

### Findings and Interpretations

**§11.6.2.0 Data and Markedness:** Fully 56.00% of the 50 prefixes examined here are of negligible productivity, i.e. none of those 28 prefixes accounts for more than 0.48% of all the prefixed items under examination. Six prefixes' productivity is very low, i.e. none accounts for more than 0.85% of the prefixed items. Another seven prefixes are of low productivity, i.e. they account for 1.00% to 1.87% of the items examined. Four prefixes are of moderate productivity, i.e. accounting for at least 3.00% and no more than 5.91% of the data. Three are highly productive and account for between 6.00% and

9.35% of the data. One is of very high productivity (10.07% of all the data). And the most productive prefix (#a+) is of supreme productivity, with some 7,944 tokens accounting for 25.11% of all the data. Of course the information content of these prefixes is usually inversely related to their frequency—the higher the prefix's frequency, the less specificity it conveys.

**§11.6.2.1** As was the case with the segmental phonemes and the deriving suffixes, a minority of the prefixes accounts for the majority of the data. The 34 prefixes of negligible and very low productivity account for 10.84% of the data; the seven of low productivity 9.81, the four moderate 17.33%, the four high 37.01%, and the one very high 10.07%. The 16 prefixes of low to supreme productivity account for 89.16% of the entire dataset.

**§11.6.2.2** Remarkably, it turns out that there is a positive correlation between the more productive (low to supreme) prefixes' segmental markedness and their frequency. The negligibly productive prefixes averaged 3.05 segments per prefix with an average of 6.68 positive specifications per prefix. Those of very low productivity have a segmental average of 3.17, and their positive specification average was 6.17. Those of low productivity averaged 3.57 segments and 7.57 posititive specificatons; those of moderate productivity, 2.50 segments and 5.50 positive specifications; high and very high productivity, 2.25 segments and 3.50 positive specifications; the supremely productive prefix had one segment with one positive specification. The more productive prefixal data best reflect the general principles of markedness: they consistently demonstrate a synergistic relationship between items' phonological complexity and their frequency of occurrence.

**§11.6.3 Allomorphy:** Prefixes' segmental allomorphy motivates five rules: Rule 11.2 deletes the final /n+ of #in+ and #kon+ before nasals, laterals, and rhotics; Rule 11.3 deletes the /n+ of #kon+ before word-initial vowels; Rule 11.4 deletes the final /z+ of #diz+ before stem-initial segments /ž, l, m, n, r, f, v/; Rule 11.5 adds a /z/ to the prefix #ab+ when it attaches to stem-initial /t/ and /k/. The remaining allomorphy was considered to be lexical in origin—the prefixes have a common source but they only appear in specific words, and the truncated or modified forms of these prefixes are historical artificts rather than productive morphemes in contemporary Portuguese.

## So What?

**§11.6.4** Prefixes combine with stems to allow Portuguese speakers to create words, and in doing this they derive words. Many are more lexical than grammatical and display almost insignificant allomorphy—especially when compared to the highly productive derivational suffixes. They do not affect their words' form class, but they are essential for Portuguese because they are instrumental in the expansion of the language's vocabulary. Prefixes contribute to this language's genius because, along with a finite set of roots and suffixes, they enable its speakers to express an infinity of concepts with a finite set of forms whose specific denotations can be so indeterminate as to be meaningless when considered alone.

## Appendix A Prefixes, Stems, and Roots: Meaning

**§11A.0** This incursion into meaning and its association with prefixation begins with Table 11A.1, which illustrates the role of prefixation in the formation of words from the roots #sɛd+, #duk+, and #plik+.[28]

28 Most of the words formed by prefixation examined here are infinitives. They represent both verbs and the myriad deverbal nominals (and, even, adverbs) derived from verbal stems and roots. Take, e.g., the verbal stem #plik++a#: derivational prefixes and suffixes create verbs (e.g. *aplica* '3rd applies'), nouns (e.g. *aplicação* 'application'), adjectives (e.g. *aplicável* 'applicable'), and adverbs (e.g. *aplicadamente* 'applicably').

Table 11A.1 Infinitives Created from Prefixes and Roots

| #sɛd+ | | | #duk+ | | | #plik+ | | |
|---|---|---|---|---|---|---|---|---|
| Prefix | Infinitive | Gloss | Prefix | Infinitive | Gloss | Prefix | Infinitive | Gloss |
| Ø | **ceder** | cede | Ø | *** | *** | Ø | **plicar** | fold |
| #a+ | **aceder** | accede | #a+ | **aduzir** | bring | #a+ | **aplicar** | apply |
| #pre+ | **preceder** | precede | #pre+ | *** | *** | #pre+ | *** | *** |
| #ante+ | **anteceder** | antecede | #ante+ | *** | *** | #ante+ | *** | *** |
| #kon+ | **conceder** | concede | #kon+ | **conduzir** | drive | #kon+ | **complicar** | complicate |
| #pro+ | **proceder** | proceed | #pro+ | **produzir** | produce | #pro+ | *** | *** |
| #retro+ | **retroceder** | go back | #retro+ | *** | *** | #retro+ | *** | *** |
| #inter+ | **interceder** | intercede | #inter+ | *** | *** | #inter+ | *** | *** |
| #sub+ | **suceder** | happen | #sub+ | *** | *** | #sub+ | **suplicar** | beg |
| #ez+ | **exceder** | exceed | #ez+ | **eduzir** | remove | #ez+ | **explicar** | explain |
| #ab+ | **absceder** | abscess | #ab+ | **abduzir** | sever | #ab+ | *** | *** |
| #tranz+ | *** | *** | #tranz+ | **traduzir** | translate | #tranz+ | *** | *** |
| #de+ | *** | *** | #de+ | **deduzir** | deduct | #de+ | *** | *** |
| #re+ | *** | *** | #re+ | **reduzir** | reduce | #re+ | **replicar** | reply |
| #se+ | *** | *** | #se+ | **seduzir** | seduce | #se+ | *** | *** |
| #intro+ | *** | *** | #intro+ | **introduzir** | introduce | #intro+ | *** | *** |
| #in+ | *** | *** | #in+ | **induzir** | induce | #in+ | **implicar** | imply |

**§11A.1.0** In Table 11A.1 15 different prefixes combine with the three roots in question to form independent words. All the roots are preceded by the boundary symbol #, which indicates that they may occur in word-initial position. The infinitives *ceder* and *plicar* (third line of Table 11A.1) are uncontraversally preceded by # since they actually occur without prefixes. The theoretically possible **ducar*, which could mean 'to lead as a duke leads', has not been documented, but this root's word-initial /d/ occurs in words like *duque* 'duke' and derivatives thereof: *ducado* 'region of a duke's authority' and *ducal* 'pertaining to a duke'. These words, plus the words *educar* 'to educate' and *ducto* 'duct' and *dúctil* 'docile' also provide evidence for the root-final /k/ of #duk+.[29]

**§11A.1.1** In analyzing Table 11A.1's two infinitives that have no prefix (i.e. *ceder* and *plicar*), one could say that the morphemes #sɛd+ and #plik+ mean something like 'give up' and 'fold', respectively. The root #duk+ may denote 'subordinate leadership'.[30] But an examination of the words formed with the different prefixes shows that sometimes combinations of prefixes and roots yield meanings that transcend whatever basic meaning one might ascribe to both the prefixes and the roots.

**§11A.1.2 The root #sɛd+:** If the root of *ceder* 'to cede' means 'give up',[31] there is some semantic relationship between *ceder* and *aceder* 'to accede' as well as between the latter infinitive and *conceder* 'to concede' since in both cases these derived infinitives suggest a 'giving up of a position or point of view'. On the other hand, whatever meanings #sɛd+ may have in words like *preceder*, *anteceder*, *proceder*, *interceder*, *suceder*, and *exceder*, the notion of 'giving in' or 'giving up' is not there.

**§11A.1.3 The root #duk+:** Contrary to #sɛd+, #duk+'s suggestion of leadership or stewardship is evident in the ten prefixed words using this root. Stretching the point somewhat, they indicate, respectively, *aduzir*, i.e. 'a leading to', *conduzir*, 'a leading with', *produzir*, ' a leading from nothing to something', *eduzir*, 'a leading out', *traduzir*, 'a leading

29 The mutation of root-final /k/ into /z/ is addressed in §14.2.1.0–2.2.

30 Dukes (i.e. *duques* #duk++e#<z#>) are held to be second in command to monarchs, unless they lead an independent duchy.

31 The *Aurélio* lists eleven different usages for the verb *ceder*: 'to transfer rights, to lend, to give in, to condescend, to surrender, to renounce, to break, to acquiesce, to give way, to decrease, to loosen'. These are, clearly, metaphorical extensions of 'to cede'.

from one framework to another', *deduzir,* 'a leading from', *seduzir,* 'a leading to one's self',[32] *introduzir,* 'a leading into something', *induzir,* 'a leading from one state of being to another', and *educar,* 'to educate' i.e. 'a leading out [from ignorance]'. Such origins and associations are metaphorical, however.

**§11A.1.4 The root #plik+:** Once more if one stretches the point one can see the metaphoric origins of the prefixed words with this root:[33] *aplicar* 'to apply' is 'to fold purposefully to one's gain', *complicar* is 'to fold repeatedly to make matters less elegant', *suplicar* is 'to fold oneself beneath someone else in petition', *explicar* is 'to take a complicated item or concept apart piece by piece'(i.e. 'to unfold'), *replicar* is 'to fold against someone's position', and *implicar* is 'to fold into'.

**§11A.1.5.0** Before considering the prefixes' meanings, examining one more root, #pon+, the root of *pôr* 'to put' will be instructive.[34] This root combines with 21 different prefixes in the formation of diverse but related words, as Table 11A.2 demonstrates:

**Table 11A.2** Formations on the Root #pon+

| Prefix | Infinitive | Gloss | Prefix | Infinitive | Gloss |
|---|---|---|---|---|---|
| Ø | **pôr** | put | #žuzta+ | **justapor*** | juxtapose |
| #a+ | **apor** | appose | #kon+ | **compor** | compose |
| #ante+ | **antepor*** | put before | #ob+ | **opor** | oppose |
| #kontra> | **contrapor*** | counter | #pɔz+ | **pospor** | postpone |

32 The prefix of *seduzir* is #se+, a form derived from the reflexive 3rd person pronoun. When people seduce others they metaphorically bring them toward themselves (to be captivated or exploited) in any number of ways. There are at least two other words where this very same #se+ is assuredly a prefix: *semostrador* 'a show-off' #se+#mɔztr++a#+dor#<e+<Ø# and *semovente* 'self propelled' #se+#mɔb++e#+nt++e#<Ø#.

33 The *Aurélio* indicates that *plicar,* in addition to indicating folding, can denote wrinkling and the writing of diacritic marks as well as the use of primes in mathematic notation. The verb *plicar* in any of these usages is rare. Indeed, *franzir* 'to wrinkle' and more native doublets *pregar* 'to nail' and *preguear* 'to fold' are more common.

34 For justification of #pon+ as the root of *pôr,* see §7.4.5.2.1 and Table 7.7e. The asterisked entries in Table 11A.2 are compound rather than derived infinitives.

Table 11A.2 Continued

| Prefix | Infinitive | Gloss | Prefix | Infinitive | Gloss |
|---|---|---|---|---|---|
| #de+ | **depor** | depose | #pre+ | **prepor** | put before |
| #diz+ | **dispor** | dispose | #pro+ | **propor** | propose |
| #entre> | **entrepor*** | separate | #re+ | **repor** | replace |
| #eztra# | **extrapor*** | discard | #soto+ | **sotopor** | omit |
| #ez+ | **expor** | expose | #sub+ | **sobpor, subpor, supor** | underestimate, put under, suppose |
| #in+ | **impor** | impose | #super+ | **superpor, sobrepor*** | superpose, overlap |
| #inter+ | **interpor*** | put between | #tranz+ | **transpor*** | transpose |
| | | | **Double Prefixes** | | |
| | 1st prefix | 2nd Prefix | Infinitve | Gloss | |
| | #kontra> | #pro+ | **contrapropor** | counterpropose | |
| | #dez+ | #kon + | **descompor** | take apart | |
| | #in+ | *#diz+* | **indispor** | perturb | |

**§11A.1.5.1 The root #pon+:** The *Aurélio* offers 70 different meanings for the infinitive *pôr*. They include: 'to place, impel, concentrate, impose, translate, swear or affirm, give up, lay eggs, decide on something, (the sun's) setting, to become'. Many of the uses are metaphoric extensions of 'to put', but some such as 'to become', 'lay eggs', or 'sun's setting' are totally idiomatic. The point here is that the derived words' stem, indeed the stem's root, even without prefixes, does not have a constant meaning. And one can see this root's indeterminate meanings in some of these derived words. For example, *depor* can mean 'to put aside, remove from power, declare in court, abdicate, express, prove'; *expor* can mean 'to put at risk, export, tell, explain, reveal'; *repor* can mean 'to put back, return, recover'; and *supor* can mean 'to hypothesize, imagine, imply, impute'. Thus, the root of all these words, #pon+, when it occurs as a word-initial morpheme or as a prefixed morpheme, does not have a definite, easily determined meaning.

**§11A.1.6.0** All this indicates roots' meanings (both when they are the sole item providing semantic content for a word and when they combine with prefixes to form new words) are not totally constant. The prefixes used in Tables 11A.1–2 do not yield anything resembling constant meanings. Table 11A.3 juxtaposes the four infinitives examined thus far, as well as words derived from them:

Table 11A.3 Prefixes and Roots

| | #sɛd+ | | #duk+ | | # plik+ | | #pon+ | |
|---|---|---|---|---|---|---|---|---|
| **Prefix** | **Infinitive** | **Gloss** | **Infinitive** | **Gloss** | **Infinitive** | **Gloss** | **Infinitive** | **Gloss** |
| Ø | **ceder** | cede | | | **plicar** | fold | **pôr** | put |
| #a+ | **aceder** | accede | **aduzir** | bring | **aplicar** | apply | **apor** | appose |
| #pre+ | **preceder** | precede | | | | | **prepor** | put before |
| #ante+ | **anteceder** | happen before | | | | | **antepor** | put before |
| #kon+ | **conceder** | concede | **conduzir** | drive | **complicar** | complicate | **compor** | compose |
| #pro+ | **proceder** | proceed | **produzir** | produce | | | **propor** | propose |
| #retro+ | **retroceder** | go back | | | | | | |
| #inter+ | **interceder** | intercede | | | | | **interpor** | interpose |
| #sub+ | **suceder** | happen | | | **suplicar** | beg | **supor** | suppose |
| #ɛz+ | **exceder** | exceed | **eduzir** | remove | **explicar** | explain | **expor** | expose |
| #tranz+ | | | **traduzir** | translate | | | **transpor** | transpose |
| #de+ | | | **deduzir** | deduct | | | **depor** | depose |
| #re+ | | | **reduzir** | reduce | **replicar** | reply | **repor** | replace |
| #se+ | | | **seduzir** | seduce | | | | |
| #intro+ | | | **introduzir** | introduce | | | | |
| #in+ | | | **induzir** | induce | **implicar** | imply | **impor** | impose |
| #diz+ | | | | | | | **dispor** | dispose |
| #ɔb+ | | | | | | | **opor** | oppose |
| #pɔz+ | | | | | | | **pospor** | postpone |
| #soto+ | | | | | | | **sotopor** | omit |
| #super+ | | | | | | | **superpor** | superpose |

**§11A.1.6.1** There are only three prefixes #a+, #kon+, and #ɛz+ that apply to all four roots. The prefix #a+ denotes a certain directionality, purpose, or goal to the stems to which it applies. The prefix #kon+ in *conceder* and *conduzir* suggests that the subject of said verbs would be involved with another entity in the action denoted. With the words *complicar* and *compor* the prefix appears to indicate addition of items or concepts to a particular state of affairs. The prefix #ɛz+ when added to #sɛd+ makes the root convey a meaning that is the diametric opposite of 'giving up'—it denotes going beyond an expectation. When it attaches to #duk+, it suggests removal from something. In *explicar*, it indicates an undoing, and in *expor* it indicates a bringing forth. There is little consistency in the meanings these prefixes have added to the roots in question.[35]

**§11A.1.6.2** The low productivity prefix #sub+, the moderately productive prefix #pro+ and the very highly productive #in+ and #re+ appear on three of the four: In the verb *suceder* the prefix #sub+ adds the notion of happening, following, triumphing, replacing, being summoned. In *proceder*, the prefix #pro+ indicates a continuation, an imperfective rather than perfective action, whereas in *produzir* it indicates a perfective creation of something, i.e. a result of some sort of action. Conversely, in *propor* this prefix suggests an incipient perfective suggestion, i.e. a beginning. The prefix #re+ when added to #duk+ indicates a diminishing, when added to #plik+ it indicates a comeback to some assertion, and with #pon+ it indicates a restoration. The prefix #in+ indicates causation with *induzir*, suggestion with *implicar*, and arbitrary authority over someone or something in *impor*.

**§11A.1.6.3** The prefixes that recur with only two of the four roots are the negligibly productive #ante+, the low productive #prɛ+ and #tranz+, and the moderately productive #de+. Consistent with its scant usage and, thus, unambiguous denotation, #ante+ indicates prior activity or placement. Likewise #prɛ+ denotes prior activity in *preceder* and *prepor*. And #tranz+ with both #duk+ and #pon+ indicates going from one set of circumstances to another. With #de+, owing to its much higher productivity (9.45 times that of #ante+, 2.15 times that of #tranz+, and 1.76 times that of #prɛ+), the meanings it adds to #duk+ and #pon+ are more vague. The verb *deduzir* can mean 'to conclude

35 Two of these prefixes (#kon+ and #ɛz+) are moderately productive, #a+ is supremely productive. See Table 11.1b.

from a set of data, diminish, provide justification', whereas *depor* can mean 'to leave off, overthrow, abandon, testify, abdicate, express, place, get to the (metaphorical) bottom of something'. Thus, the semantic relationship that #de+ has with #duk+ is very different from the one it has with #pon+. Clearly the meanings these prefixes convey as they attach to different roots can at times have tenuous semantic affinities with one another.

**§11A.1.6.4** A certain semantic alchemy obtains in the prefixation of these (and many other) roots, and this alchemy produces meanings that often transcend the sum of each different word's significant, non-inflectional, parts. In a morphophonological grammar of Portuguese, prefixed words should appear in the lexicon as idioms, and, for the purposes of this study, the 'meanings' that prefixes and the stems to which they attach are not of primary concern.[36]

## Appendix B The Grammar of Prefixal Derivation

**§11B.0** Because the rules in this chapter are so few, and because their order actually follows the order they appear (save Rule 11.1), they appear with the morphophonemic rules preceding the one phonological rule—nasal contoidal assimilation.

36 There are, however, exceptions to the notion that there can be scant consistency in the meaning of prefixed words. As Table 11A.2 demonstrates, certain prefixed words can receive additional prefixes: e.g. *contrapropor*, *descompor*, and *indispor*. Their structures are: #kontra>#pro+#pon++e#+r#+e+,#dez+#kon+#pon++e#+r#+e+,and#in+#diz+#pon++e#+r#+e+. The infinitive *exceder* #ez+#sɛd++e#+r#+e+ can acquire the morpheme #sobre>: *sobreexceder* 'to exceed even more beyond expectation'. Quite likely #re+ can be freely added to several of the prefixed words formed from the root #sɛd+, i.e. *reexceder* 'to once more exceed', *reconceder* 'to concede once more'. It can also be added to #prefix+#plik+ in words such as *reexplicar* 'to re-explain', *reaplicar* 'to reapply', *recomplicar* 'to complicate all over again'—as it can on words derived from #duk+: *reconduzir* 'to conduct once more' and *reproduzir* 'to reproduce', and from those derived from the combination of #prefix+ and the root #pon+: *recompor* 'to recompose'. Prefixes added to already prefixed words tend to have more constant meanings, although many of the words examined in this note have a semantic life of their own and have several meanings. For example, *descompor* can mean 'to upset, put in disarray, undo, undress, decompose, remove adornments, censure' and the word *decompor* can mean 'to identify constituent parts, to analyze, change, upset, rot, modify'.

**Rule 11.2 Pre-contoid Nasal Effacement (Prefixes #kon+ and #in+):**

$$\begin{bmatrix} +\text{contoid} \\ +\text{nasal} \end{bmatrix} \rightarrow \emptyset \,/\, \_\_ \; + \# \begin{bmatrix} +\text{contoid} \\ -\text{fricative} \\ -\text{occlusion} \end{bmatrix} X \#$$

Rule 11.2 deletes the final /n+ in the prefixes #in+ and #kon+ before any rule of pre-consonantal vowel nasalization or nasal assimilation takes place.

**Rule 11.3: #kon+'s Loss of /n+:**

$$\begin{bmatrix} +\text{contoid} \\ +\text{nasal} \end{bmatrix} \rightarrow \emptyset \,/\, \_\_ \; +\# \, [-\text{contoid}] \, X \#$$

Likewise, Rule 11.3, which applies to only one prefix, applies before any pre-consonantal vocalic nasalization occurs.

**Rule 11.4 Loss of /z+ in the Prefix #diz+:**

$$\begin{bmatrix} +\text{fricative} \\ -\text{high} \\ -\text{labial} \\ -\text{surd} \end{bmatrix} + \rightarrow \emptyset \,/\, \_ \; \# \begin{bmatrix} +\text{contoid} \\ -\text{occlusion} \\ \left\{ \begin{matrix} \begin{bmatrix} -\text{surd} \\ -\text{dorsal} \end{bmatrix} \\ +\text{labial} \end{matrix} \right\} \end{bmatrix}$$

Rule 11.4 uses a set of exceptions to delete the /z+ before stem-initial /ž, l, m, r, f, v/.

**Rule 11.5 The Prefix #ab+'s Acquisition of /z/:**

$$\#ab+ \rightarrow \#abz+ \ / \_\_ \begin{pmatrix} +\text{occlusion} \\ +\text{surd} \\ \text{-labial} \end{pmatrix}$$

Rule 11.5 adds a /z/ to the prefix #ab+ when it occurs before #k/ and #t/.

**Rule 11.1 Nasal Assimilation:**

$$\begin{pmatrix} +\text{nasal} \\ +\text{contoid} \end{pmatrix} \rightarrow \begin{pmatrix} \alpha\ \text{labial} \\ \beta\ \text{dorsal} \\ \gamma\ \text{palatal} \end{pmatrix} \ / \_\_ \begin{pmatrix} +\text{contoid} \\ \alpha\ \text{labial} \\ \beta\ \text{dorsal} \\ \gamma\ \text{palatal} \end{pmatrix}$$

Rule 11.1 applies to /n/ since it is the only nasal phoneme that occurs preconsonantally. It is a phonetic rule that applies after a rule that obligatorily (for most pronunciations) nasalizes all vowels that precede syllable-final /n/. After this assimilation takes place, a rule necessarily weakens syllable-final nasal contoids, and another optionally deletes them.

**§11B.1.0** The following four tables demonstrate the allomorphy of the prefixes #in+, #kon+, #diz+, and #ab+—the only ones with allmorphs that are predictable from the word-initial phonemes they precede.[37] In all cases, the stems are not analyzed since the determinant of these prefixes' allomorphy is their initial segment.

37 Chapter 12 addresses the 'prefixes' (i.e. compounding elements) that acquire (proparoxytone) stress before specific compounding elements.

**Table 11B.1** Loss of Prefix-Final /n+ (#in+ and #kon+)[a]

| | **irregular** | **corréu** | **ilimitar** |
|---|---|---|---|
| | #in+#regular# | #kon+#rɛu# | #in+#limitar# |
| **R. 11.2** | #i+#regular# | #ko+#rɛu# | #i+#limitar |
| **R. 11.3** | *** | *** | *** |
| **R. 11.4** | *** | *** | *** |
| **R. 11.5** | *** | *** | *** |
| **R. 11.1** | *** | *** | *** |
| **Ph.** | [i.r̲ə.ɣu'lar] | [ko.'r̲ɛ$^{ŭ}$] | [i.lĩ.mi.'tar] |
| | **colidir** | **imenso** | **comarca** |
| | #kon++lidir# | #in+#menso# | #kon+#marka# |
| **R. 11.2** | #ko++lidir# | #i+#menso# | #ko+#marka# |
| **R. 11.3** | *** | *** | *** |
| **R. 11.4** | *** | *** | *** |
| **R. 11.5** | *** | *** | *** |
| **R. 11.1** | *** | *** | *** |
| **Ph.** | [kŭ.li.'ðir] | [ĩ.'mẽ$^{n}$.sŭ] | [kŭ.'mar.kă] |

a The words in Table 11B.1 mean 'irregular, co-prisoner, go beyond limits, collide, immense, bailiwick'.

**§11B.1.1** The words in Table 11B.1 illustrate the loss of /n+ in the two prefixes in which it occurs as the final segment, #in+ and #kon+. Only one morphophonemic rule is necessary for words such as these to be processed by the strictly phonological section of this grammar. The forms *irregular* and *corréu* acquire their [r̲] because after # (the word-initial boundary symbol), /r/ → [r̲].

**Table 11B.2** Loss, Preservation, and Assimilation of Prefix-Final /n+ (#in+ and #kon+)[a]

| | **Loss** | | |
|---|---|---|---|
| | **inervar** | **comadre** | **coirmão** |
| | #in+#nɛrvar# | #kon+#madre# | #kon+#irmão# |
| **R. 11.2** | #i+#nɛrvar# | #ko+#madre# | *** |
| **R. 11.3** | *** | *** | #ko+#irmão# |
| **R. 11.4** | *** | *** | *** |
| **R. 11.5** | *** | *** | *** |
| **R. 11.1** | *** | *** | *** |
| **Ph.** | [ĩ.nər.'var] | [kŭ.'ma.drə] | [kŭ.ir.'mɐ̃̆$^{ŭ}$] |

*(Continued)*

Table 11B.2 Continued

| | Preserve | Assimilate | |
|---|---|---|---|
| | **inútil** | **infeliz** | **congraçar** |
| R. 11.2 | #in+#útil# | #in+#feliz# | #kon+#grasar# |
| R. 11.3 | *** | *** | *** |
| R. 11.4 | *** | *** | *** |
| R. 11.5 | *** | *** | *** |
| R. 11.1 | *** | #iŋ+#feliz# | [koŋ+#grasar# |
| Ph. | [ĩ.ˈnu.tiɫ] | [ĩ$^{m}$.fə.ˈliš] | [kõ$^{ŋ}$.grǎ.ˈsar] |

a The words in Table 11B.2 mean 'innervate, godmother (cf. *compadre* 'godfather'), first cousin (literally 'with sibling'), useless, unhappy, to reconcile'.

**§11B.1.2** Whereas the /n+ of #in+ emerges when its stem begins with a vowel, the /n+ of #kon+ disappears in that environment: cf. *coirmão* and *inútil.*

**Table 11B.3** Loss of Prefix-Final /z+ (#diz+)[a]

| | **digerir** | **dilatar** | **dimanar** |
|---|---|---|---|
| | #diz+#žerir# | #diz++latar# | #diz+#manar# |
| R. 11.2 | *** | *** | *** |
| R. 11.3 | *** | *** | *** |
| R. 11.4 | #di+#žerir# | #di++latar# | #di+#manar# |
| R. 11.5 | *** | *** | *** |
| R. 11.1 | *** | *** | *** |
| Ph. | [di.žə.ˈrir] | [di.lǎ.ˈtar] | [dĩ.mã̌.ˈnar] |
| | **direto** | **difamar** | **divergir** |
| | #diz++rɛto# | #diz++famar# | #diz++vɛržir# |
| R. 11.2 | *** | *** | *** |
| R. 11.3 | *** | *** | *** |
| R. 11.4 | #di++rɛto# | #di++famar# | #di++vɛržir# |
| R. 11.5 | *** | *** | *** |
| R. 11.1 | *** | *** | *** |
| Ph. | [di.ˈrɛ.tǔ] | [di.fã̌.ˈmar] | [di.vər.ˈžir] |

a The words in Table 11B.3 mean 'to digest, to expand, to spurt, straight, to slander, to diverge'.

**§11B.1.3** The word *direto* is obviously related to *reto* 'right (triangle), righteous'. These forms emerge with the 'multiple' [r̲] because they are word-initial. The reason *direto* contains /r/ rather than [r̲] is because the boundary affinitiy between the prefix and the stem is ++ rather than +#.

**Table 11B.4** Prefix-Final /z+ Preserved and Assimilated (#diz+), Acquisition of Prefix-Final /z/ (#ab+)[a]

| | **disopia** | **disgregar** | **distorcer** |
|---|---|---|---|
| | #diz+#ɔpia# | #diz+#gregar# | #diz+#tɔrser# |
| **R. 11.2** | *** | *** | *** |
| **R. 11.3** | | *** | *** |
| **R. 11.4** | *** | *** | *** |
| **R. 11.5** | *** | *** | *** |
| **R. 11.1** | *** | *** | *** |
| **Ph.** | [di.zŭ.ˈpi.ă] | [diž.grə.ˈɣar] | [diš.tŭr.ˈser] |
| | **abster** | **absconder** | |
| | #ab+#ter# | #ab++konder# | |
| **R. 11.2** | *** | *** | |
| **R. 11.3** | *** | *** | |
| **R. 11.4** | *** | *** | |
| **R. 11.5** | #ab+z#ter# | #ab+z+konder# | |
| **R. 11.1** | *** | *** | |
| **Ph.** | [ă.βəš.ˈter] | [ă.βəš.õ$^{n}$.ˈder] | |

a The words in Table 11B.4 mean 'defective eyesight, to come appart, to distort, to abstain, to abscond'.

**§11B.1.4** Save *abster* and *absconder*, these forms are transparent. For *abster* and *absconder*, the epenthetic /z/ is a transitional segment—neither part of the prefix nor the suffix.

# 12 Compound Nominals

## Introduction

**§12.0.0** Cunha (76) defines composition as the formation of new words through the union of two or more roots (*radicais*). He maintains that compound words ‘always’ represent unique and independent meanings that may have nothing to do with their components’ meanings. His examples are the nominals *criado-mudo* ‘dumb-waiter’, *mil-folhas* ‘napoleon’, *vitória-régia* ‘Victoria’ (a flower) and *pé-de-galinha* ‘chicken’s foot’ (i.e. crow’s feet)—three of which belie his assertion. A dumb-waiter is a piece of furniture on which a person can rest belongings and drape clothing (i.e. it functions as a servant), a napoleon is a pastry made of many (though perhaps not a thousand) leaves of dough per unit, and ‘crow’s feet’ is a metaphor for wrinkles resembling bird footprints at the corner of a person’s eye. These are all motivated metaphors. The compound *vitória-régia* is a proper noun. The data collected in writing this chapter on compound nominals indicate that such is the case with the great majority of true compound nominals: they are either motivated metaphors or proper nouns.

**§12.0.1** This chapter distinguishes between true compound nominals and others that consist of at least two meaningful elements that are neither prefixes nor suffixes. The latter forms are ‘semi-compounds’. Examples of semi-compounds include nominals such as *psicologia* ‘psychology’ and *equívoco* ‘ambiguous, mistake(n)’. Like true compounds these words’ meanings are motivated from the meanings associated with their constituent elements #psik+ ‘mind’ #lɔg++i++a# ‘study’ and #ɛk+ ‘equal’ #vɔk+<o# ‘voice’.[1] Words such as these, nonetheless, are essentially different from the examples in the previous paragraph.

**§12.0.2** For the purposes of this morphophonemic grammar, Portuguese true compound words combine two or more independent words (including prepositions) to form a new word. The meanings of true compound words are, more often than not, transparent or at least motivated. In addition, both the nominals and verbs that combine to form true compounds normally continue to bear stress on their tonic

1 The second elements in these two examples begin with # because the morphemes in them can be word-initial: e.g. *lógica* ‘logic’ and *vocal* ‘vocal’.

syllables. Minimally, their first element bears some vestige of the word-final morphological properties it has as an independent word: gender and number in nominals as well as 3rd person singular present indicative in verbs. And the relationship between or among members of true compound words may reflect the relationship they would have were they syntactically juxtaposed, i.e. they often agree in number and gender. Contrariwise, semi-compounds have only one stressed syllable, and only the second element bears suffixes indicating the entire word's gender and number.

**§12.0.3** For the most part, the formation of both true compounds and semi-compounds is lexical rather than grammatical. Thus, even though there are discernible patterns in their makeup, these patterns are not so systematic that one can account for most forms with rules that apply throughout a category, as is the case with inflection and, to a lesser extent, derivation.

**§12.0.4** The compounds and semi-compounds examined here are bona fide lexical items. The *Aurélio's* compilers include them as separate entries in that dictionary and, indeed, *pace* Cunha, from time-to-time one finds compounds whose meanings transcend the sum of their constituent parts' meanings.[2]

**§12.0.5** Notwithstanding the lexical (non-grammatical) nature of many compounds and semi-compounds, there are two types of compound words whose formation is regular: adverbs ending in *–mente* and certain diminutives ending in *–zinho*. And, even though nouns ending in *–zinho* and adverbs formed with *–mente* are grammatically formed and immediately intelligible from their constituent parts, the examples in this study (unless otherwise indicated) come from the *Aurélio* as lexical items representing specific words.

2 The criterion for including the compound words in this study comes from their appearance in the *Aurélio* as independent lexical entries. Of course not all lexical entries are words. True words have a stressed syllable and can both begin and end an utterance. The *Aurélio* includes entries for prefixes, suffixes, and morphemes (e.g. #fisio+. 'physio-') whose occurrence is constrained and which bear no stress. These entries do not figure in the tabulations of particular compounding elements' productivity—only actual words count.

## Lexical True Compounds

**§12.1.0** Lexical true compounds are those lexical items that obviously consist of at least two words (sometimes three or more, including prepositions and articles) and conform to the criteria set forth in §12.0.1: semantic motivation with or without transparency, two tonic syllables,[3] inflectional properties (gender, number, theme vowel) on both elements. There is no rule (semantic, morphological, or syntactic) for lexical compound formation; however, their formation usually reflects syntactic patterns, but in certain cases compound formation appears to flout grammatical rules of agreement.

**§12.1.1** Of the patterns Cunha (77–78) identifies for compound words, this chapter examines: nouns formed by juxtaposition: noun + noun, noun + preposition + noun, noun + adjective, adjective + noun, verb + noun as well as combinations of adverb + adjective, adverb + infinitive. Table 12.1 displays the lexical items studied here:

3 As Cunha points out (77), there are ordinary words whose compound nature has disappeared in contemporary Portuguese: e.g. *aguardente* 'brandy' literally 'burning water' *água* 'water' *ardente* 'burning' and *pernalta* 'wading bird' literally *perna* 'leg' and *alta* 'high', and *peralta* 'fop' literally *pera* 'goatee' and *alta*. Words such as these are semi-compounds since they have only one stressed syllable and appear to reflect their gender and number only word-finally since the word-initial /a/ of these adjectives causes the word-final /a/ (+a#) of the noun to disappear. Even though the final +a# of the adjectival part of these words agrees with the 1st element's [+feminine] gender, the word *peralta* applies both to male and female referents.

**Table 12.1** Sample Compounding Words[a]

| Nouns | Gloss | 1st Element | 2nd Element | Verbs | Gloss | 1st Element |
|---|---|---|---|---|---|---|
| **pau** | stick, wood | 174 | 38 | **guarda** | 3rd guards | 80 |
| **peixe** | fish | 72 | 15 | **papa** | 3rd eats | 54 |
| **pé** | foot, plant | 67 | 26 | **passa** | 3rd passes | 28 |
| **água** | water | 65 | 87 | **tira** | 3rd retrives | 19 |
| **mulher** | woman | 31 | 4 | | **Adjective** | |
| **papagaio** | parrot | 27 | 12 | **alto** | high | 30 |
| **amor** | love | 21 | 10 | | **Adverbs** | |
| **mãe** | mother | 17 | 9 | **mal** | poorly | 147 |
| **pai** | father | 15 | 1 | **bem** | well | 48 |
| **cavalo** | horse | 15 | 29 | | **Preposition** | |
| **homem** | man | 13 | 12 | **sem** | without | 15 |
| **Maria** | Maria | 12 | 5 | | **Particle** | |
| **porco** | pig | 9 | 22 | **não** | no, non- | 80 |

a The elements in Table 12.1 were chosen intuitively. Among the nouns (M=62.15, SD=59.51, Z=2.46), *pau* is the most productive and the only outlier in the set. The verbs (M=46.25, SD=27.51, Z=1.48) have no outlier. Because these elements do not constitute a complete set, it makes no sense to provide an evaluation of their relative productivity.

The left side of Table 12.1 contains the 13 nouns under scrutiny here. As compounding elements all these nouns can appear as the first or second element in compound words. The right hand side of Table 12.1 displays the other elements that can appear in compound nominals. When nouns compound with verbs, prepositions and particles, they are always the second element. With adjectives they may be either the first or second element, and when adjectives occur with adverbs they are the second element.

**§12.1.2.0** Save *papagaio* and *Maria*, the nominals chosen for this section are among the *Aurélio*'s 3,000 most common words. Of the verbs, only *papar* 'to eat' is not among the prominent 3,000, and *mal*, *sem*, and *não* do not appear there either. Every example in the tables containing these compounds appears in the *Aurélio*, which establishes their status as independent words regardless of how idioimatic, metaphorical, motivated, or transparent they may be.

**§12.1.2.1** As a morphophonological treatise, this chapter does not delve at any depth into the semantics and pragmatics involved in compound nominals' formation. Readers familiar with the Luso-Brazilian world may want to ponder these words' formation and their use as idioms (i.e. combinations of words whose meaning cannot be derived from the sum of their parts), as pet names, epithets, euphemisms, and proper nouns pertaining plants and animals. Examples come from all levels of speech: from the erudite to the folk to the jocular. When the *Aurélio* considers a word to be peculiarly Brazilian, a (B) follows it, when peculiar to Portugal a (P) follows. Both elements' gender and number are indicated in these words.

**§12.1.2.2** Table 12.2a contains compound nouns in which the nouns of Table 12.1 are the first element:

**Table 12.2a Noun-Noun Compounds**[a]

| Type 1 | | | | | | | |
|---|---|---|---|---|---|---|---|
| | 1st Element | Literal Gloss | Gloss | ±F. | P-P | P-Ø | Ø-P |
| **pau** | pau-bala (-F, +F) | wood-bullet | finger top | -F | ✓ | *** | *** |
| **água** | água-mãe (+F, +F) | water-mother | mother liquor | F | ✓ | *** | *** |
| **mulher** | mulher-dama (B) (+F,+F) | woman-lady | prostitute | F | ✓ | *** | *** |
| **papagaio** | papagaio-caboclo (B) (-F, -F) | parrot-bumpkin | parrot species | -F | ✓ | *** | *** |
| **homem** | homem-hora (-F, +F) | man-hour | man hour | -F | ✓ | *** | *** |
| **porco** | porco-espinho (-F, -F) | pig-spine | porcupine | -F | ✓ | *** | *** |
| Type 2 | | | | | | | |
| **peixe** | peixe-cabra (-F, +F) | fish-goat | sea robin | -F | ✓ | ✓ | *** |
| **Maria** | maria-fumaça (B) (+F, +F) | Maria smoke | steam locomotive | F | ✓ | ✓ | *** |
| Type 3 | | | | | | | |
| **pai** | pai-mané (B) (-F, -F) | father-Manny | stupid person | -F | ✓ | *** | ✓ |
| **mãe** | mãe-joana (B) (+F, +F) | mother-Joanne | jellyfish | F | ✓ | *** | ✓ |
| Type 4 | | | | | | | |
| **cavalo** | cavalo-vapor (-F, -F) | horse-steam | horsepower | -F | *** | ✓ | *** |
| Lacunae | | | | | | | |
| **amor** | *** | *** | *** | *** | *** | *** | *** |
| **pé** | *** | *** | *** | *** | *** | *** | *** |

a The only part of this and the subsequent tables that needs explaining are the last three columns: P-P indicates that both elements can be pluralized; P-Ø indicates that only the first element can bear the plural morpheme; and Ø-P indicates that only the second element may be inflected for plurality.

Of all the sample words, only *amor* and *pé* do not occur as first elements in noun + noun compounds. Table 12.2a shows that regardless of the second element's gender, the gender of the first element determines that of the entire word. The second noun need not agree in gender with the first (e.g. *pau-bala, peixe-cabra, homem-hora*). There are four modalities of noun+noun compound words: Type 1 compounds pluralize both elements; Type 2 compounds may pluralize only the first element or they may pluralize both; Type 3 may pluralize both elements or they may pluralize only the second element; and Type 4, whose only representative is *cavalo-vapor*, do not pluralize the second element. The pluralization of both elements in noun + noun compounds gives their second nouns near adjectival status because they agree in at least number with the first element in their words. Thus, four different (lexical) patterns underly this type of compound noun, as Table 12.2b demonstrates:

**Table 12.2b** Lexical Patterns

| | **Structure** | **Plurals** |
|---|---|---|
| **Type 1** | **#$R_1$++[±fem.]#<[αpl.]##$R_2$++[±fem.]#<[αpl.]#$_{[\alpha pl.]}$** | **P-P** |
| *e.g.* pau-bala | #pal[a]++o#<[αpl.] ##bal++a#<[αpl.]# | |
| **Type 2** | **#$R_1$++[±fem.]#<[αpl.]##$R_2$++[±fem.] #(<[αpl.]#) $_{[\alpha pl.]}$** | **P-(P)** |
| *e.g.* peixes-cabras | # peiš++e#<z##kapr++a#<z# | |
| peixes-cabra | #peiš++e#<z##kapr++a#<Ø# | |
| **Type 3** | **#$R_1$++[±fem.]#(<[αpl.]#)#$R_2$++[±fem.] #<[αpl.]#$_{[\alpha pl.]}$** | **(P)-P** |
| *e.g.* mães-joanas | #ma++e#<z##žoan+<a#<z# | |
| mãe-joanas | #ma++e##žoan+<a#<z# | |
| **Type 4** | **#$R_1$++[±fem.]#<[αpl.]##$R_2$++[±fem.]#<[-plural]#$_{[\alpha pl.]}$** | **P-Ø** |
| *e.g.* cavalo-vapor | #kaval++o#<[αpl.]##vapor#+e+<Ø# | |

a #$R_1$+ and #R+ roots and stems are not differentiated in these considerations since their morphophonology is not an issue here. However, the root #pal+ is an #$R_1$+ root, hence its loss of /l+ in compounds. In this and subsequent tables, the subscripts 1 and 2 only indicate the first and second nominal roots.

Grammatical number (i.e. [±pl.]) for compound nouns such as these will be determined by semantic and syntactic factors. When compound nouns reflect plurality on both elements, this possibility is reflected with <[αpl.]# on both. When one element's plurality is optional, parentheses around the the plural morpheme (<[αpl.]#) indicate its facultative nature. When only one element may be pluralized, only it is marked <[αpl.]#. Since the first element determines these compounds' gender, a rule can be written for this phenomenon:

**Rule 12.1 Gender in #Noun$_1$##Noun$_2$# Compounds:**

#Noun$_1$##Noun$_2$# → #Noun$_{1[\pm fem.]}$##Noun$_2$#$_{[\alpha fem.]}$

That is, simply, a compound noun consisting of two juxtaposed nouns acquires the gender of the first noun.

**§12.1.2.3** Table 12.2c contains compound nouns in which the sample nouns occur as the second element:

**Table 12.2c** Noun-Noun Compounds

| Compound | 2nd | Literal Gloss | Gloss | ±F. | P-P | P-Ø | Ø-P |
|---|---|---|---|---|---|---|---|
| bicho-pau (B) (-F,-F) | **pau** | bug-wood | an insect species | -F | ✓ | ✓ | *** |
| rede-pé (+F,-F) | **pé** | net-foot | beach net | F | ✓ | ✓ | *** |
| anu-peixe (B) (-F,-F) | **peixe** | anu-fish | a type of bird | -F | ✓ | ✓ | *** |
| *** | **água** | *** | *** | *** | *** | *** | *** |
| peixe-mulher (B) (-F,+F) | **mulher** | fish-woman | female manatee | -F | ✓ | ✓ | *** |
| *** | **papagaio** | *** | *** | *** | *** | *** | *** |
| nave-mãe (+F,+F) | **mãe** | ship-mother | mother ship | F | ✓ | ✓ | *** |
| benzinho-amor (B) (-F,-F) | **amor** | sweetie-love | a type of folk dance | -F | ✓ | *** | *** |
| bagre papai (B) (-F,-F) | **pai** | catfish daddy | white catfish | -F | ✓ | ✓ | *** |
| pau-cavalo (B) (-F,-F) | **cavalo** | wood horse | a tree species | -F | ✓ | ✓ | *** |
| mulher-homem (+F,-F) | **homem** | woman-man | lesbian | F | ✓ | ✓ | *** |
| banho-maria (-F,+F) | **Maria** | bath-maria | double boiler | -F | ✓ | ✓ | *** |
| peixe-porco (B) (-F,-F) | **porco** | fish-pig | triggerfish | -F | ✓ | ✓ | *** |

Remarkable in Table 12.2c is that all these words (save *benzinho-amor*) are Type 2 compounds—they accept plurality on both elements, or only on the 1st element. The word *benzinho-amor* is the only Type 1 compound. And, once again, in all these compounds the first element determines the compound nouns' gender. Table 12.2d displays the patterns underlying this set of compound nouns:

**Table 12.2d** Lexical Patterns

| | **Structure** | **Pl.** |
|---|---|---|
| Type 1 | **# $R_1$++[±fem.]#<[αpl.]##$R_2$++[±fem.]#<[αpl.]#** | P-P |
| *e.g.* benzinho-amor | #ben##ziɲ+<o#<[αpl.]##am++or#+e+<[αpl.]# | |
| Type 2 | **#$R_1$++[±fem.]#<[αpl.]##$R_2$++[±fem.] #(<[αpl.]#)** | P-(P) |
| *e.g.* redes-pés | #red++e#<z##pɛd++e#<z# | |
| redes-pé | #red++e#<z##pɛd++e# | |

Again, rule 12.1 accounts for the first element's determining these words' gender. Semantic factors determine these nouns' numbers, and when more than one pluralization option is possible, the particular word's lexical entry contains a set of parentheses around the number morpheme to indicate that the plural morpheme is optional on one of the two elements.

**§12.1.2.4.0** Table 12.3a presents compounds beginning with the sample nouns as the first element linked to other nouns by a preposition:

Table 12.3a Noun-Preposition-Noun Compounds

| 1st Element | Compound | Literal Gloss | Gloss | ±F. | P-P | P-Ø | Ø-P |
|---|---|---|---|---|---|---|---|
| **pau** | pau de arara (B) | stick of parrot | drought refugee | -F | *** | ✓ | *** |
| **pé** | pé de altar | foot of altar | priest's fees | -F | *** | ✓ | *** |
| **peixe** | peixe-de-briga | fish of fight | lung fish | -F | *** | ✓ | *** |
| **água** | água de flor | water of flower | orange petal water | F | *** | ✓ | *** |
| **mulher** | mulher de pulso | woman of pulse | energetic woman | F | *** | ✓ | *** |
| **papagaio** | papagaio de pirata (B) | parrot of pirate | yes man | -F | *** | ✓ | *** |
| **mãe** | mãe do corpo (B) | mother of the body | uterus | F | *** | ✓ | *** |
| **amor** | amor-de-moça (B) | love of girl | cosmos (flower) | -F | *** | ✓ | *** |
| **pai** | pai-d'égua (B) | father of mare | womanizer | -F | *** | ✓ | *** |
| **cavalo** | cavalo-de-judeu (B) | horse-of-Jew | dragonfly | -F | *** | ✓ | *** |
| **homem** | homem de palha | man of straw | straw boss | -F | *** | ✓ | *** |
| **maria** | maria-de-barro (B) | Maria-of-clay | ovenbird (f.)[a] | F | *** | ✓ | *** |
| **porco** | porco-da-terra | pig of the soil | aardvark | -F | *** | ✓ | *** |

a The male of this species is called *João de Barro* 'John of clay' (P-Ø). This name evokes the Portuguese 16th Century chronicler João de Barros.

These compounds are lexicalized combinations of nouns modified by prepositional phrases. Because their second elements are prepositional phrases, these compounds' first element determines their gender (cf. *mulher de pulso* and *pai d'égua*), and that element bears the plural morpheme. The lexical pattern underlying these compounds and the rule that determines their gender will come after displaying compounds entailing prepositions in which the sample words are the prepositional object.

**§12.1.2.4.1** Table 12.3b presents compounds in which the sample nouns appear in the second element. They are linked by a preposition to nouns that are the first element:

**Table 12.3b** Noun-Preposition-Noun Compounds

| Compound | 2nd Element | Literal | Gloss | ±F. | P-P | P-Ø | Ø-P |
|---|---|---|---|---|---|---|---|
| perna de pau (B) | **pau** | leg of wood | bad soccer player | ±F[a] | *** | ✓ | *** |
| bicho-do-pé (B) | **pé** | bug of the foot | chigoe | -F | *** | ✓ | *** |
| olho de peixe | **peixe** | eye-of-fish | white quartz | -F | *** | ✓ | *** |
| arca-d'água | **água** | chest of water | reservoir | F | *** | ✓ | *** |
| arenga de mulher (B) | **mulher** | rant of woman | mist | F | *** | ✓ | *** |
| bico de papagaio | **papagaio** | beak of parrot | adunc nose | -F | *** | ✓ | *** |
| *** | **mãe** | *** | *** | *** | *** | *** | *** |
| maçã do amor | **amor** | apple of love | candied apple | F | *** | ✓ | *** |
| *** | **pai** | *** | *** | *** | *** | *** | *** |
| unha-de-cavalo | **cavalo** | hoof of horse | a medicinal plant | +F | *** | ✓ | *** |
| jogo-do-homem (P) | **homem** | game of the man | a type of vine | -F | *** | ✓ | *** |
| mês de Maria | **maria** | month of Mary | May | -F | *** | ✓ | *** |
| focinho-de-porco | **porco** | snout of pig | a type of bird/fish | -F | *** | ✓ | *** |

a The compound *perna de pau* seems to be applicable to any (male or female) individual who performs poorly, and for that reason its gender is ±F.

Once again the same phenomena obtain: the first element determines the words' gender and can be inflected for plurality. The underlying structure of these compounds is:

$$\#R_1+\{<,+\}[\alpha\pm fem.]\#<[\beta\pm pl.]\#\#prep.>(\#det.+<[\alpha fem.]<[\alpha pl.]>)\#R_2+\{<,+\}[\pm fem]\#<[\pm pl]\#[_{\alpha fem.][\beta pl.]}$$

That is, the first noun may be [±fem.] (either inflected or derived) and it may be inflected for plurality. It is followed by a preposition which, the parentheses indicate, may (or may not) be followed by a determiner, which in turn will identify the second noun's gender (inflected or derived) and number. Table 12.3d displays the underlying structure of this type of compound using the words *unha-de-cavalo* and *porco-da-terra.*

Table 12.3c Lexical Structure: Compounds Containing Prepositions

| Noun 1 | | | Prep. | Determiner (opt) | | | Noun 2 | | |
|---|---|---|---|---|---|---|---|---|---|
| unha | | | de | | | | cavalo | | |
| #$R_1$+ | +[+fem]# | <[-pl]# | #pr> | (#det+ | <[αfem]# | <[αpl]>) | #$R_2$+ | +[αfem]# | <[-pl]# |
| #uɲ+ | +a# | <Ø# | #de> | Ø | | | #kaval | +o# | <Ø# |
| porcos | | | da | | | | terra | | |
| #$R_1$+ | <[αfem]# | <[+pl]# | #pr> | (#det+ | <[αfem]# | <[αpl]>) | #$R_2$+ | +[αfem]# | <[αpl]# |
| #pɔrk+ | <o# | <z# | de | #l+ | <a# | <Ø# | #tɛɾ̠+ | +a# | <Ø# |

Notwithstanding its final +o#, the noun *unha-de-cavalo* ('a medicinal plant') is a feminine singular noun owing to the [+feminine] gender and [-plural] number of *unha*. Conversely, *porcos-da-terra* 'aardvarks' is a non-feminine plural noun owing to the [-feminine] gender and [+plural] number of *porcos* and notwithstanding the word's final +a#, which indicates the [+feminine] gender (and non-plurality) of its second noun. Rule 12.2 accounts for these words' number and gender:

**Rule 12.2 Compound = #Noun##Prep.>(#Det.>)#Noun#:**

#$N_1$Prep.(det.)$N_2$#→ #$R_1$+{<,+}[αfem.]#<[βpl.]##prep.>(#det.>[4]) #$R_2$+{<,+}[±fem.]#<[±pl.]#$_{[\alpha fem.][\beta pl.]}$

The plus/minus sign (±) for gender (i.e. [±fem.] after the roots in question) indicates that the nominal morphemes' gender may be either feminine or non-feminine and is either lexically or grammatically assigned.

4 The rule of adjective-noun agreement (i.e. Rule 12.3 below) accounts for the forms of determiners capable of inflection. See Table 6.2 and §6.2.0–§6.2.3.2.1. Henceforth, determiners' inflection gender and number morphemes will be omitted in structural descriptions.

The signs for gender and number after the final word boundary indicate that these compound nouns' gender and number are lexically assigned according to the first noun's gender and number. The beta (β) before the first stem's plural morpheme indicates that only it is subject to the semantic and syntactic features that will cause it to reflect the entire word's plurality or lack thereof. The second element's gender and number play no part in the compound nouns' plurality or gender.[5]

**§12.1.2.4.2** Were the words in Tables 12.3a and 12.3b ordinary prepositional phrases without idiomatic meanings, they would allow, among other phenomena, pluralization of the final noun: *água de flores* would mean 'water made from different flowers'; *cavalo-de-judeus* would mean 'Jews' horse'; and *homem de palhas* would mean 'straw purveyor'. In addition, the insertion of a particular modifier between the preposition and the final noun would destroy the idiomatic meaning of these words rendering them ordinary prepositional phrases: *paus-de-grandes araras* would mean sticks of big parrots; *pé de nosso altar* would mean 'foot of our altar'. Whereas the prepositional phrases advanced here are grammatical formations, they have none of the compound words' idiomaticity.

**§12.1.2.5.0** Table 12.4a contains examples of compounds formed by combinations of the sample nouns with adjectives:

5 There is at least one compound of this nature whose gender is ambivalent. The noun *unha de fome* '(finger, toe) nail of hunger=miser' applies to both males and females.

Table 12.4a Noun-Adjective Compounds

| 1st Element | Compound | Literal | Gloss | ±F. | P-P | P-Ø | Ø-P |
|---|---|---|---|---|---|---|---|
| **pau** | pau-cheiroso | wood-fragrant | agalloch tree | -F | ✓ | *** | *** |
| **pé** | pé-cascudo (B) | foot-hooved | Devil | -F | ✓ | *** | *** |
| **peixe** | peixe-beijador | fish-kisser | kissing fish | -F | ✓ | *** | *** |
| **água** | água-bruta (B) | water-brutish | white rum | F | ✓ | *** | *** |
| **mulher** | mulher-ingrata (B) | woman-ungrateful | Amazon catfish | F | ✓ | *** | *** |
| **papagaio** | papagaio-grego | parrot-Greek | a type of parrot | -F | ✓ | *** | *** |
| **mãe** | mãe-parida (B) | mother-given-birth | French toast | F | ✓ | *** | *** |
| **amor** | amor-perfeito | love-perfect | pansy | -F | ✓ | *** | *** |
| **pai** | pai nosso | father-our | our father | -F | ✓ | *** | *** |
| **cavalo** | cavalo-marinho | horse-marine | seahorse | -F | ✓ | *** | *** |
| **homem** | homem-feito | man-finished | grown-up male | -F | ✓ | *** | *** |
| **Maria** | maria-mole (B) | Mary-soft | soft, thin-soled shoe | F | ✓ | *** | *** |
| **porco** | porco-sujo | pig-filthy | (the) Devil | -F | ✓ | *** | *** |

Again, the first element determines the entire word's gender, and, as is the case with any adjective modifying a noun, the first elements' (nouns') gender and number are reflected in the second elements' endings.

**§12.1.2.5.1** Table 12.4b contains adjectives that precede the sample nouns:

Table 12.4b Adjective-Noun Compounds

| Compound | 2nd Element | Literal Gloss | Gloss | ±F. | P-P | P-Ø | Ø-P |
|---|---|---|---|---|---|---|---|
| maneiro-pau (B) | **pau** | manageable-stick | a folk dance | -F | ✓ | *** | *** |
| *** | **pé** | *** | *** | *** | *** | *** | *** |
| meio-peixe (B) | **peixe** | half-fish | whale calf | -F | ✓ | *** | *** |
| meia-água[a] | **água** | half-water | flat roof | F | ✓ | *** | *** |
| *** | **mulher** | *** | *** | *** | *** | *** | *** |
| *** | **papagaio** | *** | *** | *** | *** | *** | *** |
| supermãe | **mãe** | super-mother | super mother | F | *** | *** | ✓ |
| feliz-amor (B) | **amor** | happy-love | a folk dance | -F | *** | *** | *** |
| nosso-pai | **pai** | our-father | travel provisions | -F | ✓ | *** | *** |
| *** | **cavalo** | *** | *** | *** | *** | *** | *** |
| rico-homem | **homem** | rich-man | high nobleman | -F | ✓ | *** | *** |
| santa-maria (B) | **Maria** | Holy-Mary | a type of foxglove | F | ✓ | *** | *** |
| *** | **porco** | *** | *** | *** | *** | *** | *** |

a The word *água* among architects refers to the configuration of roofs on buildings. This explains the motivation for referring to attic apartments as *águas-furtada*s 'stolen waters (i.e. roof)'. The word *água* also occurs in the lexical compound *verde água* 'green water', which actually means 'light (watery) green'. Its plural forms can be either *verdes-águas* or *verdes-água*—with both elements or only the first element pluralized (a type 2 compound nominal).

The five lacunae in Table 12.4b indicate that the adjective-noun pattern for compound nouns is less prevalent than all the other compound patterns examined so far. Of course the second element (the noun) determines the the adjective's gender and number. All the items, save *supermãe*, are idioms or proper nouns.

§**12.1.2.5.2** The underlying structure of these nouns parallels the common noun-adjective/adjective-noun syntagm in which adjectives modify nouns and agree in number and gender:

**#Noun##Adjective#:** #$R_1$+{<,+}α[±fem.]#<β[±pl.]# #$R_2$+<[αfem.]#<[βpl.]#

**#Adjective##Noun#:** #$R_2$+<[αfem.]#<[βpl.]# #$R_1$+{<,+}α[±fem.] #<β[±pl.]#

Table 12.4c displays specific the underlying structure of nouns and adjective compounds:

**Table 12.4c** Underlying Structure of Noun/Adjective, Adjective/Noun Compound Nouns

| Noun | | | Adjective | | |
|---|---|---|---|---|---|
| **águas** | | | **brutas** | | |
| #$R_1$+ | +[+fem.]# | <[+pl.]# [a] | #$R_2$+ | <[αfem.]# | <[αpl.]# |
| #aku+ | +a# | <z# | #brut+ | <a# | <z# |
| **Adjective** | | | **Noun** | | |
| **meia** | | | **água** | | |
| #$R_2$+ | <[αfem.]# | <[αpl.]# | #$R_1$+ | +[+fem.]# | <[-pl.]# |
| #med+ | <a# | <Ø# | #aku+ | +a# | <Ø# |
| **Noun** | | | **Adjective** | | |
| **pique** | | | **baixo** | | |
| #$R_1$+ | +[-fem.]# | <[-pl.]# | #$R_2$+ | <[αfem.]# | <[αpl.]# |
| #pik+ | +e# | <Ø# | #baiš+ | <o# | <Ø# |
| **Adjective** | | | **Noun** | | |
| **baixos** | | | **alemães** | | |
| #$R_2$+ | <[αfem.]# | <[αpl.]# | #$R_1$+ | +[-fem.]# | <[+pl.]# |
| #baiš+ | <o# | <z# | #alem+ | +an+<e+ | <z# |

a Among the sample nouns there are some whose first or second element can be lexically plural, but their plurality does not necessarily make the compound plural: *pau*: *três-paus* 'goal'; *pé*: *escalda-pés* 'foot bath'; *peixes: piolho-dos-peixes* 'aquatic parasite', *maes-do-bicho* 'feminine animal protectors'; *amores-de-negro* 'a type of plant'; *mal-de-amores* 'venereal disease'; *açoita-cavalos* 'a type of plant'; *casa-dos-homens* 'male lodge'; *três-marias* 'Orion's belt'; *mata-porcos* 'a toxic larva'.

In the first noun-adjective example, the word *água bruta* 'white rum' is pluralized so both elements are feminine and plural, as befits an adjective that modifies a feminine plural noun. The second noun-adjective example *pique-baixo* 'a game of tag' contains a [-feminine] singular noun, so the adjective, as well as the compound noun are [-feminine, -plural]. In the first Adjective-Noun example (*meia água* 'flat roof'), the adjective is inflected for [+feminine] gender, but not for plurality, since the second element is feminine but not plural. The form *baixos-alemães* 'low German terms' the gender is [-feminine] on both words, and both words are plural, as is the compound word. The rule for adjective-noun agreement can be formulated as follows:

**Rule 12.3 Adjective-Noun Agreeement:**

$$\text{Adjective} \rightarrow \#R + <[\alpha\text{fem.}]\# <[\beta\text{plural}]\ \#/ \left\{ \begin{array}{l} \#R_n + \{+ <\}[\alpha\text{fem.}] \quad <[\beta\text{pl.}]\# \ \_\_ \\ \\ \_\_\#R_n + \{+, <[\alpha\text{fem.}] \quad <[\beta\text{pl.}]\# \end{array} \right\}$$

Rule 12.3 has adjectives agreeing with nouns ($\#R_n+$) such as *água*, whose gender is lexically assigned [+fem.], or with nouns such as *menino* 'child', whose gender is semantically assigned according to its particular referent (a female or a male child).[6] There is at least one compound word in which Rule 12.3 does not obtain: *alto-falante* 'loud speaker'. Its plural is *alto-falantes*, in which the noun's plurality is indicated only by the word-final <z#. In this case, the word's first element *alto* is an adverb rather than an adjective.[7]

**§12.1.2.5.3** The lexical and idiomatic status of compounds consisting of adjectives and nouns is vouchedsafe by the same criteria invoked for

6 For this to be a syntactic rule, optional adverbs before the adjectives should appear, and there are ways of syntactically indicating the relationship between nouns and adjectives that are separated from the nouns they modify: e.g. *ramos de flores e plantas silvestres bonitos* '**pretty bouquets** of wild flowers and plants'. The adjective meaning 'pretty' *bonitos* is separated from the noun it modifies *(ramos* 'bouquets') by two [+feminine] nouns plus an adjective, but one identifies *bonitos* as modifying *ramos* because it is the only [-feminine] noun in the phrase. Adjective placements of this nature are achieved by a transformation.

7 Other compounds containing *alto*, e.g. *alto-fundo* 'high bottom (shallows)' and *alta-roda* 'high wheel (high society)', behave like adjective-noun combinations. Their plurals are: *altos-fundos* and *altas-rodas*.

the nominals formed from nouns plus prepositional phrases. That is, were one to add adverbs or adjectives to these concatentations, their idiomatic designations would no longer obtain. Whereas *homem-feito* means 'grown-up male', *homem bem feito* would mean 'well-formed man'. Whereas *mãe-parida* means 'French toast', *mãe recém parida* would indicate a mother who has recently given birth. Whereas *meio-peixe* means 'whale calf', *meio peixe frito* would mean half of a fried fish. And whereas *nosso-pai* means 'travel provisions', *nosso velho pai* would only refer to 'our old dad'.

**§12.1.2.6.0** Table 12.5a contains nominals created from conjugated verbs plus the sample nouns used for this part of the study:

**Table 12.5a** Verb-Noun Compounds

| Compound | 2nd Element | Literal | Gloss | ±F. | P-P | P-Ø | Ø-P |
|---|---|---|---|---|---|---|---|
| **quebra-pau (B)** | **pau** | breaks-wood | fracas | -F | *** | *** | ✓ |
| **alça-pé** | **pé** | raises-foot | trap | -F | *** | *** | ✓ |
| **flecha-peixe (B)** | **peixe** | 'arrows'-fish | kingfisher | -F | *** | *** | ✓ |
| *** | **água** | *** | *** | *** | *** | *** | *** |
| **esquenta-mulher (B)** | **mulher** | heats-woman | wind band | -F | *** | *** | ✓ |
| *** | **papagaio** | *** | *** | *** | *** | *** | *** |
| *** | **mãe** | *** | *** | *** | *** | *** | *** |
| *** | **amor** | *** | *** | *** | *** | *** | *** |
| *** | **pai** | *** | *** | *** | *** | *** | *** |
| **mata-cavalo (B)** | **cavalo** | kills-horse | nightshade | -F | *** | *** | ✓ |
| **capa-homem (B)** | **homem** | castrates-man | a swinging vine | -F | *** | *** | ✓ |
| **dorme-maria (B)** | **Maria** | sleeps-Maria | a type of vine | F | *** | *** | ✓ |
| **espanta-porco (B)** | **porco** | scares-pig | a type of bird | -F | *** | *** | ✓ |

Most striking in this set is the preponderance of Brazilian terms and of 1st conjugation transitive verbs. The only verb-noun compound that is [+feminine] is *dorme-maria*, which contains the only

2nd conjugation verb and is the sole term that does not consist of a transitive verb followed by a direct object.[8] All of these only allow word-final pluralization, but of course the verbs remain inflected for the 3rd person singular present indicative. Because of the considerable lacunae in this set, the next section examines cases in which selected verbs combine with nouns other than those examined up to now to form compounds.

**§12.1.2.6.1** Table 12.5b contains the four transitive verbs chosen to demonstrate verbs that regularly form compounds with nouns other than those listed in Table 12.1:

8 The *Aurélio*'s notions of transitive verbs are suspect. In the entry for *dormir* 'to sleep', the compilers include the following sentences maintaining that they contain examples of transitive uses of *dormir*: *Dormi uma deliciosa noite* 'I slept [through] a delicious night' and *Dorme [...] teu calmo sono profundo* 'Sleep your calm deep sleep', the latter a quotation from the work of António Nobre, a Portuguese poet. Neither of these uses of *dormir* is that of a truly transitive verb. Compare them with *Quero uma deliciosa noite* 'I want a delicious night' and *Envejo teu calmo sono profundo* 'I envy your calm, deep sleep'. Intransitive verbs allow noun phrases to follow them when they denote activity or times typical of the action of the verb in question: e.g. *Assobiei uma melodia* 'I whistled a melody' *Viagei o mundo inteiro* 'I traveled the whole world'. True transitive verbs will take virtually any noun as their direct object.

**Table 12.5b** Verb-Noun Compounds

| Compound | Literal | Gloss | ±F. | P-P | P-Ø | ØP |
|---|---|---|---|---|---|---|
| **guarda**-cama | keeps bed | bedspread ruffle | -F | *** | *** | ✓ |
| **guarda**-fogo | keeps fire | firewall | -F | *** | *** | ✓ |
| **guarda**-lama | keeps mud | fender | -F | *** | *** | ✓ |
| **guarda**-patrão | keeps pattern | backboard... | -F | *** | *** | ✓ |
| **papa**-jantares | eats dinners | freeloader | ±F | *** | *** | ±✓ |
| **papa**-léguas | eats leagues | wanderer | ±F | *** | *** | ±✓ |
| **papa**-missas | eats masses | zealot | ±F | *** | *** | ±✓ |
| **papa**-ovo (B) | eats egg | a snake species | +F | *** | *** | ✓ |
| **passa**-culpas | passes blames | an indulgent person | ±F | *** | *** | ±✓ |
| **passa**-piolho | passes louse | a type of beard | -F | *** | *** | ✓ |
| **passa**-moleque (B) | passes urchin | dirty trick | -F | *** | *** | ✓ |
| **passa**tempo | passes time | pastime | -F | *** | *** | ✓ |
| **tira**-testa | pulls-forehead | forehead reins | -F | *** | *** | ✓ |
| **tira**-prosa (B) | pulls prose | bully | ±F | *** | *** | ✓ |
| **tira**-nódoas | pulls blotches | spot remover | -F | *** | *** | ±✓ |
| **tira**-leite | pulls milk | breast pump | -F | *** | *** | ✓ |

The default gender in compound coinages consisting of verbs and nouns is [-feminine], yet the word *papa-ovo* is [+feminine] even though it contains no [+feminine] morpheme. Its gender may be the result of its denoting a snake, a *cobra*, a noun with a deriving [+feminine] gender morpheme +a#.[9] In addition, several of these compounds denote certain types of people: e.g. freeloaders (*papa-jantares*) and wanderers (*papa-léguas*). In these cases, they may refer to either male or female individuals, and for that reason their gender is ±F. In ordinary usage, their referents' gender would be indicated by the form ([±fem.]) of a determiner (article or demonstrative) or an obvious referent—there would be no inflection for the referent's gender on the word itself. That is, the total compound noun consisting of a verb and a noun is [-feminine]. Similarly, several of the nouns in these compounds are plurals, but the

9 Compare *cobra* #kɔbr++a# 'snake' with *cobre* #kɔbr++e# 'copper', and *cobro* #kɔbr++o# 'charge'.

compounds can refer to an individual or to a plurality, and for this reason their pluralization is [±pl.]. Those compounds identified word-finally by ✓ actually acquire <z# when they indicate plural entities, e.g. *tira-leites* and *tira-prosas*. This set contains the lowest percentage of Brazilian coinages. The underlying structure of Verb + Noun compounds is:

**#$R_v$+<Ø#[10]+TV+<Ø#<Ø##$R_n$+{<,+}[±fem.]#<[±pl.]#**

That is, the verbal root ($R_v$) is followed by the inflecting tense-mood-aspect morpheme, the theme vowel, and the 3rd person singular morpheme <Ø# followed by a noun that may be [±femine] (inflected or derived) and [±pl.]. Table 12.5c demonstrates the underlying structure of verb + noun compounds:

**Table 12.5c** Verb + Noun Compounds' Underlying Structure

| Total Compound | | | | | | | | |
|---|---|---|---|---|---|---|---|---|
| Verb | | | | Noun | | | Compound | |
| capa | | | | homem | | | [±fem.] | [±pl.] |
| Root | TMA | TV | PN | Root | ±feminine | ±plural | *** | *** |
| #kap+ | <Ø> | +a# | <Ø# | #ɔmin+ | +e+ | <Ø# | -fem. | αpl. |
| papa | | | | missas | | | [±fem.] | [±pl.] |
| Root | TMA | TV | PN | Root | ±feminine | ±plural | *** | *** |
| #pap+ | <Ø> | +a# | <Ø# | #mis+ | +a# | <z# | αfem. | αpl. |

Table 12.5c shows that these compounds have an internal structure that is coherent, but that does not directly affect the nouns' gender or number. That is, regardless of the second elements' gender, the verb-noun compounds will be [-feminine] unless, as is the case with *papa-missas*, the word refers to a living being (in this case, a human), in which case it is gender indifferent and is identified [αfemine], i.e. words of this type can denote either a male or a female. Both compounds are identified as [αpl.] because they can refer to plural entities: the word *capa-homem*, when referring to several different plants appears as

10 This position in verb structure is that of the tense-mood-aspect morpheme, which in the present indicative is <Ø#. (§13.6.0–2.)

*capa-homens* and acquires <z#. Whereas compounds such as *papa-missas* acquire <z#, this <z# evanesces because the word itself ends in <z#, which is the self-same plural suffix and is deleted because contoidal geminates do not occur in Portuguese. Rule 12.4 is a rewrite rule that identifies the structures of verb + noun compound words:

**Rule 12.4 The Formation of Noun + Verb Compound Nominals:**

$$\#\text{Verb}\#\#\text{Noun}\# \rightarrow \#R_v+<\emptyset\#+\text{TV}+<\emptyset\#\#R_n+\{<,\}[\pm\text{fem.}]\#<[\pm\text{pl.}]\#_{[\text{-fem}][\alpha\text{pl}]}$$

The subscript at the end the the nominal's structure indicates that verb+ nouns are always [-feminine] but may be singular or plural.

§**12.1.2.7.0** Table 12.6 contains compound nominals formed with the adverbs *mal* 'poorly' and *bem* 'well':

**Table 12.6** Words Formed with *Mal* and *Bem*

| Compound | Literal | Gloss | ±F. | P-P | P-Ø | Ø-P |
|---|---|---|---|---|---|---|
| mal-acabado | poorly finished | poorly finished | αF | *** | *** | ✓ |
| maldistinto | poorly distinguished | indistinct | αF | *** | *** | ✓ |
| malbaratar | to poorly cheapen | to sell at a loss | -F | *** | *** | ✓ |
| malcriadez | poorly upbringing | rudeness | F | *** | *** | ✓ |
| bem-apanhado | well-selected | attractive | αF | *** | *** | ✓ |
| bem-casado | well-married | jellyroll | -F | *** | *** | ✓ |
| benfazer | to do well | to benefit | -F | *** | *** | ✓ |
| bem-bom (B) | well-good | easy street | -F | *** | *** | ✓ |

In Table 12.6, these two adverbs attach to adjectives and to infinitives. It is of course natural that they should attach to adjectives and infinitives given that adverbs' normally modify adjectives and verbs. And of course only the second element can be pluralized in all these forms because adverbs are not inflected.

§**12.1.2.7.1.0** These adverbs' role in the formation of adjectives prevails over their formation of verbs. That is, even though *acabado*, *apanhado*, and *casado* are participial adjectives derived from the verbs *acabar* 'to finish', *apanhar* 'to select' and *casar* 'to marry' (§13.10.3.0–3), the *Aurélio* does not include verbs such as **mal-acabar*, **bem-apanhar*, or **bem-casar*. Thus, the adverbs *bem* and *mal* attach to these (participial) adjectives rather than to the verbs from which the participles are formed.

**§12.1.2.7.1.1** The word *malcriadez* is assuredly a noun derived from *malcriado* 'rude, boorish', which is itself a compound of the past participle of *criar* 'to foster', i.e. *criado* and the adverb *mal*.[11] These adverbs attach to verbs whose citation form, as tradition dictates, is the infinitive.[12] There are still more compound nominals to examine before leaving the category consisting of $word_1$ plus $word_2$.

**§12.1.2.7.2** Table 12.7 contains compounds formed with the negative particle *não* 'no' and the preposition *sem* 'without'.[13]

**Table 12.7** Compounds Formed with the Particle *Não* and the Preposition *Sem*

| Compound | Literal | Gloss | ±F. | P-P | P-Ø | Ø-P |
|---|---|---|---|---|---|---|
| não arrendondado | not rounded | unrounded | αf | *** | *** | ✓ |
| não conformismo | not conformism | non-conformism | -F | *** | *** | ✓ |
| não eu | not I | not I | -F | *** | *** | ✓ |
| não ser | not to be | non-being | -F | *** | *** | ✓ |
| | | | | | | |
| sem-abrigo (P) | without shelter | without shelter | ±F | *** | *** | ± |
| sem-vergonha | without shame | scoundrel | ±F | *** | *** | ± |
| sem-sal | without salt | insipid | ±F | *** | *** | ± |
| sem-palavra | without word | shirker | ±F | *** | *** | ± |

Among the compound lexical entries formed with *não*, adjectives will agree in both number and gender with whatever they modify. Compound nouns formed with *não* are fairly recondite terms used mainly in erudite

11 Once again, the *Aurélio* does not contain **malcriar*.

12 The verbal compounds formed with both *mal* and *bem* are tentative true lexical compounds, especially when they combine with infinitives. Since these adverbs' vowels do not reduce to [ă] and [ə] because they occur in syllables closed by /l/ and by /n/, it is not obvious that these words have two stressed elements.

13 The words formed with *não* are true compounds because *não* is a free form that can occur utterance-initially and utterance-finally and can bear stress. *Sem* is a preposition which does not bear stress and does not normally occur word-finally, so, strictly speaking, the forms beginning with *sem* are not true compounds.

discourse. Concerning those formed with *sem*, even though the *Aurélio* lists the words formed with this preposition as adjectives, they function exactly like prepositional phrases: they can modify [±fem.] and [±pl.] nouns and entities with no modification in their number and gender. The underlying structure of these compounds is

**#adverb##noun# and #prepostion>#noun#**

**Condition: Adverbs** = mal, bem, não.

§**12.1.2.8** Table 12.8 contains an overview of the compounding phenomena examined in this section:

**Table 12.8** Overall View of Nominal Compounding (Dominant Patterns)

| Compounding Elements | Gender Determination | | | Compound's Number | | |
|---|---|---|---|---|---|---|
| | 1st Element | 2nd Element | Arbitrary | P-P | P-Ø | Ø-P |
| Noun + Noun | ✓ | *** | ✓ | ✓ | (✓) | *** |
| Noun + prep + noun | ✓ | *** | ✓ | *** | ✓ | *** |
| Noun + Adjective | ✓ | *** | ✓ | ✓ | *** | *** |
| Adjective + Noun | *** | ✓ | ✓ | ✓ | *** | |
| Verb + Noun | *** | *** | -F | *** | *** | ✓ |
| Adverb + Nominal | *** | ✓ | ✓ | *** | *** | ✓ |

Section 1 (§12.1.0-2.8) shows that syntactical patterns largely obtain in the formation of compound nominals. When a motivated or somewhat transparent compound consists of a noun followed by a second noun, the second noun modifies the first noun: *pau-bala* 'wood-bullet', i.e. 'top', *pai-mané* 'father-Manny, i.e. stupid fellow', *peixe-mulher* 'fish-woman, i.e. female manatee'. Normally, both elements agree in number, but they need not agree in gender: *rede-pé* '[+F][-F], *pau-bala* [-F][+F]. In these forms, the first element determines the compound's gender. When the compound consists of two nouns linked by prepositions, the first element determines the compound's gender and bears its number marker. When adjectives combine with nouns, either post-nominally or pre-nominally, they agree in both number and gender with the noun in the compound. Verbs combining with nouns normally form [-F] nouns, and their number is expressed on the noun. Adverb plus nominal true compounds' gender and number are determined by their final (nominal) elements' gender and number. Adverb plus adjective true compounds are inflected for number and gender according to the items or beings they describe.

## Semi-compound Nominals

**§12.2.0** Both nominal elements in true compounds continue to have stressed syllables, and the first element in a true compound bears at least some vestige of the morphological properties (i.e. gender and/or number), it has as an independent word. Such is not the case with semi-compounds. They have only one stressed syllable, and, even though the first element's gender morpheme may emerge in certain semi-compounds, only the second element bears suffixes indicating the entire word's gender and number. The elements in semi-compound nouns may be actual words, but more often they consist of morphemes that are not actual words but roots of specific words. Table 12.9 contains examples of semi-compound words consisting of two independent words, of two roots, and one root and one complete word:

**Table 12.9** Sample Semi-compounds

| 2 Independent Words | | | | | |
|---|---|---|---|---|---|
| Semi-compound | Gloss | 1st Word | Gloss | 2nd Word | Gloss |
| **magnetopausa** (HL)[a] | magnetopause | **magneto** | magnet | **pausa** | pause |
| **alcoolómetro** (AH) | acohol meter | **álcool** | acohol | **metro** | meter |
| **2 Non-words (Elements)** | | | | | |
| **Semi-compound** | **Gloss** | **1st Root[b]** | **Gloss** | **2nd Root[c]** | **Gloss** |
| **ignífugo** (L) | insulator | **igni-** | fire | **-fug-** | flee |
| **terrívomo** (L) | dirt expeller | **terr-** | earth | **-vom-** | expel |
| **termostato** (H) | thermostat | **termo-** | heat | **-stato** | regulator |
| **epicarpo** (H) | husk | **epi-** | over | **-carpo** | fruit |

Table 12.9 Continued

| Element + Word | | | | | |
|---|---|---|---|---|---|
| Semi-compound | Gloss | Root[d] | Gloss | Word | Gloss |
| **locomóvel** (L) | moveable | **loc-** | place | **móvel** | moveable |
| **mirolho** (L) | sharpshooter | **mir-** | aim | **olho** | eye |
| **ortocentro** (H) | triangle peak | **orto-** | direct | **centro** | center |
| **estomalgia** (H) | mouth pain | **-stoma-** | hole | **algia** | pain |

a Part 2 (§12.2.0–5.2.1) includes the letters A, L, H in entries when the words' origin is pertinent. The letter A indicates that one element in the word is of Arabic origin; L indicates Latinate origin, and H indicates Hellenic origin. The word *magnetopausa's* first element is Hellenic, its second is Latinate. The word *alcoolómetro*'s first element is Arabic, its second is Hellenic.
b The first elements of these words appear as roots in words such as *ignição* 'ignition', *terra* 'earth', *termal* 'thermal', and *épica* 'epic'.
c The second elements in these words appear as roots in words such as *fuga* 'flight', *vomitar* 'to vomit', *estático* 'static' and *carpelo* 'carpel'.
d The first elements of these words appear as roots in words such as *local* 'local', *mira* 'aim', *ortose* 'orthodic', and *estómago* 'stomach'.

The 12 semi-compound nouns in Table 12.9 illustrate the phenomena found in the great majority of (if not all) semi-compound words: (A) Regardless of their components' status (word or root) the semi-compound has only one stressed syllable. (B) Only the second element determines (or reflects, in the case of adjectives) the complete words' gender and number. (C) Both elements need not be of the same origin: Latinate forms and Hellenic forms often combine to form semi-compounds.[14] (D) There is almost always a vowel between the first and the second element of semi-compounds. The vowel may pertain to either element, or it may arise as a transitional sound, and that transitional vowel may supplant the final vowel of the first element. (E) There is a subset of both Latinate (e.g. *–fug-* and *–vom-*) and Hellenic elements (*metro-*) that, when they occur word-finally, occasion proparoxytone stress. (F) Most semi-compound words pertain to erudite or professional and scientific vocabulary and are of relatively recent coinage. (G) Semantically, these words are transparent and motivated: in general, by knowing the meaning of their constituents, one knows, or at

14 The form *ortocentro* is Hellenic because Latin *centru* had its origin in Greek *kéntron*. Other languages may contribute elements: *kartódromo* 'go-cart track' (English) and *megablitz* 'large operation' (German).

least recognizes, semi-compounds' meanings. (H) Beyond all this, since the constituents of semi-compound words are either words themselves or roots of actual words, these elements are essentially different from prefixes and suffixes, which are restricted to stem-initial or stem-final positions, respectively.

**§12.2.1.0** Table 12.10 indicates the productivity of the Latinate and Hellenic elements in the semi-compounds examined:

**Table 12.10** Compounding Elements and Their Productivity

| | **Elements** | **Tokens** |
|---|---|---|
| Latinate 1st | 34 | 1,205 |
| Latinate 2nd | 23 | 1,334 |
| Totals: | 57 | 2,539 |
| Hellenic 1st | 112 | 7,001 |
| Hellenic 2nd | 77 | 5,254 |
| Totals: | 189 | 12,255 |
| Grand Totals: | 246 | 14,794 |

**§12.2.1.1** One cannot help but be struck by the preponderance of Hellenic elements in the formation of semi-compound nominals: they entail 3.26 times more items than their Latinate counterparts and 4.76 times as many tokens—i.e. semi-compound words appearing in the *Aurélio*. But the elements examined and the tokens accounted for do not exhaust the inventory of Portuguese semi-compound elements and the words they form. They do, however, provide sufficient data to evaluate these elements' status and productivity as well as the processes entailed in creating semi-compound words.

**§12.2.2.0 Latinate Semi-compounds:** Table 12.11a displays a set of Latinate elements found in the initial position in semi-compound words:

Table 12.11a Latinate Compounds: First Elements[a]

| Orthography | Analysis | Tokens[b] | Examples | Gloss |
|---|---|---|---|---|
| bi-<br>bis- | #bi(z)+ | 305 | **biangular** | 2 angled |
| | | (25) | **bisanual** | every other year |
| semi- | | 174 | **semiviro** | eunuch |
| multi- | #mult+ | 120 | **multifuro** | many punctures |
| | | (1) | **multangular** | many-angled |
| quadri-<br>quadra-<br>quadru- | #kuadr+ | 104 | **quadricapsular** | having 4 capsules |
| | | (7) | **quadragénio** | fortyish |
| | | (7) | **quadrupolar** | having 4 poles |
| uni- | #un+ | 101 | **unifilar** | single stranded |
| agro-<br>agri- | #agr+ | 69 | **agrotóxico** | bad for agriculture |
| | | (19) | **agricultar** | to cultivate |
| equi- | #ɛk+ | 51 | **equivalente** | equivalent |
| pluri- | #plur+ | 34 | **plurirracial** | multi-racial |
| oleo-<br>olei- | #ˈɔle++o# | 24 | **oleogravura** | oleograph |
| | | (9) | **oleicultura** | olive tree cultivation |
| ambi- | #amb+ | 22 | **ambivio** | crossroads |
| oni- | #ɔn+ | 20 | **onissapiente** | all-knowing |
| reti- | #r̠ɛt+ | 19 | **retirostro** | straight beaked |
| ferro-<br>ferri- | #fɛr̠++o# | 18 | **ferromoça** | train stewardess |
| | | (3) | **ferrimagnetismo**[*c] | ironmagnetism |
| cruci- | #kruk+ | 16 | **crucificar** | to crucify |
| igni- | #ign+ | 13 | **ignipotente** | fire master (vulcan) |
| vermi- | #vɛrm+ | 13 | **vermilingue** | long-tongued |
| loco- | #lɔk+ | 10 | **locomóvel** | moveable |
| sono- | #son+ | 10 | **sonometria*** | sound measurement |
| curvi- | #kurv+ | 9 | **curvilíneo** | curvilinear |
| morti- | #mɔrt+ | 9 | **morticínio** | natural mortality |
| olh- | #ɔλ+ | 8 | **olhiagudo** | sharp-eyed |
| sesqui - | #sɛzki+ | 8 | **sesquipedal** | 1.5 feet in length |
| calori- | #kalor+ | 7 | **caloripunctura** | puncture with heat |
| viro- | #vir+ | 7 | **virólogo*** | expert in viruses |
| avi- | #av+ | 5 | **avicultor** | bird grower |
| pisci- | #pizk+ | 5 | **piscicaptura** | fish catching |
| arbori- | #arbɔr+ | 4 | **arboriforme** | tree-shaped |
| canto- | #kant+ | 4 | **cantotomia*** | eye corner section |

(*Continued*)

Table 12.11a Continued

| Orthography | Analysis | Tokens | Examples | Gloss |
|---|---|---|---|---|
| pedi- | #pɛd+ | 4 | **pediforme** | formed like a foot |
| lingu- | #l'ingu+ | 4 | **linguífero** | having a tongue |
| ger- | #žɛr+ | 3 | **geriatria*** | geriatrics |
| capsul- | #kapsul+ | 2 | **capsulíforo*** | capsule-producing |
| vom- | #vom+ | 2 | **vomífico** | vomit inducing |
| fug- | #fug+ | 1 | **fugalaça** | long tether |

a Table 12.11a contains 34 different word-initial Latinate compounding elements (1,205 tokens). Of these elements seven (#son+, #pɛdal+, #fug+, #pɛde+, #l'ingu+, #vɔm+, and #žɛr+) also appear as second elements in Table 12.11b. In addition, #mult, #kuadr+, #kurv+, #mɔrt+, #'arbor+, and #vir+ appear in Table 12.11b even though these only occur as the second element in one semi-compound each.
b In the sections documenting allomorphs of the element under examination, the total occurrence of the form appears in boldface on the first line and the occurrences of specific allomorphs on their respective lines. For example, the element #kuadr+ appears in 104 different words as the first element. As #kuadr+a it occurs 7 times, as #kuadr+u seven times. Thus, the form #kuadr+i+ prevails with 90 tokens in the *Aurélio*. A total of 1,204 semi-compound words begins with these elements. M=35.41 tokens, SD= 62.28, and Z=2.965, which makes the form #bi(z)+ an outlier with a Z value of 4.33.
c When the second element of these semi-compound nominals is Hellenic rather than Latinate, the word bears an asterisk.

The analyses in Table 12.11a and those that follow are morphophonemic in nature, and their final + indicates that they are not complete words—they must be followed by another morpheme to emerge either as the root of a word or as the first element in a semi-compound word. The symbol # at the beginning of each transcription indicates that all items can be word-initial. Table 12.11b evaluates these Latinate Elements in first position according to their relative productivity:

**Table 12.11b** Latinate First Elements' Relative Productivity

| Negligible Productivity (2.81%) | | | Low Productivity (14.86%) | | |
|---|---|---|---|---|---|
| Element | Tokens | % | Element | Tokens | % |
| #fug+ | 1 | 0.08 | #ign+ | 13 | 1.08 |
| #kapsul+ | 2 | 0.17 | #vɛrm+ | 13 | 1.08 |
| #vom+ | 2 | 0.17 | #kruk+ | 16 | 1.32 |
| #žɛr+ | 3 | 0.25 | #fɛr̠++o# | 18 | 1.49 |
| #arbɔr+ | 4 | 0.33 | #rɛt+ | 19 | 1.58 |
| #kant+ | 4 | 0.33 | #ɔn+ | 20 | 1.66 |
| #pɛd+ | 4 | 0.33 | #amb+ | 22 | 1.83 |
| #l'ingu+ | 4 | 0.33 | #'ɔle++o# | 24 | 2.00 |
| #av+ | 5 | 0.41 | #plur+ | 34 | 2.82 |
| #pizk+ | 5 | 0.41 | Modest Productivity (9.56%) | | |
| Very Low Productivity (5.64%) | | | #ɛk+ | 51 | 4.23 |
| #kalor+ | 7 | 0.58 | #agr+ | 69 | 5.73 |
| #vir+ | 7 | 0.58 | High Productivity (26.97%) | | |
| #ɔλ+ | 8 | 0.66 | #un+ | 101 | 8.38 |
| #sɛzki+ | 8 | 0.66 | #kuadr+ | 104 | 8.63 |
| #kurv+ | 9 | 0.75 | #mult+ | 120 | 9.96 |
| #mɔrt+ | 9 | 0.75 | Very High Productivity (14.44%) | | |
| #lɔk+ | 10 | 0.83 | #semi+ | 174 | 14.44 |
| #son+ | 10 | 0.83 | Supreme (Outlier) Productivity (25.31%) | | |
| 18 -16 | | | #bi(z)+ | 305 | 25.31 |

Seven of the 34 elements account for 76.28% of all Latinate elements occurring in word-initial position. Conversely, the 18 elements of negligible or very low productivity account for 8.45% of all Latinate tokens. However, all elements (save #sezki+) in Table 12.11a can be roots or stems of actual words,[15] as Table 12.11c demonstrates:

15 The items in Table 12.11b and the remaining tables in this series demonstrate that the first and second elements can be roots of words because they are followed by deriving or inflecting suffixes, e.g. +a# (1st conjugation verb), +e# (gender morpheme), +'ari+<o# (adjective-deriving suffix), +a# [+feminine] suffix.

**Table 12.11c** Semi-compound First Elements as Roots and as Second Elements

| | Single Root Word | | Semi-compoud $2^{nd}$ Element | |
|---|---|---|---|---|
| $1^{st}$ Element | Root | Gloss | $2^{nd}$ Element | Gloss |
| #bi(z)+ | **bisar** | to repeat | *** | *** |
| #sem+ | **semelhar** | to resemble | *** | *** |
| #mult+ | **multidão** | multitude | **turbamulta** | large gathering |
| #kuadr+ | **quadrar** | to square | **miniquadro** | small painting |
| #un+ | **unir** | to unite | *** | *** |
| #agr+ | **agrário** | agrarian | *** | *** |
| #ɛk+ | **eco** | eco | *** | *** |
| #plur+ | **plural** | plural | *** | *** |
| #amb+ | **ambos** | both | *** | *** |
| #ɔn+ | **ónus** | onus | *** | *** |
| #r̠ɛt+ | **reto** | right | *** | *** |
| #kruk+ | **cruz** | cross | *** | *** |
| #ign+ | **ignição** | ignition | *** | *** |
| #vɛrm+ | **verme** | worm | *** | *** |
| #lɔk+ | **local** | local | **matrilocal** | matrilocal |
| #son+ | **som** | sound | **dulcissono** | sweet sounding |
| #kurv+ | **curva** | curve | **contracurva** | counter curve |
| #mɔrt+ | **morte** | death | **natimorto** | stillborn |
| #sɛzk+ | *** | *** | *** | *** |
| #kalor+ | **calor** | heat | *** | *** |
| #vir+ | **virus** | virus | **decênviro** | 1 of 10 rulers |
| #arbɔr+ | **arbóreo** | tree-like | **subárvore** | tree's offspring |
| #av+ | **ave** | bird | *** | *** |
| #pizk+ | **piscoso** | fishy | *** | *** |
| #kant+ | **canto** | corner | **bibliocanto** | bookend |
| #pɛd+ | **pedal** | pedal | **unipedal** | 1 footed |
| #l'ingu+ | **língua** | tongue | **fissilingue** | forked tongue |
| #žɛr+ | **gerar** | to generate | **dentígero** | having teeth |
| #kaps++ul+ | **cápsula**[a] | capsule | **bicapsular** | having 2 capsules |
| #vom+ | **vomitar** | to vomit | **fumívomo** | expelling smoke |
| #fug+ | **fugar** | to flee | **centrífugo** | centrifuge |

a The word *cápsula* is proparoxytone because the suffix +ul+ in penult position requires stress on the syllable preceding it cf. *capsa* 'cylindrical box' (Appendix 10C).

§**12.2.2.1** In addition to the data in Tables 12.11a–c showing that these word-initial elements are potential roots rather than mere prefixes, they also show that nearly half these elements (15 of 34, 44.11%) can also occur as the second element in semi-compounds. The data also indicate that for the most part the vowel that intercedes between the first and second element of these semi-compound words rarely pertains to the first element because these vowels do not follow the them when they are roots of independent words. Of the vowels that are unambiguously transitional in Table 12.11a, /i/ is preponderant.[16] Transitional /i/'s preponderance in Table 12.11a reflects its overall preponderance in Latinate semi-compound nominals (§12.2.3.2 and Table 12.13). Also in Tables 12.11a–b, some of the semi-compounds' stress is proparoxytone.

§**12.2.3.0** Table 12.12a contains Latinate semi-compounds' second elements:

**Table 12.12a** Latinate Semi-compounds: Second Element[a]

| Orthography | Transciption | Tokens | Examples | Glosses |
|---|---|---|---|---|
| -forme | #form++e# | 468 | **petaliforme** | petal formed |
| -fero* | #fεr+<[αfem.]# | 273 | **vaporífero** | vaporific |
| -cola* | +kɔl++a# | 87 | **salícola** | salt producing |
| -cultura | #cultur++a# | 78 | **apicultura** | bee raising |
| -cida | +sid++a# | 70 | **virucida** | virus killer |
| -fico* | #fik+<[αfem.]# | 65 | **vulnífico** | dangerous |
| -pede* | #pεd++e# | 61 | **solípede** | single hoofed |
| -gero* | #žεr+<[αfem.]# | 43 | **sedígero** | silk producing |
| -voro* | #vɔr+<[αfem.]# | 42 | **ratívoro** | rat eater |
| -paro* | #par+<[αfem.]# | 32 | **uriníparo** | urine producing |
| -fugo* | #fug+<[αfem.]# | 31 | **lucífugo** | flees from light |
| -lingue | #l'ingu++e# | 28 | **fissilingue** | forked tongued |
| -sono* | #son+<[αfem.]# | 21 | **raucíssono** | hoarse sounding |
| -potente | #pɔt++ent++e# | 16 | **ventripotente** | gastronome |
| -olho | #ɔλ++o# | 6 | **mirolho** | sharp shooter |

(*Continued*)

16 The /o/ in *ferromoça* is the +o# of the noun *ferro* 'iron'. And the /a/ in *fugalaça* 'long tether' is that of *fuga* 'flight'. The final element of *fugalaça* is quite likely the word *laço* 'lasso' that has acquired the [+feminine] suffix +a# owing to the [+feminine] gender of *fuga*.

Table 12.12a Continued

| Orthography | Transciption | Tokens | Examples | Glosses |
|---|---|---|---|---|
| -vomo* | #vom+<[αfem.]# | 5 | **terrívomo** | dirt expeller |
| -arbore | #ˈarbor++e# | 1 | **subárvore** | tree's offspring |
| -curva | #kurv++a# | 1 | **contracurva** | counter curve |
| -morto | #mɔrt+<[αfem.]# | 1 | **natimorto** | stillborn |
| -mult- | #mult+<[αfem]# | 1 | **turbamulta** | large gathering |
| -quadro | #quadr++o# | 1 | **miniquadro** | small painting |
| -viro | #vir+<[αfem.]# | 1 | **decênviro** | 1 of 10 rulers |

a The 22 elements in Table 12.12 occur in 1,332 different words. M=60.55 words per element, SD=108.36, Z=2.756. The first element *–forme* (Z=3.76) is an outlier. The elements followed by asterisks are those that occasion proparoxytone stress.

Once again, the transcriptions in Table 12.12a are morphophonemic; however, here the elements are morphologically complex because they include gender (either inflected or derived). Implicitly, these elements may be pluralized, i.e. <z# may be attached word-finally when semantic and syntactic circumstances require pluralization. In fact, many of these nominals are adjectives or the type of noun that indicates a living being and thus will also agree in number and gender with the entities they designate.[17] The symbol # at the beginning of specific transcriptions indicates that these items can be word-initial—either as roots or in a few cases as the first element in a semi-compound, as Table 12.12b demonstrates:

17 The gender morphemes +e# and +a# are valid for [±fem.] referents.

**Table 12.12b** Latinate Second Elements as Roots and First Elements

| | Single Root Word | | Semi-compoud 1st Element | |
|---|---|---|---|---|
| 2nd Element | Root | Gloss | 1st Element | Gloss |
| #form+ | **forma** | form | *** | *** |
| #fɛr+ | **féria** | income | *** | *** |
| #cultur+ | **cultura** | culture | *** | *** |
| +sid+ | *** | *** | *** | *** |
| #fik+ | **ficar** | to become | *** | *** |
| #pɛd+ | **pedâneo** | standing judge | **pedicura** | pedicure |
| #žɛr+ | **gerar** | to generate | *** | *** |
| #vor+ | **voraz** | voracious | *** | *** |
| #par+ | **parir** | to give birth | *** | *** |
| #fug+ | **fugaz** | ephemeral | *** | *** |
| +kol+ | *** | *** | *** | *** |
| #l'ingu+ | **linguado** | flounder | **linguiforme** | tongue-like |
| #son+ | **sonoro** | sonorous | **sonípede** | noisy walker |
| #pɔt++ent+ | **potentado** | potentate | *** | *** |
| #magnɛt+ | **magnetismo** | magnetism | **magnetopausa** | magnetopause |
| #ɔλ+ | **olhar** | facial expression | **olhalvo** | white eyed |
| #vɔm+ | **vómito** | vomitus | **vomífico** | emetic |
| #'arbor+ | **árvore** | tree | **arboriforme** | tree-shaped |
| #kurv+ | **curva** | curve | **curvicórneo** | curved horned |
| #mɔrt+ | **morto** | dead | **mortífero** | lethal |
| #mult+ | **multa**[a] | fine | **multifaceta** | multi-facet |
| #quadr+ | **quadro** | painting | **quadrifónico** | quadriphonic |
| #vir+ | **virulento** | virulent | **virólogo** | virologist |

a This word consists of the root (element) #mult+ plus the +a# ([+feminine]) deriving gender morpheme.

**§12.2.3.1** Similar to the data in Tables 12.11a–b, those in Tables 12.12a–b show that these word-final elements are not mere suffixes. Except for +kɔl++a# and +sid++a#, they all can occur as roots in independent words, and 12 of the 23 (52.17%) can actually occur as the first element in semi-compound words. In these data, /i/ is the only transitional vowel to occur between the first and second elements. In Table 12.12b's semi-compounds that do not have /i/, the vowel interceding between the first and second element is either the final –o (<o# or +o#) of the first element (*bovino* 'bovine', *electro* 'gold-silver

alloy'[18]) and the /u/ of *vírus* 'virus'.[19] In the compound using *olho* 'eye': *mirolho* the final +a# of *mira* 'aim' does not appear. Likewise, there is no final +o of *olho* when the word *alvo* 'white' follows in *olhalvo* 'white eyed'.

**§12.2.3.2** The data in the preceding paragraph as well as those in §12.2.2.1 suggest that for Latinate semi-compounds /i/ is the favored transitional vowel between their first and second elements. Going beyond the samples in Tables 12.11a–b and 12.12a–b and making an actual count of the first and second elements in Latinate semi-compounds, the data in Table 12.13 confirm that over all /i/ is the preferred transitional vowel in Latinate semi-compounds.

**Table 12.13** Latinate Transitional Vowels (2,525 Tokens)

| | /i/ | Ø | /ɔ/ | /o/ | /a/ | /u/ |
|---|---|---|---|---|---|---|
| **Totals:** | 1,986 | 323 | 150 | 32 | 24 | 10 |
| **Percentages:** | 78.65% | 12.79% | 5.94% | 1.27% | 0.95% | 0.40% |

In the entire Latinate sampling, /i/ prevails as the transitional component in 78.65% of the cases. The next most prominent transition (12.79%) is not to have a transitional vowel.

**§12.2.3.3** There are two reasons not to have an intervening vowel between the first and second elements. Either the first element ends in a vowel or a segment that can close a syllable: e.g. #bi+ *bipedal* 'bipedal' (vowel) or #pan+ *pânfobo* 'fear of everything:' (Table 12.17e) and does not need a transitional vowel to combine with a second element, or the second element may begin with a vowel, which allows (e.g. *olhalvo* 'white eyed') the first element's root to appear without its gender morpheme.[20]

---

18 The word *electro* is also a shortened form of *electrocardiograma* 'electrocardiogram'.

19 Quite likely the final /z/ (or /s/) of *virus* disappeared in *virucida* owing to the initial +s/ of +sid++a#.

20 The word *olho* 'eye' provides two cases of this phenomenon: e.g. *olho* 'eye' and *alvo* 'white' combine to form *olhalvo* 'white eyed' and *mira* 'aim' + *olho* 'eye' → *mirolho* 'sharp shooter'. In both cases, the initial vowel of the second element either allows the root to appear without a gender morpheme, or it causes the first element's final vowel to elide.

§**12.2.3.3** Since the vast majority of transitional vowels in Latinate semi-compounds is /i/, and the presence of an element-final or element-initial vowel, as well as element-final /n, l, r, z/ allows the amalgamation of first and second elements without an inserted transitional vowel, Rule 12.5 accounts for the insertion of /i/ in 78.65% of Latinate semi-compounds:

**Rule 12.5 Latinate Semi-compound /i/ Insertion Rule:**

$$\#XC_1 \;??\; CX\# \rightarrow \#XC? \begin{pmatrix} +\text{palatal} \\ +\text{high} \\ -\text{contoid} \end{pmatrix} ?CX\#$$

**Conditions:**

1. At least one boundary of the two unknown boundaries (??) must be +.
2. $C_1$ must not be /n, l, r, z/, i.e. any consonant that can close syllables.[21]

Rule 12.5 accounts for approximately 91.44% of the compound words examined here. The semi-compounds with transitional vowels other than /i/, will be entered in the lexicon, as will those few Latinate semi-compounds whose first element ends in /n, l, r, z/ and has a transitional vowel.[22]

§**12.2.4.0 Hellenic Semi-compounds:** Table 12.14a identifies and analyzes the first elements in Portuguese Hellenic semi-compound nominals.

21 For examples of semi-compound (both Latinate and Hellenic) that have no transitional vowel owing to this phenomenon (see§12.2.5.2.0).

22 In Hellenic semi-compounds, the second elements that occasion proparoxytone stress overwhelmingly favor /ˈɔ/ (§12.2.5.1.0).

**Table 12.14a** Hellenic Semi-compounds: First Element[a]

| Orthography | Analysis | Tokens | Example | -V- | Gloss |
|---|---|---|---|---|---|
| **tri-** | #tri+ | 385 | **triarca** | -Ø- | 1 of 3 rulers |
| **auto-** | #aut+ | 338 | **autolimpante***[b] | /ɔ/ | self-cleaning |
| **mono-** | #mon+ | 270 | **monodia** | /ɔ/ | song by soloist |
| **poli-** | #poli+ | 267 | **poliuria** | -Ø- | polyuria |
| **di-** | #di+ | 235 | **dimorfo** | -Ø- | formed in 2 units |
| **hidr-** | #idr+ | 229 | **hidremia** | -Ø- | excess blood water |
| **hidro-** | | (201) | **hidromante** | /ɔ/ | water witch |
| **hidra-** | | (22) | **hidradenite** | /a/ | sweat gland inflammation |
| **hipo**$_1$**-** | #ipɔ$_1$+[c] | 223 | **hipófora** | -Ø- | deep ulcer |
| **iso-** | #izɔ+ | 208 | **isopia** | -Ø- | equal vision in both eyes |
| **micro-** | #mikrɔ+ | 202 | **microdia** | -Ø- | 1 millionth of a day |
| **bio-** | #bi+ | 200 | **biocoro** | /ɔ/ | type of landscape |
| **hetero-** | #ɛter+ | 160 | **heterotélico** | /ɔ/ | purpose beyond itself |
| **foto-** | #fɔto+ | 154 | **fotossensor*** | -Ø- | light meter |
| **neo-** | #neo+ | 143 | **neomorfo** | -Ø- | newly formed |
| **tele-** | #tɛle+ | 131 | **televizinho*** | -Ø- | TV moocher |
| **aero-** | #aer+ | 126 | **aeromodelo*** | /ɔ/ | model airplane |
| **zoo-** | #zo+ | 123 | **zoobia** | /ɔ/ | vital organ functioning |
| **tetra-** | #tetra+ | 120 | **tetravô*** | -Ø- | 4$^{th}$ generation grandparent |
| **hemo-** | #em+ | 118 | **hemalopia** | /a/ | blood from eyes |
| **hema-** | | (83) | **hemocultura*** | /ɔ/ | blood culture |
| **hem-** | | (8) | **hemartrose** | -Ø- | hemorrhage at joints |
| | #em++at+ | (27) | **hematófago** | /ɔ/ | blood eater |
| **mega-** | #mega+ | 113 | **megablitz (G)**[d] | -Ø- | extreme undertaking |
| **geo-** | #žeɔ+ | 103 | **geotrópico** | -Ø- | geotropic |
| **macro-** | #makrɔ+ | 102 | **macrobjectiva*** | -Ø- | detail photography lens |

Table 12.14a Continued

| Orthography | Analysis | Tokens | Example | -V- | Gloss |
|---|---|---|---|---|---|
| poli- | #pɔli+ | 100 | **poliandria** | -Ø- | polyandry |
| electro- | #ɛlɛktr+ | 99 | **electroimã** | /ɔ/ | electromagnet |
| psico- | #psik+ | 91 | **psicossocial*** | /ɔ/ | psycho-social |
| orto- | #ort+ | 82 | **ortocentro** | /ɔ/ | orthocenter |
| antropo- | #antrop+ | 76 | **antropocoria** | /ɔ/ | planted by humans |
| meso- | #mɛz+ | 76 | **mesoleto** | /ɔ/ | mesolect |
| proto- | #prɔt+ | 74 | **protossol*** | /ɔ/ | proto-sun |
| pseudo- | # pseudɔ+ | 71 | **pseudotrabalhar*** | -Ø- | to feign work |
| termo- | #term+ | 71 | **termostato** | /ɔ/ | thermostat |
| biblio- | #bibli+ | 68 | **bibliomania** | /ɔ/ | manic book obsession |
| hemi- | #emi+ | 67 | **hemipénis** | -Ø- | paired sexual organ |
| penta- | #pent+ | 67 | **pentavalente*** | /a/ | valence of 5 |
| arqui- | #ark+ | 62 | **arquirrival*** | /i/ | arch rival |
| hexa- | #ɛks+ | 58 | **hexacampeã*** | /a/ | six time winner |
| lito- | #lit+ | 57 | **litocola** | /ɔ/ | glue for precious stones |
| deca- | #dɛk+ | 56 | **decagonal** | -Ø- | 10 angled |
| pan- | #pan+ | 56 | **panaceia** | /a/ | panacea |
| paleo- | #paleo+ | 54 | **paleoliteratura*** | -Ø- | ancient literature |
| caco- | #kak+ | 53 | **cacoepia** | /ɔ/ | bad pronunciation |
| $filo_1$- | $\#fil_1+^e$ | 52 | **filopatria*** | /ɔ/ | bound to habitat |
| oxi- | #ɔks+ | 48 | **oxígono** | /i/ | acute angle |
| logo- | #lɔg+ | 47 | **logorreia** | /ɔ/ | compulsive speaking |
| hepta- | #ɛpta+ | 45 | **heptatio** | /a/ | decathlon for women |
| magneto- | #magnɛt+ | 44 | **magnetógrafo** | /ɔ/ | magnetograph |
| odonto- | #odont+ | 43 | **odontorragia** | /ɔ/ | dental hemorrhage |
| etno- | #etn+ | 42 | **etnologia** | /ɔ/ | ethnology |
| melo- | #mɛl+ | 41 | **melodrama** | /ɔ/ | melodrama |
| tox- | #tɔks+ | 40 | **toxómano** | /ɔ/ | obsessive drug user |
| fono- | #fon+ | 39 | **fonotática** | /ɔ/ | phonotactics |
| piro- | #pir+ | 39 | **piromante** | /ɔ/ | fire diviner |
| cosmo- | #kɔzm+ | 37 | **cosmovisão*** | /ɔ/ | worldview |

(*Continued*)

Table 12.14a Continued

| Orthography | Analysis | Tokens | Example | -V- | Gloss |
|---|---|---|---|---|---|
| ptero- | #pter+ | 37 | pterópode | -ɔ- | fin-shaped feet |
| rizo- | #r̠iz+ | 37 | rizofilo | /ɔ/ | root growing leaves |
| quiro- | #kir+ | 35 | quiroplasto | /ɔ/ | piano finger guide |
| cromo- | #krom+ | 35 | cromogravura* | /ɔ/ | color engraving |
| ictio- | #ikti+ | 35 | ictiomorfo | /ɔ/ | fish formed |
| fisio- | #fizi+ | 34 | fisiogénico | /ɔ/ | physiogenic |
| panto- | #panto+ | 34 | pantogamia | -Ø- | trans-species cohabitation |
| oro- | #oro+ | 33 | orogenia | -Ø- | mountain building |
| demo- | #dem+ | 32 | demologia | -Ø- | mass psychology |
| octo- | #ɔkt+ | 32 | octolípide | /ɔ/ | eight-scaled |
| rino- | #rin+ | 32 | rinovírus* | /ɔ/ | rhino-virus |
| oftalmo- | #ɔftalm+ | 31 | oftalmalgia | -Ø- | eye pain |
| glosso- | #glɔs+ | 31 | glossónimo | /ɔ/ | language name |
| cefalo- | #s'ɛfal+ | 31 | cefalópode | /ɔ/ | cephalopod |
| topo- | #tɔp+ | 30 | toporama | /ɔ/ | a specific panorama |
| crono- | #kron+ | 29 | cronofobia | /ɔ/ | fear of aging |
| topo- | #tɔp+ | 28 | topótipo | /ɔ/ | typical of a place |
| anemo- | #anem+ | 28 | anemofilia | /ɔ/ | pollenization by wind |
| hipo$_2$- | #ip$_2$+ | 28 | hipogrifo | /ɔ/ | half-horse-half-fish |
| pato- | #pat+ | 27 | patogenia | /ɔ/ | illness development study |
| gene-<br>geno- | #žen+ | 25 | geneantropia | /e/ | treatise on human origins |
| | | (12) | genótipo | -Ø- | genotype |
| dactilo- | #d'aktil+ | 25 | dactiloteca | /ɔ/ | fingerprint archive |
| gameto- | #gam+ | 25 | gamofobia[f] | /ɔ/ | fear of marriage |
| nomo- | #nom+ | 25 | nomologia | /ɔ/ | study of nature's laws |
| miso- | #mizo+ | 24 | misofilia | -Ø- | love of filth |
| farmaco- | #f'armak+ | 24 | farmacomania | /ɔ/ | compulsive self-medication |
| grafo- | #graf+ | 24 | graforreia | /ɔ/ | compulsive writing |
| tipo- | #tip+ | 24 | tipofonia | /ɔ/ | marking a beat |
| coro- | #kɔr+ | 23 | coromania | /ɔ/ | mania for dancing |

Table 12.14a Continued

| Orthography | Analysis | Tokens | Example | -V- | Gloss |
|---|---|---|---|---|---|
| gino- | #žin+ | 23 | **ginofobia** | /ɔ/ | fear of women |
| morfo- | #morf+ | 22 | **morfogénese** | /ɔ/ | morphogenesis |
| estoma- | #ztoma+ | 21 | **estomalgia** | -Ø- | mouth pain |
| quilo- | #kil+ | 19 | **quilolitro*** | /ɔ/ | 1,000 liters |
| metro$_1$-[g] | #mɛtr$_1$+ | 19 | **metrografia** | -ɔ- | measurement treatise |
| mito$_1$-[h] | #mit+ | 18 | **mitogema** | /ɔ/ | myth topics |
| tecno- | #tɛkn+ | 18 | **tecnómino** | /ɔ/ | technical term |
| metro$_2$- | #mɛtr$_2$+ | 17 | **metrómana** | /ɔ/ | nymphomaniac |
| quilo- | #kil+ | 17 | **quilófito** | /ɔ/ | succulent plant |
| fago- | #fag+ | 17 | **fagómano** | /ɔ/ | obsessive eater |
| potamo- | #pˈɔtam+ | 17 | **potamologia** | /ɔ/ | river study |
| tecno- | #tɛkn+ | 16 | **tecnocrata** | /ɔ/ | technocrat |
| arqueo- | #arke+ | 15 | **arqueografia** | /ɔ/ | ancient site description |
| cali- | #kal+ | 15 | **calistenia** | /i/ | calisthenics |
| onomato- | #onomat+ | 13 | **onomatomancia** | /ɔ/ | personality through name |
| enea- | #enea+ | 12 | **eneafilo** | -Ø- | 9-leaved |
| pluto- | #plut++o# | 12 | **plutocrata** | -Ø- | plutocrat |
| falo- | #fal+ | 10 | **falodinia** | /ɔ/ | pain in the penis |
| sof- | #sɔf+ | 10 | **sofómono** | /ɔ/ | obsessive sophisticate |
| tomo- | #tom+ | 10 | **tomomania** | /ɔ/ | compulsive cutting |
| mito- | #mito$_2$+ | 9 | **mitocôndria** | -Ø- | mitochondria |
| trofo- | #trɔf+ | 9 | **trofobiose** | /ɔ/ | symbiotic nutrition |
| tropo- | #trɔp+ | 8 | **tropófilo** | /ɔ/ | deciduous |
| dromo- | #drom+ | 7 | **dromomania** | /ɔ/ | wanderlust |
| escopo- | #zkɔp+ | 7 | **escopófilo** | /ɔ/ | voyeur |
| gloto- | #glɔt+ | 5 | **glotólogo** | /ɔ/ | linguist |
| mano- | #man+ | 5 | **manóstato** | /ɔ/ | pressure stabilizer |
| asten+ | #aztɛn+ | 3 | **astenópia** | -Ø- | weakness in eyes |
| estato- | #ztat+ | 3 | **estatólito** | /ɔ/ | silicon balancing grain |
| fobo- | #fɔb+ | 3 | **fobofobia** | /ɔ/ | fear of phobias |

*(Continued)*

Table 12.14a Continued

| Orthography | Analysis | Tokens | Example | -V- | Gloss |
|---|---|---|---|---|---|
| glifo- | #glif+ | 2 | **glifodonte** | /ɔ/ | poison duct in tooth |
| edro | #ɛdr+ | 1 | **edrioftalmo** | /i/ | armadillo |
| lise | #liz+ | 1 | **lisérgico** | -Ø- | acidic |

a The 113 elements in Table 12.14a occur in 7,047 different words. M=62.35 words per element, SD=72.03, Z =3.425, which puts the first two elements: *tri-* (4.48) and *auto-* (3.83) in the outlier category.
b The asterisk after a particular semi-compound indicates that the second element is Latinate.
c This element #ipɔ+ (*hipo-* [1]) indicates 'low or under', whereas #ip+ (*hipo-* [2]) indicates 'equine'. The /ɔ/ in words like *hipódromo* 'race track' is an inserted vowel and pertains neither to the first nor the second element.
d A (G) follows *megablitz* because *blitz* is a German word.
e There are two compounding elements whose configuration is #fil+. This one is derived from Greek *phylos* and indicates affection or affinity, the other #fil+ derives from Greek *phy?llon* and indicates leaves or other plant life. The former is #$fil_1$+, the latter #$fil_2$+.
f Of the 25 tokens with #gam+, five have the added suffix +ɛt+, e.g. *gametófito* 'gametophyte'.
g #$mɛtr_1$+ denotes 'measurement'; #$mɛtr_2$+ designates phenomena related to the uterus.
h #$mito_1$+ is different from #$mit_2$+ as in *mitocondria* 'mitochondria'.

The transcriptions in Table 12.14a are morphophonemic, and all elements are preceded by the word boundary symbol # because they are all word-initial. Table 12.14b evaluates these elements' relative productivity:

**Table 12.14b** Hellenic Semi-compounds: First Element Productivity

| Negligible (16.39%) | | | | | | Very Low (18.83%) | | | Low | | |
|---|---|---|---|---|---|---|---|---|---|---|---|
| **Element** | **#** | **%** | **Element** | **#** | **%** | **Element** | **#** | **%** | **Element** | **#** | **%** |
| #ɛdr+ | 1 | 0.01 | #ztoma+ | 21 | 0.30 | #kɔzm+ | 37 | 0.52 | #prɔt+ | 74 | 1.05 |
| #liz+ | 1 | 0.01 | #morf+ | 22 | 0.31 | #pter+ | 37 | 0.52 | #antrop+ | 76 | 1.08 |
| #glif+ | 2 | 0.03 | #kɔr+ | 23 | 0.33 | #ṟiz+ | 37 | 0.52 | #mɛz+ | 76 | 1.08 |
| #aztɛn+ | 3 | 0.04 | #žin+ | 23 | 0.33 | #fon+ | 39 | 0.55 | #ort+ | 82 | 1.16 |
| #ztat+ | 3 | 0.04 | #mizo+ | 24 | 0.30 | #pir+ | 39 | 0.55 | #psik+ | 91 | 1.29 |
| #fɔb+ | 3 | 0.04 | #fˈarmak+ | 24 | 0.34 | #tɔks+ | 40 | 0.57 | #ɛḷɛktr+ | 99 | 1.40 |
| #glɔt+ | 5 | 0.07 | #graf+ | 24 | 0.34 | #mɛl+ | 41 | 0.58 | #pɔli+ | 100 | 1.42 |
| #man+ | 5 | 0.07 | #tip+ | 24 | 0.34 | #etn+ | 42 | 0.60 | #makrɔ+ | 102 | 1.45 |
| #drom+ | 7 | 0.09 | #žen+ | 25 | 0.35 | #odont+ | 43 | 0.61 | #žeɔ+ | 103 | 1.46 |
| #zkɔp+ | 7 | 0.09 | #dˈaktil+ | 25 | 0.35 | #magnɛt+ | 44 | 0.62 | #mega+ | 113 | 1.60 |
| #trɔp+ | 8 | 0.11 | #gam+ | 25 | 0.35 | #ɛpta+ | 45 | 0.64 | #em+ | 118 | 1.67 |
| #mito$_2$+ | 9 | 0.13 | #nom+ | 25 | 0.35 | #lɔg+ | 47 | 0.67 | #tetra+ | 120 | 1.70 |
| #trɔf+ | 9 | 0.13 | #pat+ | 27 | 0.38 | #ɔks+ | 48 | 0.68 | #zo+ | 123 | 1.75 |
| #fal+ | 10 | 0.14 | #tɔp+ | 28 | 0.40 | #fil$_1$+ | 52 | 0.74 | #aer+ | 126 | 1.79 |
| #sɔf+ | 10 | 0.14 | #anem+ | 28 | 0.40 | #kak+ | 53 | 0.75 | #tɛle+ | 131 | 1.86 |
| #tom+ | 10 | 0.14 | #ip$_2$+ | 28 | 0.40 | #paleo+ | 54 | 0.77 | #neo+ | 143 | 2.03 |
| #enea+ | 12 | 0.17 | #kron+ | 29 | 0.40 | #dɛk+ | 56 | 0.79 | #fɔtʊ+ | 154 | 2.18 |
| #plut++o# | 12 | 0.17 | #tɔp+ | 30 | 0.43 | #pan+ | 56 | 0.79 | #ɛter+ | 160 | 2.27 |
| #onomat+ | 13 | 0.18 | #ɔftalm+ | 31 | 0.44 | #lit+ | 57 | 0.81 | #bi+ | 200 | 2.84 |
| #arke+ | 15 | 0.21 | #glɔs+ | 31 | 0.44 | #ɛks+ | 58 | 0.82 | #mikrɔ+ | 202 | 2.87 |
| #kal+ | 15 | 0.21 | #sˈɛfal+ | 31 | 0.44 | #ark+ | 62 | 0.88 | #izɔ+ | 208 | 2.95 |
| #tɛkn+ | 16 | 0.22 | #dem+ | 32 | 0.45 | #emi+ | 67 | 0.95 | **Modest** | | |
| #mɛtr$_2$+ | 17 | 0.24 | #ɔkt+ | 32 | 0.45 | #pent+ | 67 | 0.95 | #ipɔ$_1$+ | 223 | 3.16 |
| #kil+ | 17 | 0.24 | #rin+ | 32 | 0.45 | #bibli+ | 68 | 0.95 | #idr+ | 229 | 3.25 |
| #fag+ | 17 | 0.24 | #oro+ | 33 | 0.47 | #term+ | 71 | 1.00 | #di+ | 235 | 3.33 |
| #pˈɔtam+ | 17 | 0.24 | #fizi+ | 34 | 0.48 | #pseudɔ+ | 71 | 1.00 | #poli+ | 267 | 3.79 |
| #mit+ | 18 | 0.25 | #panto+ | 34 | 0.48 | | | | #mon+ | 270 | 3.83 |
| #tɛkn+ | 18 | 0.25 | #kir+ | 35 | 0.40 | | | | #aut+ | 338 | 4.80 |
| #kil+ | 19 | 0.27 | #krom+ | 35 | 0.50 | | | | #tri+ | 385 | 5.46 |
| #mɛtr$_1$+ | 19 | 0.27 | #ikti+ | 35 | 0.50 | | | | | | |

**§12.2.4.1** That none of these 113 elements has a productivity greater than modest, yet two of the modestly productive elements (#aut+ and #tri+) are outliers is striking. Equally striking is that 53.10% of these elements are of negligible productivity and account for 16.39% of all the tokens. The elements of very low productivity account for 18.83% of the tokens, the low 36.90%, and the modest 27.62%. The modestly productive elements' average productivity is 3.95%, which is the highest of any of the other categories' averages.

**§12.2.4.2** All of these elements (save *pluto*) end in +, which indicates that they are not complete words—they must be followed by at least one other morpheme to emerge as words, or in the case of Table 12.13, the first elements are followed by a transitional vowel that pertains to neither the first nor the second element. The vowel /ɔ/ is the most predominant transitional vowel with 75 tokens,[23] /a/ is next with six, /i/ with four. There are 32 instances in which no vowel intercedes—either because the first element ends in a vowel (e.g. #ipɔ+ as in *hipófora*), or because the second begins with one (e.g. +ɛm++i++a# as in *hidremia*). Table 12.15 displays the overall prominence of transitional vowels in the Hellenic semi-compounds.

**Table 12.15** Hellenic Transitional Components (6,999 Tokens)

| | /ɔ/ | Ø | /a/ | /i/ | /e/ |
|---|---|---|---|---|---|
| **Totals:** | 3,674 | 2,972 | 208 | 126 | 25 |
| **Percentages:** | **52.49** | **42.46** | **2.97** | **1.80** | **0.36** |

Over all, /ɔ/ prevails as the transitional vowel in Hellenic semi-compounds, but it is not nearly as preponderant as /i/ is for Latinate semi-compounds. However, a much larger proportion of the Hellenic semi-compounds does not have a transitional vowel: (A) because the first element ends in a vowel that is not altered by the second element;[24] (B) because the second element begins with a vowel allowing a final consonant on the first element to become a syllable-onset in the resultant semi-compound; (C) because the first element ends in a consonant that can occur syllable-finally. That is, 94.95% of the Hellenic semi-compounds studed here can be accounted for by a rule similar to Rule 12.4:

23 This vowel is /ɔ/ rather than /o/ because when a second element causes it to be stressed, the vowel emerges as [ɔ]. When the vowel is not stressed, it emerges as either [o] in most Brazilian pronunciations or as [ŭ] in typically Portuguese pronunciations.

24 There is a subset of both Latinate and Hellenic second elements that occasion proparoxytone stress that falls on either the transitional vowel of semi-compounds or on the final vowel of the first element. (§12.2.5.0–2.1.)

**Rule 12.6 Hellenic Semi-compound /ɔ/ Insertion Rule:**

$$\#XC_1??CX\# \rightarrow \#XC_1? \begin{bmatrix} +\text{labial} \\ +\text{w.g.} \\ -\text{contoid} \end{bmatrix} ?CX\#_h$$

**Conditions:**

1. At least one of the two unknown boundaries (??) must be +.
2. $C_1$ must not be /n, l, r, z/, i.e. any consonant that can close syllables.

Rule 12.6 inserts /ɔ/ between the first element and second elements of a Hellenic semi-compounds (H) when the first element ends in a consonant other than /n, l, r, z/ and the second element begins with a consonant. Rules 12.5 and 12.6 can be conflated into a single rule:

**Rule 12.7 Epenthetic Vowel Insertion (Latinate and Hellenic Semi-compounds):**

$$\#XC_1??CX\# \rightarrow \#XC_1? \begin{bmatrix} -\text{contoid} \\ \left\{ \begin{matrix} \begin{bmatrix} +\text{labial} \\ +\text{w.g.} \end{bmatrix} \\ \alpha \begin{bmatrix} +\text{palatal} \\ +\text{high} \end{bmatrix} \end{matrix} \right\} \end{bmatrix} ?CX\#_{\alpha l}$$

**Conditions:**

1. At least one of the two unknown boundaries (??) must be +.
2. $C_1$ must not be /n, l, r, z/, i.e. any consonant that can close syllables.

The subscript αL indicates that Latinate semi-compounds occasion the α-prefixed member of Rule 12.7's disjunction—i.e. the high palatal non-contoid /i/, which intercedes between the two compounding elements. Those semi-compounds that are not Latinate (i.e. the Hellenic ones), have an /ɔ/ inserted.[25] The remaining, atypical, transitional vowels will appear in the lexicon with said vowels between their two elements.

**§12.2.4.3** Table 12.14b demonstrates that most of Table 12.14ă's first elements also occur as roots of independent words.

**Table 12.14b** Semi-compound First Elements as Hellenic Roots

| Root | Example | Gloss | Root | Example | Gloss |
|---|---|---|---|---|---|
| .#tri+ | **triagem** | triage | #krom+ | **croma** | tv color index |
| #aut+ | **autista** | autistic | #ikti+ | **ictíico** | relative to fish |
| #mon+ | **mónoda** | monad | #panto+ | *** | *** |
| #di+ | **díada** | dyad | #oro+ | *** | *** |
| #idr+ | **hidrante** | hydrant | #kozm+ | **cosmo** | cosmos |
| #ipɔ+ | ***a[a] | *** | #mɛgalo+ | *** | *** |
| #izo+ | *** | *** | #rin+ | *** | *** |
| #mikro+ | ***a | *** | #fizi+ | **física** | physics |
| #bi+ | **bioma** | biome | #oftalm+ | **oftalmia** | eye inflammation |
| #ɛter+ | **hetera** | prostitute | #kil+ | **quilíade** | 1 thousand |
| #fɔto+ | **foto** | photo | #anem+ | **anemona** | ubiquitous plant |
| #neo+ | **neon** | neon | #kron+ | **crónica** | chronicle |
| #tɛle+ | ***a | *** | #dɛk+ | **década** | decade |
| #aer+ | **aerar** | to air | #ɔkt+ | **octão** | 8 day interval |
| #zo+ | **zoico** | animal life | #kir+ | *** | *** |
| #tetra+ | **tetrada** | foursome | #demo+ | *** | *** |
| #žeo+ | **geode** | geode | #pat+ | **pateta** | fool |
| #makro+ | **macro** | macron | #tɔp+ | **tópico** | topical |
| #pɔli+ | **política** | politics | #mizo+ | *** | *** |
| #ɛlɛktr+ | **eléctrico** | electric | #glɔs+ | **glossário** | glossary |
| #psik+ | **psicose** | psychosis | #ip+ | **hípico** | related to horses |
| #em+ | **hemácia** | blood cell | #dˈaktil+ | **dactilite** | finger inflammation |
| #ort+ | **ortose** | orthotic | #fˈarmak+ | **farmácia** | pharmacy |

25 The classification of hybrid forms can be somewhat arbitrary: some end up being considered Latinate others Hellenic. This comes from examining each category according to first and second elements. Sometimes only second elements are of the opposite type. Sometimes second elements will only occur with first elements of the opposite type, e.g. #L#+H#, #H+#L#.

Table 12.14b Continued

| Root | Example | Gloss | Root | Example | Gloss |
|---|---|---|---|---|---|
| #antrop+ | **antropia** | human impact | #morf+ | **morfema** | morpheme |
| #mɛz+ | **mesial** | related to mean | #kɔr+ | *** | *** |
| #prɔt+ | **prótase** | content notice | #ztoma+ | **estômago** | stomach |
| #pseudo+ | *** | *** | #tip+ | **tipo** | type |
| #term+ | **termo** | thermos | #p'ɔtam+ | **potamite** | river dweller |
| #bibli+ | **bíblia** | Bible | #mit+ | **mito** | myth |
| #pent+ | **pentano** | pentane | #tɛkn+ | **técnica** | technique |
| #ɛks+ | **hexodo** | 6 electrodes | #arke+ | **arqueano** | pre-pre-cambrian |
| #lit+ | **lítico** | related to rocks | #onomat+ | **onomático** | related to names |
| #pan+ | *** | *** | #enea+ | *** | *** |
| #paleo+ | *** | *** | #plut++o# | **pluto** | wealth |
| #kak+ | **cagar** | to shit | #žin+ | **gineceu** | gynoecium |
| #fil+ | *** | *** | #kal+ | **calor** | heat |
| #ɛpta+ | **heptano** | heptane | #fal+ | **falo** | phallus |
| #odont+ | **odonite** | tooth pain | #mito+ | **mitoma** | fibrous reticule |
| #etn+ | **entia** | ethnic group | #trɔf+ | **trófico** | related to nutrition |
| #mɛl+ | **melar** | to be silly | #trɔp+ | **tropo** | trope |
| #fon+ | **fon** | phon | #ztat+ | **estático** | static |
| #pir+ | **pira** | pyre | #glif+ | **glifo** | glyph |
| #mega+ | ***a | *** | #liz+ | **lisado** | acidic suspension |
| #riz+ | **riz** | sail cable | *** | *** | *** |

a The dingbats followed by a indicate that the root may constitute an abbreviation of a longer form, e.g. *hipo* is the shortened form of *hiposulfito de sódio* 'sodium hyposulfite'.

The occurrence of these first elements as roots of independent words identifies their actual forms because deriving suffixes attach to the bare root in most cases. With the roots identified, most of the vowels interceding between the first and second elements of the words in Table 12.14a are transitional vowels.

**§12.2.4.4.0** Table 12.15a identifies and analyzes the second elements in Portuguese Hellenic semi-compounds.

Table 12.15a Hellenic Semi-compounds: Second Element[a]

| Orthography | Transcription | Tokens | Example | Gloss |
|---|---|---|---|---|
| **-logia** | #lɔg++i++a# | 531 | ****algologia**[b] | study of algae |
| **-alogia** | | (10) | **genealogia** | genealogy |
| **-ilogia** | | (6) | **braquilogia** | shorted linguistic form |
| **-metro***[c] | #mɛtr++o# | 499 | **catetómetro** | vertical distance meter |
| **-grafia** | #graf++i++a# | 345 | ***rurografia** | treatise on rural life |
| **-mano*** | #man+<[αfem.] | 292 | ***galómano** | francophile |
| **-grafo*** | #graf+<[αfem.] | 238 | **ofiógrafo** | snake specialist writer |
| **-tomia** | #tom++i++a# | 233 | **ornitomia** | bird dissection |
| **-ólogo*** | #lɔg+<[αfem.][d] | 209 | ***amazonólogo** | Amazon specialist |
| **-álogo** | | (6) | **penálogo** | penal specialist |
| **-ílogo** | | (3) | **epílogo** | epilog |
| **-fobo*** | #fɔb+<[αfem.] | 205 | ***halitófobo** | fear of one's halitosis |
| **-fobia** | #fɔb++i++a# | 199 | ***apifobia** | fear of bees |
| **-mania** | #man++i++a# | 161 | ***ablutomania** | excessive bathing |
| **-metria**[e] | #mɛtr++i++a# | 156 | ***audiometria** | hearing test |
| **-grama** | #gram++a# | 119 | ***cecograma** | braille text |
| **-filia** | #fil$_1$++i++a# | 111 | ***padrofilia** | love for priests |
| **-céfalo** | #sˈɛfalo++i++a# | 98 | **ofiocéfalo** | snake-headed |
| **-algia** | #alg++i++a# | 94 | ***nostalgia** | nostalgia |
| **-terapia** | #terap++i++a# | 91 | **fitoterapia** | plant therapy |
| **-scopia** | #ezkɔp++i++a# | 84 | **uranoscopia** | astrology |
| **-geno*** | #žen+<[αfem.]# | 82 | **tricógeno** | hair grower |
| **-ptero*** | +pter+<[αfem.]# | 80 | **quiróptero** | flying mammal |
| **-foro*** | #fɔr+<[αfem.]# | 78 | **zimóforo** | yeast transporter |
| **-mancia** | #mans++i++a# | 76 | **brizomancia** | dream divination |
| **-fago*** | #fag +<[αfem.]# | 74 | **zoófago** | eater of live prey |
| **-lise*** | #liz++e# | 74 | **fotólise** | decomposition by light |

Table 12.15a Continued

| Orthography | Transcription | Tokens | Example | Gloss |
|---|---|---|---|---|
| -génio | #žɛn+<[αfem.]# | 60 | **fitogénio** | produced by plants |
| -morfo | #morf+<[αfem.]# | 58 | **zoomorfo** | animal in appearance |
| -gono* | #gon+<[αfem.]# | 57 | **epígono** | disciple |
| -nomia | #nɔm++i++a# | 57 | ***siglonomia** | word's letters enunciated |
| -tecnia | #tɛkn+ | 55 | **aerotecnia** | air industry |
| -técnico | | (31) | **biotécnico** | biotechnical |
| -arquia | #ark++i++a# | 54 | **oligarquia** | oligarchy |
| -arca | #ark+αa# | (24) | **genearca** | $1^{st}$ of a lineage |
| -cracia | #krat++i++a# | 52 | **pornocracia** | governed by courtesans |
| -crata | #krat++a# | (22) | ***canalhocrata** | low life ruler |
| -edro | +ɛdr++o# | 52 | **plagiedro** | obliquely faceted crystal |
| -teca | #tɛk++a# | 46 | **pinoteca** | painting collection |
| -fagia | #fag++i++a# | 41 | **taquifagia** | rapid eating |
| -gamia | #gam++i++a# | 40 | **homogamia** | self-fertilization |
| -dáctilo | #dˈaktil<[αfem.]# | 37 | **didáctilo** | 2 toed |
| -fono*? | #fon+<[αfem.]# | 36 | ***lusófono** | Portuguese speaker |
| -gino* | #žin+<[αfem.]# | 34 | **andrógino** | androgynous |
| -stomo* | #ztom+<[αfem.]# | 34 | **cacóstomo** | bad pronunciation |
| -nomo* | #nɔm+<[αfem.]# | 33 | **gastrónomo** | gastronome |
| -tomo | #tom+<[αfem.]# | 30 | **ciclótomo** | surgical instrument |
| -gamo* | #gam+<[αfem.]# | 28 | **fanerógamo** | visible sexual organs |
| -tropo * | +trɔp+<[αfem.]# | 28 | **homótropo** | with similar tastes |
| -pata | #pat++a# | 26 | **homeopata** | homeopath |
| -rragia | +ṟagi++a# | 25 | **falorragia** | hemorrhage of the penis |

(*Continued*)

Table 12.15a Continued

| Orthography | Transcription | Tokens | Example | Gloss |
|---|---|---|---|---|
| -stato | +ztat++o# | 23 | higróstato | air pressure mechanism |
| -dromo* | #drom++o# | 24 | *kartódromo | go-cart track |
| -óxido | #ˈɔksid++o# | 19 | dióxido | dioxide |
| -tono* | #ton+<[αfem.]# | 19 | ecótono | ecotone |
| -rrino | #r̲in+<[αfem.]# | 17 | paquirrino | thick nose(d) |
| -agogo | +agɔg+<[αfcm.]# | 16 | hidragogo | diuretic |
| -glosso | #glɔs+<[αfem.]# | 16 | hipoglosso | below the tongue |
| -sofia | #zɔf++i++a# | 16 | mateosofia | pseudo-science |
| -glifo*? | #glif+<[αfem.]# | 15 | díglifo | two striped |
| -stoma* | #ztom++a# | 15 | citóstoma | alimentary opening |
| -oftalmo | #oftalm<[αfem.]# | 13 | lagoftalmo | inability to shut eyes |
| -peia | +pε++a# | 13 | ritmopeia | laws of rhythm |
| -antropo | #antrɔp+<[αfem.]# | 11 | filantropo | philanthropic |
| -pole* | #pɔl++e# | 10 | megalópole | megalopolis |
| -cromo | #krom+<[αfem.]# | 9 | calicromo | beautifully colored |
| -crono* | #kron+<[αfem.]# | 9 | oligócrono | short lived |
| -tóxico | #tˈɔksik+<[αfem.]# | 9 | nefrotóxico | nephro-toxic |
| -astenia | #asten++i++a# | 13 | logastenia | difficulty in reading |
| -maquia | #mak++i++a# | 8 | logomaquia | dispute over words |
| -clase* | +klaz++e# | 7 | litóclase | natural fissure in rocks |
| -coro | #kɔr+<[αfem.]# | 7 | hidrocoro | water born plant spores |
| -rrizo | #riz+<[αfem.]# | 7 | polirrizo | many rooted |

Table 12.15a Continued

| Orthography | Transcription | Tokens | Example | Gloss |
|---|---|---|---|---|
| -trofo* | #trɔf+<[αfem.]# | 7 | **pedótrofo** | child nutritionist |
| -topo* | #tɔp++o# | 6 | **isótopo** | isotope |
| -metra | #mɛtr++a# | 5 | **geómetra** | geometer |
| -pose | +pɔz++e# | 5 | **adipose** | obesity |
| -doxo | #dɔks+<[αfem.]# | 4 | **ortodoxo** | orthodox |
| -glossa | #glɔs++a# | 4 | **isoglossa** | isogloss |
| -glota | #glɔt+α<a# | 3 | **monoglota** | monolingual |
| -fármaco | #farmak++o# | 3 | **alexifármaco** | anti-venom medicine |
| -gene | #žen++e# | 3 | **oncogene** | oncogene |
| -falo | #fal++o# | 2 | **difalo** | double penis |
| -quiro | #kir+<[αfem.]# | 2 | **hecatonquiro** | 100 handed |

a Table 12.15a consists of 77 Hellenic elements (5,352 tokens) that can appear as second elements in compounds in a total of 5,352 different words: M=69.51, SD= 102.00, Z=3.292. The first two elements #log++i++a# (Z=4.52) and #mɛtr++o# (Z= 4.21) are outliers.

b An asterisk appears before semi-compounds whose first element is not Hellenic. All are Latinate save *kart* which has been borrowed from English with the initial k used to designate go-karts rather than ordinary carts such as ox-carts.

c As in Table 12.12a, the asterisk after an element indicates that the element in question occasions proparoxytone stress.

d #lɔg++i++a# and #lɔg+<[αfem.] appear in different sections of Table 12.15a owing to their suffixes: deriving in the first case, inflecting in the second—c.f. *-grafia* and *-grafo*, *-fobia* and *–fobo*, *-metro* and *-metria*, *-fobo* and *-fobia*, *-mano* and *-mania*, etc. (static nouns in the first case, noun/adjectives in the second).

e This element mainly denotes measurement, but the word *ametria* indicates 'no measurement' and 'congenital lack of a uterus', and *hidrometria* indicates both 'water measurement' and 'water in the uterus'.

The transcriptions in Table 12.15a are morphophonemic, and the elements preceded by the word boundary symbol # can be word-initial (see Table 12.15b). Element-finally all end in nominal forming suffixes, be they inflecting gender suffixes or noun- or adjective-deriving suffixes. Table 12.15b displays the productivity hierarchy of Helenic second elements:

**Table 12.15b** Hellenic Semi-compounds: Second Elements' Productivity

| 35 Negligible 7.27 | | | 13 Very Low 9.16 | | | 6 Modest 25.71 | | |
|---|---|---|---|---|---|---|---|---|
| **Element** | **#** | **%** | **Element** | **#** | **%** | **Element** | **#** | **%** |
| #fal++o# | 2 | 0.04 | #gam+<[αfem.]# | 28 | 0.52 | #fɔb++i++a# | 199 | 3.72 |
| #kir+<[αfem.]# | 2 | 0.04 | +trɔp+<[αfem.]# | 28 | 0.52 | #fɔb+<[αfem.] | 205 | 3.83 |
| #glɔt+<a# | 3 | 0.05 | #tom+<[αfem.]# | 30 | 0.56 | #lɔg+<[αfem.] | 209 | 3.90 |
| #farmak++o# | 3 | 0.05 | #nɔm+<[αfem.]# | 33 | 0.62 | #tom++i++a# | 233 | 4.35 |
| #žen++e# | 3 | 0.05 | #žin+<[αfem.]# | 34 | 0.63 | #graf+<[αfem.] | 238 | 4.45 |
| #dɔks+<[αfem.]# | 4 | 0.07 | #ztom+<[αfem.]# | 34 | 0.63 | #man+<[αfem.] | 292 | 5.46 |
| #glɔs++a# | 4 | 0.07 | #fon+<[αfem.]# | 36 | 0.67 | **3 High 25.69** | | |
| #mεtr++a# | 5 | 0.09 | #d'aktil<[αfem.]# | 37 | 0.69 | #graf++i++a# | 345 | 6.45 |
| +pɔz++e# | 5 | 0.09 | #gam++i++a# | 40 | 0.75 | #mεtr++o# | 499 | 9.32 |
| #tɔp++o# | 6 | 0.11 | #fag++i++a# | 41 | 0.77 | #lɔg++i++a# | 531 | 9.92 |
| +klaz++e# | 7 | 0.13 | #tεk++a# | 46 | 0.86 | | | |
| #kɔr+<[αfem.]# | 7 | 0.13 | #krat++i++a# | 52 | 0.97 | | | |
| #riz+<[αfem.]# | 7 | 0.13 | +εdr++o# | 52 | 0.97 | | | |
| #trɔf+<[αfem.]# | 7 | 0.13 | **20 Low 32.07** | | | | | |
| #mak++i++a# | 8 | 0.15 | #ark++i++a# | 54 | 1.01 | | | |
| #krom+<[αfem.]# | 9 | 0.17 | #tεkn+ | 55 | 1.03 | | | |
| #kron+<[αfem.]# | 9 | 0.17 | #gon+<[αfem.]# | 57 | 1.06 | | | |
| #t'ɔksik+<[αfem.]# | 9 | 0.17 | #nɔm++i++a# | 57 | 1.06 | | | |
| #pɔl++e# | 10 | 0.19 | #morf+<[αfem.]# | 58 | 1.08 | | | |
| #antrɔp+<[αfem.]# | 11 | 0.20 | #žεn+<[αfem.]# | 60 | 1.11 | | | |
| #oftalm<[αfem.]# | 13 | 0.24 | #fag +<[αfem.]# | 74 | 1.38 | | | |
| +pε++a# | 13 | 0.24 | #liz++e# | 74 | 1.38 | | | |
| #asten++i++a# | 13 | 0.24 | #mans++i++a# | 76 | 1.42 | | | |
| #glif+<[αfem.]# | 15 | 0.28 | #fɔr+<[αfem.]# | 78 | 1.46 | | | |
| #ztom++a# | 15 | 0.28 | +pter+<[αfem.]# | 80 | 1.49 | | | |
| +agɔg+<[αfem.]# | 16 | 0.30 | #žen+<[αfem.]# | 82 | 1.53 | | | |
| #glɔs+<[αfem.]# | 16 | 0.30 | #ezkɔp++i++a# | 84 | 1.57 | | | |
| #zɔf++i++a# | 16 | 0.30 | #terap++i++a# | 91 | 1.70 | | | |
| #r̲in+<[αfem.]# | 17 | 0.32 | #alg++i++a# | 94 | 1.76 | | | |
| #'ɔksid++o# | 19 | 0.35 | #s'εfalo++i++a# | 98 | 1.83 | | | |
| #ton+<[αfem.]# | 19 | 0.35 | #fil$_1$++i++a# | 111 | 2.07 | | | |
| +ztat++o# | 23 | 0.43 | #gram++a# | 119 | 2.22 | | | |
| #drom++o# | 24 | 0.45 | #mεtr++i++a# | 156 | 2.91 | | | |
| +r̲agi++a# | 25 | 0.47 | #man++i++a# | 161 | 3.00 | | | |
| #pat++a# | 26 | 0.49 | | | | | | |

The 35 negligibly productive elements (45.45% of the data) account for only 7.27% of all the tokens. Conversely, the five modest and three highly productive elements account account for 51.40% of all the tokens.

**§12.2.4.4.1** Table 12.16 contains instantiations of second position semi-compound elements that occur as roots of words.

**Table 12.16** Hellenic Second Elements: Roots and $1^{st}$ Elements

| Orthography | Morpheme | Example | Gloss | Position[a] | |
|---|---|---|---|---|---|
| -logia<br>(-logo*) | #lɔg+ | **lógico** | logical | $1^{st}$ | $2^{nd}$ |
| -metro*<br>(-metria)<br>(-metra) | #mɛtr+ | **metro** | meter | $1^{st}$ | $2^{nd}$ |
| -grafia<br>(-grafo) | #graf+ | **grafia** | writing | $1^{st}$ | $2^{nd}$ |
| -mano*<br>(-mania) | #man+ | **maníaco** | maniac | $1^{st}$ | $2^{nd}$ |
| -tomia<br>(-tomo*) | #tom+ | **tomo** | tome | $1^{st}$ | $2^{nd}$ |
| -fobo*<br>(-fobia) | #fob+ | **fobia** | phobia | $1^{st}$ | $2^{nd}$ |
| -grama | #gram+ | **grama** | gram | *** | $2^{nd}$ |
| -filia | #fil$_1$+ | **filo** | phylum | $1^{st}$ | $2^{nd}$ |
| -céfalo | #sˈɛfal+ | **cefálico** | cephalic | $1^{st}$ | $2^{nd}$ |
| -algia | #alg+ | **algia** | (any) pain | *** | $2^{nd}$ |
| -terapia | #terap+ | **terapia** | therapy | *** | $2^{nd}$ |
| -scopia | #zkɔp+ | **escopo** | scope | $1^{st}$ | $2^{nd}$ |
| -geno | #žɛn+ | **gene** | gene | $1^{st}$ | $2^{nd}$ |
| -ptero* | #pter+ | **pteroide** | wing-like | $1^{st}$ | $2^{nd}$ |
| -foro* | #fɔr+ | *** | *** | *** | $2^{nd}$ |
| -mancia | #mans+ | **mancípio** | slave | *** | $2^{nd}$ |
| -fago* | #fag+ | *** | *** | $1^{st}$ | $2^{nd}$ |
| -lise* | #liz+ | **lise** | destruction | $1^{st}$ | $2^{nd}$ |
| -morfo | #mɔrf+ | **morfema** | morpheme | $1^{st}$ | $2^{nd}$ |
| -tecnia<br>(-técnico) | #tɛkn- | **técnico** | technician | $1^{st}$ | $2^{nd}$ |

(*Continued*)

Table 12.16 Continued

| Orthography | Morpheme | Example | Gloss | Position[a] | |
|---|---|---|---|---|---|
| **-gono*** | #gɔn+ | **gónada** | gonad | *** | 2nd |
| **-edro** | #ɛdr+ | *** | *** | *** | 2nd |
| **-nomia (-nomo)** | #nɔm+ | **nome** | name | 1st | 2nd |
| **-teca** | #tɛk+ | **teca** | covering | | 2nd |
| **-gamia (-gamo*)** | #gam+ | **gameta** | gamete | 1st | 2nd |
| **-dáctilo** | #daktil+ | **dactilite** | finger pain | 1st | 2nd |
| **-gino*** | #žin+ | **ginoide** | 2 X, 1 Y[b] | 1st | 2nd |
| **-arquia (-arca)** | #ark+ | **arquivo** | archive | 1st | 2nd |
| **-cracia (-crata)** | +krat+ | *** | *** | *** | 2nd |
| **-pata** | #pat+ | **patético** | pathetic | 1st | 2nd |
| **-rragia** | #r̲ag+ | **rágada** | slender ulceration | *** | 2nd |
| **-stato** | #ztat+ | **estático** | static | 1st | 2nd |
| **-dromo*** | #drom+ | *** | *** | 1st | 2nd |
| **-tropo*** | #trɔp+ | **tropo** | trope | 1st | 2nd |
| **-óxido** | #ɔks+ | **óxido** | oxide | 1st | 2nd |
| **-rrino** | #r̲ino+ | **rinário** | nostril lips | 1st | 2nd |
| **-agogo** | #agog+ | **agoge** | sound series | | 2nd |
| **-glosso -glossa** | #glɔs+ | **glossário** | glossary | 1st | 2nd |
| **-sofia** | #sɔf+ | **sofisma** | sophism | 1st | 2nd |
| **-glifo*** | #glif+ | **glifo** | glyph | 1st | 2nd |
| **-stoma*** | #ztɔm+ | **estoma** | plant opening | 1st | 2nd |
| **-oftalmo** | #ɔftalm+ | **oftálmico** | eye related | 1st | 2nd |
| **-peia** | #pɛ+ | *** | *** | *** | 2nd |
| **-fono*** | #fon+ | **fonética** | phonetics | 1st | 2nd |
| **-pole*** | #pol+ | **político** | politic | 1st | 2nd |
| **-rrizo** | #r̲iz+ | **riz** | sail cable | 1st | 2nd |
| **-cromo** | #krɔm+ | **croma** | color data | 1st | 2nd |
| **-crono*** | #krɔn+ | **crónica** | chronicle | 1st | 2nd |
| **-tóxico** | #tɔks+ | **toxicar** | to intoxicate | 1st | 2nd |
| **-trofo*** | #trof+ | *** | *** | 1st | 2nd |
| **-astenia** | #aztɛn+ | **astenia** | weakness | 1st | 2nd |

Table 12.16 Continued

| Orthography | Morpheme | Example | Gloss | Position[a] | |
|---|---|---|---|---|---|
| -maquia | +mak+ | *** | *** | *** | 2nd |
| -clase* | #klaz+ | *** | *** | *** | 2nd |
| -coro | #kor+ | *** | *** | 1st | 2nd |
| -topo* | #tɔp+ | tópico | topic | 1st | 2nd |
| -pose | #pɔz+ | *** | *** | *** | 2nd |
| -doxo | #dɔks+ | *** | *** | 1st | 2nd |
| -glota | #glɔt+ | glote | glotis | 1st | 2nd |
| -fármaco | #fˈarmak+ | farmácia | pharmacy | 1st | 2nd |
| -falo | #fal+ | falo | phallus | 1st | 2nd |
| -quiro | #kir+ | *** | *** | 1st | 2nd |

a This section indentifies Hellenic second elements that may aslo occur as first elements in semi-compound nominals.
b Chromosomes.

In addition to demonstrating that 13 (21.31%) of its 61 elements do not provide roots for non-compound words, Table 12.16 also shows that 46 (75.41%) of these elements occur both in first and in second positions, and 15 (24.59%) occur only in the second position of compounds.

**§12.2.5.0** Paragraphs 12.2.0–4.3 demonstrate that considerable numbers of the elements (both Latinate and Hellenic) initially identified as either first or second in the formation of semi-compound words actually occur as both first and second elements in semi-compounds. This flexibility parallels the phenomena examined earlier (§12.1.0–2.8), where specific words could be either the first or second element in two word compounds. But semi-compound nominals differ from true compound nominals in two ways: their gender and number appear as suffixes on the second element, and, regardless of the number of syllables a semi-compound may have, they only have one syllable that bears primary stress.

**§12.2.5.1.0 Proparoxytone Stress:** Tables 12.17a–b contain both the Latinate and Hellenic second elements that occasion proparoxytone semi-compound words.

Table 12.17a Latinate Proparoxytone Stress-Inducing Second Elements

| | | Transitional Vowels | | | | | |
|---|---|---|---|---|---|---|---|
| Element | Example | /ˈɔ/ | /ˈi/ | /ˈɛ/ | /ˈa/ | /ˈu/ | Totals |
| #fɛr+<[αfem.]# | vaporífero | 1 | 271 | 0 | 1 | 0 | 273 |
| +kɔl++a# | salícola | 0 | 87 | 0 | 0 | 0 | 87 |
| #fik+<[αfem.]# | vulnífico | 0 | 68 | 4 | 13 | 0 | 85 |
| #pɛd++e# | solípede | 0 | 59 | 0 | 0 | 1 | 60 |
| #žɛr+<[αfem.]# | sedígero | 0 | 46 | 0 | 0 | 0 | 46 |
| #vɔr+<[αfem.]# | ratívoro | 0 | 41 | 0 | 0 | 0 | 41 |
| #par+<[αfem.]# | uriníparo | 0 | 30 | 0 | 1 | 0 | 31 |
| #fug+<[αfem.]# | lucífugo | 0 | 27 | 0 | 0 | 0 | 27 |
| #son+<[αfem.]# | raucíssono | 0 | 17 | 0 | 0 | 0 | 17 |
| #vom+<[αfem.]# | terrívomo | 0 | 6 | 0 | 0 | 0 | 6 |
| #vir+<[αfem.]# | semíviro | 0 | 2 | 2 | 0 | 0 | 4 |
| Totals: | | 1 | 654 | 6 | 15 | 1 | 677 |
| Percentages of Total: | | 0.15% | 96.6% | 0.90% | 2.20% | 0.15% | |

Table 12.17b Hellencic Proparoxytone Stress-Inducing Second Elements

| | | Transitional Vowels | | | | | |
|---|---|---|---|---|---|---|---|
| Element | Example | /ˈɔ/ | /ˈi/ | /ˈɛ/ | /ˈa/ | /ˈu/ | Totals |
| #mɛtr++o# | catetómetro | 400 | 24 | 2 | 15 | 1 | 442 |
| #man+<[αfem.] | *galómano | 265 | 21 | 2 | 0 | 0 | 288 |
| #graf+<[αfem.] | ofiógrafo | 209 | 20 | 5 | 4 | 0 | 238 |
| #lɔg+<[αfem.] | *amazonólogo | 201 | 3 | 0 | 6 | 0 | 210 |
| #fɔb+<[αfem.] | *halitófobo | 190 | 5 | 0 | 3 | 0 | 198 |
| +pter+<[αfem.]# | quiróptero | 61 | 12 | 0 | 9 | 0 | 82 |
| #žen+<[αfem.]# | tricógeno | 46 | 34 | 0 | 1 | 0 | 81 |
| #fɔr+<[αfem.]# | zimóforo | 73 | 0 | 3 | 2 | 0 | 78 |
| #fag +<[αfem.]# | zoófago | 65 | 7 | 1 | 0 | 0 | 73 |
| #liz++e# | fotólise | 45 | 0 | 0 | 21 | 0 | 66 |
| #gon+<[αfem.]# | epígono | 8 | 8 | 0 | 40 | 0 | 56 |
| #fon+<[αfem.]# | *lusófono | 17 | 30 | 0 | 1 | 1 | 49 |
| #tom+<[αfem.]# | dicótomo | 28 | 0 | 0 | 6 | 1 | 35 |
| #nɔm+<[αfem.]# | gastrónomo | 32 | 0 | 0 | 1 | 0 | 33 |
| #ztom++a# | citóstoma | 28 | 3 | 0 | 2 | 0 | 33 |
| #gam+<[αfem.]# | fanerógamo | 23 | 6 | 0 | 1 | 0 | 30 |
| #drom++o# | kartódromo | 19 | 1 | 0 | 3 | 0 | 23 |
| #žin+<[αfem.]# | andrógino | 17 | 4 | 0 | 6 | 0 | 27 |
| #ton+<[αfem.]# | ecótono | 10 | 8 | 0 | 1 | 0 | 19 |
| #glif++o# | petróglifo | 10 | 3 | 0 | 2 | 0 | 15 |

Table 12.17b Continued

| | | Transitional Vowels | | | | | |
|---|---|---|---|---|---|---|---|
| #trɔp+<[αfem.]# | **homótropo** | 7 | 1 | 0 | 3 | 0 | 11 |
| #pɔl++e# | **megalópole** | 5 | 1 | 1 | 3 | 0 | 10 |
| +klaz++e# | **litóclase** | 2 | 0 | 0 | 6 | 0 | 8 |
| #kron+<[αfem.]# | **oligócrono** | 6 | 0 | 0 | 1 | 0 | 7 |
| #trɔf+<[αfem.]# | **pedótrofo** | 7 | 0 | 0 | 0 | 0 | 7 |
| #tɔp++o# | **isótopo** | 3 | 1 | 0 | 1 | 0 | 5 |
| Totals: | | **1,777** | **192** | **14** | **138** | **3** | **2,124** |
| Percentages of Total | | 83.66% | 9.90% | 0.66% | 6.50% | 0.14% | |

Whereas the the vocabulary in these two tables are hardly common words,[26] Tables 12.17a–b demonstrate that there are at least 2,801 proparoxytone words that are created through the addition of these Latinate and Hellenic elements in the second position of semi-compound nominals. Of these words, 24.17% are Latinate whereas 75.83% are Hellenic. The great bulk (96.6%) of the vowels interceding between first and second elements in Latinate semi-compounds of this ilk are /ˈi/, and a less overwhelming but significant majority (83.66%) of vowels interceding between first and second elements in Hellenic semi-compounds are /ˈɔ/.

**§12.2.5.1.1** Tables 12.17a–b also demonstrates that other vowels may preceed these elements and receive stress. Vowels other than /ˈi/ for Latinate semi-compounds and other than /ˈɔ/ for Hellenic ones are not inserted vowels, rather they form part of the first elements of these compound words, as Tables 12.17c and 12.17d demonstrate.

26 The *Aurélio*'s 3,000 most frequent words include eight semi-compounds: *agrícola, científico, específico, magnífico, pacífico*; *fósforo, análise, metrópole*—'agricultural, scientific, specific, magnificent, pacific, match, analysis, city'.

Table 12.17c Latinate Proparoxytone Stress—Atypical Vowels

| | **Atypical Vowel /ˈɔ/** | | | |
|---|---|---|---|---|
| **2nd Element** | **Example** | **Gloss** | **1st Element** | **1st Element Gloss** |
| #fɛr+<[αfem.]# | **hilófero** | has a hilum | #il++o# | hilum |
| **2nd Element** | **Atypical Vowel /ˈa/** | | | |
| #fɛr+<[αfem.]# | **isodiáfero** | similar nuclei | #izo+#dia- | same shape |
| #fik+<[αfem.]# | **disáfico** | touch ailment | #diza+ | perturbation |
| #par+<[αfem.]# | **láparo** | baby rabbit | #lap+ | rabbit |
| **2nd Element** | **Atypical Vowel /ˈɛ/** | | | |
| #fik+<[αfem.]# | **espanéfico** | tidy | #zpan++e+ | to dust |
| #vir+<[αfem.]# | **séviro** | 1 of 6 rulers | #sɛ+ | 6 |
| **2nd Element** | **Atypical Vowel /ˈu/** | | | |
| **#pɛd+α<e#** | **quadrúpede** | quadruped | #kuadru+ | 4 |

Table 12.17d Proparoxytone Stress Hellenic Atypical Vowels

| | **Atypical Vowel /ˈi/** | | | |
|---|---|---|---|---|
| **2nd Elements** | **Example** | **Gloss** | **1st Element** | **Gloss** |
| #mɛtr++o# | **taxímetro** | taximeter | #tˈaksi# | taxi |
| #graf+<[αfem.]# | **dígrafo** | digraph | #di+ | two |
| #lɔg+<[αfem.]# | **epílogo** | epilogue | #epi+ | above |
| #fɔb+<[αfem.]# | **apífobo** | bee-phobe | #api+ | bee |
| +pter+<[αfem.]# | **díptero** | two winged | #di+ | two |
| #žen+<[αfem.]# | **ambígeno** | from two species | #ambi+ | both |
| #fag +<[αfem.]# | **taquífago** | fast eater | #taki+ | fast |
| #gon+<[αfem.]# | **polígono** | polygon | #pɔli+ | poly |
| #ztom+<o# | **dístomo** | two mouthed | #di+ | two |
| #gam+<[αfem.]# | **bígamo** | two wives | #bi+ | two |
| #drom++o# | **perídromo** | awning | #peri+ | surrounding |
| #žin+<[αfem.]# | **polígino** | multiple wives | #pɔli+ | poly |
| #ton+<[αfem.]# | **trítono** | 3 toned | #tri+ | 3 |
| #glif++o# | **tríglifo** | 3 sulci | #tri+ | 3 |
| #pɔl++e# | **trípole** | sedimentary rock | #tri+ | 3 |
| #tɔp++o# | **epítopo** | epitope | #epi+ | above |
| #trɔp+<[αfem.]# | **hemítropo** | hemitrope | #ɛmi+ | half |
| **Second Elements** | **Atypical Vowel /ˈa/** | | | |
| #mɛtr++o# | **rotâmetro** | fluid meter | #rɔt++a# | rotate[a] |

Table 12.17d Continued

| | | | | |
|---|---|---|---|---|
| #fɔr+<[αfem.]# | **adiáforo** | postponable | #adi++a# | postpone |
| #lɔg+<[αfem.]# | **análogo** | analog | #ana+ | contrary move |
| #fɔb+<[αfem.]# | **agoráfobo** | agoraphobe | #'agora# | market place |
| +pter+<[αfem.]# | **áptero** | without wings | #a+ | without |
| #liz++e# | **análise** | analysis | #ana+ | contrary move |
| #fon+<[αfem.]# | **áfono** | without speech | #a+ | without |
| #tom+<[αfem.]# | **átomo** | atom | #a+ | without |
| #nɔm+<[αfem.]# | **agorânomo** | market place magistrate | #'agora# | market place |
| #gam+<[αfem.]# | **ágamo** | non-sexual reproducer | #a+ | without |
| #drom++o# | **anádromo** | river spawning fish | #ana+ | contrary move |
| #žin+<[αfem.]# | **eneágino** | nine spiked | #eana+ | nine |
| #ton+<[αfem.]# | **átono** | atonic | #a+ | without |
| #glif+<[αfem.]#? | **áglifo** | solid snake tooth | #a+ | without |
| #trɔp+<[αfem.]# | **átropo** | nocturnal butterfly | #a+ | without |
| #pɔl++e# | **escápole** | unobligated | #ezkap+ | escape |
| +klaz++e# | **catáclase** | rock crushing | #kata+ | tumble |
| #kron+<[αfem.]# | **ácrono** | non-seasonal (plants) | #a+ | without |
| #tɔp++o# | **parátopo** | anti-antigen | #para+ | close |
| **Second Elements** | **Atypical Vowel /'ɛ/** | | | |
| #mɛtr++o# | **telémetro** | telemeter | #tɛle+ | distant |
| #man+<[αfem.] | **clopémano** | cleptomaniac | #klɔpe+ | thievery |
| #graf+<[αfem.] | **marégrafo** | tide measurer | #mar'ɛ# | tide |
| #fɔr+<[αfem.]# | **coéforo** | provider for the dead | #kɔɛ+ | dead |
| #fag +<[αfem.]# | **adéfago** | tremendously voracious | #adɛ+ | large |
| #pɔl++e# | **helépole** | wall scaler | #ɛle+ | Greek |
| **Second Elements** | **Atypical Vowel /'u/** | | | |
| #mɛtr++o# | **acúmetro** | hearing test machine | #aku+ | needle |
| #fon+<[αfem.]# | **êufono** | beautifully voiced | #eu+ | beautiful |
| #tom+<[αfem.]# | **bútomo** | ornamental plant | #bu+ | buffalo |

a The first elements of *rotâmetro* and *adiáforo* are verbal stems, cf. *rodar* 'to rotate' and *adiar* 'to put off'

Table 12.17d shows that these elements, all of which begin with consonants, cause the vowel that precedes them to acquire stress—even when the vowel is a mere prefix (#a+, e.g. *ácrono* 'non-seasonal') or the first element is a proparoxytone *ágora* 'market place' (cf. *agoráfobo* 'agoraphobe').

**§12.2.5.2.0** There is a set of semi-compound words whose first elements end in consonants, but no transitional vowel appears between the first and second elements as Table 12.17e demonstrates.

**Table 12.17e** Consonant-Final First Elements—No Vowel Insertion

| | Final /n+ | Gloss | 1st Element(s) | 2nd Element(s) |
|---|---|---|---|---|
| Latinate | íncola | habitant | #in+ | +kɔl+ɑ<a# |
| | ameríncola | Americas native | #amɛr++in+ | +kɔl+ɑ<a# |
| | cônsono | consonant | #kon+ | #son+<o# |
| | decênviro | 1 of 10 magistrates | #dɛk++en+ | #vir+<o# |
| Hellenic | pânfobo | fear of everything | #pan+ | #fɔb+<o# |
| | síncrono | synchronic | #sin+ | #krɔn+<o# |
| | síngrafo | mutually signed iou | #sin+ | #graf+<o# |
| | síntrofo | lichen parasite | #sin+ | #trɔf++o# |
| | **Final /z+** | **Gloss** | **1st Element(s)** | **2nd Element(s)** |
| Latinate | píscola | dual plows | #piz+ | +kɔl+ɑ<a# |
| | céspede | grassy clump | #sɛz+ | #pɛd++e# |
| | hóspede | guest | #ɔz+ | #pɛd++e# |
| | **Final /r/** | **Gloss** | **1st Element(s)** | **2nd Element(s)** |
| Helenic | alérgeno | allergen | #alɛr+ | #žen+<o# |
| | atérmano | thermic isolator | #a+#tɛr+ | #man+<o# |
| | **Final /l+** | **Gloss** | **1st Element(s)** | **2nd Element(s)** |
| | fotoalgrafia | photolithography | #fɔto+al+ | #graf++i++a# |

The elements preceding the final element in this set all end in the least marked consonants of the nasal, fricative, rhotic, and lateral series, i.e. those consonants that close syllables. And the vowels preceeding those consonants (except in the final example[27]) receive stress, which makes

27 Which is a paroxytone owing to the noun-deriving suffix +i++a#. A photolithographer (if such a specialty exists) could be called a **fotoálgrafo*.

them proparoxytones just like the ones examined in Tables 12.17a–d.[28] Still these data, do not mean that the element-final contoids /n, z, r, l/ are immune to vowel insertion. There are ample cases of element-final /n, z, r, l/ in Latinate and Hellenic semi-compounds that allow vowel insertion.[29] By far the easiest way to account for the exceptions in Table 12.17e would be to mark them as immune to Rule 12.6.

**§12.2.5.2.1** The final step in addressing semi-compounds is to propose a rule that causes this set to be proparoxytone. Rule 12.8 accomplishes this.

**Rule 12.8 Semi-Compound Proparoxytone Stress:**

#[-contoid] (C)# / __ #CX$_p$# → [+delayed transition]

Rule 12.8 stresses the first vowel preceding semi-compound second elements, be they Latinate or Hellenic, when they are of the class p (i.e. proparoxytone-inducing) and the word has no stressed syllable assigned in the lexicon.

## Grammatically Formed Compounds

**§12.3.0** Whereas the formation of true and semi-compound nominals is mainly a lexical matter, with some rule-governed phenomena pertinent to gender assignment, number reflection, and vowel insertion; there are two sets of totally regular true compound words—adverbs formed from adjectives followed by the word *mente* 'mind' and diminutive nominals formed by the addition of *zinho*.

**§12.3.1.0 Adverbs formed with *mente*:** Because the formation of adverbs from adjectives is almost entirely regular and because the meaning of these adverbs is the sum of their constituent parts, it is

---

28 The word *êufono* 'beautiful sound' in Table 12.17d is an exeption to Rule 12.5. The vowel preceeding #fon+<o# is /u/, but this word's intial vowel, rather than the one preceeding the second element receives the word's stress. The first vowel of *êufono* should be stressed in its lexical entry because #fon+<o# does not cause that /e/ to be stressed: (A) because it is not the vowel immediately preceding the word's second element, and (B) because when second elements cause a preceding mid vowel to be stressed, they emerge as open vowels, i.e. as /ɔ/ and /ɛ/.

29 Latinate examples include: /n+ *uriníparo* 'urine producing', /z+ *fusípede* 'fused feet, /r+ *vaporífero* 'vaporous', and /l+ *salícola* 'salt producing'. Hellenic examples include: /n+ *amazonólogo* 'Amazon student', /z+ *viscosímetro* 'viscous meter', /l+ *decibelímetro* 'decibel meter', /r+ *amperímetro* 'ampermeter'.

surprising that the *Aurélio* contains 303 adverbial entries ending in -*mente.*[30] The second element in these adverbs is the Portuguese word *mente* 'mind', the first in almost all cases is an adjective. Table 12.18 contains representative samples:

**Table 12.18** Representative Adverbs ending in –*mente*

| Adverb | Gloss | Adjective | Gloss |
|---|---|---|---|
| **chãmente** | flatly | **chão** | flat |
| **chorosamente** | weepily | **choroso** | weepy |
| **comumente** | commonly | **comum** | common |
| **facilmente** | easily | **fácil** | easy |
| **francesmente** | in a French way | **francês** | French |
| **maiormente** | mainly | **maior** | bigger |
| **somente** | only | **só** | alone |

**§12.3.1.1** Rule 12.9 indicates that adverbs can be formed from adjectives plus the lexical item *mente,* and when this happens the adjective agrees in number [-plural] and gender [+feminine] with the second element in the compound.

**Rule 12.9 Adverb Formation:**

#nominal+<[αfem.]<[αnumber]##ment++e$_{[+fem]}$#<Ø# → #adverb#

In Table 12.18, the first two adverbs bear the [+feminine] gender morpheme <a#; however, the adverbs formed from the adjectives *comum, fácil* and *maior* have no overt gender morpheme. This is because adjectives such as these modify or identify both [-feminine] and [+feminine] entities without needing to reflect their gender since their gender morpheme is +e+ (ambivalent gender), and it evanesces in these adjectives' non-plural manifestations (§6.1.5, Rule 6.2a).[31] These formations are nothing new, they are well known.

**§12.3.1.2.0** There are two entries among the *Aurélio*'s adverbs, one of which (*francesmente*) appears in Table 12.18.[32] This form is surprising

30 Indeed, among adverbs in Table 12.18, the 1975 *Aurélio* only lists *maiormente* and *somente.*

31 The adjective *só* also modifies both feminine and non-feminine entities: *Ele/Ela está só* 'He/she is alone'.

32 Among the adverbs included in the *Aurélio* the adverbs *simplesmente* and *prestesmente* 'simply, readily' are listed without feminine inflection, but the

because there is a [+feminine] reflex of the nominal in question: *francesa.*[33] Concerning words such as *burguês* 'bourgeois', *polonês* 'Polish' and *montês* 'pertinent to mountains' native speakers accept both *burguesmente* and *burguesamente*, *polonesmente* and *polonesamente*, and *montesmente*, and *montesamente*. Apparently, in addition to those adjectives that do not reflect gender, those whose pre-gender stems end in /z/ (whether or not they can be inflected for feminine gender) can appear in adverbs formed with #ment++e# without the morpheme <a#.

**§12.3.1.2.1** The stems that do not, or need not, occur inflected for [+feminine] in adverbs end in one of the four consonants that close a syllable word-internally and word-finally: /l, n, r, z/. That being the case, Rule 12.10 accounts for the loss of the gender morpheme in adverbs formed from adjectives like *burguês* and *francês* (i.e. adjectives whose pre-gender stems end in /z#):

**Rule 12.10 Optional Loss of <a# in De-adjectival Adverbs:**

$$<[+\text{feminine}]\# \rightarrow \emptyset \,/\, \begin{pmatrix} +\text{fricative} \\ -\text{labial} \\ -\text{high} \\ -\text{surd} \end{pmatrix} \# \;\_\_\; \#\text{ment}++\text{e}\#$$

Rule 12.10 optionally deletes the [+feminine] morpheme when the final segment of the pre-gender stem ends in /z#. The loss of the final /n# in adjectives like *comum* when they form adverbs comes from the process in which morpheme-final nasals are deleted before morpheme-initial nasals (see Tables 11.7–8 and Rule 11.2).

---

adjectives from which these adverbs are formed do not reflect [+feminine] with the [+feminine] morpheme <a#: *um homem simples*, *uma mulher simples* 'a simple man, a simple woman'; *um homem prestes a agir, uma mulher prestes a agir* 'man ready for action, a woman ready for action'. The adverb: *prestemente* is formed using the adjective *preste*, which also means 'ready'.

33 Foreign students are taught that the only adjective that is capable of bearing <a# but that fails to do so in the formation of regular adverbs is *português* 'Portuguese' ⇔ *portuguesmente* 'in a Portuguese fashion' (cf. *portuguesa* [+fem.]). Jucá Filho includes *francesmente* in his 1963 *Dicionário escolar das dificuldades da língua portuguesa*, but he cites the statesman Rui Barbosa to show that for this revered stylist the adjective *francês* can be inflected for [+feminine] in the adverb: *francesamente.*

**§12.3.2.2** The other surprise among the *Aurélio*'s 303 adverbs ending in *–mente* was *atoamente* 'heedlessly'. The prepositional phrase *à toa* 'heedless, not-thought-out, useless' appears in the *Aurélio* as an adjective capable of modifying nouns of both genders and numbers without inflectional adjustment[34]—which of course it can and does because it is a prepositional phrase that can be used adjectivally. Indeed, as a prepositional phrase it also performs adverbial functions: e.g. *Falei à toa* 'I spoke heedlessly'. At any rate, the adverb superficially resembles ordinary adverbs formed with *mente* because it ends with the [+feminine] morpheme +a#.[35]

**§12.3.2.3** Beyond this, and similar to the lexical true compounds, both halves of these adverbs (the adjectives and the noun *mente*) bear primary stress.[36] This is evident because the vowels that would 'reduce' atomically (/ɔ/ to [u], and /a/ to [ă]) do not do so in these adverbs. The vowel /ɔ/ in *somente* remains [ɔ] as does the second /ɔ/ in *chorosamente*, they do not reduce to [ŭ]. And the vowel /a/ in *facilmente* does not 'reduce' to [ă] in European Portuguese as it does when it is atonic in derived words such as: *facilidade* 'ease' [fă.si.li.'δa.δə].

**§12.3.2.4** Thus, what makes adverbs ending in *–mente* compound words is: (A) Both elements are words (or lexical entries) in their own right. (B) When possible, and with a rule-governed exception, the adjectival (first) element is inflected for [+feminine] gender owing to *mente*'s [+feminine] gender. And both the adjective and *mente* bear primary stress *comumente* [kũ.'mũ.'mẽ$^{n}$.tə]. Table 12.19 demonstrates the derivation of *comumente*, *finalmente*, *chorosamente*, and *somente*.[37]

---

34 Neither this phrase's classification as an adjective nor its appearance in *atoamente* are new-comers. The 1975 *Aurélio* considers *à-toa* an adjective and *à toa* an adverb, and it contains *atoamente*. The 2010 *Aurélio* does not distinguish the adverbial *à toa* from the adjectival one.

35 The ([+feminine]) word *toa* means 'tow rope' and derives from the English word 'tow'.

36 Brazilian orthography used to represent the compounding adjectives' tonicity with a grave accent when the adjective alone required an acute accent: *rápido*→*ràpidamente* 'rapid→rapidly', *fácil* → *fàcilmente*, 'easy → easily'.

37 Villalva and Gonçalves acknowledge the double stress in adverbs formed with #ment++e# and the adjective-noun agreement between their components. But they fail to recognize these adverbs' compound nature and refer to #ment++e# as a 'suffix' (177). See fn. 38 below.

Table 12.19 The Derivation of Compound Adverbs

| | comummente | finalmente |
|---|---|---|
| U.F. | #kon+#mun#+e+<Ø##ment++e#<Ø# | #fin++al#+e+<Ø##ment+ +e#<Ø# |
| R. 12.3 | #kon+#mun#+e+#ment++e# | #fin++al#+e+#ment++e# |
| R. 3.1 | #kon+#mˈun#+e+#mˈent++e# | #fin++ˈal#+e+#mˈent++e# |
| R. 6.2a | *** | #fin ++ˈal#+mˈent++e# |
| R. 6.2b | #kon+#mˈun##mˈent++e# | *** |
| R. 7.2 | #kõn+#mˈũn##mˈẽnt++e# | #fin++ˈal#+mˈẽnt++e# |
| R. 8.3 | #kõ+#mˈũ##mˈẽnt++e#[a] | #fin++ˈal#+mˈẽnt++e# |
| R. 2.3 | #kõ+#mˈũ##mˈẽnt++ĭ# | #fin++ˈal#+mˈẽnt++ĭ# |
| Ph. | [kũ.ˈmũ.ˈmẽ$^{n}$.tə] | [fĩ.ˈnaɫ.ˈmẽ$^{n}$.tə] |
| | **chorosamente** | **somente** |
| U.F. | #šɔr++ɔz+<[αfem.]#<Ø##ment++e#<Ø# | #sɔ#<Ø##ment++e#<Ø# |
| R. 12.3 | šɔr++ɔz+<a##ment++e# | #sɔ##ment++e# |
| R. 3.1 | #šɔr++ˈɔz+<a##mˈent++e# | #sˈɔ##mˈent++e# |
| R. 6.2a | *** | *** |
| R. 6.2b | *** | *** |
| R. 7.2 | #šɔr++ˈɔz+<a##mˈẽnt++e# | #sˈɔ##mˈẽnt++e# |
| R. 8.3 | #šɔr++ˈɔz+<a##mˈẽt++e# | #sˈɔ##mˈẽt++e# |
| R. 2.3 | #šŭr++ˈɔz+<ă##mˈẽt++ĭ#[b] | #sˈɔ##mˈẽt++ĭ# |
| Ph. | [šŭ.ˈrɔ.sã̆.ˈmẽ$^{n}$.tə] | [ˈsɔ.ˈmẽ$^{n}$.tə] |

a The Brazilian spelling of this word *comumente* acknowledges the loss of the stem-final /n+.

b Notice as well that nasalization of adjective-final vowels in these adverbs is non-existent owing to the word boundary ## between the adjectives and the following word #ment++e#.

Table 12.19 demonstrates that the seven rules needed to generate compound adverbs such as these are rules that have been justified for other (morpho)phonological phenomena. These compounds are juxtapositions of ordinary words that add up to something more than the sum of their constitutent parts—they are adverbs rather than nouns modified by pre-posed adjectives.

**§12.3.3.0 Compound Nouns Formed with *–zinho*:** Since the compound nature of forms ending in *zinho* has been addressed

(§10.2.2.9.0–3) the rationale for their compounding function is condensed here. Nominals ending in *zinho* are compound words because: (A) Both elements are words (or lexical entries) in their own right. That is, the form *zinho* used alone means 'person'. (B) When possible, compound nominal elements (both adjectives and nouns) can reflect both [+feminine] gender and plurality—at least vestiges thereof. And (C) both elements bear primary stress.[38] Table 12.20 demonstrates *zinho*'s role in creating compounds whose first element reflects its number and/or gender as well as compounds in which the original vowels do not reduce:

**Table 12.20** Compound Diminutives

| Diminutives Internally Inflected for Plurality | | | | |
|---|---|---|---|---|
| Nominal | | | Diminutive | |
| Word | Plural | Gloss | Singular | Plural |
| cão | cães | dog(s) | **cãozinho** | **cãezinhos** |
| algodão | algodões | cotton, types of | **algodãozinho** | **algodõezinhos** |
| hotel | hotéis | hotel(s) | **hotelzinho** | **hoteizinhos** |
| amor | amores | love(s) | **amorzinho** | **amorezinhos** |
| **Diminutives Internally Inflected for Gender** | | | | |
| [-feminine] | [+feminine} | Gloss | [-feminine] | [+feminine] |
| bom | boa | good | **bonzinho** | **boazinha** |
| ilhéu | ilhoa | islander | **ilheuzinho** | **ilhoazinha** |
| judéu | judia | Jew, Jewess | **judeuzinho** | **judiazinha** |
| leão | leoa | lion, lioness | **leãozinho** | **leoazinha** |
| **Diminutives Preserving Open Vowels** | | | | |
| café | cafés | coffee(s) | **cafezinho** | **cafezinhos** |
| só | sós | alone | **sozinho** | **sozinhos** |
| vovó | vovós | grandma(s) | **vovozinha** | **vovozinhas** |

**§12.3.3.1** In the first section of Table 12.20 whatever underlying feature emerges with the pluralization of these ordinary nouns emerges

38 Even though Villalva and Gonçalves (cf. fn. 37) acknowledge the double stress on words formed with +ziɲ+ (*dorzinha* 'slight pain' [ˈdɔr.ˈzĩ.ɲă]) and the double plurals of specific words *cãozinho* 'doggy' *cãezinhos* 'doggies', they fail to recognize the compound nature of such words (172–3) .

also in their diminutive forms: The underlying form *cão* is #kan++e# and that of *algodão* is #algodon++e#. Their endings /an++e# and /on++e# are neutralized in their singular forms (to ['ã̆ᵘ̃]) in both cases, but their pluralization causes both their original gender morpheme and their underlying vowels to emerge with nasalization coming from the intervocalic /n/ that disappears. These phenomena obtain in both these unembellished nouns and in their diminutive forms.[39] In *hotel* and *amor* pluralization causes their underlying gender morpheme +e+ to remain both in the bald forms and in the diminutives. The presence of +e+ after the /l# of *hotel* causes the intervocalic /l# to be deleted in plural forms.

**§12.3.3.2** Table 12.20's second section contains one bona fide adjective (*bom*) and two words that work equally well as either adjectives or nouns (*ilheu* and *judeu*) plus *leão* whose valence is more noun-like than the others. However, in all the [+feminine] diminutive forms both the first and second (*zinho*) elements are inflected for [+feminine] and [-feminine] gender.

**§12.3.4.0** The third section of Table 12.19 contains words whose final segment /ɛ/ and /ɔ/ is stressed in their simple (monomorphemic) forms. These vowels maintain their stress and do not reduce to [e], [ə], [ĭ] or to [o] or [ŭ] in diminutives. Table 12.21 demonstrates derivations of *cãezinhos*, *hoteizinhos*, *boazinhas*, and *cafezinhos*.

39 Owing to the general constraint that does not allow geminate contoids in Portuguese, the plural morpheme <z# disappears in the diminutive forms because it is followed by morpheme-initial #z/.

Table 12.21 The Derivation of Compound Diminutives

| | cãezinhos | hoteizinhos |
|---|---|---|
| U.F. | #kan++e+<z##ziɲ+<br><[αfem.]#<[αnumber]# | #otɛl#+e+<z##ziɲ+<br><[αfem.]#<[αnumber]# |
| R.12.3 | #kan++e+<z##ziɲ+<o#<z# | #otɛl#+e+<z##ziɲ+<o#<z# |
| R. 3.1 | #kˈan++e+<z##zˈiɲ+<o#<z# | #otˈɛl#+e+<z##zˈiɲ+<o#<z# |
| R. 7.2 | #kˈãn++e+<z##zˈiɲ+<o#<z# | #otˈɛl#+e+<z##zˈiɲ+<o#<z# |
| R. 8.3 | #kˈã++e+<z##zˈiɲ+<o#<z# | *** |
| R. 9.5 | *** | #otˈɛ#+e+<z##zˈiɲ+<o#<z# |
| R. 4.1 | #kˈã++e+#zˈiɲ+<o#<z# | #otˈɛ#+e+##zˈiɲ+<o#<z# |
| R. 2.3 | #kˈã++ĭ##zˈiɲ+<ŭ#<z# | #ŭtˈɛ#+ĭ##zˈiɲ+<ŭ#<z# |
| R. 4.4 | #kˈã++ĭ##.zˈi.ɲ+<ŭ#<z# | #ŭ.tˈɛ#+ĭ##.zˈi.ɲ+<ŭ#<z# |
| R. 9.2 | #kˈã++$^{\breve{\imath}}$##.zˈi.ɲ+<ŭ#<z# | *** |
| R. 4.5 | *** | *** |
| Ph. | [ˈkã̃$^{\tilde{\imath}}$ˈzĩ.ɲũš] | [ŭ.ˈtɛ$^{\breve{\imath}}$.ˈzĩ.ɲũš] |
| | **boazinhas** | **cafezinhos** |
| U.F. | #bo[a]+<a#<z##ziɲ+<br><[αfem.]#<[αnumber]# | #kafˈɛ#<z##ziɲ+<br><[αfem.]#<[αnumber]# |
| R.12.3 | #bo+<a#<z##ziɲ+<a#<z# | #kafˈɛ#<z##ziɲ+<o#<z# |
| R. 3.1 | #bˈo+<a#<z##zˈiɲ+<a#<z# | #kafˈɛ#<z##zˈiɲ+<o#<z# |
| R. 7.2 | *** | *** |
| R. 8.3 | *** | *** |
| R. 9.5 | *** | *** |
| R. 4.1 | #bˈo+<a##zˈiɲ+<a#<z# | #kafˈɛ##zˈiɲ+<o#<z# |
| R. 2.3 | #bˈo+<ă##zˈiɲ+<ă#<z# | #kăfˈɛ##zˈiɲ+<ŭ#<z# |
| R. 4.4[b] | # bˈo+<ă##.zˈi.ɲ+<ă#<z# | #kă.fˈɛ##.zˈi.ɲ+<ŭ#<z# |
| R. 9.2 | *** | *** |
| R. 4.5 | bˈo+<.ă##.zˈiɲ+<ă#<z# | *** |
| Ph. | [ˈbo.ă.ˈzĩ.ɲăš] | [kă.ˈfɛ.ˈzĩ.ɲũš] |

a The [+feminine] manifestation of the root #bon+ as #bo+ is lexically determined (§9.5.1.2.4.2).

b Whereas the syllabation rules (4.4 and 4.5) are subsumed in the derivations of adverbs (Table 12.19), Rule 4.4 is necessary in order to enable the progressive [+nasal] assimilation of [ĭ] to [ã] in *cãezinhos* since no syllable boundary exists between [ã] and [ĭ].

§**12.3.4.1** The second element in adverbs, *mente,* causes the preceding elements (adjectives) to agree in number and gender, but among the diminutives the opposite obtains—the first nominal causes the second to agree in number and gender. In both cases, the first and the second elements in these compounds receive primary stress. Loss of geminates ($C_1C_1 \rightarrow C$) is a generalized phenomenon in Portuguese as is atonic vowel reduction. And both the compound adverbs and the compound diminutives are forms whose meanings are transparent. The formation of adverbs using the word *mente* and of nominals using the word *zinho* exhausts the category of grammatical compounding.

## Conclusions

### Summary

**§12.4.0.0 True Compounds:** In addressing Portuguese compound nominals, this study distinguishes true compound from semi-compound words. True compounds have two separate classes: lexical compounds and grammatical compounds. Both share common features: they consist of at least two separate, full-fledged[40] words. Each word in these compounds has a stressed syllable. And both words are at least minimally inflected, i.e. for gender and often for number.

**§12.4.0.1 Semi-compounds**: These differ from true compounds by having only one primary stressed syllable and by being inflected for gender and number only at the word's end.[41] The great bulk of the semi-compounds consists of the combination of two 'elements'. In Portuguese morphology, these elements are less restricted than prefixes and suffixes and more restricted than actual words. Many of them occur both as the first and second element in different semi-compound words. Beyond this, most elements also occur as **roots** of independent words. The true compounds and the semi-compounds examined in this study appear in the *Aurélio*. The compilers of that dictionary, a major database for this study, have considered these words to be bona fide lexical items.

**§12.4.1 True Compound Formation:** To study the processes entailed in the formation of true compound nominals, this chapter examines the

40 Portuguese prepositions are not full-fledged words since they cannot occur sentence-finally.

41 Some semi-compound nouns began as true compounds, but have lost their basic characteristics (two stressed syllables, double inflection).

role of: twelve common nouns and one proper noun (Maria), four transitive verbs, one adjective, two adverbs, one preposition, and the negative particle *não* 'no'.[42] To the extent possible this chapter distinguishes specifically Brazilian and specifically Portuguese formations from those that obtain for the language as a whole. The formations examined are: noun+noun (i.e. $n_1$[43]+n, $n+n_1$), noun+preposition+noun (i.e. $n_1$+prep+n, n+prep+$n_1$), adjective+noun, noun+adjective, verb+noun, adverb+adjective, adverb+infinitive, preposition+nominal, *não*+nominal.

**§12.4.2.0 Semi-compound Elements:** The elements used in the formation of semi-compound nominals come from two sources: Latin and Greek. The 57 Latinate semi-compound elements are examined separately from the 189 elements of Hellenic (Greek) origin. There is, however, considerable mixing of origins. Many semi-compounds have one Hellenic and one Latinate element—in either first or second position.

**§12.4.2.1 Patterns:** Despite the less than totally systematic nature of compounding, certain generalizations obtain that can be accounted for with rules: gender in noun+noun combinations, gender, and number in adjective+noun combinations, vowel insertion between elements in both Latinate and Hellenic compounds, and proparoxytone stress occasioned by subsets of Latinate and Hellenic second elements. In addition to these, other patterns obtain: verb+noun true compounds are almost always [-feminine], their verb is in the 3rd person singular present indicative, and their plurals only emerge on the final noun. Preposition+noun compounds are inflected at their end, and they function as prepositional phrases, i.e. they modify both [±fem.] nouns indifferently. Nominals whose first element is *não* are inflected for gender and number on their noun. Rules are not necessary for these patterns since their lexical entries will contain indications of those peculiarities. The patterns and rules that account for these pheneomena appear in the order presented and invoked in Appendix A.

---

42 All of the items examined are common—indeed, most appear among the *Aurélio*'s 3,000 most frequent words.

43 The subscript (i.e. $\underline{n}_1$) indicates the 13 nouns (Table 12.1) chosen for this study. The non-subscribed $\underline{n}$ indicates nouns that form true compounds with the vocabulary selected for this study.

## Findings and Iterpretations

**§12.4.3.0 Lexical and Grammatical True Compounds:** The true compounds that appear in the lexicon display patterns of formation, some of which prevail, but there seems to be no overall pattern susceptible to being rule-governed. The grammatical true compounds, adverbs formed with adjectives followed by the word *mente* 'mind' and diminutives formed with the **word** *zinho* 'small being' are rule-governed. Being rule-governed, adverbs formed with *mente* and the diminutives formed with *zinho* need not appear in a lexicon—except when certain adverbs do not conform to the dominant pattern and when certain diminutives' meanings are idiomatic: e.g. *josezinho*, literally 'little Joe'' actually means 'sleeveless cape'.

**§12.4.3.1** True compound nominals are lexical items both because they sometimes become proper nouns, i.e. designators of plant and animal species, and because their meanings can transcend the sum of their constituents' meanings, e.g. *josezinho* and *amor-perfeito*, literally 'love perfect' actually 'pansy'. The basic difference between compound nominals and derived nominals is that the relationship between the denoted item or concept and the word is largely arbitrary in derived vocabulary, whereas compound words' relationship with their denotands is often motivated and transparent, to one degree or another, e.g. *pau-bala* literally 'stick bullet', actually 'a wooden top spun by one's fingers'.

**§12.4.4.0 Regularities:** True compound nominals exhibit certain regularities. Those composed of nouns (with or without prepositions) normally bear the gender of the initial noun. Noun+adjective and adjective+noun true compounds of course bear the noun's gender. Verb+noun compounds are normally [-feminine] regardless of the nouns' original gender. Adverb+adjective and *não*+nominal compounds agree in number and gender with whatever the form modifies or designates. Preposition+nominal compounds function as adjectives and, owing to their origins as prepositional phrases, modify [±fem.] nouns indifferently.

**§12.4.4.1** Pluralization in true compounds is also patterned. Most noun+noun compounds pluralize both components, but a minority pluralizes only the second. Noun+preposition+noun compounds pluralize only the first nominal. Noun+adjective compounds pluralize both words. Verb+noun, adverb+adjective, *não*+nominal compounds pluralize only the second element.

**§12.4.5.0 Hellenic and Latin Elements:** Semi-compounds' Hellenic elements far outnumber Latinate elements, and, consequently Hellenic semi-compound nominals prevail over Latinate semi-compounds.[44] As one would expect, the elements of both types are hierarchical, and in both cases most of the elements are of negligible or very low productivity. And a minority of elements accounts for a majority of the compound vocabulary. So much so that certain elements, both Latinate and Hellenic, are outliers among their fellow elements in first or second position—even though no element is ever supremely productive. The Hellenic semi-compounds are largely professional terms: scientific and medical, and of recent coinage. Considerable numbers of Latinate semi-compounds are of that ilk, but many pertain to ordinary and even jocular vocabulary. Semi-compounds' gender is determined by the gender morpheme pertaining to the second element.

**§12.4.5.1 Transitions:** Most semi-compounds have a vowel between their first and second elements. Sometimes this vowel occurs at the end of the word's first element, other times the second element begins with a vowel. However, in both Latinate and Hellenic semi-compounds, it seems that some intervening vowels pertain to neither element. They are inserted to allow these words to have normal syllable structure. Overall, Latinate semi-compounds favor /i/, Hellenic /ɔ/, and a single rule (Rule 12.6) accounts for these insertions and the lack thereof. A small minority of semi-compounds contains atypical and/or otiose transitional vowels. These semi-compounds appear in the lexicon with these vowels.

**§12.4.5.2 Proparoxytone Stress:** Finally, there is a subset of Latinate and Hellenic semi-compound elements that occasion proparoxytone stress on either the transitional vowel or on the final vowel of the first element in these words.

## So What?

**§12.4.6** Chapter 12 has shown that compounding makes a significant contribution to the noun stock of Portuguese. It is systematic to the extent that compounds are largely interpretable and of metaphoric origin, but they merit inclusion in dictionaries and lexicons, whereas syntactic

---

44 Those semi-compounds consisting of one Latinate and one Hellenic element are relatively negligible and have appeared in both the sections dealing with Latinate and Hellenic semi-compounds.

patterns using the same terms do not—except when they form idiomatic expressions. Also, distinct patterns of formation obtain both in the lexical true compounds and in the semi-compounds. These patterns include gender determination and inflection for number. The mark of a true compound is its tonic stress on both components. And, this study has shown that considerable numbers of the marked proparoxytone words receive their stress from the application of a rule—their stress need not be listed in the lexicon.

## Appendix A Compound Nominals: Structures and Rules

**§12A.0 Compounding Structures and Rules:** This section presents the compounding structures this chapter has induced from the patterns found in compound nominals as well as the rules that account for phenomena related to these structures. The structures and rules are ordered as they appear in the text. Sections §12A.1–4 consist of compound nominals that are lexical items whose formation is not rule-governed.

**§12A.1.0** The first set of compound nominals consists of juxtaposed nouns. There are four distinct patterns with the following structures:

**§12A.1.1.0 Type 1:** $\#R_1{++}[\pm fem.]\#<[\alpha pl.]\#\#R_2{++}[\pm fem.]\#<[\alpha pl.]\#_{[\alpha\ pl.]}$. This structure underlies compound nouns in which the gender of each noun is independent—neither noun need have the same gender. Conversely, the second noun's plurality, and that of the entire compound is determined by that of the first noun. Words of this nature appear in Table 12.2a. Other examples include *martelo-voador* 'capoeira maneuver', *mestre-escola* '(male) primary school teacher' and *casa-mestra* 'widest part of a ship's framework'. Their plurals are *martelos-voadores*, *mestres-escolas*, and *casas-mestras*.

**§12A.1.1.1 Type 2:** $\#R_1{++}[\pm fem.]\#<[\alpha pl.]\#\#R_2{++}[\pm fem.]\ \#(<[\alpha pl.]\#)_{[\alpha\ pl.]}$. This structure is the same as Type 1, except that these nouns' plurality appears obligatorily on the first noun and only optionally on the second. Word such as *carro-pipa* 'water truck', *guarda-marinha* 'midshipman', and *agulha-mãe* 'main needle (on a meter)' are additional examples of Type 2 true compounds.

**§12A.1.1.2 Type 3:** $\#R_1{++}[\pm fem.]\#(<[\alpha pl.]\#)\#R_2{++}[\pm fem.]\ \#<[\alpha pl.]\#_{[\alpha\ pl.]}$. These noun + noun compounds' plurality appears obligatorily on the second noun, and the first noun may or may not be inflected for plurality. Examples other than those in Table 12.2a are hard to find.

**§12A.1.1.3 Type 4:** $\#R_1{+}{+}[\pm fem.]\#<[\alpha pl.]\#\#_{R2}{+}{+}[\pm fem.]\#<[-plural]\#_{[\alpha pl.]}$. These compounds' number is only reflected on their first noun. Similar to Type 3, other examples are hard to find.

**§12A.1.1.4** For this entire set of compound nominals, only Rule 12.1 is necessary.

**Rule 12.1 Gender in $\#Noun_1\#\#Noun_2\#$ Compounds:**

$\#Noun_1\#\#Noun_2\# \rightarrow \#Noun_{1[\alpha fem.]}\#\#Noun_2\#_{[\alpha fem.]}$

The gender of the first noun in these forms determines that of the entire compound noun.

**§12A.1.2.0** The second set of compound nouns are those formed by a noun followed by a preposition followed by a second noun, which may or may not be preceded by a determiner. Their structure is: $\#R_1+\{<,+\}[\pm fem.]\#<[\pm pl]\#\#prep.>(\#det+<[\alpha fem.]<[\alpha pl]>)$[45] $\#R_2+\{<,+\}[\pm fem]\#<[\pm pl]\#_{[\alpha\ pl.]}$. In addition to the examples in Tables 12.3a and 12.3b, consider: *café da manhã* 'coffee of the morning=breakfast', *laranja de mico* 'orange of marmoset monkey=wild lily', *menina do olho*'(female) child of the eye=pupil', *menina dos olhos* '(female) child of the eyes=beloved person or thing', *nariz de burro* 'nose of donkey= double-barrelled pistol'.

**§12A.1.2.1** Rule 12.2 accounts for the gender and number of compound nouns configured as #Noun##Prep.>(#Det.>)#Noun#

**Rule 12.2:**

$\#N_1Prep.(det.)N_2\# \quad \rightarrow \quad \#R_1+\{<,+\}[\alpha fem.]\#<[\beta pl.]\#\#prep.>(\#det.>)\#R_2+\{+,<\}[\pm fem.]\#<[\pm pl.]\#_{[\alpha fem.][\beta pl.]}$

A compound noun may consist of a noun followed by preposition plus another noun, which may be preceded by a determiner. The first noun may bear either an inflecting or a deriving gender morpheme and a number morpheme. These morphemes determine the resultant compound word's number and gender. The second noun's gender is independent of that of the first noun and may be inflectional or derivational. The second noun's number is also independent from that of the first noun and of the compound noun itself. The gender and number

45 Most determiners agree in number and gender with the nouns they identify. Numbers are determiners, but only *um* 'one' and *dois* 'two' are inflected for [+feminine]: *uma* and *duas*.

of the determiner (when relevant) are determined by the second noun's number and gender.

§**12A.2.0** The next set of compound nominals are those consisting of nouns either followed by adjectives or preceded by adjectives. Their underlying structures are:

1. **Noun + Adjective:** $\#R_1+\{+,<\}\alpha[\pm\text{fem.}]\#<\beta[\pm\text{pl.}]\#\#R_2+<[\alpha\text{fem.}]\#<[\beta\text{pl.}]\#$

2. **Adjective + Noun:** $\#R_2+<[\alpha\text{fem.}]\#<[\beta\text{pl.}]\#\ \#R_1+\{+,<\}\alpha[\pm\text{fem.}]\#<\beta[\pm\text{pl.}]\#$

The adjectives are identified as $\#R_2$s with purely inflectional gender, whereas the nouns' ($\#R_1$s') gender may be inflectional or derivational. Examples other than those in Tables 12.4a and 12.4b include: *bico-doce* 'beak sweet=seduction', *alto-contraste* 'high contrast'. Their plurals are *bicos-doces* and *altos-contrastes*.

§**12A.2.1** Adjective-noun agreement in compound nouns is the same as adjective noun agreement in syntax:

**Rule 12.3 Adjective-Noun Agreeement:**

$$\text{Adjective} \rightarrow \#R+<[\alpha\text{fem.}]\#<[\beta\text{plural}]\#/ \left\{ \begin{array}{l} \#R_n+\{+<\}[\alpha\text{fem.}]\quad <[\beta\text{pl.}]\#\ \_\_ \\ \\ \_\_\#R_n+\{+,<\}[\alpha\text{fem.}]\quad <[\beta\text{pl.}]\# \end{array} \right\}$$

§**12A.2.2** The next type of compound nominals are those formed by 3rd person singular present tense verbs followed by nouns. These nouns' underlying structure is: $\boldsymbol{\#R_v<\text{Ø}\#+TV+<\text{Ø}\#<\text{Ø}\#\#R_n+\{<,+\}[\pm\text{fem.}]\#<[\pm\text{pl.}]\#}$ and the rule that generates it is:

**Rule 12.4 The Formation of Noun + Verb Compound Nominals:**

$$\#\text{Verb}\#\#\text{Noun}\# \rightarrow \#R_v+<\text{Ø}\#+TV+<\text{Ø}\#<\text{Ø}\#\#R_n+\{<,+\}[\pm\text{fem.}]\#<[\pm\text{pl.}]\#_{[\text{-fem}][\alpha\text{pl}]}$$

These nouns are mostly formed with 1st conjugation verbs transitive verbs and nouns. They are non-femine regardless of the nouns' gender, and they are pluralized by the plural morpheme on the nouns. Examples other than those in Tables 12.5a and 12.5b include: *sabe-tudo* 'know-it-all', *dorme-nenê* 'sleep child=lullaby', and *rega-bofe* 'irregate lung= party with abundant food'.

**§12A.6.0** The final type of compound nouns of a lexical nature are those formed with nouns preceded by the adverbs *bem, mal*, and *não* 'well, poorly, non' and prepositions. The adverbs and prepositions are never inflected and the nominals (nouns or adjectives) bear gender (deriving or inflectional) which turns out to be the compounds' gender. Their number is inflected according to the particular words' syntactic or semantic circumstances. Additional examples include *bem-aventurança* 'well venture=great happiness', *malfeitoria* 'evil-doing= damage', *contragosto* 'against taste=disinclination', *parabens* 'for goods=congratulations'.

**§12A.3.1** The formation of all these lexical compounds entails the use of the default stress rule:

**Rule 3.1 Paroxytone Stress:**

$$[\text{-contoid}] \rightarrow [+\text{stress}] \,/\, \#X \_ \left( \begin{bmatrix} +\text{high} \\ -\text{contoid} \end{bmatrix} \right) C_{0\text{-}4}V_{[\text{-high}]}\#(C)\#$$

**Condition:** The word has no previously assigned stress.

**§12A.4 Semi-compounds:** The next set of words addressed in this chapter are nominals formed with two elements that are rarely words but often occur as roots of nominals. The elements are mainly of Greek or Latin origin. These are essentially lexical formations with the structure:

**#Element$_1${#,+}{+, #}Element$_2${+,<}[±fem.]#<[±pl.]#** Here, internal boundaries cannot be ##, i.e. both elements are never words. Semi-compounds are stressed on only one syllable, and their gender morpheme occurs on the final element and may be deriving or inflectional. The words' number is reflected only on the final element. One semi-regular phenomena these words exhibit is the insertion of vowels between many (but not all) first and second elements, for which two rules were proposed, with a third amalgamating both types:

**Rule 12.5 Latinate Semi-compound /i/ Insertion Rule:**

$$\#XC_1\ ??\ CX\# \rightarrow \#XC? \begin{bmatrix} +\text{palatal} \\ +\text{high} \\ \text{-contoid} \end{bmatrix} ?CX\#$$

**Conditions:**

1. At least one boundary of the two unknown boundaries (??) must be +.
2. $C_1$ must not be /n, l, r, z/, i.e. any consonant that can close syllables.

**Rule 12.6 Hellenic Semi-compound /ɔ/ Insertion Rule:**

$$\#XC_1??CX\# \rightarrow \#XC_1? \begin{pmatrix} +\text{labial} \\ +\text{w.g.} \\ -\text{contoid} \end{pmatrix} ?CX\#_h$$

**Conditions:**

1. At least one of the two unknown boundaries (??) must be +.
2. $C_1$ must not be /n, l, r, z/, i.e. any consonant that can close syllables.

**Rule 12.7 Epenthetic Vowel Insertion (Latinate and Hellenic Semi-compounds)**

$$\#XC_1??CX\# \rightarrow \#XC_1? \left( \begin{matrix} -\text{contoid} \\ \left\{ \begin{matrix} \begin{pmatrix} +\text{labial} \\ +\text{w.g.} \end{pmatrix} \\ \alpha\begin{pmatrix} +\text{palatal} \\ +\text{high} \end{pmatrix} \end{matrix} \right\} \end{matrix} \right) ?CX\#_{\alpha l}$$

**Conditions:**

1. At least one of the two unknown boundaries (??) must be +.
2. $C_1$ must not be /n, l, r, z/, i.e. any consonant that can close syllables.

For examples of these phenomena see Tables 12.11a, 12.11b, 12.12a, 12.12b (Latinate compounds) and Tables 12.14a (Hellenic compounds).

A significant number of both Latinate and Hellenic compounding elements also occasion proparoxytone stress. The rule for this phenomenon is:

**Rule 12.8 Semi-compound Proparoxytone Stress:**

$\#[\text{-contoid}]\ (C)\#\ /\ \_\_\ \#CX_p\# \rightarrow [\text{+delayed transition}]$

**§12A.5.0 Grammatical True Compounds:** The final section returns to true compound words, but in this case, the words are grammatically formed.

**§12A.5.1.0 Adverb formation:** Adverbs may be coined at will by juxtaposing adjectives to the [+feminine] noun *mente* 'mind'. The rule for this is:

**Rule 12.9 Adverb Formation:**

$\#\text{nominal}+<[\alpha\text{fem.}]<[\alpha\text{pl.}]\#\#\text{ment}++e_{[+fem]}\#<\emptyset\# \rightarrow \#\text{adverb}\#$

Rule 12.9 is written as it is because this process (adjective + *mente*) forms a subset of all adverbs. Many adverbs are monomorphemic idions: e.g. *mal* 'poorly' *bem* 'well', *quando* 'when', *antes* 'before', *como* 'as'.

**§12A.5.1.1** The adjectives in compound adverbs, when possible, are inflected for [+feminine] gender, with the morpheme <a#. However, it appears that inflectable adjectives whose stem-final consonant is /z+ may occur without the [+feminine] morpheme, e.g. *portuguesmente* 'in a Portuguese way'. The rule for this is the following:

**Rule 12.10 Optional Loss of <a# in De-adjectival Adverbs:**

$$<[+\text{feminine}]\# \rightarrow \emptyset\ /\begin{pmatrix} +\text{fricative} \\ \text{-labial} \\ \text{-high} \\ \text{-surd} \end{pmatrix} +\ \_\_\ \#\text{ment}++e_{[+fem]}\#$$

**§12A.5.1.2** Since the adverbs formed from adjectives + *mente* are grammatically formed, it became possible to propose derivations for their formation, almost exclusively using rules postulated in previous chapters. In addition to Rules 12.3 and 3.1. The rules necessary for deriving adverbs are:

**Rule 6.2a Deletion of Word-Final <e+ and +e+_ after /r#, /l#, and /z#:**

$$\begin{Bmatrix} < \\ + \end{Bmatrix} \begin{pmatrix} +\text{palatal} \\ -\text{contoid} \end{pmatrix} \# \rightarrow \emptyset \;/\; \#X\,[-\text{contoid}] \begin{pmatrix} +\text{contoid} \\ -\text{surd} \\ -\text{labial} \\ -\text{high} \\ -\text{nasal} \\ -\text{occlusion} \end{pmatrix} \_\_ + <[-\text{plural}]\#$$

**Rule 6.2b Deletion of Word-Final <e+, +e+, (and +ε#) after /n#:**

$$\begin{pmatrix} -\text{contoid} \\ -\text{high} \\ -\text{delayed transition} \\ +\text{palatal} \end{pmatrix} \rightarrow \emptyset \;/\; \#\, X \begin{pmatrix} +\text{contoid} \\ +\text{nasal} \\ -\text{labial} \\ -\text{high} \end{pmatrix} \#_{[-N4]}$$

**Rule 7.2 Morphophonemic Nasalization $R_1$ Stems:**

$$[-\text{contoid}] \;/\; \_\_ \begin{pmatrix} +\text{nasal} \\ -\text{high} \\ -\text{labial} \\ +\text{contoid} \end{pmatrix} + \;/\; (X)+S \rightarrow [+\text{nasal}]_{R1}$$

**Rule 8.3 Loss of /n+:**

$$\begin{pmatrix} +\text{nasal} \\ +\text{contoid} \end{pmatrix} \rightarrow \emptyset / \begin{pmatrix} -\text{contoid} \\ +\text{nasal} \end{pmatrix} \;/\; \_\_ \;+ +\; S(<S)\#$$

**Rule 2.3 Atonic Vowel Reduction:**

$$\begin{pmatrix}\text{-contoid}\\ \text{-high}\\ \alpha\text{labial}\\ \text{-del. trans.}\end{pmatrix} \rightarrow \begin{pmatrix}\text{+wide glottis}\\ \text{-palatal}\\ \alpha\text{high}\\ \text{-low}\end{pmatrix} \;/\; \_\_\_\_ \;\left( \begin{pmatrix}\text{+contoid}\\ \left\{\begin{matrix}[\text{-lateral}]\\ [\text{-occlusion}]\\ [\text{-nasal}]\end{matrix}\right\}\end{pmatrix}\right).$$

§**12A.5.2.0** The diminutives formed with *zinho* #ziɲ+<[±fem.]#<[±pl.]#, in addition to Rules 12.3, 3.1, 7.2, 8.3, 2A.2, 2.5 also require Rules 9.5, 4.1, 9.2. and 4.5.

**Rule 9.5 The Loss of Word-Final /l# in Pluralizations:**

$$[\text{+lateral}] \;/\; \_\# \left\{\begin{matrix} < \\ + \end{matrix}\right\} \; e+ \; \# < z\# \rightarrow \varnothing$$

**Rule 4.1 Like Segment Deletion:**

$\text{Segment}_2 \rightarrow \varnothing \;/\text{Segment}_1 \; \_\_\_\_$

**Condition:** $\text{Segment}_1\text{=Segment}_2$

**Rule 9.2 Nasalization (progressive/regressive assimilation):**

$[\text{-contoid}] \rightarrow [\text{+nasal}] \;/\; .X \; \_\_\_ \; [\text{+nasal}].$

**Rule 4.4 Syllable Boundary V.CV, V.C/r/, V.C/l/:**

$$\varnothing \rightarrow \;. \;/[\text{-contoid}] \; \_\_ \; [\text{+contoid}] \left\{\begin{matrix}[\text{-contoid}]\\ C_2\end{matrix}\right\}$$

**Rule 4.5 (Syllable Boundary 3):**

$$\varnothing \rightarrow \;. \;/ \begin{pmatrix}\text{-contoid}\\ \alpha\text{high}\end{pmatrix} \_\_ \begin{pmatrix}\text{-contoid}\\ \left\{\begin{matrix}\alpha\text{high}\\ \text{+delayed transition}\end{matrix}\right\}\end{pmatrix}$$

**Rule 4.6 (Syllable Boundary 4):**

$$\emptyset \rightarrow .\ /\ C_4\_\_ \left( \begin{array}{l} +\text{contoid} \\ \left\{ \begin{array}{l} +\text{nasal} \\ +\text{occlusion} \\ +\text{fricative} \end{array} \right\} \end{array} \right)$$

# Appendix B Lexical Nominals: True Compounds and Semi-compounds

## Rules, Structures, and Derivations

**§12B.0 True Compounds:** The rules that account for the configuration of true compounds are:

**Rule 12.1 Gender in $\#\text{Noun}_1\#\#\text{Noun}_2\#$ Compounds:**

$$\#\text{Noun}_1\#\#\text{Noun}_2\# \rightarrow \#\text{Noun}_{1[\alpha\text{fem.}]}\#\#\text{Noun}_2\#_{[\alpha\text{fem.}]}$$

**Rule 12.2 $\#\text{Noun}_1\#\#\text{Preposition}>(\#\text{Det.}>)\#\text{noun}_2\#$:**

$$\#N_1\#\#\text{Prep.}>(\text{det.}>)\#N_2\# \rightarrow \#R_1+\{<,+\}[\alpha\text{fem.}]\#<[\beta\text{plur}]_1\#\#\text{prep.}>(\#\text{det.}>)\ R_2+\{<,+\}[\pm\text{fem.}]\#<[\pm\text{plur}]\#_{[\alpha\text{fem.}][\beta\text{plur}]}$$

**Rule 12.3 Adjective-Noun Agreeement:**

$$\text{Adjective} \rightarrow \#R+<[\alpha\text{fem.}]\#<[\beta\text{plural}]\ \#/ \left\{ \begin{array}{l} \#R_n+\{+<\}[\alpha\text{fem.}]\quad <[\beta\text{pl.}]\#\ \_\_ \\ \_\_\#R_n+\{+,<\}[\alpha\text{fem.}]\quad <[\beta\text{pl.}]\# \end{array} \right\}$$

**Rule 12.4 #Verb##Noun# Compounds:**

$$\#\text{Verb}\#\#\text{Noun}\# \rightarrow \#R_v+<\emptyset\#+TV+<\emptyset\#\#R_n+\{<,+\}[\pm\text{fem.}]\#<\alpha[\pm\text{pl.}]\#_{[-\text{fem.}][\alpha\text{pl}]}$$

**Rule 3.1 Paroxytone Stress:**

$$[-\text{contoid}] \rightarrow [+\text{stress}]\ /\ \#X\ \_\ \left( \begin{pmatrix} +\text{high} \\ -\text{contoid} \end{pmatrix} \right) C_{0\text{-}4}V_{[-\text{high}]}\#(C)\#$$

**Condition:** The word has no previously assigned stress.

**Rule 12.7 Epenthetic Vowel Insertion (Latinate and Hellenic Semi-compounds):**

$$\#XC_1??CX\# \rightarrow \#XC_1? \left\{ \begin{array}{c} \text{-contoid} \\ \left\{ \begin{array}{c} \left( \begin{array}{l} +\text{ labial} \\ +\text{ W.G.} \end{array} \right) \\ \alpha \left( \begin{array}{l} +\text{ palatal} \\ +\text{ high} \end{array} \right) \end{array} \right\} \end{array} \right\} ?CX\#_{\alpha l}$$

**Conditions:**

1. At least one of the two unknown boundaries (??) must be +.
2. $C_1$ must not be /n, l, r, z/, i.e. any consonant that can close syllables.

**Rule 12.8 Semi-compound Proparoxytone Stress:**

$\#[\text{-contoid}]\ (C)\#\ /\ \_\_\ \#CX_p\# \rightarrow [\text{+delayed transition}]$

## Derivations

**§12B.1.0** The following derivations illustrate the generation of lexical compounds.

**Table 12B.1** Type 1 True Compound
$\#R_1{+}{+}[\pm\text{fem.}]\#{<}[\alpha\text{pl.}]\#\ \#R_2{+}{+}[\pm\text{fem.}]\#{<}[\alpha\text{pl.}]\#_{[\alpha\text{pl.}]}$

| | (dois) homens-horas | | | | | | [αfem.] |
|---|---|---|---|---|---|---|---|
| U.F. | #ˈomin | ++e# | <z# | #ɔr+ | +a# | <[αpl.]# | |
| Agree[a] | #ˈomin | ++e# | <z# | #ɔr+ | +a# | <z# | |
| R. 12.1 | #ˈomin | ++e# | <z# | #ɔr+ | +a# | <z# | [-fem.] |
| R. 3.1 | #ˈomin | ++e# | <z# | #ˈɔr+ | +a# | <z# | |
| **Ph.** [b] | [ˈdoĭ.zˈɔ.mẽĭ.ˈzɔ.răš] | | | | | | |

Table 12B.1 Continued

| | (um) homem-hora | | | | | | [αfem.] |
|---|---|---|---|---|---|---|---|
| U.F. | #'omin | ++e# | <Ø# | #ɔr+ | +a# | <[αpl.]# | |
| Agree | #'omin | ++e# | <Ø# | #ɔr+ | +a# | <Ø# | |
| R. 12.1 | #'omin | ++e# | <Ø# | #ɔr+ | +a# | <Ø# | [-fem.] |
| R. 3.1 | #'omin | ++e# | <Ø# | #'ɔr+ | +a# | <Ø# | |
| Ph. | [ũ.'ɔ.mẽ$^{\tilde{\imath}}$.'ɔ.ră] | | | | | | |

a 'Agree' is not a rule. It registers the effect of the compound's structure. In this case, both nouns reflect the first noun's plurality.
b The mutation of the sequence /in++e+ in #'ɔmine+ to [ẽ$^{\tilde{\imath}}$] follows the assignment of stress and entails mutation (Rule 9.1a) and nasalization (Rule 9.2b) (§9.2.2.2.0–1).

**§12B.1.1** The phrases in Table 12B.1 mean 'two man hours' and 'one/a man hour'. The final column (headed [αfem.]) indicates that these nouns' gender is not pretermined. The examples illustrate the features typical of Type 1 True Compounds: Their number is expressed on both elements (Agree), but the two words that compose them need not be of the same gender. The compound word's gender is determined by the first noun in the word. And the elements receive paroxytone stress unless they are lexically stressed as is the case with #'omin++e+ 'man'.

**Table 12B.2** Type 2 True Compound
**$\#R_1$++[±fem.]#<[αpl.]##$R_2$++[±fem.]# (<[αpl.]#)$_{[\alpha pl.]}$**

| | (cinco) bombas-relógios | | | | | | [αfem.] |
|---|---|---|---|---|---|---|---|
| U.F. | #bonb | ++a# | <z# | #rel'ɔži | +o# | <[αpl.]# | |
| Agree | #bonb | ++a# | <z# | #rel'ɔži | +o# | <z# | |
| R. 12.1 | #bonb | ++a# | <z# | #rel'ɔži | +o# | <z# | [+fem.] |
| **R. 3.1** | **#b'onb** | **++a#** | **<z#** | **#rel'ɔži** | **+o#** | **<z#** | |
| Ph. | ['sĩ$^{ŋ}$.kŭ 'βõ$^{m}$.băž.ɾ̠ə.'lɔ.ži.ŭš] | | | | | | |
| | (cinco) bombas-relógio | | | | | | |
| U.F. | #bonb | ++a# | <z# | #rel'ɔži | +o# | (<[αpl.]#) | |
| Agree | #bonb | ++a# | <z# | #rel'ɔži | +o# | | |
| R. 12.1 | #bonb | ++a# | <z# | #rel'ɔži | +o# | | [+fem.] |
| R. 3.1 | #b'onb | ++a# | <z# | #rel'ɔži | +o# | | |
| Ph. | ['sĩ$^{ŋ}$.kŭ 'βõ$^{m}$.băž.ɾ̠ə.'lɔ.ži.ŭ] | | | | | | |

(*Continued*)

Table 12B.2 Continued

| | (uma) bomba-relógio | | | | | | |
|---|---|---|---|---|---|---|---|
| **U.F.** | #bonb | ++a# | <Ø# | #rel'ɔži | +o# | <[αpl.]# | |
| **Agree** | #bonb | ++a# | <Ø# | #rel'ɔži | +o# | | [+fem.] |
| **R. 12.1** | #bonb | ++a# | <Ø# | #rel'ɔži | +o# | | |
| **R. 3.1** | #bonb' | ++a# | <Ø# | #rel'ɔži | +o# | | |
| **Ph.** | (uma) 'βõ$^{m}$.bǎž.r̲ə.'lɔ.ži.ǔ] | | | | | | |

§**12B.1.2** The phrases in Table 12B.2 mean 'five time bombs' and 'one time bomb'. Like Type 1 compounds these compounds' nouns need not be of the same gender; the first determines the entire compound nouns' gender, and unstressed elements acquire stress. Different from Type 1, Type 2 compounds need be inflected for plurality only on the first word, but may be inflected on both words, hence the parentheses around the final noun's plural morpheme.

**Table 12B.3** Type 3 True Compound
#R$_1$++[±fem.]#(<[αpl.]#)#R$_2$++[±fem.]# <[αpl.]#$_{[\alpha pl.]}$

| | (dois) pais-gonçalos | | | | | | [αfem.] |
|---|---|---|---|---|---|---|---|
| **U.F.** | #pa+ | +e# | <[αpl.]# | #gonsal+ | +o# | <z# | |
| **Agree** | #pa+ | +e# | <z# | #gonsal+ | +o# | <z# | |
| **R. 12.1** | #pa+ | +e# | <z# | #gonsal+ | +o# | <z# | [-fem.] |
| **R. 3.1** | #p'a+ | +e# | <z# | #gons'al+ | +o# | <z# | |
| **Ph.** | ['do$^{ĭ}$š.'pa$^{ĭ}$ž.gõ$^{n}$.'sa.lǔš] | | | | | | |
| | **(uns) pai-gonçalos** | | | | | | **[αfem.]** |
| **U.F** | #pa+ | +e# | (<Ø#) | #gonsal+ | +o# | <z# | |
| **Agree** | *** | *** | *** | *** | *** | *** | |
| **R. 12.1** | #pa+ | +e# | (<Ø#) | #gonsal+ | +o# | <z# | [-fem.] |
| **R. 3.1** | #p'a+ | +e# | (<Ø#) | #gons'al+ | +o# | <z# | |
| **Ph.** | (uns) 'pa$^{ĭ}$.gõ$^{n}$.'sa.lǔš] | | | | | | |

§**12B.1.3** The phrases in Table 12B.3 mean 'two hen-pecked husbands, some hen-pecked husbands'. They exemplify the coupling of the words *pai* 'father' (cf. *mãe* 'mother') with proper nouns. In most cases, either or both nouns can be inflected for plurality, or only the second one need be.[46] Since the [-feminine] noun couples with [-feminine] names, there is no need for gender agreement on these forms.[47]

**Table 12B.4** Type 4 True Compound
#$R_1$++[±fem.]#<[αpl.]##$R_2$++[±fem.]# <[-plural]# $_{[\alpha pl.]}$

| | **(uns) cavalos-vapor** | | | | | | **[αfem.]** |
|---|---|---|---|---|---|---|---|
| U.F. | #caval+ | +o# | <z# | #vapor# | +e# | <Ø# | |
| Agree | *** | *** | *** | *** | *** | *** | |
| R. 12.1 | #caval+ | +o# | <z# | #vapor# | +e# | <Ø# | [-fem |
| R. 3.1 | #cav'al+ | +o# | <z# | #vap'or# | +e# | <Ø# | |
| **Ph.** | (uns) [kă.'va.lŭž.vă.'por] | | | | | | |

**§12B.1.4** This example means 'some horse-steam, i.e. some horse power'. Type 4 True compounds only allow inflection for plurality on their first noun, which also determines the resultant noun's gender.

46 There is one exception: *pai-agostinho* 'father Agostine', a proper noun identifying a passerine bird of Brazil inflected for plurality on both words.

47 The only [+feminine] example *mãe-joana* 'mother Joanne, i.e. jelllyfish' combines a gender-appropiate given name with *mãe* and can be inflected for plurality on both nouns or only on the second.

**Table 12B.5** Noun + Preposition + Noun

#R$_1$+{<,+}[αfem.]#<[βpl.]$_1$##prep.>(#det.>)R$_2$+{<,+}[±fem.]#<[±pl.]#$_{[\alpha fem.][\beta pl.]}$

| | | | | | | | | | |
|---|---|---|---|---|---|---|---|---|---|
| | **menina de cinco olhos** | | | | | | | | **[αfem.]** |
| **U.F.** | #menin+ | +a# | <Ø# | #de> | #sinko# | #ɔλ+ | +o# | <z# | |
| Agree | *** | *** | *** | *** | *** | *** | *** | *** | |
| R. 12.1 | #menin+ | +a# | <Ø# | #de> | #sinko# | #ɔλ+ | +o# | <z# | [+fem.] |
| R. 3.1 | #menˈin+ | +a# | <Ø# | #de> | #sˈinko# | #ˈɔλ+ | +o# | <z# | [+fem.] |
| Number[a] | #menˈin+ | +a# | <Ø# | #de> | #sˈinko# | #ˈɔλ+ | +o# | <z# | [-plural] |
| **Ph.** | [m$^{\tilde{\imath}}$.ˈnĩ.ă.δə.ˈsĩŋ.kŭ.ˈɔ.λŭ̃š] | | | | | | | | |
| | **meninas de cinco olhos** | | | | | | | | **[αfem.]** |
| **U.F.** | #menin+ | +a# | <z# | #de> | #sinko# | #ɔλ+ | +o# | <z# | |
| Agree | *** | *** | *** | *** | *** | *** | *** | *** | |
| R. 12.1 | #menin+ | +a# | <z# | #de> | #sinko# | #ɔλ+ | +o# | <z# | [+fem.] |
| R. 3.1 | #menˈin+ | +a# | <z# | #de> | #sˈinko# | #ˈɔλ+ | +o# | <z# | [+fem.] |
| Number | #menˈin+ | +a# | <z# | #de> | #sˈinko# | #ˈɔλ+ | +o# | <z# | [+pl.] |
| **Ph.** | [m$^{\tilde{\imath}}$.ˈnĩ.ăž.δə.ˈsĩŋ.kŭ.ˈɔ.λŭ̃š] | | | | | | | | |

a 'Number' is not a rule. It acknowledges the overall compound's number's being determined by the forms' structural descriptions.

**§12B.1.5** This phrase 'girl of five eyes' is a synonym of *palmatória* 'ferule', a switch Brazilian teachers once used to discipline students by smacking their outstretched hands. It is a typical compound of the sort #N$_1$##pre.>#(Determiner)>#N$_2$#, whose gender and number are determined by that of the first noun.

**Table 12B.6 Noun + Adjective/Adjective + Noun #R$_1$+{<,+)[αfem.]#<β[±pl.]# #R$_2$+<[αfem.]#<[βpl.]# #R$_2$+<[αfem.]#<[βpl.]# #R$_1$+{<,+)[αfem.]#<[βpl.]#**

| | | | | | | | |
|---|---|---|---|---|---|---|---|
| | **água-viva** | | | | | | **[αfem.]** |
| U.F. | #ˈagu+ | +a# | <Ø# | #viv+ | <[αfem.]# | <[αpl.]# | |
| Agree | #ˈagu+ | +a# | <Ø# | #viv+ | <a# | <Ø# | |
| R. 12.1 | #ˈagu+ | +a# | <Ø# | #viv+ | <a# | <Ø# | [+fem.] |
| R. 3.1 | #ˈagu+ | +a# | <Ø# | #vˈiv+ | <a# | <Ø# | [+fem.] |
| **Ph.** | [ˈa.ɣʷă.ˈvi.vă] | | | | | | |
| | **águas-vivas** | | | | | | **[αfem.]** |
| U.F | #ˈagu+ | +a# | <z# | #viv+ | <[αfem.]# | <[αpl.]# | |
| Agree | #ˈagu+ | +a# | <z# | #viv+ | <a# | <z# | |
| R. 12.1 | #ˈagu+ | +a# | <z# | #viv+ | <a# | <z# | [+fem.] |
| R. 3.1 | #ˈagu+ | +a# | <z# | #vˈiv+ | <a# | <z# | [+fem.] |
| **Ph.** | [ˈa.ɣʷăž.ˈvi.văš] | | | | | | |
| | **viva-voz** | | | | | | **[-fem.]** |
| U.F. | #viv+ | <[αfem.]# | <[αpl.]# | #vɔz# | +e+ | <Ø# | |
| Agree | #viv+ | <a# | <Ø# | #vɔz# | +e+ | <Ø# | |
| R. 12.1 | #viv+ | <a# | <Ø# | #vɔz# | +e+ | <Ø# | *** |
| R. 3.1 | #vˈiv+ | <a# | <Ø# | #vˈɔz# | +e+ | <Ø# | |
| **Ph.** | [ˈvi.vă.ˈvɔš] | | | | | | |
| | **vivas-vozes** | | | | | | **[-fem.]** |
| U.F | #viv+ | <[αfem.]# | <[αpl.]# | #vɔz# | +e+ | <z# | |
| Agree | #viv+ | <a# | <z# | #vɔz# | +e+ | <z# | |
| R. 12.1 | #viv+ | <a# | <z# | #vɔz# | +e+ | <z# | *** |
| R. 3.1 | #vˈiv+ | <a# | <z# | #vˈɔz# | +e+ | <z# | |
| **Ph.** | [ˈvi.văž.ˈvɔ.zeš] | | | | | | |

**§12B.1.6** The words (literally 'water live' and 'live voice') in Table 12B.6 mean 'jelly fish' (singular and plural), and 'speaker phone(s)'. They exhibit the standard adjective pattern of agreeing in number and gender with the modified noun. In the case of *água-viva*, both the adjective and noun are [+feminine], as is the compound noun. In the case of *viva-voz*, notwithstanding the [+feminine] gender of both components, the compound word is [-feminine].

**Table 12B.7** Verb + Noun
#R$_{v}$+<TMA#+TV+<Ø##R$_{n}$+{<,+}[±fem.]#<[±pl.]#

| | | | | | | | | |
|---|---|---|---|---|---|---|---|---|
| | | **quebra-luz** | | | | | | [-fem.] |
| U.F. | #kebr+ | <Ø# | +a# | <Ø# | #luz+ | +e+ | <Ø# | |
| Agree | ** | *** | *** | *** | *** | *** | *** | |
| R. 12.1 | **** | *** | *** | *** | *** | *** | *** | |
| R. 3.1 | #kˈebr+ | <Ø# | +a# | <Ø# | #lˈuz+ | +e+ | <Ø# | |
| **Ph.** | | [ˈke.βră.luš] | | | | | | |
| | | **quebra-molas** | | | | | | [-fem.] |
| U.F | #kebr+ | <Ø# | +a# | <Ø# | #mɔl+ | +a# | <z# | |
| Agree | *** | *** | *** | *** | *** | *** | *** | |
| R. 12.1 | *** | *** | *** | *** | *** | *** | *** | |
| R. 3.1 | #kˈebr+ | <Ø# | +a# | <Ø# | #mˈɔl+ | +a# | <z# | |
| **Ph.** | | [ˈke.βră.ˈmɔ.lăš] | | | | | | |

**§12B.1.7** The two compounds in Table 12B.7 mean 'visor' and 'speed bump' (literally 'breaks light' and 'breaks springs'). The verbs are 3rd person singular present indicative, as is the case with all verb+noun compounds, and their gender is [-feminine] regardless of the noun's gender. The plural of *quebra-luz* is *quebra-luzes*, whereas *quebra-molas* can be both singular or plural, which is normal for verb+noun compounds whose noun is already plural.

**Table 12B.8 Adverb/Prepostion + Noun:**
**#adverb##noun#, #Prep.>#noun#**

| | | | | | | | |
|---|---|---|---|---|---|---|---|
| | | **não-sofrer** | | | | | [αfem.] |
| U.F. | #non# | #sɔfr | +e+ | +r# | +e+ | <[±pl.# | |
| Agree | *** | *** | *** | *** | *** | | |
| R. 12.1 | #non# | #sɔfr | +e+ | +r# | +e+ | <[±pl.# | [-fem.] |
| R. 3.1 | #nˈon# | #sɔfr | +ˈe+ | +r# | +e+ | <[±pl.# | |
| **Ph.** | | [ˈnã̆$^{\tilde{u}}$.sŭ.ˈfrer] | | | | | |
| | | **sem-ventura** | | | | | [αfem.] |
| U.F | #sem> | #vent+ | +ur+ | +a# | <Ø# | | |
| Agree | *** | *** | *** | *** | | | |
| R. 12.1 | *** | *** | *** | *** | | | [+fem.] |
| R. 3.1 | #sem> | #vent+ | +ˈur+ | +a# | | | |
| **Ph.** | | [sẽ$^{\tilde{\imath}}$.vẽ$^{n}$.ˈtu.ră] | | | | | |

**§12B.1.8** The words in Table 12B.8 mean 'absence of suffering, haplessness' (literally 'no to suffer' and 'without luck'). *Não-sofrer* is [-feminine] owing to the infinitive *sofrer* and it can be pluralized (*não-sofreres*), whereas *sem-ventura* can be singular or plural and is [+feminine] owing to the gender of *ventura*.

**Table 12B.9** Semi-compounds: #element$_1$??element$_2$#

| | Semi-Compounds – Paroxytones | |
|---|---|---|
| | **globifloro** | **ortodoxo** |
| U.F. | #glɔb+#flor#<o#<[αpl.]# | #orto+#dɔks+<o#<[αpl.]# |
| R. 12.7 | #glɔb+i#flor#<o#<[αpl.]# | *** |
| R. 12.8 | *** | *** |
| R. 3.1 | #glɔb+i#flˈor#<o#<[αpl.]# | #orto+#dˈɔks+<o#<[αpl.]# |
| Ph. | [glŭ.βi.ˈflo.rŭ] | [ŭr.tŭ.ˈδɔk.sŭ] |
| | **Semi-Compounds—Proparoxytones** | |
| | **ambígeno** | **ortógrafo** |
| U.F. | #anb+#žen+<o#<[αpl.]# | #orto+#graf+<o#<[αpl.]# |
| R. 12.7 | #anb+i#žen+<o#<[αpl.]# | #ortɔ+#graf+<o#<[αpl.]# |
| R. 12.8 | #anb+ˈi#žen+i<o#<[αpl.]# | #ortˈɔ+#graf+<o#<[αpl.]# |
| R. 3.1 | *** | *** |
| Ph. | [ã$^{\tilde{m}}$.ˈbi.žẽ.nŭ] | [ŭr.ˈtɔ.ɣră.fŭ] |
| | **fumívoro** | **fagómano** |
| U.F. | #fum+#vor+<o#<[αpl.]# | #fag+#man+<o#<[αpl.]# |
| R. 12.7 | #fum+i#vor+<o#<[αpl.]# | #fag+ɔ#man+<o#<[αpl.]# |
| R. 12.8 | #fum+ˈi#vor+<o#<[αpl.]# | #fag+ˈɔ#man+<o#<[αpl.]# |
| R. 3.1 | *** | *** |
| Ph. | [fŭ.ˈmi.vŭ.rŭ] | [fă.ˈγɔ.mă.nŭ] |

**§12B.1.9.0** The top section of Table 12B.9 demonstrates the derivation of three Latinate semi-compound nominals meaning 'globule-flower, hybrid, smoke-eater'. The first element in each case ends in a consonant, which occasions Rule 12.7, the insertion of transitional /i/ between both elements. The second element in *ambígeno* and *fumívoro* are of the sort that occasion proparoxytone stress, accounted for with Rule 12.8, whereas #flor#<o# does not.

**§12B.1.9.1** The bottom section demonstrates the derivation of three Hellenic semi-compound nominals meaning 'orthodox, correct speller, insatiable eater'. The element #orto+ ending in a vowel, does not require any alteration to emerge in *ortodoxo*, whereas when it combines with the element #graf+, its final /o/ mutates to /ɔ/ (Rule 12.7) then it acquires stress (Rule 12.8). On the other hand, since the element #fag+ ends in /g+, Rule 12.7 inserts /ɔ/ between the elements, and Rule 12.8 assigns stress to the inserted /ɔ/. Because the forms here are nominals that can indicate both [+feminine] and [-feminine] as well as [±pl.] entities, their word-final gender and number morphemes are inflectional.

## Appendix C The Grammar of Grammatical Nominals

**12C.0** The following order of rules allows for the derivation of both compound adverbs and diminutive nominals:

**Rule 12.3 Adjective-Noun Agreement:**

$$\text{Adjective} \rightarrow \#R + <[\alpha\text{fem.}]\# < [\beta\text{plural}]\ \#/ \left\{ \begin{array}{l} \#R_n + \{+<\}[\alpha\text{fem.}]\ \ <[\beta\text{pl.}]\#\ \_\_ \\ \\ \_\_\_\#R_n + \{+,<[\alpha\text{fem.}]\ \ <[\beta\text{pl.}]\# \end{array} \right\}$$

**Rule 3.1 Paroxytone Stress (all derivations):**

$$[\text{-contoid}] \rightarrow [+\text{stress}]\ /\ \#X\ \_\ \ \left( \left[ \begin{array}{l} +\text{high} \\ \text{-contoid} \end{array} \right] \right) C_{0\text{-}4}V_{[\text{-high}]}\#(C)\#$$

**Condition:** The word has no previously assigned stress:

**Rule 9.5 The Loss of Word-Final /l# in Pluralizations:**

$$[+\text{lateral}]\ /\ \_\# \left\{ \begin{array}{c} < \\ \\ + \end{array} \right\}\ e+\ \#<z\# \rightarrow \varnothing$$

**Rule 6.2a Deletion of Word-Final <e+ and+e+_ after /r#, /l#, and /z#:**

$$\begin{Bmatrix} < \\ + \end{Bmatrix} \begin{pmatrix} +\text{palatal} \\ \text{-contoid} \end{pmatrix} \# \rightarrow \text{Ø} \,/\, \#\text{X}\,[\text{-contoid}] \begin{pmatrix} +\text{contoid} \\ \text{-surd} \\ \text{-labial} \\ \text{-high} \\ \text{-nasal} \\ \text{-occlusion} \end{pmatrix} \_\_ + < [\text{-plural}]\#$$

**Rule 6.2b Deletion of Word-Final <e+, +e+, (and +ɛ#) after /n#:**

$$\begin{pmatrix} \text{-contoid} \\ \text{-high} \\ \text{-delayed transition} \\ +\text{palatal} \end{pmatrix} \rightarrow \varnothing \,/\, \#\,\text{X} \begin{pmatrix} +\text{contoid} \\ +\text{nasal} \\ \text{-labial} \\ \text{-high} \end{pmatrix} \#_{[\text{-N4}]}$$

**Rule 7.2 Morphophonemic Nasalization $R_1$ Stems:**

$$[\text{-contoid}] \,/\, \begin{pmatrix} +\text{nasal} \\ \text{-high} \\ \text{-labial} \\ +\text{contoid} \end{pmatrix} +\text{R}_1 \rightarrow [+\text{nasal}] \,/\, \_\_ \; +\text{X}+\text{S}\#$$

**Rule 8.3 Loss of /n+:**

$$\begin{pmatrix} +\text{nasal} \\ +\text{contoid} \\ \text{-high} \\ \text{-labial} \end{pmatrix} \rightarrow \text{Ø}/ \begin{pmatrix} \text{-contoid} \\ +\text{nasal} \end{pmatrix} \,/\, \_\_ \; + + \; \text{S} < \text{S}\#$$

**Rule 4.1 Like Segment Deletion:**

$$\text{Segment}_2 \rightarrow \emptyset \: / \: \text{Segment}_1 \, \_\_\_\_$$

**Condition:** $\text{Segment}_1 = \text{Segment}_2$

**Rule 2.3 Atonic Vowel Reduction:**

$$\begin{pmatrix} \text{-contoid} \\ \text{-high} \\ \alpha\text{labial} \\ \text{-del. trans.} \end{pmatrix} \rightarrow \begin{pmatrix} \text{+wide glottis} \\ \text{-palatal} \\ \alpha\text{high} \\ \text{-low} \end{pmatrix} \: / \: \_\_\_\_ \: \left( \begin{pmatrix} \left\{ \begin{matrix} [\text{-nasal}] \\ [\text{-lateral}] \\ [\text{-occlusion}] \end{matrix} \right\} \\ [\text{+contoid} \end{pmatrix} \right).$$

**Rule 12.10 Optional Loss of <a# in De-Adjectival Adverbs:**

$$<[\text{+feminine}]\# \rightarrow \emptyset \: / \begin{pmatrix} \text{+fricative} \\ \text{-labial} \\ \text{-high} \\ \text{-surd} \end{pmatrix} + \: \_\_ \#\text{ment} + + \text{e}_{[+\text{fem}]}\#$$

**Rule 4.4 Syllable Boundary V.CV, V.C/r/, V.C/l/:**

$$\emptyset \rightarrow . \: /[\text{-contoid}] \, \_\_ \, [\text{+contoid}] \: \left\{ \begin{matrix} [\text{-contoid}] \\ C_2 \end{matrix} \right\}$$

**Rule 9.2b Progressive Assimilation: Vocoid:**

$$\begin{pmatrix} \text{-contoid} \\ \text{-delayed transition} \end{pmatrix} \rightarrow [\text{+nasal}] / \begin{pmatrix} \text{-contoid} \\ \text{+nasal} \end{pmatrix} \_\_\_\_$$

**Rule 4.5 Syllable Boundary V.V:**

$$\emptyset \rightarrow . \: / \begin{pmatrix} \text{-contoid} \\ \alpha\text{high} \end{pmatrix} \_\_ \begin{pmatrix} \text{-contoid} \\ \left\{ \begin{matrix} \alpha\text{high} \\ \text{+delayed transition} \end{matrix} \right\} \end{pmatrix}$$

**Rule 4.6 Syllable Boundary C.C:**

$$\emptyset \rightarrow . \,/\, C_4\_\_ \left( \begin{array}{c} +\text{contoid} \\ \left\{ \begin{array}{c} +\text{nasal} \\ +\text{occlusion} \\ +\text{fricative} \end{array} \right\} \end{array} \right)$$

**§12C.1.0** What follows are sample derivations of adverbs and diminutives using the entire set of rules in the order set above.

Table 12C.1 Compound Adverbs[a]

| | rapidamente | inferiormente |
|---|---|---|
| U.F. | #rˈapid+<o#+<Ø##ment++e#<Ø# | #inferior#+e+<Ø##ment++e#<Ø# |
| R. 12.3 | #rˈapid+<a##ment++e#<Ø# | #inferior#+e+#ment++e#<Ø# |
| R. 3.1 | #rˈapid+<a##mˈent++e#<Ø# | #inferiˈor#+e+#mˈent++e#<Ø# |
| R. 9.5 | *** | *** |
| R. 6.2a | *** | #inferiˈor##mˈent++e#<Ø# |
| R. 6.2b | *** | *** |
| R. 7.2 | *** | *** |
| R. 8.3 | *** | *** |
| R. 4.1 | *** | *** |
| R. 2.3 | #rˈapid+<ă##mˈent++ĭ#<Ø# | #inferiˈor##mˈent++ĭ<Ø# |
| R. 12.10 | *** | *** |
| R. 4.4 | #rˈa.pi.d+<ă##.mˈent++ĭ#<Ø# | #in.fe.riˈor##mˈent++ĭ<Ø# |
| R. 9.2 | *** | *** |
| R. 4.5 | *** | #infe.ri.ˈor##mˈent++ĭ<Ø# |
| R. 4.6 | #rˈa.pi.d+<ă##.mˈen.t++ĭ#<Ø# | #in.fe.ri.ˈor##.mˈen.t++ĭ<Ø# |
| Ph. | [ˈr̠a.pi.ðă.ˈmẽ$^{n}$.tə] | [ĩ$^{\text{ɱ}}$.fə.ri.ˈor.ˈmẽ$^{n}$.tə] |

a The examples mean ‘rapidly’ and’ inferiorly’.

**§12C.1.1** As in the text examples (Table 12.18), for the formation of adverbs Tables 12C.1 and 12C.2 demonstrate that adverbs’ generation entails no rule peculiar to adverb formation—they are created by Rewrite Rule 12.9 that juxtaposes adjectives to the noun *mente*.

In the case of these two adverbs, the adjective *rápido* 'rapid' is a proparoxytone and is stressed lexically—the adverb's noun receives rule-governed stress. *Rápido* agrees in number and gender with the adjectives it modifies and reflects [+feminine] gender with the suffix <a#. On the other hand, the gender morpheme of *inferior* is +e+, and is indifferent to a referent's gender, which is deleted (Rule 6.2a) in [-plural] circumstances, including the adverb-forming word *mente*.

**Table 12C.2 Compound Adverbs[a]**

| | burguesmente | simplesmente |
|---|---|---|
| U.F. | #burg++ez#<e#<Ø##ment++e#<Ø# | #sinplez##ment++e#<Ø# |
| R. 12.3 | #burg++ez#<a##ment++e#<Ø# | *** |
| R. 3.1 | #burg++ˈez#<a##mˈent++e#<Ø# | #sˈinplez##mˈent++e#<Ø# |
| R. 9.5 | *** | *** |
| R. 6.2a | *** | *** |
| R. 6.2b | *** | *** |
| R. 7.2 | #burg++ˈez#<a##mˈẽnt++e#<Ø# | #sˈĩnplez##mˈẽnt++e#<Ø# |
| R. 8.3 | *** | *** |
| R. 4.1 | *** | *** |
| R. 2.3 | #burg++ˈez#<ă##mˈẽnt++ĭ#<Ø# | #sĩnplĭz##mˈẽnt++ĭ#<Ø# |
| R. 12.10 | #burg++ˈez##mˈẽnt++e#<Ø# | *** |
| R. 4.4 | #burg++ˈez##mˈẽnt++ĭ#<Ø# | #sˈinplĭz##mˈẽnt++ĭ#<Ø# |
| R. 9.2 | *** | *** |
| R. 4.5 | *** | *** |
| R. 4.6 | #bur.g++ˈez##.mˈẽn.t++ĭ#<Ø# | #sˈin.plĭz##.mˈẽn.t++ĭ#<Ø# |
| Ph. | [bur.ˈgež.ˈmẽ$^{n}$.tə] | [ˈsĩ$^{m}$.pləž.ˈmẽ$^{n}$.tə] |

a These adverbs mean 'in a bourgeois fashion' and 'simply'.

**§12C.1.2** These adverbs are of interest because *burguês* is inflected for gender <e# [-feminine], <a# [+feminine] and number. *Simples*, on the other hand, is not inflected for gender, and its [+plural] morpheme (<z#) evanesces in all forms because it is the same phoneme as the adjective's final segment /z#. For the form *burguesmente* to emerge, it is susceptible to the specific, optional, compounding rule 12.10, which allows for the gender morpheme to evanesce, should a speaker desire. (The form *burguesamente*, containing the adjective's gender morpheme, is acceptable.)

**§12C.1.3** Tables 12C.3 and 12.4 situate the derivations in Table 12.8 among the entire gamut of rules used to form rule-governed compound adverbs and diminutives.

**Table 12C.3** Compound Adverbs (cf. Table 12.18)

| | comummente | finalmente |
|---|---|---|
| U.F. | #kon+#mun#+e+<Ø##ment++e#<Ø# | # fin ++al#+e+<Ø##ment++e#<Ø# |
| R. 12.3 | #kon+#mun#+e+#ment++e# | #fin++al#+e+#ment++e# |
| R. 3.1 | #kon+#mˈun#+e+#mˈent++e# | #fin++ˈal#+e+#mˈent++e# |
| R. 9.5 | *** | *** |
| R. 6.2a | *** | #fin ++ˈal##mˈent++e# |
| R. 6.2b | #kon+#mˈun##mˈent++e# | *** |
| R. 7.2 | #kõn+#mˈũn##mˈent++e# | *** |
| R. 8.3 | #kõ+#mˈũ##mˈent++e# | *** |
| R. 4.1 | *** | *** |
| R. 2.3 | #kõ+#mˈũ##mˈent++ĭ# | #fin++ˈal##mˈent++ĭ# |
| R.12.10 | *** | *** |
| R. 4.4 | #kõ+#.mˈũ##.mˈent++ĭ# | #fi.n++ˈal##mˈent++ĭ# |
| R. 9.2 | *** | *** |
| R. 4.5 | *** | *** |
| R. 4.6 | *** | #fi.n++ˈal##.mˈen.t++ĭ# |
| Ph. | [kũ.ˈmũ.ˈmẽ$^{n}$.tə] | [fĩ.ˈnał.ˈmẽ$^{n}$.tə] |
| | **chorosamente** | **somente** |
| U.F. | #šɔr++ɔz+<[αf.]#<Ø##ment++e#<Ø# | #sɔ#<Ø##ment++e#<Ø# |
| R. 12.3 | šɔr++ˈɔz+<a##mˈent++e# | #sɔ##ment++e# |
| R. 3.1 | #šɔr++ˈɔz+<a##mˈent++e# | #sˈɔ##mˈent++e# |
| R. 9.5 | *** | *** |
| R. 6.2a | *** | *** |
| R. 6.2b | *** | *** |
| R. 7.2 | *** | *** |
| R. 8.3 | *** | *** |
| R. 4.1 | *** | *** |
| R. 2.3 | # šŭr++ˈɔz+<ă##mˈent++ĭ# | #sˈɔ##mˈent++ĭ# |
| R. 12.10 | *** | *** |

(*Continued*)

Table 12C.3 Continued

| | | |
|---|---|---|
| R. 4.4 | #šŭ.r++ˈɔ.z+<ă##.mˈent++ĭ# | #sˈɔ##.mˈent++ĭ# |
| R. 9.2 | *** | *** |
| R. 4.5 | *** | *** |
| R. 4.6 | #šŭ.r++ˈɔ.z+<ă##.mˈen.t++ə# | #sˈɔ##.mˈen.t++ə# |
| Ph. | [šu.ˈrɔ.sã.ˈmẽ$^{n}$.tə] | [ˈsɔ.ˈmẽ$^{n}$.tə] |

§**12C.2.0** The following tables show the derivation of rule-governed diminutives within the gamut of the entire set of rules associated with rule-governed true compound diminutives.

**Table 12C.4 Compound Diminutives**[a]

| | **capitãzinhas** | **iguaizinhos** |
|---|---|---|
| U.F. | #kapit++an+<a#<z##ziɲ+<[αfem.]#<[βpl.]# | #igual#+e+<z##ziɲ+<[αfem.]#<[βpl.] |
| Agree | #kapit++an+<a#<z##ziɲ+<a#<z# | #igual#+e+<z##ziɲ+<o#<z# |
| R. 3.1 | #kapit++ˈan+<a#<z##zˈiɲ+<a#<z# | #iguˈal#+e+<z##zˈiɲ+<o#<z# |
| R. 9.5 | *** | #iguˈa#+e+<z##zˈiɲ+<o#<z# |
| R. 6.2a | *** | *** |
| R. 6.2b | *** | *** |
| R. 7.2 | #kapit++ˈãn+<a#<z##zˈiɲ+<a#<z# | *** |
| R. 8.3 | #kapit++ˈã+<a#<z##zˈiɲ +<a#<z# | *** |
| R. 4.1 | #kapit++ˈã+##zˈiɲ+<a#<z# | #iguˈa#+e+#zˈiɲ+<o#<z# |
| R. 2.3 | #kăpit++ˈã+##zˈiɲ+<ă#<z# | #iguˈa#+ĭ+#zˈiɲ+<ŭ#<z# |
| R. 12.10 | *** | *** |
| R. 4.4 | #kă.pi.t++ˈã+##.zˈi.ɲ+<ă#<z# | #i.guˈa#+ĭ.+#zˈi.ɲ+<ŭ#<z# |
| R. 9.2 | | *** |
| R. 4.5 | *** | #i.guˈ.a#+ĭ.+#zˈi.ɲ+<ŭ#<z# |
| R. 4.6 | *** | *** |
| Ph. | [kă.pi.ˈtã̃.ˈzĩ.$^{ɲ}$ăš | [i.ˈγ$^{w}$a$^{i}$ˈzĩ.$^{ɲ}$ŭš][b] |

a The words in Table 12C.4 mean 'little (female) captains' and 'exactly alike'.
b The atonic /u/ that follows /g/ becomes a labialized appendage of the /g/ before /a/. According to this derivation, this phenomenon occurs on the phonetic level, and entails the loss of the syllable boundary between the segments [g$^{w}$] and [ˈa].

§12C.2.1 The words in Table 12C.4 are of interest because of the [+feminine] gender of the first noun in *capitãzinhas* and the necessary morphophonemic processes entailed in the mutation of +an+<a# to ['ã] (and finally ['ã̃]). The adjective *iguaizinhos* entails processes in which: (A) the ambivalent gender morpheme +e+ is not deleted because the form is [+plural]; (B) the stem-final /l# is deleted because the form is [+plural]. Both *capitãzinhas* and *iguaizinhos* lose a /z/ in these forms because the first words' final <z# and *zinho*'s initial #z/ are susceptible to Rule 4.1.

**Table 12C.5 Compound Diminutives**[a]

| | maiorezinhos | florzinha |
|---|---|---|
| U.F. | #maior#+$e_{[\alpha fem]}$+β<z##ziɲ+ <[$\alpha_{fem}$]#<[βpl] | #flor#+$e_{[\alpha+fem.]}$+β<Ø##ziɲ+ <[$\alpha_{fem}$]#<[βpl] |
| Agree | #maior#+$e_{[\alpha fem]}$+β<z##ziɲ+ <o#<z# | #flor#+$e_{[\alpha+fem.]}$+β<Ø##ziɲ+<a#<Ø# |
| R. 3.1 | #mai'or#+$e_{[\alpha fem]}$+β<z##z'iɲ+ <o#<z# | #fl'or#+$e_{[\alpha+fem.]}$+β<Ø##z'iɲ+<a# |
| R. 9.5 | *** | *** |
| R. 6.2a | *** | #fl'or##z'iɲ+<a# |
| R. 6.2b | *** | *** |
| R. 7.2 | *** | *** |
| R. 8.3 | *** | *** |
| R. 4.1 | #mai'or#+$ĭ_{[\alpha fem]}$+#z'iɲ+<ŭ#<z# | *** |
| R. 2.3 | #mai'or#+$ĭ_{[\alpha fem]}$+#z'iɲ+<ŭ#<z# | #fl'or##z'iɲ+<ă# |
| R. 12.10 | *** | *** |
| R. 4.4 | #mai'or#+$ĭ_{[\alpha fem]}$+#z'iɲ+<ŭ#<z# | #fl'or##z'i.ɲ+<ă# |
| R. 9.2 | *** | *** |
| R. 4.5 | *** | #fl'or##.z'i.ɲ+<a# |
| R. 4.6 | #mai'or#+$ĭ_{[\alpha fem]}$+#z'iɲ+<ŭ#<z# | *** |
| Ph. | [ma$^{i}$.'o.rə.'zĩ.$^{ɲ}$ŭš] | ['flor.'zĩ.$^{ɲ}$ă] |

a *Maiorezinhos* is the diminutive form of the adjective *maior* 'larger, greater, adult, older'. As a diminutive it means something like 'noticeably and agreeably larger or more grown-up'. *Florzinha* means 'little flower' and transmits positive affect on the part of the user of such a word.

§**12C.2.2** These compounds are of interest because their first words end in +e+. The +e+ of *maior* is ambivalent ([±fem.]) that of *flor* is [+feminine]. They both disappear when the words are singular. Thus, Rule 6.2a accounts for the loss of +e+ in *florzinha*. Rule 6.2's failure to operate on #maior#+e+<z# owing to the adjective's plurality accounts for the emergence of +e+ in *maiorezinhos*.[48]

§**12C.2.3** As with the adverbs, the derivations of diminutive compounds found in the text appear here in the context of the entire set of rules that generate true compounds.

**Table 12C.6** Compound Diminutives

| | **cãezinhos** | **hoteizinhos** |
|---|---|---|
| **U.F.** | #kan++e+<z##ziɲ+<br><[αfem.]#<[αnumber]# | #otɛl#+e+<z##ziɲ+<br><[αfem.]#<[αnumber]# |
| **Agree** | #kan++e+<z## ziɲ+<o#<z# | #otɛl#+e+<z##ziɲ+<o#<z# |
| **R. 3.1** | #kˈan++e+<z## zˈiɲ+<o#<z# | #otˈɛl#+e+<z##zˈiɲ+<o#<z# |
| **R. 9.5** | *** | #otˈɛ#+e+<z##zˈiɲ+<o#<z# |
| **R. 6.2a** | *** | *** |
| **R. 6.2b** | *** | *** |
| **R. 7.2** | #kˈãn++e+<z## zˈiɲ+<o#<z# | *** |
| **R. 8.3** | #kˈã++e+<z## zˈiɲ+<o#<z# | *** |
| **R. 4.1** | #kˈã++e+# zˈiɲ+<o#<z# | #otˈɛ#+e+<z##zˈiɲ+<o#<z# |
| **R. 2.3** | #kˈã++ĭ## zˈiɲ+<ŭ#<z# | #ŭtˈɛ#+ĭ##zˈiɲ+<ŭ#<z# |
| **R. 12.10** | *** | *** |
| **R. 4.4** | #kˈã++ĭ##. zˈi.ɲ+<ŭ#<z# | #ŭ.tˈɛ#+ĭ##.zˈi.ɲ+<ŭ#<z# |
| **R. 9.2** | #kˈã++$^{i}$##. zˈi.ɲ+<ŭ#<z# | *** |
| **R. 4.5** | *** | *** |
| **R. 4.6** | *** | *** |
| **Ph.** | [ˈkã̆$^{i}$ˈzĩ.ɲŭš] | [ŭ.ˈtɛ$^{ĭ}$.ˈzĩ.ɲŭš] |

48 Again the morpheme's emergence is more common in European Portuguese than in Brazilian.

Table 12C.6 Continued

| | **boazinhas** | **cafezinhos** |
|---|---|---|
| **U.F.** | #bo+<a#<z##ziɲ+ <[αfem.]#<[αnumber]# | #kafˈɛ#<z##ziɲ+ <[αfem.]#<[αnumber]# |
| **Agree** | #bo+<a#<z##ziɲ+<a#<z# | #kafˈɛ#<z##ziɲ+<o#<z# |
| **R. 3.1** | #bˈo+<a#<z##zˈiɲ+<a#<z# | #kafˈɛ#<z##zˈiɲ+<o#<z# |
| **R. 9.5** | *** | *** |
| **R. 6.2a** | *** | *** |
| **R. 6.2b** | *** | *** |
| **R. 7.2** | *** | *** |
| **R. 8.3** | *** | *** |
| **R. 4.1** | #bˈo+<a##zˈiɲ+<a#<z# | #kafˈɛ##zˈiɲ+<o#<z# |
| **R. 2.3** | #bˈo+<ă##zˈiɲ+<ă#<z# | #kafˈɛ##zˈiɲ+<ŭ#<z# |
| **R. 4.4** | # bˈo+<ă##.zˈi.ɲ+<ă#<z# | #kă.fˈɛ##.zˈi.ɲ+<ŭ#<z# |
| **R. 9.2** | *** | *** |
| **R. 4.5** | *** | *** |
| **R. 4.6** | bˈo+<.ă##.zˈiɲ+<ă#<z# | *** |
| **Ph.** | [ˈbo.ă.ˈzĩ.ɲăš] | [kă.ˈfɛ.ˈzĩ.ɲŭš] |

# References


Anonymous. 2011. *The American Heritage Dictionary of the English Language*, 5th ed. Boston: Houghton Mifflin Harcourt.

Anonymous. 2018. Dicionário infopédia da língua portuguesa [em linha]. Porto: Porto Editora. www.infopedia.pt/dicionarios/lingua-portuguesa.

Azevedo, Milton M. 2005. *Portuguese, a Linguistic Introduction.* Cambridge: CUP.

Baird Ferreira, Marina and Margarida dos Anjos, (eds.). 2010. *Dicionário Aurélio da língua portuguesa.* Curitiba: Editora Positiva.

Bechara, Evanildo. 2009. *Moderna gramática portuguesa,* 37th ed. Rio: Nova Fronteira.

Brakel, Arthur. 1981. Review of *The Portuguese Language*, by Joaquim Mattoso Cámara, Tr. Anthony Naro. *Luso-Brazilian Review* 18: 206–211.

Buarque de Hollanda, Aurélio, ed. 1975. *Novo dicionário da língua portuguesa.* Rio: Nova Fronteira.

Canesin Dal Molin, Eugênio. 2013. *O terceiro tempo do trauma: Freud, Ferenczi, e os desvios de um conceito.* Master's Thesis. Instituto de Psicologia, Universidade de São Paulo, São Paulo, Brazil.

Cunha, Celso. 1970. *Gramática do português contemporâneo.* Belo Horizonte: Editora Bernardo Alves.

Delgado Martins, Maria Raquel. 1982. *Aspects de l'accent en portugais.* Hamburg: Buske.

eliza-souza.blogspot.com/2011/11/to-malzona.html, www.dicio.com.br./mauzão, www.infopedia.pt.dicionarios/lingua-portuguesa/malzão.

Houaiss, Antônio and Catherine Avery, (eds.). 1964. *The New Appleton Dictionary of the English and Portuguese Languages.* New York: Appleton-Century-Crofts.

Jucá, Cândido. 1963. *Dicionário escolar das dificuldades da língua portuguesa.* Rio: M.E.C. (Ministério de Educação e Cultura).

Mateus, Maria Helena and Ernesto d'Andrade. 2000. *The Phonology of Portuguese.* Oxford: OUP.

Mattoso Câmara, Joaquim. 1964. *Dicionário de filologia e gramática referente à língua portuguesa,* 2nd ed. Rio de Janeiro: Ozon.

Mattoso Câmara, Joaquim. 1972. *The Portuguese Language*. Trans. Anthony J. Naro. Chicago: University of Chicago Press.

Moreno, Augusto, Cardoso Júnior, and José Pedro Machado, (eds.). 1961. *António de Morais Silva: Novo dicionário compacto da língua portuguesa*, 10th ed. Lisboa: Confluência.

Pardal, Ernesto d'Andrade. 1977. *Aspects de la phonologie (generative) du portugais*. Lisboa: Instituto Nacional de Investigação Científica.

Saramago, José. 1991. *O evangelho segundo Jesus Cristo*. Lisboa: Editorial Caminho.

Schwindt, Luís Carlos and W. Leo Wetzels. 2016. The morphology and phonology of inflection. In Wetzels et al., 188–209.

Vilalva, Alina. 2009. Sobre a formação dos chamados diminutivos no português europeu. (www.clul.pt/files/alina_vilalva/2009Lisboa_diminutivos.pdf, accessed 3 February 2014).

Villalva, Alina and Carlos Alexandre Gonçalves. 2016. The phonology and morphology of word formation. In Wetzels et al., 167–187.

Wetzels, W. Leo, Sérgio Menuzzi, and João Costa, (eds.). 2016. *Handbook of Portuguese Linguistics*. Hoboken, New Jersey. Wiley.

Williams, Edwin. 1962. *From Latin to Portuguese*. Philadelphia: University of Pennsylvania Press.

# Index

AUTHORS